D0361928

Temples of
Angkor
p118

Siem Reap
p88

Northwestern
Cambodia
p204

Eastern Cambodia
p243

Phnom Penh
p34

South Coast
p158

Cambodia
Border
Crossings

THIS EDITION WRITTEN AND RESEARCHED BY

Nick Ray, Greg Bloom

welcome to Cambodia

An Empire of Temples

Contemporary Cambodia is the successor state to the mighty Khmer empire, which, during the Angkorian period, ruled much of what is now Laos, Thailand and Vietnam. The remains of this empire can be seen at the fabled temples of Angkor, monuments unrivalled in scale and grandeur in southeast Asia. The traveller's first glimpse of Angkor Wat, the ultimate expression of Khmer genius, is sublime and is matched by only a few select spots on earth, such as Machu Picchu or Petra.

The Comeback Capital

Just as Angkor is more than its wat, so too is Cambodia more than its temples. The chaotic yet charismatic capital of Phnom Penh is a hub of political intrigue, economic vitality and intellectual debate. All too often overlooked by hit-and-run tourists ticking off Angkor on a regional tour, the revitalised city is finally earning plaudits in its own right thanks to a gorgeous riverside location, a cultural renaissance, and a wining and dining scene to rival anywhere in the region.

Upcountry Adventures

Siem Reap and Phnom Penh may be the heavyweights, but to some extent they are a bubble, a world away from the Cambodia of the countryside. This is the place to experience the rhythm of rural life and time-

Ascend to the realm of the gods, Angkor Wat. Descend into the hell of the Khmer Rouge at Tuol Sleng. Thanks to a history both inspiring and depressing, Cambodia delivers an intoxicating present for adventurous visitors.

(left) Monks at Angkor Thom, Bayon (p138)
(below) Shadow-puppetry performance at the Sovanna Phum Arts Association (p73) in Phnom Penh

less landscapes of dazzling rice paddies and swaying sugar palms. The South Coast is fringed by tropical islands, with just a handful of beach huts in sight. Inland from the coast lie the Cardamom Mountains, part of a vast tropical wilderness that provides a home to elusive wildlife and is the gateway to emerging ecotourism adventures. The mighty Mekong River cuts through the country and is home to some of the region's last remaining freshwater dolphins. The northeast is a world unto itself, its wild and mountainous landscapes a home for Cambodia's ethnic minorities and an abundance of natural attractions.

The Cambodian Spirit

Despite having the eighth wonder of the world in its backyard, Cambodia's real treasure is its people. The Khmers have been to hell and back, struggling through years of bloodshed, poverty and political instability. Thanks to an unbreakable spirit and infectious optimism, they have prevailed with their smiles intact. No visitor comes away without a measure of admiration and affection for the inhabitants of this enigmatic kingdom.

›Cambodia

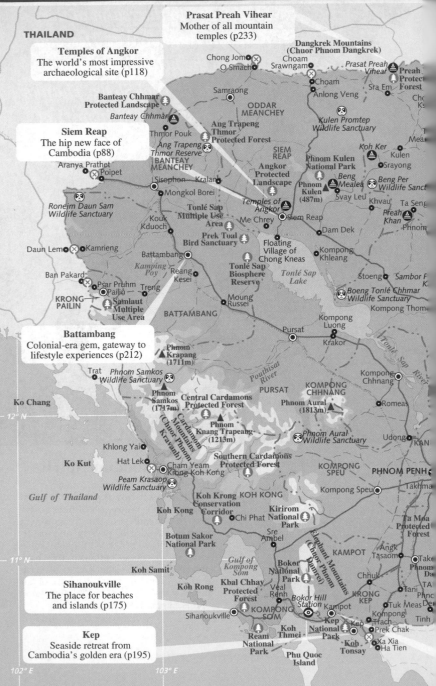

THAILAND

Prasat Preah Vihear
Mother of all mountain temples (p233)

Temples of Angkor
The world's most impressive archaeological site (p118)

**Dangkrek Mountains
(Chuor Phnom Dangkrek)**

Chong Jom
O Smach
Choam Srawngam
Prasat Preah Vihear
Preah Protec
Forest

Choam
Anlong Veng
Sra Em

Samraong

ODDAR MEANCHEY

Kulen Promtep Wildlife Sanctuary

Banteay Chhmar Protected Landscape

Banteay Chhmar

Thmor Pouk

Ang Trapeng Thmor Protected Forest

Siem Reap
The hip new face of Cambodia (p88)

Ang Trapeng Thmor Reserve

BANTEAY MEANCHEY

SIEM REAP

Koh Ker
Kulen
Srayong

Phnom Kulen National Park

Aranya Prathet
Poipet

Sisophon
Kralan

Angkor Protected Landscape

Phnom Kulen (487m)

Beng Mealea

Beng Per Wildlife Sanct

Roneim Daun Sam Wildlife Sanctuary

Mongkol Borei

Tonlé Sap Multiple Use Area

Me Chrey

Temples of Angkor

Siem Reap

Svay Leu

Khvau

Ta Seng

Preah Khan

Phnom

Kouk Kduoch

Prek Toal Bird Sanctuary

Dam Dek

Kompong Khleang

Daun Lem
Kamrieng

Battambang
Reang Kesei

Floating Village of Chong Kneas

Stoeng
Sambor F
K

Kamping Poy

Tonlé Sap Biosphere Reserve

Tonlé Sap Lake

Boeng Tonlé Chhmar Wildlife Sanctuary

Ban Pakard
Psar Pruhm
Pailin
Treng

Moung Russei

Kompong Thom

KRONG PAILIN

Samlaut Multiple Use Area

BATTAMBANG

Kompong Luong

Pursat

Kompong Chhnang

Tonlé Sap River

Battambang
Colonial-era gem, gateway to lifestyle experiences (p212)

Phnom Krapang (1711m)

Krakor

Trat
Phnom Samkos Wildlife Sanctuary

Pouthisat River

PURSAT

KOMPONG CHHNANG

Kompong Chhnang

Phnom Samkos (1717m)

Central Cardamons Protected Forest

Phnom Aural (1813m)

Romeas

Ko Chang

Cardamom Mountains (Chuor Phnom Kravanh)

Phnom Knang Trapeang (1213m)

Phnom Aural Wildlife Sanctuary

Udong

KAN

12° N

Khlong Yai

Hat Lek

Southern Cardamons Protected Forest

KOMPONG SPEU

PHNOM PENH

Ko Kut

Cham Yeam
Krong Koh Kong

Peam Krasaop Wildlife Sanctuary

Koh Krong Conservation Corridor

KOH KONG

Kompong Speu

Takhma

Gulf of Thailand

Chi Phat

Kirirom National Park

Sre Ambel

Ta Moa Protected Forest

Botum Sakor National Park

Angk Tasaom

Take
Phnom
Da

KAMPOT

11° N

Koh Samit

Gulf of Kompong Som

Bokor National Park

Elephant Mountains (Chuor Phnom Damrei)

Chhuk

Chuk

Sihanoukville
The place for beaches and islands (p175)

Koh Rong

Kbal Chhay Protected Forest

Veal Renh

Bokor Hill Station

Tani

Phnc

KRONG KEP

Kampot

Tuk Meas De

Kompong Trach

Kompong

Tinh

Sihanoukville

KOMPONG SOM

Kampot

Kep National Park

Prek Chak

Kep
Seaside retreat from Cambodia's golden era (p195)

Ream National Park

Koh Thmei

Kep

Koh Tonsay

Xa Xia
Ha Tien

Phu Quoc Island

102° E
103° E

Ratanakiri
Jungle romps and adrenaline-fuelled excursions (p258)

Mondulkiri
The wild east (p267)

Kratie
Rare dolphins in the Mekong River (p251)

Phnom Penh
The 'pearl of Asia' is back (p34)

Kampot
Laid-back little charmer, gateway to Bokor (p189)

LAOS

Preah Vihear Protected Forest

Muang Khong

Siem Pang

Nong Nok Khiene

Ko Chheuteal Thom

Trapaeng Kriel

Anlong Veng Seima

Thala Boravit

Stung Treng Ramsar Site

STUNG TRENG

Roviang

Virachey National Park

Voen Sai

RATANAKIRI

Ban Lung

O' Yadaw

Le Tanh

Bokheo

Boeng Yeak Lom

Tonlé Kong

Tonlé San

Lumphat

Lomphat Wildlife Sanctuary

Koh Nhek

Mondulkiri Protected Forest

OMPONG THOM

Phnom Prich Wildlife Sanctuary

MONDULKIRI

Sambor

Sandan

KRATIE

Kratie

Mekong River

Sen Monorom

Nam Lear Wildlife Sanctuary

Spoe Tbong

Stung Trang

Chhlong

Snoul Wildlife Sanctuary

Sre Khtum

KOMPONG CHAM

Kompong Cham

Suong

Snuol

Trapaeng Sre

Loc Ninh

Chub Krau

Trapaeng Plong

Memot

Xa Mat

VIETNAM

Prey Veng

PREY VENG

Ba Phnom

SVAY RIENG

Tay Ninh

Neak Long

Banteay Chakrey

Svay Rieng

Bavet

Moc Bai

Kaam Samnor

Khanh Binh

Chiphu

Vinh Xuong

Chau Doc

HO CHI MINH CITY (SAIGON)

Tonlé

0   50 km
0   25 miles

SOUTH CHINA SEA

107° E

108° E

10 TOP
EXPERIENCES

Siem Reap & the Temples of Angkor

1 One of the world's most magnificent sights, the temples of Angkor are so much better than the superlatives. Choose from Angkor Wat, the world's largest religious building; Bayon, one of the world's weirdest, with its immense stone faces; or Ta Prohm, where nature runs amok. Buzzing Siem Reap, with a superb selection of restaurants and bars, is the base for temple exploration. Beyond lie floating villages on the Tonlé Sap lake (p116), adrenaline-fuelled activities like quad biking and microlighting, and such cultured pursuits as cooking classes and birdwatching. Ta Prohm (p142)

Phnom Penh

2 The Cambodian capital is a chaotic yet charming city that has thrown off the shadows of the past to embrace a brighter future. Boasting one of the most beautiful riverfronts in the region, Phnom Penh is in the midst of a boom, with hip hotels, designer restaurants and funky bars ready to welcome urban explorers. Experience emotional extremes at the inspiring National Museum and the depressing Tuol Sleng prison, showcasing the best and worst of Cambodian history. Once the 'Pearl of Asia', Phnom Penh is fast regaining its shine.

ANTONY GIBLIN/LONELY PLANET IMAGES ©

RACHEL LEWIS/LONELY PLANET IMAGES ©

1

2

Sihanoukville

3 Despite a reputation for backpacker hedonism, Sihanoukville's real appeal lies in its beaches. On nearby islands like Koh Rong and Koh Rong Samloem, resorts are creating a laid-back beach-bungalow vibe. On the mainland, it's only 5km from Sihanoukville's grittier central beach, Occheuteal, to Otres Beach, still mellow and sublime despite the long-looming threat of development. More central Victory Beach, Independence Beach, Sokha Beach, and even Occheuteal and backpacker favourite Serendipity Beach all have their charms and unique personalities. Serendipity Beach (p175)

Mondulkiri

4 Eventually the endless rice fields and sugar palms that characterise the Cambodian landscape give way to rolling hills. Mondulkiri is the wild east, home to the hardy Bunong people, who still practise animism and ancestor worship. Elephants are used here, but better than riding them is visiting them at the Elephant Valley Project (p259), where you can experience 'walking with the herd'. Add thunderous waterfalls, jungle treks and black-shanked douc spotting to the mix and you have the right recipe for adventure. Bunong hill-tribe villagers in Mondulkiri (p267)

MARK KIRBY/LONELY PLANET IMAGES ©

TOM COCKREM/LONELY PLANET IMAGES ©

ampot & Kep

5 These South Coast retreats form a perfect one-two punch for those looking get beyond the beaches of Sihanoukville. aid-back Kampot, take in the wonderful onial architecture, explore the pretty river paddleboard or kayak, and day-trip to wild kor National Park. Sleepier Kep offers its fa- ous Crab Market, hiking in Kep National Park d hidden resorts to escape from it all. Crum- ng half-century-old villas in both towns offer mpses of a time when these were prime stinations for Phnom Penh's privileged few. hing village near Kampot (p189)

Battambang

6 This is the real Cambodia, far from the jet- set destinations of Phnom Penh and Siem Reap. Unfurling along the banks of the Sang- ker River, Battambang is one of the country's best-preserved colonial-era towns. Streets of French shophouses host everything from fair-trade cafes to bike excursions. Beyond the town lie the Cambodian countryside and a cluster of ancient temples (p220) – while they're not exactly Angkor Wat, they do, mer- cifully, lack the crowds. Further afield is Prek Toal Bird Sanctuary (p113), a world-class bird sanctuary. Battambang in a word? Charming.

TIM HILL/ALAMY ©

Khmer Cuisine

7 Everyone has tried Thai and Vietnamese specialities before they hit the region, but Khmer cuisine remains under the culinary radar. *Amok* (baked fish with lemongrass, chilli and coconut) is the national dish, but sumptuous seafood and fresh-fish dishes are plentiful, including Kep crab infused with Kampot pepper. It wouldn't be Asia without street snacks and Cambodia delivers everything from noodles (*mee*) and congee (*bobor*; rice porridge) to deep-fried tarantulas and roasted crickets. With subtle spices and delicate herbs, Cambodian food is an unexpected epicurean experience, see p311 for details.

Kratie

8 Gateway to the rare freshwater Irrawaddy dolphins of the Mekong River (p255), Kratie is emerging as a busy crossroads on the overland route between Phnom Penh and northeastern Cambodia or southern Laos. The town has a certain decaying colonial grandeur and boasts some of the country's best Mekong sunsets. Nearby Koh Trong island is a relaxing place to experience a homestay or explore on two wheels. North of Kratie lies the Mekong Discovery Trail, with adventures and experiences themed around the mother river, including community-based homestays, bicycle rides and boat trips.

Prasat Preah Vihear

9 The mother of all mountain temples, Prasat Preah Vihear stands majestically atop the Dangkrek Mountains, forming a controversial border post between Cambodia and Thailand (see p236). The foundation stones of the temple stretch to the edge of the cliff as it falls precipitously away to the plains below, and the views across northern Cambodia are incredible. The 300-year chronology of its construction also offers an insight into the metamorphosis of carving and sculpture during the Angkor period. It's all about location, though, and it doesn't get better than this.

TOM COCKREM/LONELY PLANET IMAGES ©

Ratanakiri

10 The setting for Colonel Kurtz's jungle camp in *Apocalypse Now*, Ratanakiri is one of Cambodia's most remote and pretty provinces. Home to Virachey National Park, one of the largest protected areas in the country, this is serious trekking country. Animal encounters here include elephants and gibbons (p261). Swimming is popular too, with jungle waterfalls and a beautiful crater lake within striking distance of provincial capital Ban Lung (p258). Home to a diverse mosaic of ethnic-minority people, Ratanakiri is a world away from lowland Cambodia.
Kinchaan waterfall (p264)

NICK RAY/LONELY PLANET IMAGES ©

10

need to know

Currency
» The Cambodian currency is the riel (r), but US dollars are universally accepted and act as a dual currency.

Language
» Khmer is the official language, but English and Chinese are also widely spoken in urban areas.

When to Go

Siem Reap
GO Nov–Mar & Jun–Aug

Sen Monorom
GO Year Round

Phnom Penh
GO Year Round

Sihanoukville
GO Nov–Jun

Kep
GO Nov–Jul

■ Tropical Climate, Wet-Dry Seasons

High Season
(Nov–Mar)
» Cool and windy, with almost Mediterranean temperatures; the best all-round time to be here.
» Book accommodation in advance during the peak Christmas and New Year period.

Shoulder
(Jul–Aug)
» Wet in most parts of Cambodia, with high humidity, but the landscapes are emerald green.
» South Coast can be busy at this time of year as Western visitors escape for summer holidays while school is out.

Low Season
(Apr–Jun & Sep–Oct)
» April and May spells hot season, when the mercury hits 40°C and visitors melt.
» September and October can be wet, but awesome storms and cloud formations accompany the deluge.

Your Daily Budget

Budget

US$20–50

» Cheap guesthouse room: US$5–10
» Local meals and street eats: US$1–2
» Local buses: US$2–3 per 100km

Midrange

US$50–150

» Air-con hotel room: US$15–50
» Decent local restaurant meal: US$5–10
» Local tour guide per day: US$25

Top End More than

US$150

» Boutique hotel or resort: US$50–500
» Gastronomic meal with drinks: US$25–50
» 4WD rental per day: US$60–120

Money

» ATMs are now widely available, including in all major tourist centres and provincial capitals. Credit cards are accepted by many hotels and restaurants in larger cities.

Visas

» A tourist visa valid for one month costs US$20 on arrival and requires one passport-sized photo. Easily extendable business visas are available for US$25.

Mobile Phones

» Roaming is possible but is generally very expensive. Local SIM cards and unlocked mobile phones are readily available.

Driving

» In keeping with the French influence, Cambodia drives on the right, although on many roads this isn't always apparent!

Websites

» **Lonely Planet** (www .lonelyplanet.com) The online authority on travel in the Mekong region.

» **Travelfish** (www .travelfish.org) Opinionated articles and reviews.

» **Andy Brouwer's Cambodia Tales** (blog .andybrouwer.co.uk) Gateway to all things Cambodian, includes a popular blog.

» **Khmer Rouge Tribunal** (www.cambo diatribunal.org) Detailed coverage of the Khmer Rouge trials.

» **Phnom Penh Post** (www.phnompenhpost .com) Cambodia's newspaper of record.

Exchange Rates

Australia	A$1	4220r
Canada	C$1	4002r
euro zone	€1	5107r
Japan	¥100	5291r
New Zealand	NZ$1	3257r
Thailand	1B	128r
UK	UK£1	6231r
USA	US$1	4058r

For current exchange rates see www.xe.com.

Important Numbers

Drop the 0 from a regional (city) code when calling Cambodia from another country.

Cambodia code	☎855
International access code	☎001
Phnom Penh	☎023
Siem Reap	☎063
Sihanoukville	☎034

Arriving in Cambodia

» **Phnom Penh Airport** Taxi to centre US$9, around 30 minutes.

» **Siem Reap Airport** Taxi to centre US$7, 15 minutes.

» **Land borders** Shared with Laos, Thailand and Vietnam; Cambodian visas available on arrival.

Travelling Responsibly

In the 20th century alone, Cambodia experienced war, genocide and famine. There are many ways to contribute to the country even during a short stay, however, by engaging with locals in markets and spending money in restaurants and outlets that assist disadvantaged locals. The following websites have more information on sustainable tourism:

Cambodia Community-Based Ecotourism Network (www.ccben.org)

ChildSafe (www.childsafe-cambodia.org) Aims to stop child-sex tourism and protect vulnerable children from exploitation.

ConCERT (www.concertcambodia.org) Connecting communities and tourism.

Mekong Discovery Trail (www.mekongdiscoverytrail.org) Community-based tourism initiatives on the upper Mekong.

Stay Another Day (www.stay-another-day.org) Ideas on day trips and project visits.

if you like...

Temples

Cambodia is home to some of the world's most spectacular temples. Angkor is the temple heavyweight thanks to monumental Angkor Wat, the enigmatic Bayon, the iconic tree roots of Ta Prohm...and the list goes on. But northwestern Cambodia is home to forgotten jungle temples and pre-Angkorian capitals.

Angkor Wat The one and only, the temple that puts all others in the shade. If they were handing out 'wonders of the world' accolades today, Angkor Wat would be first in the queue (p125).

Ta Prohm Iconic tree roots locked in a muscular embrace with ancient stones; this is the *Tomb Raider* temple where Angelina Jolie once roamed (p142).

Prasat Preah Vihear The most mountainous of all the Khmer mountain temples, it is perched imperiously on the cliff-face of the Dangkrek Mountains (p233).

Sambor Prei Kuk The pre-Angkorian capital of Isanapura was the first temple city in the Mekong region and is a chronological staging post on the road to Angkor (p240).

Islands & Beaches

Southern Cambodia boasts a lengthy and beautiful coastline with idyllic islands lurking not far offshore. Don't expect Thailand-style development; these islands have barely been discovered, making them perfect for aspiring Robinson Crusoes. Do expect beauty on par with anything southeast Asia has to offer.

Sihanoukville King of the Cambodian beach resorts, with a headland ringed by squeaky white sands. Centrally located Sokha Beach is a gem, while Otres Beach offers a more subdued vibe (p175).

Koh Rong & Koh Rong Samloem More and more resorts are cropping up on the long, lonely white-sand beaches of these neighbouring islands two hours off Sihanoukville (p171).

Koh Kong No shortage of dreamy beaches on practically uninhabited Koh Kong Island and the cluster of islands just off Botum Sakor National Park (p169).

Kep Cambodia's original beach resort, Kep was devastated by war but has resurrected itself in recent years with boutique resorts and succulent seafood (p195).

Epicurean Experiences

There is no surer way to spice up your life than with a culinary odyssey through Cambodia. Check out cutting-edge Khmer restaurants in the capital or learn the tricks of the trade with a Cambodian cooking class in the provinces. Go global with a range of menus from around the world, including Chinese, French, Indian, Italian, Lebanese, Mexican and Vietnamese.

Phnom Penh Dine to make a difference at one of Phnom Penh's many training restaurants to help the disadvantaged (p63).

Siem Reap Browse the lively restaurants of the Old Market area and choose from exotic barbecues, mod Khmer cuisine or stop-and-dip food stalls (p102).

Sihanoukville Sample succulent seafood at Cambodia's leading beach resort, including fresh crab, prawn and squid, cooked up with Kampot pepper (p181).

Battambang Discover the delights of Cambodian cooking with a cheap and cheerful cooking class in this relaxed riverside town (p215).

» Boats at the floating market near Chong Kneas (p116) on Tonlé Sap lake

Water Features

River cruises are incredibly popular along parts of the Mekong River – including luxurious options linking Siem Reap, Phnom Penh, and Ho Chi Minh City in Vietnam – and its tributaries in the northeast offer jungle excursions straight out of *Apocalypse Now*. The Tonlé Sap lake is home to otherworldly floating villages and the Prek Toal Biosphere, home to rare water birds. In the far northeast are plunging waterfalls and pristine crater lakes.

Mekong Discovery Trail See rare freshwater dolphins, cycle around remote Mekong islands or experience a local family homestay (see the box, p253).

Tonlé Sap lake Discover floating villages, bamboo skyscrapers, flooded forest and rare birdlife with a boat trip on Cambodia's Great Lake (p113).

Boeng Yeak Loam Small but perfectly formed, this jungle-clad crater lake is Cambodia's most inviting natural swimming pool (p259).

Bou Sraa Waterfall One of Cambodia's biggest set of falls, this roars out of the jungle in remote Mondulkiri Province (p271).

Off-the-Beaten-Track Adventures

If you are looking for a classic Asian adventure, then you have come to the right place. Choose from tough treks in national parks, animal encounters in remote jungle, exploring karst cave systems or motorbiking along ancient Angkor roads.

Elephant Valley Project Learn about elephants in their element by experiencing a walk with the herd in remote Mondulkiri Province (p250).

Virachey National Park Disappear for a week into the wild life-rich forest of this remote northeastern Cambodian natural treasure (p266).

Kampot Cave Pagodas Go underground at Kampot Province's cave pagodas, perfectly preserved since the 6th century in their own microclimate (p194).

Cardamom Mountains Penetrate the vast rainforests of the remote Cardamoms like an explorer of old (p164).

Motorbiking 'Route 66' to Preah Khan Follow the ancient Angkorian highway from Beng Mealea to Preah Khan temple in Preah Vihear Province (p236).

Nightlife

For some visitors, Cambodia by night is just as much fun as Cambodia by day. Join the nightshift to discover Cambodian beer gardens, hole-in-the-wall pubs, designer bars and serious nightclubs. Phnom Penh is Cambodia's nightlife capital and rumbles on 24 hours a day. Siem Reap and Sihanoukville come a close joint second.

Phnom Penh This is where Cambodia rocks. Warm up with a riverfront happy hour, crawl around the Wat Langka area and end up in a nightclub (p70).

Siem Reap There are so many bars around town that in fact that one strip has earned itself the accolade of Pub St. Stay late for the alternative Angkor sunrise (p106).

Sihanoukville Home to a hedonistic crowd, the beachfront strips of Serendipity and Occheuteal have long been party central on the coast (p184).

month by month

Top Events

1 **Khmer New Year** April

2 **Chinese New Year** January/February

3 **P'chum Ben** September/October

4 **Bon Om Tuk** October/November

5 **Angkor International Half Marathon** December

January

This is peak tourist season in Cambodia with Phnom Penh, Siem Reap and the South Coast heaving as Europeans and Americans escape the winter chill. Chinese and Vietnamese New Years sometimes fall in this month too.

Chaul Chnam Chen (Chinese New Year)

The Chinese inhabitants of Cambodia celebrate their New Year somewhere between late January and mid-February – for the Vietnamese, this is Tet. As many of Phnom Penh's businesses are run by Chinese, commerce grinds to a halt around this time and there are dragon dances all over town. Many Vietnamese living in Cambodia return to their homeland for a week or more.

February

Still one of the busiest times of year for tourist arrivals, February is also often the month for Chinese and Vietnamese New Years. Young Cambodians swoon as Valentine's Day comes around.

Giant Puppet Parade

This colourful annual fund-raising event takes place in Siem Reap. Local organisations, orphanages and businesses come together to create giant puppets in the shape of animals, deities and contemporary characters, and the whole ensemble winds its way along the Siem Reap River like a scene from the Mardi Gras.

April

This is the most important month in the calendar for Khmers, as the New Year comes in the middle of April. For tourists it's a possible month to avoid, as the mercury regularly hits 40°C.

Chaul Chnam Khmer (Khmer New Year)

This is a three-day celebration of the Khmer New Year, and it's like Christmas, New Year and a birthday all rolled into one. Cambodians make offerings at wats, clean out their homes, and exchange gifts. It is a lively time to visit the country as the Khmers go wild with water in the countryside. Throngs of Khmers flock to Angkor, and it's absolute madness at most temples, so avoid the celebration if you want a quiet, reflective Angkor experience. That said, it is nowhere near as excessive as in Thailand or Laos, so it might seem tame by comparison.

May

This is the beginning of the low season for visitors as the monsoon arrives (and lasts till August), but there may be a last blast of hot weather to welcome mango season and some delicious ripe fruits.

Chat Preah Nengkal (Royal Ploughing Ceremony)

Led by the royal family, the Royal Ploughing Ceremony is a ritual agricultural festival held to mark the traditional beginning of the rice-growing season. It takes place in early May in front of the National Museum, near the Royal Palace in Phnom Penh, and the royal oxen are said to have a nose for whether it will be a good harvest or a bad one.

⭐ Visakha Puja (Buddha Day)

A celebration of Buddha's birth, enlightenment and *parinibbana* (passing). Activities are centred on wats. The festival falls on the eighth day of the fourth moon (May or June) and is best observed at Angkor Wat, where you can see candle-lit processions of monks.

September

Traditionally the wettest month in Cambodia, September is usually a time of sporadic flooding along the Mekong. The calendar's second most important festival, P'chum Ben, usually falls in this month.

⭐ P'chum Ben (Festival of the Dead)

This festival is a kind of All Souls' Day, when respects are paid to the dead through offerings made at wats. Offerings include paper money, candles, flowers and incense, as well as food and drink, all passed through the medium of the monks. P'chum Ben lasts for several days and devout Buddhists are expected to visit seven wats during the festival. Head to the village of Vihear Sour in Kandal Province, about 35km northeast of Phnom Penh, to witness authentic bareback buffalo racing and traditional Khmer wrestling.

October

The rains often linger long into October and this has led to some major flooding in Siem Reap in recent years. However, the countryside is extraordinarily green at this time.

⭐ Bon Om Tuk (Water Festival)

Celebrating the epic victory of Jayavarman VII over the Chams, who occupied Angkor in 1177, this festival also marks the extraordinary natural phenomenon of the reversal of the current of the Tonlé Sap River. It's one of the most important festivals in the Khmer calendar and is a wonderful, chaotic time to be in Phnom Penh or Siem Reap. Boat races are held on the Tonlé Sap and Siem Reap Rivers, with each boat colourfully decorated and holding 40 rowers. As many as two million people flood the capital for the fun and frolics, so be sure to book ahead for accommodation. Sadly, this event was marred by tragedy in 2010 when a stampede developed on a bridge connecting the city with nearby Koh Pich (Diamond Island). More than 350 people died in the resulting crush.

November

November brings the dry, windy season and signals the start of the best period to be in the country (which extends through until January or February). Bon Om Tuk often comes around in November.

⭐ Angkor Photo Festival

This photo festival has become a regular on the Siem Reap calendar. Resident and regional photographers descend on the temples and team up with local youths to teach them the tricks of the trade. Photography exhibitions are staged all over town.

December

Christmas and New Year are the peak of the peak season at Angkor and leading beach resorts; book a long way ahead. Sign up for a marathon or cycle ride if you fancy doing something for charity.

🏃 Angkor Wat International Half Marathon

This has been a fixture in the Angkor calendar for 15 years. Choose from a 21km half marathon, a 10km fun run or various bicycle races and rides. It may not be as famous as the London or New York marathons, but it's hard to imagine a better backdrop to a road race than the incredible temples of Angkor.

itineraries

Whether you've got a week or a month, these itineraries provide a starting point for a journey to remember. Want more inspiration? Head online to lonelyplanet.com/thorntree to chat with other travellers.

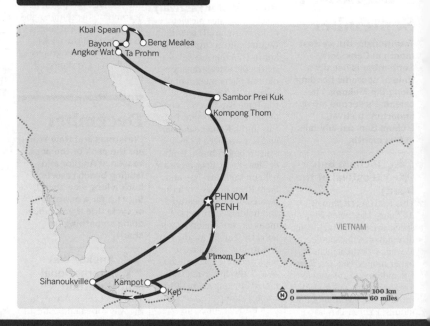

Two Weeks
Cambodia Snapshot

> This is the ultimate journey, via temples, beaches and the capital. Hit **Phnom Penh** for its impressive **National Museum** and stunning **Silver Pagoda**. There's superb shopping at the **Psar Tuol Tom Pong**, and a **night shift** that never sleeps.
>
> Take a fast boat to **Phnom Da**, then go south to the colonial-era town of **Kampot**. From here, visit Bokor Hill Station, the seaside town of **Kep** and nearby cave pagodas.
>
> Go west to **Sihanoukville**, Cambodia's beach capital, to sample the seafood, dive the nearby waters or just soak up the sun. Backtrack via Phnom Penh to **Kompong Thom** and visit the pre-Angkorian brick temples of **Sambor Prei Kuk**.
>
> Finish the trip at Angkor, a mind-blowing experience with which few sights compare. See **Angkor Wat**, perfection in stone; **Bayon**, weirdness in stone; and **Ta Prohm**, nature triumphing over stone – before venturing further afield to **Kbal Spean** or jungle-clad **Beng Mealea**.
>
> This trip can take two weeks at a steady pace or three weeks at a slow pace. Public transport serves most of this route.

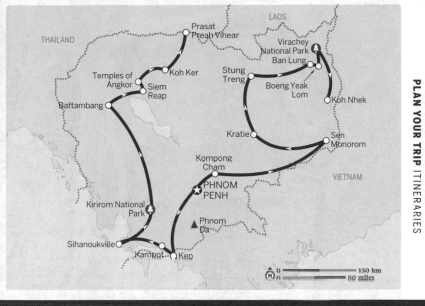

One Month
The Big One

Cambodia is a small country and even though the roads are sometimes bad and travel can be slow, most of the big hitters can be visited in a month.

Setting out from the hip capital that is **Phnom Penh**, take in the beauty of the northeast, following the Run to the Hills itinerary. Choose between **Ratanakiri Province** and the volcanic crater lake of Boeng Yeak Lom, or **Mondulkiri Province** and the original Elephant Valley Project to ensure maximum time elsewhere. The gentle hills of Mondulkiri are better for budget travellers as traversing overland is easy, while Ratanakiri makes sense for those planning an overland journey between Cambodia and Laos. Both offer new primate experiences for those that fancy a bit of monkey business along the way. Tough choice...can't decide? Flip a coin, if you can find one in this coinless country.

Head to the South Coast, taking the route outlined in the Cambodia Snapshot itinerary. Take your time and consider a few nights in **Kep** or on one of the nearby islands, and a boat trip from **Sihanoukville** to explore the up-and-coming islands off the coast. Turning back inland, check out **Kirirom National Park**, home to pine trees, black bears and some spectacular views of the Cardamom Mountains.

Then it's time to go northwest to charming **Battambang**, one of Cambodia's best-preserved colonial-era towns and a base from which to discover rural life. Take the proverbial slow boat to **Siem Reap**, passing through stunning scenery along the snaking Sangker River, and turn your attention to the **temples of Angkor**.

Visit all the greatest hits in and around Angkor, but set aside some extra time to venture further to the rival capital of **Koh Ker**, which is cloaked in thick jungle, or **Prasat Preah Vihear**, a mountain temple perched precariously atop a cliff on the Thai border.

Overlanders can run this route in reverse, setting out from Siem Reap and exiting Cambodia by river into Vietnam or Laos. Entering from Laos, divert east to Ratanakiri before heading south. Getting around is generally easy, as there are buses on the big roads, taxis on the small roads and buzzing boats on the many rivers.

» (above) Ta Prohm temple (p142), Angkor
» (left) Fishing boats, Kompong Ch (p245)

TIM HALL/GETTY IMAGES ©

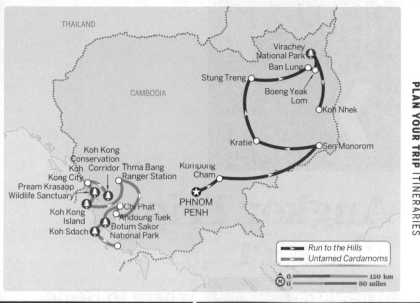

THAILAND

Virachey
National Park
Ban Lung
Stung Treng
Boeng Yeak
Lom
CAMBODIA
Koh Nhek

Kratie
Sen Monorom

Koh Kong
Conservation
Koh Corridor   Thma Bang   Kompong
Kong City   Ranger Station   Cham
Pream Krasaop
Wildlife Sanctuary
                 Chi Phat   PHNOM
Koh Kong   Andoung Tuek   PENH
Island   Botum Sakor
Koh Sdach   National Park

Run to the Hills
Untamed Cardamoms

0 ___ 150 km
0 ___ 80 miles

Two Weeks
Untamed Cardamoms

Ten Days
Run to the Hills

Get a sense of the diverse ecosystems of the Cardamom Mountains along the Koh Kong Conservation Corridor. Start at one-time smugglers' port **Koh Kong**, a good base for day trips through the pristine mangrove forests of **Peam Krasaop Wildlife Sanctuary**, and to **Koh Kong Island**, with seven unspoiled beaches. Then travel inland by moto or boat to the **Tatai River**, where ecologically sustainable accommodation is available. Drive to **Thma Bang ranger station** to explore the Areng River habitats of the endangered dragonfish and Siamese crocodile.

Continue east along NH48 to **Andoung Tuek** and cruise upriver to **Chi Phat**, a pioneering community-based ecotourism project. Return to Andoung Tuek and set your sights on the **Koh Sdach Archipelago**, off **Botum Sakor National Park**. There's accommodation on **Koh Sdach** and **Koh Tatong**, both near excellent snorkelling grounds.

A daily boat links Koh Sdach with Sihanoukville, where you can continue island hopping to the popular **Koh Rong** and **Koh Rong Samloem** or explore more ecotourism opportunities in nearby **Ream National Park**.

Northeast Cambodia, a notably much cooler region of rolling hills and secret waterfalls, is home to a patchwork of ethnic minorities.

Leaving **Phnom Penh**, pass through the bustling Mekong town of **Kompong Cham** before heading east to **Sen Monorom**, the charming capital of Mondulkiri Province. Spend a few days here to walk with the herd at the Elephant Valley Project and explore Bunong villages before heading back to the Mekong at **Kratie**, for an encounter with elusive Irrawaddy river dolphins.

Push north up the Mekong to **Stung Treng Province**, site of several budding ecotourism excursions. To the east lies **Ban Lung**, capital of Ratanakiri Province and base for an adventure to remember. From here plunge into Cambodia's most beautiful natural swimming pool at **Boeng Yeak Lom**, visit ethnic-minority villages around **Voen Sai**, or trek deep into the forests of **Virachey National Park**.

This trip is easy to manage using share taxis or pick-ups, but it's a challenge in the wet season. Experienced motorbikers can link Mondulkiri and Ratanakiri Provinces via **Koh Nhek** village on one of Cambodia's more devilish roads.

Angkor Trip Planner

When to Go

November–March Quite cool, but popular
June–August Wet season, with lush green landscapes and light crowds

Best Temple

Bayon Top for inspirational expression.

Best Bas-Reliefs

Angkor Wat Almost 1km of art cast in stone, including the Churning of the Ocean of Milk.

Best Jungle Temple

Ta Prohm Nature runs riot at the '*Tomb Raider* temple'.

Best Carvings

Banteay Srei Some of the finest carvings on earth.

Best Remote Temple

Beng Mealea The *Titanic* of temples, smothered in jungle.

Best Jungle Trek

Kbal Spean Hike through the rainforest to the River of a Thousand Lingas.

Best Lingas

Koh Ker Whether you prefer length or girth, the ones at Prasat Ling, Koh Ker, are huge.

Where to Begin

Abandoned to the jungles for centuries, the magnificent temples are set amid the region's oldest national park, with towering trees and a refreshing lack of modern development amid the audacious architecture. With such a wealth of temples, it is also possible to plan a peaceful pilgrimage here, far from the madding crowds, which really are madding at some temples at certain times of day, particularly during the peak season.

Some visitors assume they'll be quickly templed out, but the diversity of the design, which switches dramatically from one god-king to another, is fascinating. Come face to face (literally) with Bayon, one of the world's weirdest buildings; experience the excitement of the first European explorers at Ta Prohm, where nature runs riot; or follow the sacred River of a Thousand Lingas like pilgrims of old. The most vexing part is working out what to see. If any of the 'second-string' holy sites were anywhere else in the region they would have top billing. One day at Angkor? Sacrilege! Don't even consider it – there is no greater concentration of architectural riches anywhere on earth.

Admission Fees

While the cost of entry to Angkor is relatively expensive by Cambodian standards, the fees represent excellent value. Visitors have a choice of a one-day pass (US$20), a three-day pass (US$40) or a one-week pass (US$60). An improved system was introduced in 2009 that allows three-day passes to run over three non-consecutive days in a one-week period and one-week passes to last for a full month. Purchase the entry pass from the large official entrance booth on the road to Angkor Wat. The **Angkor ticket checkpoint** (Map p114) is due to move location during the lifetime of this book and will reopen near the new Apsara Authority headquarters. Passes include a digital photo snapped at the entrance booth, so queues can be slow at peak times. Visitors entering after 5pm get a free sunset, as the ticket starts from the following day. The fee includes access to all the monuments in the Siem Reap area but not the sacred mountain of Phnom Kulen or the remote complexes of Beng Mealea and Koh Ker.

Entry tickets to the temples of Angkor are controlled by local hotel chain Sokha Hotels, part of a local petroleum conglomerate called Sokimex, which, in return for administrating the site, takes 17% of the revenue. Apsara Authority (see the box, p130), the body responsible for protecting and conserving the temples, takes 68% for operating costs, and 15% goes to restoration. A South Korean company is due to take over the concession in 2012.

Most of the major temples now have uniformed guards to check the tickets, which has reduced the opportunity for scams. A pass is not required for excursions to villages around or beyond Angkor, but you still have to stop at the checkpoint to explain your movements to the guards.

Itineraries

Back in the early days of tourism, the problem of what to see and in what order came down to two basic temple itineraries: the Small (Petit) Circuit and the Big (Grand) Circuit, both marked on the Temples of Angkor map (Map p126). It's difficult to imagine that anyone follows these to the letter any more, but in their time they were an essential component of the Angkor experience and were often undertaken on the back of an elephant.

For tips on the best times to visit particular temples, the best locations for sunrise

TEMPLE-PASS WARNING!

Visitors found inside any of the main temples without a ticket will be fined a whopping US$100.

and sunset, and avoiding the hordes, see the box, p25.

Small Circuit

The 17km Small Circuit begins at Angkor Wat and heads north to Phnom Bakheng, Baksei Chamkrong and Angkor Thom, including the city wall and gates, the Bayon, the Baphuon, the Royal Enclosure, Phimeanakas, Preah Palilay, the Terrace of the Leper King, the Terrace of Elephants, the Kleangs and Prasat Suor Prat. It exits from Angkor Thom via the Victory Gate in the eastern wall, and continues to Chau Say Tevoda, Thommanon, Spean Thmor and Ta Keo. It then heads northeast of the road to Ta Nei, turns south to Ta Prohm, continues east to Banteay Kdei and Sra Srang, and finally returns to Angkor Wat via Prasat Kravan.

Big Circuit

The 26km Big Circuit is an extension of the Small Circuit: instead of exiting the walled city of Angkor Thom at the east gate, the Grand Circuit exits at the north gate and continues to Preah Khan and Preah Neak Poan, east to Ta Som, then south via the Eastern Mebon to Pre Rup. From there it heads west and then southwest on its return to Angkor Wat.

One Day

If you have only one day to visit Angkor, a good itinerary would be Angkor Wat for sunrise and then sticking around to explore the mighty temple while it's quieter. From there continue to the tree roots of Ta Prohm before breaking for lunch. In the afternoon, explore the temples within the walled city of Angkor Thom and the beauty of the Bayon in the late-afternoon light.

Two Days

A two-day itinerary allows time to include some of the other big hitters around Angkor. Spend the first day visiting petite Banteay Srei, with its fabulous carvings; stop at Banteay Samré on the return leg. In the afternoon, visit immense Preah Khan, delicate Preah Neak Poan and the tree roots of Ta Som, before taking in a sunset at Pre Rup. Spend the second day following the one-day itinerary to Angkor Wat, Ta Prohm and Angkor Thom.

Three to Five Days

If you have three to five days to explore Angkor, it's possible to see most of the important sites. One approach is to see as much as possible on the first day or two (as covered earlier) and then spend the final days combining visits to other sites such as the Roluos temples and Banteay Kdei. Better still is a gradual build-up to the most spectacular monuments. After all, if you see Angkor Wat on the first day, then a temple like Ta Keo just won't cut it. Another option is a chronological approach, starting with the earliest Angkorian temples and working steadily forwards in time to Angkor Thom, taking stock of the evolution of Khmer architecture and artistry.

It is well worth making the trip to the River of a Thousand Lingas at Kbal Spean for the chance to stretch your legs amid natural and human-made splendour, or the remote, vast and overgrown temple of Beng Mealea. Both can be combined with Banteay Srei in one long day.

One Week

Those with the time to spend a week at Angkor will be richly rewarded. Not only is it possible to fit all the temples of the region into an itinerary, but a longer stay also allows for non-temple activities, such as relaxing by a pool, indulging in a spa treatment or shopping around Siem Reap. Check out the aforementioned itineraries for some ideas on approach, but relax in the knowledge that you'll see it all. You may also want to throw in some of the more remote sites such as Koh Ker, Prasat Preah Vihear or Banteay Chhmar.

Tours

Most budget and midrange travellers not on package tours prefer to take in the temples at their own pace. However, visitors who have only a day or two at this incredible site may prefer something organised locally.

It is possible to link up with an official tour guide in Siem Reap. The **Khmer**

Angkor Tour Guides Association ($\boxed{\mathbb{J}}$063-964347; www.khmerangkortourguide.com) represents some of Angkor's authorised guides. English- or French-speaking guides can be booked from US$20 to US$30 a day; guides speaking other languages, such as Italian, German, Spanish, Japanese and Chinese, are available at a higher rate, as there are fewer of them.

For an organised tour around Angkor, check out the recommended Cambodian operators on p341. Other good Siem Reap–based companies:

Beyond (www.beyonduniqueescapes.com) Beng Mealea, Kompong Pluk, cycling trips and cooking classes.

Buffalo Trails (www.buffalotrails-cambodia .com) Ecotours and lifestyle adventures around Siem Reap.

Grasshopper Adventures (www.grasshop peradventures.com) Cycling tours around Angkor or to Beng Mealea.

Sam Veasna Center (Map p92; www.sam veasna.org) Day trips that combine birdwatching with visits to outlying temples.

Terre Cambodge (www.terrecambodge.com) Remote sites around Angkor, some by bicycle, plus boat trips on the Tonlé Sap lake.

Getting There & Around

Visitors heading to the temples of Angkor – in other words pretty much everybody coming to Cambodia – need to consider the most suitable way to travel between the temples. Many of the best-known temples are no more than a few kilometres from the walled city of Angkor Thom, which is just 8km from Siem Reap, and can be visited using anything from a car or motorcycle to a sturdy pair of walking boots. For the independent traveller, there is a daunting range of alternatives to consider.

For the ultimate Angkor experience, try a pick-and-mix approach, with a moto, *remork-moto* or car for one day to cover the remote sites, a bicycle to experience the central temples, and an exploration on foot for a spot of peace and serenity.

Transport will be more expensive to remote temples such as Banteay Srei or Beng Mealea, due to extra fuel costs.

DODGING THE CROWDS

Let's be honest: we know some of you are a little cynical when it comes to following our advice on avoiding other tourists. Sure, a lot of other travellers are carrying Lonely Planet's *Cambodia*, but bear in mind that they are a fraction of the overall numbers. Vietnamese, South Korean and Chinese travellers together accounted for around 580,000 visitors in the first six months of 2011, or more than half of all visitors. Very few, if any, are carrying the Lonely Planet, but are visiting the temples in groups of 25 to 75 people at a time. So we suggest you pay close attention to the following advice.

Angkor is on the tourist trail and is getting busier by the year but, with a little planning, it is still possible to escape the hordes. One important thing to remember, particularly when it comes to sunrise and sunset, is that places are popular for a reason, and it is worth going with the flow at least once.

It is received wisdom that as Angkor Wat faces west, one should be there for late afternoon, and in the case of the Bayon, which faces east, in the morning. Ta Prohm, most people seem to agree, can be visited in the middle of the day because of its umbrella of foliage. This is all well and good, but if you reverse the order, the temples will still look good – and you can avoid some of the crowds.

The most popular place for sunrise is Angkor Wat. Most tour groups head back to town for breakfast, so stick around and explore the temple while it's cool and quiet between 7am and 9am. Bayon sees far fewer visitors than Angkor Wat in the early hours. Sra Srang is usually pretty quiet, and sunrise here can be spectacular thanks to reflections in the extensive waters. Phnom Bakheng could be an attractive option, because the sun comes up behind Angkor Wat and you are far from the madding crowd that gathers here at sunset, but there are now strict limitations on visitor numbers each day. Ta Prohm is an alternative option, with no sight of sunrise, but a mysterious and magical atmosphere.

The definitive sunset spot is the hilltop temple of Phnom Bakheng. This was getting well out of control, with as many as 1000 tourists clambering around the small structure. However, new restrictions limit visitors to no more than 300 at any one time. It is generally better to check it out for sunrise or early morning and miss the crowds. Staying within the confines of Angkor Wat for sunset is a rewarding option, as it can be pretty peaceful when most tourists head off to Phnom Bakheng around 4.30pm or so. Pre Rup is popular with some for an authentic rural sunset over the countryside, but this is starting to get very busy. Better is the hilltop temple of Phnom Krom, which offers commanding views across Tonlé Sap lake, but involves a long drive back to town in the dark. The Western Baray takes in the sunset from the eastern end, across its vast waters, or from Western Mebon island, and is generally a quiet option.

When it comes to the most popular temples, the middle of the day is generally the quietest time. This is because the majority of the large tour groups head back to Siem Reap for lunch. It is also the hottest part of the day, which makes it tough going around relatively open temples such as Banteay Srei and the Bayon, but fine at well-covered temples such as Ta Prohm, Preah Khan and Beng Mealea, or even the bas-reliefs at Angkor Wat. The busiest times at Angkor Wat are from 6am to 7am and 3pm to 5pm; at the Bayon, from 8am to 10am; and at Banteay Srei, mid-morning and mid-afternoon. However, at other popular temples, such as Ta Prohm and Preah Khan, the crowds are harder to predict, and at most other temples in the Angkor region it's just a case of pot luck. If you pull up outside and see a car park full of tour buses, you may want to move on to somewhere quieter. The wonderful thing about Angkor is that there is always another temple to explore.

Bicycle

A great way to get around the temples, bicycles are environmentally friendly and are used by most locals. There are few hills and the roads are good, so there's no need for much cycling experience. Moving about at a slower speed, you soon find that you take in more than from out of a car window or on the back of a speeding moto.

GUIDE TO THE GUIDES

Countless books on Angkor have been written over the years, with more and more new titles coming out, reflecting Angkor's rebirth as one of the world's cultural hot spots. Here are just a few of the best:

A Guide to the Angkor Monuments (Maurice Glaize)The definitive guide, downloadable for free at www.theangkorguide.com.

A Passage Through Angkor (Mark Standen) One of the best photographic records of the temples.

A Pilgrimage to Angkor (Pierre Loti) One of the most beautifully written books on Angkor, based on the author's 1910 journey.

Ancient Angkor (Claudes Jacques) Written by one of the foremost scholars on Angkor, this is the most readable guide to the temples, with photos by Michael Freeman.

Angkor: An Introduction to the Temples (Dawn Rooney) Probably the most popular contemporary guide.

Angkor: Millennium of Glory (various authors) A fascinating introduction to the history, culture, sculpture and religion of the Angkorian period.

Angkor – Heart of an Asian Empire (Bruno Dagens) The story of the 'discovery' of Angkor, complete with lavish illustrations.

Angkor: Splendours of the Khmer Civilisation (Marilia Albanese) Beautifully photographed guide to the major temples, including some of the more remote places in northern Cambodia.

Khmer Heritage in the Old Siamese Provinces of Cambodia (Etienne Aymonier) Aymonier journeyed through Cambodia in 1901 and visited many of the major temples.

The Customs of Cambodia (Chou Ta-Kuan) The only eyewitness account of Angkor, by a Chinese emissary who spent a year at the Khmer capital in the late 13th century.

White Bicycles (www.thewhitebicycles.org; per day US$2) is supported by some guesthouses around town, with proceeds from the hire fee going towards community projects. Many guesthouses and hotels in town rent bikes for around US$1 to US$2 per day.

Some places, like Trek or Giant, offer better mountain bikes for US$7 to US$10 per day. Try **Travel Loops** (☑063-963776; www.cyclingincambodia.com; Sivatha St, Siem Reap), with Cannondale road bikes for US$5 and mountain bikes with helmet for US$10.

Car & Motorcycle

Cars are a popular choice for getting about the temples. The obvious advantage is protection from the elements, be it heavy downpours or the punishing sun. Shared between several travellers, they can also be an economical way to explore. The downside is that visitors are a little more isolated from the sights, sounds and smells as they travel between temples. A car for the day around the central temples is US$25 to US$35 and can be arranged with hotels, guesthouses and agencies in town.

Motorcycle rental in Siem Reap is currently prohibited, but some travellers bring a motorcycle from Phnom Penh. If you manage to get a bike up here, leave it at a guarded parking area or with a stallholder outside each temple; otherwise it could get stolen.

Elephant

Travelling by elephant was the traditional way to see the temples way back in the early days of tourism at Angkor, at the start of the 20th century. It is once again possible to take an elephant ride between the south gate of Angkor Thom and the Bayon (US$10) in the morning, or up to the summit of Phnom Bakheng for sunset (US$15). The elephants are owned by the **Angkor Village** (www.angkorvillage.com) resort group. Some tourists have complained about the elephants being poorly treated by handlers.

Helicopter & Hot-Air Balloon

For those with plenty of spending money, there are tourist flights around Angkor Wat

(US\$90) and the temples outside Angkor Thom (US\$150) with **Helicopters Cambodia** (✆012 814500; www.helicopterscambodia .com; 658 Hup Quan St, Siem Reap). The company also offers charters to remote temples such as Prasat Preah Vihear and Preah Khan, with prices starting at around US\$2250 per hour. Newer company **Helistar** (✆063 966072; www.helistarcambodia.com; 24 Sivatha St, Siem Reap) is another option for scenic flights and charters.

Angkor Balloon (Map p126; ✆012 759698; per person US\$15) offers a bird's-eye view of Angkor Wat. The balloon carries up to 30 people, is on a fixed line and rises 200m above the landscape.

Minibus

Minibuses are available from various hotels and travel agents around town. A 12-seat minibus costs from US\$50 per day, while a 25- or 30-seat coaster bus is around US\$80 to US\$100 per day.

Moto

Many independent travellers end up visiting the temples by moto. Moto drivers accost visitors from the moment they set foot in Siem Reap, but they often end up being knowledgeable and friendly, and good companions for a tour around the temples. They can drop you off and pick you up at allotted times and places and even tell you a bit of background about the temples as you zip around. Many of the better drivers go on to become official tour guides.

Remork-Moto

Motorcycles with twee little hooded carriages towed behind, these are also known as *remorks* or túk-túks. They are a popular way to get around Angkor as fellow travellers can still talk to each other as they explore (unlike on the back of a moto). They also offer some protection from the rain. As with moto drivers, some *remork* drivers are very good companions for a tour of the temples. Prices run from US\$10 to US\$20 for the day, depending on the destination and number of passengers.

Walking

Why not forget all these newfangled methods and simply explore on foot? There are obvious limitations to what can be seen, as some temples are just too far from Siem Reap. However, it is easy enough to walk to Angkor Wat and the temples of Angkor Thom, and this is a great way to meet up with villagers in the area. Those who want to get away from the roads should try the peaceful walk along the walls of Angkor Thom. It is about 13km in total, and offers access to several small, remote temples and some bird life. Another rewarding walk is from Ta Nei to Ta Keo through the forest. For more on trekking around the temples, see p136.

Travel with Children

Best Regions for Kids

Phnom Penh
The city has a good selection of swimming pools and even a go-kart track. Boat trips on the river should be a hit, but best of all is the nearby Phnom Tamao Wildlife Rescue Centre, with tigers, sun bears and elephants.

Siem Reap
Cambodian Cultural Village may be kitsch, but it's the right tonic after the temples. Hot-air balloons, helicopter rides, quad biking and horse riding round off the action-packed options.

Temples of Angkor
The temples may be too much for littlies but will be appreciated by older children. Kids are amazed by the jungle roots of Ta Prohm and the immense four-faced gates of Angkor Thom.

South Coast
The beaches and islands around Sihanoukville and Kep will be a big hit. The cave pagodas of Kampot will wow your wannabe Indiana Jones or Lara Croft.

Eastern Cambodia
Children are sure to appreciate the cooler climes of Mondulkiri and Ratanakiri, and attractions include thundering waterfalls and walking with elephants.

Cambodia for Kids

There's plenty to keep kids happy in Phnom Penh, Siem Reap and the South Coast, but in the smaller provincial towns the boredom factor might creep in.

Your young travel companions can live it up in Cambodia, as they are always the centre of attention and almost everybody wants to play with them. This goes double for exotic-looking foreign children from far-away lands. In short, expect your children become instant celebrities wherever they go.

Khmers are generally not backwards in coming forwards with children and this extends to pinching cheeks and patting bums. While your child might tolerate this from the Great Aunt they see once in a blue moon, they may object when it's happening a dozen times a day with random people in the street.

For the full picture on surviving and thriving while travelling, check out Lonely Planet's *Travel with Children* by Cathy Lanigan, which contains useful advice on how to cope on the road, with a focus on travel in developing countries. There is also a rundown on health precautions for kids and advice on travel during pregnancy.

Children's Highlights
Activities

» Elephant Valley Project, Mondulkiri Province – great for older children to learn about the real life of a pachyderm.

Lakes & Waterfalls

» Ratanakiri – swim in Yeak Loam, the best natural swimming pool in Cambodia, or clamber around jungle waterfalls.

Temples

» Bayon, Angkor – weird and wonderful faces to inspire building-block or meccano madness.

» Ta Prohm, Angkor – Nature run amok; the kids can imagine they're Indiana Jones or Lara Croft.

Beaches

» Sihanoukville – the number one beach spot, with soft sand, nearby peaceful islands and lots of hotels with pools.

» Kep – boutique resorts with funky pools, a jungle backdrop and accessible islands.

Planning

Amenities specially geared towards young children – such as safety seats for cars or nappy-changing facilities in public restrooms – are virtually nonexistent. It is sometimes possible to arrange a child seat if booking a regional tour through a high-end travel agent, but otherwise parents have to be extra resourceful in seeking out substitutes.

Cot beds are available in international-standard midrange and top-end hotels, but not elsewhere. However, many hotels are happy to add an extra bed or a mattress for a nominal charge. Consider investing in a sturdy hammock or two if travelling to lesser-known destinations.

Baby formula and nappies (diapers) are available at minimarts and supermarkets in the larger towns and cities. Nappy-rash cream and teething gel is sold at pharmacies. Breastfeeding in public is quite common, so there is no need to worry about crossing a cultural boundary.

Hauling around little ones can be a challenge. Pavements and footpaths are often too crowded to push a stroller, especially today's full-sized SUV versions. Instead opt for a compact umbrella pushchair that can squeeze past the storm drain and the noodle cart and that can be folded up and thrown in a *remork*.

Health & Safety

» Encourage regular hand washing

» Watch what infants and toddlers are putting into their mouths (dysentery, typhoid and hepatitis are common)

» Keep children's hydration levels up

» Regularly apply sunscreen

» Never let kids play with animals, even (especially) dogs and monkeys. Rabies is present in Cambodia, and monkeys often bite.

» Use child-friendly mosquito repellents around dusk and arrange for kids to sleep under a mozzie net in remote areas, especially in the wet season

» Guard against sandflies on beaches. If infected, sandfly bites can cause complications; use plasters and encourage children to scratch with fingers, not nails.

» The cities can be sensory overloads for young children. Be sure that your child cooperates with your safety guidelines before heading out, as it will be difficult for them to focus on your instructions amidst all the street noise.

» Pay close attention during any playtime in the sea, as there are deceptively strong currents in the wet season.

» Parts of rural Cambodia are not such good travel destinations for children, as landmines and unexploded ordnance (UXO) litter the countryside.

regions at a glance

Phnom Penh, Cambodia's resurgent capital, is the place to check the pulse of contemporary life. Siem Reap, gateway to the majestic temples of Angkor, is starting to give the capital a run for its money with sophisticated restaurants, funky bars and chic boutiques. World Heritage Site Angkor houses some of the most spectacular temples on earth.

Down on the South Coast are several up-and-coming beach resorts and a smattering of tropical islands that are very undeveloped compared to those of neighbouring countries. Northwestern Cambodia is home to Battambang, a slice of more traditional life, and several remote jungle temples. The country's Wild East is where elephants roam, waterfalls thunder and freshwater dolphins can be found.

Phnom Penh

Dining ✓✓✓
Bars ✓✓✓
Shopping ✓✓

Dining
French bistros abound, and outstanding fusion restaurants blend the best of Cambodian and European flavours. Ubiquitous Cambodian barbecues offer a more local experience.

Bars
Get started early in a breezy establishment overlooking the Mekong, move on to one of the many live-music bars, and top it off by dancing till dawn in a legendary club.

Shopping
Bring an extra bag to fill with gifts. Choose from colourful local markets where bargains abound on name-brand clothing, silks and handicrafts, or check out the impressive collections of several local and expat designers.

p34

Siem Reap

Dining ✓✓✓
Shopping ✓✓
Activities ✓✓✓

Dining
Contemporary Khmer, spiced-up street food, fine French and a whole host more, plus legendary Pub St – Siem Reap is where it's happening.

Shopping
Chic boutiques have arrived in a big way, including fashion and handicraft initiatives to help the disenfranchised. Silk scarves, replica carvings and temple rubbings head the list, but the retail-therapy opportunities are boundless.

Activities
Take to the skies by hot-air balloon, microlight or helicopter to see Angkor from a different angle. Learn the secrets of Cambodian cuisine with a cooking class. Too much work? Indulge in a massage in one of the many spas around town.

p88

Temples of Angkor

Temples ✓✓✓
Rural Life ✓✓
Quiet ✓✓

Temples

Many visitors arrive under the misconception that it's all about Angkor Wat. True, the 'city that is a temple' is one of the world's most iconic buildings, but nearby are the enigmatic faces of the Bayon, the jungle temple of Ta Prohm and the inspirational carvings of Banteay Srei.

Rural Life

The countryside surrounding the temples remains rooted in a traditional lifestyle. Explore back roads by bicycle, visit floating communities on the Tonlé Sap lake or spot rare water birds.

Quiet

Escape the crowds at the smaller temples: trek to Kbal Spean, clamber through Beng Mealea or venture to former capital Koh Ker.

p118

South Coast

Beaches ✓✓✓
Activities ✓✓✓
Dining ✓✓

Beaches

Thailand's beaches create more buzz, which suits those who make it to Cambodia's islands just fine. Here you can still have a strip of powdery sand all to yourself, or relax in a beachfront bar and ruminate on how long the secret can last.

Activities

Several national parks and other protected areas dot the region, offering trekking, mountain biking, kayaking, rock climbing and kitesurfing.

Dining

Each coastal town has its speciality. In Kep it's delectable and remarkably affordable crab. In Takeo it's lobster. In Kampot it's anything cooked with the region's famous pepper. Sihanoukville offers a more cosmopolitan experience.

p158

Northwestern Cambodia

Temples ✓✓✓
Towns ✓✓
Boat Trips ✓✓

Temples

Heard enough about Angkor Wat? Don't forget the pre-Angkorian capital of Sambor Prei Kuk, the region's first temple city, or the remote jungle temples of Preah Vihear Province.

Towns

Battambang has some of the best-preserved French architecture in the country, a lively dining scene and a beautiful riverside setting. Kompong Chhnang and Thom are well off the tourist trail and offer a slice of the real Cambodia.

Boat Trips

One of the most memorable boat rides in Cambodia links Battambang to Siem Reap following the Sangker River. Explore the largest floating village on the Tonlé Sap lake, Kompong Luong.

p204

Eastern Cambodia

Wildlife ✓✓✓
Culture ✓✓
River Life ✓✓

Wildlife

View rare freshwater river dolphins around Kratie, walk with a herd of elephants in Mondulkiri or spot primates in newly launched community-based forest treks around Mondulkiri or Ratanakiri.

Culture

Northeast Cambodia is home to a mosaic of ethnic minorities. Encounter the friendly Bunong people of Mondulkiri or venture up jungle rivers to visit the remote tribal cemeteries in Ratanakiri.

River Life

The Mekong cuts through the region's heart; along much of this length is the Mekong Discovery Trail, a community-based tourism initiative to develop homestays, lifestyle adventures and activities.

p243

Every listing is recommended by our authors, and their favourite places are listed first

Look out for these icons:

TOP CHOICE Our author's top recommendation

A green or sustainable option

FREE No payment required

On the Road

Phnom Penh

TELEPHONE CODE ☎023 / POP 2 MILLION / AREA 290 SQ KM

Includes »

Best Places to Eat

» Romdeng (p64)

» Foreign Correspondents' Club (p62)

» Van's Restaurant (p64)

» Living Room (p67)

» La Residence (p66)

Best Places to Stay

» Raffles Hotel Le Royal (p54)

» Blue Lime (p54)

» Pavilion p56)

» Number 9 Guesthouse (p56)

» The Quay (p53)

Why Go?

Phnom Penh (ភ្នំពេញ): the name can't help but conjure up an image of the exotic. The glimmering spires of the Royal Palace, the fluttering saffron of the monks' robes and the luscious location on the banks of the mighty Mekong – this is the Asia many dreamed of when first imagining their adventures overseas.

Cambodia's capital can be an assault on the senses. Motorbikes whiz through laneways without a thought for pedestrians; markets exude pungent scents; and all the while the sounds of life, of commerce, of survival, reverberate through the streets. But this is all part of the attraction.

Once the 'Pearl of Asia', Phnom Penh's shine was tarnished by the impact of war and revolution. But the city has since risen from the ashes to take its place among the hip capitals of the region, with an alluring cafe culture, bustling bars and a world-class food scene.

When to Go

Pleasant northeasterly breezes massage the riverfont from December to February, making this a pleasant time to visit, although the crowds peak during this period and some hotels jack up rates. April and May sizzle before the afternoon showers begin in June and the crowds dwindle. September is sopping, but it's an experience to wade through the capital's flooded streets. The city empties out during P'chum Ben (p17), providing glimpses of the old, traffic-free Phnom Penh. In October or November seemingly the whole country descends on the city for Bon Om Tuk (p17).

History

Legend has it that the city of Phnom Penh was founded when an old woman named Penh found four Buddha images that had come to rest on the banks of the Mekong River. She housed them on a nearby hill, and the town that grew up here came to be known as Phnom Penh (Hill of Penh).

In the 1430s, Angkor was abandoned and Phnom Penh chosen as the site of the new Cambodian capital. Angkor was poorly situated for trade and subject to attacks from the Siamese (Thai) kingdom of Ayuthaya. Phnom Penh commanded a more central position in the Khmer territories and was perfectly located for riverine trade with Laos and China, via the Mekong Delta.

By the mid-16th century, trade had turned Phnom Penh into a regional power. Indonesian and Chinese traders were drawn to the city in large numbers. A century later, however, the landlocked and increasingly isolated kingdom had become a buffer between ascendant Thais and Vietnamese. In 1772 the Thais burnt Phnom Penh to the ground. Although the city was rebuilt, Phnom Penh was buffeted by the rival intrigues of the Thai and Vietnamese courts, until the French took over in 1863. Its population is thought to have risen not much above 25,000 during this period.

The French protectorate in Cambodia gave Phnom Penh the layout we know today. They divided the city into districts or *quartiers* – the French and European traders inhabited the area north of Wat Phnom between Monivong Blvd and Tonlé Sap River. By the time the French departed in 1953, they had left many important landmarks, including the Royal Palace, National Museum, Psar Thmei (Central Market) and many impressive government ministries.

The city grew fast in the post-independence peacetime years of Sihanouk's rule. By the time he was overthrown in 1970, the population of Phnom Penh was approximately 500,000. As the Vietnam War spread into Cambodian territory, the city's population swelled with refugees and reached nearly three million in early 1975. The Khmer Rouge took the city on 17 April 1975 and, as part of its radical revolution, immediately forced the entire population into the countryside. Whole families were split up on those first fateful days of 'liberation'.

During the time of Democratic Kampuchea, many tens of thousands of former Phnom Penhois – including the vast majority of the capital's educated residents – were killed. The population of Phnom Penh during the Khmer Rouge regime was never more than about 50,000, a figure made up of senior party members, factory workers and trusted military leaders.

Repopulation of the city began when the Vietnamese arrived in 1979, although at first it was strictly controlled by the new government. During much of the 1980s, cows were more common than cars on the streets of the capital, and it was not until the government dispensed with its communist baggage at the end of the decade that Phnom Penh began to develop. The 1990s were boom years for some: along with the arrival of the UN Transitional Authority in Cambodia (Untac) came US$2 billion (much of it in salaries for expats).

Phnom Penh has really begun to change in the last decade, with roads being repaired, sewage pipes laid, parks inaugurated and riverbanks reclaimed. Business is booming in many parts of the city, with skyscrapers under development, investors rubbing their hands with the sort of glee once reserved for Bangkok or Hanoi and swanky new restaurants opening. Phnom Penh is finally on the move as a new middle class emerges to replace the thousands eliminated by the Khmer Rouge, and the elite invest their dollars at home rather than taking the risk of hiding them abroad. Phnom Penh is back, and bigger changes are set to come.

⊙ Sights

Phnom Penh is a relatively small city and easy to navigate as it is laid out in a numbered grid, a little like New York City. The most important cultural sights can be visited on foot and are located near the riverfront in the most beautiful part of the city. Most other sights are also fairly central – walking distance or just a short *remork* (túk-túk) ride from the riverfront.

Royal Palace & Silver Pagoda   PALACE
(Map p38; Samdech Sothearos Blvd; admission incl camera/video 25,000r; ⊙8-11am & 2-5pm) With its classic Khmer roofs and ornate gilding, the Royal Palace dominates the diminutive skyline of Phnom Penh. It is a striking structure near the riverfront, bearing a remarkable likeness to its counterpart in Bangkok.

Being the official residence of King Sihamoni, parts of the massive compound are

Phnom Penh Highlights

1 Discovering the world's finest collection of Khmer sculpture at the stunning **National Museum** (p39)

2 Being dazzled by the 5000 silver floor tiles of the **Silver Pagoda** (p38), part of the Royal Palace

3 Delving into the dark side of Cambodian history with visits to the **Tuol Sleng Museum** (p40) and the **Killing Fields** (p41), essential to understanding the pain of the past

4 Checking out the huge dome of **Psar Thmei** (p75), the art-deco masterpiece that is Phnom Penh's central market

5 Putting your hands in the air like you just don't care during public **aerobics sessions** (p46) at another landmark, Olympic Stadium

6 Experiencing Phnom Penh's legendary nightlife with a happy-hour cocktail, a local meal and a crawl through the city's **lively bars** (p70)

7 Shopping till you drop (of heat exhaustion) at bounteous **Russian Market** (p75)

closed to the public. Visitors are only allowed to visit the palace's Silver Pagoda and its surrounding compound. However, photography is not permitted inside the pagoda itself. Visitors need to wear shorts that reach to the knee, and T-shirts or blouses that reach to the elbow; otherwise they will have to rent an appropriate covering. The palace gets very busy on Sundays when countryside Khmers come to pay their respects, but this can be a fun way to experience the place, thronging with locals.

Chan Chaya Pavilion

Performances of classical Cambodian dance were once staged in the Chan Chaya Pavilion, through which guests enter the grounds of the Royal Palace. This pavilion is sometimes lit up at night to commemorate festivals or anniversaries.

Throne Hall

The Throne Hall, topped by a 59m-high tower inspired by the Bayon at Angkor, was inaugurated in 1919 by King Sisowath. The Throne Hall is used for coronations and ceremonies such as the presentation of credentials by diplomats. Many of the items once displayed here were destroyed by the Khmer Rouge. In the courtyard is a curious iron house given to King Norodom by Napoleon III of France, hardly designed with the Cambodian climate in mind.

Silver Pagoda

The Silver Pagoda is named in honour of the floor, which is covered with more than 5000 silver tiles weighing 1kg each, adding up to five tonnes of gleaming silver. You can sneak a peek at some of the 5000 tiles near the entrance – most are covered for their protection. It is also known as Wat Preah Keo (Pagoda of the Emerald Buddha). It was originally constructed of wood in 1892 during the rule of King Norodom, who was apparently inspired by Bangkok's Wat Phra Keo, and was rebuilt in 1962.

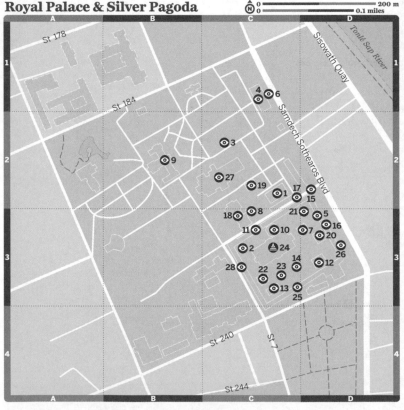

Royal Palace & Silver Pagoda

The Silver Pagoda was preserved by the Khmer Rouge to demonstrate its concern for the conservation of Cambodia's cultural riches to the outside world. Although more than half of the pagoda's contents were lost, stolen or destroyed in the turmoil that followed the Vietnamese invasion, what remains is spectacular. This is one of the few places in Cambodia where bejewelled objects embodying some of the brilliance and richness of Khmer civilisation can still be seen.

The staircase leading to the Silver Pagoda is made of Italian marble. Inside, the Emerald Buddha, believed to be made of Baccarat crystal, sits on a gilded pedestal high atop the dais. In front of the dais stands a life-sized gold Buddha decorated with 9584 diamonds, the largest of which, set in the crown, is a whopping 25 carats. Created in the palace workshops around 1907, the gold Buddha weighs in at 90kg.

Along the walls of the pagoda are examples of extraordinary Khmer artisanship, including intricate masks used in classical dance and dozens of gold Buddhas. The many precious gifts given to Cambodia's monarchs by foreign heads of state appear rather spiritless when displayed next to such diverse and exuberant Khmer art.

The classic Indian epic of the *Ramayana* (known as the *Reamker* in Cambodia) is depicted on a beautiful and extensive mural enclosing the pagoda compound, created around 1900; the story begins just south of the east gate and includes vivid images of the battle of Lanka.

Other structures to be found in the complex (listed clockwise from the north gate) include the *mondap* (library), which once housed richly decorated sacred texts written on palm leaves (now moved to the safety of air-conditioned storage); the shrine of King Norodom (r 1860–1904); an equestrian statue of King Norodom; the shrine of King Ang Duong (r 1845–59); a pavilion housing a huge footprint of the Buddha; Phnom Mondap, an artificial hill with a structure containing a bronze footprint of the Buddha from Sri Lanka; a shrine dedicated to one of Prince Sihanouk's daughters; a pavilion for celebrations held by the royal family; the shrine of Prince Sihanouk's father, King Norodom Suramarit (r 1955–60); and a bell tower, whose bell is rung to order the gates to be opened or closed.

National Museum of Cambodia   MUSEUM
(សារមន្ទីរជាតិ; Map p48; www.cambodiamuseum.info; cnr St 13 & St 178; admission US$3, camera/video US$1/3, ☉8am–5pm) Located just north of the Royal Palace, the National Museum of Cambodia is housed in a graceful terracotta structure of traditional design (built 1917–20), with an inviting courtyard garden. The museum is home to the world's finest collection of Khmer sculpture – a millennium's worth and more of masterful Khmer design.

The museum comprises four pavilions, facing the pretty garden. Most visitors start left and continue in a clockwise, chronological direction. The first significant sculpture to greet visitors is a large fragment – including the relatively intact head, shoulders and

Royal Palace & Silver Pagoda

⊙ **Sights**

two arms – of an immense bronze reclining Vishnu statue recovered from the Western Mebon temple near Angkor Wat in 1936.

Continue into the left pavilion, where the pre-Angkorian collection begins. It illustrates the journey from the human form of Indian sculpture to the more divine form of Khmer sculpture from the 5th to 8th centuries. Highlights include an imposing eight-armed Vishnu statue from the 6th or 7th century found at Phnom Da (p202), and a staring Harihara, combining the attributes of Shiva and Vishnu. The Angkor collection includes several striking statues of Shiva from the 9th, 10th and 11th centuries, a giant pair of wrestling monkeys, a beautiful 12th-century stele (stone) from Oddar Meanchey inscribed with scenes from the life of Shiva, and the sublime statue of a seated Jayavarman VII (r 1181–1219), his head bowed slightly in a meditative pose.

The museum also contains displays of pottery and bronzes dating from the pre-Angkorian periods of Funan and Chenla (4th to 9th centuries), the Indravarman period (9th and 10th centuries) and the classical Angkorian period (10th to 14th centuries), as well as more recent works such as a beautiful wooden royal barge.

Unfortunately, it is not possible to photograph the collection – only the courtyard. English-, French- and Japanese-speaking guides (US$5 to US$7) are available. A comprehensive booklet, *The New Guide to the National Museum,* is available at the front desk (US$10), while the smaller *Khmer Art* *in Stone* covers some of the signature pieces (US$2).

Tuol Sleng Museum   MUSEUM
(សារមន្ទីរទួលស្លែង; Map p43; St 113; admission US$2, video US$5; ⊙7am-6pm) In 1975, Tuol Svay Prey High School was taken over by Pol Pot's security forces and turned into a prison known as Security Prison 21 (S-21). This soon became the largest centre of detention and torture in the country. Between 1975 and 1978 more than 17,000 people held at S-21 were taken to the killing fields of Choeung Ek.

S-21 has been turned into the Tuol Sleng Museum, which serves as a testament to the crimes of the Khmer Rouge.

Like the Nazis, the Khmer Rouge leaders were meticulous in keeping records of their barbarism. Each prisoner who passed through S-21 was photographed, sometimes before and after torture. The museum displays include room after room of harrowing black-and-white photographs; virtually all of the men, women and children pictured were later killed. You can tell which year a picture was taken by the style of number-board that appears on the prisoner's chest. Several foreigners from Australia, New Zealand and the USA were also held at S-21 before being murdered. It is worth paying US$2 to have a guide show you around, as they can tell you the stories behind some of the people in the photographs.

As the Khmer Rouge 'revolution' reached ever greater heights of insanity, it began

PHNOM PENH IN...

One Day

Start early to observe the aerobics sessions on the riverfront, then grab breakfast before venturing into the **Royal Palace**. Next is the **National Museum** and the world's most wondrous collection of Khmer sculpture. After lunch at **Friends** restaurant, check out the funky architecture of **Psar Thmei**, but save the heavy shopping for **Russian Market**. Take a deep breath and continue to **Tuol Sleng Museum**. Sobering indeed – it may be time for a happy-hour drink to reflect on the highs and lows of the day, and then a night out on the town.

Two Days

Start the first day as per the one-day itinerary, but leave the entire afternoon for browsing and shopping in the markets. Wind up with a sunset cruise on the **Mekong River**, offering a beautiful view over the Royal Palace. Start day two with a walking tour of the centre, or just wander around **Wat Phnom**, where Khmers pray for luck. Have lunch at **Boddhi Tree Umma**, then venture across the street to the Tuol Sleng Museum before continuing on to the **Killing Fields of Choeung Ek**. It is a grim afternoon, but essential for understanding just how far Cambodia has come in the intervening years.

devouring its own. Generations of torturers and executioners who worked here were in turn killed by those who took their places. During early 1977, when the party purges of Eastern Zone cadres were getting underway, S-21 claimed an average of 100 victims a day.

When the Vietnamese army liberated Phnom Penh in early 1979, there were only seven prisoners alive at S-21, all of whom had used their skills, such as painting or photography, to stay alive. Fourteen others had been tortured to death as Vietnamese forces were closing in on the city. Photographs of their gruesome deaths are on display in the rooms where their decomposing corpses were found. Their graves are nearby in the courtyard.

Altogether, a visit to Tuol Sleng is a profoundly depressing experience. The sheer ordinariness of the place makes it even more horrific; the suburban setting, the plain school buildings, the grassy playing area where children kick around balls juxtaposed with rusted beds, instruments of torture and wall after wall of disturbing portraits. It demonstrates the darkest side of the human spirit that lurks within us all. Tuol Sleng is not for the squeamish.

Behind many of the displays at Tuol Sleng is the **Documentation Center of Cambodia** (DC-Cam; www.dccam.org). DC-Cam was established in 1995 through Yale University's **Cambodian Genocide Program** (www.yale.edu/cgp) to research and document the crimes of the Khmer Rouge. It became an independent organisation in 1997 and researchers have spent years translating confessions and paperwork from Tuol Sleng, mapping mass graves, and preserving evidence of Khmer Rouge crimes.

French-Cambodian director Rithy Panh's 1996 film *Bophana* tells the true story of Hout Bophana, a beautiful young woman, and Ly Sitha, a regional Khmer Rouge leader, who fall in love but are made to pay for this 'crime' with imprisonment and execution at S-21 prison. It is well worth investing an hour to watch this powerful documentary, which is screened here at 10am and 3pm daily.

Killing Fields of Choeung Ek   MUSEUM
(វាលពិឃាតជើងឯក; admission incl audio tour US$5; ⊙7.30am-5.30pm) Between 1975 and 1978 about 17,000 men, women, children and infants who had been detained and tortured at S-21 were transported to the extermination camp of Choeung Ek. They were often bludgeoned to death to avoid wasting precious bullets.

The remains of 8985 people, many of whom were bound and blindfolded, were exhumed in 1980 from mass graves in this one-time longan orchard; 43 of the 129 communal graves here have been left untouched. Fragments of human bone and bits of cloth are scattered around the disinterred pits. More than 8000 skulls, arranged by sex and age, are visible behind the clear glass panels of the Memorial Stupa, which was erected in 1988. It is a peaceful place today, masking the horrors that unfolded here less than three decades ago.

Admission to the Killing Fields includes an excellent audio tour, available in several languages. Introduced in 2011, the tour includes stories by those who survived the Khmer Rouge, plus a chilling account by Choeung Ek guard and executioner Him Huy about some of the techniques they used to kill innocent prisoners and defenceless women and children.

There is a museum here with some interesting information on the Khmer Rouge leadership and the ongoing trial (see p297). A memorial ceremony is held annually at Choeung Ek on 9 May.

To get to the Killing Fields of Choeung Ek, take Monireth Blvd southwest out of the city. The site is well signposted in English about 7.5km from the bridge near St 271. Most people arrive by bicycle, moto or *remork*. Don't pay more than US$10 for a *remork* (riders will ask US$15 to US$20), and a few dollars less is probably doable.

Wat Phnom   TEMPLE
(វត្តភ្នំ; Map p48; temple admission US$1, museum admission US$2; ⊙7am-6.30pm) Set on top of a 27m-high tree-covered knoll, Wat Phnom is on the only 'hill' in town. According to legend, the first pagoda on this site was erected in 1373 to house four statues of Buddha deposited here by the waters of the Mekong River and discovered by Madame Penh. The main entrance to Wat Phnom is via the grand eastern staircase, which is guarded by lions and *naga* (mythical serpent) balustrades.

Today, many people come here to pray for good luck and success in school exams or business affairs. When a wish is granted, the faithful return to deliver on the offering promised, such as a garland of jasmine flowers or a bunch of bananas, of which the spirits are said to be especially fond.

The *vihara* (temple sanctuary) was rebuilt in 1434, 1806, 1894 and 1926. West of the *vihara* is a huge stupa containing the ashes of King Ponhea Yat (r 1405–67). In a pavilion on the southern side of the passage between the *vihara* and the stupa is a statue of a smiling and rather plump Madame Penh.

A bit to the north of and below the *vihara* is an eclectic shrine dedicated to the genie Preah Chau, who is especially revered by the Vietnamese. On either side of the entrance to the central altar containing a statue of Preah Chau are guardian spirits bearing iron bats. In the chamber to the right of the statue (if you are looking at it) are drawings of Confucius, as well as two Chinese-style figures of the sages Thang Cheng (on the right) and Thang Thay (on the left).

Down the hill from the *vihara* in the northwest corner of the complex is a **museum** (admission US$2; ☺7am-6pm) with some old statues and historical artefacts, which can probably be skipped if you've been to the National Museum.

If you show up at Wat Phnom before it officially opens at 7am, you may be able to wander around the grounds for free – or a guard may attempt to extract some money from you.

Wat Phnom can be a bit of a circus, with beggars, street urchins, women selling drinks and children selling birds in cages (you pay to set the bird free, but the birds are trained to return to their cage afterwards). Fortunately it's all high-spirited stuff. Phnom Penh's only resident elephant, Sambo, has been retired from his duties of circling Wat Phnom with tourists on his back. At research time it remained unclear whether a replacement would be sought.

Wat Ounalom   TEMPLE
(វត្តឧណ្ណាលោម; Map p48; Samdech Sothearos Blvd; admission free; ☺6am-6pm) This wat is

---

WARNING: MONKEY BUSINESS AROUND WAT PHNOM

There are large troupes of macaques living around Wat Phnom and they can be aggressive when they see people with food. They have been known to bite children on occasion, so keep a good distance even if your children want to see the 'cute' monkeys.

---

the headquarters of Cambodian Buddhism. It was founded in 1443 and comprises 44 structures. It received a battering during the Pol Pot era, but today the wat has come back to life. The head of the country's Buddhist brotherhood lives here, along with a large number of monks.

On the 2nd floor of the main building, to the left of the dais, is a statue of Huot Tat, fourth patriarch of Cambodian Buddhism, who was killed by Pol Pot. The statue, made in 1971 when the patriarch was 80 years old, was thrown in the Mekong by the Khmer Rouge to show that Buddhism was no longer the driving force in Cambodia. It was retrieved after 1979. To the right of the dais is a statue of a former patriarch of the Thummayuth sect, to which the royal family belongs.

On the 3rd floor of the building is a marble Buddha of Burmese origin that was broken into pieces by the Khmer Rouge and later reassembled. In front of the dais, to either side, are two glass cases containing flags – each 20m long – used during Buddhist festivals and celebrations.

Behind the main building is a stupa containing an eyebrow hair of Buddha with an inscription in Pali (an ancient Indian language) over the entrance.

Olympic Stadium   LANDMARK
(Map p43; near cnr Sihanouk & Monireth Blvds) Known collectively as the National Sports Complex, the Olympic Stadium is a striking example of 1960s Khmer architecture and includes a sports arena and facilities for boxing, gymnastics, volleyball and other sports. Turn up after 5pm to see countless football matches, *pétanque* duels or badminton games.

FREE **Wat Moha Montrei**   TEMPLE
(វត្តមហាមន្ត្រី; Map p43; Sihanouk Blvd) Situated close to the Olympic Stadium, Wat Moha Montrei was named in honour of one of King Monivong's ministers, Chakrue Ponn, who initiated the founding of the pagoda (*moha montrei* means 'the great minister'). The cement *vihara,* topped with a 35m-high tower, was completed in 1970. Between 1975 and 1979, it was used by the Khmer Rouge to store rice and corn.

Check out the assorted Cambodian touches incorporated into the wall murals of the *vihara,* which tell the story of Buddha. The angels accompanying Buddha to heaven are dressed as classical Khmer dancers and the

South Phnom Penh

0 500 m
0 0.25 miles

Tonlé Sap River

See North Phnom Penh Map (p48)

To Kith Eng (300m);
Paramount Express
Angkor

Jawaharlal Blvd

Sisowath Quay

Royal Palace

Samdech Sotheros Blvd

Samdech Sotheros Blvd

National Assembly

Australian Embassy

Reclaimed Land

To Sofitel Phnom Penh
Phokeethra (300m)

To Watthar-Artisans (300m); Cambodia
Angkor Airlines (350m); Myanmar Embassy (400m);
Japanese Embassy (800m); Sofitel (1.1km);
Malaysian Embassy (1.5km); Monivong Bridge (2km)

Norodom Blvd

Norodom Blvd

GOLDEN ST AREA

See Enlargement

BOEING KANG KANG DISTRICT

Monivong Blvd

Monivong Blvd

German Embassy

Singaporean Embassy

Suramarit Blvd

Wat Botum Park

Sihanouk Blvd

Tuol Sleng Museum

GOLDEN ST AREA

Enlargement

Sihanouk Blvd

Monireth Blvd

South Phnom Penh

⦿ Top Sights
Tuol Sleng Museum...............................C4

◎ Sights
1 Cambodia Living Arts.............................F3
2 Cambodia-Vietnam Friendship
   Monument...F2
3 Independence Monument.....................E2
4 Olympic Stadium..................................B2
5 Prayuvong Buddha Factories.............F3
6 Wat Botum..F2
7 Wat Moha Montrei...............................B3

⊕ Activities, Courses & Tours
Cambodian Cooking Class..........(see 72)
8 Children's Playground..........................F2
9 Dream Land..G2
   Flicks..(see 97)
10 Kundalini Yoga....................................D4
11 Monkey Business................................E1
12 NatuRāj Yoga.......................................D3
   Spa Bliss....................................(see 100)
13 The Place...B4
14 Wat Langka...B3

⊜ Sleeping
15 Anise..B3
16 Blue Dog Guesthouse..........................B4
17 Boddhi Tree Aram...............................F2
18 Boddhi Tree Umma..............................C4
   Capitol Guesthouse.................(see 113)
19 Circa 51...E2
20 Fairyland Guesthouse.........................C2
21 Golden Gate Hotel...............................B3
22 Golden Mekong Hotel..........................E1
23 Himawari...G2
24 Hotel Cambodiana................................G2
25 Hotel Nine..F3
26 Imperial Garden...................................G2
27 Kabiki..E2
28 Khmer Surin Boutique
   Guesthouse.......................................A4
29 Lazy Gecko Guest House.....................G2

30 Mad Monkey..E3
31 Manor House...E2
32 Mini Banana..B4
33 Mystéres & Mekong.............................F2
   Narin Guesthouse.....................(see 40)
34 New Golden Bridge Hotel....................B3
35 Number Nine Guesthouse...................G2
36 Pavilion...F2
37 Smiley's Hotel.......................................C2
38 Spring Guesthouse..............................C2
39 Star Wood Inn......................................C2
40 Tat Guesthouse....................................C2
41 The 240...E2
42 The 252...D2
43 Top Banana Guesthouse.....................B4
44 Town View Hotel..................................C2
45 Villa Langka...E3
46 Villa Paradiso......................................D2
47 Willow...F3

⊗ Eating
48 Aussie XL..B4
49 Boat Noodle Restaurant......................F3
   Boddhi Tree Umma Restaurant...(see 18)
   Cafe Fresco BKK.........................(see 65)
50 Café Soleil...A4
   Capital Restaurant....................(see 113)
51 Chayyam...B4
52 Chinese Noodle/China
   Restaurant..D3
53 City Mall...A2
54 Comme a la Maison.............................A4
55 Curry Noodle Stalls............................F2
56 Ebony Tree...F3
57 Flavours of India.................................A3
   Freebird.......................................(see 72)
58 Friendly House....................................D4
59 Hagar..D4
60 Java Café..F3
61 K'nyay...F2
62 Ko Ko Ro...F3
63 La Residence...E1
64 Le Jardin...E4

assembled officials wear the white military uniforms of the Sihanouk period.

Independence Monument MONUMENT
(វិមានឯករាជ្យ; Map p43; cnr Norodom & Sihanouk Blvds) Modelled on the central tower of Angkor Wat, Independence Monument was built in 1958 to commemorate the country's independence from France in 1953. It also serves as a memorial to Cambodia's war dead (at least those that the current government chooses to remember). Wreaths are laid here on national holidays.

Nearby, in Wat Botum Park opposite photogenic **Wat Botum** (Map p43; btwn Sts 7 & 19), is the optimistically named **Cambodia-Vietnam Friendship Monument** (Map p43; Wat Botum Park), built to a Vietnamese (and rather communist) design in 1979. Concerts are often held in the park, which springs to life with aerobics, football and *takraw* (foot juggling with a rattan ball) enthusiasts after 5pm.

French Embassy LANDMARK
(Map p36; 1 Monivong Blvd) Located at the northern end of Monivong Blvd, the French embassy played a significant role in the dramas that unfolded after the fall of Phnom Penh on 17 April 1975. About 800 foreigners and 600 Cambodians took refuge in the embassy. Within 48 hours, the Khmer Rouge informed the French vice-consul that the new government did not recognise diplomatic privileges and that if all the Cambodians in the compound were not handed over, the lives of the foreigners inside would also be forfeited. Cambodian women married to foreigners could stay; Cambodian men married to foreign women could not. Foreigners wept as servants, colleagues, friends, lovers and husbands were escorted out of the

embassy gates. At the end of the month the foreigners were expelled from Cambodia by truck. Many of the Cambodians were never seen again. Today a high whitewashed wall surrounds the massive complex and the French have returned to Cambodia in a big way, promoting French language and culture in their former colony.

Prayuvong Buddha Factories BUDDHIST
(Map p43; btwn St 308 & St 310) In order to replace the countless Buddhas and ritual objects smashed by the Khmer Rouge, a whole neighbourhood of private workshops making cement Buddhas, *naga* and small stupas has grown up on the grounds of Wat Prayuvong. While the graceless cement figures painted in gaudy colours are hardly works of art, they are an effort by the Cambodian people to restore Buddhism to a place of honour in their culture. The Prayuvong Buddha factories are about 300m south of the Independence Monument.

National Library LANDMARK
(Bibliothèque Nationale; Map p48; St 92; ⊗8-11am & 2-5pm Mon-Fri) The National Library is in a graceful old building constructed in 1924, near Wat Phnom. During its rule, the Khmer Rouge turned the building into a stable and destroyed most of the books. Many were thrown out into the streets, where they were picked up by people, some of whom donated them back to the library after 1979; others used them as food wrappings.

🏃 Activities

Aerobics (Line Dancing)

Every morning at the crack of dawn, and again at dusk, Cambodians gather in several pockets throughout the city to participate in quirky and colourful aerobics sessions. This quintessential Cambodian phenomenon sees a ring-leader, equipped with boom box and microphone, whip protégés into shape with a mix of 1980s-Soviet-style calisthenics and *Thriller*-inspired line-dancing moves. It's favoured by middle-aged Khmer women, but you'll see both sexes and all ages participating, and tourists are more than welcome.

There are a few good places to join in the fun or just observe. Olympic Stadium is probably the best spot because of the sheer volume of participants. Here several instructors compete for clients and the upper level of the grandstand becomes a cacophony of competing boom boxes.

The riverfront usually sees some action – the patch opposite Blue Pumpkin (Map p48) at the terminus of St 144 is a good bet. Another popular place that usually sees several groups getting their collective freaks on is Wat Botum Park (Map p43) along Samdech Sothearos Blvd.

Boat Cruises

Boat trips on the Tonlé Sap or Mekong Rivers are very popular with visitors. Sunset cruises are ideal, the burning sun sinking slowly behind the glistening spires of the Royal Palace. Local **tourist boats** are available for hire on the riverfront in Phnom Penh and can usually be arranged on the spot for between US$10 and US$20 an hour, depending on negotiations and numbers. It is also possible to charter them further afield to Koh Dach (see p83).

Bowling

Superbowl BOWLING
(Parkway Sq, Mao Tse Toung Blvd; per hr US$9, shoe hire US$1) The only bowling alley in town. Hourly rates are per lane, with any number of bowlers.

Cooking Courses

Cambodian Cooking Class COOKING COURSE
(Map p43; ☎012 524801; www.cambodian-cooking -class.com; booking office on 67 St 240, classes near Russian embassy; half/full day US$12.50/20; ⊗closed Sun) Learn the art of Khmer cuisine through Frizz Restaurant. Reserve ahead.

Cycling

You can hire a bike and go it alone – Koh Dach is a doable DIY trip – or opt for something more organised with or without a guide through one of the companies below. Vicious Cycle and Off-Road Cambodia both run daily tours to Udong or the Mekong islands, departing by 8am.

Off-Road Cambodia CYCLING
(Map p52; ☎012 555123; www.cyclingoffroad.com; 18 St 360) Quality Trek mountain bikes go for US$7 per day at this tiny bike shop.

Vicious Cycle CYCLING
(Map p48; ☎012 462165; www.grasshopper adventures.com; 23 St 144; bicycles per day US$4-8) Plenty of quality mountain and other bikes available, including a couple of family bikes with kiddie seats for US$10. DIY cyclers should request a map of local bicycle routes. Vicious represents Grasshopper Adventures here.

THE SHOOTING RANGES

Shooting ranges have long been a popular activity for gung-ho travellers visiting Cambodia. Cambodia's lack of law enforcement and culture of impunity allowed visitors to do pretty much anything they wanted in the bad old days. A number of military bases near Phnom Penh were transformed into shooting ranges and rapidly became popular with tourists wanting to try their luck with an AK-47, M-60 or B-40 grenade launcher. The government periodically launched crackdowns, but the business continued largely unabated.

And so the show goes on. The most popular one is located just beyond the go-cart track in Kambol district off NH4. Visitors can try out a range of weapons, but most of the machine guns work out at about US$1 a bullet. Handguns are available at the lower end, while at the other extreme it is possible to try shooting a B-40 rocket-propelled grenade launcher (US$350).

There have been rumours that it is possible to shoot live animals, such as a chicken or cow, at these places. Naturally, we in no way endorse such behaviour.

2Cycle Cambodia CYCLING
(off Map p36; ☑015 696376; www.2cyclecambodia .com) Venture across the Mekong River on a local ferry in front of the Imperial Garden Hotel and you'll find bikes for hire just a short stroll from the ferry pier. Local-ish mountain bikes cost US$2 per hour to US$6 for the day, and smaller bikes are available for children. Book the day before you plan to ride. This is a great way to escape the city without pedalling through traffic. The countryside is very beautiful. 2Cycle can arrange village homestays if you want to turn this into a multiple-day trip.

Fitness Centres & Swimming

The fancier fitness centres have swimming pools, gyms and sometimes tennis courts, and you can pay a bit extra to use them all. Top-end hotels with fitness centres and good pools include the Himawari, the Cambodiana and Imperial Garden. All three charge US$10 to use both the pool and gym (tack on US$3 at weekends), and US$7 to use just the pool (tack on a dollar or two at weekends).

Moving up the ladder, the new Sofitel wins the prize for best gym (walk-in US$15), while the Hotel Le Royal has a rambling resort-style pool (admission weekday/weekend incl gym US$20/30).

Some pool-equipped boutique hotels will let you swim if you buy a few bucks' worth of grub or cocktails, but increasingly these hotels are closing their doors to walk-in guests. Holdouts at the time of research included Little Garden, Hotel Nine and the 252, but keep in mind that the pools at these places are pretty small – more for dipping and cooling off than for doing laps.

Other options for swimming and/or pumping iron:

Long Beach Plaza Hotel SWIMMING POOL
(Map p36; 3 St 280; US$1) A bargain for a lap-sized pool.

Muscle Fitness GYM
(Map p52; cnr Sts 95 & 386; per session US$3; ⊙6am-9pm) The 'NGO gym' is a pretty good deal considering the range of equipment, although the air-con is somewhat dysfunctional.

The Place GYM
(Map p43; ☑999799; 11 St 51; per day US$15, 10 sessions US$75; ⊙6am-10pm) This is absolutely state of the art, with myriad machines, a big pool and a range of cardio classes.

Sokhan Fitness Club GYM
(Parkway Sq, 113 Mao Tse Toung Blvd; walk-in US$6; ⊙5.30am-10pm) Has an indoor pool, steam bath, sauna and gym, and is half-price before 2pm.

Go-Carting
Kambol Kart Raceway GO CARTS
(☑012 232332; per 10min US$12) Kambol Kart Raceway is a professional circuit in a rural setting just outside of Phnom Penh. Prices include helmets and racing suits. It's about 2km off the road to Sihanoukville. Look for a hard-to-spot sign on the right, 8km beyond the airport; if you hit the toll booth, you've gone too far.

Golf
If you can't survive without a swing, contact **Royal Cambodia Phnom Penh Golf Club** (☑011 353703; off NH4; per round weekend/weekday US$79/59, shoe/club hire US$7/10),

North Phnom Penh

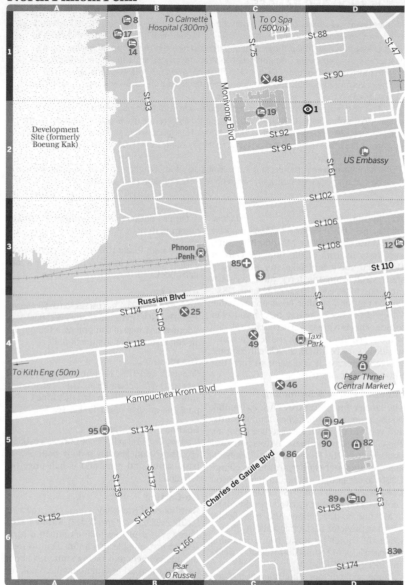

which is considerably overpriced considering the poor level of upkeep, or the better-maintained **Cambodia Golf & Country Club** (☑363666; NH4; weekend/weekday US$48/45). Both are beyond the airport on NH4 - the latter down an access road about 3km west of the airport, the former closer to the highway about 30km beyond the airport.

Massage & Spas

There are plenty of massage parlours in Phnom Penh, but some are purveying

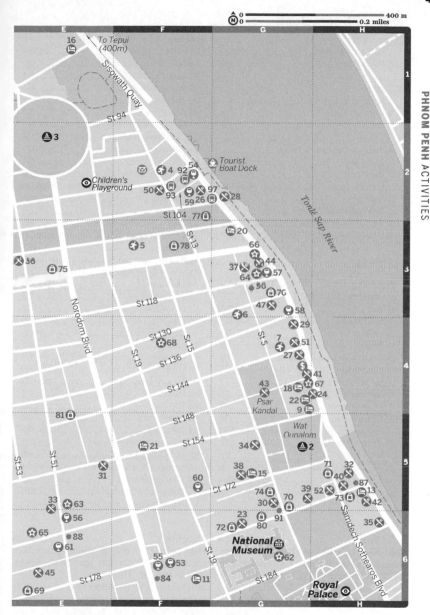

'naughty' massages. However, there are also now a lot of legitimate massage centres and a number of superb spas for that pampering palace experience. Some of the leading addresses:

Spa Bliss SPA

(Map p43; 215754; http://blissspacambodia.com; 29 St 240; massages from US$22) One of the most established spas in town, set in a lovely old French house on popular 240.

North Phnom Penh

Bodia Spa SPA

(Map p48; ☎226199; www.bodia-spa.com; cnr Samdech Sothearos Blvd & St 178; massages from US$26; ⊙10am-midnight) About the best rubdowns in town, in a Zen-like setting (albeit with some street noise).

O Spa SPA

(off Map p48; ☎992405; www.ospacambodia.com; 4B St 75; body massages from US$20; ⊙11am-9pm) An oasis of calm with rejuvenating hot-stone massage, plus Balinese and Thai treatments, and virtually no street noise.

Daughters FOOT SPA

(Map p48; ☎077 657678; www.daughtersofcambodia.org; St 178; 1hr foot spa US$10; ⊙9am-5.30pm Mon-Sat) Hand and food massages administered by participants in this NGO's vocational training program for at-risk women. Shorter (15- to 30-minute) treatments available.

Nail Bar MASSAGE, SALON

(Map p48; www.mithsamlanh.org; Friends n' Stuff store, 215 St 13; massages US$4/7 for 30/60min; ⊙11am-9pm) Cheap manicures, pedicures, foot massages, hand massages and nail painting, all to help Mith Samlanh train street children in a new vocation.

Seeing Hands Massage MASSAGE
Riverside (Map p48; 12 St 13); St 108 (Map p48; 34 St 108; 8am-9pm) Helps you ease those aches and pains; helps blind masseurs stay self-sufficient. Massages average US$7 per hour, making it one of the best-value massages in the capital. Several other cooperatives around town.

Meditation & Yoga
There's naturally plenty of meditating going on at any given wat, and some hold regular sessions that are open to the public. Free one-hour Vipassana meditation sessions take place in the central *vihara* of **Wat Langka** (Map p43; cnr St 51 & Sihanouk Blvd) at 6pm on Mondays, Thursdays and Saturdays, and on Sunday morning at 8am. Warning: if you've never done it before, an hour will seem like an eternity. It's OK to just do 20 or 30 minutes.

The following studios hold regular yoga classes – check their websites for schedules. All offer discounts for multiple classes and memberships.

Russian Market Area

Kundalini Yoga YOGA
(Map p43; ☎089 897609; www.kundaliniyogacam bodia.org; 204 St 322) Early morning and early evening kundalini yoga and pilates classes for US$9.

NatuRāj Yoga YOGA
(Map p43; ☎012 739419; www.yogacambodia.com; 52 St 302) Popular yoga studio with a range of classes from US$9.

Flicks YOGA
(Map p43; ☎097 8967827; www.theflicks-cambo dia.com; 39B St 95) Classes here are US$5 for a 60-minute session.

Running
A good opportunity to meet local expatriates is via the Hash House Harriers (www .p2h3.com), usually referred to simply as 'the Hash'. A run/walk takes place every Sunday. Participants meet in front of Phnom Penh train station (Map p48) at 2.15pm. The fee of

US$5 includes refreshments (mainly a lot of beer) at the end.

☞ Tours
If you want an organised city tour, most of the leading guesthouses and travel agencies (p78) can arrange one for about US$6 per person, not including entrance fees. What follows are some interesting niche tours in and around Phnom Penh.

Khmer Architecture Tours ARCHITECTURE TOUR (www.ka-tours.org). Those interested in the new-wave Khmer architecture from the Sangkum era (1953–70) should look no further. These introductory tours take in some of the most prominent buildings in the city and take place on foot or by *cyclo,* usually starting at 8.30am every other weekend. The website also includes a DIY map of the most popular walking tour. For more on this landmark architecture, pick up a copy of

Russian Market Area

Cultures of Independence (2001) or *Building Cambodia: New Khmer Architecture 1953-70* (2006).

Cyclo Centre   CYCLO TOUR
(Map p48; ☑ 012 518762; www.cyclo.org.uk; 95 St 158) Dedicated to supporting cyclo drivers in Phnom Penh, these tours are a great way to see the sights. Themed trips such as pub crawls or cultural tours are also available. Prices run from US$2.50 an hour to US$10 for a full day.

Kingdom Brewery   BREWERY TOUR
(off Map p48; ☑430180; 1748 National Highway 5; ☺8am-noon & 1-5pm) It costs just US$6 to tour the facilities of Kingdom Brewery. Tours include all-you-can-drink beer and you don't even have to book ahead – just show up. It's exactly 1km north of the Japanese Bridge on NH5.

Nature Cambodia   QUAD BIKING TOUR
(☑012 676381; www.nature-cambodia.com) Offers quad biking in the countryside around Phnom Penh. The quads are automatic, and so are easy to handle for beginners, and prices are pretty affordable at US$25 per bike (maximum two passengers) for two hours or US$55 for a half day. Despite its proximity to the capital, this is rural Cambodia and very beautiful. Longer trips and jeep tours are also available. Follow signs to Choeung Ek and it is about 300m before the entrance. Call ahead as numbers are limited.

🛏 Sleeping

Accommodation in Phnom Penh, as in the rest of the country, is terrific value no matter your budget and there are hundreds of guesthouses and hotels to choose from. All midrange and top-end hotels listed include breakfast and have non-smoking rooms.

CENTRE NORTH (RIVERFRONT)

While the idea of roosting riverfront has obvious appeal to many, you'll find better value elsewhere. Also keep in mind that hotels along the river tend to be noisy, and most budget rooms are windowless or face away from the river. A few prime options exist at the top end, but budget and midrange travellers are advised to sleep off-river.

TOP CHOICE The Quay   BOUTIQUE HOTEL $$$
(Map p48; ☑224894; www.thequayhotel.com; 277 Sisowath Quay; r/ste US$90/170; ✿@☎) Cambodia's first carbon-neutral hotel, the Quay is a temple of contemporary style right on the riverfront. The river-view panoramic suites, with balconies done right, are the beds of choice, as they are far more spacious than the still-stylish but dark rooms at the rear. Ascend to the roof-top Chow bar to catch breezes off the Tonlé Sap.

**Foreign Correspondents'
Club**   BOUTIQUE HOTEL $$
(Map p48; ☑210142; www.fcccambodia.com; 363 Sisowath Quay; std/deluxe r US$78/106; ✿☎) This landmark location is a fine place to

recapture the heady days of the war correspondents. The eight rooms are delightfully finished in wood and include fine art, top-of-the-line furniture and DVD players. The deluxe rooms have lovely balconies with prime river views.

Amanjaya Pancam Hotel   BOUTIQUE HOTEL $$$
(Map p48; ☑219579; www.amanjaya.com; 1 St 154; r US$155-250; ❄@🛜) One of Phnom Penh's original Asian Zen–style boutiques, Amanjaya boasts a superb riverfront location and spacious, stylish rooms with dark-wood floors, elegant Khmer drapes and tropical furnishings.

Paddy Rice   BOUTIQUE HOTEL $$
(Map p48; ☑990321; www.paddyrice.net; 213 Sisowath Quay; r US$45-65; ❄@🛜) Most of the US$45 rooms have no windows, but upgrade to the US$65 riverfront rooms and you are in business, with a great-looking room and a spacious balcony loaded with furniture. Do keep in mind that you're over a popular Irish bar here, so it won't be the quietest option.

River 108   BOUTIQUE HOTEL $$$
(Map p48; ☑218785; www.river108.com; 2 St 108; ste without/with balcony US$85/105; ❄@🛜) This hip boutique hotel near the riverfront has a chic chintz look to it. Rooms include flat-screen TVs and ample bathrooms, plus some have partial-river-view terraces.

Ohana Hotel   HOTEL $$
(Map p48; ☑211425; www.hotelcastle.com.kh; 4 St 148; r from US$65; ❄@🛜🏊) Not quite on the riverfront, but more than makes up for it with smart business-like rooms and a swimming pool.

Bougainvillier Hotel   HOTEL $$
(Map p48; ☑220528; www.bougainvillierhotel .com; 277G Sisowath Quay; r/ste from US$72/136; ❄@🛜) Khmer-style high-rise has big rooms filled with big shiny furniture, disappointing balconies and leopard prints in the lobby.

CENTRE NORTH (OFF-RIVER)
You'll get much better deals staying off the river, including a handful of delectable boutique hotels. All eyes are on St 172 as a potential heir apparent to Boeng Kak Lake as the prime backpacker district. Do be aware that in general the north-central area is grittier than the neighbourhoods to the south, and there are pockets of sleaze on several streets running west from the river – St 104 and St 136 being the main examples.

TOP CHOICE Raffles Hotel Le Royal   HISTORIC HOTEL $$$
(Map p48; ☑981888; www.raffles.com; cnr Monivong Blvd & St 92; r from US$200; ❄@🛜🏊) From the golden age of travel, this is one of Asia's grand old palaces, belonging in the illustrious company of the Oriental in Bangkok and Raffles in Singapore. This classic colonial-era property is Phnom Penh's leading address, with a heritage to match its service and style. Indulgent diversions include two swimming pools, a gym, spa, bars and restaurants with lavish food and drink. Between 1970 and 1975 many famous journalists working in Phnom Penh stayed here.

TOP CHOICE Blue Lime   BOUTIQUE HOTEL $$
(Map p48; ☑222260; www.bluelime.asia; 42 St 19z; r US$40-75; ❄@🛜🏊) The follow-up act of the

---

CAMBODIAN FIGHT CLUB

The whole world knows about *muay Thai* (Thai boxing) and the sport of kickboxing, but what is not so well known is that this contact sport probably originated in Cambodia. *Pradal serey* (literally 'free fighting') is Cambodia's very own version of kickboxing and it is possible to see some fights in Phnom Penh. Popular Cambodian TV channel CTN hosts live bouts at 2pm on Saturday and Sunday out at its main studio on National Hwy 5. It is about 4km north of the Chruoy Changvar Bridge. Entry is free and there is usually a rowdy local crowd surreptitiously betting on the fights. Most bouts are ended by a violent elbow move and there is a lot more ducking and diving than with other kickboxing genres.

An even older martial art is *bokator*, or *labokatao*, which some say dates back to the time of Angkor. It translates as 'pounding a lion' and was originally conceived for battlefield confrontations. Weapons include bamboo staffs and short sticks, as well as the *krama* in certain situations. Grand Master San Kim Sean operates the **Bokator Academy** (off Map p36; www.bokatorcambodia.com; 1671 NH2) in Phnom Penh and offers **lessons** (per person US$5; ⊙hourly 5.30-7.30pm Mon-Fri, 5-7pm Sat & Sun).

team behind the Pavilion outdoes its predecessor with smart, minimalist rooms and a leafy pool area done just right. The pricier rooms have private plunge pools, four-poster beds and contemporary concrete love seats. You don't lose too much with the equally appealing cheaper rooms upstairs in the main building. No kids.

Billabong BOUTIQUE HOTEL **$$**
(Map p48; ☎223703; www.thebillabonghotel.com; 5 St 158; d US$36-70, tr US$85; ❄@🛜≋) Near Psar Thmei but an oasis of calm by comparison, Billabong has a big open courtyard and 20 rooms set around a large swimming pool. Standard rooms are smallish, so it's better to invest in the pool-view rooms for space and style. Wi-fi costs extra.

Royal Guesthouse BACKPACKER **$**
(Map p48; ☎218026; 91 St 154; s US$6-12, d US$8-13, tr US$15; ❄@🛜) This old-timer has some smarter rooms that verge on the flashpacker side, with sparkling bathrooms and tasteful decoration. It's run by a friendly family with travel info aplenty.

Me Mate's Place BACKPACKER **$$**
(Map p48; ☎5002497; www.matesplace.com; 5 St 90; dm US$9, r US$20-24; ❄@🛜) This is a smart little guesthouse bar on a quiet strip north of Wat Phnom. The spartan private rooms have (unfortunately unfurnished) balconies and glass shower stalls, while the four- and six-bed dorms are equipped with air-con and wide, sturdy bunk beds.

Encounters BACKPACKER **$**
(Map p48; ☎089 530185; www.socambodia.com; 89-91 St 108; dm US$4-6.50, r US$12; ❄@🛜) Formerly Nomads, Encounters specialises in cheap dorms that come with fan or air-con, co-ed or single-sex, and include access to safety lockers and free laundry. Just two private rooms. Reliable travel info available thanks to Cambo-experienced host Martin.

Last Home BACKPACKER **$**
(Map p48; ☎6921009; 21 St 172; r with fan US$7-10, with air-con US$15-20; ❄@🛜) This four-storey walk-up was the first budget guesthouse to plant its flag on up-and-coming St 172. It has a loyal following among regular visitors. Rooms are size-over-substance affairs – you can squeeze three or four people into some of them.

BOENG KAK AREA

This was backpacker central – a lakeside version of Bangkok's Khao San Rd – until Boeng Kak (ie, the lake) was completely filled in with sand in 2011 as part of a massive development project. This caused most guesthouses to close or move elsewhere, but three holdouts remained and seemed to be doing OK at the time of research. A semblance of the crusty old backpacker spirit survives here, but it's unclear how long it will last.

Grand View Guesthouse BACKPACKER **$**
(Map p48; ☎430766; www.grandview.netfirms.com; 4 St 93; r US$4-10, ❄@🛜) Tall, skinny structure with unrivalled views of the sandlot formerly known as Boeng Kak.

11 Happy Guesthouse BACKPACKER **$**
(Map p48; ☎6301231, 012 999921; www.happy11ghcambodia.com; 11 St 93; s US$3, d US$5-10; ❄@🛜) Also known as Simon's. The friendly, informative staff here put smiles on backpackers' faces with cheap laundry, a cosy hangout area and good rooms at these prices. Shoot for a room in the main building.

Number 10 Lakeside Guesthouse BACKPACKER **$**
(Map p48; ☎012 970989; 10 St 93; s/d with fan US$4/6, with air-con US$8/12; ❄@🛜) Longtime stalwart with some bargain rooms with shared bathroom, or bigger rooms with hot water and cable TV.

CENTRE SOUTH (NORODOM EAST)

The hotels in this zone are ideally positioned – on or within walking distance of the river, close to the Royal Palace and well south of the chaos and girlie bars of the north-central area. Walk-in backpackers can target up-and-coming St 258, which has a clutch

> **HAVE YOUR SAY**
>
> Found a fantastic restaurant that you're longing to share with the world? Disagree with our recommendations? Or just want to talk about your most recent trip?
>
> Whatever your reason, head to lonelyplanet.com, where you can post a review, ask or answer a question on the Thorntree forum, comment on a blog, or share your photos and tips on Groups. Or you can simply spend time chatting with like-minded travellers. So go on, have your say.

PHNOM PENH FOR CHILDREN

With its chaotic traffic, lack of public parks, and open sewers, at first glance Phnom Penh is not the most child-friendly city in Asia. However, there are a few little gems that help to pass the time in the capital. Plus, kids love *remork* rides!

Most sights will be overwhelming for younger children, but the Royal Palace and Wat Phnom are interesting places to explore.

Phnom Penh has two excellent children's indoor playrooms (bring socks) with elaborate slides, bouncy castles and the like: **Monkey Business** (Map p43; 3rd fl, Paragon Shopping Centre, St 214; child US$3-6, adult free; ⊙9am-8pm) and at amusement park **Dream Land** (Map p43; www.dreamland.com.kh; Sisowath Quay; admission US$5; ⊙9am-8pm). Monkey Business has a cafe with wi-fi on hand so that you can do your business while the kids are theirs. Dream Land adds a ferris wheel and carousel, among a host of rides.

Decent outdoor playgrounds are northwest of the Cambodia-Vietnam Friendship Memorial in Wat Botum Park (Map p43), and just south of Wat Phnom (Map p48).

Phnom Penh Water Park (✆881008; Russian Blvd; weekends/weekdays US$4/3; ⊙8am-5pm), with its slides and wave pool, is a definite hit with the young-uns and a world away from bustling downtown Phnom Penh, but it's pretty dirty compared with the hotel pools. There is also a small fairground here.

Many of the restaurants and cafes are child-friendly, but there are a few specifically aimed at families, including Le Jardin (p67) and Living Room (p67), while Fresco's Boeng Keng Kang (BKK) locale has a kiddies' corner.

The most interesting attraction is beyond the city limits and makes a good day trip: Phnom Tamao Wildlife Rescue Centre (p86), a rescue centre for Cambodia's incredible wildlife. The huge enclosures here include tigers, elephants and bears.

of guesthouses with rooms in the US$5 to US$10 range.

TOP CHOICE **Pavilion** BOUTIQUE HOTEL $$
(Map p43; ✆222280; www.thepavilion.asia; 227 St 19; r US$50-90; ✳@🛜🏊) Housed in an elegant French villa, this immensely popular and atmospheric place helped popularise the Phnom Penh poolside boutique hotel. Furnishings show a Chinese-Khmer touch and some rooms have pool views. Expanded into a second contemporary building next door, some of the newer rooms include a private plunge pool. No children allowed.

TOP CHOICE **Number 9 Guesthouse** GUESTHOUSE $
(Map p43; ✆984999; 7C St 258; www.number9 hotel.com; s/d/tw/tr US$15/20/25/25; ✳@🛜🏊) Oh, how times change. Rising from the lakeside ashes of backpackersville and propelling Ph 258 into flashpackersville, this is something. Smart rooms, flat-screen TVs, an ultra-trendy bar-restaurant and rooftop jacuzzi. Shoot for the twin rooms, which have heaps of extra space.

The 240 BOUTIQUE HOTEL $$
(Map p43; ✆218450; www.the240.asia; 83 St 240; r US$45-55; ✳@🛜) The Pavilion group scores another hit. There's no garden courtyard or swimming pool, but a few of the rooms have private plunge pools and guests are licensed to swim at sister hotels Kabiki and Pavilion. Healthy organic restaurant Naturae is downstairs.

Willow BOUTIQUE HOTEL $$
(Map p43; ✆996256; www.thewillowpp.com; 1 St 21; r US$45-77; ✳🛜) Another fashionable boutique, the Willow has seven spacious rooms in a splendid 1960s villa. Also known for its build-your-own-sandwich bar.

Kabiki BOUTIQUE HOTEL $$
(Map p43; ✆222290; www.thekabiki.com; 22 St 264; r US$50-75; ✳@🛜🏊) The most family-friendly place in town, the Kabiki offers an extensive garden and an inviting swimming pool with a kiddie pool. Family rooms include bunks and most rooms have a private garden terrace.

Lazy Gecko Guest House BACKPACKER $
(Map p43; ✆078 786025; St 258; d with fan/air-con from US$5/12; ✳@🛜) Well-known as a cafe in its lakeside days, it tacked on an equally appealing guesthouse upon moving to its new location amid the backpacker haunts of St 258. The large rooms, with flat-screen TVs,

are some of the best in town at this price range, albeit they're not well lit.

Boddhi Tree Aram
BOUTIQUE HOTEL $$

(Map p43; ☑211376; www.boddhitree.com; 70 St 244; s/d US$78/82; ✳@♠⊜) Those on a bigger budget than Boddhi Tree Umma (p59) might consider this elegant place with stylish rooms in two neighbouring colonial villas. Rates include use of the great pool at the Himawari Hotel.

Hotel Cambodiana
HISTORIC HOTEL $$$

(Map p43; ☑426288; www.hotelcambodiana.com .kh; 313 Sisowath Quay; r/ste from US$110/180; ✳@♠⊜) A real Phnom Penh landmark, the Cambodiana has large, well-appointed rooms that are heavy on fabrics with 1980s patterns. The unfinished hotel was used as a military base by the Lon Nol government, and by 1975 thousands of refugees from the countryside sheltered under its concrete roof.

Himawari
SERVICED APARTMENTS $$$

(Map p43; ☑214555; www.himawarihotel.com; 313 Sisowath Quay; r/apt from US$155/193; ✳@♠⊜) Another property offering serviced apartments as well as rooms, Himawari has a great location on the banks of the Mekong. Definitely request a nonsmoking room, as smokers have left their stamp on some rooms.

Mystéres & Mekong
BOUTIQUE HOTEL $$

(Map p43; ☑210274; www.mysteres-mekong.com; 70 St 244; r/ste from US$78/112; ✳@♠) The lush pool area, surrounded by wicker chaise longues, is the main selling point. Rooms are divided between an old and a new building. They have lovely four-poster beds and TVs, but there's nowhere to sit in the standard rooms. Better value exists in this genre.

Imperial Garden
SERVICED APARTMENTS $$$

(Map p43; ☑219991; www.imperialgarden-hotel .com; 315 Sisowath Quay; d/apt incl breakfast from US$120/250; ✳@♠⊜) Rooms here are a bit pricey but big discounts are usually available if you ask. Rooms have outstanding river views, while apartments are off-river, closer to the road.

Sofitel Phnom Penh Phokeethra
LUXURY HOTEL $$$

(off Map p43; ☑999200; www.sofitel.com; 26 Sothearos Blvd; r from US$145; ✳@♠⊜) Phnom Penh's latest five-star property boasts spacious rooms and a gazillion facilities, including numerous tennis courts and several

restaurants, but feels somewhat large and impersonal.

Hotel Nine
BOUTIQUE HOTEL $$

(Map p43; ☑215964; www.hotel-nine.com; 48 St 9; r US$55-75; ✳@♠⊜) This new white-washed hotel was just getting its sea legs when we checked in. It has a nice little pool, cosy beds and attractive minimalist rooms but is a tad overpriced compared with other boutique hotels of this ilk.

Golden Mekong Hotel
HOTEL $$

(Map p43; ☑211721; www.goldenmekonghotel.com; 205A St 19; r US$15-20; ✳@♠) Atmospheric hotel behind the Royal Palace offering a good deal for the standard and comfort provided.

CENTRE SOUTH (NORODOM WEST & PSAR O RUSSEI)
This area is centrally located just north of Phnom Penh's main east west axis – Sihanouk Blvd. It includes the most popular budget accommodation area, which starts near Psar O Russei and heads south towards Sihanouk Blvd along a network of backstreets just west of Monivong Blvd. The Psar O Russei area is a mix of high-rise hotels and backpacker-oriented guesthouses. The hotels are particularly appealing – you won't come close to finding better US$15 air-con elsewhere in the centre.

TOP CHOICE Narin Guesthouse
GUESTHOUSE $

(Map p43; ☑099 881133; touchnarrin@hotmail. com; 50 St 125; r with fan/air-con US$10/15; ✳@♠) One of the stalwarts of the Phnom Penh guesthouse scene (we first stayed here back in 1995), Narin has recently been given a makeover. Rooms are smart, bathrooms smarter still and the price is nice. There is a super-relaxed open-air restaurant-terrace for taking some time out.

TOP CHOICE Smiley's Hotel
HOTEL $

(Map p43; ☑012 365959; smileyhotel.pp@gmail. com; 37 St 125; s US$6, d with fan/air-con US$10/15; ✳@♠) A migrant from Siem Reap, Smiley's is a huge new seven-storey hotel with a choice of 40 spacious rooms that border on chic. An absolutely stupendous deal. Includes a lift.

Manor House
GUESTHOUSE $$

(Map p43; ☑992566; www.manorhousecambodia .com; 21 St 262; s/d from US$42/49; ✳@♠⊜) Set in a small villa, this gay-friendly guesthouse offers artfully decorated rooms and a narrow swimming pool. The standard rooms are well-appointed but smallish and cluttered, so upgrade if you want more room to stretch out. Kids aren't allowed.

The 252 BOUTIQUE HOTEL $$
(Map p43; ☑998252; www.the-252.com; 19 St 152; r US$45-55; ✳☎🖥) Just a tick down from Blue Lime and Pavilion in style and comfort, it's nonetheless terrific value. The attractive lime-striped rooms are a tad small for hangin', but around the pool prime lounging spots lurk. The charismatic French owner makes guests feel welcome.

Circa 51 BOUTIQUE HOTEL $$
(Map p43; ☑012 585714; www.circa51.com; 155 St 222; s US$45, d US$55-90; ✳☎🖥) Lovers of '60s new Khmer architecture will adore the stark, white-washed ambience of Circa 51. Touches like original checkerboard-tile floors will seem arty or just old, depending on your tastes. Extras in all rooms include DVD players, flat-screen TVs and silk robes. The pool area is a tad overexposed.

Villa Paradiso BOUTIQUE HOTEL $$
(Map p43; ☑213720; www.thevillaparadiso.com; 27 St 222; s/d from US$55/65; ✳@☎🖥) They go a bit over the top with the themed rooms ('Japanese', 'colonial'), but it's hard to argue with the result: lavish rooms with loads of hangout space and eye-catching accoutrements like silk curtains, ceramic sinks and tiled bathtubs. It has a fine spa and a pool area that could use a few more tables. Kids under 12 are not allowed.

Town View Hotel HOTEL $
(Map p43; ☑992949; 30 St 111; www.townviewhotel.com; d US$15; ✳@☎) Another fantastic value hotel in the Psar O Russei area. All rooms include cable TV, minibar, sparkling bathrooms and a choice of king or twin beds, plus there's a lift.

Fairyland Guesthouse HOTEL $
(Map p43; ☑214510; fairylandhotel@yahoo.com; 99 St 141; r US$13-15; ✳@☎) This towering guesthouse has large, bright rooms, decent linen, smart bathrooms and a lift. You can squeeze three into the more expensive rooms, which include a queen and single bed.

Star Wood Inn HOTEL $$
(Map p43; ☑223253; www.starwood-inn.com; 74 St 141; r US$15; ✳@☎) More clean and sleek rooms for a ridiculously low price here. Rooms have either twin or king beds with attractive runners, and include unique tiled

mosaics of bikini-clad women in the bathrooms. No lift.

Tat Guesthouse BACKPACKER $
(Map p43; ☑099 801000; tatguesthouse@yahoo.com; 52 St 125; s/d without bathroom US$3/6, d with bathroom US$7-12; ✳@☎) A friendly, family-run place with cheap and cheerful rooms, plus a breezy rooftop hangout area.

Spring Guesthouse BACKPACKER $
(Map p43; ☑222155; 34 St 111; r with fan US$6-9, with air-con & hot water US$10; ✳@☎) This five-storey walk-up was the first of a new generation of smart guesthouses in this area. It offers bright, spotless rooms with cable TV and loads of travel info.

Capitol Guesthouse GUESTHOUSE $
(Map p43; ☑724104; www.capitolkh.com; 14 St 182; s US$3-8, d US$5-10; ✳@☎) The original guesthouse in town has several annexes with bargain-basement rooms and a bustling cafe with travel info. The cheapest rooms lack windows.

CENTRE SOUTH (BKK AREA)

Popular among NGO workers and other expats, the Boeng Keng Kang (BKK) district southwest of Independence Monument has developed into something of a flashpacker district, with an expanding selection of fine midrange hotels to go with a wealth of trendy bars and restaurants, plus a few good hostels. Many of the hotels are centred on St 278, dubbed the 'Golden Mile' or 'Golden St' because of the preponderance of hotels that feature 'Golden' in their name. There is little to choose between the hotels on this strip, as all offer air-con, cable TV, fridge, hot water and free laundry for US$15 to US$20. Golden St is less than a 10-minute *remork* ride from the riverfront.

TOP CHOICE Khmer Surin Boutique Guesthouse BOUTIQUE HOTEL $$
(Map p43; ☑012 731909; www.khmersurin.com.kh; 11A St 57; r US$50-60; ✳☎) This guesthouse was recently tacked onto the long-running restaurant of the same name in a sumptuous villa near Golden St (St 278). The result is spectacular indeed. Rooms come with four-poster beds, leafy and lavish balconies, and loads of antique furniture, not to mention bathrooms that would put most four-star properties to shame. With all the museum-quality furniture lying around, rooms might seem busy to some.

TOP CHOICE **Top Banana Guesthouse** BACKPACKER $
(Map p43; ☏012 885572; www.topbanana.biz; 9 St 278; r US$6-15; ❋@🛜) A great location high above Golden St, comfy open-air chill-out area and popular bar make this the Penh's top backpacker crash pad. Cheap rooms don't come with hot water, but the more expensive ones include brisk air-con. Book way ahead.

Villa Langka BOUTIQUE HOTEL $$
(Map p43; ☏726771; www.villalangka.com; 14 St 282; r US$44-121; ❋@🛜☀) One of the first players in the poolside-boutique-hotel game, it's now firmly cemented as a Phnom Penh favourite. Rooms ooze post-modern panache. People complain that it has become too big and impersonal – 45 rooms at last count – but the flip side is more variety. The open-plan bathrooms are among the nicest in Phnom Penh.

Anise HOTEL $$
(Map p43; ☏222522; 2C St 278; www.anisehotel.com.kh; s US$37-57, d US$47-67; ❋🛜) If the leafy boutique hotel around pool isn't the thing for you, Anise is the best midrange high-rise in town. Indigenous textiles and lovely wood trim add character to rooms that already boast extras like DVD players. Pricier rooms are gargantuan. Free laundry.

Boddhi Tree Umma GUESTHOUSE $
(Map p43; www.boddhitree.com; 50 St 113; r with fan & shared bathroom US$14-18, with air-con incl breakfast from US$31; ❋@🛜) Some might be spooked by the location opposite Tuol Sleng, but it's a wonderfully atmospheric place. There is a divine restaurant in the verdant garden.

Little Garden BOUTIQUE HOTEL $$
(Map p52; ☏217871; www.littlegarden.asia; 8A St 398; r US$30-40; ❋@🛜☀) A bit like the Pavilion in miniature, it's priced better than most of the poolside boutique hotels. The location south of the centre will appeal to those looking for quiet, and it's an easy five-minute moto ride to buzzing Golden St (St 278). Only six rooms here, and they are lovely, as is the compact pool area.

Mad Monkey BACKPACKER $
(Map p43; ☏987093; www.phnompenhhostels.com; 26 St 302; dm US$7, r without/with bathroom US$14/16; ❋@🛜) The spacious dorms here have air-con and lockers and sleep six to eight in double-wide bunk beds. The private rooms are homey enough but lack TVs, and windows open to the corridor. Popular downstairs restaurant and rooftop bar above quiet St 302.

New Golden Bridge Guesthouse HOTEL $
(Map p43; ☏721396; www.goldenbridgehtl.com; 7 St 278; s/d/tr US$15/18/20; ❋@🛜) It's close, but this is our favourite among the 'Golden' hotels. Rooms are huge if a bit dark, with clean linen, low bamboo beds, desks, fine bathrooms and no funky smells like in some of its neighbours.

Golden Gate Hotel HOTEL $$
(Map p43; 012 737319; www.goldengatehotels.com; 9 St 278; d incl breakfast US$20-35, ste/tr US$45/50; ❋@🛜) Big, functional, affordable and perfectly placed smack dab in the middle of Golden St. Perfect for big groups.

Blue Dog Guesthouse BACKPACKER $
(Map p43; ☏012 658075; bluedogguesthouse@gmail.com; 13 St 51; r per person US$5; @🛜) Location and price are right, plus there's a delightful common area/restaurant, so you don't have to spend too much time in the basic rooms. Recently opened a slightly spiffier annex, Red Dog, just down the street.

Mini Banana BACKPACKER $
(Map p43; ☏726854; http://mini.topbanana.biz; 136 St 51; dm US$4, r with shared/private bathroom from US$8/10; ❋@🛜) Top Banana's sister hostel is like the Top Banana of old: laid-back and sleepy. Just a few private rooms here along with a sweltering seven-bed dorm under an A-frame roof.

Long Thaily HOTEL $
(Map p52; d with fan US$6, d/tw with air-con US$10/15; ❋🛜) Rooms in this new high-rise are big and immaculate – you won't find better value in this price range, and it even has a lift. The Russian Market location is great for shopaholics.

✖️ Eating

For foodies, Phnom Penh is a real delight, boasting a superb selection of restaurants that showcase the best in Khmer cooking, as well as the greatest hits from world cuisine such as Chinese, Vietnamese, Thai, Indian, French, Italian, Spanish, Mexican and more. Visitors to Phnom Penh are quite literally spoilt for choice these days.

Some travellers get into the habit of hunkering down on their guesthouse balcony, encouraged by proprietors talking up the dangers of Phnom Penh. Don't do it, as a culinary adventure awaits...

ANTONY GIBLIN/LONELY PLANET IMAGES ©

AUSTIN BUSH/LONELY PLANET IMAGES ©

. Buddhist monks
he saffron robes worn by young men doing
heir stint in the sangha are a common sight in
Phnom Penh

2. Suburban Agriculture
A farmer tends his rice fields, north of the city

3. Colonial Architecture
The Unesco headquarters is housed in a restored French villa in downtown Phnom Penh

4. Rush Hour
A family on the move in the capital

PETER STUCKINGS/LONELY PLANET IMAGES ©

ℹ BAKED GOODIES

Most of the city's finest hotels also operate bakery outlets with extravagant pastries, but prices are higher than in cafes or restaurants. Drop in after 6pm when they offer a 50% discount, and gorge away. Hotel Cambodiana has the best selection. The larger supermarkets also stock their own range of breads and cakes, freshly baked on the premises.

Check out *Drinking and Dining*, produced by **Pocket Guide Cambodia** (www .cambodiapocketguide.com), for various restaurant delivery menus and additional listings.

CENTRE NORTH (RIVERFRONT)

TOP CHOICE Foreign Correspondents' Club
FUSION $$$

(FCC; Map p48; ☎210142; www.fcccambodia.com; 363 Sisowath Quay; mains US$5-15; ⏱6am-midnight; ☎☜) A PP institution, the 'F', as expats call it, is housed in a colonial gem with great views and cool breezes. The Asian and international dishes are delicious. One of those must-see places in Cambodia, almost everyone swings by for a drink – happy hour is 5pm to 7pm.

TOP CHOICE Fish
SEAFOOD $$

(Map p48; ☎222685; cnr Sts 108 & Sisowath Quay; mains US$5-15; ☒☜) No prizes for guessing the speciality of the house. Fish serves some of the best fish and chips in town, as well as sophisticated seafood creations, such as the superb antipasti and a bouillabaisse. Stylish and fun.

Metro
FUSION $$$

(Map p48; ☎222275; 271 St 148; large plates US$7-22; ⏱9am-midnight; ☒☜) Metro is the trendiest spot on the riverfront strip thanks to a striking design and an adventurous menu. Small plates are for sampling and include beef with red ants and tequila black-pepper prawns, while large plates include steaks and soy-roasted chicken. Also does a mean eggs Benedict.

Rahu
SUSHI $$$

(Map p48; ☎215179; 159 Sisowath Quay; mains US$4-18; ⏱5pm-1am; ☒) The sushi at this hip new joint run by the Metro folks is some of the best in town and comes half price after 11pm – we gorged like grizzlies on raw fish

for under US$10 per person. The rest of the menu is practically identical to Metro's.

Cafe Fresco Riverside
CAFE $$

(Map p48; ☎217041; 363 Sisowath Quay; mains US$3-10; ⏱6am-9pm; ☒☜) A chic cafe under the FCC, the highlights are the ice cream and the US$5 lunch special, which includes a premade sandwich and a fresh-squeezed juice or smoothie (about an US$8 value). A second branch is further south on St 306 in the trendy BKK district.

Blue Pumpkin
CAFE $$

(Map p48; 245 Sisowath Quay; dishes US$2.50-6; ⏱6am-11pm; ☒☜) The beloved Siem Reap cafe with the alluring white upholstery has open its doors in Phnom Penh and proved a smashing success. Healthy breakfasts, pastas and sandwiches lead the menu, and you can watch the nightly aerobics spectacle on the riverfront as you eat.

Riverhouse Asian Bistro
FUSION $$$

(Map p48; ☎212302; cnr St 110 & Sisowath Quay; mains US$5-15; ⏱8am-2am; ☒☜) A contemporary dining space with a menu that runs the gamut from tapas (duck wraps, spicy prawns) to imported steaks and original mains like barracuda fish and chips and tornadoes of salmon.

Khmer Borane Restaurant
CAMBODIAN $$

(Map p48; 389 Sisowath Quay; mains US$4-5.50) A great little restaurant for traditional Khmer recipes; choose from *trey kor* (steamed fish with sugar palm) or *lok lak* (fried diced beef with a salt, pepper and lemon dip).

Pop Café
ITALIAN $$

(Map p48; ☎012 562892; 371 Sisowath Quay; pasta dishes US$6-9; ⏱11am-1.45pm & 6-10pm; ☒) Owner Giorgio welcomes diners as if you are coming to his own home for dinner, making this a popular spot for authentic Italian cooking. Thin-crust pizzas, homemade pastas and tasty gnocchi, it could be Roma.

Cantina
MEXICAN $$

(Map p48; 347 Sisowath Quay; mains US$3-6; ⏱2.30-11pm, closed Sat) This is the spot for tostadas, fajitas and other Mexican favourites, all freshly prepared. It's also a journo hangout and a lively bar with professional margaritas and tequilas.

Tepui
INTERNATIONAL $$$

(off Map p48; ☎991514; 45 Sisowath Quay; mains US$12-17; ⏱6-10pm Tue-Sun) Housed in the Chinese House, one of the city's true colonial-era masterpieces, Tepui is worth a visit for the ambience alone. Creative specials supplement the diminutive menu, which includes South American– and Mediterranean-influenced mains like red snapper, duck and a succulent rib-eye steak.

La Croisette INTERNATIONAL **$$**
(Map p48; ☎220554; 241 Sisowath Quay; mains US$5-18; ⊗7am-1am; 🖼🛜) The stylish Croisette is a popular riverfront spot with a good range of Italian food plus hearty steaks, lamb chops and even some Cambodian offerings.

Beirut MIDDLE EASTERN **$**
(Map p48; ☎720011; 117 Sisowath Quay; dishes US$2.50-3.50; ⊗9am-11pm; 🖼🚗) Lilliputian eatery with super deals on wraps, kebabs and saucy appetisers like *hummus* with pita bread, plus *shisha* pipes (hookahs) for US$8. Keep in mind that river views are obstructed up here.

¡Viva! MEXICAN **$**
(Map p48; ☎093 678 888; 111 Sisowath Quay; dishes US$4.50-6; ⊗10am-11.30pm; 🖼🖼) It doesn't look like much, but this recent Siem Reap import instantly raised the bar for Mexican food

---

GOOD-CAUSE DINING

There are several restaurants around town that are run by aid organisations to help fund their social programs in Cambodia. These are worth seeking out, as the proceeds of a hearty meal go towards helping Cambodia's recovery and allow restaurant staff to gain valuable work experience.

Centre North

Friends (Map p48; ☎012 802 072; www.friends-international.org; 215 St 13; tapas US$2-5, mains from US$6; ⊗11am-9pm; 🖼) One of Phnom Penh's best-loved restaurants, this place is a must, with tasty tapas bites, heavenly smoothies and creative cocktails. It offers former street children a head start in the hospitality industry.

Sugar 'n Spice Cafe (Map p48; www.daughtersofcambodia.org; 65 St 178; sandwiches US$3.50-4; ⊗9am-6pm Mon-Sat; 🖼🛜) This busy and attractive cafe on the top floor of the Daughters visitors' centre features sandwiches, salads, smoothies, coffee and baked goods served by former sex workers being trained by Daughters to reintegrate into society.

Ebony Tree (Map p43; St 29 cnr St 294; mains US$3.50-6; ⊗11am-midnight, to 2am weekends; 🚗) A stylish little cafe serving health shakes, vegetarian treats and Khmer food. Forty per cent of the profits go to the Apsara Arts Association (p73).

Veiyo Tonlé (Map p48; 237 Sisowath Quay; mains US$3.75-6.50; ⊗7am-11.30pm; 🛜) A little restaurant on the breezy riverfront, the menu here is mainly Khmer and Italian cuisine, including yummy pizzas. Some proceeds go towards helping a local orphanage.

Centre South

Café Yejj (Map p52; 92A St 432; www.yejj.com; mains US$3.50-6; 🖼🛜🚗; ⊗7am-9pm) An air-con escape from Russian Market (walk upstairs), this bistro-style cafe uses many organic ingredients to prepare pastas, salads, sandwiches and burritos. Promotes fair trade and responsible employment.

Hagar Main Restaurant (Map p43; www.hagarcatering.com; 44 St 310; mains US$4.50-12; ⊗7am-8pm; 🖼🛜); St 163 (9 St 163) The all-you-can-eat Asian fusion lunch buffet costs US$6.50 and all proceeds go towards assisting destitute or abused women. If you can't afford that, the branch on St 163 charges only US$2.50 for its Cambodian lunch buffet.

Le Lotus Blanc (Map p43; 152 St 51; mains US$6; ⊗closed Sun) This upscale diner acts as a training centre for youths who previously scoured the city dump. Run by French NGO Pour un Sourire d'Enfant (For the Smile of a Child), it serves classy Western and Khmer cuisine.

Le Rit's (Map p43; 71 St 240; mains US$2-7) The three-course lunches and dinners (US$6) are a relaxing experience in the well-groomed garden. Dishes are available in cheaper 'small' portions. Proceeds assist disadvantaged women to re-enter the workplace.

in Phnom Penh. A bucket of margaritas costs US$5. It's on the same strip as Beirut, and is flanked by Indian and pizza restaurants.

Bopha Phnom Penh Restaurant
CAMBODIAN $$$
(Map p48; Sisowath Quay; mains US$6.50-15) Also known as Titanic, it's right on the river and designed to impress, with Angkorian-style carvings and heavy furniture. The menu is thick with the exotic, especially water buffalo, and there's a Western menu for the less adventurous.

Happy Herb Pizza
PIZZA $$
(Map p48; ☎362349; 345 Sisowath Quay; pizzas US$4-8; ☺8am-11pm; ☎) No, happy doesn't mean it comes with free toppings; it means pizza à la ganja. The non-marijuana pizzas are also pretty good, but don't involve the free trip. Good place to sip a cheap beer as well. Delivery available.

Kandal House
INTERNATIONAL $$
(Map p48; 239B Sisowath Quay; mains US$4-6; ☎) Blink and you'll miss it, this riverfront restaurant turns out delicious *amok* and other Cambodian faves, plus homemade pastas, salads and soups. Anchor draught available in pints.

Anjali/Karma Cafe
CAFE $$
(Map p48; 273 Sisowath Quay; mains US$3-6; ☺7am-late) Twin-sister restaurants practically under one roof. The prices are more than reasonable for this part of town. Anjali has some Indian offerings; otherwise, they share an identical menu – pub grub and some Asian highlights.

El Mundo
CAFE $
(Map p48; 219 Sisowath Quay; mains US$3-5; ☎) A mellow riverfront establishment with a range of global food and pastries, plus an upstairs lounge for movies at 7.30pm daily.

CENTRE NORTH (OFF RIVER)

TOP CHOICE Romdeng
CAMBODIAN $$
(Map p48; ☎092 219565; 74 St 174; mains US$4-7; ☺11am-9pm; ☎) Set in a gorgeous colonial villa with a small pool, the elegant Romdeng specialises in Cambodian country fare and offers a staggering choice of traditional Khmer recipes, including the legendary deep-fried spiders. It's part of the Friends' extended family (see p63).

TOP CHOICE Van's Restaurant
FRENCH $$$
(Map p48; ☎722067; 5 St 13; mains US$8-40; ☺11.30am-2.30pm & 5-10.30pm; ✲) Located

in one of the city's grandest buildings, the former Banque Indochine, you can still see the old vault doors en route to the refined dining room upstairs. Dishes are presented with decorative flourish and menu highlights include foie-gras ravioli, tender veal and boneless quail. Set lunches available for US$15, including a glass of wine.

TOP CHOICE Le Wok
FUSION $$$
(Map p48; ☎092 821857; 33 St 178; mains US$7-15) The name says it all – French flair with an Asian flavour. Choose from a tempting menu of regular meals, plus some more daring specials like snail cassoulet or scallop salad.

Lemongrass
THAI $$
(Map p48; ☎012 996707; 14 St 130; mains US$3.50-9; ☺9am-midnight; ✲☎) A higher-class Thai restaurant with a fair selection of Khmer classics. The prices are pretty reasonable given the look of the place. Splurge for the ocean tiger prawns in red curry.

Tell Restaurant
SWISS, GERMAN $$$
(Map p48; ☎430650; 13 St 90; mains US$8-25; ☺11am-2pm & 5-10.30pm Mon-Fri, 11am-10.30pm Sat & Sun; ✲) With fondues and *raclettes* (melted cheese with vegetables), this restaurant brings a Swiss touch to the Wat Phnom area. Portions are generous and dishes include a selection of tenderised meats.

Sher-e-Punjab
INDIAN $$
(Map p48; ☎992901; 16 St 130; mains US$3-6; ☺11am-11pm; ☎) The top spot for a curry fix according to many members of Phnom Penh's Indian community; the tandoori dishes are particularly good. Even the prawn dishes cost under US$6.

La Marmite
FRENCH $$
(Map p48; ☎012 391746; 80 St 108; mains US$4.50-12; ☺11am-2pm & 6-10.30pm; ✲) Traditional French bistro with classic Gallic flavours. Choose from daily specials such as Andouillette chitterlings or go with the regular menu, which includes tender *tournedos* and duck.

La Patate
BELGIAN $$
(Map p48; ☎012 840522; 14 St 5; mains US$2-4; ☺9am-2am) Come here for hearty Belgian fare and gourmet coffee ground by corpulent, moustachioed chef/host Didier. Meat dishes arrive swimming in one of several rich sauces. If you're really hungry, try the foot-long 'bazooka burger' on a king-sized bed of Phnom Penh's best fries.

Kith Eng Restaurant   CAMBODIAN $$
(off Map p43; ☑092 751688; 33B St 169; mains US$3-5; ⊙7am-8.30pm) The family of the late Tuol Sleng artist Vann Nath (see p85) continues to run the restaurant he founded. The food is traditional Khmer. An attached art gallery features his famous paintings.

Genova   ITALIAN $$
(Map p48; ☑012 390039; 19 St 154; mains US$4-7; ⊙10.30am-10.30pm) An authentic Italian streetside trattoria in the heart of Phnom Penh? You betcha. Friendly proprietor Roberto puts plenty of TLC into his pint-sized eatery, and the delicious food is a fine value. Linguini in the 'best pesto in Cambodia' is the house speciality.

Le Bistrot de Paris   FRENCH $$
(Map p48; ☑092 448945; 52 St 51; mains US$3.50-7; ⊙8am-11pm) This is the French version of Genova, only a bit more of a hole-in-the-wall, with a few tables tossed haphazardly on the sidewalk of bar-packed St 57. Food is French bistro fare all the way, served with a choice of four excellent sauces.

Kebab   QUICK EATS $
(Map p48; St 51; wraps US$2.50-3; ⊙9pm-6am; ☑) One of several shacks that exist solely to provide late-night edibles to St 57 bar crawlers, this is the pick of the bunch, best known for its veggie falafel wraps. Opposite Heart of Darkness.

Sam Doo Restaurant   CHINESE $$
(Map p48; 56-58 Kampuchea Krom Blvd; mains US$2.60-10; ⊙7am-3am; ☒) Many Chinese Khmers swear this has the best food in town. Choose from spicy morning glory, signature 'Sam Doo fried rice', *trey chamhoy* (steamed fish with soy sauce and ginger) and fresh seafood. It's open late and has delicious dim sum.

Anaora   FRENCH $$
(Map p48; 57 St 178; mains US$4.50-14; ⊙10.30am-10.30pm; ☞) Friendly family-run French bistro specialising in *galettes* (non-sweet crêpes) and saucy beef dishes, plus a few Cambodian options.

Laughing Fatman   BACKPACKER CAFE $
(Map p48; St 172; mains US$2-6) This is a welcoming place with cheap food and big breakfasts, formerly Oh My Buddha – 'New name, same body', the corpulent owner joked.

Warung Bali   INDONESIAN $
(Map p48; 25 St 178; dishes US$1.50-3; ⊙9am-9pm) Here you'll encounter spicy Indonesian favourites like fish in sweet soy bean sauce and beef *rendang* (beef cooked in coconut milk and spices). It's busy and fragrant.

Lucky Pho   VIETNAMESE $
(Map p48; 11 St 178; mains from US$2-4; ⊙8am-9pm) Great location near the riverfront for good *pho*, the noodle soup that keeps Vietnam moving forward, plus dirt-cheap fried rice and fried noodles.

Sorya Food Court   FAST FOOD $
(Map p48; St 63) The top-floor food court is a more sanitised way to experience a variety of local fare. Also up here is McDonald's imitator **BB World** (burgers from US$1.75; ☒☞).

Thai Huot Supermarket   SUPERMARKET $
(Map p48; 103 Monivong Blvd; ⊙7.30am-8.30pm) This is the place for French travellers who are missing home, as it stocks many French products, including Bonne Maman jam and Hérnaff paté.

Bayon Market   SUPERMARKET $
(Map p48; 33 34 Russian Blvd; ⊙8am 9pm) Carries a good range of products, including some nice surprises that don't turn up elsewhere in the city.

CENTRE SOUTH (NORODOM EAST)

TOP CHOICE **Shop**   CAFE $$
(Map p43; 39 St 240; mains US$3.50-6; ⊙7am-7pm, to 3pm Sun; ☞☑) If you are craving the local

FLOWER POWER

Anyone who spends a night or two on the town in Phnom Penh will soon be familiar with young girls and boys hovering around popular bars and restaurants to sell decorative flowers. The kids are incredibly sweet and most people succumb to their charms and buy a flower or two. All these late nights for young children might not be so bad if they were benefiting from their hard-earned cash, but usually they are not. Look down the road and there will be a moto driver with an ice bucket full of these flowers waiting to ferry the children to another popular spot. Yet again, the charms of children are exploited for the benefit of adults who should know better but are too poor to worry about it. Think twice before buying from them, as the child probably won't reap the reward.

PHNOM PENH EATING

deli back home, make for this haven, which has a changing selection of sandwiches and salads with healthy and creative ingredients like wild lentils, wild 'shrooms and lamb meat. The pastries, cakes and chocolates are delectable and worth the indulgence.

Java Café   CAFE $$
(Map p43; www.javaarts.org; 56 Sihanouk Blvd; mains US$3.50-7; ✱📶✐) Consistently popular thanks to a breezy balcony and a creative menu that includes crisp salads, delicious homemade sandwiches, burgers (do try the vegetarian burger) and excellent coffee from several continents. The upstairs doubles as an art gallery, the downstairs as a bakery.

K'nyay   VEGAN $$
(Map p43; 25K Suramarit Blvd; mains US$5-6; ⏰noon-9pm Mon-Fri, 7am-9pm Sat; 📶✐) A stylish little Cambodian restaurant that is hidden away from the main road in a leafy colonial villa. The menu includes a generous selection of vegetarian and vegan options and original health shakes. Ask them to spice it up.

Yi Sang   CHINESE $$
Almond Hotel (Map p43; 128 Samdech Sothearos Blvd; mains US$3-20; 📶); Riverfront (Map p43; Sisowath Quay; 📶) Yi Sang is all about contemporary Chinese cuisine. The menu includes live seafood, or at least recently alive, plus just about the best dim sum in town (available before 5pm only). The riverfront location, with an abbreviated menu, is one of the best places in the city for a relaxing sunset cocktail.

Origami   JAPANESE $$$
(Map p43; ☎012 968095; 88 Samdech Sothearos Blvd; set menus US$8-30; ⏰11.30am-2pm & 6-10pm Mon-Sat; ✱) This outstanding Japanese eatery takes the art of Japanese food to another level. Set menus include beautifully presented sushi, sashimi (US$15) and tempura boxes. The *Kobe* set is a favourite.

Malis   CAMBODIAN $$
(Map p43; ☎221022; 136 Norodom Blvd; mains US$4-15) The leading Khmer restaurant in the Cambodian capital, Malis is a chic place to dine al fresco. The original menu includes beef in bamboo strips, sand goby with ginger, and traditional soups and salads. Popular for a boutique breakfast, as the menu is a good deal at US$1.50 to US$3.

Naturae   ORGANIC $$
(Map p43; 83 St 240; wraps US$5.50; ⏰7am-9pm; 📶✐) Delightful spot with delicious all-organic salads and wraps and grass growing in the tables, plus a health-food store on the premises.

Freebird   AMERICAN $$
(Map p43; 69 St 240; mains US$5-15; ✱📶) An American-style bar-diner with a great selection of burgers, wraps, salads and Tex-Mex. The steak 'n' cheese sandwich and the chilli con carne are highlights.

Pho 24   VIETNAMESE $
(Map p43; cnr Samdech Sothearos & Sihanouk Blvds; noodle soups US$3.30-4.30; ⏰6.45am-9pm; ✱) Big bowls of *pho* in a tidy and blissfully air-conditioned space.

Morning Glory   THAI $$
(Map p43; 57 St 240; mains US$3-4; ⏰10am-10pm; ✱📶) A superb deal for Thai food this good. It also has Indonesian and Filipino food on the menu.

Villa Khmer   CAMBODIAN $
(Map p43; 215 St 294; meals US$2.50-4; ✱) The US$2.50 all-you-can eat lunch buffet, with a selection of Cambodian favourites that rotates daily, is a steal given the attractive open-air space. Classic Khmer menu at other times; 'small' dishes feed two.

Boat Noodle Restaurant   THAI $$
(Map p43; ☎012 200426; St 294; mains US$3-4; ⏰7am-9pm) Stately wooden house festooned with antiques exudes old-school ambience and serves decent-value Thai and Cambodian food.

CENTRE SOUTH (NORODOM WEST & PSAR O RUSSEI)

TOP CHOICE La Residence   FRENCH $$$
(Map p43; ☎224582; 22 St 214; mains US$12-48, set lunches US$15-29; ⏰lunch Mon-Fri, dinner Sat & Sun; ✱) Princess Marie's daughter Ratana has converted part of the family home into this classy contemporary restaurant. Pass through the immense wooden doors and enjoy fine French food, including a foie gras speciality menu and superb seafood, plus a great Café de Paris steak.

TOP CHOICE Sleuk Chark   CAMBODIAN $$
(Map p43; 165 St 51; mains US$3-10; ⏰10.30am-3pm & 5-10pm; ✱) This place doesn't look much from the street, but venture inside for a dining experience that includes a zesty

frogs legs and quails eggs in a sugar palm and black pepper clay pot or a fish egg soup. Or test your taste buds with fried spiders or beef with red ants.

TOP CHOICE **The Vegetarian** VEGETARIAN $
(Map p43; 11 St 200; mains US$1-1.50; ☺10am-8pm; ☑) This may well be the best value in Phnom Penh. All dishes are under US$2, and it doesn't skimp on portions either. Noodles and fried rice are the specialities.

Mama Restaurant BACKPACKER CAFE $
(Map p43; 10C St 111; mains US$1.50-3.50; ☺7am-9pm) The menu at this long-running hole-in-the-wall in the backpacker district south of Psar O Russei includes a bit of Khmer, Thai, French and even African.

Capitol Restaurant BACKPACKER CAFE $
(Map p43; 14 St 182; mains US$1-2; ☺6am-9pm) Another Psar O Russei option, it's popular for a reason – namely really cheap food and a good selection of both Western and Khmer favourites. Breakfasts are an especially good deal.

City Mall FOOD COURT $
(Map p43; City Mall, Monireth Blvd; ☺9am-9pm; ☑) Large food court next to Legend Cinema on the top floor of Phnom Penh's newest mall.

Lucky Supermarket SUPERMARKET $
(Map p43; City Mall, Monireth Blvd; ☺8am-9pm) The sprawling City Mall branch of Lucky is the king of supermarkets.

CENTRE SOUTH (BKK AREA)

TOP CHOICE **Living Room** CAFE $$
(Map p43; 9 St 306; mains US$3.50-7; ☺7am-8.30pm; ☑☎☑) Family-friendly place in an atmospheric colonial house with a wonderfully healthy menu and fresh fruit drinks to die for (try the mango passion smoothie). The veggie and non-veggie plates (US$6), which mix four or five snacks and dips, are highly recommended. Garden seating available, and there's a small air-conditioned room upstairs.

TOP CHOICE **Boddhi Tree Umma Restaurant** FUSION $
(Map p43; ☑211397; 50 St 113; mains US$4-6; ☺7am-9pm; ☎) This is heaven compared to the hell of Tuol Sleng across the road. The lush garden is the perfect place to seek solace and silence after the torture museum. The impressive menu includes fusion fla-

vours, Asian dishes, sandwiches and salads, innovative shakes and tempting desserts.

TOP CHOICE **Taste Budz** INDIAN $$
(Map p43; ☑092 961554; 13E St 282; mains US$3-6; ☺10am-10pm; ☑) As the preponderance of Indian expats eating lunch here indicates, this is the most toothsome of Phnom Penh's many Indian restaurants. The speciality is Kerala (South Indian) cuisine. The spicy *kedai* dishes are divine. Order *porotta* (flatbread) on the side and dig in (with your hands, naturally).

Le Jardin CAFE $$
(Map p43; 16 St 360; mains US$3.50-6; ☺closed Mon) Taking full advantage of a garden laden with jackfruit trees, this family-oriented cafe has a sandpit and a play house. Snacks and salads for adults, pastas and titbits for kids.

Sonoma Oyster Bar SEAFOOD $$
(Map p43; ☑222361; 159 St 278; oyster platters US$6.50-8.50; ☺5-11pm; ☑) Scallops and steaks are among other tempting options. It's tiny – reservations recommended.

Yumi FUSION $$
(Map p43; ☑092 163903; 29a St 288; meals US$7-10; ☺noon-2.30pm & 6-10.30pm Mon-Sat) With a compact menu of refreshingly original tapas and other light Asian fare, it's the perfect spot for a late dinner before a night out on nearby St 278.

Chayyam THAI $$
(Map p43; 8A St 278; mains US$4-6) It has some of the best Thai food in the city, along with Khmer specialities, conveniently located in the heart of Golden St. Traditional Khmer dances take place some nights.

Ocean SEAFOOD $$$
(Map p43; ☑017 766690; 11 St 288; mains US$5-15; ☺noon-2pm & 6-10pm Mon-Sat, 6-10pm Sun) Another seafood speciality restaurant, Ocean's menu is predominantly Mediterranean and includes a tempting selection of fish and crustaceans.

Samaky FUSION $$
(Map p43; 9 St 51; mains US$4-12; ☺7am-11.30pm; ☎) You can 'make your own steak' here – choose a cut and a sauce. Exciting fusion dishes include flavourful stuffed calamari and a range of tapas. Samaky employs waiters brought up through Friends and similar programs to train at-risk Cambodians.

GOING LOCAL

Khmer Barbecues & Soup Restaurants

After dark, Khmer eateries scattered across town illuminate their Angkor Beer signs, hailing locals in for fine fare and generous jugs of draught beer. Don't be shy, and heed the call – the food is great and the atmosphere lively.

The speciality at most of these places is grilled strips of meat or seafood, but they also serve fried noodles and rice, curries and other pan-fried faves along with some veggie options.

Many of these places also offer *phnom pleung* (hill of fire), which amounts to cook-your-own meat over a personal barbecue. One good block for Khmer barbecues is on St 13 between St 154 and St 172 (Map p48). Another speciality is *soup chhnang dei* (cook-your-own soup in a clay pot), which are great fun if you go in a group. Other diners will often help with protocol, as it is important to cook things in the right order so as not to overcook half the ingredients and eat the rest raw.

A few recommended local eateries:

City 360 (Map p52; City Villa, cnr St 71 & 360; mains US$1.50-2.50; ⏰10.30am-1.30pm & 4pm-midnight) Here you can cook your own meat *phnom pleung* and wash it down with US$5 towers of draught beer.

Red Cow (Map p43; 126 Norodom Blvd; mains US$2-3; mains US$3-5; ⏰4-11pm) Grills up everything imaginable – eel, eggplant, frog, goat, pig and quail – along with curries and other traditional Khmer dishes.

Sovanna (Map p43; 2C St 21; mains US$2-3; ⏰4-11pm) Always jumping with locals and even a smattering of expats who have made this their barbecue of choice.

Master Suki (Map p48; 7th fl, Sorya Shopping Centre; soup from US$5) It may be a Japanese concept, but it has a very Khmer touch and is a great way to try soup *chhnang dei*, with photos to help choose the ingredients. Great views as well.

Street Fare & Markets

Street fare is not quite as familiar or user-friendly as in, say, Bangkok. But if you're a little adventurous and want to save boatloads of money, look no further. Breakfast is when the street-side eateries really get hopping, as most Cambodian men eat out for breakfast. Look for bums on seats and you can't go wrong.

Phnom Penh's many markets all have large central eating areas where stalls serve up local faves like noodle soup and fried noodles, as well as decidedly more exotic specialities, many spiced up with insects. Most dishes cost a reasonable 4000r to 6000r.

Aussie XL INTERNATIONAL **$$**
(Map p43; 205A St 51; mains US$3-10; ⏰11am-11pm) The name is telling – this is a place for serious fill-ups. Super-sized fish, lamb, chicken, beef and about every other type of burger imaginable is available. Weekends sometimes see pigs roasted on spits.

Comme a la Maison FRENCH **$$**
(Map p43; 13 St 57; mains US$5-10; ⏰6am-10.30pm) Something of an upmarket French deli, it has a compact menu of provincial French fare, plus pizza and pasta and enticing weekly specials. An on-site bakery makes this a good spot for an early *petit dejeuner*.

Flavours of India INDIAN **$$**
(Map p43; ☎990455; 158 St 63; mains US$4-6; ⏰9.30am-10.30pm; ✴🌐) Another eatery popular with the South Asian community, it specialises in North Indian and Nepalese cuisine. Ask them to spice it up or they will spice it down for tourists.

Tom Yum Kung THAI **$**
(Map p43; 10 St 278; mains US$2.50-3.50; 🌐) Some of the best Thai food in this part of town and it's priced right.

Café Soleil VEGETARIAN **$**
(Map p43; St 22D St 278; mains US$2-4; 🌐🍽) New spot with cheap-as-chips vego dishes like fried noodles, pumpkin curry, hummus and salads.

Nike Pizza ITALIAN **$**
(Map p43; St 63; dishes US$3-4.50; ⏰10am-10pm) The burly calzones (US$3.50) are the high-

If the markets are just too hot or claustrophobic for your taste, look out for the mobile street sellers carrying their wares on their shoulders or wheeling it around in small carts.

The best markets for breakfast and lunch are Psar Thmei (Map p48), Russian Market (Map p52) and Psar O Russei (Map p43). Psar Kandal (Map p48), just off the riverfont between Sts 144 & 154, gets going a little later and is an early-evening option. Another popular all-day option is a row of curry noodle stalls opposite Wat Botum Park (Map p43).

Over the Bridge

The reconstruction of the Chruoy Changvar Bridge (Japanese Bridge) spanning the Tonlé Sap River created a restaurant boom on the river's east bank. There are dozens of restaurants lining the highway – from the decidedly downmarket to the obviously over-the-top – but most are interesting places for a very Cambodian night out. Most charge about US$3 to US$10 a dish (with around 300 dishes to choose from). Heading north, the restaurants start to appear about 1km from the bridge. The larger places on NH6 include a resident band and the amps are often cranked up to 11 – remember to sit a fair distance from the stage. A row of slightly more subdued restaurants line the west bank of the Mekong River about 4km north of the bridge. To get to these you have to follow the small river road that parallels the NH6 – turn right off the highway anywhere beyond Mother-In-Law House 2 to access this road.

Places come in and out of favour, but following are some of the consistently popular. All have English menus. A moto should cost about US$2 or so each way from the city centre.

Boeung Meas The music is loud and the decor tacky, but this huge restaurant is a fine place for a real Khmer experience. Karaoke, seafood (including river lobster) and fine sunset views.

Mother-In-Law House 2 About 200m beyond Boeung Meas, this delightfully named establishment has a huge menu of Cambodian, Vietnamese and Chinese food, served in bushy thatch-roofed pavilions facing the sunset.

Chamkar Nornaung This one is a bit further along, on the Mekong River about 350m south of the main ferry to Koh Dach (Silk Island). It's a good lunch option after a morning on Koh Dach, with little pavilions out over the river.

Rum Chang Restaurant Long one of the best places for authentic Khmer food, Rum Chang has no band and the location overlooking the Mekong is very breezy. It's on the river road 700m south of the Ko Dach ferry.

light at this pint-sized budget Italian joint, along with charcoal-fired thin-crust pizza and the usual range of pastas and salads.

Chinese Noodle/China Restaurant — CHINESE $
(Map p43; 553 Monivong Blvd; mains US$1.50-2.50) Twin bargain eateries popular among locals and expats alike. Chinese Noodle is all about – what else – noodles, with anything from duck to pig stomach. China Restaurant is famous for its dumpling-like pork buns.

Friendly House — CAMBODIAN $
(Map p43; 203 St 310; mains US$1-1.75; ☺8am-9pm) It's not a BBQ, but it draws a mostly local crowd who appreciate affordable Cambodian and Vietnamese dishes like lemongrass chicken and fried noodles with seafood.

Lucky Burger — FAST FOOD $
(Map p43; 160 Sihanouk Blvd; burgers US$1.80; ☺8am-9pm; 🌐) Among the local fast-food chains, this is one of the most established. Don't expect McDonald's, but at least the ingredients are fresh.

Lucky Supermarket — SUPERMARKET $
(Map p43; 160 Sihanouk Blvd; ☺7am-9pm) The leading supermarket chain in town, with a professional deli counter.

RUSSIAN MARKET AREA
There is nothing better than an ice coffee or fresh fruit shake after surviving the scrum that is the Russian Market. Most of these are within spitting distance of the market, but don't try it, as you won't be popular with the locals. Also, see Cafe Yejj (p63).

Sumatra INDONESIAN $
(Map p52; 35 St 456; mains US$1-3; ☺10am-8.30pm; 🖉) The vegetarian dishes, which average about US$1.50, are absolutely ridiculous value, although big eaters may have to order two. The spicy *balado* (tomato and chilli sauce) dishes are good. Seating is on a leafy garden patio under a tin roof.

Spring Vale JAPANESE $$
(Map p52; 27 St 450; mains US$3-5; ☺11.30am-3pm Mon-Thu, 11.30am-7pm Fri & Sat) Relaxing corner lunch stop with a tidy menu of creative Japanese dishes, including affordable sushi.

Jars of Clay CAFE $
(Map p52; 39B St 155; cakes US$1.50, mains US$3-4.75; ☺7.30am-9pm Mon-Sat; 🖳🖃) Thirst-quenching drinks, light bites and home-baked cakes, plus welcome air-conditioning on a hot day.

Sisters BAKERY $
(Map p52; 26B St 446; sandwiches US$2.50-3.50; ☺7am-6pm) Tiny little place that punches above its weight with light bites, all-day breakfasts and excellent homemade cakes, including a zesty lemon meringue pie.

Coffee Korner CAFE $
(Map p52; 172 St 155; mains US$3.50-10; ☺7.30am-9pm) Lively corner cafe with an encyclopaedic menu of international and Asian food. Meals lean toward heavy and calorific; burgers and eggy breakfasts feature prominently.

🍷 Drinking

Phnom Penh has some great bars and it's definitely worth at least one big night on the town. Many venues are clustered along the riverfront, but one or two of the best are tucked away in the backstreets. 'Golden St' (St 278) is another popular bar strip. Most bars are open until midnight and beyond.

Keep an eye out for happy hours around town, as these include two-for-one offers and the like and can save quite a bit of cash. Several of the leading hotels, a few of which are listed below, have great happy hours that are worth the diversion.

Among the restaurants that double as bars, the FCC is the one can't-miss of the bunch, especially during happy hour.

TOP CHOICE Elephant Bar BAR
(Map p48; St 92; ☺2pm-midnight) Few places are more atmospheric than this sophisticated bar at the Raffles Hotel Le Royal. It has been drawing journalists, politicos, and the rich and famous for more than 80 years. There are half-price happy hours between 4pm and 9pm, plus accompanying snacks and a pool table.

Chow BAR
(Map p48; 277 Sisowath Quay; ☺7am-11pm) If you prefer to be on the river, head up to Quay hotel's swanky rooftop lounge, which has views, cooling breezes, a plunge pool and happy hours (half price) from 5pm to 7pm. The cocktail list is arguably the most creative in town, including zesty infusions like ginger and lemon grass.

Zeppelin Café BAR
(Map p48; 109 St 51; ☺6.30pm-late) Who says vinyl is dead? It lives on in the Cambodian capital, thanks to the owner of this old-school rock bar manning the turntables every night.

Top Banana BAR
(Map p43; 9 St 278) There's no question where the top backpacker party spot in Phnom Penh is. The rooftop bar of this guesthouse goes off practically every night of the week – sometimes with spontaneous dancing into the wee hours.

Rubies BAR
(Map p43; cnr Sts 240 & 19; ☺10am-late, closed Mon) Small bar, big personality. Hip bartenders mix cool cocktails and the expat masses flock. The bar is lined with wood and spills out onto the pavement on weekends. Dubs itself a wine bar but beer and cocktails are just as popular.

Paddy Rice IRISH
(Map p48; 213 Sisowath Quay; ☺24hr) A real jack of all trades – good pub grub, big screens for sports viewing, and occasional live music – Wednesday is open-mic night. All this in a perfect riverside location.

Elsewhere BAR
(Map p43; 2 St 278; ☺8am-late) With ambient vibes, a great drinks menu and two plunge pools for punters, it's sedate by day but sexy by night. Hit the happy hours from 4pm to 8pm and forget your worries over an 'amnesia' cocktail.

Le Moon BAR
(Map p48; 1 St 154) Another hotel bar, the Amanjaya's rooftop offering scores points for atmosphere and views, but service is spotty. Bring patience.

Mekong River Restaurant BAR-RESTAURANT
(Map p48; cnr St 118 & Sisowath Quay; ☺24hr) All-day happy hour means US$0.75 draft beers from 7am to midnight, plus a restaurant that stays open until the wee hours while most riverfront kitchens shut down around 10pm.

Blue Chili BAR
(Map p48; 36 St 178; ☺6pm-late) The owner of this gay-friendly bar stages his own drag show every Friday and Saturday at 10.30pm.

Bouchon WINE BAR
(Map p43; 3/4 St 246; ☺4pm-midnight; ❋) Bouchon has a great selection of French wines, plus patés and other French nibbles, in a contemporary space on a quiet side street opposite the Himawari Hotel. A glass of house red costs US$3.50.

Green Vespa IRISH PUB
(Map p43; 95 Sisowath Quay; ☺6am-11pm) A favourite watering hole for local expats, the Vespa has a huge drinks collection, including some serious single malts. It's become a dining destination in its own right thanks to its original hearty pub fare and great selection of sophisticated specials.

Le Sauvignon WINE BAR
(Map p43; 6B St 302; ☺noon-midnight Tue-Sun) Elegant wine bar with a popular outdoor patio in the NGO district. Afternoons are tea time.

Score SPORTS BAR
(Map p43; ☎221357; 5 St 282; ☺8am-late) With its ginormous screen, this spacious bar is best place to watch the big game – although there's too much glare on the screen during daylight hours. They open early for night games in the US, and serve good breakfasts. Several pool tables tempt those who would rather play than watch.

Gym Bar SPORTS BAR
(Map p48; 42 St 178; ☺11am-late) The only workout going on here is raising glasses. This top sports bar, with ample big and small screens, was undergoing a management change and a major revamp when we visited.

Pickled Parrot SPORTS BAR
(Map p48; 4 St 104; ☺24hr) One of the few bars in town where you can wash up any time of the day and find a fellow drinker supping a beer, this is a friendly air-con spot with big screens, a pool table, cheap drinks and plenty of channels. Not a hostess bar, unlike many others in this strip.

Dodo Rhum House BAR
(Map p48; 42C St 178; ☺5pm-late) Specialising in homemade flavoured rums, this friendly bar also offers an excellent fish fillet and other French favourites.

Rainbow Bar BAR
(Map p48; 36 St 172) Laid-back, gay-friendly bar.

Howie Bar BAR
(Map p48; 32 St 51; ☺7pm-6am) Friendly and fun place that is the perfect spillover when the Heart of Darkness is packed.

☆ Entertainment

For news on what's happening here while you are in town, grab a copy of *This Week,* a new weekly listings guide produced by online listings and information source **Lady Penh** (www.ladypenh.com). The Friday issue of the *Phnom Penh Post,* which includes the *7 Days* magazine supplement, also has weekly entertainment listings, as does the Friday edition of *Cambodia Daily. AsiaLife* is a free monthly with entertainment features and some listings.

Live Music

Phnom Penh boasts a surprisingly active music scene, with several talented expat and mixed Khmer-expat bands, most of whom play quite a bit of original music in addition to covers spanning all genres imaginable.

Equinox BAR
(Map p43; 3A St 278; ☺7am-late) At the heart of the action on St 278, this is a popular place with a lively outdoor bar downstairs and bands upstairs from Thursday to Saturday. Works well as just a bar on other nights.

Memphis Pub MUSIC BAR
(Map p48; 3 St 118; ☺4pm-late, closed Sun) It's not closed, it just has soundproof doors. Memphis has a decent house cover band and frequently attracts more diverse acts. There's an open-mic jam session on Monday night.

Sharky MUSIC BAR
(Map p48; www.sharkybarblog.com; 126 St 130; ☺5pm-late) An old-school Phnom Penh hangout long famous for billiards and babes, Sharky's has done a good job of redirecting some of its focus towards quality live music.

Riverside Bistro BAR
(Map p48; 273 Sisowath Quay; ☺7am-midnight; ☺☎) A popular bar-restaurant with pool tables and live music from 8.30pm Wednesday

to Saturday, plus an open-mic night on Sunday.

Nightclubs

There aren't many out-and-out nightclubs in Phnom Penh and the few that there are tend to be playgrounds of the privileged, attracting children of the country's political elite who aren't always the best-behaved people to hang out with. The volume is normally cranked up to 11 and drinks are pretty expensive. Don't expect a crowd until well after 10pm.

Heart of Darkness NIGHTCLUB
(Map p48; 26 St 51; ⊙8pm-late) This Phnom Penh institution with the alluring Angkor theme has evolved into a nightclub more than a bar. It goes off every night of the week, attracting all – and we mean all – sorts. Still, everybody should stop in at least once just to bask in the aura of the place.

Pontoon NIGHTCLUB
(Map p48; 80 St 172; www.pontoonclub.com; admission US$3-5 weekends, free weekdays; ⊙9.30pm-late) After floating around from pier to pier for a few years (hence the name), the city's premier nightclub has finally found a permanent home on *terra firma*. It draws top local DJs and occasional big foreign acts. Thursday is gay-friendly night, with a 1am lady-boy show.

Riverhouse Lounge NIGHTCLUB
(Map p48; cnr St 110 & Sisowath Quay; ⊙4pm-2am) This atmospheric lounge bar has DJs and live music through the week, and really goes off on weekends. It's chic and cool, adding up to the place where the hip young Khmers hang out.

Rock NIGHTCLUB
(Map p52; Monivong Blvd; admission depends on event; ⊙until late) If you want a more authentic local experience, Rock is your best bet. Looks like a gigantic Home Depot, but Khmers go crazy for the place, complete with karaoke rooms and all.

Mao's Club NIGHTCLUB
(Map p48; cnr Sisowath Quay & St 108; ⊙8pm-late) In an attractive colonial-era space, Mao's was recently converted from bar to nightclub. It has the setting to succeed but time will tell.

Spark NIGHTCLUB
(Parkway Sq, Mao Tse Toung Blvd; admission depends on event; ⊙until late) Owned by the daughter of Prime Minister Hun Sen; security should be tight.

Film

Phnom Penh has two state-of-the-art cineplexes that show movies exclusively in English, plus two excellent expat-oriented boutique movie houses that have bars and a range of other activities on offer. Guesthouses in backpacker zones like Boeng Kak and St 258 also show movies every night.

⟨TOP CHOICE⟩ **Meta House** CINEMA
(Map p43; 37 Samdech Sothearos Blvd; www.meta-house.com; ⊙4pm-midnight Tue-Sun; ☎) This German-run open-air theatre screens arthouse films, documentaries and shorts from Cambodia and around the world nightly at 7pm. Films are sometimes followed by Q&As with those involved. Order German sausages, pizza and beer to supplement your viewing experience.

Flicks CINEMA
(Map p43; ☎097 8967827; www.theflicks-cambodia.com; 39B St 95; tickets US$3.50; ✱☎) It shows at least two movies a day in an uber-comfortable air-conditioned screening room. You can watch both on one ticket. Kids' matinees on weekends.

Legend Cinema CINEMA
(Map p43; www.legend-cinemas.com; 3rd fl, City Mall, Monorith Blvd; tickets US$3-5; ✱) Large Western-style theatre.

The Cineplex CINEMA
(Map p48; Sorya Shopping Centre; tickets US$4-6; ✱) Large theatre screens Western blockbusters on the top floor of Phnom Penh's premier shopping mall.

Bophana Centre CINEMA, ARCHIVE
(Map p43; ☎992174; www.bophana.org; 64 St 200; admission free) Established by Cambodian-French filmmaker Rithy Panh, this is an audiovisual resource for filmmakers and researchers, and visitors can explore its archive of old photographs and films and attend free film screenings on Saturdays at 4pm.

French Cultural Centre CINEMA
(Map p43; www.ccf-cambodge.org; 218 St 184) Has frequent movie screenings in French during the week, usually kicking off at 6.30pm.

Mekong River Restaurant CINEMA
(Map p48; cnr St 118 & Sisowath Quay) Screens two original films in English or French, one covering the Khmer Rouge and the other

on the subject of landmines. Showings are hourly from 11am to 9pm and cost US$3.

Classical Dance & Arts

🎭**Apsara Arts Association**　DANCE
(Map p36; ☎012 979335; www.apsara-art.org; 71 St 598; tickets US$6-7) Alternate performances of classical dance and folk dance are held most Saturdays at 7pm (call to confirm). Visitors are also welcome from 7.30am to 10.30am and from 2pm to 5pm Monday to Saturday to watch the students in training (suggested donation: US$3). However, it is important to remember that this is a training school – noise and flash photography should be kept to a minimum. It's in Tuol Kork district, in the far north of the city.

🎭**Sovanna Phum Arts Association**　SHADOW PUPPETS
(off Map p52; ☎987564; www.shadow-puppets .org; 166 St 99, btwn Sts 484 & 498; adult/child

LOCAL KNOWLEDGE

ARN CHORN-POND, MUSICIAN

Arn Chorn-Pond is the founder of **Cambodian Living Arts** (CLA; Map p43; ☎986032; www.cambodianlivingarts.org; 128 G9 Samdech Sothearos), an organisation dedicated to reviving traditional music, dance and other Cambodian art forms that were nearly lost during the Khmer Rouge years. Arn himself almost didn't survive that dark time. His parents ran a respected traditional opera company in Battambang. This made them immediate targets of the Khmer Rouge, which slaughtered more than 90% of performing artists, according to Arn. Twenty-five members of Arn's immediate family, including five of his eight siblings, were killed.

But the Khmer Rouge needed to keep some musicians around to play their revolutionary hymns. Arn was among several children in Battambang recruited to dance and play the flute and the *khim* (a traditional Cambodian string instrument) at a local killing temple.

'They killed three kids who were slow to learn,' Arn says. 'I was a fast learner because I had music in my blood. If there was no music at that time, I probably would have been killed. Music saved my life.'

At the killing temple, Arn witnessed all sorts of atrocities. The Khmer Rouge made him play music to drown out the sounds of the screams. In the late 1970s, at the age of 12, Arn was forced to trade in his *khim* for a gun as he was recruited into the beleaguered Khmer Rouge army. He eventually managed to escape over the border to a refugee camp in Thailand, where he was ultimately adopted along with several other refugees by an American family from New Hampshire.

When Arn returned to Cambodia several years later, people in Battambang still recognized him as 'that little boy who played the *khim*'. Since its establishment in 1998, Cambodian Living Arts has supported elder Cambodian musicians to train scores of young and mostly at-risk Cambodians in traditional music, dance and other forms.

Arn shared with us his top five places for cultural connections in Phnom Penh. In addition to these, the CLA runs cultural tours for tourists in both Phnom Penh and in other provinces - see the website for details.

Amrita Performing Arts (www.amritaperformingarts.org) 'They work with traditional Apsara dancers to create new stories, and are working closely with CLA to organise the "Season of Cambodia" in New York in 2013.'

Apsara Arts Association (p73) 'A great family-run organisation that's working with a new generation of kids to preserve forms like Apsara and traditional folk dance.'

CLA's Folk Dance Troupe 'They perform every Thursday in front of the National Museum.'

CLA's Yike Class (65 Samdech Sothearos Blvd) 'These daily traditional-opera classes for at-risk youth are run by master theatre performer Ieng Sithul and are open to tourists. Many of the kids here would be prostitutes if not for this class.'

Sovann Phum (p73) 'They do a great job creating new stories and new dances out of old Cambodian traditional forms.'

US$5/3) Regular traditional shadow-puppet performances and occasional classical dance and traditional drum shows are held here at 7.30pm every Friday and Saturday night. Audience members are invited to try their hand at the shadow puppets after the 50-minute performance. Classes are available here in the art of shadow puppetry, puppet making, classical and folk dance, and traditional Khmer musical instruments.

Chatomuk Theatre   THEATRE
(Map p43; Sisowath Quay) Check the flyer out front for information on performances at the Chatomuk Theatre, just north of the Hotel Cambodiana. Officially, it has been turned into a government conference centre, but it regularly plays host to cultural performances.

🛍 Shopping

There is some great shopping to be had in Phnom Penh, but don't forget to bargain in the markets or you'll have your 'head shaved', local-speak for being ripped off. Most markets are open from around 6.30am to 5.30pm. Some shops keep shorter hours

by opening later, while tourist-oriented stores often stay open into the evening.

A few stores surrounding Russian Market specialise in higher quality clothing, mostly made in Vietnam, that is almost guaranteed to be authentic. It costs a bit more but still retails for a fraction of what you'd pay back home (eg, a name-brand Gortex ski jacket for US$100).

As well as the markets, there are now some shopping malls in Phnom Penh. While these may not be quite as glamorous as the likes of the Siam Paragon in Bangkok, they are good places to browse thanks to the air-conditioning. **Sorya Shopping Centre** (Map p48; cnr Sts 63 & 154) is currently pick of the crop with a good range of shops and superb views over the more traditional Psar Thmei.

There are several boutiques specialising in silk furnishings and stylish clothing, as well as glam accessories. Many are conveniently located on St 240, Cambodia's answer to London's King's Rd.

Plenty of shops sell locally produced paintings along St 178, opposite the Royal University of Fine Arts between streets 13 and 19. With a new generation of artists

---

SHOPPING TO HELP CAMBODIA

There are a host of tasteful shops selling handicrafts and textiles to raise money for projects to assist disadvantaged Cambodians. These are a good place to spend some dollars, as it helps to put a little bit back into the country.

Cambodian Handicraft Association (CHA; Map p43; 56 St 113; ☺8am-7pm) This well-stocked showroom and workshop sells fine handmade silk clothing, scarves, toys and bags produced by land-mine and polio disabled.

Daughters (Map p48; www.daughtersofcambodia.org; 65 St 178; ☺9am-6pm Mon-Sat) Daughters is an NGO that runs a range of programs to train and assist former prostitutes and victims of sex trafficking. The fashionable clothes, bags and accessories here are made with eco-friendly cotton and natural dyes by program participants.

Friends n' Stuff (Map p48; 215 St 13; ☺11am-9pm) The closest thing to a charity shop or thrift store in Phnom Penh, with a good range of new and secondhand products sold to generate money to help street children.

Mekong Blue (Map p48; www.bluesilk.org; 9 St 130; ☺7.30am-7pm) Phnom Penh boutique for Stung Treng's best-known silk cooperative to empower women. Produces beautiful scarves and shawls.

Mekong Quilts (Map p43; ☏219607; www.mekong-quilts.org; 49 St 240; ☺9am-7pm) An incredible queen-/king-sized quilt costs from US$353/377 for silk, US$180/230 for cotton. Helps women in remote rural villages.

Nyemo Main store (Map p43; www.nyemo.com; 71 St 240; ☺7am-10pm); Outlet store (Map p52; Russian Market; ☺8am-5pm) In Le Rit's restaurant and with a branch at Russian Market, Nyemo focuses on quality silk and soft toys for children. It helps vulnerable women return to work.

Rajana Main store (Map p52; www.rajanacrafts.org; 170 St 450; ☺7am-5.30pm Mon-Fri, 10.30am-5pm Sun); Market store (Map p52; Russian Market) One of the best all-around handicrafts stores,

coming up, the selection is much stronger than it once was. Do bargain. Lots of reproduction busts of famous Angkorian sculptures are available along this stretch – great for the mantelpiece back home.

There are several galleries and art spaces of note to seek out around the city.

Psar Thmei
MARKET

(ផ្សារថ្មី; Central Market; Map p48; St 53) A landmark building in the capital, the art-deco Psar Thmei is often called the Central Market, a reference to its location and size. The huge domed hall resembles a Babylonian ziggurat and some claim it ranks as one of the 10 largest domes in the world. The design allows for maximum ventilation, and even on a sweltering day the central hall is cool and airy. The market was recently renovated with assistance from the French government and is looking in fine fettle these days.

The market has four wings filled with stalls selling gold and silver jewellery, antique coins, dodgy watches, clothing and other such items. For photographers, the fresh food section affords many opportunities. For a local lunch, there are a host of food stalls located on the western side, which faces Monivong Blvd.

Psar Thmei is undoubtedly the best market for browsing. However, it has a reputation among Cambodians for overcharging on most products.

Russian Market
MARKET

(ផ្សារទួលទំពូង; Psar Tuol Tong Pong; Map p52; south of Mao Tse Toung Blvd) Known to foreigners as Russian Market (Russians shopped here during the 1980s), this sweltering bazaar (and the stores surrounding it) is the place to shop for souvenirs and discounted Western name-brand clothing. We can't vouch for the authenticity of everything, but along with plenty of knock-offs you will find genuine articles stitched in local factories that has found its way to the market. You'll pay as little as 10% of the price you'll pay back home for brands like Banana Republic, Billabong, Calvin Klein, Colombia, Gap, Gant and Next.

Russian Market also has a large range of handicrafts and antiquities (many fake), including miniature Buddhas, woodcarvings, betel-nut boxes, silks, silver jewellery, musical instruments and so on. Bargain hard,

Rajana aims to promote fair wages and training. It has a beautiful selection of cards, some quirky metalware products, quality jewellery, bamboo crafts, lovely shirts, gorgeous wall hangings, pepper, candles – you name it.

Sobbhana (Map p48; www.sobbhana.org; 23 St 144; ☺8am-noon & 1-5.30pm) Established by Princess Marie, the Sobbhana Foundation is a not-for-profit organisation training women in traditional weaving. Beautiful silks in a stylish boutique.

Tabitha (Map p43; 239 St 360; ☺8am-6pm Mon-Sat) A leading NGO shop with a good collection of silk bags, tableware, bedroom decorations and children's toys. Proceeds go towards rural community development, such as well drilling.

Peace Handicrafts (Map p52; www.peacehandicraft.com; 39C St 155; ☺7.30am-6pm) Carries an impressive range of souvenirs, including affordable Buddha heads and other statues, stationary and silks. Provides training and employment opportunities to landmine victims and other disabled people.

Rehab Craft Workshop (Map p43; ☎726801; 10A St 322; ☺8am-5pm Mon-Fri); Store (Map p43; 1 St 278; ☺9am-9pm) Sells carvings, weavings, wallets, jewellery and bags, all produced in their workshop by disabled artisans. The workshop is open to visitors – call ahead to schedule a visit.

Villageworks (Map p43; www.villageworks.com; 118 St 113; ☺8am-5pm) Opposite Tuol Sleng Museum, this shop has the inevitable silk and bags, as well as coconut-shell utensils made by poor and disadvantaged artisans in Kompong Thom province.

Watthan Artisans (off Map p43; www.wac.khmerproducts.com; 180 Norodom Blvd; ☺8am-5pm) Located at the entrance to Wat Than, it sells silk and other products, including wonderful contemporary hand bags, made by a project-supported cooperative of landmine and polio victims. You can visit the on-site woodworking and weaving workshops.

as thousands of tourists pass through here each month.

This is the one market all visitors should come to at least once during a trip to Phnom Penh.

Psar O Russei   MARKET

(ផ្សារអូរ៉ូស្សី; Map p43; St 182) Much bigger than either Psar Thmei or Russian Market, Psar O Russei sells foodstuffs, costume jewellery, imported toiletries, secondhand clothes and everything else you can imagine from hundreds of stalls. The market is housed in a huge labyrinth of a building that looks like a shopping mall from the outside.

Psar Olympic   MARKET

(Map p43; btwn Sts 286 & 298) Items for sale include bicycle parts, clothes, electronics and assorted edibles. This is quite a modern market set in a covered location.

Night Market   MARKET

(Psar Reatrey; Map p48; St 108 & Sisowath Quay; ☺5pm-11pm Fri-Sun) A cooler al-fresco version of Russian Market, this night market takes place every Friday, Saturday and Sunday evening, if rain doesn't stop play. Bargain vigorously, as prices can be on the high side. Interestingly, it's probably more popular with Khmers than foreigners.

Psar Chaa   MARKET

(Map p48; St 108) This is a scruffy place that deals in household goods, clothes and jewellery. There are small restaurants, food vendors and jewellery stalls, as well as some good fresh-fruit stalls outside.

WExport   CLOTHES

Four Seasons (Map p43; Sihanouk Blvd; ☺7am-7pm); Winter (Map p52; St 155; ☺8am-7pm); Summer (Map p52; St 155; ☺7am-7pm) This is the biggest of the overrun outlets, with an impressive winter collection, plenty of kiddie clothing and a prominent main branch in the centre of town. A lifetime 20% discount kicks in if you spend US$250.

Ambre   SILK

(Map p48; 37 St 178; ☺10am-6pm) Leading Cambodian fashion designer Romyda Keth has turned this striking French-era mansion into an ideal showcase for her stunning silk collection.

Artisans d'Angkor   HANDICRAFTS

(Map p48; 12 St 13; ☺9am-6pm) Newly opened Phnom Penh branch of the venerable Siem Reap sculpture and silk specialist.

Bliss Boutique   CLOTHING

(Map p43; 29 St 240; ☺9am-9pm) Casual dresses, blouses and men's shirts made of wonderfully airy materials, plus silks and other textiles.

Couleurs d'Asie   ACCESSORIES

(Map p43; www.couleursdasie.net; 33 St 240; ☺8am-7pm) Great place for gift shopping, with lots of kids' clothes, silks, creams, chunky jewelry and brick-like bars of soap.

Kambuja   CLOTHING

(Map p48; 165 St 110; ☺9am-8pm) Blending the best of East and West, the Cambodian and American designers focus on female fashion but also produce some quality embroidered men's shirts.

Spicy Green Mango   CLOTHING

BKK (Map p43; 4A St 278; www.spicygreenmango .com; ☺9am-9pm); Riverside (Map p48; 29 St 178; ☺9.30am-9.30pm) *The* place to shop for original and creative kids' clothes, plus quality T-shirts and a hippyesque adult female line.

Subtyl   CLOTHING

(Map p43; www.subtyl.com; 43 St 240; ☺9am-7pm Mon-Sat, 9.30am-5pm Sun) French-run boutique offering stylish accessories and clothes, plus the Chilli Kids line for hip youngsters.

Tuol Sleng Shoes   SHOES

(Map p43; 136 St 143) Scary name, but there's nothing scary about the price of these custom-made handmade shoes. Neighbouring Beautiful Shoes is another good option.

Waterlily   ACCESSORIES

(Map p43; 37 St 240; ☺9am-7pm Mon-Fri, 9am-5pm Sat) Strikingly original bags, jewellery, art and dolls, all made from recycled materials.

Asasax Art Gallery   GALLERY

(Map p48; 192 St 178; ☺8am-7.30pm) High-end gallery featuring the striking work of artist Asasax.

French Cultural Centre   GALLERY

(Map p43; www.ccf-cambodge.org; 218 St 184; ☺11am-7pm Mon-Sat) Regularly hosts topnotch art and architecture exhibitions in its large gallery.

Reyum   GALLERY

(Map p48; www.reyum.org; 47 St 178) Under renovation when we dropped by, this nonprofit institute of arts and culture is expanding to include a bookshop and space for guest lectures, art classes for tourists, and exhibitions on all aspects of Cambodian culture. Also offers tours to a major ceramics studio outside town.

Bohr's Books BOOKS
(Map p48; 5 Samdech Sothearos Blvd; ⊙8am-8pm) Secondhand bookshop near the riverfront with a great selection of novels and nonfiction.

Citadel Knives KNIVES
(Map p48; ☎217617; www.knives-citadel.com; 10 St 110; ⊙9am-10pm) Premium knives and swords, locally produced.

D's Books BOOKS
Norodom East (Map p43; 79 St 240; ⊙9am-9pm); Riverfront (Map p48; 7 St 178; ⊙9am-9pm) The largest chain of secondhand bookshops in the capital, with a good range of titles.

Monument Books BOOKS
(Map p43; 111 Norodom Blvd; ⊙7am-8pm) The best-stocked bookshop in town, with almost every Cambodia-related book available, good maps and lots of LP titles, plus a wi-fi enabled branch of Blue Pumpkin cafe on site.

ℹ Information

Dangers & Annoyances

Phnom Penh is not as dangerous as people imagine, but it is important to take care. Armed robberies do sometimes occur, but statistically you would be very unlucky to be a victim.

Should you become the victim of a robbery, do not panic and do not, under any circumstances, struggle. Calmly raise your hands and let your attacker take what they want. *Do not* reach for your pockets, as the assailant may think you are reaching for a gun. Do not carry a bag at night, because it is more likely to make you a target.

It pays to be cautious in crowded bars or nightclubs frequented by the Khmer elite. Many pampered children hang out in popular places, bringing their bodyguards along for good luck. If trouble starts, and if they have bodyguards with them, it will only end in tears, big tears.

If you ride your own motorbike during the day, some police may try to fine you for the most trivial of offences, such as turning left in violation of a no-left-turn sign. At their most audacious, they may try to get you for riding with your headlights on during the day although, worryingly, it does not seem to be illegal for Cambodians to travel without their headlights on at night. The police will most likely demand US$5 from you and threaten to take you to the police station for an official US$20 fine if you do not pay. If you are patient with them and smile, you can usually get away with handing over

US$1. The trick is not to stop in the first place by not catching their eye.

The riverfront area of Phnom Penh, particularly places with outdoor seating, attracts many beggars, as do Psar Thmei and Russian Market. Generally, however, there is little in the way of push and shove.

Flooding is a major problem in the wet season (June to October), and heavy downpours see some streets turn into canals for a few hours.

Emergency

In the event of a medical emergency it may be necessary to be evacuated to Bangkok. See p78 for details of medical services in Phnom Penh.

Emergency numbers:
Ambulance (☎119, in English 724891)
Fire (☎118 in Khmer)
Police (☎117)

Internet Access

Phnom Penh is now well and truly wired, with prices dropping to less than US$0.50 per hour. Internet cafes are all over the city and you'll find plenty of computer terminals on the main backpacker strips – St 258, St 278, St 172 and Boeng Kak. Most internet cafes are set up for Skype or similar services, and offer cheap VOIP calls as well.

Most hotels and many cafes and restaurants offer wi-fi connections, usually free.

Media

Phnom Penh has two excellent English-language newspapers – the *Cambodia Daily* and the

---

BAG SNATCHING

Bag snatching has become a real problem in Phnom Penh and foreigners are often targeted. Hot spots include the riverfront and busy areas around popular markets, but there is no real pattern and the speeding motorbike thieves can strike any time, any place. In 2007 this ended in tragedy for a young French woman who was dragged from a speeding moto into the path of a vehicle. Try to wear close-fitting bags such as backpacks that don't dangle from the body temptingly. Don't hang expensive cameras around the neck and keep things close to the body and out of sight, particularly when walking in the road, crossing the road or travelling by moto, *remork* or *cyclo*. These guys are real pros and only need one chance.

Phnom Penh Post (www.phnompenhpost.com), both widely circulated. They mix original local-news content with international stories pulled from wire services. *AsiaLife* (www.asialife cambodia.com) is a monthly listings mag full of features targeted at Phnom Penh's expat community. The *Phnom Penh Visitors Guide* (www.canbypublications.com) is brimming with useful information on the capital and beyond, plus detailed maps of the entire city.

Medical Services

It is important to be aware of the difference between a clinic and a hospital in Phnom Penh. Clinics are good for most situations, but in a genuine emergency it is best to make for one of the hospitals.

Calmette Hospital (off Map p48; ☑426948; 3 Monivong Blvd; ⊘24hr) French-administered and the best of the local hospitals.

International SOS Medical Centre (Map p43; ☑216911; www.internationalsos.com; 161 St 51; ⊘8am-5.30pm Mon-Fri, 8am-noon Sat, emergency 24hr) One of the best medical services around town, but with prices to match. Also has a resident foreign dentist.

Naga Clinic (Map p43; ☑211300; www.naga clinic.com; 11 St 254; ⊘24hr) A French-run clinic for reliable consultations.

Pharmacie de la Gare (Map p48; ☑430205; 81 Monivong Blvd; ⊘7am-9pm Mon-Sat, 7am-5pm Sun) A pharmacy with English- and French-speaking consultants.

Royal Rattanak Hospital (☑991000; www.royalrattanakhospital.com; 11 St 592; ⊘24hr) International hospital affiliated with Bangkok Hospital and boasting top facilities. Expensive.

Tropical & Travellers Medical Clinic (Map p48; ☑306802; www.travellersmedicalclinic.com; 88 St 108) Well-regarded British-run clinic.

U-Care Pharmacy (Map p48; ☑222399; 26 Samdech Sothearos Blvd; ⊘8am-10pm) International-style pharmacy with a convenient location near the river.

Money

Those looking to change cash into riel need look no further than jewellery stalls around the markets of Phnom Penh. Central Market and Russian Market are the most convenient.

A number of upmarket hotels offer money-changing services, although this is usually reserved for their guests.

The main cluster of banks is found along the avenue formed by Sts 110 and 114, Cambodia's very own answer to Wall St.

ANZ Royal Bank (Map p48; 265 Sisowath Quay; ⊘8.30am-4pm Mon-Fri, 8.30am-noon Sat) ANZ has ATMs galore all over town, including at supermarkets and petrol stations, but there is a US$4 charge per transaction. This branch cashes US$ travellers cheques (2%).

Canadia Bank (Map p48; cnr St 110 & Monivong Blvd; ⊘8am-3.30pm Mon-Fri, 8-11.30am Sat) Changes travellers cheques of several currencies for a 2% commission, plus free cash advances on MasterCard and Visa. Canadia Bank ATMs around town incur no transaction charges. Canadia Bank also represents MoneyGram.

Foreign Trade Bank (Map p48; 3 St 114; ⊘8am-4pm Mon-Fri) Lowest commission in town on US-dollar travellers cheques at 1%. Can also arrange international money transfers.

CAB Bank (Map p48; 263 Sisowath Quay; ⊘7.30am-9pm) Convenient hours and location; cashes travellers cheques denominated in a range of currencies. There's also a Western Union office here (one of several in the city).

Post

Central post office (Map p48; St 13; ⊘7am-7pm) A landmark, it's in a charming building just east of Wat Phnom.

Post office (Map p43; cnr Monivong & Sihanouk Blvds; ⊘7am-5.30pm)

Tourist Information

Visitor Information Centre (Map p43; Sisowath Quay; ⊘8am-5.30pm) Located on the riverfront near the Chatomuk Theatre; while it doesn't carry a whole lot of information, it does offer free internet access on a solitary computer, free wi-fi, air-con and clean bathrooms. It can also arrange a guide.

ChildSafe (Map p48; www.childsafe-cambodia .org; 186 St 174; ⊘8am-5pm Mon-Fri) This drop-in centre and office for the ChildSafe campaign aims to raise awareness among visitors about the problems of child begging, sex tourism and more. It also distributes a good city map listing ChildSafe network centres and member hotels and organisations.

Travel Agencies

There are plenty of travel agents around town. The following are good bets for air tickets and all manner of domestic excursions, and can also arrange local transport and tour guides in multiple languages.

Exotissimo (Map p48; ☑218948; www.exotissimo.com; 66 Norodom Blvd) Runs tours all over Cambodia and the Mekong region.

Hanuman Travel (Map p43; ☑218356; www.hanumantravel.com; 12 St 310) Guides in several languages, tours and more, all over the country.

Palm Tours (Map p43; ☑726291; www.palm tours.biz; 1B St 278; ⊘8am-7pm) Great option

CHILD PROSTITUTION

The sexual abuse of children by foreign paedophiles is a serious problem in Cambodia. Paedophilia is a crime in Cambodia and several foreigners have served or are serving jail sentences. There is no such thing as an isolation unit for sex offenders in Cambodia. Countries such as Australia, France, Germany, the UK and the USA have also introduced much-needed legislation that sees nationals prosecuted in their home country for having under-age sex abroad.

This child abuse is slowly but surely being combated, although in a country as poor as Cambodia, money can tempt people into selling babies for adoption and children for sex. The trafficking of innocent children has many shapes and forms, and the sex trade is just the thin end of the wedge. Poor parents have been known to rent out their children as beggars, labourers or sellers; many child prostitutes in Cambodia are Vietnamese and have been sold into the business by family back in Vietnam. Once in the trade, it is difficult to escape a life of violence and abuse. Drugs are also being used to keep children dependent on their pimps, with bosses giving out *yama* (a dirty meta-amphetamine) or heroin to dull their senses.

Paedophilia is not unique to Western societies and it is a big problem with Asian tourists as well. The problem is that some of the home governments don't treat it as seriously as some of their Western counterparts. Even more problematic is the domestic industry of virgin-buying in Cambodia, founded on the superstition that taking a virgin will enhance one's power. Even if NGOs succeed in putting off Western paedophiles, confronting local traditions may be a greater challenge.

Visitors can do their bit by keeping an eye out for any suspicious behaviour on the part of foreigners. Don't ignore it – pass on any relevant information such as the name and nationality of the individual to the embassy concerned. There is also a **Cambodian hotline** (023-997919) and a confidential **ChildSafe Hotline** (012 311112; www.childsafe-cambodia.org). When booking into a hotel or jumping on transport, look out for the ChildSafe logo, as each establishment or driver who earns this logo supports an end to child sex tourism and has undergone child protection training. **End Child Prostitution and Trafficking** (Ecpat; www.ecpat.org) is a global network aimed at stopping child prostitution, child pornography and the trafficking of children for sexual purposes, and has affiliates in most Western countries.

for bus tickets and the like in the heart of the action on St 278.

PTM Travel & Tours (Map p48; 364768; www.ptm-travel.com; 200 Monivong Blvd; 8am-5.30pm Mon-Sat) Good bet for outgoing air tickets.

STS Mobile Ticket Agency (Map p48; Sisowath Quay; 8.30am-8.30pm) Convenient sidewalk-based vendor posts a transparent price list for day trips and transport. You can find better *remork* prices on your own, but prices here aren't too bad if you don't care to negotiate.

ⓘ Getting There & Away

Air

For information on international and domestic air services to/from Phnom Penh, see p339.

Boat

There are numerous fast-boat companies that operate from the **tourist boat dock** (Map p48; Sisowath Quay) at the eastern end of St 104. This area has been touted for redevelopment as a marina, but it is unlikely to happen in the very near future.

Boats go to Siem Reap via Tonlé Sap River and then Tonlé Sap Lake, but there are no services up the Mekong from Phnom Penh. For details on the international boat services connecting Phnom Penh with Chau Doc and the Mekong Delta in Vietnam, see p350.

The fast boats to Siem Reap (US$35, five to six hours) aren't as popular as they used to be. When it costs just US$6 for an air-conditioned bus or US$35 to be bundled on the roof of a boat, it is not hard to see why. It is better to save your boat experience for elsewhere in Cambodia.

Several companies have daily services departing at 7am and usually take it in turns to make the run. The first stretch of the journey along the river is scenic, but once the boat hits the lake, the fun is over as it is a vast inland sea with not a village in sight. In the dry season, the boats are very small and sometimes overcrowded.

Bus

Bus services have improved dramatically with the advent of revitalised roads in Cambodia, and most major towns are now accessible by air-conditioned bus from Phnom Penh. Most buses leave from company offices, which are generally clustered around Psar Thmei or located near St 104 at the northern end of Sisowath Quay. Buying tickets in advance is a good idea to ensure a seat, although it's not always necessary.

The most popular destination, Siem Reap, is served by all bus companies. It costs US$5 to US$6 to get there and takes about seven hours during the day (a bit less at night), compared with five hours in a private car. Neak Krohorm has speedier minibuses to Siem Reap (US$8, 5½ hours). Sok Sokha runs a somewhat upmarket service, with free hotel pick-up and just one stop (US$8, six hours).

See the individual destination chapters in this book for fares, duration and frequency information to other Cambodian cities. Most of the long-distance buses drop off and pick up in major towns along the way, such as Kompong Thom en route to Siem Reap or Pursat on the way to Battambang. However, full fare is usually charged anyway.

Another popular bus route is to Ho Chi Minh City, which costs about US$10 and takes six to eight hours depending on the border crossing and traffic in Ho Chi Minh City. The border crossing is usually hassle free, but in the event of a logjam you are better off using Vietnamese companies (such as Sapaco or Mai Linh) travelling to Ho Chi Minh City, and using one of the Cambodia companies in the other direction. For more details on this and other Vietnamese border crossings, see p350.

Most departures to the destinations listed below are during the day, with trips fizzling out by mid-afternoon to all but the most popular destinations (Siem Reap, Sihanoukville). However, several companies run night buses to Siem Reap, and Virak Buntham runs late-night trips to Battambang, Ho Chi Minh City, Poipet and Sihanoukville as well.

Destinations:

BANGKOK (WITH A BUS CHANGE AT THAI BORDER) Capitol Tour, GST, Phnom Penh Sorya (via Poipet); Virak Buntham (via Cham Yeam)

BATTAMBANG Capitol Tour, GST, Paramount Angkor (both terminals), Phnom Penh Sorya, Rith Mony, Virak Buntham

HA TIEN (VIETNAM, FOR PHU QUAC) Virak Buntham

HO CHI MINH CITY Capitol Tour, GST, Mai Linh, Mekong Express, Phnom Penh Sorya, Rith Mony, Sapaco, Virak Buntham

KAMPOT Capitol Tour, Hua Lian, Paramount Angkor (main terminal), Phnom Penh Sorya

KEP Capitol Tour, Hua Lian, Phnom Penh Sorya,

KOH KONG Phnom Penh Sorya, Rith Mony, Virak Buntham

KOMPONG CHAM Capitol Tour, GST, Paramount Angkor (main terminal), Phnom Penh Sorya, Rith Mony

KOMPONG CHNNANG Phnom Penh Sorya

KRATIE GST, Paramount Angkor (main terminal), Phnom Penh Sorya, Rith Mony

MONDULKIRI (SEN MONOROM) GST, Paramount Angkor (main terminal), Rith Mony

PAKSE (LAOS) Paramount Angkor (main terminal), Phnom Penh Sorya, Rith Mony

POIPET Capitol Tour, GST, Paramount Angkor (both terminals), Phnom Penh Sorya, Rith Mony, Virak Buntham

RATTANAKIRI (BAN LUNG) GST, Paramount Angkor (main terminal), Phnom Penh Sorya, Rith Mony

SIEM REAP Capitol Tour, GST, Mekong Express, Neak Krorhorm, Paramount Angkor (both terminals), Phnom Penh Sorya, Rith Mony, Sok Sokha, Virak Buntham

SIHANOUKVILLE Capitol Tour, GST, Mekong Express, Paramount Angkor (both terminals), Phnom Penh Sorya, Rith Mony, Virak Buntham

SRA EM (FOR PRASAT PREAH VIHEAR) GST, Paramount Angkor (both terminals), Phnom Penh Sorya, Rith Mony

STUNG TRENG GST, Paramount Angkor (main terminal), Phnom Penh Sorya, Rith Mony

TAKEO Phnom Penh Sorya

TBENG MEANCHEY GST, Phnom Penh Sorya

TRAT/KO CHANG (THAILAND) Virak Buntham

Leading bus companies:

Capitol Tour (Map p43; ☎217627; 14 St 182)

GST (Map p48; ☎218114; Psar Thmei area)

Hua Lian (Map p43; ☎223025; Monireth Blvd & Olympic Stadium)

Mai Linh (Map p43; ☎211888; 391 Sihanouk Blvd)

Mekong Express (Map p48; ☎427518; 87 Sisowath Quay)

Neak Krorhorm (Map p48; ☎092 966669; 4 St 108)

Paramount Angkor Express main terminal (Map p43; ☎015 818737; www.paramountangkorexpress.com; St 169) riverfront terminal (Map p48; ☎427567; 24 St 102)

Phnom Penh Sorya (Map p48; ☎210359; Psar Thmei area)

Rith Mony (Map p48; ☎6966667; cnr Sts 134 & 139)

Sapaco (Map p43; ☎210300; www.sapacotourist.com; Sihanouk Blvd)

Sok Sokha (Map p48; ☎991414; 7 St 106)
Virak Buntham (Map p48; ☎016 786270; St 106)

Share Taxi, Minibus & Pick-up

Share taxis, pick-ups and minibuses leave Phnom Penh for destinations all over the country, but have lost a lot of ground to cheaper and more comfortable buses as the road network continues to improve. Taxis to Kampot, Kep and Takeo leave from Psar Dang Kor (Map p36), while minibuses and taxis for most other places leave from the northwest corner of Psar Thmei (Map p48). Vehicles for the Vietnam border leave from Chbah Ampeau taxi park (off Map p52) on the eastern side of Monivong Bridge in the south of town.

Different vehicles run different routes depending on the quality of the road, but the fast shared taxis are more popular than the overcrowded minibuses. However, you may have to wait awhile (possibly until the next day if you arrive in the afternoon) before the taxi fills up, or pay for the vacant seats yourself.

The following are approximate prices for an entire shared taxi; divide it by the number of passengers (usually five to seven) to determine the price you'll pay. You'll have to pay for two seats if you want the entire front seat.

SIHANOUKVILLE US$50, four hours
KAMPOT US$35, three hours
KEP US$40, three hours
KOH KONG US$55, 4½ hours
KOMPONG THOM US$35, 2½ hours
SIEM REAP US$60, five hours
BATTAMBANG US$50, four hours
PURSAT US$35, three hours
KOMPONG CHAM US$25, two hours
KRATIE US$50, five hours
TAKEO US$25, 1¾ hours
VIETNAM BORDER US$50, three hours

Minibuses aren't much fun and are best avoided when there are larger air-con buses or faster share taxis available, which is pretty much everywhere. See the individual entries in the Eastern Cambodia chapter for details of 'express minibuses' connecting Ban Lung and Stung Treng with Phnom Penh.

Train

There are currently no passenger services operating on the Cambodian rail network, but this should be seen as a blessing in disguise, given that the trains are extremely slow, travelling at about 20km/h. Yes, for a few minutes at least, you can outrun the train!

Just for reference, Phnom Penh's train station (Map p48) is located at the western end of St 106 and St 108, in a grand old colonial-era building that is a shambles inside. The railway is being overhauled and has been reopened to cargo services, so there may be the option of passenger services by 2013 or so.

🛈 Getting Around

Being such a small city, Phnom Penh is quite easy to get around, although traffic is getting worse by the year and traffic jams are common around the morning and evening rush hour, particularly around the two main north–south boulevards, Monivong and Norodom.

To/From the Airport

Phnom Penh International Airport (off Map p36) is 7km west of central Phnom Penh, via Russian Blvd.

An official booth outside the airport arrivals area arranges taxis/*remorks* to anywhere in the city for a flat US$9/7. You can get a *remork* for $US4 and a moto for half that if you walk one minute out to the street. Heading to the airport from central Phnom Penh, a taxi/*remork*/moto will cost about US$9/4/2. The journey usually takes about 30 minutes.

Bicycle

It is possible to hire bicycles at some of the guesthouses around town for about US$1 to US$2 a day, but take a look at the chaotic traffic conditions before venturing forth. Once you get used to the anarchy, it can be a fun way to get around.

Car & Motorcycle

Exploring Phnom Penh and the surrounding areas on a motorbike is a very liberating experience if you are used to chaotic traffic conditions.

There are numerous motorbike hire places around town. A 100cc Honda costs from US$4 to US$7 per day and 250cc dirt bikes run from US$10 to US$30 per day. You'll have to leave your passport – a driver's license or other form of ID won't do. Remember you usually get what you pay for when choosing a steel steed.

A Cambodia license isn't a bad idea if you'll be doing extensive riding. Motorbike rental shops can arrange to get you one for about US$40. Otherwise you technically need an international license to drive in Cambodia (although a small bribe gets you out of most infractions if you don't have one). If you want to purchase insurance (available at motorbike rental shops for about US$22 per month), you'll need an international or Cambodian license. Remember to lock your bike, as motorbike theft is common.

Car hire is available through travel agencies, guesthouses and hotels in Phnom Penh. Everything from cars (from US$25) to 4WDs (from US$60) are available for travelling around the city, but prices rise if you venture beyond.

PHNOM PENH GETTING AROUND

The following are popular motorcycle rental shops:

Angkor Motorcycles (Map p48; ☎012 722098; 92 St 51) Huge selection of trail bikes (day/week rentals US$15/100), plus motorbikes at US$5 to US$7 per day.

Little Bikes (Map p48; ☎017 329338; 178 St 13) High-quality trail bikes from US$18, and 125cc bikes for US$6/30 per day/week.

Lucky! Lucky! (Map p43; ☎212788; 413 Monivong Blvd) Motorbikes are US$5 per day, or US$3 to US$4 for multiple days. Trail bikes from US$13.

New! New! (Map p43; ☎012 855 488; 417 Monivong Blvd) Cheapest bikes in town. Motorbikes start at US$4 per day, trail bikes from US$10.

Vannak Bikes Rental (Map p48; 46 St 130) Has high-performance trail bikes up to 600cc for US$15 to US$30 per day, and smaller motorbikes for US$5 to US$7.

Serious off-roaders may want to talk to one of the specialists. See p344 for details on dirt-bike-touring companies. The following companies are based in Phnom Penh:

Riverside Moto (Map p48; ☎223588; 30 St 118) This place specialises in upcountry touring, has well-serviced trail bikes (from US$13) and can provide a tool kit and spares.

Two Wheels Only (Map p52; ☎012 200513; www.twocambodia.com; 34L St 368) Two leads motorcycle tours and has well-maintained bikes available to rent (motorbike/trail bike per day US$5/25).

Harley Tours Cambodia (☎012 948529; www.harleycambodia.com) For those looking for a little more muscle on the road, Harley Tours organise Harley rides around Phnom Penh, including overnights to places like Kompong Cham or Kep. Day rental is available, but prices are similar to luxury-car rental back home.

Cyclo

They are still common on the streets of Phnom Penh, but *cyclos* have lost a lot of ground to the moto. Travelling by *cyclo* is a more relaxing way to see the sights in the centre of town, but they are just too slow for going from one end of the city to another. For a day of sightseeing, expect to pay around US$8 to US$10 depending on exactly where you go and how many hours of pedalling it includes. Late at night, *cyclos* would have to be considered a security hazard for all but the shortest of journeys, but most drivers are asleep in their *cyclos* at this time anyway. Costs are generally similar to moto fares, although negotiate if picking one up at popular spots around town.

It's also possible to arrange a *cyclo* tour through the Cyclo Centre (see p53).

Moto

In areas frequented by foreigners, moto drivers generally speak English and sometimes a little French. Elsewhere around town it can be difficult to find anyone who understands where you want to go – see the boxed text, p82. Most short trips are about 1000r to 2000r and more again at night, although if you want to get from one end of the city to the other, you have to pay up to US$1. Prices were once rarely negotiated in advance when taking rides, but with so many tourists paying over the odds, it may be sensible to discuss the price first. For those staying in a luxury hotel, negotiation is essential. Likewise, night owls taking a moto home from popular drinking holes should definitely negotiate to avoid an expensive surprise.

Many of the moto drivers who wait outside the popular guesthouses and hotels have good English and are able to act as guides for a daily rate of about US$8 to US$10 depending on the destinations.

Remork-moto

Also commonly known as túk-túks, *remorks* are motorbikes with carriages and are now pretty

---

WE'RE ON A ROAD TO NOWHERE

Taking a ride on a *remork-moto*, moto or *cyclo* is not as easy as it looks. Drivers who loiter around guesthouses, hotels, restaurants and bars may speak streetwise English and know the city well, but elsewhere the knowledge and understanding required to get you to your destination dries up fast. Flag one down on the street or grab one from outside the market, and you could end up pretty much anywhere in the city. You name your destination, and they nod confidently, eager for the extra money a foreigner may bring, but not having the first clue of where you want to go. They start driving or pedalling furiously down the road and await your instructions. You don't give them any instructions, as you think they know where they are going. Before you realise it, you are halfway to Sihanoukville or Siem Reap. The moral of the story is always carry a map of Phnom Penh and keep a close eye on the driver unless he speaks enough English to understand where on earth you want to go.

popular around Phnom Penh. They come in every shape and size from China, India and Thailand, plus the home-grown variety such as those pioneered in Siem Reap. Average fares are about double those of motos, and increase if you pack on the passengers.

Taxi

Taxis are cheap at 3000r per kilometre but don't expect to flag one down on the street. Call **Global Meter Taxi** (☑011 311888), **Choice Taxi** (☑888023) or **Taxi Vantha** (☑012 855000; www.taxivantha.com) for a pickup.

AROUND PHNOM PENH

There are several attractions around Phnom Penh that make good day trips. Kien Svay and Koh Dach are the easiest trips and are best done by mountain bike, moto or *remork*.

The Angkorian temple of Tonlé Bati, Phnom Tamao Wildlife Rescue Centre and the hilltop pagoda of Phnom Chisor are near each other off NH2. You can easily combine two of these into one trip (all three might be a stretch). These can also be built into a journey south to either Takeo or Kampot.

Udong, once the capital of Cambodia, is a separate half-day trip and can be combined with a visit to Kompong Chhnang, known for being a 'genuine' Cambodian town. Kirirom National Park lies further afield, about halfway to Sihanoukville off NH4.

Kien Svay

Kien Svay is a very popular picnic area on a small tributary of the Mekong. Hundreds of bamboo huts have been built over the water and Khmers love to come here on the weekend and sit around gossiping and munching.

Kien Svay is a peculiarly Cambodian institution, mixing the universal love of picnicking by the water with the unique Khmer fondness for lounging about on mats. It works like this: for 5000r an hour, picnickers rent an area on a raised open hut covered with reed mats. Be sure to agree on the price *before* you rent a space.

All sorts of food is sold at Kien Svay, although it is necessary to bargain to ensure a fair price. Prices generally seem reasonable thanks to the massive competition – there are perhaps 50 or more sellers here. Popular dishes include grilled chicken and fish, river lobster and fresh fruit. The area is pretty deserted during the week, but this can make it a calmer time to picnic.

❶ Getting There & Away

Kien Svay is a district in Kandal Province, and the actual picnic spot is just before the small town of Koki, about 15km east of Phnom Penh. To get here from Phnom Penh, turn left off NH1, which links Phnom Penh with Ho Chi Minh City, through a wat-style gate at a point 15km east of the Monivong Bridge. You will know you are on the right track if you see plenty of beggars and hundreds of cars. Buses regularly depart for Kien Svay from Psar Thmei and cost just 4000r. A round-trip moto should cost about US$5.

Koh Dach

Known as 'Silk Island' by foreigners, this is actually a pair of islands lying in the Mekong River about 5km NE of the Japanese Friendship Bridge. They make for an easy half-day DIY excursion for those who want to experience the 'real Cambodia'. The hustle and bustle of Phnom Penh feels light years away here.

The name derives from the preponderance of silk weavers who inhabit the islands. When you arrive by ferry, you'll undoubtedly be approached by one or more smiling women who speak a bit of English and will invite you to their house to observe weavers in action and – they hope – buy some *kramas*, sarongs or other silk items. If you are in the market for silk, you might follow them and have a look. Otherwise, feel free to smile back and politely decline their offer – you'll see plenty of weavers as you journey around the islands.

Other attractions include a few colourful modern temple complexes and the rural scenery.

❶ Getting There & Around

Remork drivers offer half-day tours to Koh Dach; US$10 should do it, but they have been known to charge as much as US$40. Scheduled boat trips from the tourist boat dock are another option. Otherwise, hire a mountain bike or motorbike and go it alone. Ferries cross the Mekong in three places and cost 500r per person, plus 500r per bike. The southernmost ferry crossing is the most convenient; it takes you to the larger, closer island. Cross the Japanese Bridge and follow NH6 for 4.3km, then turn right at the Goal

Sun Hotel & KTV complex. You immediately hit a small river road that parallels the Mekong. Turn left and follow it north for about 200m until you see the ferry crossing. Once there you are just a short cycle ride from a bridge that links the two islands. The smaller island (technically named Koh Okhna Tey, or Mekong Island) has better infrastructure, including a paved main road; the larger island is more rustic and remote feeling, especially as you venture north.

Udong ភ្នំឧដុង្គ

Udong (the Victorious) served as the capital of Cambodia under several sovereigns between 1618 and 1866, during which time 'victorious' was an optimistic epithet, as Cambodia was in terminal decline. A number of kings, including King Norodom, were crowned here. The main attractions today are the twin humps of **Phnom Udong**, which have several stupas on them. Both ends of the ridge have good views of the Cambodian countryside dotted with innumerable sugar palm trees. Phnom Udong is not a leading attraction, but for those with the time it's worth the visit.

The larger main ridge – the one you'll approach first if approaching from NH5 – is known as Phnom Preah Reach Throap (Hill of the Royal Fortune). It is so named because a 16th-century Khmer king is said to have hidden the national treasury here during a war with the Thais.

At the base of the stairs leading up to the ridge, close to the road, is a **memorial** to the victims of Pol Pot, which contains the bones of some of the people who were buried in approximately 100 mass graves, each containing about a dozen bodies. Instruments of torture were unearthed along with the bones when a number of the pits were disinterred in 1981 and 1982. Just north of the memorial is a **pavilion** decorated with graphic murals depicting Khmer Rouge atrocities.

Ascending the stairs, the first structure you come to at the top of the ridge is a modern temple containing a relic of the Buddha, believed to be an eyebrow hair, which was relocated from the blue stupa in front of Phnom Penh railway station in 2002. Follow the path behind this stupa along the ridge and you'll come to a line of three large stupas. The first (northwesternmost) is **Damrei Sam Poan**, built by King Chey Chetha II (r 1618–26) for the ashes of his predecessor, King Soriyopor. The second stupa, **Ang Doung**, is decorated with coloured tiles; it was built in 1891 by King Norodom to house the ashes of his father, King Ang Duong (r 1845–59), but some say King Ang Duong was in fact buried next to the Silver Pagoda in Phnom Penh. The last stupa is **Mak Proum**, the final resting place of King Monivong (r 1927–41). Decorated with *garudas* (mythical half-man, half-bird creatures), floral designs and elephants, it has four faces on top.

Bushwhack your way along the trail beyond Mak Proum and you'll come to a line of three small *viharas*. The first is **Vihear Prak Neak**, its cracked walls topped with a thatched roof. Inside this *vihara* is a seated Buddha who is guarded by a *naga* (*prak neak* means 'protected by a *naga*'). The second structure also has a seated Buddha inside. The third structure is **Vihear Preah Keo**, a brick-roofed structure that contains a statue of Preah Ko, the sacred bull; the original statue was carried away by the Thais long ago.

Another 120m or so along is the most impressive structure on Phnom Preah Reach Throap, **Vihear Preah Ath Roes**. The *vihara* and the statue of Buddha, dedicated in 1911 by King Sisowath, were blown up by the Khmer Rouge in 1977; only sections of the walls, the bases of eight enormous columns and the right arm and part of the right side of the original Buddha statue remain. The Buddha has been reconstructed and the roof has now been rebuilt.

Southeast of the large ridge, the smaller ridge has two structures and several stupas on top. **Ta San Mosque** faces westward towards Mecca. Across the plains to the south of the mosque you can see **Phnom Vihear Leu**, a small hill on which a *vihara* (temple sanctuary) stands between two white poles. To the right of the *vihara* is a building used as a prison under Pol Pot's rule. To the left of the *vihara* and below it is a pagoda known as **Arey Ka Sap**.

🛏 Sleeping & Eating

There is a **Cambodia Vipassana Dhura Buddhist Meditation Centre** (contact Mrs Kim Simoeun ☑012 221505; www.cambodia vipassanacenter.com) at Udong and it is possible for foreigners to stay here and practise meditation with experienced monks or nuns. The rooms are fairly comfortable by monastic standards, but they're not always kept that clean. There is no fixed price for a meditative retreat here, but a figure of US$20 for a day, including lunch, or US$30

VANN NATH: PORTRAIT OF THE ARTIST

The late Cambodian artist Vann Nath is famous the world over for his depictions of Khmer Rouge torture scenes at Phnom Penh's notorious S-21 Security Prison, where he was one of only seven survivors. He died in 2011, but many of his works remain on display at the prison, which is now the Tuol Sleng Museum.

Vann Nath was born in Battambang in 1946 and took up painting as a teenager, finding work as a sign painter and artist for cinema posters. Like many Cambodians, his life was turned upside down by the Khmer Rouge takeover and he found himself evacuated to the countryside along with other urban Cambodians. On 7 January 1978, he was taken to S-21 prison, aged 32 years, and spent the next year living in hellish surrounds, as thousands perished around him.

The Vietnamese brought Vann Nath back to S-21 from 1980 to 1982 to paint the famous images we see today. He was still painting right up until the end of his life, and many of his later works can be seen (and bought) at his family's Kith Eng Restaurant (p65). In the wake of his death, fellow prisoners Chum Mey and Bou Meng are the last remaining survivors of S-21.

In an interview with Vann Nath not long before he passed away, we asked what it feels like to see Tuol Sleng as a tourist attraction today.

'We must think of the souls of those who died there. These souls died without hope, without light, without a future. They had no life. So I paint my scenes to tell the world the stories of those who did not survive.' He added that he felt duty-bound to tell the world what happened, recalling a pledge he made back in 1978 when first incarcerated: 'We were taken up to a holding room on the 1st floor. We agreed that whoever survives would need to tell the families of the victims how they met their fate.'

How did it feel to return to the scene of such personal horrors? 'The first time I went back was a real struggle, as everything looked the same as before. I could hardly speak or move.' On the Khmer Rouge tribunal for surviving leaders, Vann Nath offered the following: 'As a person who represents thousands of dead prisoners, I am not sure the tribunal will deliver enough justice for the dead. Based on human rights it may be fair, but the Khmer Rouge was about human wrongs as well. If we talk about human feeling, then we want more than this, but we must ask ourselves what is fair. If we demand too much justice then it becomes revenge. I just hope the court will deliver justice fairly.'

with an overnight stay is what one of the French-speaking nuns suggested in the past. The electricity usually stops at 8pm, but you may be able to request the generator be turned on for an extra donation.

There are plenty of food stalls around the base of Udong.

ⓘ Getting There & Away

Udong is 41km from the capital. To get there take a Phnom Penh Sorya bus bound for Kompong Chhnang (10,000r, one hour to Udong). It will drop you off at the access road to Phnom Udong, and from there it's 3km (4000r by moto). Other bus companies also make the trip to Udong. To return to Phnom Penh flag down a bus on NH5 or take a moto (US$6 to US$10, depending on your haggling skills).

If going it alone, head north out of Phnom Penh on NH5 and turn left (south) at the signposted archway.

A taxi for the day trip from Phnom Penh will cost around US$40. Moto drivers also run people to Udong for about US$15 or so for the day, but compared with the bus this isn't the most pleasant way to go, as the road is pretty busy and very dusty.

Tonlé Bati   ទន្លេបាទី

Tonlé Bati (admission US$3) is the collective name for a pair of old Angkorian-era temples and a popular lakeside picnic area. Anyone who has already experienced the mighty temples of Angkor can probably survive without a visit, but if Angkor is yet to come, these attractive temples are worth the detour.

TA PROHM   ទ័ព្រះ
The laterite temple of Ta Prohm was built by King Jayavarman VII (r 1181–1219) on the site of an ancient 6th-century Khmer shrine.

Today the ruined temple is surrounded by colourful flowers and plants, affording some great photo opportunities.

The main sanctuary consists of five chambers, each containing a modern buddha. The facades of the chambers contain intricate and well-preserved bas-reliefs. In the central chamber is a linga (phallic symbol) that shows signs of the destruction wrought by the Khmer Rouge.

YEAY PEAU

Yeay Peau temple, named after King Prohm's mother, is 150m north of Ta Prohm in the grounds of a modern pagoda. Legend has it that Peau gave birth to a son, Prohm. When Prohm discovered his father was King Preah Ket Mealea, he set off to live with the king. After a few years, he returned to his mother but did not recognise her and, taken by her beauty, asked her to become his wife. He refused to believe Peau's protests that she was his mother. To put off his advances, she suggested a contest…for the outcome of this legend, see p248.

LAKEFRONT

About 300m northwest of Ta Prohm, a long, narrow peninsula juts into Tonlé Bati. The lakefront here is lined with floating pavilions that you can rent for the day for US$1. Bring a picnic or order food from one of several little restaurants – fixed food and drink prices are printed on the reverse of the entry ticket. You can swim in the lake or hire an innertube for 2000r. The views (and breezes) across the lake are pretty inviting. Tonlé Bati fills up with locals at weekends, but during the week it's quiet.

ⓘ Getting There & Away

The access road heading to Tonlé Bati is signposted on the right on NH2 30km south of Independence Monument in Phnom Penh. The entrance to the complex is 1.8km from the highway.

Most people hire private transport to get here. Figure on US$10/20 return for a moto/ *remork* from Phnom Penh, or US$35 for a taxi. Another option is to take a Takeo-bound Phnom Penh Sorya bus (three daily) and jump off at the access road. Returning to Phnom Penh can be problematic, however. The best advice is to buy a ticket in advance on the infrequent Takeo–Phnom Penh bus, or take your chances flagging it down (it won't stop if there's no space). Otherwise, hire a moto.

Phnom Tamao Wildlife Rescue Centre ភ្នំតាម៉ៅ

This wonderful **wildlife sanctuary** (www .cambodianwildliferescue.org; admission US$5) for rescued animals is home to gibbons, sun bears, elephants, tigers, lions, deer and a massive bird enclosure. They were all taken from poachers or abusive owners and receive care and shelter here as part of a sustainable breeding program. Wherever possible animals are released back into the wild once they have recovered, The centre operates breeding programs for a number of globally threatened species.

The sanctuary occupies a vast site south of the capital and its animals are kept in excellent conditions by Southeast Asian standards, with plenty of room to roam in enclosures that have been improved and expanded over the years with help from international wildlife NGOs. Spread out as it is, it feels like a zoo crossed with a safari park.

The centre is home to the world's largest captive collections of pileated gibbons and Malayan sun bears, as well as other rarities such as Siamese crocodiles and greater adjutant storks. Other popular enclosures include huge areas for the large tiger population, and there are elephants that sometimes take part in activities such as painting. You'll also find a walk-through area with macaques and deer, and a huge aviary.

Cambodia's wildlife is usually very difficult to spot, as larger mammals inhabit remote areas of the country. Phnom Tamao is the perfect place to discover more about the incredible variety of animals in Cambodia. If you don't like zoos, you might not like this wildlife sanctuary, but remember that these animals have been rescued from traffickers and poachers and need a home. Visitors that come here will be doing their own small bit to help in the protection and survival of Cambodia's varied and wonderful wildlife.

Free the Bears (www.freethebears.org.au; vol unteercambodia.ftb@gmail.com) operates a Bear Keeper for a Day program to allow students and adults with a genuine interest in wildlife a better understanding of the Asian black bear and Malayan sun bear. Participants have no contact with the bears, but learn the ins-and-outs of caring for the nearly 90 bears being looked after here.

Betelnut Jeep Tours (☏012 619924; www .betelnuttours.com; per person US$33) offers day trips here, departing at 10am on Tuesday,

Thursday and Saturday, including entry, a guided tour, lunch and a chance to meet some of the residents.

❶ Getting There & Away

The access road to Phnom Tamao is clearly signposted on the right 6.5km south of the turnoff to Tonlé Bati on NH2. The sanctuary is 5km from the highway on an incredibly dusty road often lined with elderly beggars.

To get here follow the directions to Tonlé Bati (figure on a few extra dollars for private transport). If coming by bus ask to be let off at the turnoff, where motos await to whisk you to the sanctuary.

Phnom Chisor

A temple from the Angkorian era, **Phnom Chisor** (admission US$3, levied at the summit) is set upon a solitary hill in Takeo Province, offering superb views of the countryside. Try to get to Phnom Chisor early in the morning or late in the afternoon, as it is an uncomfortable climb in the heat of the midday sun.

The main temple stands on the eastern side of the hilltop. Constructed of laterite and brick with carved sandstone lintels, the complex is surrounded by the partially ruined walls of a 2.5m-wide gallery with windows. Inscriptions found here date from the 11th century, when this site was known as Suryagiri.

On the plain to the west of Phnom Chisor are the sanctuaries of **Sen Thmol**, just below Phnom Chisor, **Sen Ravang** and the former sacred pond of **Tonlé Om**. All three of these features form a straight line from Phnom Chisor in the direction of Angkor. During rituals held here 900 years ago, the king, his Brahmans and their entourage would climb a monumental 400 steps to Suryagiri from this direction.

If you haven't got the stamina for an overland adventure to Preah Vihear (p233) or Phnom Bayong (p202), this is the next best thing for a temple with a view. Near the main temple is a modern Buddhist *vihara* that is used by resident monks.

❶ Getting There & Away

The eastward-bound access road to Phnom Chisor is signposted (in Khmer) on the left 12km south of the Phnom Tamao turnoff on NH2. The temple is 4.5km from the highway – motos wait at the turnoff.

To get here follow the directions for Tonlé Bati and Phnom Tamao, adding yet

another few dollars if you are hiring private transport.

Kirirom National Park
ឧទ្យានជាតិគីរីរម្យ

You can really get away from it all at this lush elevated **park** (admission US$5) just a two-hour drive southwest of Phnom Penh. Winding walking trails lead to cascading wet-season waterfalls and cliffs with amazing views of the Cardamom Mountains, and there's some great mountain-biking to be done if you're adventurous.

Or you could just relax and forget about the outside world for a few days at **Kirirom Hillside Resort** (☑016 590999; www.kirirom resort.com; room/bungalow US$50/65; ❉@✉) near the park entrance. With plastic dinosaurs, it's tacky at first, but scattered around the grounds are some great Scandinavian-style bungalows in various shapes and sizes (these are preferable to the rooms in the main lodge). The pool has a lovely setting with the hills of Kirirom as a backdrop and is open to nonguests for US$5 per day.

Nearby are camping and basic budget sleeping options, and a **Community-Based Ecotourism program** (admission adult/child US$3/1) 10km from the park entrance in Chambok commune, where attractions include a 40m-high waterfall, traditional ox-cart rides and nature walks. About 1km from the Chambok commune entrance is a restaurant and information centre where you pay your entrance fee. From here it's a 2km or 3km walk to a series of three waterfalls. The second waterfall has a swimming hole. The third one is the impressive 40m-high waterfall.

For a more substantial walk, consider hooking up with a ranger (about US$5) for a two-hour hike up to **Phnom Dat Chivit** (End of the Life Mountain), where an abrupt cliff face offers an unbroken view of the **Elephant Mountains** and **Cardamom Mountains** to the west.

❶ Getting There & Away

Kirirom National Park is roughly equidistant between Phnom Penh and Sihanoukville on NH4. From the highway turnoff it's about 8km to the resort via an access road. Unless you have your own transport, it is not that easy to get here. A taxi from either city is about US$60, or have a bus drop you off at the turnoff and take a moto.

Siem Reap

TELEPHONE CODE ☎063 / POP (TOWN) 125,000 / AREA 10,299 SQ KM

Why Go?

The life-support system for the temples of Angkor, Siem Reap (*see*-em ree-*ep;* ស៉ៀមរាប) was always destined for great things. It has reinvented itself as the epicentre of cool Cambodia, with everything from backpacker party pads to hip hotels, world-class wining and dining, and sumptuous spas.

This is good news for the long-suffering Khmers riding the wave, but it can make the town a little bling in places. Authentic it is not, although just a short distance away lies Siem Reap Province and the real Cambodia of rural beauty. Explore floating villages and rare-bird sanctuaries or just cycle (or quad bike or pony trek) through the paddies as an antidote to the bustle of town.

Angkor is a place to be savoured, not rushed, and this is the base to plan your adventures. Still think three days at the temples is enough? Think again, with Siem Reap on the doorstep.

Best Places to Eat

» Cuisine Wat Damnak (p105)
» Green Star (p105)
» Abacus (p105)
» Blue Pumpkin (p104)
» Pub St Food Stalls (p102)

Best Places to Stay

» Villa Medamrei (p97)
» La Résidence d'Angkor (p99)
» Shadow of Angkor Guesthouse (p97)
» Frangipani Villa Hotel (p100)
» European Guesthouse (p100)

When to Go

Peak season is November to March, a good time to avoid if you want to dodge the crowds. April and May can be shockingly hot, which makes exploring hard work and the countryside barren. The wet-season months are generally OK, as you can set your watch by the late-afternoon showers. However, the town centre has been under water for long periods in October during the past few years.

Fixtures in the calendar include February's Giant Puppet Parade and the Bon Om Tuk (Water Festival) in October/November.

History

Siem Reap was little more than a village when French explorers discovered Angkor in the 19th century. With the return of Angkor to Cambodian – or should that be French – control in 1907, Siem Reap began to grow, absorbing the first wave of tourists. The Grand Hotel d'Angkor opened its doors in 1929 and the temples of Angkor remained one of Asia's leading draws until the late 1960s, luring luminaries such as Charlie Chaplin and Jackie Kennedy. With the advent of war and the Khmer Rouge, Siem Reap entered a long slumber from which it only began to awaken in the mid-1990s.

Tourism is the lifeblood of Siem Reap and, without careful management, it could become Siem Reapolinos, the not-so-Costa-del-Culture of southeast Asia. However, there are promising signs that developers are learning from the mistakes that have blighted other regional hot spots, with

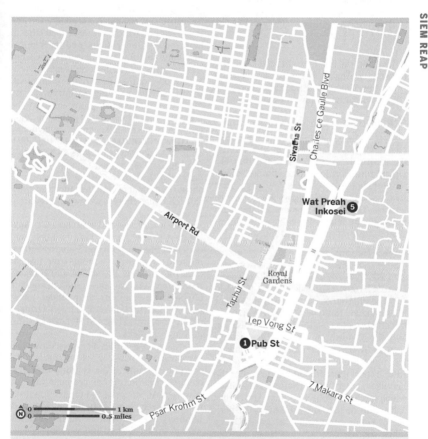

Siem Reap Highlights

❶ Diving into **Pub St** (p106), the drinking capital of Siem Reap, and discover nearby restaurants and bars

❷ Exploring the flooded forest of **Kompong Pluk** (p116), an incredible village of bamboo skyscrapers

❸ Encountering some of the world's rarest large water birds at **Prek Toal Bird Sanctuary** (p113)

❹ Learning the secrets of Khmer cuisine with a **cooking course** (p95),

the perfect way to impress friends back home

❺ Discovering the quiet temples of Angkor hidden away in the modern pagodas of **Wat Athvea** (p94) and **Wat Preah Inkosei** (p94)

WHAT'S IN A NAME?

The name Siem Reap means 'Siamese Defeated', hardly the most tactful name for a major city near Thailand. Imagine Birmingham with the name 'Germany Defeated'? The empire of Angkor once included much of modern-day Thailand, but there's a touch of irony about the name, given that Thailand ultimately defeated Cambodia, and controlled Siem Reap and Angkor from 1794 to 1907.

restrictions on hotel height and bus size. Either way, Angkor is centre stage on the world travel map right now, and there's no going back for its supply line, Siem Reap.

◉ Sights

Visitors come to Siem Reap to see the temples of Angkor. The sights in and around the town pale in comparison, but they are a good diversion for those who find themselves templed out after a few days. That said, some of the modern sights are...yet more temples. The modern pagodas around Siem Reap offer an interesting contrast to the ancient sandstone structures of Angkor.

Angkor National Museum   MUSEUM
(Map p92; ☑966601; www.angkornationalmuseum
.com; 968 Charles de Gaulle Blvd; adult/child under
1.2m US$12/6; ☺8.30am-6pm, to 6.30pm 1 Oct-30
Apr) Looming large on the road to Angkor is the Angkor National Museum, a state-of-the-art showpiece on the Khmer civilisation and the majesty of Angkor. Displays are themed by era, religion and royalty as visitors move through the impressive galleries. After a short presentation, visitors enter the Zen-like 'Gallery of a Thousand Buddhas', which has a fine collection of images. Other collections include the pre-Angkorian periods of Funan and Chenla, the great Khmer kings, Angkor Wat, Angkor Thom and the inscriptions.

Presentations include touch-screen video, epic commentary and the chance to experience a panoramic sunrise at Angkor Wat, but for all the technology there seems less sculpture on display than in the National Museum in Phnom Penh. However, it remains a very useful experience for first-time visitors to put the story of Angkor and the Khmer empire in context before exploring

the temples. The US$12 admission fee is a little high, given that US$20 buys admission to all the temples at Angkor. Visitors also have to pay a US$2 camera fee, but can't snap everywhere, and an audio tour is available for US$3. Attached to the museum is a 'Cultural Mall', lined with shops, galleries and cafes, but this hasn't really taken off and sees few visitors.

⬚ Les Chantiers Écoles   ARTISANAL SCHOOL
(Map p92) Siem Reap is the epicentre of the drive to revitalise Cambodian traditional culture, which was dealt such a harsh blow by the Khmer Rouge and the years of instability that followed its rule. Les Chantiers Écoles is a school specialising in teaching wood- and stone-carving techniques, traditional silk painting, lacquerware and more to impoverished youngsters. On the premises the school has a beautiful shop called Artisans d'Angkor (p109), which sells everything from stone and wood reproductions of Angkorian-era statues to household furnishings. Free guided tours are available daily from 7.30am to 5.30pm to learn more about traditional techniques. Tucked down a side road, the school is well signposted from Sivatha St.

There's also a second shop opposite Angkor Wat in the Angkor Cafe building, and outlets at Phnom Penh and Siem Reap international airports. Some profits from sales go back into funding the school and bringing more teenagers into the training program, although the majority shareholder (50%) is now Société Concessionaire d'Aeroport (SCA), a privately owned, French-run airport-management company.

Les Chantiers Écoles also maintains a **silk farm** (off Map p114), which produces some of the best work in the country, including clothing, interior-design products and accessories. All stages of the production process can be seen here, from the cultivation of mulberry trees through the nurturing of silk worms to the dyeing and weaving of silk. Free tours are available daily between 7am and 5pm and there is a free shuttle bus departing from Les Chantiers Écoles at 9.30am and 1.30pm. The farm is about 16km west of Siem Reap, just off the road to Sisophon in the village of Puok.

⬚ Khmer Ceramics Centre   CERAMICS
(Map p114; ☑092-476689; www.khmerceramics
.com; Charles de Gaulle Blvd; ☺8am-7.30pm) Lo-

cated on the road to the temples, this ceramics centre is dedicated to reviving the Khmer tradition of pottery, which was an intricate art during the time of Angkor. It's possible to visit and try your hand at the potter's wheel, and courses in traditional techniques are available from US$15 to US$30. There are plenty of elegant items on sale and the centre is working with **Heritage Watch** (www .heritagewatch.org) to offer a sustainable livelihood to remote villagers.

Shadow Puppets
SHADOW PUPPETS

The creation of leather *sbei tuoi* (shadow puppets) is a traditional Khmer art form, and the figures make a memorable souvenir. Characters include gods and demons from the *Reamker,* as well as exquisite elephants with intricate armour. These are a very Cambodian keepsake. The **House of Peace Association** (Map p114), about 4km down NH6 on the way to the airport, makes these puppets; small pieces start at US$15, while larger ones can be as much as US$150. A second workshop is located at Wat Preah Inkosei. It's possible to watch a shadow-puppet show at La Noria Restaurant (p108).

Miniature Replicas of Angkor's Temples
MINIATURES

(Map p92; admission US$1.50) One of the more quirky places in town is the garden of a local master sculptor, which houses miniature replicas of Angkor Wat, the Bayon, Banteay Srei and other temples. It is a bluffer's way to get that aerial shot of Angkor without chartering a helicopter, although the astute might question the presence of oversized insects in the shot. There is also a display of scale miniatures at Preah Ko Temple (see the box, p148).

Cambodian Cultural Village
CULTURAL VILLAGE

(Map p114; ☎963836; www.cambodianculturalvillage.com; Airport Rd; adult/child under 1.1m US$9/free; ☺8am-7pm) It may be kitsch, it may be kooky, but it's very popular with Cambodians and provides a diversion for families travelling with children. This is the Cambodian Cultural Village, which tries to represent all of Cambodia in a whirlwind tour of recreated houses and villages. The visit begins with a wax museum and includes homes of the Cham, Chinese, Kreung and Khmer people, as well as miniature replicas of landmark buildings in Cambodia. There are dance shows and performances throughout the day, but it still doesn't add up to a turn-on for most foreign visitors, unless they have the kids in tow. It's located about midway between Siem Reap and the airport.

Banteay Srey Butterfly Centre
BUTTERFLY PARK

(off Map p114; ☎011 348460; www.angkorbutterfly.com; adult/child US$4/2; ☺9am-5pm daily) The Banteay Srey Butterfly Centre is a worthwhile place to include on a trip to Banteay Srei and the Cambodia Landmine Museum. The largest fully enclosed butterfly centre in southeast Asia, it has more than 30 species of Cambodian butterflies fluttering about. It is a good experience for children, as they can

SIEM REAP SIGHTS

DON'T MISS

THE CAMBODIA LANDMINE MUSEUM

Established by DIY de-miner Aki Ra, the **Cambodia Landmine Museum** (off Map p114; ☎012 598951; www.cambodialandminemuseum.org; admission US$2; ☺7.30am-5pm) is very popular with travellers thanks to its informative displays on the curse of landmines in Cambodia. The museum includes an extensive collection of mines, mortars, guns and weaponry used during the civil war. The site includes a mock minefield so that visitors can attempt to spot the deactivated mines. Not only a weapon of war, landmines are a weapon against peace, and proceeds from the museum are ploughed into mine-awareness campaigns and support an on-site orphanage, rehabilitation centre and training facility. The museum is about 25km from Siem Reap via Banteay Srei and is easily combined with a visit to Banteay Srei temple, about 6km beyond.

For those wanting to learn more about the after-effects of an amputation, it is possible to visit the **Physical Rehabilitation Centre** (Map p92; ☺8am-noon & 2-5pm Mon-Fri), run by **Handicap International** (www.handicapinternational.be). There are informative displays including a variety of homemade prosthetics that it has replaced with international-standard artificial limbs, plus it's possible to meet some of the locals receiving assistance here.

Siem Reap

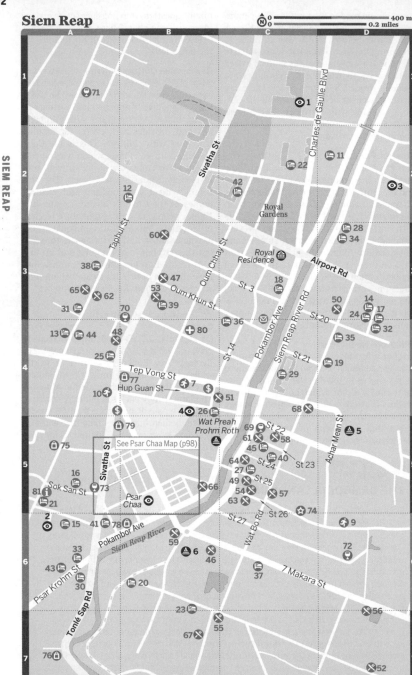

SIEM REAP

0 — 400 m
0 — 0.2 miles

Siem Reap

SIEM REAP

see the whole process from egg to caterpillar to cocoon to butterfly. The centre is trying to provide a sustainable living for the rural poor and most of the butterflies are farmed around Phnom Kulen. It's located about 7km before Banteay Srei on the left-hand side of the road.

Wat Bo   TEMPLE
(Map p92; ☺6am-6pm) This is one of the town's oldest temples and has a collection of well-preserved wall paintings from the late 19th century depicting the *Reamker*, Cambodia's interpretation of the *Ramayana*.

Wat Preah Inkosei   TEMPLE
(Map p114; ☺6am-6pm) This wat is built on the site of an early Angkorian brick temple north of town, which still stands today at the rear of the compound.

Wat Athvea   TEMPLE
(Map p126; ☺6am-6pm) South of the city centre, Wat Athvea is an attractive pagoda on the site of an ancient temple. The old temple is still in very good condition and sees far fewer visitors than the main temples in the Angkor area, making it a peaceful spot in the late afternoon.

Wat Thmei   TEMPLE
(Map p114; ☺6am-6pm) On the left fork of the road to Angkor Wat, Wat Thmei has a small memorial stupa containing the skulls and bones of victims of the Khmer Rouge. It also has plenty of young monks eager to practise their English.

Wat Dam Nak   TEMPLE
(Map p92; ☺6am-6pm) Formerly a royal palace during the reign of King Sisowath, hence the name *dam nak* (palace), today the structure is home to the **Centre for Khmer Studies** (www.khmerstudies.org), an independent institution promoting a greater understanding of Khmer culture with a drop-in research library on site.

🏃 Activities

It's hot work clambering about the temples and there's no better way to wind down than a dip in a swimming pool. Pay by the day at most hotels for use of the pool and/or gym, ranging from just US$5 at some of the mid-range hotels to US$20 at the five-star palaces. More and more of the cheaper hotels and resorts are putting in pools and this can be a worthwhile splash for weary travellers.

Locals like to swim in the waters of the Western Baray (p147) at the weekend.

Foot massage is a big hit in Siem Reap – not surprising given all those steep stairways at the temples. There are half a dozen or more places offering a massage for about US$6 to US$8 an hour on the strip running northwest of Psar Chaa. Some are more authentic than others, so dip your toe in first before selling your sole.

For an alternative foot massage, brave the waters of Dr Fish: you dip your feet into a paddling pool full of cleaner fish, which nibble away at your dead skin. It's heaven for some, tickly as hell for others. The original was housed in the Angkor Night Market, but copycats have sprung up all over town, including a dozen or so tanks around Pub St and Psar Chaa.

Phokheetra Country Club   GOLF
(off Map p114; ☎964600; www.sofitel.com; green fees US$100) This club hosts a tournament on the Asian tour annually and includes an ancient Angkor bridge amid its manicured fairways and greens.

Angkor Golf Resort   GOLF
(Map p114; ☎761139; www.angkor-golf.com; green fees US$100) This world-class course was designed by celebrated British golfer Nick Faldo and is world class.

Happy Ranch   HORSE RIDING
(Map p114; ☎012 920002; www.thehappyranch .com; 1hr/half-day ride US$22/64) Forget the Wild West and try your hand at riding in the Wild East. Happy Ranch offers the chance to explore Siem Reap on horseback, taking in surrounding villages and secluded temples. This is a calm way to experience the countryside, far from the traffic and crowds elsewhere. Popular rides take in Wat Athvea, a modern pagoda with an ancient temple on its grounds, and Wat Chedi (Map p126), a temple set on a flood plain near the Tonlé Sap lake. Riding lessons are also available for children and beginners. Book direct for the best prices.

🖋 Seeing Hands Massage 4   MASSAGE
(Map p92; ☎012 836487; 324 Sivatha St; per hr fan/air-con US$5/7) Seeing Hands trains blind people in the art of massage. Watch out for copycats, as some of these are just exploiting the blind for profit.

🖋 Krousar Thmey   MASSAGE
(Map p114; massage US$7) Massage by the blind in the same location as its free Tonlé Sap Exhibition.

NAVIGATING SIEM REAP

Siem Reap is still a small town at heart and is easy enough to navigate. The centre is around Psar Chaa (Old Market) and accommodation is spread throughout town. National Hwy 6 (NH6) cuts across the northern part of town, passing Psar Leu (Main Market) in the east of town and the Royal Residence and the Grand Hotel d'Angkor in the centre, and then heads to the airport and beyond to the Thai border. Siem Reap River (Stung Siem Reap) flows north–south through the centre of town, and has enough bridges that you won't have to worry too much about being on the wrong side. As in Phnom Penh, however, street numbering is haphazard to say the least, so take care when hunting down specific addresses.

Angkor Wat and Angkor Thom are only 6km and 8km north of town respectively – see the map, p126, for the location of all the leading temples.

Buses and share taxis usually drop passengers off at the bus station/taxi park about 3km east of the town centre, from where it's a short moto or *remork-moto* (túk-túk) ride to nearby guesthouses and hotels. Fast boats from Phnom Penh and Battambang arrive at Phnom Krom, about 11km south of town, and most places to stay include a free transfer by moto or minibus. Siem Reap International Airport is 7km west of town and there are plenty of taxis and motos available for transfers to the town centre.

Quad Adventure Cambodia   QUAD BIKING
(Map p92, ☐092-787210, www.quadventurecambodia.com; rides US$28-165) All-terrain biking is alive and well in Siem Reap thanks to this outfit. For those who haven't tried it, all-terrain biking is serious fun and all rides include a short introductory lesson. Rides around Siem Reap involve rice fields at sunset, pretty temples, and back roads through traditional villages where children wave and shout. Quad Adventure Cambodia is well signposted in the Wat Dam Nak area.

Flomo Adventure Tours   QUAD BIKING
(Map p92; ☐964586; www.flomoadventuretours.com; rides US$50-190) This newcomer offers revved-up buggy adventures for those wanting to cover a bit more distance. Complete with roll-bars and rally-style safety belts, Flomo has two-hour trips around the Western Baray (from US$50), four-hour trips towards the Tonlé Sap lake (from US$80) and several full-day options (from US$140) including the holy mountain of Phnom Kulen, the River of a Thousand Lingas at Kbal Spean and the jungle ruin of Beng Mealea.

Bodia Spa   SPA
(Map p98; ☐761593; www.bodia-spa.com; Pithnou St; ☉10am-midnight) Sophisticated spa near Psar Chaa offering a full range of scrubs, rubs and natural remedies, including its own line of herbal products.

Bodytune   SPA
(Map p98; ☐764141; www.bodytune.co.th; 293 Pokambor Ave; ☉10am-10pm) A lavish outpost of a popular Thai spa, this is a fine place to relax and unwind on the riverfront.

Frangipani   SPA
(Map p92; ☐964391; www.frangipanisiemreap.com; 615 Hup Guan St; ☉10am-10pm) This delightful hideaway offers massage and a whole range of spa treatments.

Aqua Sydney   SWIMMING
(Map p114; 7 Makara St; swimming US$3; ☉9am-late) Has a large pool and a lively little bar-restaurant.

🎓 Courses

Cooking classes have really taken off in Siem Reap with a number of restaurants and hotels now offering an introduction to the secrets of Cambodian cooking, including many of the top-end places. Some classes with a good reputation are listed below.

Angkor Palm   COOKING CLASS
(Map p98; Pithnou St; 1/2/3 dishes US$10/15/20) Informal cooking classes held from 8am to 5pm.

Cooks in Tuk Tuks   COOKING CLASS
(Map p114; ☐963400; www.therivergarden.info; per person US$25) Starts at 10am daily with a visit to Psar Leu market, then returns to the River Garden for a professional class.

🔖 **Le Tigre de Papier**   COOKING CLASS
(Map p92; Pub St; per person US$12) Starts at 10am daily and includes a visit to the market. Proceeds go to supporting Sala Bai Hotel

and Restaurant School (see the box, p103), making it great value and a good cause.

Tours

Most visitors are in Siem Reap to tour the temples of Angkor. See p24 for more on temple tours and p341 for a list of recommended Cambodian tour operators.

The beautiful countryside is perfect for two-wheeled adventures. Some of the companies promoting bike tours are listed below.

Travel Loops   BICYCLE TOUR
(www.travelloops.com; per person US$20) All-day ride taking in the countryside near the Tonlé Sap lake and the Western Baray, before passing through Angkor Thom and back to town.

Grasshopper Adventures   BICYCLE TOUR
(www.grasshopperadventures.com; per person US$25) Rides around the Siem Reap countryside, plus a dedicated temple tour on two wheels.

Pure Countryside Cycling Tour BICYCLE TOUR
(www.pureforkids.org; per person US$22) Long half-day tour that takes in local life around Siem Reap, including lunch with a local family. All proceeds go towards supporting Pure educational and vocational-training projects.

Sleeping

Siem Reap has the best range of accommodation in Cambodia. A vast number of family-run guesthouses charging US$3 to US$20 a room cater for budget travellers, while those looking for midrange accommodation can choose upmarket guesthouses or small hotels from US$20 per room.

Touts for budget guesthouses wait at the taxi park, Phnom Krom (where the fast boat from Phnom Penh docks) and at the airport. Even if you've not yet decided where to stay in Siem Reap, don't be surprised to see a noticeboard displaying your name, as most guesthouses in Phnom Penh either have partners up here or sell your name on to another guesthouse. This system usually involves a free ride into town. There's no obligation to stay at the guesthouse if you don't like the look of it, but the 'free lift' might suddenly cost US$1 or more.

There are plenty of great midrange deals available thanks to an explosion in quality boutique accommodation. Most rates include a free transfer from the airport or boat dock.

Many top end hotels levy an additional 10% government tax, 2% tourist tax, and sometimes an extra 10% for service, but breakfast is included. It's essential to book ahead at most places from November to March, particularly for the glamorous spots.

In the low season (April to September), it may be possible to negotiate discounts at some of these places. Top-end hotels usually publish high- and low-season rates.

The places listed below are just a selection of our favourites. There are many more good places around town that we simply don't have the room to cover, so the lack of a listing here doesn't mean it's not a decent place to stay.

Commission scams abound in Siem Reap, so keep your antennae up. See Dangers & Annoyances, p111, for more details.

PSAR CHAA AREA

This is the liveliest part of town, brimming with restaurants, bars and boutiques. Staying here can be a lot of fun, but it's not the quietest part of town.

SIEM REAP FOR CHILDREN

Siem Reap is a great city for children these days thanks to a range of activities beyond the temples. Many of the temples themselves will appeal to older children, particularly the Indiana Jones atmosphere of Ta Prohm and Beng Mealea, the sheer size and scale of Angkor Wat or the weird faces at the Bayon.

Other activities that might be popular include boat trips on the Tonlé Sap to visit other-worldly villages (p116), swimming at a hotel or resort, pottery classes at the Khmer Ceramics Centre (p90), exploring the countryside on horseback or quad bike, goofing around at the Cambodian Cultural Village, exploring the Angkor Butterfly Centre, or just enjoying the cafes and restaurants of Siem Reap at a leisurely pace. Ice-cream shops might be popular, if a little naughty, while the local barbecue restaurants are always enjoyably interactive for older children.

Shadow of Angkor Guesthouse GUESTHOUSE $$

(Map p98; ☑964774; www.shadowofangkor.com; 353 Pokambor Ave; r US$15-25; ❋@❋) In a grand old French-era building overlooking the river, this friendly, 15-room place offers affordable air-con in a superb setting. Newer annexe across the river includes a swimming pool.

Ivy Guesthouse 2 GUESTHOUSE $

(Map p92; ☑012 602930; www.ivy-guesthouse .com; r US$6-15; ❋@❋) An inviting guesthouse with a chill-out area and bar, the Ivy is a lively place to stay. The restaurant is as good as it gets among the guesthouses in town, with a huge vegetarian selection.

Golden Banana Boutique BOUTIQUE HOTEL $$

(Map p92; ☑761259; www.goldenbanana.Info; r US$55-109; ❋@❋❋) The Golden Banana has peeled off into two incarnations and the attractive boutique is the destination of choice. The duplex suites are set on two floors with swing chairs and a pool view. Some include a rain shower and alfresco tub. Gay-friendly.

EI8HT Rooms GUESTHOUSE $

(Map p92; ☑969788; www.ei8htrooms.com; r US$12-24; ❋@❋) A smart, gay-friendly guesthouse with boutique touches, bright silks, DVD players and free internet. So popular, there are 16 rooms now set in two buildings.

Steung Siem Reap Hotel HOTEL $$

(Map p98; ☑965167; www.steungsiemreaphotel .com; r from US$63; ❋@❋❋) In keeping with the French-colonial air around Psar Chaa, this hotel has high ceilings, louvre shutters and wrought-iron balconies. Three-star rooms feature smart wooden trim. The location is hard to beat.

Prohm Roth Guesthouse GUESTHOUSE $

(Map p98; ☑012 466495; www.prohmroth-guest house.com; r US$9-25; ❋@❋) Central, yet tucked away down a side street which runs parallel to Wat Preah Prohm Roth, this is a friendly place. Free pick-up from airport, port or bus station.

Mandalay Inn GUESTHOUSE $

(Map p92; ☑761662; www.mandalayinn.com; r US$7-18; ❋@❋) This smart guesthouse promises Burmese hospitality meets Khmer smiles, offering spotless rooms plus free wi-fi and a rooftop 'gym'.

Popular Guesthouse GUESTHOUSE $

(Map p92; ☑963578; www.popularguesthouse .com; r US$3-14; ❋@❋) Popular by name, popular by nature, this extensive guesthouse has more than 70 well-tended rooms. There's a rooftop restaurant with delicious food.

Neth Socheata Hotel HOTEL $$

(Map p98; ☑963294; www.nethsocheatahotel.com; r US$22-60; ❋@❋) This place has a likeable location in the warren of alleys to the east of the market. Tasteful furnishings, sparkling bathrooms and free wi-fi add up to an affordable deal.

Molly Malone's Guesthouse GUESTHOUSE $$

(Map p98; ☑963533; www.mollymalonescambodia .com; Pub St; r US$20-35; ❋@❋) If you want to be in the heart of the action, this smart B&B above a popular Irish pub (p107) has a small selection of guestrooms, creatively finished with four-poster beds.

Terrasse des Elephants BOUTIQUE HOTEL $$

(Map p92; ☑380117; www.terrasse-des-elephants .com; s/d from US$66/71; ❋@❋❋) This place has a kitsch Angkor theme, including bas-reliefs in the bedroom and ornate Bayon-themed bathrooms, complete with four faces. The rooftop pool and garden are a nice surprise.

SIVATHA ST AREA

The area to the west of Sivatha St includes a good selection of budget guesthouses and midrange boutique hotels.

TOP CHOICE Villa Medamrei BOUTIQUE HOTEL $$

(Map p92; ☑763636; www.villamedamrei.com; r US$22-35; ❋@❋) The eye-catching exterior sets the tone for a stylish and affordable boutique stay. Cheaper rooms are smaller, but all include flat-screen TV and bright silk decor. Some rooms include a small garden or balcony and all come with a complimentary breakfast.

My Home Tropical Garden Villa HOTEL $

(Map p114; ☑760035; www.myhomecambodia .com; r US$14-26; ❋@❋❋) Offering hotel standards at guesthouse prices, this is a fine place to rest your head. The decor includes some soft silks and the furnishings are tasteful, plus there's a decent little swimming pool.

Cashew Nut Guesthouse GUESTHOUSE $

(Map p114; ☑092 815975; thecashewnut.com; Wat Bo Rd; r US$9-20; ❋@❋) A lively new place run by a self-proclaimed 'nutter' who previously worked as a tour leader for Intrepid. Artful decoration and slick service propel

Psar Chaa

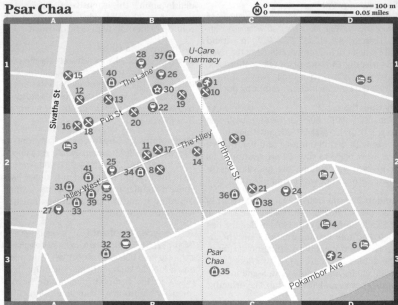

this into boutique backpacker orbit, plus breakfast is included.

Hotel de la Paix   LUXURY HOTEL $$$
(Map p92; ☎966000; www.hoteldelapaixangkor .com; Sivatha St; r from US$200; ❋@🕸🏊) This place is all about funky, contemporary design, trendy interiors and minimalist style. Rooms include open-plan bathrooms and iPods, plus house restaurant Meric serves up cutting-edge cuisine. Huge renovations underway during 2012.

Le Tigre   HOTEL $$
(Map p114; ☎966100; www.letigrehotel.com; r US$35-45; ❋@🕸🏊) This is a chic little hotel offering extra touches like minibar and flat-screen TV. Facilities include an inviting pool and even a jacuzzi. Breakfast included.

Golden Temple Villa   HOTEL $
(Map p92; ☎012 943459; www.goldentemplevilla .com; r US$13-23; ❋@🕸) Independent travellers love this place thanks to its funky, colourful decor and fun outlook. There's a bar-restaurant downstairs, plus free internet. The new Golden Temple Hotel offers the four-star high life.

Garden Village   GUESTHOUSE $
(Map p114; ☎012 217373; www.gardenvillageguest house.com; dm US$1, r US$6-13; ❋@🕸) This old-fashioned backpacker hang-out offers some of the cheapest beds in town and is a good place to meet travellers. Options among its 70 rooms include eight-bed dorms and US$3 cubicles with shared bathroom. The rooftop bar is a draw around sunset.

🌿 Sala Bai Hotel & Restaurant School   HOTEL $$
(Map p92; ☎963329; www.salabai.com; Taphul St; r US$15-30; ❋@🕸) Immerse yourself in the intimate surrounds of this training-school hotel, where the super staff are ever helpful. Rooms include silk wall hangings, woven throw pillows and wicker wardrobes.

Villa Siem Reap   HOTEL $$
(Map p92; ☎761036; www.thevillasiemreap.com; Taphul St; r US$20-55; ❋@🕸) Homely service in intimate surrounds make this a popular place for flashpackers. Rooms are nicely finished and include a safe and a minibar. Responsible tours are available to some of the far-flung sights.

Encore Angkor Guesthouse   HOTEL $$
(Map p92; ☎969400; www.encoreangkor.com; 456 Sok San St; r US$20-50; ❋@🕸) The stylish lobby sets the tone for a budget boutique experience. Rooms include oversized beds and

Psar Chaa

SIEM REAP SLEEPING

an in-room safe. Its motto is 'just don't tell anyone', but we had to go and spoil it.

Auberge Mont Royal HOTEL $$
(Map p92; ☎964044; www.auberge-mont-royal.com; r US$29-70; ❋@☎☂) Set in a classic colonial-style villa, the Auberge has smart rooms at a smart price, with the swimming pool and spa making it a cut above other offerings in this price bracket.

Mommy's Guesthouse GUESTHOUSE $
(Map p92; ☎012 941755; mommy_guesthouse@yahoo.com; r US$5-15; ❋@☎) A warm and welcoming, family-run place, this 13-room villa has large rooms with air-con, as well as cheap digs with cold showers. The owners really go out of their way to assist travellers.

Smiley Guesthouse GUESTHOUSE $
(Map p92; ☎012 852955; www.smileyguesthouse.com; r US$8-21; ❋@☎) One of the first guest-houses to undergo a hotel-tastic makeover almost a decade ago, this place has more than 70 rooms set around a garden courtyard.

RIVERFRONT & ROYAL GARDENS
The smart end of town, this is where the royal residence is to be found, along with many of the luxury hotels and boutique resorts.

TOP CHOICE La Résidence d'Angkor BOUTIQUE RESORT $$$
(Map p92; ☎963390; www.residencedangkor.com; Stung Siem Reap St; r from US$280; ❋@☎☂) The 54 wood-appointed rooms, among the most tasteful and inviting in town, come with verandas and huge Jacuzzi-sized tubs. The gorgeous swimming pool is perfect for laps. The new wing is ultra-contemporary, as is the sumptuous Kong Kea Spa.

Shinta Mani
BOUTIQUE HOTEL **$$$**

(Map p92; ☑761998; www.shintamani.com; Oum Khun St; r from US$120; ❄@🖥🛜) Established as a training institute to give disadvantaged youth a helping hand into the tourism industry, the hotel has rooms featuring designer bathrooms and sleigh beds, as well as a small pool. Shinta Mani has won several international awards for responsible tourism practices. Reopening in 2012 after a long makeover.

FCC Angkor
BOUTIQUE HOTEL **$$$**

(Map p92; ☑760280; www.fcccambodia.com; Pokambor Ave; r from US$135; ❄@🖥🛜) This funky property is a member of Design Hotels and wouldn't look out of place in any chic European capital. However, there are Khmer touches, and rooms feature large bath-tubs, Cambodian silks and wi-fi throughout. The black-tiled swimming pool and Visaya Spa complete the picture.

Victoria Angkor Hotel
HOTEL **$$$**

(Map p92; ☑760428; www.victoriahotels-asia.com; r from US$155; ❄@🖥🛜) The Victoria is a popular choice for those craving the French touch in Indochine. The classy lobby is the perfect introduction to one of the most impressive courtyard pools in town. The rooms are well finished and many include a striking pool view.

Grand Hotel d'Angkor
HISTORIC HOTEL **$$$**

(Map p92; ☑963888; www.raffles.com; r from US$260; ❄@🖥🛜) The hotel with history on its side, this place has been welcoming guests since 1929, including Charlie Chaplin, Charles de Gaulle, Jackie Kennedy and Bill Clinton. Ensconced in such opulent surroundings, you can imagine what it was like to be a tourist in colonial days. Rooms include classic colonial-era touches and a dizzying array of bathroom gifts.

Amansara
LUXURY HOTEL **$$$**

(Map p92; ☑760333; www.amanresorts.com; r from US$850; ❄@🖥🛜) Set in the old guest villa of Norodom Sihanouk, the suites here are among the largest in town and some include a private plunge pool. Rates include tours around the main Angkor temples. Former guests already include a who's who of the rich and famous, like Angelina Jolie and Brad Pitt.

WAT BO AREA

This up-and-coming area features socially responsible guesthouses, as well as some hip boutique hotels. There is a great guesthouse ghetto in a backstreet running parallel to the north end of Wat Bo Rd, which is good for on-the-spot browsing.

⭐ Frangipani Villa Hotel
BOUTIQUE HOTEL **$$**

(Map p92; ☑999930; www.frangipanihotel.com; Wat Bo Rd; r US$40-60; ❄@🖥🛜) The Siem Reap outpost of the growing Frangipani empire, this is chic boutique on the cheap. Rooms include stylish touches like flat-screen TVs, and there's an inviting pool.

Babel Guesthouse
GUESTHOUSE **$$**

(Map p92; ☑965474; www.babelsiemreap.hostel .com; r US$16-27; ❄@🛜) An upmarket guesthouse with a relaxing tropical garden; the service and presentation are a cut above the nearby budget places and rates include breakfast. Under Norwegian ownership, this place is a strong supporter of responsible tourism.

European Guesthouse
GUESTHOUSE **$**

(Map p92; ☑012 582237; www.european-guest house.com; r US$8-18; ❄@🛜) Scandinavian run, the European is a member of local NGO networks Childsafe and ConCERT and supports projects like the White Bicycles. Fun and friendly, the rooms are well presented and the garden a good place to relax. Breakfast is included.

Seven Candles Guesthouse
GUESTHOUSE **$**

(Map p92; ☑963380; www.sevencandlesguest house.com; 307 Wat Bo Rd; r US$10-20; ❄@🛜) A good-cause guesthouse; its profits help a local foundation that seeks to promote education to rural communities. Rooms include hot water, TV and fridge.

Viroth's Hotel
BOUTIQUE HOTEL **$$$**

(Map p92; ☑761720; www.viroth-hotel.com; r from US$80; ❄@🖥🛜) Minimalist and modern, this small boutique property has seven rooms finished in contemporary chic. Facilities include a pool, a hot tub and free wi-fi.

Soria Moria Hotel
BOUTIQUE HOTEL **$$**

(Map p92; ☑964768; www.thesoriamoria.com; Wat Bo Rd; r US$40-65; ❄@🖥🛜) A hotel with a heart, promoting local causes to help the community, this boutique place has attractive rooms with smart bathroom fittings. Fusion restaurant downstairs, sky hot tub upstairs.

Karavansara   BOUTIQUE HOTEL **$$$**
(Map p92; ☑760678; www.karavansara.com; 25 Acha Sva St; r from US$87; ✳@☎⚛) Set in an iconic building from Cambodia's new architecture heyday, this boutique hotel offers tasteful rooms and, across the road, larger apartments for families. The restaurant is set in a delightful relocated traditional house.

Men's Resort & Spa   BOUTIQUE HOTEL **$$**
(Map p114; ☑963503; www.mens-resort.com; r US$49-90; ✳@☎⚛) The latest gay resort among a growing scene in Siem Reap, this is designed along slick minimalist lines. Rooms include funky artworks and the hideaway premises includes a pool and spa.

La Noria Guesthouse   BOUTIQUE GUESTHOUSE **$$**
(Map p92; ☑964242; www.lanoriaangkor.com; r US$44; ✳@☎⚛) Lovely La Noria is set in a lush tropical garden with a pretty swimming pool. Rooms have a traditional trim and include a veranda but no TV or fridge.

Happy Guesthouse   GUESTHOUSE **$**
(Map p92; ☑012 960879; www.angkorhotels.com/happy; r US$5-11; ✳@☎) This place will really make you happy thanks to welcoming owners who speak very good English *et un peu de Français*. Great-value rooms and free internet.

Mother Home Guesthouse   GUESTHOUSE **$$**
(Map p92; ☑760302; www.motherhomeguesthouse.com; r US$18-27; ✳@☎) A somewhat smarter place in the guesthouse strip, offering clean, spacious rooms, plus free use of bicycles and internet.

Siem Reap Hostel   BACKPACKERS **$**
(Map p92; ☑964660; www.thesiemreaphostel.com; 10 Makara St; dm US$6, r US$15-36; ✳@☎⚛) Angkor's first full-on backpacker hostel is pretty slick. The dorms are well tended and the rooms are definitely flashpacker, and they include breakfast too. There is a lively bar-restaurant and a covered pool.

Green Village Palace   GUESTHOUSE **$$**
(off Map p92; ☑760623; www.greenvillagepalace.com; Wat Dam Nak St; r US$15-30; ✳@☎⚛) It really is quite palatial for this sort of money, as the smart rooms include sweeping silks, plus TV and fridge. There's also a small swimming pool and a gym.

Rosy Guesthouse   GUESTHOUSE **$**
(Map p92; ☑965059; www.rosyguesthouse.com; Stung Siem Reap Rd; r US$8-30; ✳) A British-

owned establishment whose 15 rooms come with TV and DVD, but the four cheapest are small and have shared bathrooms. Has a lively pub downstairs.

FURTHER AFIELD
Don't shy away from venturing further afield, as some of the most memorable boutique hotels lie hidden beyond.

Pavillon Indochine   BOUTIQUE HOTEL **$$**
(Map p114; ☑012 849681; www.pavillon-indochine.com; r US$50-55, ste US$70-85; ✳@☎⚛) The Pavillon offers charming colonial-chic rooms set around a small swimming pool. The trim includes Asian antiques, billowing mosquito nets and a safe.

HanumanAlaya   BOUTIQUE HOTEL **$$**
(Map p114; ☑760582; www.hanumanalaya.com; r US$60-100; ✳@☎⚛) A blissful boutique retreat, HanumanAlaya is set around a lush garden and pretty swimming pool. Rooms are decorated with antiques and handicrafts but include modern touches like cable TV, minibar and safe. It also includes a garden spa and Reahoo Restaurant, popular for authentic Khmer flavours.

1961   BOUTIQUE HOTEL **$$**
(Map p114; ☑966961; www.the1961.com; r US$30; ✳@☎) Part hotel, part art gallery and creative space, this is a memorable little hotel themed around the Cold War era. The key year was 1961, and rooms are named after the Norodoms, the Kennedys and famous Khmer architect Vann Molyvann. We like the Norodoms, complete with royal pop art and movie posters.

Samar Villas & Spa   BOUTIQUE RESORT **$$$**
(Map p114; ☑762449; www.samarvillas.com; r US$160-300; ✳@☎⚛) The most boutique of many boutique places in Siem Reap, the Samar offers sumptuous all-wooden suites, each with individual taste and character. Rates include a daily shave for gents and a hand massage for women.

River Garden   BOUTIQUE HOTEL **$$**
(Map p114; ☑963400; www.therivergarden.info; r US$55-99; ✳@☎⚛) Invitingly set amid a verdant garden, this wooden resort has a small selection of atmospheric rooms, some with large balconies and deep baths. Renowned for its 'cooks in túk-túks' culinary class (p95).

Heritage Suites   BOUTIQUE HOTEL **$$$**
(Map p114; ☑969100; www.relaischateaux.com/heritage; r from US$200; ✳@☎⚛) Designed in

SIEM REAP SLEEPING

TOP FIVE: LOW-SEASON DEALS

A number of hotels offer enticing deals in the low season (mid-April to mid-October). Here are some of the most popular:

Lotus Angkor Hotel (Map p114; ☑965555; www.lotusangkor.com; Airport Rd; r from US$50; ✵@🛜⊠) Popular with tour groups thanks to smart rooms and a full-size pool.

Somadevi Angkor Hotel (Map p92; ☑967666; www.somadeviangkor.com; Sivatha St; r from US$50; ✵@🛜⊠) Huge hotel just off the main drag with smart, spacious rooms and a large T-shaped pool.

Angkorland Hotel (Map p92; ☑760544; www.angkorland.com; Taphul St; r from US$59; ✵@⊠) Big hotel with a heavy wood finish and a large courtyard pool.

Borei Angkor Resort & Spa (Map p114; ☑964406; www.boreiangkor.com; NH6 East; r from US$60; ✵@🛜⊠) Popular resort within walking distance of the town centre.

Angkor Home Hotel (Map p114; ☑969797; www.angkorhomehotel.com; r from US$79; ✵@🛜⊠) Swish hotel off Airport Rd with elegant rooms and a large pool.

the colonial style, the suites here are spectacular and open plan, many including a small garden and freestanding bathtub. Lanterns Restaurant here is highly regarded.

Lotus Lodge
HOTEL $$
(Map p114; ☑966140; www.lotus-lodge.com; r US$13-29; ✵@🛜⊠) A good deal for those wanting a peaceful retreat after a day at the temples. Rooms are clean and comfortable, plus there's a spacious swimming pool. Free bikes and evening shuttles.

Earthwalkers
HOSTEL $
(Map p114; ☑012 967901; www.earthwalkers.no; dm US$5, s/d from US$12/15; ✵@🛜⊠) One of the first hostels in town, Earthwalkers is popular thanks to the signature 'footprint' swimming pool. Dorms include breakfast, and private rooms come with fan or air-con to suit all budgets. It's off NH6.

Paul Dubrule Hotel & Tourism School
HOTEL $$
(Map p114; ☑963673; www.ecolepauldubrule.org; NH6; r US$20-35; ✵@🛜) Paul Dubrule cofounded the Accor hotel group, so it's no surprise that his four-room training hotel offers smart rooms and slick service. A great deal.

Eating

The dining scene in Siem Reap is something to savour, offering a superb selection of street food, Asian eateries and sumptuous restaurants. The range encompasses something from every continent, with new temptations constantly on offer. Sample the subtleties of Khmer cuisine in town, or simply indulge in home comforts or gastronomic delights prior to – or after – hitting the remote provinces.

Tourist numbers mean many top restaurants are heaving during high season. But with so many places to choose from, keep walking and you'll find somewhere more tranquil. Quite a lot of restaurants work with tour groups to some degree. If you prefer to avoid places with tour groups, it's better to stick to the Psar Chaa area and explore on foot. The restaurants reviewed here represent just a fraction of the food on offer.

Some of the budget guesthouses have good menus offering a selection of local dishes and Western meals; while it's easy to order in-house food, it hardly counts as the full Siem Reap experience. Several of the midrange hotels and all the top-end places have restaurants, some excellent. For details on dinner and a performance of classical dance, as featured at several hotels and restaurants around town, see Entertainment (p108).

For more on the lunch options available in and around Angkor, see p131.

The Alley is wall-to-wall with good Cambodian restaurants, many of which are family owned. Most have 'Khmer' in the name and offer cheap beers and meal deals. Take a stroll and see what takes your fancy.

PUB ST & AROUND

Pub St may not seem the most relaxing dining venue, particularly by night, but the alleys and lanes that criss-cross the area reveal some atmospheric places.

Pub St Food Stalls
CAMBODIAN $
(Map p98; mains US$1-3; ⊙5pm-2am) Every evening a cluster of stalls sets up shop at

the western end of Pub St. Outdoor kitchens and plastic chairs are the order of the day, but the meals are a real bargain, including freshly barbecued skewers of meat, fish and seafood.

Khmer Kitchen Restaurant   CAMBODIAN **$**
(Map p98; The Alley; mains US$2-5; ☺11am-10pm) Can't get no (culinary) satisfaction? Then follow in the footsteps of Sir Mick Jagger and try this popular place, which offers an affordable selection of Khmer and Thai favourites, including feisty curries.

Le Tigre de Papier   INTERNATIONAL **$$**
(Map p98; Pub St; mains US$2-9; ☺24hr; 🛜) One of the best all-rounders in Siem Reap, the popular Tigre serves up authentic Khmer food, great Italian dishes and a selection of favourites from most other corners of the globe. Doubles as a popular bar by night, with frontage on both Pub St and the Alley.

Chamkar   VEGETARIAN **$$**
(Map p98; The Alley; mains US$4-8; ☺11am-11pm, closed lunch Sun; ✳) The name translates as 'farm' and the ingredients must be coming from a pretty impressive organic vegetable supplier given the creative dishes on the

menu here. Asian flavours predominate, such as stuffed pumpkin or vegetable kebabs in black pepper sauce.

Cambodian BBQ   BARBECUE **$$**
(Map p98; The Alley; mains US$5-9; ☺11am-11pm) Crocodile, snake, ostrich and kangaroo meat add an exotic twist to the traditional *phnom pleung* (hill of fire) grills. It has spawned a dozen or more copycats in the surrounding streets, many of which offer discount specials.

Amok   CAMBODIAN **$$**
(Map p98; The Alley; mains US$4-9; ☺5-11pm; 🛜) The name pays homage to Cambodia's national dish, *amok* (or *amok*), and this is indeed a fine place to try baked fish curry in banana leaf or, better still, an *amoc* tasting platter with four varieties. It is in the heart of the Alley.

Il Forno   ITALIAN **$$**
(Map p98; The Lane; mains US$4-12; ☺11am-11pm; 🛜) Fans of fine Italian cuisine will be delighted to know that there is, as the name suggests, a full-blown brick oven in this cosy little *trattoria*. The menu includes fresh

---

TOP FIVE: DINING FOR A CAUSE

These are some good restaurants that support worthy causes or assist in the training of Cambodia's future hospitality staff with a subsidised ticket into the tourism industry. If you dine at the training places, it gives the trainees a good opportunity to hone their skills with real customers.

Butterflies Garden Restaurant (Map p92; www.butterfliesofangkor.com; mains US$3-8; ☺8am-10pm) Set in a blooming garden that provides a backdrop for hundreds of butterflies, this is dining with a difference. The menu includes Khmer flavours, some classics from home and indulgent desserts. Supports good causes, including Cambodian Living Arts and communities affected by HIV/AIDS.

Common Grounds (Map p92; 719 St 14; light meals US$3-5; ☺7am-10pm; @🛜) Sophisticated international cafe akin to Starbucks. Great coffee, homemade cakes, light bites, and free wi-fi *and* internet terminals. Offers free computer classes and English classes for Cambodians, and supports good causes.

Les Jardins des Delices (Map p114; Paul Dubrule Hotel & Tourism School, NH6; set lunch US$12; ☺noon-2pm Mon-Fri) Enjoy Sofitel standards at an affordable price, with a three-course meal of Asian and Western food prepared by students training in the culinary arts.

Sala Bai Hotel and Restaurant School (Map p92; www.salabai.com; set lunch US$8; ☺7-9am & noon-2pm Mon-Fri) This school trains young Khmers in the art of hospitality and serves an affordable menu of Western and Cambodian cuisine.

Singing Tree Café (Map p98; www.singingtreecafe.com; mains US$2-5; ☺closed Mon) Relocated in the chic shopping strip that is Alley West, this small pavement cafe is the perfect place to wind down after some retail therapy with scrumptious muffins, creative coffees and original health foods.

antipasti, authentic pizzas and some home-cooked Italian dishes.

🏷️**n.y.d.c.** CAFE $
(Map p98; The Alley; meals US$3-5; ⊙6am-10pm; 📶) NYC-style deli with subs, sandwiches and wraps, plus tall coffees. Twenty per cent of profits goes to support family care around Siem Reap, so it's all for a good cause.

AHA FUSION $$
(Map p98; The Alley; tapas US$3-10; ❀📶) A trendy little tapas emporium and wine bar with a variety of tasting platters, including cheese, veggie, Khmer, classic and contemporary. Inventive cuisine.

Soup Dragon ASIAN, INTERNATIONAL $$
(Map p98; Pub St; Vietnamese mains US$2-10; ⊙6am-11pm; 📶) This three-level restaurant has a split personality: the ground floor serves up cheap, classic Asian breakfasts, while upstairs serves a diverse menu of Asian and international dishes, including Italian and Moroccan.

Red Piano INTERNATIONAL $
(Map p98; Pub St; mains US$3-6; 📶) Strikingly set in a restored colonial gem, Red Piano has a big balcony for watching the action unfold below. The menu has a reliable selection of Asian and international food, all at decent prices. Former celebrity guest Angelina Jolie has a cocktail named in her honour.

Sushi Bar Koh Kong JAPANESE $$
(Map p98; Pub St; meals US$3-12; ⊙5-11pm) The first sushi bar to open in the heart of old Siem Reap, much of the seafood is locally sourced in Cambodia from – wait for it, Koh Kong – and prices are tempting for Japanese cuisine.

Samsara INDIAN $$
(Map p98; The Alley; mains US$5-10 ⊙11am-11pm) Under the same team as the old Kama Sutra, Samsara offers authentic Indian flavours in contemporary surrounds. It is particularly renowned for its mutton curries, prepared with New Zealand's finest lamb.

PSAR CHAA AREA

🔝**Blue Pumpkin** INTERNATIONAL $
(Map p98; Pithnou St; mains US$2-6; ⊙6am-10pm; ❀📶) Downstairs it could be any old cafe, albeit with a delightful selection of cakes, breads and homemade ice cream. Upstairs is another world of white minimalism, with beds to lounge on and free wi-fi. Light bites,

great sandwiches, filling specials and divine shakes, this place is the real deal.

Cafe Central INTERNATIONAL $
(Map p98; ⊙7am-late; 📶) A popular spot looking across to the market, this is as central as it gets. The eclectic menu includes generous all-day breakfasts, good-value pizzas, a selection of seven burgers and a diverse choice of mains from lemongrass chicken to steak and Guinness pie.

Angkor Palm CAMBODIAN $
(Map p98; Pithnou St; mains US$3-8; ⊙10am-10pm) This popular restaurant offers the authentic taste of Cambodia. Even Khmers rave about the legendary *amoc* (baked fish in banana leaf) here, and it offers a great-value sampling platter for just US$7.50. Cooking classes available.

Psar Chaa CAMBODIAN $
(Map p98; mains US$1.50-3; ⊙7am-9pm) When it comes to cheap Khmer eats, Psar Chaa itself has plenty of food stalls on the northwest side, all with signs and menus in English. These are atmospheric places for a local meal at local-ish prices. Some dishes are on display, others are freshly flash fried to order, but most are wholesome and filling.

F for Falafel INTERNATIONAL $
(Map p98; mains US$2.50-5; ⊙7am-10pm) Falafel fever has come to Siem Reap in the shape of this cosy streetside diner. Choose a half falafel combo with fries and a soft drink for US$3.50, or a range of healthy shakes and salads.

Viva MEXICAN $
(Map p98; Pithnou St; mains US$2-6; ⊙7am-late) Spice up your life with Mexican food and margaritas at this long-running place, which has expanded to include a guesthouse. Lively location.

SIVATHA ST AREA

Le Malraux FRENCH-ASIAN $$
(Map p98; Sivatha St; mains US$5-12; ⊙7am-midnight) A good spot for gastronomes, this classy art-deco cafe-restaurant offers fine French food. Try the combination salmon tartar and carpaccio to start, followed by a quality cut from the selection of steaks. The Cognac and Armagnac selection is to die for. Asian dishes also available.

Curry Walla INDIAN $
(Map p92; Sivatha St; mains US$2-5; ⊙10.30am-11pm) For good-value Indian food, this place is hard to beat. The *thalis* (set meals) are a

bargain and the owner knows his share of spicy specials from the subcontinent.

Barrio FRENCH $$
(Map p92; Sivatha St; mains US$4-10; ⊙11am-11pm) One of the longest-running French bistros in town, it is popular with European expats thanks to its Gallic menu and continental vibe.

WAT BO AREA

TOP
CHOICE Green Star CAMBODIAN $
(Map p92; mains US$2-6; ⊙lunch & dinner) Tucked away in a quiet street behind Wat Damnak is this appealing not-for-profit restaurant supporting former street kids in Siem Reap. Authentic Khmer dishes include spicy duck, lemongrass eel and succulent frog. Blackboard specials change regularly.

Alliance Cafe FRENCH, ASIAN $$
(Map p92; mains US$3.50-16; ⊙10am-11pm) Set in an attractive French colonial–era villa, this classy French restaurant also pays homage to its Cambodian context with some original Asian recipes. Choose from set menus such as Asian Tradition and Alliance Passion for just US$14. Doubles as an art venue.

Le Café CAFE $
(Map p92; snacks US$2-4; ⊙7.30am-9pm, 🖥) Run in partnership with the Paul Dubrule Hotel & Tourism School (p102), this cafe brings five-star sandwiches, salads and shakes to the French Cultural Centre.

Kholene INTERNATIONAL $$
(Map p92; Wat Bo Rd; mains US$3-15; ⊙11am-2pm & 5-10.30pm) French in orientation, Kholene also offers Italian dining and some Khmer teasers. Tuna tartar with ginger and green mango is a delight, as is salmon in a lemongrass cream sauce. Happy hour from 5pm till 7pm daily. Two-for-one pizzas.

Square 24 CAMBODIAN $$
(Map p92; St 24; mains US$4-10; ⊙11.30am-late) A newly built (2011), stylish venue for contemporary Khmer and Asian cuisine. Billowing silks flutter around the open-plan architecture, making it ideal for a balmy evening.

Viroth's Restaurant CAMBODIAN $
(Map p92; Wat Bo Rd; mains US$4-8; ⊙lunch & dinner) A sophisticated garden restaurant near Wat Bo, this is where Khmer cuisine meets Balinese design. It's popular with tour groups but still manages to retain an element of intimacy.

Chivit Thai THAI $
(Map p92; 130 Wat Bo Rd; mains US$3-8; ⊙7am-10pm) The most atmospheric Thai place in town, this is set in a beautiful wooden villa surrounded by a lush garden. Choose between floor dining on Thai cushions or table dining. The food includes a delicious *laab* (spicy Thai salad with fish or meat).

El Camino MEXICAN $$
(Map p92; St 26; mains US$4-9; ⊙11am-late) New Mexican cantina located in a stylish premises near the east bank of the Siem Reap River. Choose from contemporary Mex-like tequila-flamed meats or traditional tacos and burritos.

Moloppor Cafe JAPANESE, INTERNATIONAL $
(Map p92; Siem Reap River Rd; mains US$1-4; ⊙10am-11pm) One of the cheapest deals in Siem Reap, it offers Japanese, Asian and Italian dishes at almost giveaway prices for what is a real restaurant. Nice location offering river views.

AROUND SIEM REAP

TOP
CHOICE Cuisine Wat Damnak CAMBODIAN $$$
(Map p92; Sivatha Blvd; set menus from US$18; ⊙dinner) Opened in April 2011 in a traditional wooden house, this is the latest restaurant from Siem Reap celeb chef Johannes Rivieres. The menu delivers the ultimate contemporary Khmer dining experience. Seasonal set menus are incredible value for the calibre of the dishes.

Abacus FRENCH $$$
(Map p114; mains US$8-20; ⊙11am-late; ❋🖥) The finest French dining in town is found here, with steaks in black-truffle sauce, succulent lamb and superb seafood, including tuna *maguro*. Dine in the garden or the cool interior. The menu includes some beautifully presented Khmer dishes. Off Airport Rd.

Sugar Palm CAMBODIAN $$
(Map p92; Taphul St; mains US$5-9; ⊙11am-late; 🖥) Set in a beautiful wooden house in the west of town, the Sugar Palm is the place to sample traditional flavours infused with herbs and spices, including delicious '*char kreung*' (curried lemongrass) dishes. Owner Kethana showed celebrity chef Gordon Ramsay how to prepare *amoc*.

FCC Angkor INTERNATIONAL $$
(Map p92; mains US$5-15; ⊙7am-midnight; 🖥) This landmark building draws people in from the riverside thanks to a reflective

pool, torchlit dining and a garden bar. Inside, the colonial chic continues with lounge chairs and an open kitchen turning out a range of Asian and international food.

Touich
CAMBODIAN $

(Map p114; mains US$2.50-8; ☺dinner) Hidden away but worth the search, this is a traditional Khmer restaurant set in the backstreet suburbs of Wat Preah Inkosei. The menu includes regional specialities and seafood such as Mekong prawns and Koh Kong red snapper. Check the blog to avoid getting lost at http://the-touich-restaurant-bar.blogspot.com.

Kanell
INTERNATIONAL $$

(Map p92; 7 Makara St; mains US$5-15 ☺11am-midnight; 🛜🏊) Set in a handsome Khmer villa on the edge of town, Kanell offers extensive gardens and a swimming pool for those seeking to dine and unwind. The menu includes French-accented dishes, plus some Cambodian favourites.

Tangram Garden
INTERNATIONAL $

(Map p92; mains US$4-8; ☺lunch & dinner; 🛜) A new al-fresco garden restaurant in a quiet suburb near Wat Damnak, Tangram Garden specialises in barbecue grills, as well as Khmer staples. Atmospheric at night, there's also a small children's playground here to keep it family-friendly.

L'Oasi Italiana
ITALIAN $$

(Map p114; meals US$4-10; ☺6-10pm Mon, 11am-2pm & 6-10pm Tue-Sun) This really is something of an oasis, hidden away in a forest near Wat Preah Inkosei. Expats swear by the gnocchi and homemade pasta, including ravioli with porcini mushrooms.

Vitking House
VEGETARIAN $

(Map p114; 7 Makara St; mains US$1-2; ☺7am-9pm; 🍴) Popular with students from the nearby university, this is one of the cheapest vegie spots in town, with sizzling platters of shitake mushrooms and noodles. Worth the detour.

Madame Butterfly
ASIAN $$

(Map p114; Airport Rd; mains US$4-10; ☺6-11pm) This traditional wooden house has been sumptuously decorated with fine silks and billowing drapes. Lovely atmosphere, but sometimes dampened by the sheer number of tour groups who come to sample the Asian and Khmer cuisine.

Self-Catering

The markets are well stocked with fruit and fresh bread. For more substantial treats, like cheese and chocolate, try the local supermarkets. Eating in the market usually works out cheaper than self-catering, but some folks like to make up a picnic for longer days on the road.

Try the following:

Angkor Market
SUPERMARKET $

(Map p92; Sivatha St) The best all-round supermarket in town, this place has a steady supply of international treats.

Lucky Market
SUPERMARKET $

(Map p92; Sivatha St) Part of a big shopping mall on Sivatha St, this is the biggest supermarket in town.

🍷 Drinking

The transformation from sleepy overgrown village to an international destination for the jet set has been dramatic and Siem Reap is now firmly on the nightlife map of southeast Asia. By night it feels more like a beach town than a cultural capital. The Psar Chaa area is a good hunting ground, with one street even earning the moniker 'Pub St', where you can dive in and crawl out. Pub St is closed to traffic every evening.

Great spots running parallel to Pub St include the Alley, to the south, where the volume control is just a little lower, plus a series of smaller lanes to the north. There are plenty more places around town, so make sure you plan at least one big night out.

CRAVING ICE CREAM?

After a hot day exploring the temples, there's nothing quite like an ice-cream fix and Siem Reap delivers some superb surprises:

Blue Pumpkin (Map p98; Pithnou St; cones US$1.50; ☺6am-10pm) Homemade ice cream in original tropical flavours from ginger to passionfruit.

Cafe de la Paix (Map p92; Hotel de la Paix, Sivatha St; cones US$2; ☺6am-10pm) Velvety ice creams including Mars Bar flavour and tangy sorbets.

Swenson's Ice Cream (Map p92; Pokambor Ave; cones US$1.25; ☺9am-9pm) One of America's favourites has become one of Siem Reap's favourites. Located in the Angkor Trade Centre.

Most of the bars here have happy hours, but so do some of the fancier hotels, which is a good way to sample the high life even if you're not staying at those places, although the atmosphere can be a little austere.

As well as the selection of bars below, some of the aforementioned restaurants double as lively bars by night, including atmospheric Abacus (p105), Aqua Sydney (p95) with its tempting swimming pool, classic FCC Angkor (p105), the popular Red Piano (p104) and the rooftop Soup Dragon (p104), which donates 7% of the take to the Angkor Children's Hospital, so you're helping someone else's health, if not your own.

Warehouse   BAR
(Map p98; ⊙10.30am-3am; 📷) This lively bar opposite Psar Chaa has long been popular with resident expats and travellers in Siem Reap. Top tunes, table football, a pool table and devilish drinks keep them coming until the early hours.

Laundry Bar   BAR, CLUB
(Map p98; ⊙6pm-late) One of the most alluring bars in town thanks to low lighting and discerning decor, this is the place to come for electronica and ambient sounds. It heaves on weekends or when guest DJs crank up the volume. Happy hour until 9pm.

Miss Wong   COCKTAIL LOUNGE
(Map p98; The Lane; ⊙6pm-late) Miss Wong carries you back to the chic of 1920s Shanghai. The cocktails are a draw here, making it a cool place to while away an evening. Gay-friendly and extremely popular with the well-heeled expat crowd.

Nest   COCKTAIL LOUNGE
(Map p92; Sivatha St; ⊙4pm-late) A memorable bar thanks to its sweeping sail-like shelters and stylish seating, this place has one of the most creative cocktail lists in town. Curl up in a sleigh bed and relax for the night. Also has an impressive menu of fusion and international cuisine should the munchies strike.

Angkor What?   DIVE BAR
(Map p98; Pub St; ⊙6pm-late) Siem Reap's original bar claims to have been promoting irresponsible drinking since 1998. The happy hour (to 9pm) lightens the mood for later when everyone's bouncing along to indie anthems, sometimes on the tables, sometimes under them.

Silk Garden   BAR
(Map p98; The Lane; ⊙3pm-late) Hidden away in the maze of lanes, this is a relaxing place

---

THE CAMBODIAN BEER GARDEN EXPERIENCE

There are dozens of beer gardens around Siem Reap that cater to young Cambodians working in the tourism industry. These can be a great experience for cheap beer, local snacks and getting to know some Cambodians beyond your driver or guide. All serve up ice-cold beer, some served in 3L beer towers complete with chiller. They can be a bit laddish by Cambodian standards, so solo female travellers might want to hook up with a traveller crowd before venturing forth.

The best strip is just north of Airport Rd from the first set of traffic lights after Sivatha St. **Trey Kon** (Map p92; ⊙5pm-late) is one of the best of the bunch, with a huge circular bar, regular football on big screens and mighty beer towers. Wander around this area to see where the local are hanging out.

---

to sink some drinks away from the pandemonium of Pub St. Little garden, silk drapes and a chill-out area upstairs.

Linga Bar   COCKTAIL LOUNGE
(Map p98; The Alley; ⊙5pm-late) This chic gay bar attracts all comers thanks to a relaxed atmosphere, a cracking cocktail list and some big beats, which draw a dancing crowd later into the night.

🖉 Joe-to-Go   CAFE
(Map p98; ⊙7am-9.30pm) If you need coffee coursing through your veins to tackle the temples, then head here. Gourmet coffees, shakes and light bites, with proceeds supporting street children.

Molly Malone's   IRISH PUB
(Map p98; Pub St; ⊙7.30am-midnight) Siem Reap's original Irish pub brings the sparkle of the Emerald Isle to homesick Irish and a whole host of honorary Dubliners. Serves up Powers whiskey, Guinness and excellent pub grub.

Temple Club   BAR
(Map p98; Pub St; ⊙10am-late) The only worshipping going on at this temple is 'all hail the ale'. This place starts moving early and doesn't stop, but it's not for the hard of hearing as the music is permanently cranked up

to 11. Dangerous happy hours from 10am to 10pm.

Chilli Si-Dang   WINE BAR
(Map p92; Siem Reap River Rd; ☺7am-late; 🛜)
Boasting a tranquil riverside location and balcony views, this is a relaxed wine bar from which to quaff some vintages or sample some cocktails. Friday happy hour includes all cocktails at US$2.75.

X Bar   BAR
(Map p92; Sivatha St; ☺4pm-sunrise) One of *the* late-night spots in town, X Bar draws revellers for the witching hour when other places are closing up. Early-evening movies on the big screen, pool tables and even a skateboard pipe…if you're not too hammered.

Villa Anjuna   BAR
(Map p92; St 27; ☺7am-late) It feels like you've stumbled upon a hippie retreat in '60s California when you first rock up here. The pop-art garden includes psychedelic painted Bayon faces and coconut palms, as well as a full-size tee-pee tent. Weekend and full-moon parties.

Picasso   TAPAS BAR
(Map p98; Alley West; ☺4pm-midnight) A tiny tapas bar in the up-and-coming Alley West area, this is a convivial spot for a bit of over-the-counter banter. With only 10 stools, expect spillover into the street, especially once the cheap sangria, worldly wines and cheap Tiger bottles start flowing.

☆ Entertainment

Several restaurants and hotels offer cultural performances during the evening, and for many visitors such shows offer the only opportunity to see Cambodian classical dance. While they may be aimed at tourists and are nowhere near as sophisticated as a performance of the Royal Ballet in Phnom Penh, to the untrained eye it is nonetheless graceful and alluring. Prices usually include a buffet meal. Look out for special performances to support cultural organisations and orphanages, as these can be a good way to assist the local community.

Temple Club   DANCE
(Map p92; Pub St) Free traditional dance show upstairs from 7.30pm, providing punters order some food and drink from the very reasonably priced menu.

Dining Room   DANCE
(Map p92; ☺free performance Tue, Thu & Sat) The stylish restaurant (mains US$15 to US$50)

at La Résidence d'Angkor offers an impressive performance and you can dine à la carte in the garden.

🖋 Acodo Orphanage   DANCE
(off Map p92; 🖉012 734306; www.acodo.org; admission free) Offers a free traditional dance show every night at 6.30pm. Donations are very welcome. It's signposted on the road to the Tonlé Sap lake.

🖋 Beatocello   CLASSICAL MUSIC
(Map p114; www.beatocello.com; ☺7.15pm Sat) Better known as Dr Beat Richner, Beatocello performs cello compositions at Jayavarman VII Children's Hospital. Entry is free, but donations are welcome, as they assist the hospital in offering free medical treatment to the children of Cambodia.

🖋 La Noria Restaurant   SHADOW PUPPETRY
(Map p92; 🖉964242; show US$6, mains US$4-8) For something a bit different, try the Wednesday-evening shadow-puppet show with classical dance at La Noria. Part of the fee is donated to a charity supporting local children.

Apsara Theatre   DANCE
(Map p92; www.angkorvillage.com/theatre.php; admission US$25) The setting is a striking wooden pavilion finished in the style of a wat, but the set menu is less inspiring. There are two shows per night and it's packed to the rafters with tour groups.

🔒 Shopping

Much of what you see on sale in the markets of Siem Reap can also be purchased from children and vendors throughout the temple area. Some people get fed up with the endless sales pitches as they navigate the ancient wonders, while others enjoy the banter and a chance to interact with Cambodian people. It's often children out selling, and some visitors will argue that they should be at school instead. However, most do attend school at least half of the time, joining for morning or afternoon classes, alternating with siblings.

Items touted at the temples include postcards, T-shirts, temple bas-relief rubbings, curious musical instruments, ornamental knives and crossbows – the last may raise a few eyebrows with customs should you try to take one home! Be sure to bargain, as overcharging is pretty common.

TOP 10: SHOPPING FOR A CAUSE

Several shops support Cambodia's disabled and disenfranchised through their production process or their profits. Consider spending some money at one of these worthy places:

Artisans d'Angkor (Map p92; www.artisansdangkor.com; ⊙7.30am-6.30pm) High-quality reproduction carvings and exquisite silks are available. Impoverished youngsters are trained in the arts of their ancestors at Les Chantiers Écoles (see p90).

iiDA (Map p98; www.iidadesigns.com; Alley West; ⊙11am-10pm) Vintage and timeless fashion finished in local fabrics. Supports sustainable employment for local women, including education and healthcare initiatives.

IKTT (Map p92; Tonlé Sap Rd; ⊙9am-5pm) A traditional wooden house that is home to the Institute for Khmer Traditional Textiles. Fine *kramas*, scarves, throws and more.

Krousar Thmey (Map p114; www.krousar-thmey.org; Charles de Gaulle Blvd; ⊙8am-5.30pm) Small shop selling shadow puppets, traditional scarves, paintings and postcards, all to assist blind children in Cambodia.

Mekong Quilts (Map p92; www.mekong-quilts.org; 5 Sivatha St; ⊙8am-10pm) Handmade bed covers, quilts, home accessories and more in cotton, linen and silk. Supports women from poor rural areas and helps them earn money within their community.

Nyemo (Map p92; www.nyemo.com; Angkor Night Market; ⊙4pm-midnight) Silk products such as cushions, hangings and throws, plus children's toys. Proceeds are used to help HIV/AIDS sufferers and vulnerable women generally.

Rajana (Map p92; www.rajanacrafts.org; Sivatha St; ⊙9am-9pm, closed Sun) Sells quirky wooden and metalwork objects, well-designed silver jewellery and handmade cards. Rajana promotes fair trade and employment opportunities for Cambodians.

Samatoa (Map p98; www.samatoa.com; Pithnou St; ⊙8am-11pm) Designer clothes finished in silk with the option of a tailored fit in 48 hours. Promotes fair trade and responsible employment.

Senteurs d'Angkor (Map p98; Pithnou St; ⊙8.30am-9.30pm) Opposite Psar Chaa, this shop has an eclectic collection of silk and carvings, as well as a superb range of traditional beauty products and spices, all made locally. It targets rural poor and disadvantaged for jobs and training, and sources local products from farmers. Visit its **Botanic Garden** (Map p114; ⊙7.30am-5.30pm) on Airport Rd, a sort of Willy Wonka's for the senses.

Smateria (Map p98; www.smateria.com; Alley West; ⊙10am-10pm) Recycling rocks here, with funky bags made from construction nets, plastic bags, motorbike seat covers and more. Fair-trade enterprise employing some disabled Cambodians.

SIEM REAP SHOPPING

Cheap books on Angkor and Cambodia are hawked by kids around the temples, and by amputees trying to make a new start in Siem Reap. Be aware that many are illegal photocopies and the print quality is poor.

Psar Chaa   MARKET

(Old Market; Map p98) When it comes to shopping in town, Psar Chaa is well stocked with anything you may want to buy, and lots you don't. Silverware, silk, wood carvings, stone carvings, Buddhas, paintings, rubbings, notes and coins, T-shirts, table mats...the list goes on. There are bargains to be had if you haggle patiently and humorously. Avoid buying old stone carvings that vendors claim are from Angkor.

Whether or not they are real, buying these artefacts serves only to encourage their plunder and they will usually be confiscated by customs.

Angkor Night Market   MARKET

(Map p92; ⊙4pm-midnight) Near Sivatha St, this is a popular place on the Siem Reap shopping scene. It's packed with stalls selling a variety of handicrafts, souvenirs and silks and is well worth a browse to take advantage of cooler temperatures. It's also possible to chill out in the Island Bar, indulge in a Dr Fish massage or watch a 3-D event movie (US$3) about the Khmer Rouge or the scourge of landmines.

Bambou Indochine   CLOTHING
(Map p98; Alley West; ☺10am-10pm) Original clothing designs inspired by Indochina. A cut above the average souvenir T-shirts.

Diwo Gallery   ART GALLERY
(www.tdiwo.com; Wat Svay District; ☺9am-6pm) French photographer and writer Thierry Diwo's collection of art photography from around Angkor and high-quality replica bronze, stone and wood sculptures.

Eric Raisina Workshop   FASHION
(Map p114; www.ericraisina.com; Wat Thmei area; ☺by appointment) Renowned designer Eric Raisina brings a unique cocktail of influences to his couture. Born in Madagascar, raised in France and resident in Cambodia, he offers a striking collection of clothing and accessories.

Jasmine   FASHION
(Map p92; Pokambor Ave; ☺9am-10pm) Located in FCC Angkor, this boutique produces stylish silk clothing for any occasion.

McDermott Gallery   PHOTOGRAPHY
(Map p98; www.mcdermottgallery.com; The Alley; ☺10am-10pm) These are the famous images you have seen of Angkor. Calendars, cards and striking sepia images of the temples, plus regular exhibitions.

Rogue   MUSIC
(Map p98; Pithnou St; ☺10am-10pm) Dedicated to selling iPods, downloads, accessories and T-shirts.

Three Seasons   FASHION
(Map p98; The Lane; ☺10am-10pm) Three shops in one at this new place, including Elsewhere, Zoco and Keo Kjay, a fair-trade fashion enterprise helping HIV-positive women earn a living.

Wanderlust   FASHION
(Map p98; Alley West; ☺8am-10pm) Small designer boutique with fun and funky fashion and accessories, in an old house that looks straight out of Provence.

Blue Apsara   BOOKS
(Map p98) Longest-running secondhand bookstore in town, with a good selection of English, French and German titles. Psar Chaa area.

D's Books   BOOKS
(Map p98; Pithnou St; ☺9am-10pm) The largest chain of secondhand bookshops in Cambo-

dia, this is conveniently located for night browsing.

Monument Books   BOOKS
(Map p92; Pokambor Ave) Well-stocked new bookstore near Psar Chaa, with an additional branch at the airport.

❶ Information

Pick up a copy of the *Siem Reap Angkor Visitors Guide* (www.canbypublications.com), which is packed with listings and comes out quarterly. Check out *Drinking and Dining* for the low-down on bars and restaurants, or *Out and About* for shops and services, both produced by **Pocket Guide Cambodia** (www.cambodiapocket guide.com) and widely available.

Emergency
Tourist police (Map p114; ☎097-7780013) Located at the main ticket checkpoint for the Angkor area, this is the place to come and lodge a complaint if you encounter any serious problems while in Siem Reap.

Internet Access
Internet shops have spread through town like wildfire and your nearest online fix will never be far away. Prices are US$0.50 to US$1 per hour and most places also offer cheap internet-based telephone calls. The greatest concentration is along Sivatha St and around the Psar Chaa area. Many guesthouses and hotels also offer free access for guests. Many of the leading restaurants and bars, as well as many midrange hotels, offer free wi-fi.

Medical Services
Siem Reap now has an international-standard hospital for emergencies. However, any serious complications will still require relocation to Bangkok.
Angkor Children's Hospital (Map p92; ☎963409; ☺24hr) This international-standard paediatric hospital is the place to take your children if they fall sick. Will also assist adults in an emergency for up to 24 hours. Donations accepted.
Royal Angkor International Hospital (Map p114; ☎761888; www.royalangkorhospital .com; Airport Rd) A new international facility; affiliated with the Bangkok Hospital, so very expensive.
U-Care Pharmacy (Map p98; Pithnou St; ☺8am-9pm) Smart pharmacy and shop like Boots in Thailand (and the UK). English spoken.

Money
For cash exchanges, markets (usually at jewellery stalls or dedicated money-changing stalls) are faster and less bureaucratic than the banks.

ANZ Royal Bank (Map p92; Achar Mean St) Credit-card advances and can change travellers cheques in most major currencies. Several branches and many ATMs (US$4 per withdrawal) around town.

Canadia Bank (Map p92; Sivatha St) Offers free credit-card cash advances and changes travellers cheques in most major currencies at a 2% commission. International ATM with no transaction fees.

Post
Main post office (Map p92; ☺7am-5.30pm) Services are more reliable these days, but it doesn't hurt to see your stamps franked. Includes a branch of EMS express mail.

Dangers & Annoyances
Siem Reap is a pretty safe city, even at night. However, if you rent a bike, don't keep your bag in the basket, as it will be easy pickings for a drive-by snatch. Likewise, lone females should try to walk home with travelling companions when leaving late-night spots, particularly if heading through poorly lit areas.

There are a lot of commission scams in Siem Reap that involve certain guesthouses and small hotels paying moto and taxi drivers to deliver guests. Ways to avoid these scams include booking ahead via the internet and arranging a pick-up, or sticking with a partner guesthouse if you are coming from Phnom Penh. Alternatively, just go with the flow and negotiate with the hotel or guesthouse on arrival.

For more on the commission scams facing those travelling to Siem Reap by land from Bangkok, see the box, p350.

There are a lot of beggars around town and some visitors quickly develop beggar fatigue. However, try to remember that with no social-security network and no government support, life is pretty tough for the poorest of the poor in Cambodia. In the case of children, it is often better not to encourage begging, but, if you are compelled to help, then offer food, as money usually ends up being passed on to someone else. These days the problem is less serious, as many have been retrained to sell books or postcards to tourists instead of simply begging.

Out at the remote temple sites beyond Angkor, stick to clearly marked trails. There are still landmines at locations such as Phnom Kulen and Koh Ker.

Telephone & Fax
Making international calls is straightforward. The cheapest way is to use the major internet cafes, with calls starting at about US$0.10 per minute, but there can be some delay. The cheapest 'unblemished' calls can be arranged with one of the many private booths advertising these telephone services. Hotels impose hefty surcharges on calls, so check the rates before you dial.

Tourist Information
It's hard to believe given the sheer number of tourists passing through Siem Reap, but there isn't a dedicated official tourism office in the town. Guesthouses and hotels are often a more reliable source of information, as are fellow travellers who have been in town for a few days.

❶ Getting There & Away
Air
There are direct international flights from Siem Reap to Bangkok in Thailand; Vientiane, Luang Prabang and Pakse in Laos; Ho Chi Minh City (Saigon), Hanoi and Danang in Vietnam; Hong Kong; Kuala Lumpur in Malaysia; Kunming in China; Seoul in South Korea; Singapore; Taipei in Taiwan; and Yangon in Myanmar. For more information on international flights to and from Siem Reap, see p339.

Domestic links are currently limited to Phnom Penh (from US$63 one way) and, finally, Sihanoukville (from US$85 one way, and only Cambodia Angkor Airways currently operates these routes. Cheaper specials are sometimes offered, but these are usually restricted to Cambodian nationals. Demand for seats is high during peak season, so book as far in advance as possible. The flights to Sihanoukville only began operation in December 2011 so may just be available during high season.

Airline offices around town:

Bangkok Airways (☎380191; www.bangkokair.com)

Cambodia Angkor Air (☎964488; www.cambodiaangkorair.com)

China Eastern Airlines (☎965229; www.ce-air.com)

SUPPORTING RESPONSIBLE TOURISM IN SIEM REAP
Many travellers passing through Siem Reap are interested in contributing something to the communities they visit as they explore the temples and surrounding areas. **ConCERT** (Map p92; ☎963511; www.concertcambodia.org; 560 Phum Stoeung Thmey; ☺9am-5pm Mon-Fri) is a Siem Reap–based organisation that is working to build bridges between tourists and good-cause projects in the Siem Reap-Angkor area. It offers information on anything from ecotourism initiatives to volunteering opportunities.

TRANSPORT CONNECTIONS FROM SIEM REAP

DESTINATION	CAR & MOTORBIKE	BUS	BOAT	AIR
Phnom Penh	5hr	6hr, US$5-11, frequent	5hr, US$35, 7am	30min, 3 daily, from US$90
Kompong Thom	2hr	2½hr, US$5, frequent	N/A	N/A
Battambang	3hr	4hr, US$4-5, regular	6-8hr, US$20, 7am	N/A
Poipet	3hr	4hr, US$4-5, regular	N/A	N/A
Bangkok	8hr	10hr, US$12-15, frequent	N/A	1hr, from US$144, 5 daily

Jetstar Asia (☎964388; www.jetstarasia.com)

Lao Airlines (☎963283; www.laoairlines.com)

Malaysia Airlines (☎964135; www.malaysia-airlines.com)

Myanmar Airways International (☎969121; www.maiair.com)

Siem Reap Airways (☎380191; www.siemreapairways.com)

Vietnam Airlines (☎964488; www.vietnamairlines.com)

Boat

There are daily express boat services between Siem Reap and Phnom Penh (US$35, five to six hours) or Battambang (US$20, four to eight hours or more, depending on the season). The boat to Phnom Penh is a bit of a rip-off these days, given it is just as fast by road and less than one-fifth of the price. The Battambang trip is seriously scenic, but breakdowns are *very* common. See the Phnom Penh (p79) and Battambang (p219) listings for more details.

Boats from Siem Reap leave from the floating village of Chong Kneas near Phnom Krom, 11km south of Siem Reap. The boats dock in different places at different times of the year; when the lake recedes in the dry season, both the port and floating village move with it. An all-weather road has improved access around the lake area, but the main road out to the lake takes a pummelling in the annual October floods.

Most of the guesthouses in town sell boat tickets. Buying the ticket from a guesthouse usually includes a moto or minibus ride to the port. Otherwise, a moto out here costs about US$1 to US$2, a *remork-moto* about US$5 and a taxi about US$10.

Bus

The road linking Siem Reap to Phnom Penh is in good condition, and air-con buses thunder up and down daily. The road west to Sisophon, Thailand and Battambang has been completely rebuilt and is in great condition.

All buses depart from the bus station/taxi park (Map p114), which is 3km east of town and about 200m south of NH6. Tickets are available at guesthouses, hotels, bus offices, travel agencies and ticket kiosks. Some bus companies send a minibus around to pick up passengers at their place of lodging. Most departures to Phnom Penh are between 7am and 1pm; buses to other destinations generally leave early in the morning. Upon arrival in Siem Reap, be prepared for a rugby scrum of eager moto drivers when getting off the bus.

A number of bus companies serve Siem Reap, and all have booths or offices out at the bus station. Some also have offices in the downtown area in the vicinity of Psar Chaa and Sivatha St.

Some of the most popular:

Capitol Tour (☎963883) Serves Phnom Penh, Poipet, Battambang and Bangkok.

GST (☎092-905016) Serves Phnom Penh, Anlong Veng and Sra Em (for Prasat Preah Vihear).

Gold VIP (☎632 7600) Express minibuses to Phnom Penh.

Mekong Express (☎963662) Serves Phnom Penh and Ho Chi Minh City.

Neak Kror Horm (☎964924) Phnom Penh and Poipet.

Paramount Angkor Express (☎966469) Serves Phnom Penh, Sisophon and Battambang.

Phnom Penh Sorya (☎012 235618) Serves Phnom Penh, Poipet and Battambang.

Rith Mony (☎012 344377) Serves Phnom Penh and Kompong Cham.

Tickets to Phnom Penh (six hours), via NH6, cost US$5 to US$11, depending on the level of service (air-con, comfy seats, a toilet, a hostess) and whether there's a hotel pick-up. Many companies charge the same price to Kompong Thom as they do to Phnom Penh. Several companies offer direct services to Kompong Cham (US$6, five or six hours), Battambang (US$3.75, three hours), Sisophon (US$3.75, two hours) and Poipet (US$3.75, three hours). GST has a bus to Anlong Veng (US$4, two hours) and on to Sra Em (for Prasat Preah Vihear; US$10, four hours, 7am). There are no through buses to Ho Chi Minh City, but it is possible to change in Phnom Penh.

Car, Share Taxi, Minibus & Pick-up

As well as buses, share taxis and other vehicles operate some of the main routes and these can be a little quicker than buses.

Destinations include Phnom Penh (US$10, five hours), Kompong Thom (US$5, two hours), Sisophon (US$5, two hours) and Poipet (US$7, three hours). To get to the temple of Banteay Chhmar, head to Sisophon and arrange onward transport there. For details on getting to Anlong Veng, see p231.

For more on the overland trip between Bangkok and Siem Reap, see the box, p350.

ℹ Getting Around

For more on transport around Angkor, see p24. Following are insights into the most common forms of transport used for getting around Siem Reap.

To/From the Airport

Siem Reap International Airport is 7km from the town centre. Many hotels and guesthouses in Siem Reap offer a free airport pick-up service with advance bookings. Official taxis are available next to the terminal for US$7. A trip to the city centre on the back of a moto is US$2. Remork-motos are available for about US$5, depending on the hotel or guesthouse location.

Bicycle

Some of the guesthouses around town hire out bicycles, as do a few shops around Psar Chaa, usually for US$1 to US$2 a day. Try to support the **White Bicycles** (www.thewhitebicycles.org) project to help the local community (see p25).

Car & Motorcycle

Most hotels and guesthouses can organise car hire for the day, with a going rate of US$25 and up. Upmarket hotels may charge more. Foreigners are forbidden to rent motorcycles in and around Siem Reap. If you want to get around on your own motorcycle, you need to hire one in Phnom Penh and ride it to Siem Reap. For details on dirt-bike tours to remote temples, see p343.

Moto

A moto with a driver will cost about US$8 to US$10 per day. The average cost for a short trip within town is 2000r or so, more to places strung out along the roads to Angkor or the airport. It is probably best to negotiate in advance these days, as with the tourism boom a lot of drivers have got into the habit of overcharging.

Remork-Moto

Remork-motos are sweet little motorcycles with carriages (commonly called túk-túks around town), and are a nice way for couples to get about Siem Reap, although drivers like to inflate the prices. Try for US$1 on trips around town, although drivers may charge US$2 for a trip to the edges of town at night. Prices rise when you pile in more people.

AROUND SIEM REAP

Prek Toal Bird Sanctuary
ជីវរកបក្សីប្រែកទល

Prek Toal is one of three biospheres on Tonlé Sap lake, and this stunning bird sanctuary makes Prek Toal the most worthwhile and straightforward of the three to visit. It is an ornithologist's fantasy, with a significant number of rare breeds gathered in one small area, including the huge lesser and greater adjutant storks, the milky stork and the spot-billed pelican. Even the uninitiated will be impressed, as these birds have a huge wingspan and build enormous nests.

Visitors during the dry season (December to April) will find the concentration of birds like something out of a Hitchcock film. It is also possible to visit from September, but the concentrations may be lower. As water starts to dry up elsewhere, the birds congregate here. Serious twitchers know that the best time to see birds is early morning or late afternoon and this means an early start or an overnight at Prek Toal's environment office, where there are basic beds for US$15/20 per single/double.

Two ecotourism companies arrange trips out to Prek Toal. **Sam Veasna Center** (Map p92; ☎963710; www.samveasna.org), in the Wat Bo area of Siem Reap, offers trips to Prek Toal that contribute to the conservation of the area. Sam Veasna uses ecotourism to provide an income for local communities in return for a ban on hunting and cutting down the forest. The trips cost about US$98 per person for a group of five or more, with additional charges for smaller groups. **Osmose** (☎012 832812; www.osmosetonlesap.net) also runs organised day trips to Prek Toal. The day trips cost US$95 per person with a minimum group of four.

Around Siem Reap

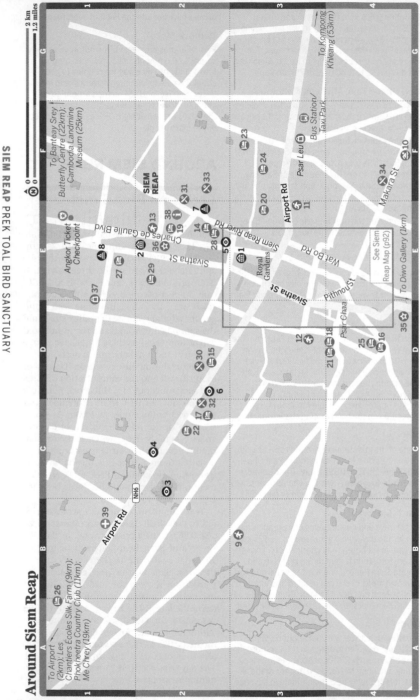

2 km
1.2 miles

To Banteay Srey
Butterfly Centre (22km);
Cambodia Landmine
Museum (25km)

To Kompong
Khleang (53km)

SIEM REAP

Angkor Ticket
Checkpoint

Charles de Gaulle Blvd

Sivatha St

Siem Reap River Rd

Airport Rd

Psar Leu

Bus Station/
Taxi Park

Makara St

To Diwo Gallery (1km)

See Siem
Reap Map (p92)

Wat Bo Rd

Royal
Gardens

Sivatha St

Pithnou St

Psar Chaa

Airport Rd

NH6

To Airport
(2km); Les
Chantiers Ecoles Silk Farm (9km);
Prokheetra Country Club (11km);
Me Chrey (19km)

Around Siem Reap

Tours include transport, entrance fees, guides, breakfast, lunch and water. Binoculars are available on request, plus the Sam Veasna Center has spotting scopes. Both outfits can arrange overnight trips for serious enthusiasts. Some proceeds from the tours go towards educating children and villagers about the importance of the birds and the unique flooded-forest environment, and the trip includes a visit to one of the local communities. Day trips include a hotel pick-up around 6am and a return by nightfall.

Sunscreen and head protection are essential, as it can get very hot in the dry season. The guides are equipped with booklets with the bird names in English, but they speak little English themselves, hence the advantage of travelling with the Sam Veasna Center or Osmose (both of which can provide English-speaking guides).

Getting to the sanctuary under your own steam requires you to take a 20-minute moto (US$2 or so) or taxi (US$10 one way) ride to the floating village of Chong Kneas (depending on the time of day additional fees may have to be paid at the new port) and then a boat to the environment office (around US$55 return, one hour each way). From here, a small boat (US$30 including a guide) will take you into the sanctuary, which is about one hour further on.

Ang Trapeng Thmor Reserve

គំបាមព ទខេត ព្ញ ង៉្យ ហាជេ!

This **bird sanctuary** (admission US$10) is just across the border in the Phnom Srok region of Banteay Meanchey Province, about 100km from Siem Reap. It's one of only two places in the world where it's possible to see the extremely rare sarus crane, as depicted on bas-reliefs at Bayon. These grey-feathered birds have immensely long legs and striking red heads. The reserve is based around a reservoir created by forced labour during the Khmer Rouge regime, and facilities are very basic, but it is an incredibly beautiful place. Bring your own binoculars, however, as none are available.

To reach here, follow the road to Sisophon for about 72km before turning north at Prey Mon. It's 22km to the site, passing through some famous silk-weaving villages. The Sam Veasna Center (p113) arranges birding trips (US$100 per person with a group of four) out here, which is probably the easiest way to undertake the trip. It also arranges specialist birding trips to remote parts of northwestern Cambodia in partnership with the **Wildlife Conservation Society** (www.wcs .org); see the box, p237.

Floating Village of Chong Kneas ភូមិបណ្តែតចុងគ្នាស

This famous floating village is now extremely popular with visitors wanting a break from the temples, and is an easy excursion to arrange yourself. If you want something a bit more peaceful, try venturing to one of the other Tonlé Sap villages further afield. Visitors arriving by boat from Phnom Penh or Battambang get a sneak preview, as the floating village is near Phnom Krom, where the boat docks. It is very scenic in the warm light of early morning or late afternoon and can be combined with a view of the sunset from the hilltop temple of Phnom Krom (p148). The downside is that tour groups tend to take over, and boats end up chugging up and down the channels in convoy. Avoid the crowds by asking your boat driver to take you down some back channels.

Visitors should stop at the **Gecko Centre** (www.tsbr-ed.org; 8.30am-5.30pm), an informative exhibition that is located in the floating village and helps to unlock the secrets of the Tonlé Sap. It has displays on flora and fauna of the area, as well as information on communities living around the lake.

The village moves depending on the season and you will need to rent a boat to get around it properly. A joint-venture cooperative called Sou Ching has fixed boat prices at US$11 per person, plus a US$2 entrance fee, to visit the floating village.

One of the best ways to visit for the time being is to hook up with the **Tara Boat** (092-957765; www.taraboat.com), which offers all-inclusive trips with a meal aboard its converted cargo boat. Prices include transfers, entry fees, local boats, a tour guide and a two-course meal, starting from US$27 for a lunch to US$33 for a sunset dinner.

Getting to the floating village from Siem Reap costs US$2 by moto each way (more if the driver waits), or US$15 or so by taxi. The trip takes 20 minutes. Or rent a bicycle in town and just pedal out here, as it is a leisurely 11km through pretty villages and rice fields.

Kompong Pluk ព្រែលិចទឹកកំពង់ភ្លុក

More memorable than Chong Kneas, but harder to reach, is the village of **Kompong Pluk** (admission US$2), an other-worldly place built on soaring stilts. Nearby is a flooded forest, inundated every year when the lake rises to take the Mekong's overflow. As the lake drops, the petrified trees are revealed. Exploring this area by wooden dugout in the wet season is very atmospheric. The village itself is a friendly place, where most of the houses are built on stilts of about 6m or 7m high, almost bamboo skyscrapers. It looks like it's straight out of a film set.

There are two ways to get to Kompong Pluk. One is to come via the floating village of Chong Kneas, where a boat (1¼ hours) can be arranged from US$55 return, and the other is to come via the small town of Roluos by a combination of road (about US$7 by moto or US$20 by taxi) and boat (US$8). However, an all-weather elevated access road is under construction and will be completed some time during the life of this book. It is rumoured to be another toll road, which means a private company will start levying charges to visit Kompong Pluk. All said, the road-and-boat route will take up to two hours, but it depends on the season – sometimes it's more by road, sometimes more by boat. The new road may well bring the access time to less than one hour. Tara Boat also offers day trips here for US$60 per person.

Kompong Khleang កំពង់ឃ្លាំង

One of the largest communities on the Tonlé Sap, Kompong Khleang is more of a town than the other villages, and comes complete with several ornate pagodas. As in Kompong Pluk, most of the houses here are built on towering stilts to allow for a dramatic change in water level. Few tourists visit here compared with the floating villages closer to Siem Reap, but that might be a reason to visit in itself. There is only a small floating community on the lake itself, but the stilted town is an interesting place to browse for an hour or two. A boat trip around the town and out to the lake is about US$20 for a couple of hours. It is not that difficult to reach from Siem Reap thanks to an all-weather road via the junction town of Dam Dek, but the trip will cost about US$40 return by taxi.

Me Chrey ⵎⵎⵎ

One of the more recently 'discovered' floating villages, this **community** (admission US$1) lies midway between Siem Reap and Prek Toal. It is one of the smaller villages in the area but sees far fewer tourists than busy Chong Kneas. Me Chrey moves with the water level and is prettier during the wet season, when houses are anchored around an island pagoda. It is located to the south of Puok district, about 25km from Siem Reap. Arrange transport by road for about US$8 for a moto or US$25 for a taxi before switching to a boat (US$13 for fewer than 10 people) to explore the area.

Temples of Angkor

Best Temples for Sunrise or Sunset

» Angkor Wat (p125)
» Bayon (p136)
» Phnom Bakheng (p141)
» Pre Rup (p146)
» Sra Srang (p143)

Best Temples for Film Buffs

» Angkor Wat (p125)
» Bayon (p136)
» Beng Mealea (p153)
» East Gate of Angkor Thom (p135)
» Ta Prohm (p142)

Why Go?

Welcome to heaven on earth. Angkor is the earthly representation of Mt Meru, the Mt Olympus of the Hindu faith and the abode of ancient gods. The temples are the perfect fusion of creative ambition and spiritual devotion. The Cambodian 'god-kings' of old each strove to better their ancestors in size, scale and symmetry, culminating in the world's largest religious building, Angkor Wat.

The temples of Angkor are a source of inspiration and national pride to all Khmers as they struggle to rebuild their lives after years of terror and trauma. Today, the temples are a point of pilgrimage for all Cambodians, and no traveller to the region will want to miss their extravagant beauty. Angkor is one of the world's foremost ancient sites, with the epic proportions of the Great Wall of China, the detail and intricacy of the Taj Mahal and the symbolism and symmetry of the pyramids, all rolled into one.

When to Go

Avoid the sweltering temperatures of March to May. November to February is the best time of year to travel, but this is no secret, so it coincides with peak season. And peak season really is mountainous in this day and age, where more than two million visitors a year descend on Angkor. The summer months of July and August can be a surprisingly rewarding time, as the landscape is emerald green, the moats overflowing with water and the moss and lichen in bright contrast to the grey sandstone.

Plan a dawn-to-dusk itinerary with a long, leisurely lunch to avoid the heat of the midday sun. Alternatively, plan to explore the temples through lunch, when it can be considerably quieter than the peak morning and afternoon visit times. However, it will be hot as hell and the light is not that conducive to photography.

The Angkor Wat International Half Marathon takes place annually in December, including the option of bicycle rides for those not into running.

History

The Angkorian period spans more than 600 years from AD 802 to 1432. This incredible age saw the construction of the temples of Angkor and the consolidation of the Khmer empire's position as one of the great powers in southeast Asia. This era encompasses periods of decline and revival, and wars with rival powers in Vietnam, Thailand and Myanmar. This brief history deals only with the periods that produced the temples that can be seen at Angkor.

The hundreds of temples surviving today are but the sacred skeleton of the vast political, religious and social centre of Cambodia's ancient Khmer empire, a city that,

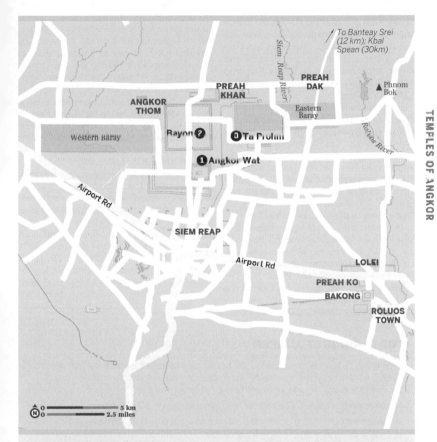

Angkor Highlights

❶ Seeing the sun rise over the holiest of holies, **Angkor Wat** (p125), the world's largest religious building

❷ Contemplating the serenity and splendour of **Bayon** (p136), its 216 enigmatic faces staring out into the jungle

❸ Witnessing nature reclaiming the stones at the mysterious ruin of **Ta Prohm** (p142), the *Tomb Raider* temple

❹ Staring in wonder at the delicate carvings adorning **Banteay Srei** (p149), the finest seen at Angkor

❺ Trekking deep into the jungle to discover the River of a Thousand Lingas at **Kbal Spean** (p152)

❻ Exploring the tangled vines, crumbling corridors and jumbled sandstone blocks of **Beng Mealea** (p153)

❼ Getting off the beaten path with a visit to the 10th-century capital of **Koh Ker** (p154), with its striking step pyramid of Prasat Thom

at its zenith, boasted a population of one million when London was a small town of 50,000. The houses, public buildings and palaces of Angkor were constructed of wood – now long decayed – because the right to dwell in structures of brick or stone was reserved for the gods.

AN EMPIRE IS BORN

The Angkorian period began with the rule of Jayavarman II (r 802–50). He was the first to unify Cambodia's competing kingdoms before the birth of Angkor. His court was situated at various locations, including Phnom Kulen, 40km northeast of Angkor Wat, and Roluos (known then as Hariharalaya), 13km east of Siem Reap.

Jayavarman II proclaimed himself a *devaraja* (god-king), the earthly representative of the Hindu god Shiva, and built a 'temple-mountain' at Phnom Kulen, symbolising Shiva's dwelling place of Mt Meru, the holy mountain at the centre of the universe. This set a precedent that became a dominant feature of the Angkorian period and accounts for the staggering architectural productivity of the Khmers at this time.

Indravarman I (r 877–89) is believed to have been a usurper, and probably inherited the mantle of *devaraja* through conquest. He built a 6.5-sq-km *baray* (reservoir) at Roluos and established Preah Ko. The *baray* was the first stage of an irrigation system that created a hydraulic city, the ancient Khmers mastering the cycle of nature to water their lands. Form and function worked together in harmony, as the *baray* also had religious significance, representing the oceans surrounding Mt Meru. Indravarman's final work was Bakong, a pyramidal representation of Mt Meru.

Indravarman I's son Yasovarman I (r 889–910) looked further afield to celebrate his divinity and glory in a temple-mountain of his own. He first built Lolei on an artificial island in the *baray* established by his father, before beginning work on the Bakheng. Today this hill is known as Phnom Bakheng, a favoured spot for viewing the sunset over Angkor Wat. A raised highway was constructed to connect Phnom Bakheng with Roluos, 16km to the southeast, and a large *baray* was constructed to the east of Phnom Bakheng. Today it is known as the Eastern Baray but has entirely silted up. Yasovarman I also established the temple-mountains of Phnom Krom and Phnom Bok.

After the death of Yasovarman I, power briefly shifted from the Angkor region to Koh Ker, around 80km to the northeast, under another usurper king, Jayavarman IV (r 924–42). In AD 944 power returned again to Angkor under the leadership of Rajendravarman II (r 944–68), who built the Eastern Mebon and Pre Rup. The reign of his son Jayavarman V (r 968–1001) produced the temples Ta Keo and Banteay Srei, the latter built by a brahman rather than the king.

TOP 10 KINGS OF ANGKOR

A mind-numbing array of kings ruled the Khmer empire from the 9th to the 14th centuries AD. All of their names include the word 'varman', which means 'armour' or 'protector'. Forget the small fry and focus on the big fish in our Top 10:

Jayavarman II (r 802–50) Founder of the Khmer empire in AD 802.

Indravarman I (r 877–89) Builder of the first *baray* (reservoir), Preah Ko and Bakong.

Yasovarman I (r 889–910) Moved the capital to Angkor and built Lolei and Phnom Bakheng.

Jayavarman IV (r 924–42) Usurper king who moved the capital to Koh Ker.

Rajendravarman II (r 944–68) Builder of Eastern Mebon, Pre Rup and Phimeanakas.

Jayavarman V (r 968–1001) Oversaw construction of Ta Keo and Banteay Srei.

Suryavarman I (r 1002–49) Expanded the empire into much of Laos and Thailand.

Udayadityavarman II (r 1049–65) Builder of the pyramidal Baphuon and the Western Mebon.

Suryavarman II (r 1112–52) Legendary builder of Angkor Wat and Beng Mealea.

Jayavarman VII (r 1181–1219) The king of the god-kings, building Angkor Thom, Preah Khan and Ta Prohm.

THE GOLDEN AGE OF ANGKOR

The temples that are now the highlight of a visit to Angkor – Angkor Wat and those in and around the walled city of Angkor Thom – were built during the golden age or classical period. While this period is marked by fits of remarkable productivity, it was also a time of turmoil, conquests and setbacks. The great city of Angkor Thom owes its existence to the fact that the old city of Angkor, which stood on the same site, was destroyed during the Cham invasion of 1177.

Suryavarman I (r 1002–49) was a usurper to the throne who won the day through strategic alliances and military conquests. Although he adopted the Hindu cult of the god-king, he is thought to have come from a Mahayana Buddhist tradition and may even have sponsored the growth of Buddhism in Cambodia. Buddhist sculpture certainly became more commonplace in the Angkor region during his time.

Little physical evidence of Suryavarman I's reign remains at Angkor, but his military exploits brought much of central Thailand and southern-central Laos under the control of Angkor. His son Udayadityavarman II (r 1049–65) embarked on further military expeditions, extending the empire once more, and building Baphuon and the Western Mebon. Many major cities in the Mekong region were important Khmer settlements in the 11th and 12th centuries, including the Lao capital of Vientiane and the Thai city of Lopburi.

From 1066 until the end of the century, Angkor was again divided as rival factions contested the throne. The first important monarch of this new era was Suryavarman II (r 1112–52), who unified Cambodia and extended Khmer influence to Malaya and Burma (Myanmar). He also set himself apart religiously from earlier kings through his devotion to the Hindu deity Vishnu, to whom he consecrated the largest and arguably most magnificent of all the Angkorian temples, Angkor Wat.

The reign of Suryavarman II and the construction of Angkor Wat signifies one of the high-water marks of Khmer civilisation. However, there were signs that decline was lurking. It is thought that the hydraulic system of reservoirs and canals that supported the agriculture of Angkor had by this time been pushed beyond its limits, and was slowly starting to silt up due to overpopulation and deforestation. The construction of Angkor Wat was a major strain on resources,

TEMPLE ADDICTS

The god-kings of Angkor were dedicated builders. Each king was expected to dedicate a temple to his patron god, most commonly Shiva or Vishnu during the time of Angkor. Then there were the ancestors, including mother, father, and grandparents (both maternal and paternal), which meant another half dozen temples or more. Finally there was the mausoleum or king's temple, intended to deify the monarch and project his power, and each of these had to be bigger and better than one's predecessor. This accounts for the staggering architectural productivity of the Khmers at this time and the epic evolution of temple architecture.

and, on top of this, Suryavarman II led a disastrous campaign against the Dai Viet (Vietnamese) late in his reign, during the course of which he was killed in battle.

ENTER JAYAVARMAN VII

In 1177 the Chams of southern Vietnam, then the Kingdom of Champa and long annexed by the Khmer empire, rose up and sacked Angkor. This attack caught the Khmers completely by surprise, as it came via sea, river and lake rather than the traditional land routes. The Chams burnt the wooden city and plundered its wealth. Four years later Jayavarman VII (r 1181–1219) struck back, emphatically driving the Chams out of Cambodia and reclaiming Angkor.

Jayavarman VII's reign has given scholars much to debate. It represents a radical departure from the reigns of his predecessors. For centuries the fount of royal divinity had reposed in the Hindu deity Shiva (and, occasionally, Vishnu). Jayavarman VII adopted Mahayana Buddhism and looked to Avalokiteshvara, the Bodhisattva of Compassion, for patronage during his reign. In doing so he may well have been converting to a religion that already enjoyed wide popular support among his subjects. It may also be that the destruction of Angkor was such a blow to royal divinity that a new religious foundation was thought to be needed.

During his reign, Jayavarman VII embarked on a dizzying array of temple projects that centred on Baphuon, which was the site of the capital city destroyed

TEMPLES OF ANGKOR

by the Chams. Angkor Thom, Jayavarman VII's new city, was surrounded by walls and a moat, which became another component of Angkor's complex irrigation system. The centrepiece of Angkor Thom was Bayon, the temple-mountain studded with faces that, along with Angkor Wat, is the most famous of Cambodia's temples. Other temples built during his reign include Ta Prohm, Banteay Kdei and Preah Khan. Further away, he rebuilt vast temple complexes, such as Banteay Chhmar and Preah Khan in Preah Vihear Province, making him by far the most prolific builder of Angkor's many kings.

Jayavarman VII also embarked on a major public-works program, building roads, schools and hospitals across the empire. Remains of many of these roads and their magnificent bridges can be seen across Cambodia. Spean Praptos at Kompong Kdei, 65km southeast of Siem Reap on National Hwy 6 (NH6), is the most famous, but there are many more lost in the forest on the old Angkorian road to the great Preah Khan, including the now accessible Spean Ta Ong, about 28km east of Beng Mealea near the village of Khvau.

After the death of Jayavarman VII around 1219, the Khmer empire went into decline. The state religion reverted to Hinduism for a century or more and outbreaks of iconoclasm saw Buddhist sculpture adorning the Hindu temples vandalised or altered. The Thais sacked Angkor in 1351, and again with devastating efficiency in 1431. The glorious Siamese capital of Ayuthaya, which enjoyed a golden age from the 14th to the 18th centuries, was in many ways a re-creation of the glories of Angkor from which the Thai conquerors drew inspiration. The Khmer court moved to Phnom Penh, only to return fleetingly to Angkor in the 16th century; in the meantime, it was abandoned to pilgrims, holy men and the elements.

ANGKOR REDISCOVERED

The French 'discovery' of Angkor in the 1860s made an international splash and created a great deal of outside interest in Cambodia. But 'discovery', with all the romance it implied, was something of a misnomer. When French explorer Henri Mouhot first stumbled across Angkor Wat on his Royal Geographic Society expedition, it included a wealthy, working monastery with monks and slaves. Moreover, Portuguese travellers in the 16th century encountered Angkor, referring to it as the Walled City. Diego do Couto produced an accurate description of Angkor in 1614, but it was not published until 1958. A 17th-century Japanese pilgrim drew a detailed plan of Angkor Wat, though he mistakenly recalled that he had seen it in India.

Still, it was the publication of *Voyage à Siam et dans le Cambodge* by Mouhot, post-

LOCAL KNOWLEDGE

PROFESSOR ANG CHOULEAN

What is the most important Khmer temple? Angkor Thom is the most striking and challenging for archaeologists, since it was a living city, humans and gods co-habiting there.

What is the most important archaeological site in Cambodia? Sambor Prei Kuk is among the most important for its homogeneity given the period and its artistic style.

Who is the most important king in Cambodian history? Suryavarman I, who had a real political vision which can be measured by the monuments he built, such as Preah Vihear and Wat Phu.

What is your position on the debate between romance and restoration at Ta Prohm? It is a matter of balance. The trees are most impressive, but maintaining the monument is our duty.

Which other civilisation interests you greatly? Japanese civilisation, as it is so different from Khmer civilisation, allowing me to better understand mine.

Professor Ang Choulean is one of Cambodia's leading experts on anthropology and archaeology and a renowned scholar on Cambodian history. He was recently awarded the 2011 Grand Fukuoka Prize for his outstanding contribution to Asian culture, and we caught up with him at the presentation ceremony at the Japanese Embassy in Phnom Penh.

humously released in 1868, that first brought Angkor to the public eye. Although the explorer himself made no such claims, by the 1870s he was being celebrated as the discoverer of the lost temple-city of Cambodia. In fact, a French missionary known as Charles-Emile Bouillevaux had visited Angkor 10 years before Mouhot and had published an account of his own findings. However, the Bouillevaux account was roundly ignored and it was Mouhot's account, with its rich descriptions and tantalising pen-and-ink colour sketches of the temples, that turned the ruins into an international obsession.

Soon after Mouhot, other adventurers and explorers began to arrive. Scottish photographer John Thomson took the first photographs of the temples in 1866. He was the first Westerner to posit the idea that they were symbolic representations of the mythical Mt Meru. French architect Lucien Fournereau travelled to Angkor in 1887 and produced plans and meticulously executed cross-sections that were to stand as the best available until the 1960s.

From this time, Angkor became the target of French-financed expeditions and, in 1901, the École Française d'Extrême-Orient (EFEO; www.efeo.fr) began a long association with Angkor by funding an expedition to Bayon. In 1907 Angkor was returned to Cambodia, having been under Thai control for more than a century, and the EFEO took responsibility for clearing and restoring the whole site. In the same year, the first foreign tourists arrived in Angkor - an unprecedented 200 of them in three months. Angkor had been 'rescued' from the jungle and was assuming its place in the modern world.

Archaeology of Angkor

With the exception of Angkor Wat, which was restored for use as a Buddhist shrine in the 16th century by the Khmer royalty, the temples of Angkor were left to the jungle for many centuries. The majority of temples are made of sandstone, which tends to dissolve when in prolonged contact with dampness. Bat droppings took their toll, as did sporadic pilfering of sculptures and cut stones. At some monuments, such as Ta Prohm, the jungle had stealthily waged an all-out invasion, and plant life could only be removed at great risk to the structures it now supported in its web of roots.

Initial attempts to clear Angkor under the aegis of the EFEO were fraught with technical difficulties and theoretical disputes. On a technical front, the jungle tended to grow back as soon as it was cleared; on a theoretical front, scholars debated the extent to which temples should be restored and whether later additions, such as Buddha images in Hindu temples, should be removed.

It was not until the 1920s that a solution was found, known as anastylosis. This was the method the Dutch had used to restore Borobudur in Java. Put simply, it was a way of reconstructing monuments using the original materials and in keeping with the original form of the structure. New materials were permitted only where the originals could not be found, and were to be used discreetly. An example of this method can be seen on the causeway leading to the entrance of Angkor Wat, as the right-hand side was originally restored by the French.

The first major restoration job was carried out on Banteay Srei in 1930. It was deemed such a success that many more extensive restoration projects were undertaken elsewhere around Angkor, culminating in the massive Angkor Wat restoration in the 1960s. Large cranes and earth-moving machines were brought in, and the operation was backed by a veritable army of surveying equipment.

The Khmer Rouge victory and Cambodia's subsequent slide into an intractable civil war resulted in far less damage to Angkor than many had assumed, as EFEO and Ministry of Culture teams had removed many of the statues from the temple sites for protection. Nevertheless, turmoil in Cambodia resulted in a long interruption of restoration work, allowing the jungle to resume its assault on the monuments. The illegal trade of *objets d'art* on the world art market has also been a major threat to Angkor, although it is the more remote sites that have been targeted recently. Angkor has been under the jurisdiction of the UN Educational Scientific and Cultural Organization (Unesco) since 1992 as a World Heritage Site, and international and local efforts continue to preserve and reconstruct the monuments. In a sign of real progress, Angkor was removed from Unesco's endangered list in 2003.

Many of Angkor's secrets remain to be discovered, as most of the work at the temples has concentrated on restoration efforts above ground rather than archaeological digs and surveys below. Underground is where the real story of Angkor and its people lies - the inscriptions on the temples give us only a partial picture of the gods to whom each structure was dedicated, and the kings who built them.

To learn more about Unesco's activities at Angkor, visit http://whc.Unesco.org, or take a virtual tour of Angkor in 360 degrees at www.world-heritage-tour.org. For a great online photographic resource on the temples of Angkor, look no further than www .angkor-ruins.com, a Japanese website with an English translation.

Architectural Styles

From the time of the earliest Angkorian monuments at Roluos, Khmer architecture was continually evolving, often from the rule of one king to the next. Archaeologists therefore divide the monuments of Angkor into nine periods, named after the foremost example of each period's architectural style.

The evolution of Khmer architecture was based on a central theme of the temple-mountain, preferably set on a real hill (but an artificial hill was allowed if there weren't any mountains to hand). The earlier a temple was constructed, the more closely it adheres to this fundamental idea. Essentially, the mountain was represented by a tower mounted on a tiered base. At the summit was the central sanctuary, usually with an open door to the east, and three false doors at the remaining cardinal points of the compass. For Indian Hindus, the Himalayas represent Mt Meru, the home of the gods, while the Khmer kings of old adopted Phnom Kulen as their symbolic Mt Meru.

By the time of the Bakheng period, this layout was being embellished. The summit of the central tower was crowned with five 'peaks' – four at the points of the compass and one in the centre. Even Angkor Wat features this layout, though on a grandiose scale. Other features that came to be favoured include an entry tower and a causeway lined with *naga* (mythical serpent) balustrades leading up to the temple.

As the temples grew in ambition, the central tower became a less prominent feature, although it remained the focus of the temple. Later temples saw the central tower flanked by courtyards and richly decorated galleries. Smaller towers were placed on gates and on the corners of walls, their overall number often of religious or astrological significance.

These refinements and additions eventually culminated in Angkor Wat, which effectively showcases the evolution of Angkorian architecture. The architecture of the Bayon period breaks with tradition in temples such as Ta Prohm and Preah Khan. In these temples, the horizontal layout of the galleries, corridors and courtyards seems to completely eclipse the central tower.

The curious narrowness of the corridors and doorways in these structures can be explained by the fact that Angkorian architects never mastered the flying buttress to build a full arch. They engineered arches by laying blocks on top of each other, until they met at a central point; known as false arches, they can only support very short spans.

Most of the major sandstone blocks around Angkor include small circular holes. These originally held wooden stakes that were used to lift and position the stones during construction before being sawn off.

Orientation

Heading north from Siem Reap, Angkor Wat is the first major temple, followed by the walled city of Angkor Thom. To the east and west of this city are two vast former reservoirs (the eastern reservoir now completely

ARCHITECTURAL STYLES AT ANGKOR

STYLE	DATE
Preah Ko	875-893
Bakheng	893-920
Koh Ker	921-945
Pre Rup	947-965
Banteay Srei	967-1000
Kleang	965-1010
Baphuon	1010-1080
Angkor Wat	1100-1175
Bayon	1177-1230

MOTIFS, SYMBOLS & CHARACTERS AROUND ANGKOR

The temples of Angkor are intricately carved with myths and legends, symbols and signs, and a cast of characters in the thousands. Deciphering them can be quite a challenge, so here we've highlighted some of the most commonly seen around the majestic temples. For more help understanding the carvings of Angkor, pick up a copy of *Images of the Gods* by Vittorio Roveda.

Apsaras Heavenly nymphs or goddesses, also known as *devadas;* these beautiful female forms decorate the walls of many temples.

Asuras These devils feature extensively in representations of the Churning of the Ocean of Milk, such as at Angkor Wat.

Devas The 'good gods' in the creation myth of the Churning of the Ocean of Milk.

Flame The flame motif is found flanking steps and doorways and is intended to purify pilgrims as they enter the temple.

Garuda Vehicle of Vishnu; this half-man, half-bird creature features in some temples and was combined with his old enemy the *nagas* to promote religious unity under Jayavarman VII.

Kala The temple guardian appointed by Shiva; he had such an appetite that he devoured his own body and appears only as a giant head above doorways. Also known as Rehu.

Linga A phallic symbol of fertility, *lingas* would have originally been located within the towers of most Hindu temples.

Lotus Another symbol of purity, the lotus features extensively in the shape of towers, the shape of steps to entrances and in decoration.

Makara A giant sea serpent with a reticulated jaw; features on the corner of pediments, spewing forth a *naga* or some other creature.

Naga The multiheaded serpent, half-brother and enemy of *garudas*. Controls the rains and, therefore, the prosperity of the kingdom; seen on causeways, doorways and roofs. The seven-headed *naga*, a feature at many temples, represents the rainbow, which acts as a bridge between heaven and earth.

Nandi The mount of Shiva; there are several statues of Nandi dotted about the temples, although many have been damaged or stolen by looters.

Rishi A Hindu wise man or ascetic, also known as *essai;* these bearded characters are often seen sitting cross-legged at the base of pillars or flanking walls.

Vine Yet another symbol of purity, the vine graces doorways and lintels and is meant to help cleanse the visitor on their journey to this heaven on earth, the abode of the gods.

Yama God of death who presides over the underworld and passes judgment on whether people continue to heaven or hell.

Yoni Female fertility symbol that is combined with the *linga* to produce holy water infused with fertility.

dried up), which once helped to feed the huge population. Further east are temples including Ta Prohm, Banteay Kdei and Pre Rup. North of Angkor Thom is Preah Khan and way beyond in the northeast, Banteay Srei, Kbal Spean, Phnom Kulen and Beng Mealea. To the southeast of Siem Reap is the early Angkorian Roluos Group of Temples.

Maps

There are several free maps covering Angkor, including the *Siem Reap Angkor 3D Map,* available at certain hotels, guesthouses and restaurants in town. River Books of Thailand publishes a fold-out *Angkor Map,* which is one of the more detailed offerings available.

ANGKOR WAT

The traveller's first glimpse of Angkor Wat (អង្គរវត្ត), the ultimate expression of Khmer genius, is simply staggering and is matched

Temples of Angkor

TEMPLES OF ANGKOR ANGKOR WAT

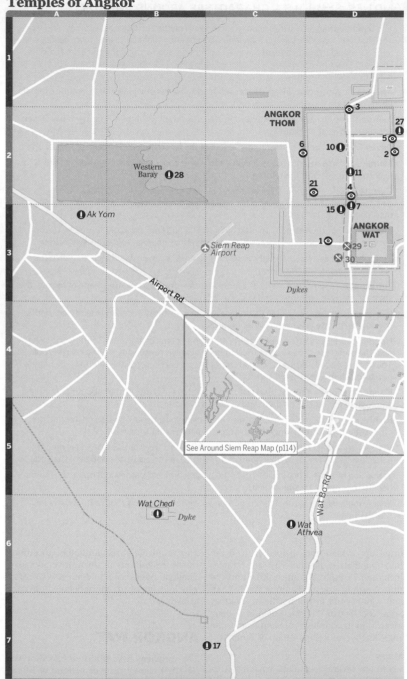

ANGKOR THOM

Western Baray

① 28

① Ak Yom

⚑ Siem Reap Airport

Airport Rd

Dykes

③ 3

① 27

⑥ 6
① 10
⑥ 5
⑥ 2

① 11

⑥ 21
⑥ 4

① 15 **①** 7

ANGKOR WAT

⑥ 1 **⊗** 29

⊗ 30

See Around Siem Reap Map (p114)

Wat Bo Rd

Wat Chedi
① — Dyke

① Wat Athvea

① 17

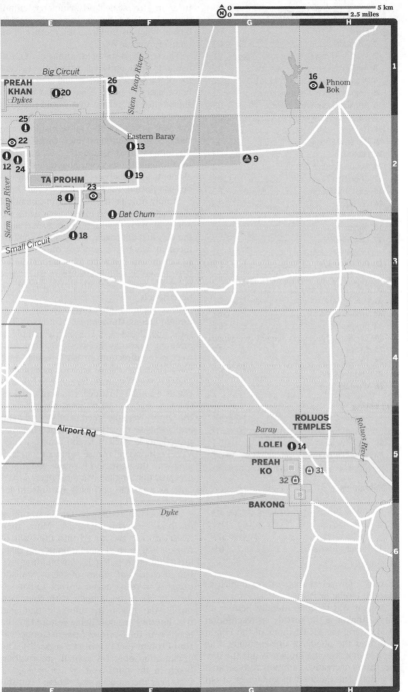

Temples of Angkor

by only a few select spots on earth such as Macchu Picchu or Petra.

Angkor Wat is, quite literally, heaven on earth. Angkor is the earthly representation of Mt Meru, the Mt Olympus of the Hindu faith and the abode of ancient gods. The 'temple that is a city', Angkor Wat is the perfect fusion of creative ambition and spiritual devotion. The Cambodian god-kings of old each strove to better their ancestors' struc-

tures in size, scale and symmetry, culminating in what is believed to be the world's largest religious building, the mother of all temples, Angkor Wat.

The temple is the heart and soul of Cambodia. It is the national symbol, the epicentre of Khmer civilisation and a source of fierce national pride. Soaring skyward and surrounded by a moat that would make its European castle counterparts blush, Angkor Wat is one of the most inspired and spectacular monuments ever conceived by the human mind. Unlike the other Angkor monuments, it was never abandoned to the elements and has been in virtually continuous use since it was built.

Simply unique, it is a stunning blend of spirituality and symmetry, an enduring example of man's devotion to his gods. Relish the very first approach, as that spine-tickling moment when you emerge on the inner causeway will rarely be felt again. It is the best-preserved temple at Angkor, and repeat visits are rewarded with previously unnoticed details.

There is much about Angkor Wat that is unique among the temples of Angkor. The most significant fact is that the temple is oriented towards the west. Symbolically, west is the direction of death, which once led a large number of scholars to conclude that Angkor Wat must have existed primarily as a tomb. This idea was supported by the fact that the magnificent bas-reliefs of the temple were designed to be viewed in an anticlockwise direction, a practice that has precedents in ancient Hindu funerary rites. Vishnu, however, is also frequently associated with the west, and it is now commonly accepted that Angkor Wat most likely served both as a temple and as a mausoleum for Suryavarman II.

Angkor Wat is famous for its beguiling *apsaras* (heavenly nymphs). More than 3000 *apsaras* are carved into the walls of Angkor Wat, each of them unique, and there are 37 different hairstyles for budding stylists to check out. Many of these exquisite *apsaras* were damaged during Indian efforts to clean the temples with chemicals during the 1980s, the ultimate bad acid trip, but they are now being restored by the teams with the **German Apsara Conservation Project** (GACP; www.gacp-angkor.de). The organisation operates a small information booth in the northwest corner of Angkor Wat, near the modern wat, where beautiful black-and-white postcards and images of Angkor are available.

Symbolism

Visitors to Angkor Wat are struck by its imposing grandeur and, at close quarters, its fascinating decorative flourishes and extensive bas-reliefs. Holy men at the time of Angkor must have revelled in its multilayered levels of meaning in much the same way a contemporary literary scholar might delight in James Joyce's *Ulysses*.

Eleanor Mannikka explains in her book *Angkor Wat: Time, Space and Kingship* that the spatial dimensions of Angkor Wat parallel the lengths of the four ages (Yuga) of classical Hindu thought. Thus the visitor to Angkor Wat who walks the causeway to the main entrance and through the courtyards to the final main tower, which once contained a statue of Vishnu, is metaphorically travelling back to the first age of the creation of the universe.

Like the other temple-mountains of Angkor, Angkor Wat also replicates the spatial universe in miniature. The central tower is Mt Meru, with its surrounding smaller peaks, bounded in turn by continents (the lower courtyards) and the oceans (the moat). The seven-headed *naga* becomes a symbolic rainbow bridge for man to reach the abode of the gods.

While Suryavarman II may have planned Angkor Wat as his funerary temple or mausoleum, he was never buried there as he died in battle during a failed expedition to subdue the Dai Viet (Vietnamese).

Architectural Layout

Angkor Wat is surrounded by a 190m-wide moat, which forms a giant rectangle measuring 1.5km by 1.3km. From the west, a sandstone causeway crosses the moat. The sandstone blocks from which Angkor Wat was built were quarried more than 50km away (from the holy mountain of Phnom Kulen) and floated down the Siem Reap River on rafts. The logistics of such an operation are mind-blowing, consuming the labour of thousands – an unbelievable feat given the lack of cranes and trucks that we take for granted in contemporary construction projects. According to inscriptions, the construction of Angkor Wat involved 300,000 workers and 6000 elephants, yet it was still not fully completed.

The rectangular outer wall, which measures 1025m by 800m, has a gate on each side, but the main entrance, a 235m-wide porch richly decorated with carvings and sculptures, is on the western side. There is a

Angkor Wat

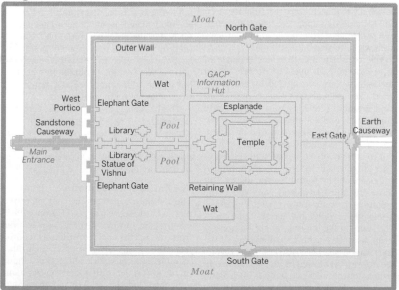

HIDDEN RICHES, POLITICAL HITCHES

Angkor Conservation (Map p114) is a Ministry of Culture compound on the banks of the Siem Reap River, about 400m east of the Sofitel Phokheetra Royal Angkor Hotel. The compound houses more than 5000 statues, *lingas* (phallic symbols) and inscribed stelae, stored here to protect them from the wanton looting that has blighted hundreds of sites around Angkor. The finest statuary is hidden away inside Angkor Conservation's warehouses, meticulously numbered and catalogued. Unfortunately, without the right contacts, trying to get a peek at the statues is a lost cause. Some of the statuary is now on public display in the Angkor National Museum in Siem Reap, but it is only a fraction of the collection.

Formerly housed at Angkor Conservation, but now going it alone in an impressive headquarters on one of the main roads to Angkor, is **Apsara Authority** (Authority for Protection & Management of Angkor & the Region of Siem Reap; www.autoriteapsara.org). This organisation is responsible for the research, protection and conservation of cultural heritage around Angkor, as well as urban planning in Siem Reap and tourism development in the region. Quite a mandate, quite a challenge – especially now that the government is taking such a keen interest in its work. Angkor is a money-spinner; it remains to be seen whether Apsara will be empowered to put preservation before profits.

statue of Vishnu, 3.25m in height and hewn from a single block of sandstone, located in the right-hand tower. Vishnu's eight arms hold a mace, a spear, a disc, a conch and other items. You may also see locks of hair lying about. These are offerings both from young people preparing to get married and from pilgrims giving thanks for their good fortune.

An avenue, 475m long and 9.5m wide and lined with *naga* balustrades, leads from the main entrance to the central temple, passing between two graceful libraries (the northern one restored by a Japanese team) and then two pools, the northern one a popular spot from which to watch the sun rise.

The central temple complex consists of three storeys, each made of laterite, which enclose a square surrounded by intricately interlinked galleries. The Gallery of a Thousand Buddhas (Preah Poan) used to house hundreds of Buddha images before the war, but many of these were removed or stolen, leaving just the handful we see today.

The corners of the second and third storeys are marked by towers, each topped with symbolic lotus-bud towers. Rising 31m above the third level and 55m above the ground is the central tower, which gives the whole grand ensemble its sublime unity. The stairs to the upper level are immensely steep, because reaching the kingdom of the gods was no easy task. Also known as Bakan, the upper level of Angkor Wat was closed to visitors for several years, but it is once again open to a limited number per day with a queuing system. This means it is once again possible to complete the pilgrimage with an ascent to the summit: savour the cooling breeze, take in the extensive views and then find a quiet corner in which to contemplate the symmetry and symbolism of this Everest of temples.

Bas-Reliefs

Stretching around the outside of the central temple complex is an 800m-long series of intricate and astonishing bas-reliefs. The following is a brief description of the epic events depicted on the panels. They are described in the order in which you'll come to them if you begin on the western side and keep the bas-reliefs to your left. The majority of them were completed in the 12th century, but in the 16th century several new reliefs were added to unfinished panels.

The bas-reliefs at Angkor Wat were once sheltered by the cloister's wooden roof, which long ago rotted away except for one original beam in the western half of the north gallery. The other roofed sections are reconstructions.

The Battle of Kurukshetra

The southern portion of the west gallery depicts a battle scene from the Hindu *Mahabharata* epic, in which the Kauravas (coming from the north) and the Pandavas (coming from the south) advance upon each other, meeting in furious battle. Infantry are shown on the lowest tier, with officers on elephants, and chiefs on the second and third tiers.

Some of the more interesting details (from left to right): a dead chief lying on a pile of arrows, surrounded by his grieving parents and troops; a warrior on an elephant who, by putting down his weapon, has accepted defeat; and a mortally wounded officer, falling from his carriage into the arms of his soldiers. Over the centuries, some sections have been polished (by the millions of hands that fall upon them) to look like black marble. The portico at the southwestern corner is decorated with sculptures representing characters from the *Ramayana*.

The Army of Suryavarman II

The remarkable western section of the south gallery depicts a triumphal battle march of Suryavarman II's army. In the southwestern corner about 2m from the floor is Suryavarman II on an elephant, wearing the royal tiara and armed with a battleaxe; he is shaded by 15 parasols and fanned by legions of servants. Check out this image of the king

and compare him with the image of Rama in the northern gallery and you'll notice an uncanny likeness that helped reinforce the aura of the god-king.

Further on is a procession of well-armed soldiers and officers on horseback; among them are bold and warlike chiefs on elephants. Just before the end of this panel is the rather disorderly Siamese mercenary army, with their long headdresses and ragged marching, at that time allied with the Khmers in their conflict with the Chams. The Khmer troops have square breastplates and are armed with spears; the Thais wear skirts and carry tridents.

The rectangular holes seen in the Army of Suryavarman II relief were created when, so the story goes, Thai soldiers removed pieces of the scene containing inscriptions that reportedly gave clues to the location of the golden treasures of Suryavarman II, later buried during the reign of Jayavarman VII.

ANGKORIN' FOR LUNCH

Many of the tour groups buzzing around Angkor head back to Siem Reap for lunch. This is as good a reason as any to stick around the temples, taking advantage of the lack of crowds to explore some popular sites and enjoy a local lunch at one of the many stalls. Almost all the major temples have some sort of nourishment available beyond the walls. Anyone travelling with a moto or *remork-moto* (túk-túk) should ask the driver for tips on cheap eats, as these guys eat around the temples every day. They know the best spots, at the best price, and should be able to sort you out (assuming you are getting along well).

The most extensive selection of restaurants is lined up opposite the entrance to Angkor Wat. It includes several restaurants, such as Khmer Angkor Restaurant (Map p126) and Angkor Reach Restaurant (Map p126), with dishes ranging from US$3 to US$6. There is also now a handy branch of **Blue Pumpkin** (Map p126; Angkor Cafe; dishes US$2-5; 🐾) turning out sandwiches, salads and ice creams, as well as the usual divine fruit shakes, all to take away if required. **Chez Sophea** (Map p126; ☎012 858003; meals US$10-20) offers barbecued meats and fish, accompanied by a cracking homemade salad, but prices are at the high end.

There are dozens of local noodle stalls just north of Angkor Thom's Terrace of the Leper King, which are a good spot for a quick bite to eat. Other central temples with food available include Ta Prohm, Preah Khan and Ta Keo. There is also a cluster of welcoming Khmer restaurants located along the northern shore of Sra Srang.

Further afield, Banteay Srei has several small restaurants, complete with ornate wood furnishings cut from Cambodia's forests. Further north at Kbal Spean, food stalls at the bottom of the hill can cook up fried rice or a noodle soup, plus there is the inviting **Borey Sovann Restaurant** (meals US$3-6), which is a great place to wind down before or after an ascent. There are also stop-and-dip stalls (dishes US$1 to US$3) near the entrance to Beng Mealea temple.

Water and soft drinks are available throughout the temple area, and many sellers lurk outside the temples, ready to pounce with offers of cold drinks. Sometimes they ask at just the right moment; on other occasions it is the 27th time in an hour that you've been approached and you are ready to scream. Try not to – you'll scare your fellow travellers and lose face with the locals.

Temples of Angkor

THREE-DAY EXPLORATION

The temple complex at Angkor is simply enormous and the superlatives don't do it justice. This is the site of the world's largest religious building, a multitude of temples and a vast, long-abandoned walled city that was arguably Southeast Asia's first metropolis, long before Bangkok and Singapore got in on the action.

Starting at the Roluos group of temples, one of the earliest capitals of Angkor, move on to the big circuit, which includes the Buddhist-Hindu fusion temple of **1 Preah Khan** and the ornate water temple of **2 Neak Poan**.

On the second day downsize to the small circuit, starting with an atmospheric dawn visit to **3 Ta Prohm**, before continuing to the temple pyramid of Ta Keo, the Buddhist monastery of Banteay Kdei and the immense royal bathing pond of **4 Sra Srang**.

Next venture further afield to Banteay Srei temple, the jewel in the crown of Angkorian art, and Beng Mealea, a remote jungle temple.

Saving the biggest and best until last, experience sunrise at **5 Angkor Wat** and stick around for breakfast in the temple to discover its amazing architecture without the crowds. In the afternoon, explore **6 Angkor Thom**, an immense complex that is home to the enigmatic **7 Bayon**.

Three days around Angkor? That's just for starters.

TOP TIPS

» **Dodging the Crowds** Early morning at Ta Prohm, post sunrise at Angkor Wat and lunchtime at Banteay Srei does the trick.

» **Extended Explorations** Three-day passes can now be used on non-consecutive days over the period of a week but be sure to request this.

Bayon
The surreal state temple of legendary king Jayavarman VII, where 216 faces bear down on pilgrims, asserting religious and regal authority.

Terrace of Leper K

Preah Palilay

Phimeanakas Temple

Tep P.

West Gate Angkor Thom

Baphuon Temple

Terrac of the Elephan

7

South Gate Angkor Thom

Phnom Bakheng

Baksei Chamrong

5

Angkor Wat
The world's largest religious building. Experience sunrise at the holiest of holies, then explore the beautiful bas-reliefs – devotion etched in stone.

Angkor Thom

The last great capital of the Khmer empire conceals a wealth of temples and its epic proportions would have inspired and terrified in equal measure.

Preah Khan

A fusion temple dedicated to Buddha, Brahma, Shiva and Vishnu; the immense corridors are like an unending hall of mirrors.

Neak Poan

If Vegas ever adopts the Angkor theme, this will be the swimming pool, a petite tower set in a lake, surrounded by four smaller ponds.

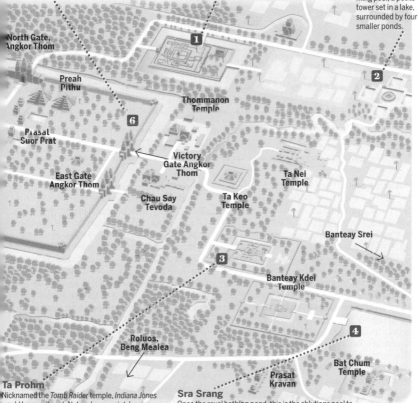

North Gate, Angkor Thom

Preah Pithu

Thommanon Temple

Prasat Suor Prat

East Gate Angkor Thom

Victory Gate Angkor Thom

Chau Say Tevoda

Ta Keo Temple

Ta Nei Temple

Banteay Srei

Banteay Kdei Temple

Roluos, Beng Mealea

Bat Chum Temple

Prasat Kravan

Ta Prohm

Nicknamed the *Tomb Raider* temple, *Indiana Jones* would be equally apt. Nature has run riot, leaving iconic tree roots strangling the surviving stones.

Sra Srang

Once the royal bathing pond, this is the ablutions pool to beat all ablutions pools and makes a good stop for sunset.

Angkor Wat Central Structure

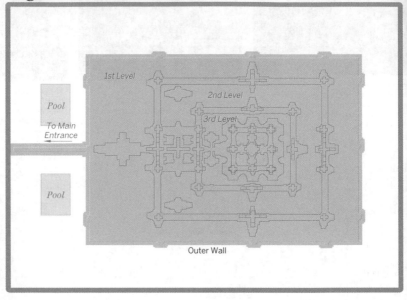

1st Level

2nd Level

3rd Level

Pool

To Main
Entrance

Pool

Outer Wall

Heaven & Hell

The eastern half of the south gallery depicts the punishments and rewards of the 37 heavens and 32 hells. On the left, the upper and middle tiers show fine gentlemen and ladies proceeding towards 18-armed Yama (the judge of the dead) seated on a bull; below him are his assistants, Dharma and Sitragupta. On the lower tier, devils drag the wicked along the road to hell. To Yama's right, the tableau is divided into two parts by a horizontal line of *garudas*: above, the elect dwell in beautiful mansions, served by women and attendants; below, the condemned suffer horrible tortures that might have inspired the Khmer Rouge. The ceiling in this section was restored by the French in the 1930s.

Churning of the Ocean of Milk

The southern section of the east gallery is decorated by the most famous of the bas-relief scenes at Angkor Wat, the Churning of the Ocean of Milk. This brilliantly executed carving depicts 88 *asuras* on the left, and 92 *devas,* with crested helmets, churning up the sea to extract from it the elixir of immortality. The demons hold the head of the serpent Vasuki and the gods hold its tail. At the centre of the sea, Vasuki is coiled around Mt Mandala, which turns and churns up the water in the

tug of war between the demons and the gods. Vishnu, incarnated as a huge turtle, lends his shell to serve as the base and pivot of Mt Mandala. Brahma, Shiva, Hanuman (the monkey god) and Lakshmi (the goddess of beauty) all make appearances, while overhead a host of heavenly female spirits sing and dance in encouragement. Luckily for us, the gods won through, as the *apsaras* above were too much for the hot-blooded devils to take. Restoration work on this incredible panel by the World Monuments Fund (WMF; www.wmf.org) was completed in January 2012.

The Elephant Gate

This gate, which has no stairway, was used by the king and others for mounting and dismounting elephants directly from the gallery. North of the gate is a Khmer inscription recording the erection of a nearby stupa in the 18th century.

Vishnu Conquers the Demons

The northern section of the east gallery shows a furious and desperate encounter between Vishnu, riding on a *garuda*, and innumerable devils. Needless to say, he slays all comers. This gallery was completed at a later date, most likely in the 16th century, and the later carving is notably inferior to the original work from the 12th century.

Krishna & the Demon King

The eastern section of the north gallery shows Vishnu incarnated as Krishna riding a *garuda*. He confronts a burning walled city, the residence of Bana, the demon king. The *garuda* puts out the fire and Bana is captured. In the final scene Krishna kneels before Shiva and asks that Bana's life be spared.

Battle of the Gods & the Demons

The western section of the north gallery depicts the battle between the 21 gods of the Brahmanic pantheon and various demons. The gods are featured with their traditional attributes and mounts. Vishnu has four arms and is seated on a *garuda*, while Shiva rides a sacred goose.

Battle of Lanka

The northern half of the west gallery shows scenes from the *Ramayana*. In the Battle of Lanka, Rama (on the shoulders of Hanuman), along with his army of monkeys, battles 10-headed, 20-armed Ravana, captor of Rama's beautiful wife Sita. Ravana rides a chariot drawn by monsters and commands an army of giants.

ANGKOR THOM

It is hard to imagine any building bigger or more beautiful than Angkor Wat, but in Angkor Thom (អង្គរធំ) the sum of the parts add up to a greater whole. Aptly named, the fortified city of Angkor Thom is indeed a 'Great City' on an epic scale. The last great capital of the Khmer empire, and set over 10 sq km, Angkor Thom took monumental to a whole new level. It was built in part as a reaction to the surprise sacking of Angkor by the Chams, after Jayavarman VII (r 1181–1219) decided that his empire would never again be vulnerable at home. Beyond the formidable walls is a massive moat that would have stopped all but the hardiest invaders in their tracks. At the city's height,

Central Area of Angkor Thom

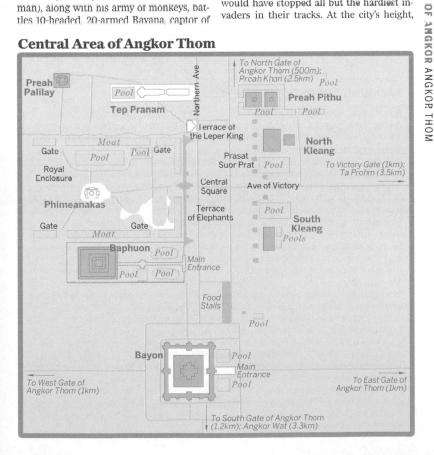

it may have supported a population of one million people in the surrounding region. Centred on Bayon, the mesmerising, if mind-bending, state temple, Angkor Thom is enclosed by a *jayagiri* (square wall) 8m high and 12km in length and encircled by a 100m-wide *jayasindhu* (moat). This architectural layout is yet another expression of Mt Meru surrounded by the oceans.

It is the gates that grab you first, flanked by a vast representation of the Churning of the Ocean of Milk, 54 demons and 54 gods engaged in an epic tug of war on the causeway. Each gate towers above the visitor, the magnanimous faces of the Bodhisattva Avalokiteshvara staring out over the kingdom. Imagine being a peasant in the 13th century approaching the forbidding capital for the first time. It would have been an awe-inspiring yet unsettling experience to enter such a gateway and come face to face with the divine power of the god-kings.

The south gate is most popular with visitors, as it has been fully restored and many of the heads (mostly copies) remain in place. The gate is on the main road into Angkor

Thom from Angkor Wat, and it gets very busy. More peaceful are the east and west gates, found at the end of dirt trails. The east gate was used as a location in *Tomb Raider,* where the bad guys broke into the 'tomb' by pulling down a giant (polystyrene!) *apsara*. The causeway at the west gate of Angkor Thom has completely collapsed, leaving a jumble of ancient stones sticking out of the soil, like victims of a terrible historical pile-up.

In the centre of the walled enclosure are the city's most important monuments, including Bayon, Baphuon, the Royal Enclosure, Phimeanakas and the Terrace of Elephants.

Bayon បាយ័ន

Unique, even among its cherished contemporaries, Bayon is the mesmerising if mind-bending state temple of Cambodia's legendary king, Jayavarman VII. Its architectural audacity epitomises the creative genius and inflated ego of this enigmatic figure. It's a place of stooped corridors, precipitous flights of stairs and, best of all, a collection of 54 Gothic-style towers decorated

TREKKING AROUND THE TEMPLES

Spread over a vast area of the steamy tropical lowlands of Cambodia, the temples of Angkor aren't the ideal candidates to tackle on foot. However, the area is blanketed in mature forest, offering plenty of shade, and following back roads into temples is the perfect way to leave behind the crowds.

Angkor Thom is the top trekking spot thanks to its manageable size and plenty of rewarding temples within its walls. Starting out at the spectacular south gate of Angkor Thom, admire the immense representation of the Churning of the Ocean of Milk before bidding farewell to the masses and their motorised transport. Ascend the wall of this ancient city and then head west, enjoying views of the vast moat to the left and the thick jungle to the right. It is often possible to see forest birds along this route, as it is very peaceful. Reaching the southwest corner, admire Prasat Chrung, one of four identical temples marking the corners of the city. Head down below to see the water outlet of Run Ta Dev, as this once powerful city was criss-crossed by canals in its heyday.

Back on the gargantuan wall, continue to the west gate, looking out for a view to the immense Western Baray on your left. Descend at the west gate and admire the artistry of the central tower. Wander east along the path into the heart of Angkor Thom, but don't be diverted by the beauty of Bayon, as this is best saved until last.

Veer north into Baphuon and wander to the back of what some have called the 'world's largest jigsaw puzzle'. Pass through the small temple of Phimeanakas and the former royal palace compound, an area of towering trees, tumbling walls and atmospheric foliage. Continue further north to petite but pretty Preah Palilay.

It's time to make for the mainstream with a walk through the Terrace of the Leper King and along the front of the royal viewing gallery, the Terrace of Elephants. If there is time, you may want to zigzag east to visit the laterite towers of Prasat Suor Prat. Otherwise, continue to the top billing of Bayon: weird yet wonderful, this is one of the most enigmatic of the temples at Angkor. Take your time to decipher the bas-reliefs before venturing up to the legendary faces of the upper level.

Bayon

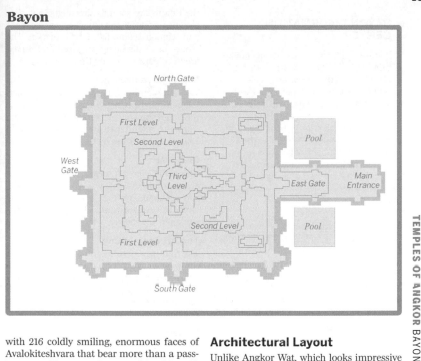

with 216 coldly smiling, enormous faces of Avalokiteshvara that bear more than a passing resemblance to the great king himself. These huge heads glare down from every angle, exuding power and control with a hint of humanity – this was precisely the blend required to hold sway over such a vast empire, ensuring the disparate and far-flung population yielded to his magnanimous will. As you walk around, a dozen or more of the heads are visible at any one time – full face or in profile, almost level with your eyes or staring down from up high.

Bayon is now known to have been built by Jayavarman VII, though for many years its origins were unknown. Shrouded in dense jungle, it also took researchers some time to realise that it stands in the exact centre of the city of Angkor Thom. There is still much mystery associated with Bayon – such as its exact function and symbolism – and this seems only appropriate for a monument whose signature is an enigmatic smiling face.

The eastward orientation of Bayon leads most people to visit early in the morning, preferably just after sunrise, when the sun inches upwards, lighting face after face. Bayon, however, looks equally good in the late afternoon. A Japanese team is restoring several outer areas of the temple.

Architectural Layout

Unlike Angkor Wat, which looks impressive from all angles, Bayon looks rather like a glorified pile of rubble from a distance. It's only when you enter the temple and make your way up to the third level that its magic becomes apparent.

The basic structure of Bayon is a simple three levels, which correspond more or less to three distinct phases of building. This is because Jayavarman VII began construction of this temple at an advanced age, so he was never confident it would be completed. Each time one phase was completed, he moved on to the next. The first two levels are square and adorned with bas-reliefs. They lead up to a third, circular level, with the towers and their faces.

Some say that the Khmer empire was divided into 54 provinces at the time of Bayon's construction, hence the all-seeing eyes of Avalokiteshvara (or Jayavarman VII) keeping watch on the kingdom's outlying subjects.

Bas-Reliefs

Angkor Wat's bas-reliefs may grab the headlines, but Bayon's are even more extensive, decorated with 1.2km of extraordinary carvings depicting more than 11,000 figures. The famous carvings on the outer wall of the

BAYON INFORMATION CENTER

The **Bayon Information Center** (Map p114; ☎092-165083; www.angkor-jsa.org/bic; admission US$2; ☺8am-4pm Tue, Wed & Fri-Sun) is a well-presented and informative exhibition on the history of the Khmer empire and the restoration projects around Angkor, including some short documentary films. Set in the beautiful compound of the Japanese government team for Safeguarding Angkor (JSA), it's a big saving on the Angkor National Museum.

first level show vivid scenes of everyday life in 12th-century Cambodia. The bas-reliefs on the second level do not have the epic proportions of those on the first level and tend to be fragmented. The reliefs described are those on the first level. The sequence assumes that you enter Bayon from the east and view the reliefs in a clockwise direction.

Chams on the Run

Just south of the east gate is a three-level panorama. On the first tier, Khmer soldiers march off to battle – check out the elephants and the oxcarts, which are almost exactly like those still used in Cambodia today. The second tier depicts coffins being carried back from the battlefield. In the centre of the third tier, Jayavarman VII, shaded by parasols, is shown on horseback followed by legions of concubines (to the left).

Linga Worship

The first panel north of the southeastern corner shows Hindus praying to a *linga* (phallic symbol). This image was probably originally a Buddha, later modified by a Hindu king.

Naval Battle

The next panel has some of the best-carved reliefs. The scenes depict a naval battle between the Khmers and the Chams (the latter with head coverings), and everyday life around Tonlé Sap lake, where the battle was fought. Look for images of people picking lice from each other's hair, of hunters and, towards the western end of the panel, a woman giving birth.

The Chams Vanquished

In the next panel, scenes from daily life continue and the battle shifts to the shore, where the Chams are soundly thrashed. Scenes include two people playing chess, a cockfight and women selling fish in the market. The scenes of meals being prepared and served are in celebration of the Khmer victory.

Military Procession

The last section of the south gallery, depicting a military procession, is unfinished, as is the panel showing elephants being led down from the mountains. Brahmans have been chased up two trees by tigers.

Civil War

This panel depicts scenes that some scholars maintain is a civil war. Groups of people, some armed, confront each other, and the violence escalates until elephants and warriors join the melee.

The All-Seeing King

The fighting continues on a smaller scale in the next panel. An antelope is being swallowed by a gargantuan fish; among the smaller fish is a prawn, under which an inscription proclaims that the king will seek out those in hiding.

Victory Parade

This panel depicts a procession that includes the king (carrying a bow). Presumably it is a celebration of his victory.

The Circus Comes to Town

At the western corner of the northern wall is a Khmer circus. A strongman holds three dwarfs, and a man on his back is spinning a wheel with his feet; above is a group of tightrope walkers. To the right of the circus, the royal court watches from a terrace, below which is a procession of animals. Some of the reliefs in this section remain unfinished.

A Land of Plenty

The two rivers, one next to the doorpost and the other a few metres to the right, are teeming with fish.

The Chams Retreat

On the lowest level of this unfinished three-tiered scene, the Cham armies are being defeated and expelled from the Khmer kingdom. The next panel depicts the Cham armies advancing, and the badly deteriorated panel shows the Chams (on the left) chasing the Khmers.

The Sacking of Angkor

This panel shows the war of 1177, when the Khmers were defeated by the Chams, and

Angkor was pillaged. The wounded Khmer king is being lowered from the back of an elephant and a wounded Khmer general is being carried on a hammock suspended from a pole. Directly above, despairing Khmers are getting drunk. The Chams (on the right) are in hot pursuit of their vanquished enemy.

The Chams Enter Angkor

This panel depicts another meeting of the two armies. Notice the flag bearers among the Cham troops (on the right). The Chams were defeated in the war, which ended in 1181, as depicted on the first panel in the sequence.

Baphuon ប្រាពួន

Baphuon was the centre of EFEO restoration efforts when the civil war erupted, and work paused for a quarter of a century. The temple was taken apart piece by piece, in keeping with the anastylosis method of renovation, but all the records were destroyed during the Khmer Rouge years, leaving experts with 300,000 stones to put back into place. The EFEO resumed restoration work in 1995, and continues its efforts today. Baphuon is approached by a 200m elevated walkway made of sandstone, and the central structure is 43m high. Clamber under the elevated causeway leading to Baphuon for an incredible view of the hundreds of pillars supporting it.

In its heyday, Baphuon would have been one of the most spectacular of Angkor's tem-

WHEN NATURE CALLS

Angkor is now blessed with some of the finest public toilets in Asia. Designed in wooden chalets and complete with amenities such as electronic flush, they wouldn't be out of place in a fancy hotel. The trouble is that the guardians often choose not to run the generators that power the toilets, meaning it is pretty dark inside the cubicles (but, thankfully, you can flush manually, too!). Entrance is free if you show your Angkor pass; and the toilets are found near most of the major temples.

Remember, in remote areas, don't stray off the path – being seen in a compromising position is infinitely better than stepping on a landmine.

THE RECLINING BUDDHA OF BAPHUON

On the western side of Baphuon, the retaining wall of the second level was fashioned – apparently in the 15th or 16th century – into a reclining Buddha about 60m in length. The unfinished figure is difficult to make out, but the head is on the northern side of the wall and the gate is where the hips should be; to the left of the gate protrudes an arm. When it comes to the legs and feet – the latter are entirely gone – imagination must suffice. This huge project, undertaken by the Buddhist faithful 500 years ago, reinforces the notion that Angkor was never entirely abandoned.

ples. Located 200m northwest of Bayon, it's a pyramidal representation of mythical Mt Meru. Construction probably began under Suryavarman I and was later completed by Udayadityavarman II. It marked the centre of the capital that existed before the construction of Angkor Thom.

Royal Enclosure & Phimeanakas ភិមានអាកាស

Phimeanakas stands close to the centre of a walled area that once housed the royal palace. There's very little left of the palace today except for two sandstone pools near the northern wall. Once the site of royal ablutions, these are now used as swimming holes by local children. The royal enclosure is fronted to the east by the Terrace of Elephants. Construction of the palace began under Rajendravarman II, although it was used by Jayavarman V and Udayadityavarman I. It was later added to and embellished by Jayavarman VII and his successors.

Phimeanakas means 'Celestial Palace', and some scholars say that it was once topped by a golden spire. Today it only hints at its former splendour and looks a little worse for wear. The temple is another pyramidal representation of Mt Meru, with three levels. Most of the decorative features are broken or have disappeared. Still, it is worth clambering up to the second and third levels for good views of Baphuon.

The northwestern wall of the Royal Enclosure is very atmospheric, with immense trees and jungle vines cloaking the outer side, easily visible on a forest walk from Preah Palilay to Phimeanakas.

Preah Palilay   ព្រះបាលិទ្បៃ

Preah Palilay is located about 200m north of the Royal Enclosure's northern wall. It was erected during the rule of Jayavarman VII and originally housed a Buddha, which has long since vanished. Sadly, the immense trees that used to loom large over the temple have been cut down, removing some of the romance of the place in the process.

Tep Pranam   ទេព្យប្រណម្យ

Tep Pranam, an 82m by 34m cruciform Buddhist terrace 150m east of Preah Palilay, was once the base of a pagoda of lightweight construction. Nearby is a Buddha that's 4.5m high, but it's a reconstruction of the original. A group of Buddhist nuns lives in a wooden structure close by.

Preah Pithu   ព្រះពិធូ

Preah Pithu, which is across Northern Ave from Tep Pranam, is a group of 12th-century Hindu and Buddhist temples enclosed by a wall. It includes some beautifully decorated terraces and guardian animals in the form of elephants and lions.

Terrace of the Leper King   ទីលានព្រះគម្លង់

The Terrace of the Leper King is just north of the Terrace of Elephants. Dating from the late 12th century, it is a 7m-high platform, on top of which stands a nude, though sexless, statue. It is yet another of Angkor's mysteries. The original of the statue is held at Phnom Penh's National Museum, and various theories have been advanced to explain its meaning. Legend has it that at least two of the Angkor kings had leprosy, and the statue may represent one of them. Another theory – a more likely explanation – is that the statue is of Yama, the god of death, and that the Terrace of the Leper King housed the royal crematorium.

The front retaining walls of the terrace are decorated with at least five tiers of meticulously executed carvings of seated *apsaras;* other figures include kings wearing pointed diadems, armed with short double-edged swords and accompanied by the court and princesses, the latter adorned with beautiful rows of pearls.

On the southern side of the Terrace of the Leper King (facing the Terrace of Elephants), there is access to the front wall of a hidden terrace that was covered up when the outer structure was built – a terrace within a terrace. The four tiers of *apsaras* and other figures, including *nagas,* look as fresh as if they had been carved yesterday, thanks to being covered up for centuries. Some of the figures carry fearsome expressions. As you follow the inner wall of the Terrace of the Leper King, notice the increasingly rough chisel marks on the figures, an indication that this wall was never completed, like many of the temples at Angkor.

Terrace of Elephants   ទីលានជល់ដំរី

The 350m-long Terrace of Elephants was used as a giant viewing stand for public ceremonies and served as a base for the king's grand audience hall. As you stand here, try to imagine the pomp and grandeur of the Khmer empire at its height, with infantry, cavalry, horse-drawn chariots and elephants parading across Central Sq in a colourful procession, pennants and standards aloft. Looking on is the god-king, crowned with a gold diadem, shaded by multi-tiered parasols and attended by mandarins and handmaidens bearing gold and silver utensils.

The Terrace of Elephants has five piers extending towards the Central Sq – three in the centre and one at each end. The middle section of the retaining wall is decorated with life-size *garudas* and lions; towards either end are the two parts of the famous parade of elephants, complete with their Khmer mahouts.

Kleangs & Prasat Suor Prat   ឃ្លាំង ប្រាសាទសួរប្រត

Along the east side of Central Sq are two groups of buildings, called Kleangs. The North Kleang and the South Kleang may at one time have been palaces. The North Kleang has been dated from the period of Jayavarman V.

Along Central Sq in front of the two Kleangs are 12 laterite towers – 10 in a row and two more at right angles facing the Ave of Victory – known as the Prasat Suor Prat, meaning 'Temple of the Tightrope Dancers'. Archaeologists believe the towers, which form an honour guard along Central Sq, were constructed by Jayavarman VII. It is likely that each one originally contained either a *linga* or a statue. It is said artists performed for the king on tightropes or rope bridges strung between these towers.

According to Chinese emissary Chou Ta-Kuan, the towers of Prasat Suor Prat were also used for public trials of sorts – during a dispute the two parties would be made to sit inside two towers, one party eventually succumbing to illness and proven guilty.

AROUND ANGKOR THOM

Baksei Chamkrong បក្សីចាំក្រុង

Located southwest of the south gate of Angkor Thom, Baksei Chamkrong is one of the few brick edifices in the immediate vicinity of Angkor. A well-proportioned though petite temple, it was once decorated with a covering of lime mortar. Like virtually all of the structures of Angkor, it opens to the east. In the early 10th century, Harshavarman I erected five statues in this temple: two of Shiva, one of Vishnu and two of Devi.

Phnom Bakheng ភ្នំបាក់ខែង

Located around 400m south of Angkor Thom, the main attraction at Phnom Ba-

kheng is the sunset view over Angkor Wat. For many years, the whole affair turned into something of a circus, with crowds of tourists ascending the slopes of the hill and jockeying for space once on top. However, numbers have now been restricted to just 300 visitors at any one time. In practice, this means arriving pretty early (4pm) for sunset to guarantee a spot. Some prefer to visit in the early morning, when it's cool (and crowds are light), to climb the hill. That said, the sunset over the Western Baray is very impressive from here.

Phnom Bakheng also lays claim to being home to the first of the temple-mountains built in the vicinity of Angkor. Yasovarman I chose Phnom Bakheng over the Roluos area, where the earlier capital (and temple mountains) had been located.

The temple-mountain has five tiers, with seven levels (including the base and the summit). At the base are or were 44 towers. Each of the five tiers had 12 towers. The summit of the temple has four towers at the cardinal points of the compass as well as a central sanctuary. All of these numbers are of symbolic significance. The seven levels, for example, represent the seven Hindu heavens, while the total number of towers, excluding the central sanctuary, is 108, a particularly auspicious number and one that correlates to the lunar calendar.

It is possible to arrange an elephant ride up the hill (US$15 one way). Try to book in advance, however, as the rides are very popular with tour groups.

To get a decent picture of Angkor Wat in the warm glow of the late-afternoon sun from the summit of Phnom Bakheng, you

TEMPLES OF ANGKOR BAKSEI CHAMKRONG

Phnom Bakheng

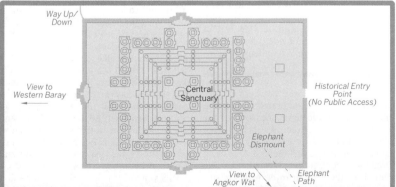

Way Up/ Down

View to Western Baray

Central Sanctuary

Historical Entry Point (No Public Access)

Elephant Dismount

View to Angkor Wat

Elephant Path

will need at least a 300mm lens, as the temple is 1.3km away.

Chau Say Tevoda
ចៅសាយទេវិតា

Just east of Angkor Thom's east gate is Chau Say Tevoda. It was probably built during the second quarter of the 12th century, under the reign of Suryavarman II, and dedicated to Shiva and Vishnu. It has been renovated by the Chinese to bring it up to the condition of its twin temple, Thommanon.

Thommanon
ធម្មនន

Thommanon is just north of Chau Say Tevoda. Although unique, the temple complements its neighbour, as it was built to a similar design around the same time. It was also dedicated to Shiva and Vishnu. Thommanon is in good condition thanks to extensive work by the EFEO in the 1960s.

Spean Thmor
ស្ពានថ្ម

Spean Thmor (Stone Bridge), of which an arch and several piers remain, is 200m east of Thommanon. Jayavarman VII constructed many roads with these immense stone bridges spanning watercourses. This is the only large bridge remaining in the immediate vicinity of Angkor. It vividly highlights how the water level has changed course over the centuries and may offer another clue to the collapse of Angkor's extensive irrigation system. Just north of Spean Thmor is a large water wheel.

There are more-spectacular examples of these ancient bridges elsewhere in Siem Reap Province, such as Spean Praptos, with 19 arches, in Kompong Kdei on NH6 from Phnom Penh; and Spean Ta Ong, a 77m bridge with a beautiful *naga*, forgotten in the forest about 28km east of Beng Mealea.

Ta Keo
តាកែវ

Ta Keo is a stark, undecorated temple that undoubtedly would have been one of the finest of Angkor's structures, had it been finished. Built by Jayavarman V, it was dedicated to Shiva and was the first Angkorian monument built entirely of sandstone. The summit of the central tower, which is surrounded by four lower towers, is almost 50m high. The four towers at the corners of a square and a fifth tower in the centre is typical of many Angkorian temple-mountains.

No one is certain why work was never completed, but a likely cause may have been the death of Jayavarman V. Others contend that the hard sandstone was impossible to carve and that explains the lack of decoration. According to inscriptions, Ta Keo was struck by lightning during construction, which may have been a bad omen and led to its abandonment.

Ta Nei
តានី

Ta Nei, 800m north of Ta Keo, was built by Jayavarman VII. There is something of the spirit of Ta Prohm here, albeit on a lesser scale, with moss and tentacle-like roots covering outer areas of this small temple. The number of visitors is also on a lesser scale, making it very atmospheric. It now houses the training unit of Apsara Authority (see the box, p130) and can be accessed by walking across the French-built dam. To get to the dam, take the long track on the left, just after the Victory Gate of Angkor Thom when coming from Siem Reap. It is possible to walk from Ta Nei to Ta Keo through the forest, a guaranteed way to leave the crowds behind.

Ta Prohm
តាព្រហ្ម

Ta Prohm is undoubtedly the most atmospheric ruin at Angkor and should be high on the hit list of every visitor. Its appeal lies in the fact that, unlike the other monuments of Angkor, it has been swallowed by the jungle, and looks very much the way most of the monuments of Angkor appeared when European explorers first stumbled upon them. Well, that's the theory, but in fact the jungle is pegged back and only the largest trees are left in place, making it manicured rather than raw like Beng Mealea. Still, a visit to Ta Prohm is a unique, other-worldly experience. The temple is cloaked in dappled shadow, its crumbling towers and walls locked in the slow, muscular embrace of vast root systems. If Angkor Wat, Bayon and other temples are testament to the genius of the ancient Khmers, Ta Prohm reminds us equally of the awesome fecundity and power of the jungle. There is a poetic cycle to this venerable ruin, with humanity first conquering nature to rapidly create, and

Ta Prohm

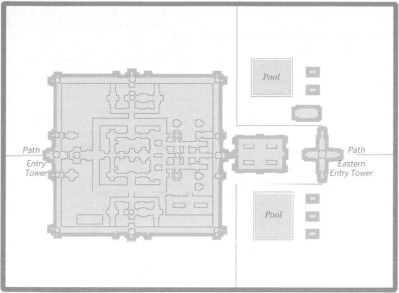

nature once again conquering humanity to slowly destroy.

Built from 1186 and originally known as Rajavihara (Monastery of the King), Ta Prohm was a Buddhist temple dedicated to the mother of Jayavarman VII. It is one of the few temples in the Angkor region where an inscription provides information about the temple's dependents and inhabitants. Almost 80,000 people were required to maintain or attend at the temple, among them more than 2700 officials and 615 dancers.

Ta Prohm is a temple of towers, closed courtyards and narrow corridors. Many of the corridors are impassable, clogged with jumbled piles of delicately carved stone blocks dislodged by the roots of long-decayed trees. Bas-reliefs on bulging walls are carpeted with lichen, moss and creeping plants, and shrubs sprout from the roofs of monumental porches. Trees, hundreds of years old, tower overhead, their leaves filtering the sunlight and casting a greenish pall over the whole scene.

The most popular of the many strangulating root formations is that on the inside of the easternmost *gopura* (entrance pavilion) of the central enclosure, nicknamed the Crocodile Tree. One of the most famous spots in Ta Prohm is the so-called 'Tomb *Raider* tree', where Angelina Jolie's Lara Croft picked a jasmine flower before falling through the earth into Pinewood Studios.

It used to be possible to climb onto the damaged galleries, but this is now prohibited, to protect both temple and visitor. Many of these precariously balanced stones weigh a tonne or more and would do some serious damage if they came down.

Banteay Kdei & Sra Srang
បន្ទាយក្ដី និង ស្រះស្រង់

Banteay Kdei, a massive Buddhist monastery from the latter part of the 12th century, is surrounded by four concentric walls. The outer wall measures 500m by 700m. Each of its four entrances is decorated with *garudas*, which hold aloft one of Jayavarman VII's favourite themes: the four faces of Avalokiteshvara. The inside of the central tower was never finished and much of the temple is in a ruinous state due to hasty construction. It is considerably less busy than nearby Ta Prohm and this alone can justify a visit.

East of Banteay Kdei is an earlier basin, Sra Srang (Pool of Ablutions), measuring 800m by 400m, reserved for the king and his consorts. A tiny island in the middle once bore a wooden temple, of which only the stone base remains. This is a beautiful body of water from which to take in a quiet sunrise.

Prasat Kravan

ប្រាសាទក្រវ៉ាន់

Uninspiring from the outside, the interior brick carvings concealed within its towers are Prasat Kravan's hidden treasure. The five brick towers here, which are arranged in a north–south line and oriented to the east, were built for Hindu worship in AD 921. The structure is unusual in that it was not constructed by royalty; this accounts for its slightly distant location, away from the centre of the capital. Prasat Kravan is just south of the road between Angkor Wat and Banteay Kdei.

Prasat Kravan was partially restored in 1968, returning the brick carvings to their former glory. The images of Vishnu in the largest central tower show the eight-armed deity on the back wall, taking the three gigantic steps with which he reclaimed the world on the left wall (see the box, p147); and riding a *garuda* on the right wall. The northernmost tower displays bas-reliefs of Vishnu's consort, Lakshmi.

Preah Khan

ព្រះខន្ធ

The temple of Preah Khan (Sacred Sword) is one of the largest complexes at Angkor – a maze of vaulted corridors, fine carvings and lichen-clad stonework. It is a good counterpoint to Ta Prohm and generally sees slightly fewer visitors. Preah Khan was built by Jayavarman VII and probably served as his temporary residence while Angkor Thom was being built. Like Ta Prohm it is a place of towered enclosures and shoulder-hugging corridors. Unlike Ta Prohm, however, the temple of Preah Khan is in a reasonable state of preservation thanks to the ongoing restoration efforts of the World Monuments Fund.

The central sanctuary of the temple was dedicated in AD 1191 and a large stone stela tells us much about Preah Khan's role as a centre for worship and learning. Originally located within the first eastern enclosure, this stela is now housed safely at Angkor Conservation. The temple was dedicated to 515 divinities and during the course of a year 18 major festivals took place here, requiring a team of thousands just to maintain the place.

Preah Khan covers a very large area, but the temple itself is within a rectangular enclosing wall of around 700m by 800m. Four processional walkways approach the gates of the temple, and these are bordered by another stunning depiction of the Churning of the Ocean of Milk, as in the approach to Angkor Thom, although most of the heads have disappeared. From the central sanctuary, four long, vaulted galleries extend in the cardinal directions. Many of the interior walls of Preah Khan were once coated with plaster that was held in place by holes in the stone. Today, many delicate reliefs remain, including *rishi* and *apsara* carvings.

The main entrance to Preah Khan is in the east, but most tourists enter at the west gate near the main road, walk the length of the temple to the east gate before doubling back to the central sanctuary, and exit at the north gate. Approaching from the west, there is little clue to nature's genius, but on the outer retaining wall of the east gate is a pair of trees with monstrous roots embracing, one still reaching for the sky. There is also a curious Grecian-style two-storey structure in the temple grounds, the pur-

---

ON LOCATION WITH TOMB RAIDER

Several sequences for *Tomb Raider,* starring Angelina Jolie as Lara Croft, were shot around the temples of Angkor. The Cambodia shoot opened at Phnom Bakheng, with Lara looking through binoculars for the mysterious temple. The baddies were already trying to break in through the east gate of Angkor Thom by pulling down a giant polystyrene *apsara*. Reunited with her custom Land Rover, Lara made a few laps around Bayon before discovering a back way into the temple from Ta Prohm. After battling a living statue and dodging Daniel Craig (aka 007) by diving off the waterfall at Phnom Kulen, she emerged in a floating market in front of Angkor Wat, as you do. She came ashore here before borrowing a mobile phone from a local monk and venturing into the Gallery of a Thousand Buddhas, where she was healed by the abbot.

Preah Khan

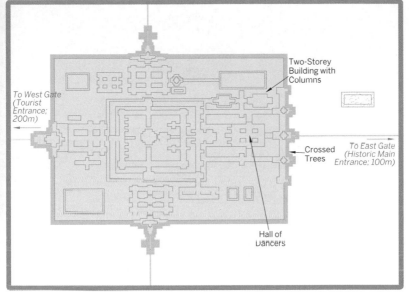

To West Gate (Tourist Entrance; 200m)

Two-Storey Building with Columns

Crossed Trees

To East Gate (Historic Main Entrance; 100m)

Hall of Dancers

pose of which is unknown, but it looks like an exile from Athens. Another option is to enter from the north and exit from the east.

Preah Khan is a genuine fusion temple, the eastern entrance dedicated to Mahayana Buddhism with equal-sized doors, and the other cardinal directions dedicated to Shiva, Vishnu and Brahma with successively smaller doors, emphasising the unequal nature of Hinduism.

Preah Neak Poan
ព្រះនាគព័ន្ធ

The Buddhist temple of Preah Neak Poan (Temple of the Intertwined Nagas) is a petite yet perfect temple constructed by – not him again, surely! – Jayavarman VII in the late 12th century. It has a large square pool surrounded by four smaller square pools. In the middle of the central pool is a circular 'island' encircled by the two *nagas* whose intertwined tails give the temple its name. It's a safe bet that if an 'Encore Angkor' casino is eventually developed in Las Vegas or Macau, Preah Neak Poan will provide the blueprint for the ultimate swimming complex.

In the pool around the central island there were once four statues, but only one

remains, reconstructed from the debris by the French archaeologists who cleared the site. The curious figure has the body of a horse supported by a tangle of human legs. It relates to a legend that Avalokiteshvara once saved a group of shipwrecked followers from an island of ghouls by transforming into a flying horse. A beautiful replica of this statue decorates the main roundabout at Siem Reap International Airport.

Water once flowed from the central pool into the four peripheral pools via ornamental spouts, which can still be seen in the pavilions at each axis of the pool. The spouts are in the form of an elephant's head, a horse's head, a lion's head and a human head. The pool was used for ritual purification rites.

Preah Neak Poan was once in the centre of a huge 3km-by-900m *baray* serving Preah Khan, known as Jayatataka, once again partially filled with water due to a new opening in the dyke road.

Ta Som
តាសោម

Ta Som, which stands to the east of Preah Neak Poan, is yet another of the late-12th-century Buddhist temples of Jayavarman VII, the Donald Trump of ancient Cambodia.

Preah Neak Poan

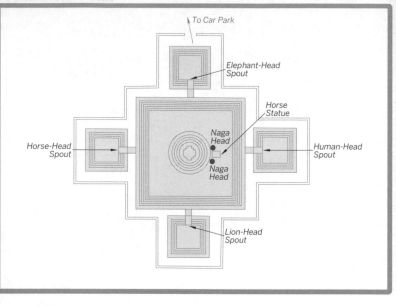

The most impressive feature at Ta Som is the huge tree completely overwhelming the eastern *gopura,* providing one of the most popular photo opportunities in the Angkor area.

Eastern Baray & Eastern Mebon
បារាយខាងត្រើត
មេបុណ្យខាងកើត

The enormous one-time reservoir known as the Eastern Baray was excavated by Yaso-varman I, who marked its four corners with stelae. This basin, now entirely dried up, was the most important of the public works of Yasodharapura, Yasovarman I's capital, and is 7km by 1.8km. It was originally fed by the Siem Reap River.

The Hindu temple known as the East-ern Mebon, erected by Rajendravarman II, would have been situated on an islet in the centre of the Eastern Baray reservoir, but is now very much on dry land. This temple is like a smaller version of Pre Rup, which was built 15 to 20 years later and lies to the south. The temple-mountain form is topped off by the now familiar quintet of towers. The elaborate brick shrines are dot-ted with neatly arranged holes, which at-tached the original plasterwork. The base of the temple is guarded at its corners by perfectly carved stone figures of elephants, many of which are still in a very good state of preservation.

The Eastern Mebon is flanked by earthen ramps, a clue that this temple was never finished and a good visual guide to how the temples were constructed.

Pre Rup
ប្រែរូប

Pre Rup, built by Rajendravarman II, is about 1km south of the Eastern Mebon. Like its nearby predecessor, the temple consists of a pyramid-shaped temple-mountain with the uppermost of the three tiers carrying five lotus towers. The brick sanctuaries were also once decorated with a plaster coat-ing, fragments of which still remain on the southwestern tower; there are some amaz-ingly detailed lintel carvings here. Several of the outermost eastern towers are perilously close to collapse and are propped up by an army of wooden supports.

Pre Rup means 'Turning the Body' and refers to a traditional method of cremation in which a corpse's outline is traced in the cinders, first in one direction and then in the other; this suggests that the temple may have served as an early royal crematorium.

Pre Rup is one of the most popular sunset spots around Angkor, as the view over the surrounding rice fields of the Eastern Baray is beautiful, although some lofty trees are starting to obscure it somewhat. However, it does get pretty crowded these days.

Banteay Samré បន្ទាយសំរែ

Banteay Samré dates from the same period as Angkor Wat and was built by Suryavarman II. The temple is in a fairly healthy state of preservation due to some extensive renovation work, although its isolation has resulted in some looting during the past few decades. The area consists of a central temple with four wings, preceded by a hall and also accompanied by two libraries, the southern one remarkably well preserved. The whole ensemble is enclosed by two large concentric walls around what would have been the unique feature of an inner moat, sadly now dry.

Banteay Samré is 400m east of the Eastern Baray. A visit here can be combined with a trip to Banteay Srei or Phnom Bok.

Western Baray & Western Mebon បារាយណ៍ខាងលិច និងមេបុណ្យខាងលិច

The Western Baray, measuring an incredible 8km by 2.3km, was excavated by hand to provide water for the intensive cultivation of lands around Angkor. Just for the record, these enormous *barays* weren't dug out, rather huge dykes were built up around the edges. In the centre of the Western Baray is the ruin of the Western Mebon temple, where the giant bronze statue of Vishnu (now in the National Museum) was found. The Western Mebon is accessible by boat (US$10 for the boat) from the dam on the southern shore.

The Western Baray is the main local swimming pool around Siem Reap. There is a small beach of sorts at the western extreme (complete with picnic huts and inner tubes for rent), which attracts plenty of Khmers at weekends.

ROLUOS TEMPLES

The monuments of Roluos (រលួស), which served as Indravarman I's capital, Hariharalaya, are among the earliest large, permanent temples built by the Khmers and mark the dawn of Khmer classical art. Before the construction of Roluos, generally only lighter (and less durable) construction materials such as brick were employed.

The temples can be found 13km east of Siem Reap along NH6 near the modern-day town of Roluos.

Preah Ko ព្រះគោ

Preah Ko was erected by Indravarman I in the late 9th century, and was dedicated to Shiva. The six *prasats* (stone halls), aligned in two rows and decorated with carved sandstone and plaster reliefs, face east; the central tower of the front row is a great deal larger than the other towers. Preah Ko has some of the best surviving examples of plasterwork seen at Angkor and is currently under restoration by a German team. There are elaborate inscriptions in the ancient Hindu language of Sanskrit on the doorposts of each tower.

The towers of Preah Ko (Sacred Ox) feature three *nandis* (sacred oxen), all of whom look like a few steaks have been sliced off them over the years. Preah Ko was dedicated by Indravarman I to his deified ancestors in AD 880. The front towers relate to male ancestors or gods, the rear towers to female ancestors or goddesses. Lions guard the steps up to the temple.

THE LONG STRIDER

One of Vishnu's best-loved incarnations was when he appeared as the dwarf Vamana, and proceeded to reclaim the world from the evil demon king Bali. The dwarf politely asked the demon king for a comfortable patch of ground upon which to meditate, saying that the patch need only be big enough so that he could easily walk across it in three paces. The demon agreed, only to see the dwarf swell into a mighty giant who strode across the universe in three enormous steps. From this legend, depicted at Prasat Kravan, Vishnu is sometimes known as the 'long strider'.

GOOD-CAUSE PROJECTS AROUND ROLUOS

Several good-cause initiatives have sprung up around the Roluos area. Look out for **Prolung Khmer** (www.prolungkhmer.blogspot.com) on the road between Preah Ko and Bakong. It's a weaving centre producing stylish cotton *kramas*, set up as a training collaboration between Cambodia and Japan. Also here is the Lo-Yuyu ceramics workshop, producing traditional Angkorian-style pottery.

Right opposite Preah Ko is **Little Angels**, a small orphanage-based project producing traditional leather puppets, and the **Khmer Group Art of Weaving**, turning out silk and cotton scarves on traditional looms. Also here is **Dy Proeung Master Sculptor** (donations accepted), who has created scale replicas of Preah Ko, Bakong and Lolei, plus Angkor Wat, Preah Vihear and Banteay Srei for good measure.

Bakong   ប្រាគង

Bakong is the largest and most interesting of the Roluos Group of Temples, and has an active Buddhist monastery just to the north of the east entrance. It was built and dedicated to Shiva by Indravarman I. It's a representation of Mt Meru, and it served as the city's central temple. The east-facing complex consists of a five-tier central pyramid of sandstone, 60m square at the base, flanked by eight towers (or their remains) of brick and sandstone and by other minor sanctuaries. A number of the eight towers below the upper central tower are still partly covered by their original plasterwork.

The complex is enclosed by three concentric walls and a moat. There are well-preserved statues of stone elephants on each corner of the first three levels of the central temple. There are 12 stupas – three to each side – on the third tier. The sanctuary on the fifth level of Bakong temple was a later addition during the reign of Suryavarman II, in the style of Angkor Wat's central tower.

On the grounds of the temple, there is also a very old wat, dating back a century or more, which has recently been restored.

Lolei   លលៃ

The four brick towers of Lolei, an almost exact replica of the towers of Preah Ko (although in much worse shape), were built on an islet in the centre of a large reservoir – now rice fields – by Yasovarman I, the founder of the first city at Angkor. The sandstone carvings in the niches of the temples are worth a look and there are Sanskrit inscriptions on the doorposts. According to one of the inscriptions, the four towers were dedicated by Yasovarman I to his mother,

his father and his maternal grandparents on 12 July 893.

AROUND ANGKOR

Phnom Krom   ភ្នំក្រោម

The temple of Phnom Krom, 12km south of Siem Reap on a hill overlooking Tonlé Sap lake, dates from the reign of Yasovarman I in the late 9th or early 10th century. The name means 'Lower Hill' and is a reference to its geographic location in relation to its sister temples of Phnom Bakheng and Phnom Bok. The three towers, dedicated (from north to south) to Vishnu, Shiva and Brahma, are in a ruined state, but Phnom Krom remains one of the more tranquil spots from which to view the sunset, complete with an active wat. The fast boats from Phnom Penh dock near here, but it is not possible to see the temple from beneath the hill. If coming here by moto or car, try to get the driver to take you to the summit, as it is a long, hot climb otherwise.

It is now necessary to have an Angkor pass to visit the temple at the summit of Phnom Krom, so don't come all the way out here without one, as the guards won't allow you access to the summit of the hill.

Phnom Bok   ភ្នំប៊ុក

Making up the triumvirate of temple-mountains built by Yasovarman I in the late 9th or early 10th century, this peaceful but remote location sees few visitors. The small temple is in reasonable shape and includes two frangipani trees growing out of a pair of ruined towers – they look like some sort of extravagant haircut when in full flower.

However, it is the views of Phnom Kulen to the north and the plains of Angkor to the south from this 212m hill that make it worth the trip. The remains of a 5m *linga* are also visible at the opposite end of the hill and it's believed there were similar *linga* at Phnom Bakheng and Phnom Krom. Unfortunately, it is not a sensible place for sunrise or sunset, as it would require a long journey in the dark.

There is a long, winding trail snaking up the hill at Phnom Bok, which takes about 20 minutes to climb, plus a faster cement staircase, but the latter is fairly exposed. Avoid the heat of the middle of the day and carry plenty of water, which can be purchased locally.

Phnom Bok is about 25km from Siem Reap and is clearly visible from the road to Banteay Srei. It is accessible by continuing east on the road to Banteay Samré for another 6km. It is possible to loop back to Siem Reap via the temples of Roluos by heading south instead of west on the return journey, and gain some rewarding glimpses of the countryside.

Chau Srei Vibol ចៅស្រីវិបុល

This petite hilltop temple used to see few visitors, as it was difficult to access, but new roads have put it on the temple map at last. The central sanctuary is in a ruined state but is nicely complemented by the construction of a modern wat nearby. Surrounding the base of the hill are laterite walls, each with a small entrance hall in reasonable condition. To get here, turn east off the Roluos to Anlong Veng highway at a point about 8km north of NH6, or 5km south of Phnom Bok. There is a small sign (easy to miss) that marks the turn. Locals are friendly and helpful should you find yourself lost.

Banteay Srei បន្ទាយស្រី

The art gallery of Angkor, Banteay Srei is considered by many to be the jewel in the crown of Angkorian artisanship. A Hindu temple dedicated to Shiva, it is cut from stone of a pinkish hue and includes some of the finest stone carving seen anywhere on earth. It is one of the smallest sites at Angkor, but what it lacks in size it makes up for in stature. It is wonderfully well preserved and many of its carvings are three-dimensional. Banteay Srei means 'Citadel of the Women' and it is said that it must have been built by a woman, as the elaborate carvings are supposedly too fine for the hand of a man.

Construction on Banteay Srei began in AD 967 and it is one of the few temples around Angkor to be commissioned not by a king but by a brahman, who may have been a tutor to Jayavarman V. The temple is square and has entrances at the east and west, the east approached by a causeway. Of interest are the lavishly decorated libraries and the three central towers, which are decorated with male and female divinities and beautiful filigree relief work.

Classic carvings at Banteay Srei include delicate women with lotus flowers in hand and traditional skirts clearly visible, as well as breathtaking recreations of scenes from the epic *Ramayana* adorning the library pediments (carved inlays above a lintel). However, the sum of the parts is no greater than the whole – almost every inch of these interior buildings is covered in decoration. Standing watch over such perfect creations are the mythical guardians, all of which are copies of originals stored in the National Museum.

Banteay Srei was the first major temple restoration undertaken by the EFEO in 1930 using the anastylosis method. The project, as evidenced today, was a major success and soon led to other larger projects such as the restoration of Bayon. Banteay Srei is also the first to have been given a full makeover in terms of facilities, with a large car park, a designated dining and shopping area, clear visitor information and a state-of-the-art exhibition on the history of the temple and its restoration.

When Banteay Srei was first rediscovered, it was assumed to be from the 13th or 14th centuries, as it was thought that the refined carving must have come at the end of the Angkor period. It was later dated to AD 967, from inscriptions found at the site.

In 1923 Frenchman André Malraux was arrested in Phnom Penh for attempting to steal several of Banteay Srei's major statues and pieces of sculpture. Ironically, Malraux was later appointed Minister of Culture under Charles de Gaulle.

Banteay Srei is 21km northeast of Bayon or about 32km from Siem Reap. It is well signposted and the road is surfaced all the way – a trip from Siem Reap should take

CHRISTER FREDRIKSSON/LONELY PLANET IMAGES ©

NICKOLAY VINOKUROV/LONELY PLANET IMAGES ©

IGNACIO PALACIOS/LONELY PLANET IMAGES ©

**. An elephant's eye view of Bayon
(p136)**
's possible to take an elephant from the south
ate of Angkor Thom to Bayon, but some
avellers have raised questions over how well
e animals are treated (p26)

. Koh Ker temples (p154)
rasat Neung Khmao, an ancient Khmer temple
the 10th-century capital of Koh Ker

. Faces of Bayon (p136)
tony-faced expressions of interest – the
amous faces of Bayon

. Apsara dancers in Siem Reap
epresentations of apsaras appear in many
tone bas-reliefs throughout Angkorian
emples (p125)

about 45 minutes. Moto and *remork-moto* drivers will want a bit of extra cash to come out here, so agree on a sum first. It is possible to combine a visit to Banteay Srei with a trip to the River of a Thousand Lingas at Kbal Spean and Beng Mealea, or to Banteay Samré and Phnom Bok.

LANDMINE ALERT!

At no point during a visit to Kbal Spean or Phnom Kulen should you leave well-trodden paths, as there may be landmines in the area.

Kbal Spean ក្បាលស្ពាន

A spectacularly carved riverbed, Kbal Spean is set deep in the jungle to the northeast of Angkor. More commonly referred to in English as the 'River of a Thousand Lingas', the name actually means 'bridgehead', a reference to the natural rock bridge at the site. Lingas have been elaborately carved into the riverbed, and images of Hindu deities are dotted about the area. Kbal Spean was 'discovered' in 1969, when EFEO ethnologist Jean Boulbet was shown the area by a local hermit; the area was soon off-limits due to the civil war, only becoming safe again in 1998.

It is a 2km uphill walk to the carvings, along a pretty path that winds its way up into the jungle, passing by some interesting boulder formations along the way. Carry plenty of water up the hill, as there is none available beyond the parking area. The path eventually splits to the waterfall or the river carvings. There is an impressive carving of Vishnu on the upper section of the river, followed by a series of carvings at the bridgehead itself, some of which have been tragically hacked off in the past few years. This area is now roped off to protect the carvings from further damage.

Following the river down, there are several more impressive carvings of Vishnu, and Shiva with his consort Uma, and further downstream hundreds of *lingas* appear on the riverbed. At the top of the waterfall are many animal images, including a cow and a frog, and a path winds around the boulders to a wooden staircase leading down to the base of the falls. Visitors between January and May will be disappointed to see very little water here. The best time to visit is between July and December. When exploring Kbal Spean it is best to start with the river carvings and work back down to the waterfall to cool off.

Near the base of the hill is the **Angkor Centre for Conservation of Biodiversity** (www.accb-cambodia.org), committed to rescuing, rehabilitating and reintroducing threatened wildlife. Tours of the centre can be arranged daily at 1pm. Species currently under protection here include pileated gibbon, silvered langur, slow loris, civet cat and leopard cat.

Kbal Spean is about 50km northeast of Siem Reap or about 18km beyond the temple of Banteay Srei. The road is now excellent, as it forms part of the new road north from NH6 to Anlong Veng and the Thai border, so it takes just one hour from town.

Moto drivers will no doubt want a bit of extra money to take you here – a few extra dollars should do, or US$12 to US$15 for the day, including a trip to Banteay Srei. Likewise, *remork-moto* drivers will probably up the price to US$20 or more. A surcharge is also levied to come out here by car. Admission to Kbal Spean is included in the general Angkor pass; the last entry to the site is at 3.30pm.

Phnom Kulen ភ្នំគូលែន

Considered by Khmers to be the most sacred mountain in Cambodia, Phnom Kulen is a popular place of pilgrimage on weekends and during festivals. It played a significant role in the history of the Khmer empire, as it was from here in AD 802 that Jayavarman II proclaimed himself a *devaraja* (god-king) and announced independence from Java, giving birth to the Cambodian kingdom. There is a small wat (Wat Preah Ang Thom) at the summit of the mountain, which houses a large **reclining Buddha** carved into the sandstone boulder upon which it is built. Nearby is a large **waterfall** and above it are smaller bathing areas and a number of carvings in the riverbed, including numerous *lingas*. A private businessman bulldozed a road up here a decade ago and charges a US$20 toll per foreign visitor, an ambitious fee compared with what you get for your money at Angkor. None of the toll goes towards preserving the site.

The road winds its way through some spectacular jungle scenery, emerging on the plateau after a 20km ascent. The road eventually splits: the left fork leads to the picnic spot, waterfalls and ruins of a 9th-century temple; the right fork continues over a bridge and some riverbed carvings to the reclining Buddha. This is the focal point of a pilgrimage here for Khmer people, so it is important to take off your shoes and any head covering before climbing the stairs to the sanctuary. The views from the 487m peak are tremendous, as you can see right across the forested plateau.

The waterfall is an attractive spot but could be much more beautiful were it not for all the litter left here by families picnicking at the weekend. Near the top of the waterfall is a jungle-clad temple known as **Prasat Krau Romeas**, dating from the 9th century.

There are plenty of other Angkorian sites on Phnom Kulen, including as many as 20 minor temples around the plateau, the most important of which is **Prasat Rong Chen**, the first pyramid or temple mountain to be constructed in the Angkor area. Most impressive of all are the giant stone animals or guardians of the mountain, known as **Sra Damrei** (Elephant Pond). These are very difficult to get to, with the route passing through mined sections of the mountain (stick to the path!) and the trail impassable in the wet season. The few people who make it, however, are rewarded with a life-size replica of a stone elephant – a full 4m long and 3m tall – and smaller statues of lions, a frog and a cow. These were constructed on the southern face of the mountain and from here there are spectacular views across the plains below. Getting to Sra Damrei requires taking a moto from Wat Preah Ang Thom for about 12km on very rough trails through thick forest before arriving at a sheer rock face. From here it is a 1km walk to the animals through the forest. Don't try to find it on your own; expect to pay the moto driver about US$8 to US$10 (with some hard negotiating) and carry plenty of water.

Phnom Kulen is a huge plateau around 50km from Siem Reap and about 15km from Banteay Srei. To get here on the new toll road, take the well-signposted right fork just before Banteay Srei village and go straight ahead at the crossroads. Just before the road starts to climb the mountain, there is a barrier and it is here that the US$20 charge is levied. It is possible to buy a cheaper entrance ticket to Phnom Kulen for US$12 from the City Angkor Hotel in Siem Reap. It is only possible to go up Phnom Kulen before 11am and only possible to come down after midday, to avoid vehicles meeting on the narrow road. There are plenty of small restaurants and food stalls located near the waterfall or in the small village near Wat Preah Ang Thom.

Moto drivers are likely to want about US$20 or more to bring you out here, and rented cars will hit passengers with a surcharge, more than double the going rate for Angkor; forget coming by *remork-moto* as the hill climb is just too tough.

Beng Mealea បឹងមាលា

One of the most mysterious temples at Angkor, Beng Mealea is a spectacular sight to behold as nature has well and truly run riot. Built to the same floor plan as Angkor Wat, this titanic of temples is Angkor's ultimate Indiana Jones experience. Built in the 12th century under Suryavarman II, Beng Mealea is enclosed by a massive moat measuring 1.2km by 900m, part of which is now dried up.

The temple used to be utterly consumed by jungle, but some of the dense foliage has been cut back and cleaned up in recent years. Entering from the south, visitors wend their way over piles of finely chiselled sandstone blocks, through long, dark chambers and between hanging vines. The central tower has completely collapsed, but hidden away among the rubble and foliage are several impressive carvings, as well as a well-preserved library in the northeastern quadrant. The temple is a special place and it is worth taking the time to explore it thoroughly – Apsara caretakers can show where rock-hopping and climbing is permitted. The large wooden walkway to and around the centre was originally constructed for the filming of Jean-Jacques Annaud's *Two Brothers* (2004), set in 1930s French Indochina and starring two tiger cubs. The filming included 20 tigers of all ages for continuity throughout the story.

HARMONY FARM

There is a small orphanage in Beng Mealea village called **Harmony Farm** (www.harmonyfarmcambodia.org) and staff are able to show visitors around. Volunteers are welcome for English-speaking classes or longer stays.

Beng Mealea

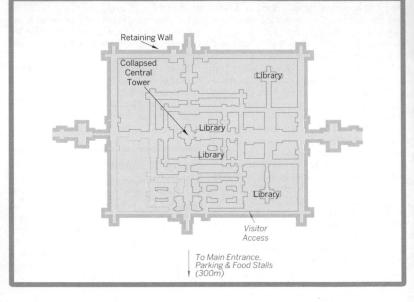

Retaining Wall

Collapsed Central Tower

Library

Library

Library

Library

Visitor Access

To Main Entrance, Parking & Food Stalls (300m)

There are several very basic, unmarked family homestays a few hundred metres behind the restaurants opposite the temple entrance. The best restaurant is **Romduol Angkor II** (mains US$5), a sister restaurant to the Romduol Angkor near Sra Srang. Wholesome Cambodian food is on offer, plus ice-cold drinks.

It costs US$5 to visit Beng Mealea and there are additional small charges for transport – make sure you work out in advance with the driver or guide who is paying this.

Beng Mealea is about 40km east of Bayon (as the crow flies) and 6.5km southeast of Phnom Kulen. By road it is about 68km (one hour by car, longer by moto or *remork-moto*) from Siem Reap. For independent travellers, it makes sense to undertake a long day trip combining Beng Mealea, Kbal Spean and Banteay Srei.

The shortest route is via the junction town of Dam Dek, located on NH6 about 37km from Siem Reap in the direction of Phnom Penh. Turn north immediately after the market and continue on this road for 31km. The entrance to the temple lies just beyond the left-hand turn to Koh Ker.

Beng Mealea is at the centre of an ancient Angkorian road connecting Angkor Thom and Preah Khan in Preah Vihear Province,

now evocatively numbered NH66. A small Angkorian bridge just west of Chau Srei Vibol temple is the only remaining trace of the old Angkorian road between Beng Mealea and Angkor Thom; between Beng Mealea and Preah Khan there are at least 10 bridges abandoned in the forest. This is a way for extreme adventurers to get to Preah Khan temple (p236); however, don't undertake this journey lightly.

REMOTE ANGKORIAN SITES

Information on the following remote Angkorian sites is found in the Northwestern Cambodia chapter: Banteay Chhmar (p228), Preah Khan (p235) and Prasat Preah Vihear (p233).

Koh Ker   កោះកេរ្ដិ៍

Abandoned for centuries to the forests of the north, **Koh Ker** (admission US$10), capital of the Angkorian empire from AD 928 to AD 944, was long one of Cambodia's most remote and inaccessible temple complexes. Now, since the opening of a toll road from Dam Dek (via Beng Mealea), Koh Ker

Koh Ker

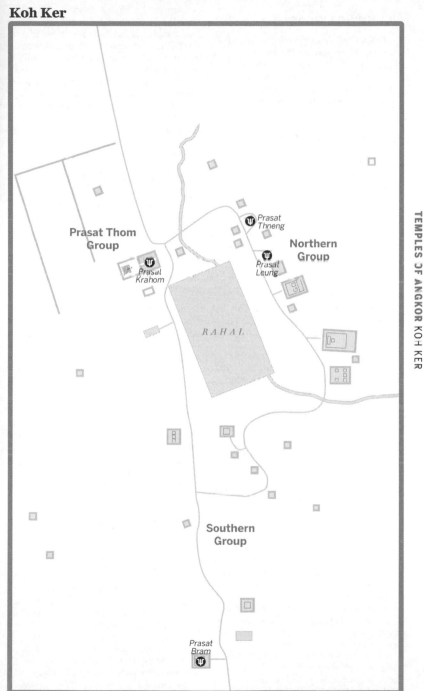

Prasat Thom Group

Prasat Krahom

Prasat Thneng

Prasat Leung

Northern Group

R A H A L

Southern Group

Prasat Bram

CUNNING LINGAS

Fertility symbols are prominent around the temples of Angkor. The *linga* is a phallic symbol and would have originally been located within the towers of most Hindu temples. It sits inside a *yoni*, the female fertility symbol, combining to produce holy water, charged with the sexual energy of creation. Brahmans poured the water over the *linga* and it drained through the *yoni* and out of the temples through elaborate gutters to anoint the pilgrims outside.

(pronounced ko-*kaye*) is within day-trip distance of Siem Reap. But to really appreciate the temples – the ensemble has 42 major structures in an area that measures 9km by 4km – it's necessary to spend at least one night.

Several of the most impressive sculptures in the National Museum come from Koh Ker, including the huge *garuda* that greets visitors in the entrance hall and a unique carving depicting a pair of wrestling monkey-kings.

Most visitors start at **Prasat Krahom** (Red Temple), the second-largest structure at Koh Ker, named for the red bricks from which it is constructed. Sadly, none of the carved lions for which this temple was once known remain, though there's still plenty to see – stone archways and galleries lean hither and thither and impressive stone carvings grace lintels and doorposts. A *naga*-flanked causeway and a series of sanctuaries, libraries and gates lead past trees and vegetation-covered ponds. Just west of Prasat Krahom, at the far western end of a half-fallen colonnade, are the remains (most of the head) of a statue of Nandin.

The principal monument at Koh Ker is **Prasat Thom** (Prasat Kompeng), a 55m-wide, 40m-high sandstone-faced pyramid with seven tiers. This striking structure, just west of Prasat Krahom, looks like it could almost be a Mayan site somewhere on the Yucatan Peninsula. Currently, the staircase to the top remains closed for safety reasons, as it is crumbling apart in places. Some 40 inscriptions, dating from 932 to 1010, have been found here.

South of this central group is a 1185m-by-548m *baray* known as the **Rahal**. It is fed by Stung Sen, which supplied water to irrigate the land in this arid area.

Some of the largest Shiva *linga* (phallic symbols) in Cambodia can still be seen in four temples about 1km northeast of Prasat Thom. The largest is found in **Prasat Thneng**, while **Prasat Leung** is similarly well endowed.

Among the many other temples that are found around Koh Ker, **Prasat Bram** is a real highlight. It consists of a collection of brick towers, at least two of which have been completely smothered by voracious strangler figs; the probing roots cut through the brickwork like liquid mercury.

🛏 Sleeping & Eating

If you bring a mosquito net (there's malaria out here) and a hammock (there are also snakes), it's possible to sleep near Prasat Krahom. Nearby are a few small **eateries** (⊙daylight hours) run by the wives of the policemen stationed here.

Nearby Srayong has a few eateries at both the old and the new markets, Psar Chaa and Psar Thmei.

Mom Morokod Koh Ker
Guesthouse   GUESTHOUSE $
(☑011 935114; r from US$10) About 200m south of the Koh Ker toll plaza, which is 8km south of Prasat Krahom, this quiet guesthouse has 11 clean, spacious rooms with elaborately carved wooden doors, painted wood-plank walls and bathrooms.

Ponloeu Preah Chan
Guesthouse   GUESTHOUSE $
(☑012 489058; r US$5) Located in the nearby village of Srayong, this friendly, family-run guesthouse has 14 rooms with bare walls, glassless windows, mosquito nets and barely enough space for a double bed. Toilets and

LANDMINE ALERT!

Many of the Koh Ker temples were mined during the war, but by 2008 most had been cleared: de-mining teams reported removing from the area a total of 1382 mines and 1,447,212 pieces of exploded and unexploded ordnance. However, considering what's at stake, it's best to err on the side of caution. Do not stray from previously trodden paths or wander off into the forest, as there may be landmines within a few hundred metres of the temples.

showers are out back. One room includes its own squat toilet.

ⓘ Getting There & Away

Koh Ker is 127km northeast of Siem Reap (2½ hours by car) and 72km west of Tbeng Meanchey (two hours). The toll road from Dam Dek, paved only as far as the Preah Vihear Province line, passes by Beng Mealea, 61km southwest of Koh Ker; one-day excursions from Siem Reap often visit both temple complexes. Admission fees are collected at the toll barrier near Beng Mealea if travelling from Siem Reap; make sure you get a proper printed receipt.

From Siem Reap, hiring a private car for a day trip to Koh Ker costs about US$80. There's no public transport to Koh Ker, although a few pick-ups (10,000r) link Srayong, 10km south of Prasat Krahom, with Siem Reap. It might also be possible to take one of the share taxis that link Siem Reap with Tbeng Meanchey and get off at Srayong.

South Coast

ELEV 0-1800M / POP 1.8 MILLION / AREA 27,817 SQ KM

Best Places to Eat

» Sailing Club (p199)

» Rikitikitavi (p192)

» Chez Claude (p183)

» Kimly Restaurant (p198)

» Holy Cow (p183)

Best Places to Stay

» Lazy Beach (p172)

» Mushroom Point (p181)

» Vine Retreat (p197)

» Les Manguiers (p192)

» Independence Hotel (p180)

Why Go?

Ever wonder what Southern Thailand was like decades ago, before the crowds arrived? The South Coast of Cambodia might provide some clues. The country's coastline is tiny compared with its northern neighbour's, but it remains practically deserted save for a clutch of fabulously diverse coastal towns: Koh Kong (the cowboy border town), Sihanoukville (the brash temptress), Kampot (the suave French colonialist) and Kep (the faded monarch).

Around these cities you won't find much besides jungle, a few truly idyllic islands and long stretches of powdery sand marred only by your footprints. Developers have long been drooling over the potential of this richly ecodiverse area, but most large-scale projects have been slow to materialise. Small resort owners have moved in, establishing little colonies of coolness on patches of paradise along the coastline. Inland, legitimate ecotourism initiatives tempt adventurous and responsible travellers.

When to Go

December, January and February are the coolest months. It starts heating up in March, and temps build to a crescendo in April before the monsoon rains start in May (a little earlier than elsewhere in Cambodia) and end in November (a little later than elsewhere). The rains tend to be steadier and more severe on the South Coast than elsewhere, but don't let this disrupt your travel plans. The scenery is lush and beautiful in the rainy season and the clouds provide welcome respite from the searing sun.

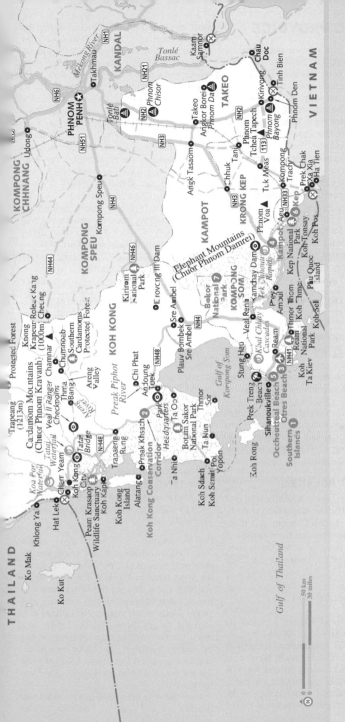

South Coast Highlights

1 Drifting idly among the magical **southern islands** (p168), home to low-key resorts and lonely white beaches

2 Exploring the pristine rainforests, mangrove-lined

rivers and remote waterfalls of the **Koh Kong Conservation Corridor** (p164), now opening up to ecotourism

3 Chilling on Sihanoukville's mellow **Otres Beach** (p131),

where exertion consists of yet another cocktail run

4 Kicking back in **Kampot** (p189), a charming river town with some of Cambodia's best-preserved French architecture

5 Partying on **Ochheuteal Beach** (p175), one of southeast Asia's top backpacker spots

6 Sampling remote islands and fresh seafood around **Kep**

(p195), the midcentury mecca of Cambodia's jet set

7 Visiting fog-enveloped **Bokor National Park** (p194), with its abandoned casino and (sometimes) breathtaking views

KOH KONG PROVINCE

Cambodia's vast and sparsely populated far southwestern province (ខេត្តកោះកុង) shelters some of the country's most remarkable and important natural sites.

Until recently the entire province was effectively cut off from the rest of the country because of dreadful roads. The capital city of Koh Kong (Krong Koh Kong) was easier to visit from Thailand, the Thai baht was king and the vast majority of foreigners in town were sex tourists on visa runs from Pattaya. That has all changed as National Hwy 48 (NH48) is now paved, bus connections to Phnom Penh are frequent, and stricter Thai visa rules keep the riff-raff out.

The best base for exploring the province's untamed jungle and coastline, spread out along the Koh Kong Conservation Corridor, is the riverine town of Koh Kong, 8km from the Thai border. From here, motorboats can whisk you to rushing waterfalls, secluded islands, sandy coves and Venice-like fishers' villages on stilts.

Koh Kong City ក្រុងកោះកុង

📞 035 / POP 29,500

Once Cambodia's Wild West, its isolated frontier economy dominated by smuggling, prostitution and gambling, Koh Kong is striding towards respectability as ecotourists scare the sleaze away. It's a sleepy town on the banks of the Koh Poi River, which spills into the Gulf of Thailand a few kilometres south of the centre.

👁 Sights & Activities

Koh Kong's main draw is adventures in and around the Cardamom Mountains and the Koh Kong Conservation Corridor, but there are a few diversions around town as well. If you want a dip, the pool at the Oasis Bungalow Resort is open to nonguests for US$3 a day.

📷 Peam Krasaop Wildlife Sanctuary   MANGROVES

Anchored to alluvial islands – some no larger than a house – this 260-sq-km sanctuary's millions of magnificent mangroves protect the coast from erosion, serve as a vital breeding and feeding ground for fish, shrimp and shellfish, and provide a home to myriad birds. The area, which is part of the Koh Kong Conservation Corridor, is all the

more valuable from an ecological standpoint because similar forests in Thailand have been trashed by short-sighted development.

To get a feel for the delicate mangrove ecosystem – and to understand how mangrove roots can stop a tsunami dead in its tracks – head to the 600m-long concrete mangrove walk (admission 5000r; ⏰6.30am-6pm), which wends its way above the briny waters to a 15m observation tower. If you're lucky you'll come upon cavorting monkeys with a fondness for fizzy drinks. The walk begins at the sanctuary entrance, about 5.5km southeast of the city centre. A moto/ *remork* costs US$5/10 return.

Unfortunately, a new resort has built 30 stilted bungalows amid the mangroves near the sanctuary entrance. The resort is a shrine to wood-crete that falls well short of blending with the beauty of the surroundings.

You can avoid confronting this eyesore by hiring a motorboat to take you through the sanctuary. Wooden boats are available for hire near the observation tower (per hour US$10), but a better plan is to head into the park's interior on a boat tour out of Koh Kong (see p161).

On a boat tour you'll have a chance to visit fishing hamlets whose residents use spindly traps to catch fish, which they keep alive till market time in partly submerged nets attached to floating wooden frames. Further out, on some of the more remote mangrove islands, you pass isolated little beaches where you can land and lounge alongside fearless hermit crabs.

Much of Peam Krasaop is on the prestigious Ramsar List of Wetlands of International Importance (www.ramsar.org). The area's habitats and fisheries are threatened by the large-scale dredging of sand for Singapore (p324).

Koh Yor Beach   BEACH

This long wind-swept beach is on the far (western) side of the peninsula that forms the west bank of the Koh Poi River opposite Koh Kong. It's not the world's prettiest beach, but it offers good shell-collecting and you're pretty much guaranteed to have it to yourself. To get there cross the bridge that spans the river north of the town centre, pay the toll on the other side (1200r for a moto) and look for a left turn about 1.5km beyond the toll booth. The beach is about 6km from the turn-off.

Sun worshippers will discover additional beaches on the Gulf of Thailand further

Koh Kong City

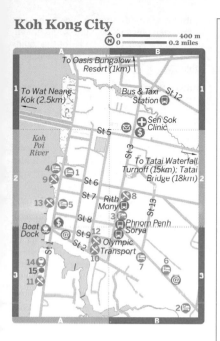

Koh Kong City

Sleeping
1 Asian Hotel...A2
2 Blue Moon Guesthouse.......................B3
3 Dugout Hotel B2
4 Koh Kong City Hotel A2
5 Koh Kong Guesthouse A2
6 Paddy's Bamboo Guesthouse.............B3
7 Rasmey Buntam Guesthouse............B3

Eating
Asian Hotel Minimart...................(see 1)
8 Baan Peakmai B2
Blue Moon Shop...........................(see 2)
9 Café Laurent A2
10 Fruit Stalls...A3
Ice Cream Shop ....(see 5)
11 Le Phnom..A3
12 Psar Leu A3
13 Riverfront Food Carts........................A2

Drinking
14 Aqua Sunset Bar..................................A3
Paddy's Bamboo Pub..................(see 6)

Transport
15 Dive Inn..A3
Virak-Buntham Bus Office..........(see 3)

north near the Thai border and the gaudy Koh Kong Resort & Casino.

Tours

Boat tours are excellent way to view Koh Kong's many coastal attractions. English-speaking Teur (☏016 278668) hangs around the boat dock (cnr Sts 1 & 9) and can help you hire six-passenger (40-horsepower) and three-passenger (15-horsepower) outboards (speedboats). Sample prices for big/small boats:

Koh Kong Island western beaches US$80/50

Around Koh Kong Island US$120/90

Peam Krasaop Wildlife Sanctuary US$40/30

The most popular tour is to Koh Kong Island (full day per person including lunch and snorkelling equipment US$25, or overnight for US$55). Trips take in some of the mangroves of Peam Krasaop Wildlife Sanctuary, and there's a good chance of spotting Irrawaddy dolphins early in the morning on these trips. Overnight trips involve beach camping or a homestay on the island. Note that tours do not take place in the rainy season (July to early October) because of strong onshore (southwesterly) breezes. However,

private boat trips to Peam Krasaop are possible year-round.

As tours become more popular, garbage is beginning to pile up on some of the island's western beaches – mainly the fault of irresponsible boatmen and tour operators. The following companies are trustworthy. All run overland trips in the Cardamom Mountains as well as boat tours. Paddy's Bamboo Guest House is also reliable for tours.

Blue Moon Guesthouse BOAT, JUNGLE TOUR
(☏012 575741; bluemoonkohkong@yahoo.com) Mr Neat offers boat trips and rainforest overnights in a hammock (US$33 per person).

Jungle Cross OFF-ROAD, JUNGLE TOUR
(☏015 601633; St 1; www.junglecross.com) Nick specialises in dirt-bike and jeep safaris deep into the Cardamoms, with riverside camping in hammocks. Also runs trekking tours to more remote bits of the Cardamoms, with transport by jeep to the launch point. The office is at the Dive Inn.

Koh Kong Eco Tours BOAT, JUNGLE TOUR
(☏012 707719; oasisresort@netkhmer.com; St 3) Rithy's excursions include excellent Koh

DON'T MISS

WAT NEANG KOK

A rocky promontory on the right (western) bank of the estuary is decorated with **life-size statues** demonstrating the violent punishments that await sinners in the Buddhist hell. This graphic tableau belongs to **Wat Neang Kok**, a Buddhist temple. To get there, cross the bridge, turn right 600m past the toll booth (motos 1200r), and proceed 150m beyond the temple to the statues.

Kong Island boat tours, birdwatching and jungle treks in the Cardamoms (two days and one night for US$35 per person, one day US$20 per person).

🛏 Sleeping

Koh Kong is becoming a popular holiday destination for Khmers, so hotels fill up – and raise their rates – during Cambodian holidays. You'll need to spend US$15 if you want a room with hot water.

The Tatai River, 18km east of town, has some appealing eco-accommodation options.

TOP CHOICE **Oasis Bungalow Resort**   RESORT $$
(☎092 228342, 016 331556; http://oasisresort .netkhmer.com; d/tr US$25/30; ❄⌨) In a quiet rural area 2km north of the centre, this oasis of calm has a gorgeous infinity pool with views of the Cardamoms and five cheerful, spacious bungalows with all the amenities. There's a no-sex-tourist policy, which one hopes will be continued by the new owners (it was being sold at the time of research). Blue signs point the way from Acleda Bank.

Koh Kong City Hotel   HOTEL $$
(☎936777; http://kkcthotel.netkhmer.com; St 1; d US$15-20; ❄@⌨) Ludicrous value for what you get: huge bathroom, two double beds, 50 TV channels, full complement of toiletries, free water and – in the US$20 rooms – glorious river views.

Asian Hotel   HOTEL $$
(☎936667; www.asiankohkong.com; St 1; r US$15-20; ❄@⌨) A virtual clone of the newer City Hotel across the street, only with views of City Hotel instead of the river.

Dugout Hotel   GUESTHOUSE $
(☎936220; thedugouthotel@yahoo.com; St 3; r with fan/air-con US$10/14; ❄⌨) Smack in the centre of town, it's another nice value, just a small step down in cleanliness and amenities from the Asian Hotel. Five of the rooms are arrayed around a small pool and all have cable TV.

Paddy's Bamboo Guesthouse   GUESTHOUSE $
(☎015 533223, 097 8483841; ppkohkong@gmail. com; dm US$2; r US$4-6; ⌨) Paddy's targets backpackers with a dormitory (planned), basic rooms, a balcony for chillin' and a pool table. Shoot for the wood-floored rooms upstairs with shared bathrooms. Paddy is also a good source of travel info and can arrange boat tours and other excursions.

Koh Kong Guesthouse   GUESTHOUSE $
(☎015 522005; St 1; d without/with bathroom US$5/6; ⌨) This budget choice has woody rooms sharing a bathroom upstairs off an appealing common area with river views and floor pillows. The concrete rooms downstairs are less appealing.

Blue Moon Guesthouse   GUESTHOUSE $
(☎012 575741; bluemoonkohkong@yahoo.com; r with fan/air-con US$6/10; ❄⌨) Nine neat, clean rooms with spiffy furnishings and hot water line a long, narrow courtyard. It's off the street so peace is a real possibility.

Rasmey Buntam Guesthouse   GUESTHOUSE $
(☎016 372528; r with fan/air-con from US$6/13; ❄@⌨) A Khmer-style place with big rooms with shiny tiles and too much air freshener.

🍴 Eating & Drinking

The best cheap food stalls are in the southeast corner of Psar Leu (the market); fruit stalls can be found near the southwest corner. Riverfront food carts sell noodles and cans of beer for 2000r to 3000r. Hotels with notable restaurants include the Asian Hotel and Oasis Bungalow Resort.

TOP CHOICE **Café Laurent**   INTERNATIONAL $$
(St 1; mains US$4-7; ⏰7am-midnight; ❄⌨) This chic, French-style cafe and restaurant has an old Citroën Deux Chevaux out front and refined Western and Khmer cuisine inside. Throw in seating in over-water pavilions and it's a slam dunk as Koh Kong's top restaurant.

Le Phnom   CAMBODIAN $
(St 1; bahn chhev US$1.25-1.50, meals US$2-4; ⏰9am-10pm) *Banh chhev* – meat, herbs and other goodies wrapped inside a pancake wrapped inside a lettuce leaf and hand-dipped in sweet sauce – is the speciality at

this authentic Khmer eatery. The giggling waitresses will teach you how to prepare it. Three *banh chhev* will feed two healthy eaters. Other 'small' dishes here feed two.

Crab Shack
CRAB SHACK $$
(Koh Yor Beach; mains US$3-5) A family-run place over the bridge on Koh Yor, it's known for perfect sunsets and heaping portions of fried crab with pepper (by request).

Ice Cream Shop
CAFE $
(St 1; mains US$2-4) Popular Bob's Bar has moved to the riverfront under a new moniker. Don't be fooled by the name, though: while the ice cream, imported from Thailand, is great, it's mainly a bar and restaurant.

Baan Peakmai
THAI $
(St 6; mains 8000-15,000r; ◎9am-9pm; ☑) One of the best restaurants in town, this open-air Thai place has a monster menu with two dozen vegetarian choices and a fair spread of seafood.

Paddy's Bamboo Pub
PUB
(mains US$2-3) Across the road from its namesake guesthouse, Paddy's angles for the backpacker market with US$1 beers and affordable Khmer food.

Aqua Sunset Bar
PUB
(St 1; snacks & sandwiches US$2-4) It's mystifyingly quiet given its attractive wood decor, pool table and breezy riverside locale. Nonetheless, a worthy spot for a sundowner.

Self-Catering

Asian Hotel Minimart
SELF-CATERING
(St 1; ◎7am-11pm) Snacks and drinks.

Blue Moon Shop
SELF-CATERING
(◎7am-9pm) Western meats and many other goodies.

❶ Information

Internet Access
Mary Internet (St 2; per hr 40 baht; ◎7am or 8am-9pm) Has five computers.

Resmey Angkor Computer Centre (per hr 3000r; ◎8am-9pm) Internet cafe.

Medical Services
In a medical emergency, evacuation to Thailand via the Cham Yeam-Hat Lek border crossing is possible 24 hours a day. In Thailand there's a hospital in Trat, 92km from the border.

Sen Sok Clinic (☑012 555060; kkpao@camintel.com; St 3 cnr St 5; ◎24hr) Has doctors who speak English and French.

Money
Thai baht are widely used so there's no urgent need to change baht into dollars or riel. To do so, use one of the many 'Hello' mobile-phone shops around Psar Leu – look for blue-and-yellow signs and glass counters with little piles of banknotes inside.

Acleda Bank (cnr Sts 3 & 5) ATM accepts Visa cards.

Canadia Bank (St 1) New bank with ATM accepting most Western plastic.

Ratha Exchange (St 2; ◎7am-5pm) A reliable exchange shop – look for the two gold-painted Chinese lions out front.

Tourist Information
Guesthouses, hotels and pubs are the best places to get the local low-down. You can also look for the free *Koh Kong Visitors Guide,* which is mostly advertisements.

❶ Getting There & Away
Koh Kong is on NH48, 220km northwest of Sihanoukville and 290km west of Phnom Penh. It's linked to the Thai border by a paved toll road that begins on the other side of the 1.9km bridge over the Koh Poi River.

Bus
Most buses drop you off at Koh Kong's unpaved **bus station** (St 12), on the northeast edge of town, where motos and *remorks* await, eager to overcharge tourists. Don't pay more than US$1/2 (preferably less) for the three-minute moto/*remork* ride into the centre. Pick-ups are at the company offices in town. Bus companies usually offer free transfer by *remork* from your guesthouse to their respective offices.

Rith Mony (☑012 640344; St 3), **Olympic Transport** (☑011 363678; St 3), **Phnom Penh Sorya** (☑077 563447; St 3) and **Virak Buntham** (☑089 998760; St 3) each run two or three buses to Phnom Penh (US$7, five hours, last trip is Rith Mony's 2pm bus) and one or two trips to Sihanoukville (US$7, four hours). Most Sihanoukville trips involve a transfer, but Rith Mony and Virak Buntham have direct buses around 8am.

Morning trips to Kampot (US$12, five hours) and Kep (US$14, four to five hours) with Rith Mony and Virak Buntham involve a vehicle change or two. The same two companies offer midday trips to Bangkok with a bus change at the border (US$20, eight hours). Those go via Koh Chang (US$14 including ferry).

Taxi
From the taxi lot next to the bus station, shared taxis head to Phnom Penh (US$11, 3½ hours) and occasionally to Sihanoukville (US$10, three hours) and Andoung Tuek (US$5). As with

anywhere your best chance for a ride is in the morning. Travel agents can easily set you up with shared or private taxi (to Phnom Penh/Sihanoukville US$55/50).

Hiring your own taxi to or from the Thai border costs about US$8 (plus 2400r for the toll), while a moto/remork will set you back US$3/6.

ℹ Getting Around

Bicycle

Paddy's Bamboo Guesthouse, Koh Kong Eco Tours and **Dive Inn** (St 1) rent out bicycles for US$1 to US$2 per day. Motorbike hire is available from most guesthouses and from Koh Kong Eco Tours for US$5.

Car, Moto & Motorbike

Short moto rides within the centre are 2000r; remorks are double that.

Most guesthouses and tour companies hire out 100cc or 125cc motorbikes (per day US$4 to US$6).

Koh Kong Conservation Corridor

Stretching along both sides of NH48 from Koh Kong to the Gulf of Kompong Som (the bay northwest of Sihanoukville), the Koh Kong Conservation Corridor encompasses many of Cambodia's most outstanding natural sites, including the southern reaches of the fabled Cardamom Mountains, an area of breathtaking beauty and astonishing biodiversity.

The Cardamoms cover 20,000 sq km of southwestern Cambodia. Their remote peaks – up to 1800m high – and 18 major

SOUTH COAST KOH KONG CONSERVATION CORRIDOR

waterways are home to at least 59 globally threatened animal species, including tigers, Asian elephants, bears, Siamese crocodiles (p167), pangolins (p164) and eight species of tortoise and turtle.

The second-largest virgin rainforest on mainland southeast Asia, the Cardamoms are one of only two sites in the region where unbroken forests still connect mountain summits with the sea (the other is in Myanmar). Some highland areas receive up to 5m of rain a year. Conservationists hope the Cardamoms will someday be declared a Unesco World Heritage Forest.

While forests and coastlines elsewhere in southeast Asia were being ravaged by developers and well-connected logging companies, the Cardamom Mountains and the adjacent mangrove forests were protected from the worst ecological outrages by their sheer remoteness and, at least in part, by Cambodia's long civil war. As a result, much of the area is still in pretty good shape, ecologically speaking, so the potential for ecotourism is huge – akin, some say, to that of Kenya's game reserves or Costa Rica's national parks.

The next few years will be critical in determining the future of the Cardamom Mountains. NGOs such as **Conservation International** (CI; www.conservation.org), **Fauna & Flora International** (FFI; www.fauna-flora.org) and the **Wildlife Alliance** (www.wildlifealliance.org), and teams of armed enforcement rangers, are working to help protect the area's 16 distinct ecosystems from loggers and poachers. Ecotourism, too, can play a role in providing local people with sustainable alternatives to logging and poaching.

TATAI RIVER & WATERFALL

About 18km east of Koh Kong on the NH48, the Phun Daung (Tatai) Bridge spans the Tatai River (Stung Tatai). Nestled in a lushly forested gorge upstream from the bridge is the **Tatai Waterfall**, a thundering set of rapids in the wet season, plunging over a 4m rock shelf. Water levels drop in the dry season, but you can swim year-round in refreshing pools around the waterfall. The water is fairly pure, as it comes down from the high Cardamoms, where there are very few human settlements.

🛏 Sleeping

The Tatai River has two marvellous eco-accommodation options that are well worth a couple of days or more.

END OF THE LINE FOR THE PANGOLIN?

In China and Vietnam, the meat of the Malayan (Sunda) pangolin – a kind of nocturnal anteater whose only food is ants and termites – is considered a delicacy, and the creature's blood and scales are believed to have healing powers. As a result, villagers in the Cardamom Mountains, who often hunt with dogs, are paid a whopping US$40 per kilo for live pangolins (the price rises to US$70 in Vietnam and US$100 in China) and pangolin populations have been in freefall. Enforcement rangers are doing their best to crack down on poaching before it's too late.

Rainbow Lodge RESORT $$
(☎099 744321, 012 160 2585; www.rainbowlodge
cambodia.com; s/d incl all meals US$40/65) This
supremely tranquil ecolodge has seven frill-
free bungalows with bathroom, fan and
mosquito net. Solar panels provide electri-
city; the wash water arrived as rain. Activi-
ties include kayaking, a sunset river cruise, a
day trek and overnight camping. It's situated
10 minutes upriver from the Tatai Bridge,
just a short kayak away from the waterfall.
Access is by boat; call ahead for free pick-up
at the bridge.

Four Rivers Floating Ecolodge RESORT $$$
(☎035 690 0650, 097 643 4032; www.ecolodges
.asia; s/d incl breakfast May-Sep US$97/118, Oct-
Apr US$119/139; ☎) Boasting 'top-of-the-line
luxury in harmony with Mother Nature',
this ecoresort's 17 South African–made tent-
ed villas – each with 45 sq metres, special
septic tanks and partial solar power – float
on a branch of the Tatai River estuary 6km
downriver from NH48. Access is by boat (20
minutes) from the western (Koh Kong) side
of the Tatai Bridge.

ⓘ Getting There & Away
You can access the Tatai Waterfall by car or
motorbike. The clearly marked turn-off is on the
NH48 about 15km southeast of Koh Kong, or
2.8km northwest of the Tatai Bridge. From the
highway it's about 2km to the falls along a rough
access road. There's a stream crossing about
halfway you may have to cross it on foot and
walk the last kilometre at the height of the wet
season.

From Koh Kong, a half-day moto/*remork* excursion to Tatai Waterfall costs US$10/15 return, or
less to go one-way to the bridge. If travelling by
public transport from Phnom Penh to one of the
resorts, tell the driver to let you off at the bridge.

KOH KONG ISLAND កោះគង
Cambodia's largest island towers over seas
so crystal clear you can make out individual
grains of sand in a couple of metres of water.
The island has seven beaches, all of them
along the Western coast. Unfortunately,
they're becoming increasingly polluted as
irresponsible tour operators fail to properly
dispose of waste. Hopefully the situation can
be reversed, as the island is a real jewel.

Several of the beaches – lined with coconut palms and lush vegetation, just as you'd
expect in a tropical paradise – are at the
mouths of little streams. At the **sixth beach**
from the north, a narrow channel leads to a
genuine *Gilligan's Island*-style lagoon.

On Koh Kong Island's eastern side, half
a dozen forested hills – the highest towering 407m above the sea – drop steeply to
the mangrove-lined coast. The Venice-like
fishing village of **Alatang**, with its stilted
houses and colourful fishing boats, is on the
southeast coast facing the northwest corner
of Botum Sakor National Park.

It's forbidden to explore the thickly forested interior, and there are no resorts, but
overnight camping and homestay options
are available with a guide (see p161).

ⓘ Getting There & Away
Koh Kong Island lies about 25km south of Koh
Kong City. The most practical way to get there
is on a boat tour from Koh Kong City (see p161).
In theory you could also get here by private boat
from Koh Sdach.

**CENTRAL CARDAMOMS PROTECTED
FOREST**
The Central Cardamoms Protected Forest
(CCPF; 4013 sq km) encompasses three of
southeast Asia's most threatened ecosystems: lowland evergreen forests, riparian
forests and wetlands.

The rangers and military police who protect this vast area from illegal hunting and
logging, with the help of Conservation International, are based at eight strategically
sited ranger stations, including one in Thma
Bang, where they run a bare-bones **guest
house** (per person US$5) with about 12 double
rooms and electricity from 6pm to 9pm. The
rangers' cook can prepare meals for US$2.
Bring warm clothes, as the temperature can
drop as low as 10°C.

Mostly covered with dense rainforest,
Thma Bang is perfect for birdwatching or
hiking – perhaps to a waterfall – with a local guide (rangers can help you find one).
The nearby **Areng Valley**, some of whose
inhabitants belong to the Khmer Daeum
minority community, is home to Asian elephants and the dragonfish (Asian arowana),
almost extinct in the wild, and the world's
most important population of critically endangered wild Siamese crocodiles (p167),
toothy critters up to 3.5m long who don't eat
people. The valley and its fauna are under
threat from a huge Chinese-built hydroelectric dam which, if constructed, will dis-
place 1500 people, flood 90 to 120 sq km of
land and inundate an important elephant-
migration route. Government proponents
of the dam counter that this and several additional Chinese-funded dams being built in

Cambodia will provide much-needed electricity to a power-starved country.

From December to May, the truly intrepid can accompany an armed enforcement-ranger patrol on the eight-day trek from Thma Bang north to Kravanh, or from Chamnar (linked to Thma Bang by road) over the mountains to Kravanh, a five- or six-day affair.

An easier, year-round option is the three- or four-day hike from Chumnoab, east of Thma Bang, eastwards to Roleak Kang Cheung, linked to Kompong Speu by road. Between the two is Knong Krapeur (1000m), set amid high-elevation grassland and pines. Inhabited five centuries ago, the area is known for its giant ceramic funeral jars, still filled with human bones.

There's no reservation system in Thma Bang; just show up and arrange trekking and accommodation on the spot.

❶ Getting There & Away

The southern reaches of the CCPF are easiest to reach from the south. The road to Thma Bang from NH48 has been widened and it now takes only about an hour to drive from Koh Kong. Turn off NH48 about 10km east of the Tatai River bridge at the Veal II (Veal Pii) ranger checkpoint.

Thma Bang is linked to Chi Phat by a difficult trail that can be handled by motorbike, but just barely and only in the dry season.

An improving road, passable by Toyota Camry or motorbike in the dry season, goes north through the Cardamoms to Pursat, Pailin and Battambang, passing by remote mountain towns such as Veal Veng, O Som (where there's a ranger station) and Promoui (the main town in the Phnom Samkos Wildlife Sanctuary). Near Koh Kong, the turn-off is on the old road to Phnom Penh past the airport, a few hundred metres beyond the army base. Going south, share taxis link Pursat with Promoui, where it should be possible to hire a moto for the long trip to Koh Kong.

The CCPF's northern sections (see p212) are accessible from Pursat.

BOTUM SAKOR NATIONAL PARK

Occupying almost the entirety of the 35km-wide peninsula west across the Gulf of Kompong Som from Sihanoukville, this 1834-sq-km national park, encircled by mangroves and beaches, is home to a profusion of wildlife, including elephants, deer, leopards and sun bears.

Alas, Botum Sakor appears to be a national park in name only. A US$5 billion Chinese-run tourism project will see the western third of the park developed into seven resort-like 'cities'. Launched in 2010, the project will take 30 years to complete, but already during our visit construction crews were kicking up huge plumes of dust and smoke as they laid a four-lane (at least) divided highway through the heart of the park.

Meanwhile, Cambodian businessman Ly Yong Phat has been granted a concession to develop a large central swath of the park.

That leaves the eastern third of the peninsula as the only viable area to visit. Boats can be hired in Andoung Tuek to take you up into four mangrove-lined streams that are – for the time being at least – rich with wildlife, including the pileated gibbon, long-tailed macaque and black-shanked douc langur: **Ta Op**, the largest, on the east coast; **Ta Nun** in the middle of the south coast; and **Ta Nhi** and **Preak Khsach** on the east coast.

At the **park headquarters** (☎099 374797, 081 414988), on NH48, 3.5km west of Andoung Tuek, you can arrange a hike with a ranger (US$5 a day) or a boat excursion out of Andoung Tuek.

The new four-lane highway, which begins 6km west of Andoung Tuek, provides improved access to the Koh Sdach Archipelago.

Trail bikers and intrepid moto riders might opt to bypass the new highway and take the rugged road around the park's east coast via the scenic fishing village of Thmor Sor, which is largely built on stilts. There's a basic guesthouse in Thmor Sor.

ANDOUNG TUEK   អណ្ដូងទឹក

This unassuming little town on the banks of the Preak Piphot River is at the crossroads of several of Koh Kong Province's prime adventures. Cambodia's signature ecotourism program, Chi Phat, is a couple of hours upstream by boat. The headquarters of Botum Sakor National Park is just west of town.

If you arrive in town late and are stranded, the extremely basic **Botum Sakor Guesthouse** (☎016 732731; r with/without bathroom US$6/5), 250m west of the bridge, has six slightly musty rooms with bright pink mosquito nets and sinkless bathrooms.

❶ Getting There & Away

Andoung Tuek is on NH48, 98km from Koh Kong. All buses travelling between Koh Kong and Phnom Penh or Sihanoukville pass through here. Share taxis passing through Andoung Tuek tend to be full.

For boats and motorbikes to Chi Phat, see p168. There is no public transport on the new highway through Botum Sakor National Park.

THE COMEBACK CROC

The Siamese crocodile (Crocodylus siamensis) was thought to be 'effectively extinct in the wild' until small viable populations were discovered in the Cardamom Mountains in 2000. Today, Flora & Fauna International (FFI) believes that about 250 Siamese crocs survive in the wild, mostly in the southwestern Cardamom Mountains.

FFI led the expeditions to rediscover the Siamese crocodile and runs a captive breeding program at Phnom Tamao Wildlife Rescue Centre. Genetic testing carried out in late 2009 determined that 35 of the 69 rescued crocodiles living at Phnom Tamao are purebred Siamese. FFI also collects croc eggs from river nesting sights and brings them to hatch at protected sites where they'll have a better chance of survival.

While there's evidence that FFI's efforts have helped stabilise the Siamese croc population, a new threat has emerged in the Cardamoms in the form of planned Chinese-built hydroelectric dams in two of the crocs' last Cardamoms habitats – Stung Atay and the Areng Valley. FFI has teamed up with Australia Zoo to rescue as many crocs as possible from the dam construction site before it's too late.

The Siamese crocodile is still classified as 'critically endangered' on the **IUCN Red List** (www.iucnredlist.org). Almost all the critters on Cambodia's 1000-plus croc farms are hybrids, their lineage mixed with that of the larger Australian saltwater crocodiles (Crocodylus porosus) – despite their name, also native to Cambodia and other coastal areas of Southeast Asia.

CHI PHAT   ជីតាំ់

In an effort to protect the southern Cardamom Mountains from poaching, logging and land grabbing by turning the rainforest into a source of jobs and income for local people, the **Wildlife Alliance** (www.wildlifealliance.org) has launched a multiphase project to transform the **Southern Cardamoms Protected Forest** (1443 sq km), whose southern boundary is NH48 between Koh Kong and Andoung Tuek, into a world-class ecotourism destination.

Once notorious for its loggers and poachers, the river village of Chi Phat (population 550 families) is now home to the Wildlife Alliance's pioneering **community-based ecotourism project** (CBET), offering travellers a unique opportunity to explore the Cardamoms ecosystems while contributing to their protection.

A variety of outdoor adventure activities are on offer. Visitors can take one- to five-day (four-night) **treks** through the jungle, go sunrise birdwatching by kayak, hire motos or mountain bikes to visit several nearby waterfalls and shoot (with a camera) monkeys and hornbills with a former poacher as a guide. Destinations include an area with mysterious, ancient **burial jars**; and – 45km away – the Areng Valley (p165). On overnight trips you sleep in hammocks or at one of four campsites set up by the Wildlife Alliance, equipped with ecotoilets, solar-powered electric light and either hammocks or field beds.

Of particular interest are the multiday **mountain-bike safaris** deep into the Cardamoms and the **sunrise birdwatching** trip. The latter involves an early wakeup call and a 1½-hour longtail boat ride before you jump in the kayaks and paddle along the placid **Stung Proat**, an unlogged tributary of the Preak Piphot River. Silver langurs, long-tailed macaques, greater hornbills and other rainforest creatures can often be seen along the banks of Stung Proat. Gibbons are hard to spot, but can often be heard calling to each other through the forest canopy.

All of this is controlled through the exceptionally organised **CBET office** (☎092-720 925; www.ecoadventurecambodia.com; ecotourism@wildlifealliance.org), a two-minute walk from the river pier in Chi Phat. Stop by the office when you arrive to get your housing assignment and book your tours for the upcoming days. The office has wi-fi, 24-hour electricity and a good restaurant serving both meat and vegetarian Khmer food.

Prices for all tours are extremely reasonable – usually less than US$35 per person per day for groups of two or more, including lunch, transport and equipment. All-inclusive multiday trips cost a bit more per day. All tours require guides, most of whom once worked as poachers and loggers.

🛏 Sleeping

Chi Phat's CBET project has 12 family-run **guesthouses** (d US$5) and nine **homestays** (s/d US$3/4). Some of these places are in town, others are out in the countryside, surrounded by orchards. In addition there's a fancier guesthouse, the **Sothun Lodge** (r US$15-20), on a small island in the middle of a river. It has a delightful bar on a platform overlooking the river, and simple but sturdy en-suite bungalows with two double beds, a few extras like towels, balconies and real showers.

All bookings are made through the CBET office. You can choose whether you want a guesthouse or a homestay, but unless you are staying in the Sothun Lodge you can't choose a specific establishment (the CBET office will assign one for you).

There's not a huge difference between the guesthouses and the homestays. Rooms – inspected monthly by the CBET committee – come with mosquito nets, cotton sheets, foam mattresses, free filtered water and a laminated sheet on local customs. Most guesthouses and one homestay are connected to the town's 24-hour electricity grid. The others have 12V fans powered either by generator (from 6pm to 10pm) or rechargeable car battery. Toilets (Western or squat) and showers (a rainwater cistern with a plastic bucket) are outside, but are clean and commodious.

At one guesthouse, the enterprising owners distil rice liqueur potent enough to be flammable. They're so proud of their product that you'll be offered a tumbler no matter when you visit – even if it's 8am, as it was when we dropped by.

ⓘ Information
At the boat dock in Andoung Tuek and in nearby coffee shops, scammers sometimes accost travellers, purveying misinformation, offering bogus tourist services and demanding spurious payments. For reliable information, contact the CBET office or check out its website.

ⓘ Getting There & Away
Chi Phat is on the Preak Piphot River 21km up-river from Andoung Tuek. Call the CBET office to arrange a longtail boat (US$25 for a four-passenger boat, two hours) or moto (US$5 to US$7, 45 minutes) in Andoung Tuek. The boats are far more atmospheric and relaxing, especially late in the day or early in the morning when the light is sublime and the birds are out.

The CBET office works only with local boatmen who have been trained in safety standards and whose boats have been remodelled to offer tourists a degree of comfort. The meeting point for CBET-sanctioned boats is underneath the bridge, on the eastern (ie toward Phnom Penh) bank of the river.

You'll find unsanctioned boats on the other side. These tend to be loaded with produce and sometimes other people, and thus are a more colourful means of transport, but you'll have to haggle on a price (obviously, don't pay more than US$25).

The road to Chi Phat is unsealed but in pretty good shape, and you can easily drive there with your own car.

TRAPAENG RUNG
The Wildlife Alliance's second community-based ecotourism initiative is modelled on its flourishing initial project in nearby Chi Phat. Same deal here: guests can choose from an array of participant homestays while making full- to several-day forays into the surrounding forest by foot, mountain bike or kayak.

One major difference here is access: Trapaeng Rung is right on the NH48 about 35km east of Koh Kong, making it much easier to get to than Chi Phat. It's also smaller and more local than its counterpart in Chi Phat, with a stronger emphasis on 'cultural tourism' (handicraft workshops, noodle-making lessons). And there's no central canteen like at the CBET office in Chi Phat – you eat what the locals eat in small restaurants or in their homes.

At the time of research seven homestays were signed up for the project in Trapaeng Rung proper, each with two rooms that cost US$3/5 for one/two persons. Additionally there's one homestay on the river about 40 minutes away from the town – this one is favoured by kayakers and is by request only.

To get sorted, drop by the project's **Community Based Ecotourism office** (CBET; ☏035 690 0815), which is right on the NH48 about 800m south (ie on the Phnom Penh side) of the bridge over the Areng River. They'll assign you a homestay and take your order for the next day's tour.

To get here follow the directions to Andoung Tuek and just tell your driver to drop you off in Trapaeng Rung instead of Andoung Tuek.

THE SOUTHERN ISLANDS

They may lack the cachet of Southern Thailand, but the two dozen or so islands that dot the Cambodian coast offer a lazy, undiscovered quality that their Thai counterparts lack. Until recently all signs pointed to the whole lot of them being pawned off to well-

CHI PHAT: AN ECOTOURISM CASE STUDY

Chi Phat's 550 families have long supplemented their meagre agricultural income with products from the nearby forests. Gathering nontimber forest products (known in development lingo as NTFPs) and small quantities of firewood can be ecologically sustainable, but around Chi Phat the wholesale forest destruction carried out during 'the logging time' – the anarchic 1990s – left the whole ecosystem, and the villagers' livelihoods, way out of whack. For many, poaching endangered animals became a way of life.

When the **Wildlife Alliance** (www.wildlifealliance.org) came on the scene in 2002 in a last-ditch effort to save the southern Cardamoms, local villagers and outsiders were encroaching on protected land, destroying the forest by illegal logging, and hunting endangered animals for local consumption and sale on the black market. The only way to prevent ecological catastrophe – and, among other things, to save macaques from being trapped, sold for US$60 and shipped to Vietnam to be eaten – was to send in teams of enforcement rangers to crack down on 'forestry and wildlife crimes'.

But enforcing the law impinged on local people's ability to earn money to feed their children (or buy motorbikes), generating a great deal of resentment. Many didn't see that environmental degradation – caused, in part, by their own unsustainable activities – would leave them far worse off in a few years' time, though most everyone noticed that animals were getting harder and harder to find.

The Wildlife Alliance realised that in order to save the Cardamoms, it needed the cooperation of locals, and that such cooperation would be forthcoming only if income-generating alternatives to poaching and logging were available. In such a remote area, one of the only resources is the forest itself, and one of the few ways to earn money from plants and animals without destroying them is ecotourism.

Thus the Wildlife Alliance launched what's known in NGO parlance as a community-based ecotourism (CBET) project. The first step was empowering the local community. A committee of 14 elected representatives was established to assess positive and negative impacts (eg of contact with Western culture), set goals and manage the project. Many of those who joined as 'stakeholders' were former loggers and wildlife traders.

Today the Chi Phat CBET project is flourishing. The initially sceptical locals have warmed to the idea and are beginning to see forest conservation in a different light. The income generated from ecotourism – income that goes into both the villagers' pockets and a community development fund – is starting to make a real difference. Chi Phat is seen as a model for other CBET projects, and delegations from around Cambodia now come here to see how it's done.

connected foreign investors for unchecked development. Instead, pretty much the opposite has happened. The global recession scared away the big boys, paving the way for lighter weights to move in with rustic resorts targeting backpackers.

This is paradise the way you dreamt it: endless crescents of powdered, sugary-soft sand, hammocks swaying in the breeze, photogenic fishing villages on stilts, technicolour sunsets and the patter of raindrops on thatch as you slumber. It seems too good to last, so enjoy it while it does.

❶ Getting There & Away

This section covers the main habitable islands between the Koh Kong Conservation Corridor and Ream National Park. The logical jumping-off point for any of them is Sihanoukville. Scheduled boat services link Sihanoukville with Koh Rong and Koh Sdach (buy an open-ended ticket in case you never want to leave). Other islands are reached by private boats, usually owned by the resort for which you are destined.

The Koh Sdach Archipelago is accessible overland from Koh Kong or even Phnom Penh via the new four-lane highway that cuts through Botum Sakor National Park.

Cambodia's largest island, Koh Kong Island, has no accommodation and is best visited from Koh Kong. It is covered as part of the Koh Kong Conservation Corridor on p165. Busier Koh Tonsay (Rabbit Island), off Kep, is covered on p196.

Koh Sdach Archipelago
កោះស្តេច

Just off Botum Sakor National Park's southwest tip, this is a modest archipelago of 12 small islands, most of them uninhabited. Basing yourself at one of the two islands with accommodation – **Koh Sdach** (King Island) and **Koh Totang** – you can spend a day or two exploring the other islands, some of which have utterly isolated beaches and good snorkelling. Most island-hopping tours target **Koh Ampil**, which is a cluster of three tiny islands surrounding a spit of sand, and the long white beaches on either side of **Koh Smach**.

The only village of any size is on Koh Sdach, which is just 10 minutes by outboard (speedboat) from the point where the new four-lane highway terminates on the mainland. This highway makes the archipelago infinitely easier to access, but as it's part of a huge tourism development, it may permanently change the southwest coast of Botum Sakor, once known for virgin beaches backed by virgin forest.

Fortunately, the islands appear to be largely excluded from the development agenda, and existing resorts are far enough from the mainland that the commotion will be out of earshot, if not completely out of eyeshot. The two main resorts here are a special breed – barely visited, well managed and far from run-of-the-mill. Koh Sdach has 24-hour electricity.

🛌 Sleeping

🏝 **Nomad's Land**   RESORT $$
(nomadslandcambodia@hotmail.com; Koh Totang; bungalows US$15-35) It's hard to imagine a more chilled out place than Nomad's. Owner Karim has serious Zen cred, hosting periodic yoga retreats and making this the greenest resort in the islands. The five bungalows have solar panels, and the toilets (all shared except for one) are waterless. The sturdy bungalows are funky for these parts. Some are split-level and they have loads of shelving, decent mirrors and beds facing the sea. There's a basic US$15 A-frame for those who prefer to rough it. The resort sits on a lovely stretch of white beach on Koh Totang, a speck of an island about 20 minutes from Koh Sdach by outboard. Karim and his partner spend June to November in Switzerland and close the resort during that time.

Belinda Beach Lovely Resort   RESORT $$$
(☏017 517517, 011 517517; www.belindabeach.com; Koh Sdach; r incl breakfast US$120; ❀☷) Belinda's lacks the brilliant beach that would normally be de rigueur for a resort of this price tag, yet it somehow makes up for it

through its other attributes and the charm of the owner, Benoit, a Belgian. Benoit cooks ridiculously good food (three-course dinner US$16) and leads post-dinner trivia sessions that involve shots of absinthe – or cookies for teetotallers and kids. After dinner, depending on the clientele, he'll either leave you alone or get the disco ball out and get a rogue dance party started (we were dancing on the bar). The four rooms are in a pair of duplex concrete cottages that are by far the most stylish and best appointed in the islands (for under US$1000, at least). Fuss: no hot water or soap in the bathrooms.

Mean Chey Guesthouse   GUESTHOUSE $
(☏011 983806; Koh Sdach; r US$7.50) Super-budget travellers will have to settle for this simple guesthouse close to the main fishing village on the northwest side of Koh Sdach. Accommodation is in 15 powder-blue concrete cottages with basic beds, TVs and soaps in the bathrooms. The Yvonne restaurant on the premises has lovely views of the neighbouring islands and serves French and Khmer food. Part-time caretaker Didier is here in the high season and runs affordable island-hopping tours that include a fresh-grilled-fish lunch.

ℹ Getting There & Away

There are two ways to get to the archipelago. The easiest and cheapest way, for now, is on a boat from Sihanoukville to Koh Sdach. The main 'passenger' ferry (it's more like small cargo boat with a few local passengers) leaves Sihanoukville's port area daily between noon and 2pm (US$10, 4½ hours with a stop or two along the way). The return leg departs at 8pm. There's also a much bigger cargo boat that stops at Koh Sdach roughly every other day on its run from Sihanoukville to Thailand. It's slower, costs only US$5, and departs Sihanoukville around 8pm. The return trip from Koh Sdach departs around 3am.

The other method is to travel overland via the new Chinese highway to the village of Poi Yopon on the mainland opposite Koh Sdach. This takes an investment in private transport. A car from Phnom Penh will cost at least US$120 until they get the highway paved. A cheaper option is to get off the bus where the highway starts, 6km west of Andoung Tuek on the NH48. From here moto drivers will take you to Poi Yopon for US$15 to US$20, depending on your negotiating skills. It's a blazing fast two-hour moto ride over a dirt road that may be sealed by the time you read this.

Hiring an outboard from Poi Yopon to Koh Sdach/Koh Totang costs US$10/15.

ℹ️ Getting Around

For island hopping, all of the resorts have boats of their own or can arrange for boats to take you throughout the archipelago and to the beaches of Botum Sakor National Park.

Koh Rong & Koh Rong Samloem

Moving south from the Koh Sdach Archipelago, you'll eventually run into these large neighbouring islands. They share more than confusingly similar names. Both are deceptively large islands with heavily forested interiors populated by an incredible variety of bird and other wildlife, some of it endemic. And both have several head-turning beaches that in terms of sheer brilliance would give anything in Thailand a run for its money.

That's not to say they are exactly the same. The larger island, **Koh Rong**, is the only island in Southern Cambodia that shows any hint of becoming more than a place to escape civilization entirely. Koh Tui, the village on Koh Rong's southeast foot, has a growing range of accommodation options, plus a bar where you might find a crew of drinkers until, who knows, midnight or so.

In the late 2000s developers laid out plans to turn Koh Rong into a Cambodian version of Thailand's Koh Samui, complete with a paved ring road, scores of resorts and an airport. Those plans have been slow to materialise, and for now Koh Rong remains a quintessential backpacker paradise.

Koh Rong Samloem has no such visions of tourism grandeur. A horseshoe-shaped, 10km-long island embracing Saracen Bay to the east, its three resorts are nowhere near each other and require separate transport to reach. The old French road network is overgrown, but you can fish, snorkel and take short treks. The island's amazing wildlife ranges from macaques, black squirrels and sea eagles to oversized salamanders, lizards and iguanas. Choose resorts carefully here as you won't have the option of sauntering down the beach to find something better.

🏖️ Beaches

You're spoilt for choice on Koh Rong. **Koh Tui Beach**, also called Pinetree Beach, extends for about 1km northeast from the pier in Koh Tui and gets lonelier and lovelier the further out you go. Rounding the headland (near Treehouse Bungalows) and continuing northeast, you can walk at least another hour along the sand and encounter little more than hermit crabs.

On the back (west) side of the island is a 7km stretch of the finest white sand, dubbed **Sok San Beach** after the fishing village at its northern end. There are simple resorts at the extreme north and south ends of this beach, with virtually nothing in between.

Koh Rong Samloem's best beach, **Lazy Beach**, is unfortunately off-limits to outsiders, but circumnavigate the island by boat and you'll find no shortage of similarly idyllic expanses of white sand.

🏃 Activities

Talk to **Frank Fortune** (📱015 703805; kohrong activities@gmail.com) at the pier in Koh Rong about **deep-sea fishing** opportunities and **island-hopping** trips that include lunch plus optional snorkelling and **sea kayaking**. He has a sturdy slow boat for big groups and a zippy little 15-horsepower outboard, plus a Zodiac with twin 60-horsepower engines.

On Koh Rong, you can walk 1½ hours from the main beach to Sok San Beach via a somewhat rigorous jungle track; bring bug spray and consider footwear other than flip-flops. Talk to Gil at Paradise Resort about other **hiking** options in the jungle of Koh Rong.

On Koh Rong Samloem, it's a relatively easy walk between Lazy Beach and Saracen Bay via the island's narrow waist, or you can take a guide at Lazy Beach and walk two hours to a lighthouse on a hill overlooking the ocean at the island's extreme southern tip, which is also a prime nesting spot for sea eagles.

There's good **snorkelling** around on both islands; resorts rent out gear for about US$5 per day. The islands also have some of Cambodia's best **diving**. Most dive trips are organised out of Sihanoukville. The Dive Shop has an office at the main pier in Koh Rong.

Several resorts hire out **sea kayaks** for about US$5/8 per hour for a single/tandem kayak. From Koh Tui Beach on Koh Rong, it's a 30-minute paddle out to an idyllic island topped by a wat just offshore. With your own sea kayak you could have a go at circling either of the islands, sleeping on deserted beaches along the way.

🛏️ Sleeping

As a rule resorts run their electricity only at night until about 10.30pm or so, which means no air-con and no fan, but most of the year you should be OK without it. All resorts provide mosquito nets and all tap water is cold.

Budget travellers who prefer not to book ahead should head to Koh Tui village on Koh Rong, where on either side of the pier locals run homestays and basic guesthouses with rooms for as little as US$5. These places should have vacancies for walk-in guests outside of major holiday periods.

Lazy Beach RESORT $$

(☎016 214211, 017 456536; www.lazybeachcambodia.com; Koh Rong Samloem, office on Serendipity St, Sihanoukville; bungalows US$40) Alone on the southwest coast of Koh Rong Samloem, the 16 bungalows at this idyllic getaway front one of the must stunning beaches you'll find anywhere. They have balconies and hammocks outside, and spiffy stone-floor bathrooms and duelling queen-size beds inside. The restaurant–common area is one of the area's best and is loaded up with books and board games, making it a good fit for families. Our only fuss is the lack of aquatic activities on offer – some sea kayaks would be a good idea. Play ping pong and badminton instead.

Treehouse Bungalows RESORT $$

(☎016 594177, in Sihanoukville 034 934744; www.treehouse-island.com; Koh Tui, Koh Rong, office on road to Serendipity, Sihanoukville; bungalows US$18-30) Treehouse is on a secluded cove around a small headland just northeast of Koh Tui, about a 15-minute beach walk from the pier. The sand here is a sublime golden hue, in contrast to the blinding white of Koh Tui Beach, and some of the island's best snorkelling is among the rocks that dot the shoreline. There are five pricier 'treehouses' – raised bungalows with prime sea views – and seven standalone bungalows nestled in the canopy at the back. They are delightfully rustic, with sturdy beds, clean private bathrooms and sea-facing balconies with hammocks. The bigger bungalows can sleep four in two large beds. Nonguests should drop by to sample the delicious wood-fired pizza.

Monkey Island RESORT $$

(☎081 830992; swoopingpenguin@yahoo.co.uk; Koh Tui Beach, Koh Rong, office at Monkey Republic, Sihanoukville; bungalow without/with bathroom US$18/25) Loosely associated with Sihanoukville backpacker haven Monkey Republic (some owners have stakes in both), Monkey Island is a good choice if you are looking for a semblance of action. While far from raucous, the bar does at least show a

pulse on most evenings, with hip tunes, hip bartenders and at least a few folks showing up to socialise. They run their generator as late as midnight, depending on the crowd. Bungalows have two double beds and can sleep four. The cheaper ones are down by the beach, while the pricier ones are at the back.

Paradise Bungalows RESORT $$

(☎092 548883, 078 300354; www.paradise-bungalows.com; Koh Tui Beach, Koh Rong, office at Boun Travel, road to Serendipity, Sihanoukville; bungalows US$20-60) This is the most upscale of the options on Koh Rong's main beach, with its restaurant set up on a hill under a soaring canopy. The 16 bungalows leave little to be desired, although the cheaper ones, curiously, don't face the ocean. The US$30 rooms are set way up on the hill with sweeping sea views, while the US$40 and US$60 rooms are on the beachfront and practically lapped by waves at high tide. The food is scrumptious – definitely drop by to eat if you aren't staying here.

Song Saa RESORT $$$

(☎023 686 0360 in Phnom Penh; http://songsaa.com; villas from US$1350; ✳@🛜☀) The South Coast's first ultra-luxury property occupies a private island just off the east coast of Koh Rong. The over-water and jungle villas are honeymoon-ready. Opulence pure, if you can afford it.

🏆 M'Pay Bay RESORT $$

(☎016 596111; www.kohrongsamloem.com; Koh Rong Samloem, office at Island Divers, road to Serendipity, Sihanoukville; bungalows US$20) A cluster of five simple bungalows nestled amid mangroves in a fishing village on the north side of Koh Rong Samloem, M'Pay Bay is all about living in harmony with nature. Efforts are made to limit waste, and management takes pains to ensure that the local fishing village benefits from tourism. From the resort it's a short walk south through the mangroves to a long crescent beach sweeping around a bay. The resort shares space with Marine Conservation Cambodia, which houses foreign volunteers in an adjacent cluster of bungalows. M'Pay Bay is only a 20-minute boat ride from Koh Rong, so it's a good choice if you want to experience both islands.

Broken Heart Guesthouse RESORT $$

(☎097 764 9424; www.bhgh.info; Sok San Beach, Koh Rong; dm US$10, bungalows without/with bathroom from US$10/25) For full castaway effect, look no further than this quirky, electricity-free retreat at the far southern end of Sok San Beach. The rickety bungalows are hidden in the maze-like canopy above the beach; most have delicious sea views. Bathrooms are rudimentary with scoop showers. You can walk here through the jungle from Koh Rong's main beach, or take a boat.

Pura Vida   RESORT $$
(☑097 518 1930; http://puravida.asia, Koh Tui, Koh Rong; r US$40-50) This Italian-run place was just opening when we visited. It sits alone on a seemingly endless stretch of white sand about a 30-minute walk beyond Treehouse Bungalows (beware, this involves wading chest-deep through an estuary at high tide), or a 15-minute boat ride from the pier. There are a few standalone bungalows plus some rooms above the restaurant, all large and brimming with Italian panache.

Freedom Island Bungalows   RESORT $$
(☑in Sihanoukville 034 633 3830; freedom_cambodia@yahoo.com; Koh Rong Samloem; r US$35) This lonely resort is all by itself at the north end of Koh Rong Samloem's Saracen Bay. It aspires to be slightly more upscale than most island retreats, leading to some curious choices like wall-to-wall carpeting and sliding glass doors. On the plus side, it has a pleasant hang-out area and is so little known that you might have the entire place to yourself. A small group could easily rent out all of the bungalows – four at research time, with plans to add more.

Coco Bungalow   RESORT $$
(☑081 466880; Koh Tui Beach, Koh Rong; bungalows US$15-40) This place is close to the village and the pier, so it does not offer quite as much privacy as others on this stretch, but you are nonetheless just a stumble away from your own private patch of sand. The nine solid-wood bungalows have two beds and sleep three to four people. Cheaper bungalows share bathrooms, while pricier digs are up on the hill with prime views.

Angkor Chum   GUESTHOUSE $$
(☑078 559959; Sok San Beach, Koh Rong; bungalows/r US$15/20) Angkor Chum consists of four solid bungalows raised over the high-tide mark at the extreme northern end of Sok San Beach (it's owned by the chief of Sok San village). There's no restaurant or services – dine at one of several basic eateries in the village. Sok San village is a good hour-long walk along uninterrupted beach from Broken Heart Guesthouse, or arrive by boat.

Sok San Beach Bungalows   RESORT $$
(☑099 605255, 097 677 2424; Sok San Beach, Koh Rong; bungalows/r US$15/20) Just south of Angkor Chum is this decidedly run-down option. The bungalows look like they would blow away in a gale; the sweltering rooms in a central structure are in only slightly better shape. You're paying for the setting here.

Mango Lounge   GUESTHOUSE $
(☑016 405010; Koh Tui Beach, Koh Rong; d with shared bathroom US$10) Rudy, the German owner of Paradise Bungalows, also runs this backpacker-oriented guesthouse near Koh Rong's pier. It has five simple rooms upstairs, and a bar downstairs that gets going every once in a while until midnight or so.

❶ Getting There & Away

If you are going anywhere besides the Koh Tui area on Koh Rong, make arrangements through your resort, most of which run daily trips to Sihanoukville for about US$20 return.

For Koh Tui, Treehouse Bungalows runs two daily boats to/from the port area in Sihanoukville. Guests of other resorts are accepted on these trips. There's a big boat and a small boat (you may want to avoid the latter in heavy seas). The big boat leaves Sihanoukville daily at 1pm and the next morning at 8am. The smaller boat leaves Sihanoukville daily at 8am and returns the same day at 4pm. It costs US$7.50 each way and takes about 2¼ hours in flat seas (longer in rough waters).

Frank Fortune (☑015 703805; kohrongactivities@gmail.com) lives at the pier in Koh Rong and can pick you up in one of his boats for about US$100 to US$150 depending on which boat you use. His six-passenger Zodiac can make the trip to Sihanoukville in well under an hour.

Koh Russei

Less than an hour by boat from Sihanoukville, tiny Koh Russei (Bamboo Island) was recently cleared of most resorts in preparation for a high-end development that has yet to materialise. Just one resort remained at the time of research, on a pretty beach at the back of the island, backpacker-friendly **Koh Ru** (☑012 388860; koh_ru@yahoo.com; office at Ocean Walk Inn, Serendipity St, Sihanoukville; dm/bungalows US$3/15). The bungalows are rudimentary and share bathrooms with scoop showers. You get a few hours of electricity after sunset. The daily boat out here costs US$10 return.

Koh Ta Kiev

Koh Ta Kiev, a delightful little island just off Ream National Park, is something of a black hole for resorts. New resorts open and then close with frightening regularity. Ask around Sihanoukville to see if anything is operating on Koh Ta Kiev. You'd do well to stay out here, as there's a wide white beach on the northwest side along with some pretty forest walks.

This may be a moot point, as the entire island has been leased to a French company to be converted into a top-end resort. It remained unclear at the time of research if and when this project might get under way.

Koh Ta Kiev, along with Koh Russei and some smaller uninhabited islands in the area, appears on most island-hopping itineraries out of Sihanoukville.

Koh Thmei

Moving east toward the Vietnamese island of Phu Quoc, the large island of Koh Thmei is part of Ream National Park. There's only one resort on the island, German-managed **Koh Thmei Resort** (☑097 737 0400, 089 897830;

www.koh-thmei-resort.com; bungalows US$15). It's a real gem and fantastic value, with super-simple bungalows that are just right for the setting. The resort sits on a great beach, and you can easily walk to several more, plus go sea kayaking or snorkelling (visibility varies). Khmer meals are surprisingly good and cost US$6.

Getting here is difficult and requires private transport overland to the mainland fishing village of Koh Kchhang; turn off the NH4 in the town of Bat Kokir, about 12km east of Sihanoukville airport. From Koh Kchhang the resort is a 1¼-hour boat ride (six-passenger boat US$12.50).

KOMPONG SOM PROVINCE

Sandwiched between Kampot and Koh Kong Provinces, this diminutive province (ខេត្តកំពង់សោម) is dominated by its main city, the dynamic port of Sihanoukville. Besides the surrounding islands, natural sites include Ream National Park, 18km east of Sihanoukville, and the Kbal Chhay Cascades.

THE LAST BATTLE OF THE VIETNAM WAR

The final bloody confrontation of the Vietnam War took place off the coast of Sihanoukville.

On 12 May 1975, two weeks after the fall of Saigon, Khmer Rouge forces, using captured US-made Swift boats, seized an American merchant ship, the SS *Mayagüez* (named after a city in Puerto Rico) while it was on a routine voyage from Hong Kong to Thailand. The vessel was anchored 50km southwest of Sihanoukville off **Koh Tang** – now a popular scuba-diving destination – while the 39 crew members were taken to Sihanoukville.

Determined to show resolve in the face of this 'act of piracy', President Gerald Ford ordered that the ship and its crew be freed. Naval planes from the US aircraft carrier *Coral Sea* bombed Sihanoukville's oil refinery and the Ream airbase, and Marines prepared for their first hostile boarding of a ship at sea since 1826.

On 15 May, Marines stormed aboard the *Mayagüez* like swashbuckling pirates but found it deserted. In parallel, airborne Marine units landed on Koh Tang. Thought to be lightly defended, the island turned out to have been fortified in anticipation of a Vietnamese attack (Vietnam also claimed the island). In the course of the assault, most of the US helicopters were destroyed or damaged and 15 Americans were killed.

Unbeknownst to the Americans, early on 15 May the Khmer Rouge had placed the crew of the *Mayagüez* aboard a Thai fishing boat and set it adrift – but the men weren't discovered by US ships until after the assault on Koh Tang had begun. In the chaotic withdrawal from the island, three Marines were accidentally left behind and, it is believed, later executed by the Khmer Rouge.

The Vietnam War Memorial in Washington DC, lists American war dead chronologically, which is why the names of the Marines who perished in the 'Mayagüez' Incident' appear at the bottom of the very last panel.

Sihanoukville

ក្រុងព្រះសីហនុ

☑034 / POP 221,000

Surrounded by white-sand beaches and undeveloped tropical islands, Sihanoukville (Krong Preah Sihanouk), also known as Kompong Som, is Cambodia's most happening beach destination. Visitor numbers have risen steadily in recent years – and stand to skyrocket now that flights from Siem Reap have been initiated.

For the time being, despite the boomtown rents, the city and its sandy bits remain pretty laid-back. While backpackers continue to flock to the party scene of Serendipity Beach, more subdued Otres Beach, south of town, has made a comeback. That and the emergence of the southern islands as cradles of castaway cool give non-backpackers a reason to visit.

None of Sihanoukville's beaches would qualify as southeast Asia's finest, but it's easy to have stretches of casuarina- and coconut palm–shaded sand to yourself, especially if you venture outside the centre.

Named in honour of the then-king, Sihanoukville was hacked out of the jungle in the late 1950s to create Cambodia's first and only deep-water port, strategically vital because it meant that the country's international trade no longer had to pass through Vietnam's Mekong Delta.

◎ Sights

Wat Leu   TEMPLE
(off Map p182) Spectacular views of almost the entire city – and gorgeous sunset panoramas – await at Wat Leu (Wat Chhnothean), situated on a peaceful, forested hilltop 1.5km northwest of the city centre (next to three red-and-white radio telecom towers). The small museum opens for groups.

From the city centre, a moto ride due north up the hill costs US$1 to 6000r. Remorks have to take the long way around and ask US$5 (give them US$3).

Monkeys   MONKEYS
On most days in the late afternoon, three troupes of tame monkeys gather on 2 Thnou St, behind and on the chain-link fence enclosing the grounds of the Independence Hotel (Map p176), hoping to score peanuts and bananas from passing humans. Locals often stop by with their kids, generating a great deal of mirth and mutual interprimate admiration.

🏖 Beaches

Sihanoukville's beaches all have wildly different characters, offering something for just about everyone. The most isolated are a short moto ride away in Ream National Park (p188).

Occheuteal Beach   BEACH
(Map p184) This 4km-long beach is by far Sihanoukville's most popular. Sunset views and a string of mellow beach bars make it a great place for happy hour, but you'll likely want to avoid it during the day, when it's too busy with vendors, beggars and nuisances like jet skis. It also gets packed, especially at weekends, and it's far from clean – note the rivulets of wastewater that flow from the shacks into the surf.

You can escape the mayhem by walking down to the southern section of the beach, ultimately slated to become another exclusive Sokha resort complex but for now pretty empty.

A rocky strip at the northwestern end of Occheuteal has emerged as a happy, easygoing travellers' hang-out known as Serendipity Beach. At the atmospheric resort bar-restaurants, waves lap just a few metres from the tables – very romantic, especially at sundown and in the evening.

Otres Beach   BEACH
At the southern end of Occheuteal Beach, go up and over the small headland, Phnom Som Nak Sdach (Hill of the King's Palace), and you'll get to gloriously quiet Otres Beach, a seemingly infinite strip of casuarinas and almost-empty sand that can just about give southern Thailand a run for its money.

Developers have long been eyeing Otres Beach, and in 2010 a stretch of resorts was forcibly removed. But as of early 2012 developers had yet to build on the land they claimed and Otres was making a comeback.

When we visited, resorts and beach bars were springing up at such a rapid rate that Otres seemed in danger of losing its 'mellow' tag. Even so, Otres has cleaner water and is more relaxed than anything in Sihanoukville proper, and is lengthy enough that finding your own patch of private sand is not a challenge (just walk south).

Otres also has an expanding range of activities on offer. At the north end of the beach (near where you arrive from Sihanoukville) you'll find Hurricane Windsurfing (☑017 471604; www.windsurf-cambodia.com),

Sihanoukville

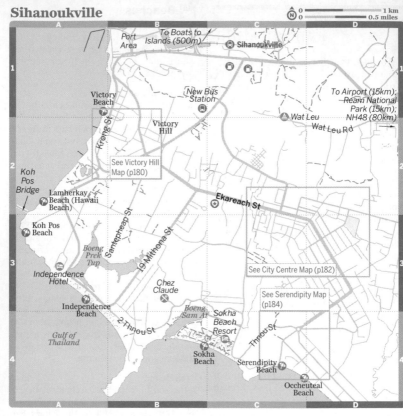

which rents out paddle boards (per hour US$7), windsurfers (basic/high-performance boards per hour US$9/20), sea kayaks (single/tandem per hour US$4/6) and skim boards (try bungee skim boarding). Otres Beach sometimes gets surf from May to October; you can rent surfboards and body boards here too.

About 700m south near the main cluster of guesthouses you'll find **Blue Lagoon Kitesurf Centre** (☎085 511145), which was just starting up when we dropped by. It's located at Sunlord Seagarden resort. Owner Andy also runs daily **boat tours** to four islands (per person US$15 including breakfast, lunch, snorkelling and a drink or two).

Way down at the beach's sleepy southern terminus, 2.5km south of Sunlord Seagarden, is **Otres Nautica** (☎092 230065), a laid-back, French-run outfit that rents tandem sea kayaks (per hour US$4) and Hobie Cat sailing catamarans (per hour US$10) that

you can take out to nearby islands. It also has a boat for snorkelling or island-hopping excursions.

Otres Beach is about 5km south of the Serendipity area. It's a US$2/5 moto/*remork* ride to get here (more at night). If going it alone, follow the road southeast along the beach and skirt the closed section; motorbikes can drive up and over the headland, but cars and *remorks* have to detour a bit inland. From the city centre, you can take Omui St from Psar Leu east out of town for 5km.

Sokha Beach   BEACH
(Map p176) Midway between Independence and Serendipity lies Sihanoukville's prettiest beach, 1.5km-long Sokha Beach. Its fine-crystal-like sand squeaks loudly when you walk on it. The eastern end of Sokha Beach is open to the public and rarely crowded. The rest is part of the exclusive Sokha Beach Resort. Tourists are welcome to enjoy the

sand near Sokha but are expected to buy something to drink or eat. You might even duck into the resort to use the pool (US$4).

Victory Beach BEACH
(Map p176) The hippy buzz is gone, but under Russian management, Victory Beach has found a new niche as a refuge for expats who aren't in the mood for Occheuteal's busy backpacker scene. Clean, hassle-free and family-friendly, the area and its midrange beach eateries get very quiet after sundown – despite the best efforts of Airport bar (p184).

Lamherkay Beach BEACH
(Map p176) About 1.5km southwest of Victory Beach, next to a shady grove, is Lamherkay Beach, also known as Hawaii Beach. It's hugely popular with car-owning Khmers on weekends and holidays but quiet on weekdays. Koh Pos (Koh Pos; Snake Island), the island 800m offshore, has been leased by Russians with big resort plans, which explains the flashy new bridge linking it with the mainland. It's currently a bridge to nowhere, as work on the actual resort appears to have stalled.

Independence Beach BEACH
(Map p176) Northwest of Sokha Beach, Independence Beach (7-Chann Beach) has mostly been taken over by a gargantuan new property development. The only open section is beneath the classic hotel for which the beach is named.

🏃 Activities

The diving near Sihanoukville isn't the best in southeast Asia, but there are reefs and fish to be ogled and it gets better the further you go out. Just don't expect anything on par with the western Gulf of Thailand or the Andaman Sea.

Most serious trips will hit Koh Rong Samloem, while overnight trips target the distant islands of Koh Tang and Koh Prins. Overnight trips cost about US$85 per day including two daily dives, food, accommodation on an island and equipment. Two-tank dives out of Sihanoukville average US$70 including equipment. PADI open-water courses average about US$300 to US$350 – very competitive by world standards.

Marine Conservation Cambodia (MCC; www.marineconservationcambodia.org) is working to protect the area's reefs and coastal breeding grounds and occasionally has volunteer positions available at its base near M'Pay Bay Bungalows on Koh Rong Samloem.

Most of the dive operators have some sort of presence on Koh Rong or Koh Rong Samloem – either bungalows or an office-restaurant where you can take pit stops.

Dive Shop DIVING
(Map p184; ☏933664; www.diveshopcambodia .com; road to Serendipity) PADI five-star dive centre offering National Geographic Diver certification. It has a dive shop on Koh Rong and works closely with Paradise Bungalows.

EcoSea Dive DIVING
(Map p184; ☏012 606646; 934631; www.ecosea dive.com; road to Serendipity) Offers PADI and SSI courses.

Frogmen DIVING
(Map p184; ☏097 585 1579; Serendipity St) Popular with a French clientele.

Island Divers DIVING
(Map p184; ☏086 494716; www.islandscubadiv ingcambodia.com; Rd to Serendipity) Based at the Safety Stop guesthouse, Island Divers is closely aligned with MCC (they use the same boats).

Scuba Nation DIVING
(Map p184; ☏012 604680; www.divecambodia .com; Serendipity St) Has a comfortable boat for liveaboard trips, and runs Cambodia's first PADI five-star National Geographic dive centre and its first five-star instructor-development centre.

Relax SPA
(Map p184; ☏011 686987; road to Serendipity; per hr from US$10; ⊙10am-9.30pm) English-owned and managed, this place's Khmer, lavender, jasmine-oil and foot massages get great reviews, plus facials, pedicures and waxing.

Seeing Hands Massage 3 MASSAGE
(Map p182; ☏012 799016; 95 Ekareach St; per hr US$6; ⊙8am-9pm; ⊛) The two masseurs and four masseuses who work here, some of them English-speaking, are blind.

Starfish Bakery & Café MASSAGE
(Map p182; ☏012 952011; 62 7 Makara St, City Centre; per hr US$6-10; ⊙7am-6pm) Blind and disabled masseuses, trained by Western massage therapists, perform Khmer, Thai, oil, foot and Indian head massages. Profits go towards social projects.

Fitness Resort · GYM

(off Map p182; ☑015 620534; www.fitness-siha
noukville.com; Boray Kamakor St; per day US$4, incl
a class US$5; ☺6am-8pm Mon-Sat, to noon Sun)
A funky French-run complex in a villa 2km
northwest of the bus station with a huge
open-air gym (165 machines), free weights,
aerobics, and Khmer and Thai boxing classes (US$4). It's between the city centre and
the bus station, about 600m southeast of
Mittapheap Kampuchea Soviet St.

🍃 Courses

Traditional Khmer Cookery
Classes · COOKING COURSE

(off Map p182; ☑092 738615; www.cambodiacook
eryclasses.com; 335 Ekareach St; half-/full-day
courses per person US$15/25; ☺Mon-Sat) Teach-
es traditional culinary techniques in classes
with no more than eight participants. Spe-
cialties include squid with Kampot pepper,
whole steamed fish with sweet-and-sour
sauce, and pomelo salad with prawns. Reserve a day ahead.

☞ Tours

Popular day tours go to some of the closer
islands and to Ream National Park (per person US$20). You can also hire a boat and
make your own way to the islands – most
travel agencies and guesthouses can arrange
a boat. Figure on US$50 for a boat to Koh
Ta Kiev from Occheuteal, a bit less for Koh
Russei. You'll save money going from Otres
Beach, where boats are available through
Sunlord Seagarden and a few other places.

Booze cruises were gaining traction during our visit. Bar-nightclub JJ's Playground
was among the outfits offering backpackers
the chance to board a yacht and spend the
day getting sloshed under the sun. Reports
are that many a drunk has ended up in the
water; don't drown or you might ruin it for
everybody else.

In addition to the following, Eco-Trek
Tours (see p187) also does boat and Ream
National Park trips.

Ravuth Travel · BOAT TOUR

(Map p184; ☑012 439292; www.servicestravel.info;
Serendipity Beach) Located at Coasters Resort,
Ravuth is one of several operations running
daily trips to Koh Ta Kiev/Koh Russei (per
person US$15/20), with stops at smaller
islands, departing at 9am. Tours include
breakfast, a seafood barbecue lunch and
snorkelling equipment.

Suntours · BOAT TOUR

(☑016 396201; www.suntours-cambodia.com)
The slightly more upscale day and overnight
island cruises around Koh Rong Samloem
offered by Suntours, with departures from
Victory Beach, get rave reviews.

Stray Dogs of Asia · MOTORCYCLE TRIP

(Map p184; ☑017 810125; Occheuteal St; www
.straydogasia.com; tours US$100) Runs all-day
countryside dirt-bike tours that take in
some of the natural attractions around Sihanoukville. Expensive, but the quality is high.

🛏 Sleeping

It's all about location in Sihanoukville, as
each region has its own very distinct character and attracts a different type of clientele. Prices quoted are for the high season
(approximately November to March). Rates
drop during the rainy season, especially on
pricier Serendipity Beach proper, but skyrocket on Khmer holidays at some establishments. Ask your resort about free bus
transfers. Mozzie nets are the norm.

SERENDIPITY & OCCHEUTEAL

It's hard to imagine a more mellow place
than Serendipity Beach, where a string of
resorts have names like Cloud 9, Aquarium
and Tranquility. You get the picture. Grab
that hookah and pen verse.

Unfortunately, the buzz is partly killed
by late-night noise from the nearby clubs.
The din isn't too bad, especially the further
east you go, but light sleepers may want to
bunk elsewhere. Also note that you're paying a premium on Serendipity Beach for the
waterfront locale.

From Serendipity Beach, Serendipity St
runs up the hill to the road to Serendipity,
which connects to Ekareach St at the Golden
Lions Roundabout. The road to Serendipity is the main backpacker hang-out. There
are some excellent midrange hotels on the
streets running southeast from the road to
Serendipity.

⌐TOP⌐ Cove · RESORT $$
CHOICE

(Map p184; ☑012 380296; www.thecovebeach.com;
Serendipity Beach; r with fan incl breakfast US$26-
34, with air-con US$33-35; ❋⚛) It's close, but
this is probably the best all-around choice
on Serendipity Beach, with a variety of hillside bungalows and a bar lapped by waves.
Most bungalows face the sea and all have
balconies and hammocks. The pricier air-con
rooms are way up top in a concrete row.

Above Us Only Sky
RESORT $$

(Map p184; ☏089 822318; www.aboveusonlysky
-cambodia.com; Serendipity Beach; r incl breakfast
with fan/air-con US$65/70; ❄🛜) The bunga-
lows are attractively minimalist inside, but
chances are you'll be hangin' on the cosy
balcony, where satellite chairs stare sea-
ward. The bar perched over the rocks by the
seashore is a gem. The four rooms are the
fanciest on this stretch, if a tad overpriced.

Cloud 9
RESORT $$

(Map p184; ☏012 479365; www.cloud9bungalows
.com; Serendipity Beach; r US$25-40, 🛜) The last
place on Serendipity Beach is a fine choice,
and not just because it's furthest removed
from the club noise. It has a cosy tropical bar
and seven rustic, Khmer-style bungalows
with fans, glassless windows and ocean-view
balconies.

Roof Resort
HOTEL $$

(Map p184; ☏934281; www.reefresort.com.kh; Rd
to Serendipity; d incl breakfast US$35-50; ❄🛜🏊)
The apex of comfort and style in the Seren-
dipity area. A good choice if you're doing
business around here or can't live without
your mod-cons. The 14 good-sized rooms af-
ford views of a 12.5m pool, surrounded by
a patio and lots of luscious purple orchids.

Orchidée Guesthouse
HOTEL $$

(Map p184; ☏933639; www.orchidee-guesthouse
.com; 23 Tola St; d incl breakfast US$23-28, tr US$30-
40; ❄@🛜🏊) A delightful 10m pool sur-
rounded by chairs and palms is the centrepiece of this restful place. The well-kept
rooms – some poolside, others bungalow-
style – have contemporary flair in addition
to more extras than you would expect. A real
find if you're happy off the beach.

Big Easy
HOSTEL $

(Map p184; ☏081 943930; www.thebigeasy.asia;
road to Serendipity; dm/d US$3/9; 🛜) The erst-
while Cool Banana went slightly upscale
when it changed its name. Prices are still
right, but there's better food and a more
sophisticated vibe than at other backpacker
establishments on this strip.

Serendipity Beach Resort
HOTEL $$$

(Map p184; ☏938888; www.serendipitybeach
resort.com; Serendipity St; ❄@🛜🏊) We can't
say what price they'll settle on (they had a
US$30 opening promo when we were there),
but anything under US$100 would be good
value for this location and this level of com-
fort. The rooms are practically four-star

standard, even if the service is far from it,
and the pool is immense. A high-rise, it's a
bit of an eyesore looming over Serendipity
Beach. Curiously, there's no lift.

Monkey Republic
HOSTEL $

(Map p184; ☏012 490290; http://monkeyrepublic
.info; road to Serendipity; dm US$3, r US$10; @🛜)
A favourite of the young backpacker crowd,
Monkey Republic has an eight-bed dorm
room and several dozen bright-blue bun-
galows set around two banana-tree-shaded
courtyards.

Mick & Craig's
GUESTHOUSE $

(Map p184; ☏012 727740; www.mickandcraigs
.com; road to Serendipity; r with fan/air-con from
US$8/15; ❄🛜) Set behind its popular restau-
rant, Mick & Craig's 17 neat, pastel rooms
are straightforward and practical. Excellent
value.

Beach Road Hotel
HOTEL $

(Map p184; ☏017 827677; www.beachroad-hotel
.com; road to Serendipity; r with fan/air-con from
US$15/20; ❄🛜🏊) Well located and efficient-
ly run, Beach Road has 76 modern rooms,
some set around the pool. They're clean and
well kept but have a few quirks (sneeze-in-
ducing air freshener, hard pillows).

New Sea View Villa
HOTEL $

(Map p184; ☏092 759753; www.sihanoukville
-hotel.com; Serendipity St; d with fan/air-con from
US$15/20; ❄🛜) Known more for its food,
New Sea View also has serviceable rooms.

Coolabah Resort
HOTEL $$

(Map p184; ☏017 678218; www.coolabah-hotel
.com; Mithona St; r US$45-65; ❄@🛜) Another
decent midranger up on the hill.

Malibu Bungalows
RESORT $$

(Map p184; ☏012 733334; www.malibu-bungalows
.com; s/d incl breakfast from US$40/45; ❄🛜) Of-
fers a measure of seclusion and bungalows
that descend a hillside to within a stone's
throw of the waterline, but maintenance is
an issue.

Utopia
HOSTEL $

(Map p184; ☏934319; www.utopiacambodia.com; cnr
road to Serendipity & Mithona St; dm with fan/air-con
US$2/3; @🛜🏊) Dorm beds don't come any
cheaper than at this backpacker party palace.
They're cramped but have free lockers.

VICTORY HILL & BEACH
Victory Hill (Weather Station Hill, also
known as 'The Hill'), once a backpacker

Victory Hill

Victory Hill

🛏 Sleeping

🍴 Eating

🍷 Drinking

haven, is up the hill from Victory Beach. It has lost its hippie vibe – most of the lodgers now are middle-aged males or Russians – but the area still has the cheapest rooms. The best options are down the hill toward Victory Beach, isolated from the hullabaloo of the Hill's mildly sleazy main strip.

Bungalow Village   HOSTEL $
(Map p180; ☏012 490293; bungalowvillage@hotmail.com; r with fan/air-con US$6/15) Recently taken over by a French-Belgian couple, this classic backpacker hang-out is just 200m from Victory Beach and has an old-fashioned chill-out zone where you can lounge on boulders like a lizard. The nine basic wood bungalows are leaky so you'll need those mosquito nets.

Mealy Chenda   HOSTEL $$
(Map p180; ☏933472; www.mealychenda.com; r with fan US$7-9, with air-con US$15-25; ❊🎧) The clean and spacious air-con rooms in this

old classic are a fine deal. It has survived through several Victory Hill transformations over the decades.

Sunset Garden Guesthouse   GUESTHOUSE $
(Map p180; ☏012 562004; s/d with fan US$5/7, d with air-con US$15; ❊) Run by an eccentric Khmer woman, this spotless, family-run hostelry, in an Italianate house surrounded by a medicinal-herb garden, has 14 spacious, spotless rooms.

CITY CENTRE
The shabby city centre, spread out along and north of Ekareach St, is preferred by many long-termers because it's cheap and it's removed from the traveller scene. It's also a tad more convenient if you're travelling by public transport. Most banks and businesses are here too, as is Sihanoukville's main market.

Pagoda Rocks   BOUTIQUE $$
(off Map p182; ☏077 524275; www.pagodarocks.com; Wat Leu Area; r US$45-50; ❊🎧🖥) If you're going to stay far away from the beach you might as well stay at the best. Pagoda Rocks has a swanky eating/hang-out area, a blissful infinity pool with prime views of the port area and smart cottages. Unfortunately, getting here is a huge hassle if you don't have your own wheels; *remork* drivers demand US$5 one way. Tell your driver 'Wat Leu'.

Small Hotel   HOTEL $
(Map p182; ☏934330; www.thesmallhotel.info; r US$15-18; ❊@🎧) Run by a cheerful, clued-in Swedish-Khmer couple, this guesthouse is as cosy as sitting in front of a fireplace on a snowy Scandinavian night. The 11 rooms lack the immense character of the lobby but are spotless and have hot water, fridge and TV.

Geckozy Guesthouse   GUESTHOUSE $
(Map p182; ☏012 495825; www.geckozy-guesthouse.com; r US$6-8; 🎧) Six basic rooms in an old wooden house on a quiet side street.

INDEPENDENCE BEACH
Independence Hotel   HOTEL $$$
(Map p176; ☏934300; www.independencehotel.net; 2 Thnou St; r from US$160; ❊@🎧🖥) Opened in 1963, this striking seven-storey hotel still has the jet-set feel of Sihanouk's movie-star heyday. After years of neglect, it was reopened in 2007. If features classic rooms with sea views, some more modern rooms in separate wings around the landscaped gardens, and

a few brand-new bungalows overlooking the water, one with a private plunge pool.

SOKHA BEACH

Sokha Beach Resort
RESORT $$$

(Map p176; 935999; www.sokhahotels.com; 2 Thnou St; r/ste from US$171/210; ✳@⌂≋) This opulent Khmer-style complex has a 1.5km private beach, a huge pool with its own tiny tropical island, and a children's playground. Service is not up to true ultra-luxury standards. It recently doubled in size to almost 400 rooms and tacked on a prominent casino, turning off some families. Promotional rates are available online.

OTRES BEACH

Otres is a place for serious chilling. Most guesthouses are in a cluster about 1km south of Otres' northern terminus. About 2.5km of empty beach (the land slated for eventual development) separates this cluster from a smaller, more isolated colony of resorts at the far southern end of the beach. Target the southernmost colony if your goal is complete escape.

TOP CHOICE Mushroom Point
HOSTEL $

(078 509079, 097 712 4365; mushroompoint. otres@gmail.com; dm US$7-10, s/d US$15/25; ⌂) The open-air dorm over the restaurant in the shape of – what else? – a mushroom wins the award for most awesome dorm room in Cambodia. Even those averse to communal living will be content in their mosquito-net-draped pods, good for two. The 'shroom-shaped private bungalows and food get high marks too. It's across the road from the beach.

Cinderella
RESORT $

(092 612035; s/d without bathroom $5/9, bungalows US$15) Way down in the southernmost resort colony, this is your spot if you just want some alone time. The beach is a bit dishevelled here and the A-frame cottages basic, but you can't argue with the beachfront setting. Castaways Beach Bar next door has wi-fi.

Done Right
HOSTEL $

(088 667 8668, 097 936 1441; s/d without bathroom $5/9, bungalows US$15) Space-age, eco-friendly bungalows known as 'geodomes' are done right here – a bit like concrete yurts, with skylights in lieu of windows. Above the restaurant are nine simple rooms with clapboard walls and lino floors. It's next to Mushroom Point.

Papa Pippo
RESORT $

(010 359725; info@papapippo.com; r without/with bathroom from US$$15/25; ☎) Located beachfront in the main resort cluster, Papa Pippo brings a bit of Italian flair to Otres Beach. The cute bungalows are a small step up in comfort from most other Otres options, with bushy thatched roofs and walls, and concrete floors. There's not much in them besides a bed, however. The open-air bar area is also appealing.

Sunlord Seagarden
RESORT $

(097 723 2319, 081 464746; bungalows with shared bathroom US$10) On the beach next to Papa Pippo, this is a good choice for active sorts as they have a boat for hire and there's a kitesurfing centre on premises. Bungalows are simple affairs with thatched roofs and concrete floors.

🍴 Eating

Sihanoukville's centre of culinary gravity has shifted to the Serendipity area, but the main drag of Victory Hill still has some good-value restaurants. The gritty commercial centre also holds a few pleasant surprises.

SERENDIPITY & OCCHEUTEAL

For romance, nothing beats dining on the water, either at one of the resorts at Serendipity Beach or – more cheaply – in one of the shacks along adjacent Occheuteal Beach. Two blocks inland, 12 Tola St is developing into a restaurant zone, with a plethora of barbecue places in the evening.

TOP CHOICE New Sea View Villa
INTERNATIONAL $$

(Map p184; 092-759753; Serendipity St; mains US$4-10; ⊙8am-4pm & 6-10pm) New Sea View is renowned for serving up some of city's tastiest cuisine at any time of day, but target dinner when the candles come out, the menu changes and the top chef is in action. Specialties include wasabi prawns, baked scallops in wine sauce, *magret* of duck in raspberry sauce and, for dessert, tiramisu and crème brûlée.

TOP CHOICE Sandan
CAMBODIAN $$

(Map p184; 452 4000; 2 Thnou St; mains US$4-10; ⊙dinner Mon-Sat) This brand-new eatery is loosely modelled on the beloved Phnom Penh restaurant Romdeng (p64). It's an extension of the vocational-training programs for at-risk Cambodians run by local NGO M'lop Tapang; 30 trainees were under apprenticeship at the restaurant when we

City Centre

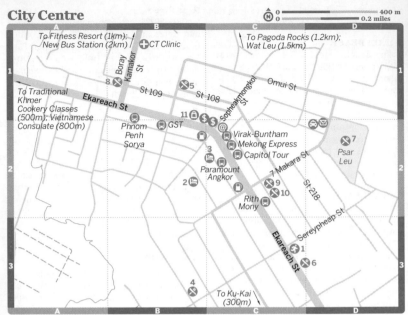

dropped by. As at Romdeng, the menu features creative Cambodian cuisine targeted at a slightly upscale clientele. There's a kids' play area and occasional cultural shows.

Kurin
BARBECUE $

(Map p184; Occheuteal Beach; mains US$2.50-4) Kurin's generous mixed seafood grill, fantastic value at US$4, separates it from the pack of barbecue shacks lining Occheuteul Beach. If you aren't up for surf, order turf – a heaping platter of various grilled meats for US$3. It's sandwiched between Dolphin Shack and Sessions.

Marco Polo
ITALIAN $$

(Map p184; ☑092 920866; Thnou St; mains US$3-8; ⊘lunch & dinner) The best Italian food for miles around is created by the Italian owner and chef of Marco Polo. The pasta dishes are perfectly al dente and the thin-crust pizzas emerging from the wood-fired oven are divine (one pizza is more than enough for one person).

Happa
JAPANESE $$

(Map p184; road to Serendipity; mains US$4-7; ⊘5pm-midnight) Authentic teppan-yaki with a variety of sauce options is tastefully served amid tropical decor with Japanese touches.

K2
INDIAN $

(Map p184; ☑011 304447; Occheuteal Beach; mains US$2-4) Run by a fellow from Gujarat, this basic beachside eatery serves inexpensive Pakistani, Indian and Mogul cuisine, including vegie and halal-meat options. Delivery available.

Happy Herb Pizza
WEED PIZZA $$

(Map p184; ☑012 632198; 23 Tola St; small/medium/large from US$4/7/9.50) Serves Khmer dishes (US$1.50 to US$3) and 23 kinds of pizza, all available 'happy' (ie ganja-fortified). Free delivery.

Grand Kampuchea
CAMBODIAN $$

(Map p184; 23 Tola St; mains US$2.50-5) This popular outdoor eatery serves some of the best amok (baked fish with lemongrass-based kreung paste, coconut and chilli in banana leaf) in town, succulent grilled marlin and other sea beasts, and bargain loc lak (peppery stir-fried beef cubes).

VICTORY HILL & BEACH

Even if you're staying elsewhere in town, it's worth checking out this area for its quirks and good-value cuisine.

Tutti Frutti
FRENCH $

(Map p180; mains US$3-6) On the Victory Hill main drag, this is a seriously good deal,

City Centre

with tasty Khmer mains to supplement rich French offerings like beef burgundy, steak tartar and *steak haché oeuf au cheval* (egg on beefsteak). The continental breakfast costs US$2.75 and includes a fruit shake.

Snake House RUSSIAN $$
(Map p180; ☎012-673805; mains US$3.50-9.50; ☺8am-11pm) Snake House serves authentic Russian dishes, sushi and seafood to diners seated at glass-topped tables with live serpents inside. Also has a bar, a guesthouse, various other caged and leashed critters, and a crocodile farm (US$3; free for diners) – one false step and the crocs will eat as well as you did. The absolute epitome of bizarre – only a Russian could dream this up.

Brown's ENGLISH $
(Map p180; Victory Beach; mains US$2.50-5; ☺9am-8.30pm) Right on the sand. Popular for its Asian dishes and burgers. It's next to a friendly Russian-owned bar.

CITY CENTRE
For Sihanoukville's cheapest dining, head to the **food stalls** in and around **Psar Leu** (Map p182; 7 Makara St; ☺7am-9pm) – the vendors across the street, next to the Kampot taxis, are open 24 hours. Options include barbecue chicken, rice porridge or noodles with chicken. More stalls are at the smaller and slightly more expensive **Psar Pinechikam** (Map p182; Boray Kamakor St).

TOP CHOICE ⁄ Holy Cow ORGANIC $$
(Map p182; 83 Ekareach St; mains US$2.50-4.50; ☺8.30am-11pm; ☎✎) Options at this chic-funky cafe-restaurant include bagels with cream cheese, pasta, sandwiches on homemade bread and a good selection of vegie options, including two vegan desserts, both involving chocolate.

Ku-Kai JAPANESE $$
(off Map p182; ☎097 697 1327; 144 7 Makara St; mains US$2-5; ☺5-9pm Tue-Sun) On a side street midway between Serendipity and the city centre, this is a real find, with a delightful ambience and superb light Japanese fare, including tempura dishes and a nightly sashimi special featuring the catch of the day (12 pieces for just US$2.75). It also serves a smattering of Western dishes.

Cabbage Farm Restaurant CAMBODIAN $
(Map p182; small/large mains 8000r/15,000r; ☺11am-10pm) Known to locals as Chom Ka Spey, it gets rave reviews for its seafood and spicy seasonings. An authentic Khmer dining experience. A sign in English on Sereypheap St points the way.

✎ Starfish Bakery & Café ORGANIC $$
(Map p182; www.starfishcambodia.org; behind 62 / Makara St; sandwiches US$3.50-4.50; ☺7am-6pm; ✎) This relaxing, NGO-run garden cafe specialises in filling Western breakfasts and healthy, innovative sandwiches heavy on Mexican and Middle Eastern flavours. Add a cookie and drink to your sandwich for $1. Income goes to sustainable-development projects.

Gelato Italiano ICE CREAM
(Map p182; 49 7 Makara St; Italian ice per scoop 75¢; ☺8am-9pm; ☀) Run by students from Sihanoukville's Don Bosco Hotel School, this Italian-style cafe specialises in gelatos (Italian ices) and also serves various coffee drinks and light meals in a bright, airy space.

Samudera Supermarket SUPERMARKET $
(Map p182; 64 7 Makara St; ☺6am-10pm) Has a good selection of fruit, vegies and Western favourites, including cheese and wine.

OTHER AREAS
TOP CHOICE ⁄ Chez Claude FRENCH $$
(Map p176; ☎934100; www.claudecambodge.com; above 2 Thnou St; mains US$5.50-14) Dou Dou and Claude are your hosts at this all-wood eyrie – perched high above Sokha Beach –

Serendipity

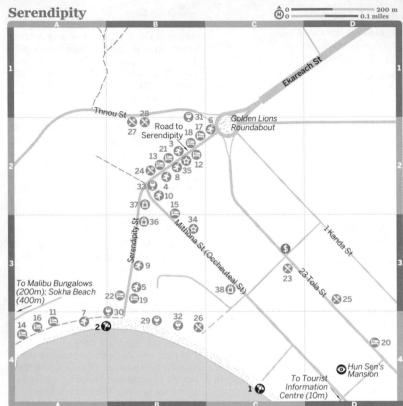

with outstanding French, Vietnamese and Cambodian cuisine, especially seafood. Order paella 48 hours in advance. Access is via an innovative tractor-pulled cable car that would make MacGyver proud.

Treasure Island   CHINESE $
(Koh Pos Beach; mains US$3.50-5.50; ⊙9am-10pm) This 'Hong Kong–style' seafoodery serves the best fish in town. Most everything is fresh and housed in tanks – just point to what you want and the staff will pluck it out. It looks shambolic, but the isolated location on windy Koh Pos Beach is wonderful.

🍷 Drinking

There's no shortage of venues to quaff locally brewed Angkor Beer, available on draught for as little as US$0.50.

Occheuteal Beach is lined with beach bars that are perfect for sundowners, although the beggars on Occheuteal are particularly active at sunset. Hit Serendipity Beach for a more laid-back scene (although the resorts here just miss the sunset).

A few longstanding regular bars remain amid the girlie bars of Victory Hill, while nearby Victory Beach is another good spot to claw a cocktail and take in the sunset.

The late-night action is seaside around the pier dividing Occheuteal and Serendipity beaches.

Sessions   BEACH BAR
(Map p184; Occheuteal Beach) A superb music selection makes Sessions the top sundowner bar on Occheuteal Beach. The crowd of expats and backpackers assembled usually lingers well into the evening before the hard-core partiers move on to Dolphin Shack and JJ's.

JJ's Playground   BEACH BAR
(Map p184; Serendipity Beach) For a while now JJ's has been the go-to spot for those seek-

Serendipity

ing pure late-night debauchery. Have an absinthe shot to get you going.

Dolphin Shack   BEACH BAR
(Map p184; Occheuteal Beach) Like JJ's, it has a host of specials designed to get you drunk fast, and bevies of beautiful backpackers pouring drinks and passing out flyers. It peaks earlier than JJ's.

Utopia   BAR
(Map p184; cnr road to Serendipity & Mithona St; ☺24hr) The prime backpacker warm-up bar, it tends to get a bit sleazy as the night wears on. The crowd usually moves down to the beach around midnight when they turn the music down. Shoot for 25c-beer hour (frequent).

Retox Bar   BAR
(Map p180) This poster- and album cover–plastered pub on the Victory Hill main drag often has live music (from 8.30pm) and jam sessions (instruments available).

Reggae Bar   BAR
(Map p184; Thnou St) It has more Marley on the walls than we've seen in quite some time

(owner Dell is an avid collector) and a clientele diligently paying homage.

Airport   BAR
(Map p180; Victory Beach) Another bizarro Russian concept, the gimmick in this huge bar under a beachfront hangar is an Antonov An-24. Ascend to the cockpit and have a drink. It purports to morph into a disco – 'fashionable disco flights', trumpets the calling card – but it rarely shows much of a pulse late at night. That's a shame because this place has serious party potential.

Monkey Republic   BAR
(Map p184; road to Serendipity) The bar and upstairs chill-out area are ideal for meeting other travellers.

☆ Entertainment

Top Cat Cinema   CINEMA
(Map p184; ☎012 790630; road to Serendipity; tickets US$3.50; ☺11am-3am) This minicinema shows films on an 8m high-def screen (for groups of at least six) or on large flat-screen TVs (for smaller groups). Has cosy satellite

chairs and powerful air-con, and can arrange happy pizza delivery (best for Cheech and Chong flicks).

Galaxy Cinema CINEMA
(Map p184; 📞017 721677; Occheuteal St; tickets US$3) A newer cinema in the vein of Top Cat, it has regular screenings starting at 7pm or you can rent it out for private viewings.

🛍 Shopping

Funky restaurant Holy Cow sells some fashionable clothing upstairs.

M'lop Tapang Gift Shop TEXTILES
(Map p184; www.mloptapang.org; Serendipity St) Run by a local NGO that works with at-risk children, this shop sells good-quality bags, scarves and T-shirts made by street kids (and their families) so that they can attend school instead of peddling on the beach. Several other handicrafts shops are right nearby.

Starfish HANDICRAFTS
(Map p182; www.starfishcambodia.org; behind 62 7 Makara St; ⏱7am-6pm) On the premises of the bakery of the same name, the silks and other gifts sold here support a sustainable livelihood for poor local families.

Cambodia Children's Painting Project ART
(Map p184; www.letuscreate.org; Serendipity St) Another NGO that works with underprivileged kids; you can buy small paintings (US$4) and postcards here. The volunteer backpackers are happy to tell you more about the project.

Q&A BOOKS
(Map p184; Mithona St; ⏱7.30am-7.30pm) A pleasant secondhand bookshop behind Occheuteal Beach, with 8000 titles in over 20 languages.

Mr Heinz BOOKS
(Map p182; 219 Ekareach St; ⏱9am-6pm) Stocks 6500 books in over 10 languages, including lots of used English paperbacks.

ℹ Information

Dangers & Annoyances
Theft is a problem on Occheuteal Beach, so leave your valuables in your room. It's often children who do the deed, sometimes in conjunction with adults. Arriving in a team, one or more will distract you while another lifts whatever valuables are lying on your towel. Or they'll strike when you're out swimming.

Even if you aren't robbed you'll probably tire of the steady stream of beggars, many of them children or amputees, on Occheuteal Beach. NGO M'lop Tapang, which exists to improve the welfare of street kids, advises to never give money or food to children begging on the beach.

As in Phnom Penh, drive-by bag snatchings occasionally happen and are especially dangerous when you're riding a moto. Hold your shoulder bags tightly in front of you, especially at night.

At night, men and especially women should avoid walking alone along dark, isolated beaches and roads.

The currents off Occheuteal can be deceptively strong, especially during the wet season.

One annoyance for locals is underdressed foreigners wandering about town. Cambodia is not Thailand; Khmers are generally more conservative than their neighbours. Just look at the Cambodians frolicking in the sea – most are fully dressed. Wearing bikinis on the beach is fine, but cover up elsewhere. Topless or nude bathing is a definite no-no.

Internet Access
The city centre's many **internet shops** (per hr 4000r) are on Ekareach St near the corner of Sopheakmongkol St. Many guesthouses and shops along the road to Serendipity have a few public internet terminals. Internet outfits are sprinkled along the road to Serendipity and can also be found at Ravuth Travel on Serendipity Beach and near K2 restaurant on Occheuteal Beach. On Victory Hill, try **TTS Internet Service** (Map p180; Ekareach St, Victory Hill; per hr 4000r; ⏱7.30am-11pm).

Medical Services
CT Clinic (Map p182; 📞936666, 081 886666; 47 Boray Kamakor St; ⏱24hr for emergencies) The best medical clinic in town. Can administer rabies shots and snake serum.

Money
Sihanoukville's banks – all with ATMs – are in the city centre along Ekareach St. ATMs can also be found around Serendipity and at Victory Hill.
ANZ Royal Bank (Map p182; 215 Ekareach St)
ANZ Royal Bank ATM (Map p184; 23 Tola St) In front of the Golden Sand Resort.
Canadia Bank (Map p182; 197 Ekareach St) No fees on ATM withdrawals.

Post
Post office (Map p182; 19 7 Makara St) Over the road from Psar Leu.

Tourist Information
Tourist Information Centre (Map p184; Occheuteal St; ⏱9am-11.30pm & 2-5pm Mon-Sat) Don't expect much out of Sihanoukville's tourist information centres. The best is this

one just off Occheuteal Beach. It has brochures and can help you with hotel reservations (just in case you can't find a room in one of Sihanoukville's 75,000 hotels).

Travel Agencies

Ana Travel (☎016 499915; www.anatraveland tours.com; road to Serendipity; ⊙8am-10pm) Handles Cambodia visa extensions (for one/ three/six/12 months US$50/85/160/295) and arranges Vietnam visas in one hour (US$45 plus US$3 service charge).

Eco-Trek Tours (☎012 987073; ecotrektours cambodia@yahoo.com; road to Serendipity; ⊙8am-10pm) Associated with the knowledgeable folks at Mick and Craig's guesthouse, this travel agency has information on just about anything. It also hires out mountain bikes (per day US$2) and can direct you to good rides.

Visas

For help extending a Cambodian visa, contact Ana Travel.

Vietnamese consulate (Map p176, ☎934039, 310 Ekareach St; ⊙8am-noon & 2-4pm Mon-Sat) Issues some of the world's speediest Vietnamese visas (US$45/90/120 for one/ three/six months), often on the spot. Bring a passport photo.

❶ Getting There & Away

National Highway 4 (NH4), which links Sihanoukville to Phnom Penh (230km), is in excellent condition, but because of heavy truck traffic and the prevalence of high-speed overtaking on blind corners, this is one of Cambodia's most dangerous highways; it's doubly dicey around dusk and at night.

NH3 to Kampot (105km) and NH48 to Koh Kong (220km) and the Thailand border (230km) are also in tip-top shape.

Air

Temple-beach combo holidays are now possible with the launch in late 2011 of direct flights between Siem Reap and Sihanoukville (US$85). These thrice-weekly flights were launched on a trial basis by **Cambodia Angkor Airlines** (www .cambodiaangkorair.com). If they are successful one can expect more routes to be opened – most likely to Phnom Penh and possibly to international destinations such as Ho Chi Minh City, Bangkok and Vietnam's Phu Quoc Island.

The airport is 15km east of town, just off the NH4. Figure on US$5/7 for a one-way moto/ *remork*.

Bus

All of the major bus companies have frequent connections with Phnom Penh (US$3.75 to $6, four hours) from early morning until at least 2pm, after which trips are sporadic. The cheapest is Capitol Tour. Virak Buntham runs the last trip at 8.30pm, while Capitol Tour, GST and Paramount Angkor have late-afternoon trips.

Bookings made through hotels and travel agencies incur a commission. Most travel agents only work with two or three bus companies, so ask around if you need to leave at a different time than what's being offered.

Virak Buntham and Kampot Tours & Travel run minibuses to Kampot (US$6, 1½ hours), that continue to Kep (US$10, 2½ hours) and Ha Tien in Vietnam (US$16, five hours). Travel agents can arrange hotel pick-ups. See p351 for details on crossing the border with Vietnam at Prek Chak.

Virak Buntham and Rith Mony have morning buses to Bangkok (US$25, change buses on the Thai side) via Koh Kong (US$7, four hours). Paramount Angkor has daily services to Koh Kong, Siem Reap, Battambang and Saigon. GST has a night bus to Siem Reap and day buses to Battambang and Saigon. Virak Buntham also has a night bus to Siem Reap (US$18, nine hours).

Most bus departures originate at the company terminals on Ekareach St and stop at the **new bus station** (Map p176; Mittapheap Kampuchea Soviet St) on the way out of town.

Bus companies:

Capitol Tour (Map p182; ☎934042; Ekareach St)

Kampot Tours & Travel (☎in Kampot 092 125556)

GST (Map p182; ☎6339666; Ekareach St)

Mekong Express (Map p182; ☎934189; Ekareach St)

Paramount Angkor (Map p182; ☎017 525366; Ekareach St)

Phnom Penh Sorya (Map p182; ☎933888; Ekareach St)

Rith Mony (Map p182; ☎012 644585; Ekareach St)

Virak Buntham (Map p182; ☎016 754358; Ekareach St)

Share Taxi

Cramped share taxis (US$6 per person, US$45 per car) and minibuses (15,000r) to Phnom Penh depart from the new bus station until about 8pm. Avoid the minibuses if you value things like comfort and your life. Hotels can arrange taxis to Phnom Penh for US$50 to US$60 (about four hours).

Share taxis to Kampot (US$5, 1½ hours) leave mornings only from an open lot across 7 Makara St from Psar Leu. This lot and the new bus station are good places to look for rides to Koh Kong or the Thai border. If nobody's sharing, expect to pay US$45 to US$60 to the Thai border.

❶ Getting Around

To/From the Bus Station

Arriving in Sihanoukville, buses stop at the bus terminal, then most (but not all) continue to their central terminals. Prices to the Serendipity Beach area from the new bus station are fixed at a pricey US$2/6 for a moto/*remork*, so continue to the centre if possible and get a cheaper, shorter *remork* ride from there.

Bicycle

Bicycles can be hired from many guesthouses for about US$1.50 a day, or try Eco-Trek Tours (p187) for mountain bikes.

Moto & Remork

Sihanoukville's moto drivers are notorious for aggressively touting passers-by and – more than anywhere else in Cambodia – shamelessly trying to overcharge, so haggle hard (with a smile) over the price before setting out.

A moto/*remork* should cost about US$1/2 from the centre to Serendipity, Occheuteal and Victory Beaches and Victory Hill. *Remorks* from Serendipity to Victory Hill/Beach should cost US$2 to US$3 (they like to ask US$5 for this trip).

Motorbikes can be rented from many guesthouses for US$5 to US$7 a day. For fund-raising purposes, the police sometimes 'crack down' on foreign drivers. Common violations: no driver's licence, no helmet, and no wing mirrors and – everybody's favourite – driving with the lights on during the day.

Hiring a moto (including the driver) for the day costs US$10 plus petrol; a *remork* is about US$20 a day.

Around Sihanoukville

REAM NATIONAL PARK ឧទ្យានជាតិរាម

Just 15km east of Sihanoukville, this large park offers good trekking in primary forest, invigorating boat trips through coastal mangroves and long stretches of unspoilt beach. This is an easy escape for those looking to flee the crowds of Sihanoukville.

The park is home to breeding populations of several regionally and globally endangered birds of prey, including the Brahminy kite, grey-headed fish eagle and white-bellied sea eagle – look for them soaring over **Prek Toeuk Sap Estuary**. Endangered birds that feed on the mudflats include the lesser adjutant, milky stork and painted stork.

Despite its protected status, Ream is gravely endangered by planned tourist development, especially along its coastline. By visiting, you can demonstrate that the park, in its natural state, is not only priceless to humanity but also a valuable economic resource for Sihanoukville.

◉ Sights & Activities

Jungle walks led by rangers – most, but not all, speak English – are easy to arrange (hiking unaccompanied is not allowed) at **park headquarters** (☑016 767686, 012 875096; ☉7am-5pm), opposite the airport entrance. Two-hour walks in the forest behind the headquarters cost US$6 per person. Four- to six-hour treks further into the park's mountainous interior cost US$10 per person. It's best (but not obligatory) to phone ahead. The income generated goes to help protect the park.

Somewhat more popular are ranger-led **boat trips** through the mangrove channels of the Prek Toeuk Sap Estuary. These leave from the coastal Prek Toeuk Sap ranger station, which is about 3km east of the park HQ along the NH4 – the rangers at HQ will help you get there and arrange for a boat to be waiting for you. From the Prek Toeuk Sap station it's a one-hour boat ride (US$35 return for one to three persons) to the fishing village of **Ta Ben**. Full-day trips (US$50 per group) continue another hour east to the village of Andoung Toeuk, where a path leads 25 minutes through the jungle to **Koh Sampoach Beach**, the park's finest.

It's possible to overnight near Andoung Toeuk in an overwater **bungalow** (per person US$5) with outside toilets and no electricity; meals are available from villagers. The bungalow is at the ranger post known as **Dolphin Station** because, from December to April, you can often spot dolphins, especially in the morning. Bring your own snorkelling gear on trips out here.

To get to some **deserted beaches** on your own, drive south from the park HQ and the airport for about 9km along a sealed road until you get to Ream Naval Base. Jog left around the base and follow the dirt roads to a series of long white beaches lined with casuarina trees. Keep walking east along these beaches and eventually you'll get to Koh Sampoach Beach.

Ream National Park's territory includes two islands with some fine snorkelling, **Koh Thmei** (p174) and – just off Vietnam's Phu Quoc Island – **Koh Seh**, which is best accessed from Koh Thmei.

🛏 Sleeping

Ream Beach Guesthouse   GUESTHOUSE **$**
(☑097 727 4510; r US$10-15; ☏) The park's only guesthouse is on the water in a village

SINS OF COMMISSION, SINS OF OMISSION

At Sihanoukville's new bus station, only members of the official 'motodup association' (read: cartel) are allowed to pick up arriving passengers (independent drivers sent to fetch someone must show their charge's name). As a result, you may be quoted inflated prices for onward local transport. Bargaining is likely to be futile – if you don't agree to the set price (usually 8000r to the beaches) no one else will take you. You can try walking out to the street, but there's not a whole lot of traffic in this part of town. You may also have trouble shaking the possibly persistent driver the cartel has assigned you according to a rotation system. Confrontations between independents and cartel drivers sometimes develop. The situation with remorks – ideal for travel with a big pack – is similar. The set price for remorks to the Serendipity area is US$6.

Many guesthouses pay US$2 to moto drivers who bring them customers, but some places pay drivers far higher sums – US$4 or even US$5 – to send custom their way, so if you've just arrived, getting your moto guy to take you where you want may turn into a battle of wills. If your chosen hostelry is one that won't ante up, don't be surprised to hear that it's closed, has contaminated water or is 'full of prostitutes'.

about 2km before the naval base. When we dropped by it had just been taken over by an Italian-Uzbek couple, who were hard at work sprucing up the somewhat dark basement rooms, and building an outdoor restaurant to take advantage of the prime sunset views. They have one kayak that guests can use for free. Koh Ta Kiev (p174) is just offshore.

ⓘ Getting There & Around

Sihanoukville travel agencies offer day trips to the park for about US$20, including a boat ride, a jungle walk and lunch.

Ream National Park is a breeze to get to – just follow the NH4 east to the airport turn-off, which is 15km from the Cambrew junction at the junction of NH4 and Wat Leu Rd. Go right and drive 500m to the park HQ. Continue south along this road to get to Ream Navy Base.

A return trip from Sihanoukville by moto should cost US$7 to US$15, a remork US$15 to US$20. The price depends on how well the driver speaks English and how long you stay.

KBAL CHHAY CASCADES

Thanks to their appearance in *Pos Keng Kong* (The Giant Snake; 2000), the most successful Cambodian film of the post–civil war era, these **cascades** (admission US$1) on the Prek Toeuk Sap River draw huge numbers of domestic tourists. That's why there are so many **picnicking platforms** (per day 5000r, more on holidays).

From the parking area, a rough log **toll bridge** (for locals/tourists 300r/500r) leads to several miniature sandy coves, more lounging areas and some perilous rapids. The best spot for a safe, refreshing dip, by children as

well as adults, is across another bridge, on the far bank of a cool, crystal-clear tributary of the brown-tinted main river. Not much water flows here in the dry season.

To get here, head east along NH4 for 5.5km from the Cambrew junction and then, at the sign, north along a wide dirt road for 8km. By moto/*remork* a return trip should cost US$7/15.

KAMPOT PROVINCE

Kampot Province (ខេត្តកំពត) has emerged as one of Cambodia's most alluring destinations thanks to a hard-to-beat combination of old colonial architecture, abundant natural attractions and easy intraregional transport. Enchanted visitors often end up staying in the sleepy, atmospheric provincial capital of Kampot rather longer than planned.

The province is renowned for producing some of the world's finest pepper (see p193). Durian haters be warned: Kampot is also Cambodia's main producer of this odoriferous fruit.

Kampot   កំពត

📞 033 / POP 33,000

Ever more visitors are being seduced, gently, by the charming riverside town of Kampot, with its relaxed atmosphere and one of Cambodia's finest (though run-down) ensembles of French colonial architecture. Eclipsed as a port when Sihanoukville was founded in 1959, Kampot makes an excellent base for exploring Bokor National Park and the verdant coast east towards Vietnam, including Kep and several superb cave-temples. Not on offer here: a beach.

◉ Sights

The most enjoyable activity is strolling along the riverside promenade and along streets lined with decrepit French-era shophouses. Some of the best colonial architecture can be found in the triangle delineated by the central Durian Roundabout, the post office and the **old French bridge**, which is quite a sight: destroyed during the Khmer Rouge's rise to power, it has been repaired in a mishmash of styles. The **old cinema** (7 Makara St), **Kampot Prison** and the **old governor's mansion** – the latter two are very French – are worth a look (from the outside).

Kampot Traditional Music School   MUSIC
(☺6-9pm Mon-Fri) Visitors are welcome to observe training sessions and/or performances every evening at this school that trains orphaned and disabled children in traditional music and dance.

🏃 Activities

Long lazy, Kampot now has several guesthouses that actively promote a range of mostly water-based activities. Olly's is the paddle-board specialist and also hires out windsurfers. Les Manguieres does river kayaks. And Villa Vedici is a jack of all trades, with kitesurfing and wakeboarding (and foosball) among many pursuits.

Seeing Hands Massage 5   MASSAGE
(per hr US$4; ☺7am-11pm) Blind masseurs and masseuses offer soothing bliss.

☞ Tours

Some of the riverside places send boats out on evening **firefly watching tours**. Many a sceptic has returned from these trips in awe. Best on a starry night when the phosphorescence peaks.

The big tour is Bokor Hill Station (p195), which everybody and their grandmother offers. Excursions also hit the pepper farms and other sights in the countryside around Kampot and nearby Kep.

Kampot Dreamtime Tours   SIGHTSEEING, BOAT TOUR
(☏089 908417; www.kampotluxurytours.com) Runs upmarket countryside trips in air-con vans (per person US$35) and wine-

and-cheese river cruises in a boat formerly owned by King Norodom Sihanouk.

Sok Lim Tours   SIGHTSEEING TOUR
(☏012 719872, 012 796919; www.soklimtours .com) Kampot's oldest and largest outfit, well regarded all around. Has trained pepper-plantation guides.

Kampot Tours & Travel   SIGHTSEEING TOUR
(☏633 5556, 092 125556) Its van fleet can get you a shared ride to just about anywhere; also does the standard area excursions.

Captain Chim's   BOAT TOUR
(☏012 321043) Sunset cruises on a traditional boat cost US$5 per head and include a cold beer.

🛏 Sleeping

Generally people prefer staying out of town on the river, but the charming city proper certainly has its merits. After a chilly day atop Bokor, a hot shower might be a welcome treat.

CITY PROPER

[TOP CHOICE] **La Java Bleue**   BOUTIQUE HOTEL **$$**
(☏667 6679; www.lajavableue-kampot.com; r incl breakfast US$45; ❀☞) Newly opened in the centre of town, it's a colonial gem with three large rooms decorated with exquisite furniture. You're just a pleasant two-minute stroll from the river here.

Rikitikitavi   BOUTIQUE HOTEL **$$**
(☏012 235102; www.rikitikitavi-kampot.com; River Rd; r incl breakfast US$40-45; ❀☞) Rikitikitavi has six of the classiest and cleanest rooms in town. They have stunning wood floors and beams, four-poster beds and elegant mirrors, plus flat-screen TVs and DVD players.

Bokor Mountain Lodge   HISTORIC HOTEL **$$**
(☏932314; www.bokorlodge.com; River Rd; r in back/front incl breakfast US$30/40; ❀@☞) In an imposing century-old colonial building facing the river, it's a bit torn and frayed these days, but undeniably charismatic. Pricier rooms come with a river view. The bar has live music on Sunday.

Mea Culpa   GUESTHOUSE **$$**
(☏012 504769; www.meaculpakampot.com; r US$20-25; ❀☞) Behind the governor's mansion in a palatial villa, the 10 spacious rooms come with big windows, a DVD library and free tea and coffee, plus the best pizza in town, from a wood-fired oven.

Kampot

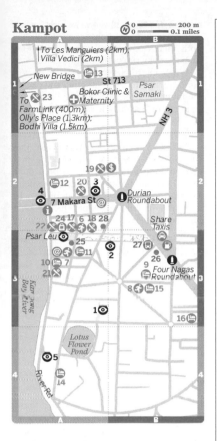

To Les Manguiers (2km);
Villa Vedici (2km)

New Bridge

St 713

Psar
Samaki

Bokor Clinic &
Maternity

To
FarmLink (400m);
Olly's Place (1.3km);
Bodhi Villa (1.5km)

NH 3

7 Makara St

Durian
Roundabout

Share
Taxis

Psar Leu

Four Nagas
Roundabout

Kampong Bay River

Lotus
Flower
Pond

River Rd

Kampot

Sights
1 Kampot Prison A3
2 Kampot Traditional Music
School...B3
3 Old Cinema A2
4 Old French Bridge.................................A2
5 Old Governor's Mansion A4

Activities, Courses & Tours
Captain Chim's............................(see 17)
6 Kampot Dreamtime Tours A2
7 Seeing Hands Massage 5.....................A3
8 Sok Lim Tours B3

Sleeping
9 Blissful Guesthouse.............................B3
10 Bokor Mountain Lodge A3
11 La Java Bleue...A3
12 Little Garden...A2
13 Long Villa Guesthouse A1
14 Mea Culpa..A4
15 Orchid Guesthouse...............................B3
Rikitikitavi ....(see 21)
16 Ta Eng..B3

Eating
17 Captain Chim's......................................A2
18 Epic Arts Café..A2
19 Fruit Stalls & Little Eateries................A2
20 Night Market...A2
21 Rikitikitavi A3
22 Rusty Keyhole A2
23 Ta Ouv Restaurant...............................A1

Shopping
24 Kepler's Kampot Books A2

Transport
Capitol Tour..................................(see 26)
Hua Lian ....(see 27)
25 Kampot Tours & Travel.........................A3
26 Paramount Angkor B3
27 Phnom Penh Sorya...............................B3
28 Sean Ly..A2

Blissful Guesthouse   GUESTHOUSE $
(092 494331; www.blissfulguesthouse.com; 3-bed drm US$2, r without/with bathroom US$4/8) An old-time backpacker vibe lives on at this atmospheric wooden house. Has a popular bar-restaurant and slightly shabby rooms.

Orchid Guest House   GUESTHOUSE $
(092 226996; orchidguesthousekampot@yahoo.com; r with fan/air-con US$5/15, bungalows US$10; ✳@✿) Set in a manicured garden, this hostelry has comfortable air-con rooms, less comfortable fan rooms and three bungalows by a fish pond toward the back.

Little Garden   GUESTHOUSE $
(012-256901; River Rd; d with fan/air-con from US$8/15) This high-rise punches above its weight, with clean and cared-for rooms in addition to a prime riverfront location.

Ta Eng   GUESTHOUSE $
(012 330058; r US$5-10; @✿) On a street lined with 1960s row houses, Ta Eng is the best of the Khmer-style high-rises thanks to squeaky-clean rooms and friendly family ownership.

Long Villa Guesthouse   GUESTHOUSE $
(012 210820; longvillaguesthouse@yahoo.com; 75 St 713; r with fan/air-con from US$5/10; @✿✳) A family-run travellers' sanctuary with 15 smallish, good-value rooms.

OUT OF TOWN
The out-of-town places aren't *that* far out of town – usually under a 10-minute *remork*

SOUTH COAST KAMPOT

ride from the centre. All of them are on the river and have over-water pavilions or docks to facilitate swimming. New resorts are opening fast on the west bank of the river near Bodhi Villa and Olly's.

Les Manguiers `TOP CHOICE` RIVER RESORT **$$**
(📞092 330050; www.mangokampot.com; r US$10-17, bungalows US$25-44; @🛜) This rambling, family-friendly garden complex, smack dab on the river 2km north of the new bridge, is rich with activities, including kayaking (single/tandem US$4/6 for two hours), swimming, firefly-watching boat trips, badminton and pétanque. You can jump into the water from one of four over-water gazebos. The rooms and tasteful wooden bungalows all come with fan and cold water. Meals are served *table d'hôte* style.

Olly's Place HOSTEL **$**
(📞092 605837; www.ollysplacekampot.com; r US$3-7; 🛜) Over on the west side of the river you'll find this mellow retreat, run by French-speaking Belgian Olly. The thatched bungalows and basic rooms are silly-good value considering the relaxed vibe and plum location. Use of windsurfers and paddle boards is free.

Bodhi Villa HOSTEL **$**
(📞012 728884; www.bodhivilla.com; dm US$2.50-3, r US$5-12; 🛜) Near Olly's, Bodhi is popular with Phnom Penh expats on weekends, when huge parties often erupt. At other times it's a peaceful hideaway on the river with a good waterfront chill-out bar and a variety of rooms, including one floating bungalow. It has a fully equipped digital recording studio and live music every Friday from 7.30pm, plus a speedboat for hire.

Villa Vedici RIVER RESORT **$$**
(📞089 290714; www.villavedici.com; r/guesthouses US$25/90; ✳@🛜🏊) Villa Vedici is a playground for kids and adults alike – along with kitesurfing and a speedboat for water-skiing and wakeboarding, it has Playstation on a gargantuan flat-screen in the main building's airy living room. In addition to four functional rooms in the main building, there's a guesthouse that sleeps eight, plus one bungalow on the river.

🍴 Eating & Drinking

Quite a few restaurants line River Rd south of the old French bridge. There are **fruit stalls and little eateries** (⊘7am-10pm) next to the Canadia Bank and, nearby, a **night market** (7 Makara St; ⊘4pm-midnight) where options include chicken rice soup (4000r). Both places have Khmer desserts (1000r) such as sticky rice with coconut sauce.

A few guesthouses are worthy of your dime – Blissful Guesthouse and Bokor Mountain Lodge have Sunday roasts, or head out to Les Manguiers.

Rikitikitavi `TOP CHOICE` FUSION **$$**
(📞012 235102; www.rikitikitavi-kampot.com; River Rd; mains US$5-8; 🛜📞) Named after the mongoose in Rudyard Kipling's *The Jungle Book*, this riverfront terrace restaurant matches its guesthouse in style and ambience. It's known for its Kampot pepper chicken, burritos, slow-cooked curry and salads.

Rusty Keyhole FUSION **$$**
(📞092 758536; River Rd; small/large/extra-large ribs US$5/7.50/10; ⊘8am-11pm Nov-May, 11am-11pm Jun-Oct; 🛜) Popular riverfront bar-restaurant serving widely praised food. Order the famous ribs in advance – they sell out.

Epic Arts Café 🍴 CAFE **$**
(www.epicarts.org.uk; mains US$2-4; ⊘7am-6pm; 🛜) A great place for breakfast, homemade cakes or tea, this mellow eatery is staffed by deaf and disabled young people. Profits fund arts workshops for disabled Cambodians.

Captain Chim's CAFE **$**
(mains US$1-3) Kampot's best budget eats are here. Best known for breakfast, Khmer faves like *loc lak* will fill you up any time of day. Ask about Cambodian cooking classes.

Ta Ouv Restaurant CAMBODIAN **$**
(River Rd; mains US$4; ⊘10am-2pm & 6-10pm) Built on stilts over the river by the new bridge, it specialises in seafood (crab with peppercorns is a favourite), with plenty of other meat and vegie options.

Green House BAR
(Kampot River West Bank; mains US$3-5) An intriguing new addition to the Kampot scene, it occupies the former house of Snowy's (aka Maxine's), a legendary Phnom Penh bar that closed in 2011. The house was transported here by truck. It's in a secluded spot on the river, 4.5km north of Bodhi Villa.

🛍 Shopping

Kepler's Kampot Books BOOKS
(⊘8am-8pm) Secondhand books plus pepper, *kramas* (scarves) and fine T-shirts.

ℹ Information

The free and often hilarious *Kampot Survival Guide* takes a tongue-in-cheek look at local expat life, and there's also the free *Coastal* guide to Kampot and Kep, with adverts and info on local businesses.

Internet Access

There's a strip of copy shops with internet access southwest of the Durian roundabout on 7 Makara St.

Medical Services

Bokor Clinic & Maternity (☎932289; consultation US$10; ☺emergency 24hr, consultation 7am-noon & 2-6pm) The best medical clinic in town, with four English-speaking doctors and ultrasound, X-ray and ECG machines.

Money

Canadia Bank Has an ATM with no transaction fees and turbo air con.

Tourist Information

Tourist Information Centre (☎6555541, 012 462286; lonelyguide@gmail.com; River Rd; ☺7am-7pm) Led by the knowledgeable Mr Pov, Kampot's new tourist office is the main point of contact for assembling groups for Bokor National Park trips. Also doles out free advice and can also arrange transport to area attractions like caves, falls and Kompong Trach.

ℹ Getting There & Away

Kampot, on NH3, is 148km southwest of Phnom Penh, 105km east of Sihanoukville and 25km northwest of Kep.

Paramount Angkor, Capitol Tour, Phnom Penh Sorya and Hua Lian sell tickets from offices opposite the Total gas station near the Four Nagas Roundabout. All have two or three daily trips to Phnom Penh (US$3.50 to US$4.50, four hours), the last of which depart at 1pm; some go via Kep (US$2, 45 minutes). Across the street you can catch share taxis (US$6), packed-to-the-gills minibuses (16,000r) and private taxis (US$40) to Phnom Penh. Sorya also has daily trips to Siem Reap and Battambang.

Share taxis to Sihanoukville cost US$5 and a private taxi from the taxi lot is US$30. Daily Kampot Tours & Travel and Virak Buntham minibuses go west to Sihanoukville (US$6, 1½ hours) and Koh Kong (US$13, four to five hours with a bus transfer); and east to Ha Tien, Vietnam (US$10, 2½ hours). Guesthouses can arrange tickets and pick-ups.

A moto/*remork*/taxi to Kep should run about US$8/12/20.

ℹ Getting Around

A moto ride in town costs 2000r (3000r in the evening); *remorks* cost about US$1. To get to the riverside guesthouses outside of town it should cost about 10,000/6000r for a moto/*remork*.

KAMPOT PEPPER

Before Cambodia's civil war, no Paris restaurant worth its salt would be without pepper from Kampot Province, but the country's pepper farms were all but destroyed by the Khmer Rouge, who believed in growing rice, not spice.

Today, thanks to a group of eco-entrepreneurs and foodies who are passionate about pepper, Kampot-grown peppercorns, delicate and aromatic but packing a powerful punch, are making a comeback.

Kampot pepper is grown on family farms that dot Phnom Voa and nearby valleys, northwest of Kompong Trach, where the unique climate and farmers' fidelity to labour-intensive growing techniques produce particularly pungent peppercorns. In fact, Kampot pepper is so extraordinary that it's about to become Cambodia's first-ever product to receive a 'geographical indication' (GI), just like French cheeses. Increased sales have made a huge difference for Kampot's pepper families and especially for the girls who were able to get married because their parents could finally afford the dowry.

Peppercorns are picked from February to May. Black pepper is plucked from the trees when the corns are starting to turn yellow and turns black during sun-drying; red pepper is picked when the fruit is completely mature; and mild white pepper is soaked in water to remove the husks. September to February is the season for green pepper, whose sprigs have to be eaten almost immediately after harvesting – the Crab Market restaurants of Kep are one of the best places to experience its gentle freshness.

A packet of pepper makes an excellent souvenir or gift: the corns are lightweight and unbreakable, and if stored properly – that is, *not* ground! – will stay fresh for years. In Kampot, you can purchase pouches of peerless pepper, and see pepper being dried and sorted, at **FarmLink** (☎6902354; www.farmlink-cambodia.com; ☺8-11am & 2-5pm Mon-Fri), one of the pioneers of GI pepper production. It's just over the New Bridge; take the first right and look for it on the left.

Bicycles can be hired or borrowed for free from many guesthouses, which can also arrange motorbike hire, or try the following:

Captain Chim's Motorbike hire for US$4 per day.

Sean Ly (☑012 944687; ◷7am-9pm) Rents 125cc bikes for US$4 a day and 250cc trail bikes for US$12.

Around Kampot

The limestone hills east towards Kep are honeycombed with caves. Phnom Chhnork, surrounded by blazingly green countryside, is a real gem and can easily be visited in an afternoon along with Phnom Sorsia.

PHNOM CHHNORK   ភ្នំល្ងៀក

The base of **Phnom Chhnork** (admission US$1) is a short walk through the rice fields from Wat Ang Sdok, where a monk will collect the entry fee and a gaggle of friendly local kids, some with precociously fluent English, will offer their services as guides.

A well-tended staircase with 203 steps leads up the hillside and down into a cavern as graceful as a Gothic cathedral. There you'll be greeted by a **stalactite elephant**, with a second elephant outlined on the flat cliff face to the right. Tiny chirping bats live up near two natural chimneys that soar towards the blue sky, partly blocked by foliage of an impossibly green hue.

Inside the cave's main chamber stands a remarkable 7th-century (Funan-era) **brick temple**, dedicated to Shiva. The temple's brickwork is in superb condition thanks to the protection afforded by the cave. Poke your head inside and check out the ancient stalactite that serves as a *linga*. A slippery passage, flooded in the rainy season, leads through the hill.

Phnom Chhnork occupies a bucolic site surrounded by a quilt of rice paddies and meticulously tended vegetable plots (tomato, cucumber, lettuce, cabbage, mint). The view from up top, and the walk to and from the wat, is especially magical in the late afternoon.

To get to Phnom Chhnork turn left off the NH33 about 5.5km east of Kampot. Look for a sign reading 'Phnom Chhngok Resort' across the road from a Cham mosque. From the turn-off it's 6km to the cave on a bumpy road. A return moto/*remork* ride from Kampot costs about US$6/10.

PHNOM SORSIA   ភ្នំសូរសៀ

Not quite as magical as Phnom Chhnork, **Phnom Sorsia** (Phnom Sia; admission free) has a gaudily painted modern temple and several natural caves.

From the parking area in front of the school, a stairway leads up the hillside to a colourful temple. From there, steps lead left up to **Rung Damrey Saa** (White Elephant Cave). A slippery, sloping staircase where one false step will send you into the abyss leads down and then up and then out through a hole in the other side. Exit the cave and follow the path to the right, which leads back to the temple.

From the colourful temple, steps angle up to the right to the **Bat Cave**. Inside, countless bats flutter and chirp overhead, flying out to the forest and back through a narrow natural chimney. Locals use bamboo poles to hunt the creatures by swatting them out of the air. The circuit ends near a hilltop **stupa** with impressive views.

The turn-off to Phnom Sorsia is on NH33 13.5km southeast of Kampot and 1.3km northwest of the White Horse Roundabout near Kep. Look for a sign reading 'Phnom Sorsia Resort' – from there a dirt road leads about 1km northeast through the rice fields.

TEK CHHOUU ZOO

This privately owned **zoo** (adult/child 16,000/1500r), 8km north of Kampot on the west bank of the Kampot River, has seen better days, but it lets you get *much* closer to the animals – including two elephants you can greet by shaking their trunks – than Western zoos. The animals, most of them rescued from the wildlife trade, appear healthy (some of the monkeys, of half a dozen species, have babies) but sad – and look like they'll appreciate the food your admission fee will buy. The entrance is marked by twin statues of roaring tigers.

TEK CHHOUU RAPIDS   ទឹកឈូរ

Hugely popular with locals, these modest rapids are surrounded by local eateries and – a prerequisite for any proper Khmer day out – picknicking platforms.

About 5km upriver, Cambodia's largest dam, the Chinese-built **Kamchay hydroelectric dam**, was opened in late 2011. Vital stats: 115m high, 568m wide, 193.2MW. The US$280-million project flooded small parts of Bokor National Park.

Bokor National Park

This 1581-sq-km **national park** (Preah Monivong National Park; admission US$5) is famed for its abandoned French hill station, refreshingly cool climate and lush primary rainforest. Threatened animals that live in the park include the tiger (photographed in the last decade with camera traps), leopard, Indian elephant, Asiatic black bear, Malayan sun bear, pileated gibbon, pig-tailed macaque, slow loris and pangolin.

A new road up to the old hill station has been completed and is open to the public, while an ambitious resort project at the summit, including a golf course and casino, was well under way when we visited. The big construction works undoubtedly spoil the ambience at the hill station, but the day and overnight treks that have long been a staple of tourism in the park remain popular.

History

In the early 1920s the French – ever eager to escape the lowland heat – established a hill station atop Phnom Bokor (1080m), known for its dramatic vistas of the coastal plain one vertical kilometre below – and for frequent pea-soup fogs.

The hill station was twice abandoned to the howling winds: first when Vietnamese and Khmer Issarak (Free Khmer) forces overran it in the late 1940s while fighting for independence from France, and again in 1972, when the Lon Nol regime left it to the Khmer Rouge forces that were steadily taking over the countryside. Because of its commanding position, the site was strategically important to all sides during the civil war and was one location the Vietnamese really had to fight for during their 1979 invasion. For several months, the Khmer Rouge held out in the Catholic church while the Vietnamese shot at them from the Bokor Palace, 500m away.

The hill station became a ghost town, its once-grand buildings turned into eerie, windowless shells. Over time they became carpeted with a bright-orange lichen that gives them an other-worldly cast. On cold, foggy days it can get pretty creepy up here as mists drop visibility to nothing and the wind keens through abandoned buildings. Appropriate, then, that the foggy showdown that ends the Matt Dillon crime thriller *City of Ghosts* (2002) was filmed here.

⊙ Sights

Bokor Hill Station   HILL STATION
The key sights of the hill station (ស្ថានីយ័ន្តំបូរគោ), such as the **Bokor Palace**, a grand hotel that opened in 1925, were undergoing

renovations when we visited and will become part of the new resort city.

The squat belfry of the Romanesque-style **Catholic church** still holds aloft its cross, and fragments of glass brick cling to the corners of the nave windows; one side window holds the barest outline of a rusty crucifix. It's easy to imagine a small crowd of French colonials in formal dress assembled here for Sunday Mass. The subdividing walls inside were built by the Khmer Rouge. A bit up the hill, a sheer drop overlooks virgin rainforest.

Other Phnom Bokor sights include lichen-caked **Wat Sampeau Moi Roi** (Five Boats Wat), which offers tremendous views over the jungle to the coastline below, including Vietnam's Phu Quoc Island. Wild monkeys like to hang out around the wat.

From the wat an 11km trail (four or five hours) leads to two-tiered **Popokvil Falls**.

❶ Getting There & Away

To visit the park you can take private transport up the new road, or you can join an organised tour. The standard full-day tour takes you up to the hill station and involves a bit of on-road driving, a bit of off-road driving and a bit of trekking. First you'll be driven 7km to the ranger station west of Kampot. There you'll jump into the ranger's truck and drive about 30 minutes before getting out to start the trekking leg of your journey. After you walk for 1¼ hours, the ranger truck again picks you up and takes you the remaining 1½ hours to the top.

The standard tour costs US$25 per person (minimum four people) and includes all transport, food, an English-speaking guide, water and the park entry fee. Bring your own protection against mosquitoes, leeches, snakes and rain. It's usually easy to hook up with a group through the Tourist Information Centre in Kampot or any travel agent or guesthouse.

Variations on the standard tour, including overnight trips, are theoretically still possible, but sleeping at the hill station is less appealing because of the construction. Bring warm clothes if you're staying overnight as temperatures can plummet as low as 12°C at night in the coldest months (December to February).

The Sam Veasna Center (p341) can organise birding trips to Bokor.

Kep   កែប

📞 036 / POP 35,000

The seaside resort of Kep-del-Mer (Krong Kep, also spelled Kaeb), is a province-level municipality that consists of little more than a small peninsula facing Bokor National

Park and Vietnam's Phu Quoc Island. Famed for its spectacular sunsets and splendid seafood, it was founded as a colonial retreat for the French elite in 1908.

In the 1960s, Cambodian high rollers continued the tradition, but Khmer Rouge rule brought evacuation, followed, in the 1980s, by systematic looting. Today, scores of Kep's luxurious prewar villas remain blackened shells, relics of a once-great (or at least rich and flashy) civilisation that met a sudden and violent end.

Some find Kep a bit soulless because it lacks a centre and accommodation options are spread out all over the place. Others revel in its sleepy vibe, content to relax at their resort, nibble on crab at the famed Crab Market and poke around the mildewed shells of modernist villas, which still give the town a sort of post-apocalyptic feel.

⊙ Sights

Koh Tonsay   ISLAND

Just off Kep, Koh Tonsay (Rabbit Island; កោះទន្សាយ; population 25 families) has the nicest beaches of any Kep-area island – except Phu Quoc, whose loss to Vietnam is still bitterly resented. It's so named because locals say it resembles a rabbit, an example of what too much local brew can do to your imagination. If you like rusticity, come now before the island is changed forever by development.

At the 250m-long, tree-lined **main beach**, which faces west towards the setting sun, you can dine on seafood, lounge around on raised bamboo platforms and overnight in family-run clusters of rudimentary bungalows for US$5 per day.

Many people say Rabbit Island is a 'tropical paradise', but don't expect the sanitised resort version – this one has shorefront flotsam, flies, chickens, packs of dogs and wandering cows.

Other Kep-area islands include **Koh Pos** (Snake Island; about 30 minutes past Rabbit Island), which has a deserted beach and fine snorkelling but no overnight accommodation (getting out there costs US$40 to US$50 for an all-day trip by 10-person boat); and small, beachless **Koh Svai** (Mango Island), whose summit offers nice views.

Boats to Rabbit Island (25 minutes) leave from a pier 2.7km east of the Kep Beach roundabout. Your guesthouse can arrange to get you on a boat for US$10 per person return – make it clear which day you want to

be picked up. A scheduled trip departs daily at 9am for the same price. A private boat arranged at the pier costs US$30 one way for up to seven passengers.

Kep National Park   NATIONAL PARK

(admission 4000r) The interior of Kep peninsula is occupied by Kep National Park, degraded in recent years by illegal logging but finally guarded by a complement of rangers. An 8km circuit around the park, navigable by foot or mountain bike, starts at the park entrance behind Veranda Natural Resort. Fuel up and grab a map of the park at the **Led Zep Cafe** (⊗9.30am-6pm), which is on the trail 300m into the walk. The map is also reprinted in the *Coastal* Kep and Kampot guide.

Led Zep Cafe has also created quirky yellow signs that point the way from the main trail to walking paths leading into the interior of the park. One such path, dubbed Stairway to Heaven, starts directly behind the Beach House guesthouse overlooking Kep Beach. It leads 800m up the hill to a pagoda, a nunnery and – 400m further on – Sunset Rock, with superb views.

Villas   HISTORIC BUILDINGS

From the Northern Roundabout, NH33A heads north past the mildewed shells of handsome mid-20th-century villas that speak of happier, carefree times – and of the terrible years of Khmer Rouge rule and civil war. Built according to the precepts of the modernist style, with clean lines, lots of horizontals and little adornment, they once played host to glittering jet-set parties and may do so again someday, though for the time being many shelter squatters (and, some say, ghosts). Don't get your hopes up about buying one – they were all snapped up for a song in the mid-1990s by well-connected speculators.

🏖 Beaches

Most of Kep's beaches are too shallow and rocky to make for good swimming. You can swim off the beach or the jetty at the Sailing Club, but the water is particularly shallow here.

Kep Beach   BEACH

Centrally located, this is the best beach in town, but it's still somewhat pebbly and tends to fill up with locals on weekends. The eastern end of the shaded **promenade** along the beach is marked by **Sela Cham P'dey**, a statue that depicts a nude fisher's wife waiting expectantly for her husband to return.

Coconut Beach   BEACH
(Chhne Derm Dont) Has dining platforms and eateries. Begins a few hundred metres southeast of Kep Beach, just past the **giant crab statue**.

🏃 Activities

For swimming, you might be better off at one of the resort pools; Kep Lodge and Veranda Natural Resort have good ones that are free if you order some food.

Sailing Club   WATER SPORTS
Open to all, the club hires out sea kayaks, Hobie Cats and windsurfers.

👉 Tours

Kep makes a good base for visiting several delightful cave-temples, including Wat Kiri Sela near Kompong Trach, and Phnom Chhnork and Phnom Sorsia on the road to Kampot. Guesthouses and travel agencies offer half- and full-day tours that take in a few of these sights and usually a pepper plantation, or you could hire an English-speaking *remork* driver and tailor your own countryside tour for about US$20 per day.

🛏 Sleeping

Kep meanders along the shoreline for a good 5km, with the resorts situated at intervals along its length. The ostensible centre is around the Kep Beach Roundabout and Kep Beach, but there isn't much happening there. Some of the best options are not on the water but on the other side of the highway in the hills leading up to Kep National Park.

Rooms at all midrange and top-end places listed include breakfast.

TOP CHOICE Vine Retreat   LODGE $$
(☑011 706231; www.thevineretreat.com; d US$25-45; @🛜🏊) This socially responsible ecolodge is near Chamcar Bei village, 13km northeast of Kep, inside the geographical indication zone for Kampot pepper. The eight comfortable rooms, with solar hot water and decent mattresses, look out on an organic farm and a naturally filtered swimming pond; the top floor has a quiet chill-out area. Divine set meals average US$11. To get there from the White Horse Roundabout, head east for 3.5km to a well-marked turn-off on the left. The resort is 2.8km from the turn-off.

Kep Lodge   RESORT $$
(☑092 435330; www.keplodge.com; r US$15-38; @🛜🏊) A friendly place whose bungalows have thatch roofs, tile floors and verandas. The grounds are lush, the common area relaxing, and the restaurant overlooking the pool serves great food and has very nice sunset views. The one US$15 bungalow is often booked out. The turn-off to Kep Lodge is 600m north of the northern roundabout towards Kampot.

Le Bout du Monde   BOUTIQUE HOTEL $$$
(☑011 964181; http://leboutdumonde.new.fr; r US$20-85; 🛜) The French-owned 'end of the earth', the highest up of all the hillside resorts, has a dozen gorgeous bungalows with wraparound verandas, Angkorian sculptures, beautiful wood furniture and stone-walled bathrooms. The view from the restaurant is Kep's best.

🌿 Jasmine Valley   RESORT $$
(☑097 7917635; www.jasminevalley.com; r US$24-64; 🛜🏊) The funky bungalows here are raised dramatically amid dense jungle foliage just below Kep National Park. There are good hikes around, and green credits include solar power and a natural swimming pool complete with pond critters. It's about 2.5km in from the Rabbit Island pier (follow the signs). A moto/*remork* from the Crab Market should cost US$2/3.

Veranda Natural Resort   RESORT $$
(☑012 888619; www.veranda-resort.com; d/tr from US$60/68; ❄🛜🏊) This rambling colony of hillside bungalows built of wood, bamboo and stone and connected by a maze of stilted walkways is a memorable spot for a romantic getaway. Check out a few rooms because they vary wildly. The food is excellent and sunset views from the restaurant pavilion stunning. It's constantly expanding and constantly raising prices.

Tree Top Bungalows   HOSTEL $
(☑012 515191; khmertreetop@hotmail.com; r US$4-25; @🛜) The highlights here are the towering stilted bamboo 'treehouse' bungalows with sea views; each pair shares a bathroom. Otherwise unspectacular. Cool off at neighbouring Kep Lodge's pool.

Knai Bang Chatt   RESORT $$$
(☑078 888556; www.knaibangchatt.com; r US$165-325; ❄@🛜🏊) This ultrachic 11-room boutique hotel, occupying three waterfront villas from the 1960s, has a beachside infinity pool

Kep

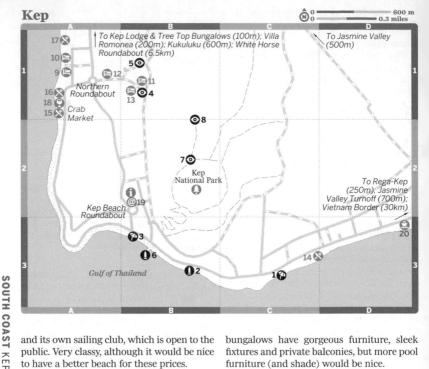

N ⊙ 0   600 m
0   0.3 miles

To Kep Lodge & Tree Top Bungalows (100m); Villa Romonea (200m); Kukuluku (600m); White Horse Roundabout (6.5km)

To Jasmine Valley (500m)

Northern Roundabout

Crab Market

Kep National Park

To Rega-Kep (250m); Jasmine Valley Turnoff (700m); Vietnam Border (30km)

Kep Beach Roundabout

Gulf of Thailand

SOUTH COAST KEP

and its own sailing club, which is open to the public. Very classy, although it would be nice to have a better beach for these prices.

Villa Romonea   BOUTIQUE **$$$**
(☑012-879486; http://villaromonea.com; r US$100-125; ❋@🛜🏊) This modernist 1960s villa has been beautifully restored and converted into an evocative guesthouse with six rooms. Right on the water, it's often booked out by groups on weekends, but it's a real gem, private and with a great pool.

Rega-Kep   GUESTHOUSE **$**
(☑088 9595130; keprega@hotmail.com; off NH33A; r with fan/air-con US$12/17; ❋🛜) Hidden on a side street near the Rabbit Island pier, Rega-Kep has 10 tasteful and well-appointed rooms set around a tropical courtyard. Excellent value considering Kep prices.

Kukuluku Beach Club   HOSTEL **$**
(☑6300150; www.kukuluku-beachclub.com; dm US$3.50-5, d with fan/air-con US$10/20; 🛜) Tiny pool and ordinary rooms, but great for meeting travellers and partying on weekends, when it sometimes imports live music (and expat crowds) from Phnom Penh.

Raingsey   RESORT **$$**
(☑011 558197; www.raingsey-bungalow-kep.com; d with fan/air-con US$35/45; ❋🛜🏊) Rooms and

bungalows have gorgeous furniture, sleek fixtures and private balconies, but more pool furniture (and shade) would be nice.

Kep Seaside Guesthouse   HOTEL **$**
(☑012 684241; r with fan/air-con from US$7/15; ❋🛜) This three-storey place is a bit decrepit, but you can't argue with the location, right on the water (although beachless) next to exclusive Knai Bang Chatt.

🍴 Eating & Drinking

Eating at the Crab Market, a row of wooden waterfront shacks by a wet fish market, is a quintessential Kep experience – for best results order crabs fried with Kampot pepper. Crabs are kept alive in pens tethered a few metres off the pebbly beach. You can dine at one of the shacks or buy crab for 35,000r a kilo and have your guesthouse prepare it.

The crab shacks also serve prawns, squid, fish and terrestrial offerings. For finer dining, the best restaurants are at the resorts – Le Bout du Monde, Kep Lodge and (especially) Veranda Natural Resort are a few of the best, and have great views to boot.

TOP CHOICE Kimly Restaurant   CRAB SHACK **$$**
(Crab Market; mains US$2.50-7; ⊙9am-10pm) The longest running and – despite the tacky decor – still the best of the Crab Market eater-

Kep

ies. It does crab every which way – 27 ways, to be exact, all US$6 to US$7, or supersize it for an extra two bucks. The Kampot pepper crab is truly mouth-watering.

TOP CHOICE Sailing Club FUSION $$
(mains US$5-12; ⊙10am-10pm; ⊛) With a small beach, a breezy bar in a New England–style pavilion and a wooden jetty poking out into the Gulf of Thailand, this is one of Cambodia's top sundowner spots – make a point to stop by at least for a drink. The Asian fusion food is excellent and you can get your crab fix here too. It's run by neighbouring luxury resort Knai Bang Chatt but is open to all and lacks any hint of attitude, and the prices are reasonable too, especially at happy hour.

Breezes FUSION $$
(NH33A; mains US$5-10; ⊙9am-9pm) Just 10m from the water line, this Dutch-owned res-

taurant out toward the Rabbit Island pier boasts sleek furnishings, excellent food and fine views of Rabbit Island. Dishes are Asian (not necessarily Khmer), Western and fusion.

La Baraka ITALIAN $$
(Crab Market; mains US$4.50-5.50) A French-run pizzeria with an upstairs chill-out area and a new seaside terrace.

Toucan BAR
(Crab Market; snacks US$3-5; ⊛) This is the best spot for a drink (or five) once the sun goes down. It has a pool table and usually a few punters propping up the bar until midnight or so (that's late night for Kep).

ℹ Information

As in Kampot, the best source of information and maps is the *Coastal* guide to Kampot and Kep. Kep does not have any banks or ATMs.
Green House (⌨089-440161; per hr US$1) A travel agency with internet access.
Kep Information Office (⌨097 7998777; pheng_say@yahoo.com; Kep Beach) Host Pheng is a font of information on buses and borders.
Rith Travel Center (⌨016 789994; www.rith travel.com; Crab Market) Specialises in island tours and handles bus tickets.

ℹ Getting There & Away

Kep is 25km from Kampot and 41km from the Prek Chak-Xa Xia border crossing to Vietnam. Phnom Penh Sorya Transport, Capitol Express and Hua Lian buses link the town with Kampot (US$2, 45 minutes) and Phnom Penh (US$4, four hours, last trips at 2pm). Stops are on request but usually include the northern round-about and Kep Beach; guesthouses have details. A private taxi to Phnom Penh (2½ hours) costs US$40 to US$45, to Kampot US$20.

See p351 for details on getting across the Vietnamese border to Ha Tien (Vietnam).

Virak Buntham's Ha Tien–Sihanoukville bus rumbles through Kep, and Kampot Tours & Travel can also get you to Sihanoukville (US$10, 2½ hours). You can also board Virak Buntham's Kampot–Siem Reap night bus in Kep.

A moto/*remork* to Kampot runs about US$8/12; private taxis are US$15 to US$20. Drivers hang out at the northern and Kep Beach roundabouts.

Motorbike rental is US$5 to US$7 per day; ask your guesthouse or any travel agency.

Around Kep

WAT KIRI SELA វត្តគីរីសិលា
Near the town of Kompong Trach, 28km north of Kep, you'll find this **Buddhist temple**

(admission US$1) at the foot of **Phnom Kompong Trach**, a dramatic karst formation riddled with over 100 caverns and passageways. From the wat, an underground passage leads to the centre of a fishbowl-like karst formation, surrounded by vine-draped cliffs and open to the sky. Various stalactite-laden caves shelter reclining Buddhas and miniature Buddhist shrines. There's major **rock-climbing** (www.rockclimbingincambodia .com) opportunities around here.

Friendly local kids with torches (flashlights), eager to put their evening-school English to use, are eager (overeager?) to serve as guides; make sure you tip them if you use them.

It may be possible to hire a **bamboo train** (see p219) behind Phnom Kompong Trach – the guides at Wat Kiri Sela know who to contact.

❶ Getting There & Away

Kompong Trach, on NH33 18km north of the Prek Chak-Xa Xia border crossing to Vietnam, is 28km northeast of Kep. Kompong Trach makes an easy day trip from Kep or Kampot, or you can hop off the bus on the way to/from Phnom Penh. Getting back on the bus can be difficult, as buses between Phnom Penh and Kampot often don't have space.

To get to Wat Kiri Sela, take the dirt road opposite the Acleda Bank, on NH33 in the centre of town, for 2km.

TAKEO PROVINCE

Often referred to as 'the cradle of Cambodian civilisation', Takeo Province (ខេត្តតាកែវ) was part of what Chinese annals called 'water Chenla', no doubt a reference to the extensive annual floods that still blanket much of the area. Today, this impoverished rural province is a backwater that gets few tourists. Those who do make it here get some of Cambodia's most ancient and fascinating temples virtually to themselves.

The temples of Tonlé Bati and Phnom Chisor lie in Takeo but are usually visited as day trips from Phnom Penh, hence they are covered in 'Around Phnom Penh' (p83).

Takeo

តាកែវ

☏ 032 / POP 39,000

There's not much happening at all in the quiet, lakeside provincial capital, but it makes a good base from which to take a zippy motorboat ride to the pre-Angkorian temples of Angkor Borei and Phnom Da. The main attraction in town is eating fresh-

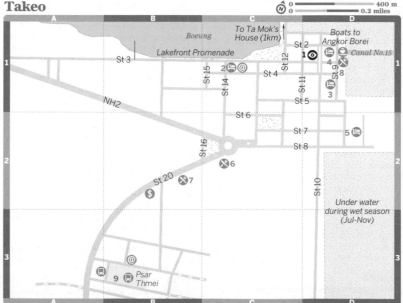

Takeo

water lobster on the waterfront (rainy season only).

Sights & Activities

Some attractive French-era shophouses line the streets around **Psar Nat**, a concrete monstrosity built after the overthrow of the Khmer Rouge, but it's nothing compared to Kampot.

Ta Mok's House   HISTORIC BUILDING
A pleasant stroll via a 150m-long railings-free bridge north of the centre takes you to the house of Takeo Province's most notorious native son, Ta Mok – aka 'The Butcher' – the Khmer Rouge commander of the Southwestern Zone, where he presided over horrific atrocities. Ta Mok's House is now occupied by a police training facility, but you can wander around the grounds. (He also had a residence near Anlong Veng – see p229.)

Sleeping

There's very little to distinguish Takeo's Khmer-style guesthouses, so your main concern should be location. Shoot for St 9 east of Psar Nat, which is lakeside during the rainy season and near the departure point for boats to the temples.

Daunkeo Guest House   GUESTHOUSE $
(012 711442; www.daunkeoguesthouse.com; St 9; d with fan/air-con from US$5/10; ❄️🛜) It's a step up from the run of the mill Takeo fare. Rooms actually have desks and are cleaner and larger than most, with nicer beds and bathrooms, plus working wi-fi.

Takeo

⊙ Sights
1 Psar Nat D1

⊜ Sleeping
2 Boeung Takeo Guesthouse C1
3 Daunkeo Guesthouse D1
4 Phnom Da Guesthouse D1
5 Suon Soben Guesthouse D2

⊗ Eating
6 Food Stalls C2
7 Kuy Teay Chhnang B2
  Psar Nat .... (see 1)
8 Stung Takeo D1

⊙ Transport
9 Psar Thmei B3

Suon Soben Guesthouse   HOTEL $
(016 337071; St 9; r US$15-20; ❄️🛜) This is about the only place in town that's not a generic high-rise. In a somewhat random location on the seasonal lake, it consists mainly of drive-up motel-style rooms. They are fairly standard but throw you bones like flat-screen TVs and refrigerators.

Boeung Takeo Guesthouse   GUESTHOUSE $
(931306; St 3; r with fan/air-con US$5/10; ❄️🛜) The selling point here is the delightful common balcony overlooking the lake, which offers a nice escape from the slightly run-down rooms. St 3 is not the quietest street in town.

Phnom Da Guesthouse   GUESTHOUSE $
(016 826083; St 9; r with fan/air-con US$5/10; ❄️) Facing the lake, this family-run hostelry has a mix of windowed and windowless rooms that have TVs but lack furniture, plus a small hang-out area with watery views.

Eating & Drinking

There are food stalls around Independence Monument. In the evening, this is the place to snack on Cambodian desserts or enjoy a *tukalok* (fruit shake).

TOP CHOICE **Stung Takeo**   CAMBODIAN $
(St 9; lobster dishes from US$3) Perched over the seasonal lake, this is the place to come for remarkably good – and remarkably affordable – freshwater lobster. The season for these toothsome creatures is approximately August to November. It has an English menu with other seafood offerings as well as chicken and beef. It's easily Takeo's best restaurant in terms of both food and ambience. Don't confuse it with similarly named Raeksmay Steong Takeo next door, or Ly Ly Steung Takao nearby.

Psar Nat   MARKET $
(St 10; 6am-about 8pm) The food court here has a dozen stalls that are great for coffee, breakfast soup (2000r), *num kong* (delectably chewy Khmer doughnuts; 200r) and *num kroch* (fried dumplings filled with beans and palm sugar).

Kuy Teay Chhnang   CAMBODIAN $
(NH2; 6am-7pm) This popular eatery, whose name means 'delicious noodles', specialises in early-morning Chinese soups (5000r), a lip-smacking way to begin the day. There's no English sign, look for a fake-brick facade.

No English menu either, but the manager speaks English and can help you out.

ℹ Information

Boeung Takeo Internet (per hr 1500r; St 3; ⏱6.30am-7pm) Internet access.
Canadia Bank (NH2) Has a 24-hour ATM that takes most forms of plastic.
Takeo Tourism (📱931323; ⏱7.30-11am & 2-5pm Mon-Fri, also open Sat & Sun) May be able to arrange an English-speaking guide (US$15 to US$20) to the temples.

ℹ Getting There & Around

Takeo is on NH2 77km south of Phnom Penh, 40km north of Kirivong and 48km north of the Phnom Den-Tinh Bien border crossing to Vietnam.

Phnom Penh Sorya Transport is the only company serving Phnom Penh (10,000r, 2¼ hours), with four small buses daily to/from a lot in front of **Psar Thmei** (Central Market; NH2). If you miss those you'll have to take a shared taxi (US$25 for the whole taxi, 15,000r for a seat). These leave from the same lot throughout the day, but you may have to wait longer or hire your own taxi in the afternoon.

Occasional share taxis (10,000r), minivans (5000r) and slower trailers pulled by motorbikes (the latter can hold at least 15 Cambodians and a foreigner – albeit not comfortably) make the 45-minute trip down to Kirivong, or hire a moto for US$10. To get to the Phnom Den-Tinh Bien border crossing to Vietnam, go to Kirivong and switch to a moto (US$2) for the final 8km. A private taxi to Kirivong is US$20, plus US$5 more to the border.

To get to Kep or Kampot by public transport, you need to go to Angk Tasaom, the chaotic transport junction 13km west of Takeo on NH3. Southbound buses pass through here, although there's no guarantee they'll have space. At Angk Tasaom you can also pick up share taxis and minibuses to Kampot and Kep. To get from Takeo to Angk Tasaom, hop on a trailer pulled by a motorbike (2000r) from Psar Thmei, a *remork* (US$5) from Psar Thmei or the hospital, or a moto (US$2) wherever you spot one.

Around Takeo

ANGKOR BOREI & PHNOM DA
អង្គរបុរី និង ភ្នំដា

The 20km open-air motorboat ride along Canal No 15, dug in the 1880s, to the impoverished riverine townlet of Angkor Borei is one of Cambodia's great thrill rides. Angkor Borei is home to a small **archaeological museum** (admission US$1; ⏱8am-4.30pm) fea-

turing locally discovered Funan- and Chenla-era artefacts. The boat then continues for 15 minutes to **Phnom Da** (admission US$2), spectacularly isolated Mont-St-Michel-style by annual floods, which is topped by a temple whose foundations date from the 6th century (the temple itself was rebuilt in the 11th century).

Angkor Borei, which can also be reached year-round via a circuitous land route from the north, was known as Vyadhapura when it served as the capital of 'water Chenla' in the 8th century. Angkor Borei was also an important centre during the earlier Funan period (1st to 6th centuries), when Indian religion and culture were carried to the Mekong Delta by traders, artisans and priests from India (the great maritime trade route between India and China passed by the Mekong Delta). The earliest datable Khmer inscription (AD 611) was discovered at Angkor Borei, which is surrounded by a 5.7km moated wall that hints at its past greatness. The town was bombed during the Vietnam War.

The twin hills of Phnom Da shelter five artificial **caves**, used for centuries as Hindu and Buddhist shrines and, during the Vietnam War, as hideouts by the Viet Cong. Exceptionally, the temple entrance faces due north; the other three sides have blind doors decorated with bas-relief *nagas*. The finest carvings have been taken to museums in Angkor Borei, Phnom Penh and Paris.

Nearby, on a second hillock, is 8m-high **Wat Asram Moha Russei**, a restored Hindu sanctuary that probably dates from around AD 700.

ℹ Getting There & Away

Hiring a boat for the trip at Takeo's dock costs US$40 return for up to four people. The canal leading out to Angkor Borei is clearly delineated in the dry season but surrounded by flooded rice fields the rest of the year. In the rainy season the water can get rough in the afternoon, so it's a good idea to head out early.

You can travel by moto from Takeo to Phnom Da in the dry season only for about US$3 return.

PHNOM BAYONG & ENVIRONS ភ្នំបាយ័ង

Affording breathtaking views of Vietnam's pancake-flat Mekong Delta, the cliff-ringed summit of Phnom Bayong (313m) is graced by a 7th-century **Chenla temple** built to celebrate a victory over Funan. The *linga* originally in the inner chamber is now in Paris' Musée Guimet, but a number of flora- and fauna-themed **bas-relief panels** can still be seen, for example on the lintels of the three false doorways and carved into the brickwork.

The sweltering grunt up to the temple takes about 1½ hours (bring plenty of water), or you can hire a moto in Kirivong to take you up in less than 20 minutes (US$10). It's a treacherous path, which explains the high price.

Kirivong town has a few basic guesthouses should you need a bed.

About 28km west along the Phnom Bayong access road (Hwy 113) is **Phnom Tchea Tapech**, whose summit is marked by a 14m-high standing Buddha inaugurated in 2006. It is reached by a monumental staircase.

Gentle **Kirivong Waterfall** (Chruos Phaok Waterfall) is reached by a 1.5km access road that begins about 1km south of Kirivong. Market stalls here sell the area's most famous products: topaz and quartz, either cut like gems or carved into tiny Buddhas and *nagas*. This area is popular with locals.

❶ Getting There & Away

Phnom Bayong is about 3km west of the northern edge of Kirivong town; the turn-off is marked by a painted panel depicting the temple.

Kirivong town is on NH2 40km south of Takeo and 8km north of the Phnom Den-Tinh Bien border crossing. From Takeo, a moto to Kirivong costs about US$10 (US$15 return).

Infrequent minibuses and share taxis to Phnom Penh (via Takeo) leave from Kirivong's Ton Lop Market on NH2 in the centre of town.

To get to the Vietnam border, a moto (US$2) from Kirivong is your best bet. Coming *from* the border, you may have to ask the Cambodian border officials to call a moto or taxi to pick you up.

Northwestern Cambodia

POP 3.75 MILLION / AREA 71,157 SQ KM

Best Places to Eat & Drink

» Riverside Balcony Bar (p218)

» Gecko Café (p217)

» Fresh Eats Café (p217)

» Community Villa (p210)

» Isanborei Community Restaurant (p240)

Best Places to Stay

» Bambu Hotel (p216)

» Sambor Village Hotel (p238)

» Chhaya Hotel & Apartments (p216)

» Banteay Chhmar Homestay (p229)

» Bamboo Guesthouse (p223)

Why Go?

Offering both highway accessibility and outback adventure, northwestern Cambodia stretches from the Cardamom Mountains to the Dangkrek Mountains. In the centre lies the unique Tonlé Sap lake (p320).

Battambang draws visitors with its classic colonial architecture, and a host of sights beyond the town. Kompong Thom is also popular as a gateway to the pre-Angkorian temples of Sambor Prei Kuk.

Northwestern Cambodia offers some of the country's most inspired temples including spectacular Prasat Preah Vihear, and Banteay Chhmar, currently under consideration for Unesco World Heritage Site status.

The Cardamom Mountains, in the far southwest, are home to pristine jungle and rare wildlife, while the forests and marshes of Preah Vihear and Kompong Thom Provinces provide an ideal habitat for endangered birds such as the giant ibis.

When to Go

The dry 'cool' months of November to February are the ideal time to explore the northwest. The June to October wet season needn't be a washout if you're sticking to major destinations such as Battambang, but it's hard work exploring the remote temples of Preah Vihear Province in these conditions.

Anyone planning the scenic boat ride from Siem Reap to Battambang should consider a wet-season visit, as it will be a smoother run. During the dry season, water levels drop. Four hours becomes eight hours or more.

ⓘ Getting There & Away

Northwestern Cambodia shares several international border crossings with Thailand. The most popular is the Poipet–Aranya Prathet (p348), 48km west of Sisophon and 153km west of Siem Reap. Psar Pruhm–Ban Pakard (p349), 22km west of Pailin and 102km southwest of Battambang is another option in the west of Cambodia. There are a couple of remote and seldom used northern borders, including the Choam–Choam Sa Ngam (p349) border, 16km north of Anlong Veng and 134km north of Siem Reap; and the O Smach–Chong Jom (p349) border, a punishing 120km north of Kralanh.

Within Cambodia, the obvious gateways to the region are Siem Reap and Phnom Penh. In the dry season, the fabled forest trail from Koh Kong Province, on the Gulf of Thailand, north through the Cardamoms to Pursat is not quite as daunting it was a few years back. The jungle track linking Thala Boravit (across the Mekong from Stung Treng; see p257) with Tbeng Meanchey is being upgraded to a road as we write.

ⓘ Getting Around

South of the lake, NH5 connects Phnom Penh with Kompong Chhnang, Kompong Luong, Pursat, Battambang, Sisophon and the Poipet–Aranya Prathet border crossing to Thailand. North of the lake, NH6 links Phnom Penh with Kompong Thom, Siem Reap and Sisophon.

Doing a loop north of Angkor along Cambodia's northern border with Thailand – from Sisophon (on NH5 and NH6) to Banteay Chhmar, Samraong, Anlong Veng, Sra Em (near Prasat Preah Vihear), Tbeng Meanchey and Kompong Thom (on NH6), or vice versa – is getting easier by the year, though it's still a challenge in the wet, when the trip could be dubbed 'the Churning of the Ocean of Mud'. This route passes minefields and goes through areas so remote they're still being homesteaded. The lingering border tensions with Thailand in the northwestern region have spurred some major improvements in roads and transport connections in this area.

A memorable, if slow, boat service links Siem Reap with Battambang.

KOMPONG CHHNANG PROVINCE

Kompong Chhnang Province (ខេត្តកំពង់ឆ្នាំង) is a relatively wealthy province thanks to its proximity to the capital and its fishing and agricultural industries, supported by abundant water resources.

Kompong Chhnang
កំពង់ឆ្នាំង

♫026 / POP 45,000

Kompong Chhnang (Clay Pot Port) is a tale of two cities: the sleepy centre dating back to the colonial area, arrayed around a huge park, and the bustling dockside on the Tonlé Sap River. Nearby sights include two floating villages, a hamlet famous for its distinctive pottery and some drop-dead gorgeous countryside, typically Cambodian in its union of verdant rice fields and towering sugar palms.

⊙ Sights & Activities

FLOATING VILLAGES

A short sail from Kompong Chhnang's waterfront, on the Tonlé Sap River, leads to a couple of colourful floating villages: **Phoum Kandal**, which has neighbourhoods to the east and northwest; and **Chong Kos**, beyond Phoum Kandal. Much less commercial than Kompong Luong (p211), they have all the amenities of a mainland village – houses, machine-tool shops, vegetable vendors, a mosque, a petrol station – except that almost everything floats. Many of the residents are ethnic Vietnamese.

To get a waterborne look at the floating villages, you can take a **boat trip** (☏012 878331; foreigner/Khmer US$2.50/1.50, minimum 10 people) from the Tourism Port. Chartering an entire vessel is US$20 per hour.

A cheaper, quieter and more ecological option, available about 300m to the northwest, is to get around like the floating villagers do on a **wooden boat** (per hr US$5) of the sort that's rowed standing up.

For a discount river cruise, you can hop on a **passenger ferry** (1000r, 30 minutes, departures at 8.30am, 11am, 1.30pm and 4pm) to Kompong Lang District, about 6km away on the other side of the Tonlé Sap River. The vessels dock 100m northwest of the Tourism Port.

Also across the Tonlé Sap River are several rather dilapidated brick-built **temples** dating from the Chenla period, including **Prasat Srei**.

ONDONG ROSSEY & PHNOM SANTUK

The quiet village of **Ondong Rossey**, where the area's famous red pottery is made under every house, is a delightful 7km ride west of town through serene rice fields dotted with sugar palms, many with bamboo ladders

NORTHWESTERN CAMBODIA KOMPONG CHHNANG

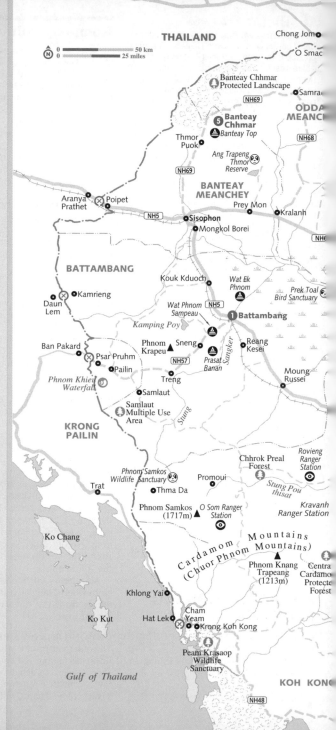

North-western Cambodia Highlights

1 Soaking up the colonial-tinged charms of the riverside town of **Battambang** (p212), surrounded by lush countryside and hilltop temples

2 Making an adventurous overland pilgrimage to the majestic mountain-top temple of **Prasat Preah Vihear** (p233)

3 Exploring the backwaters of the colourful floating village of **Kompong Luong** (p211), the largest floating community on Tonlé Sap lake

4 Exploring Southeast Asia's first temple city, the impressive pre-Angkorian ruins of **Sambor Prei Kuk** (p240)

5 Putting something back into the community with an overnight homestay at **Banteay Chmar** (p228), a massive 12th-century complex with the signature faces of Avalokiteshvara

Kompong Chhnang

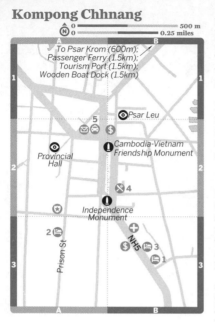

To Psar Krom (600m);
Passenger Ferry (1.5km);
Tourism Port (1.5km);
Wooden Boat Dock (1.5km)

Psar Leu

Cambodia-Vietnam
Friendship Monument

Provincial
Hall

Independence
Monument

Prison St

NH5

Kompong Chhnang

Sleeping
1 Asia Hotel..B3
2 Sokha Guesthouse A3
3 Sovannphum Hotel...........................B3

Eating
4 Mittapheap Restaurant.......................B2

Transport
5 Bus & Taxi Station A2

running up the trunk. The unpainted pots, decorated with etched or appliqué designs, are either turned with a foot-spun wheel (for small pieces) or banged into shape with a heavy wooden spatula (for large ones).

The golden-hued mud piled up in the yards is quarried at nearby **Phnom Krang Dai Meas** and pounded into fine clay before being shaped and fired; only at the last stage does it acquire a pinkish hue. Pieces can be purchased at the **Pottery Development Center**.

In Kompong Chhnang, shops selling Ondong Rossey **pottery** can be found along NH5 several kilometres towards Battambang from town.

A visit to Ondong Rossey can be combined with **Phnom Santuk**, a rocky hillock behind Wat Santuk, which is a few kilometres southwest of Kompong Chhnang. The boulder-strewn summit affords fine views of the countryside, including the Tonlé Sap, 20km to the north.

By bicycle or moto, combining Ondong Rossey and Phnom Santuk makes for a rewarding circuit, especially early in the morning or late in the afternoon. There are no road signs, so it's a good idea to go with a local.

Sleeping & Eating

Sokha Guesthouse
GUESTHOUSE $
(☏988622; Prison St; r US$8-15; 🌬) Set in a shady garden, this 30-room family pad offers the most charming accommodation in town, including fan triples for US$10. Situated a very long block west of Independence Monument.

Asia Hotel
HOTEL $
(☏989666; thydaasia@gmail.com; NH5; r US$6-25; 🌬@🤶) One of a cluster of smart new places on the main road to Phnom Penh. Fan rooms are a bargain for their size and comfort. Upgrade yourself to VIP status for just US$18.

Sovannphum Hotel
HOTEL $
(☏989333; sovannphumkpchotel@yahoo.com; NH5; r with fan/air-con from US$7/13; 🌬@🤶) Spotless and well-run, this is a popular spot for the NGO crowd. Has 30 good-sized rooms with modern bathrooms, a restaurant and wi-fi.

Mittapheap Restaurant
CAMBODIAN $
(NH5; mains 8000-20,000r; ⏰5am-9pm) Looking out over Independence Monument, this is one of the few real restaurants in town. Service is not exactly slick, but the Cambodian dishes are tasty enough.

There are plenty of food stalls at the two markets, Psar Leu and Psar Krom.

Information

The city centre is anchored by Psar Leu (Central Market), which is two blocks west of the Acleda Bank and the bus and taxi station. Independence Monument is 500m south of the bank and the waterfront 3km northeast.

Acleda Bank (NH5) Near the Cambodia-Vietnam Friendship Monument. Has an ATM that handles Visa cash advances.

Canadia Bank (NH5) Has an ATM with no charge for withdrawals.

ℹ️ Getting There & Away

Kompong Chhnang is 91km north of Phnom Penh, 93km southeast of Pursat and 198km southeast of Battambang.

Bus

On NH5 you can try to flag down a bus heading to Phnom Penh, but buses travelling to Pursat and Battambang are often full.

Phnom Penh Sorya (☑016 400031; www .ppsoryatransport.com) has frequent buses to Phnom Penh (12,000r, two hours), Battambang (20,000r, two hours) and Poipet (25,000r, five hours).

Other bus companies operating services between Phnom Penh and Battambang include Capitol Tour, Neak Kror Horm, Paramount Angkor Express and Rith Mony.

Taxi

The easiest and fastest way to get to Phnom Penh is by share taxi (15,000r, 1½ hours), which wait both at the bus and taxi station, and on the waterfront, near the ferry to Kompong Lang District. Share taxis do not generally serve destinations to the northwest, such as Battambang.

ℹ️ Getting Around

Moto rides cost about 2000r for short hops around town, US$5 to US$7 for a half-day trip and US$10 for an all-day (7am to 5pm) excursion. The Sovannphum Hotel has *remorks* (US$10 return to the old airport).

Sokha Guesthouse rents bicycles (US$1 a day) and motorbikes (US$6 a day).

PURSAT PROVINCE

Pursat Province (ខេត្តពោធិ៍សាត់), Cambodia's fourth-largest, stretches from the remote forests of Phnom Samkos, on the Thai border, eastwards to the fishing villages and marshes of Tonlé Sap lake. Famed for its oranges it encompasses the northern reaches of the Cardamom Mountains, linked with the town of Pursat by disreputable roads.

Pursat   ពោធិ៍សាត់

☑052 / POP 38,000

The provincial capital, known for its marble carvers, is no beauty, but makes a good base for a day trip to the floating village of Kompong Luong (p211) or an expedition into the

WORTH A TRIP

THE KHMER ROUGE AIRPORT

The Khmer Rouge were not known as great builders, but in 1977 and 1978, slave labourers built an airfield using cement of such high quality that even today the 2440m run way and access roads look like they were paved just last week.

No one knows for sure, but it seems that Kompong Chhnang airport (IATA code KZC), never operational under the Khmer Rouge, was intended to serve as a base for launching air attacks against Vietnam. Chinese engineers oversaw the work of tens of thousands of Cambodians suspected of disloyalty to the Khmer Rouge. Anyone unable to work was killed, often with a blow to the head delivered with a bamboo rod. In early 1979, as Vietnamese forces approached, almost the entire workforce was executed. Estimates of the number of victims, buried nearby in mass graves, range from 10,000 to 50,000.

In the late 1990s, a plan to turn the airport into a cargo hub for air-courier companies came to nought. These days, local teenagers come out here to tool around on their motorbikes, do doughnuts and drag race, while cows graze between the taxiway and the runway. On sunny days the sun creates convincing mirages.

On an anonymous slope a few kilometres away, the Khmer Rouge dug a **cave** – said to be 3km deep – apparently for the purpose of storing weapons flown in from China. Now home to swirling bats, it can be explored with a torch (flashlight) but, lacking ventilation, gets very hot and humid.

On a hillside near a cluster of bullet-pocked cement barracks, stripped of anything of value, is a massive cement water tank. Inside it's a remarkable echo chamber.

The airport is about 12km west of town. Take NH5 towards Battambang for 7km and then turn left onto a concrete road. Some of the moto (motorcycle taxi) and *remorkmoto* (túk-túk) drivers in Kompong Chhnang know the way.

Pursat

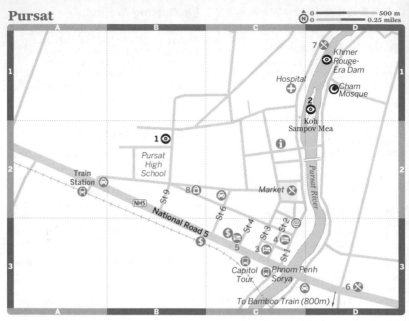

wilds of the Central Cardamoms Protected Forest (p212).

Sights & Activities

Koh Sampov Meas (Golden Ship Island) is a bit of a local landmark, complete with manicured lawns and Khmer-style pavilions. It's the place to see and be seen towards sunset as young locals drop by for **aerobics** (☺classes from 5pm), a snack, or a game of badminton.

Bun Rany Hun Sen Development Centre (St 9; ☺7-11am & 2-5pm Mon-Fri & Sat morning) teaches cloth and mat weaving, sewing, marble carving and other artisanal skills to young people, and markets the items they make. Travellers are welcome to visit classes.

Sleeping & Eating

Pursat Century Hotel   HOTEL **$**
(☎951446; NH5; pursatcenturyhotel@yahoo.com; r with fan/air-con from US$7/15; ❄@☎) This multistorey establishment has set new standards for Pursat. The 110 rooms offer two-star comfort, including (cue contented sleep) imported linens.

Phnom Pech Hotel   HOTEL **$**
(☎951515; St 1; r US$6-18; ❄☎) A long-running local hotel, rooms here are spacious and

clean. The friendly management speaks English and free wi-fi is on tap.

New Toun Sour Hotel   HOTEL **$**
(☎951506; thansourthmey@yahoo.com; St 2; r US$6-15; ❄❄☎) This hotel, popular with the NGO crowd, has 41 large and inviting rooms. The restaurant has great French fries but at prices slightly higher than local joints.

Community Villa   CAMBODIAN **$**
(NH5; mains 8000-22,000r; ☺7am-10pm) Run by a Cambodian NGO that gives job skills to at-risk young people, this place serves Khmer dishes, including ginger fish, salads, and the best pancakes and *tukalok* (fruit shakes) in town. A small gift shop sells *krama* (checked scarves), wallets and purses made by rural women.

Magic Fish Restaurant   CAMBODIAN **$**
(Tep Machha Restaurant; St 1; mains 5000-15,000r; ☺10am-9pm or later) Just north of the Khmer Rouge-era dam, this riverside place has tasty Khmer dishes and great river views.

Information

Pursat's main commercial street, north-south St 3, is two blocks west of St 1, which runs along the river. Both streets are perpendicular to NH5.

Pursat

Acleda Bank (NH5) Has an ATM that handles Visa cash advances.

Canadia Bank (NH5) Has an ATM with free withdrawals.

Department of Tourism (012 838854; 7-11am & 2-5pm Mon-Fri) Has a few handouts and displays on province highlights on the walls.

Pheng Ky Computer (St 1; per hr US$1; 6am-8pm) Internet access.

Getting There & Around

Pursat is 105km southeast of Battambang and 188km northwest of Phnom Penh along NH5.

Buses pass through Pursat virtually all day long, shuttling between Poipet (20,000r) and Battambang (15,000r, 1½ hours) to the northwest, and Kompong Chhnang and Phnom Penh (20,000r, four hours) to the southeast. A few direct services head to Siem Reap (35,000r, five hours) and Kompong Cham (35,000r). Bus companies with Pursat offices include **Capitol Tour** (951650) and **Phnom Penh Sorya** (012 687565; www.ppsoryatransport.com).

Pick-ups (outside/inside 10,000r/15,000r) and share taxis (20,000r, four hours) to the remote Cardamoms town of Promoui (Veal Veng) leave from next to the old market, Psar Chaa.

Phnom Pech Hotel rents out bicycles (US$2.50 a day) and motorbikes (US$8) and can arrange a round-trip moto/taxi trip to Kompong Luong for US$10/30.

Kompong Luong កំពង់ល្ពង់

POP 10,000

Kompong Luong has all the amenities you'd expect to find in an oversized fishing village – except that here everything floats on water. The result is a partly ethnic-Vietnamese

Venice without the dry land. The cafes, shops, chicken coops, fish ponds, ice-making factory, crocodile farm and karaoke bars are kept from sinking by boat hulls, barrels or bunches of bamboo, as are the Vietnamese pagoda, the blue-roofed church and the colourful houses. In the dry season, when water levels drop and Tonlé Sap shrinks, the entire aquapolis is towed, boat by boat, a few kilometres north.

The population of this fascinating and picturesque village is partly Vietnamese, so – reflecting their ambiguous status in Cambodian society – you may find the welcome here slightly more subdued than in most rural Cambodian towns, at least from adults. Khmer Rouge massacres of Vietnamese villagers living around Tonlé Sap lake were commonplace during the first half of the 1990s, and even as late as 1998 more than 20 Vietnamese were killed in a pogrom near Kompong Chhnang.

Homestays (per night US$6) are available with local families and meals are available for US$1 to US$2 per person. This is an interesting way to discover what everyday life is really like on the water.

Getting There & Around

Kompong Luong is between 39km and 44km east of Pursat, depending on the time of year. From Pursat, round-trip transport options include moto (US$7 to US$10, 45 minutes) and private taxi (US$30 return). The turn-off from NH5 is in Krakor next to the Sokimex petrol station.

At the dock, the official tourist rate to charter a four-passenger wooden motorboat (complete with lifejackets) around Kompong Luong is US$7 per hour for one to three passengers (US$10 for four to five). If there are enough takers for the large boat, it costs just US$2 per person.

Northern Cardamom Mountains

As the Central Cardamoms Protected Forest (CCPF) and adjacent wildlife sanctuaries slowly open up to ecotourism, Pursat is emerging as the Cardamoms' northern gateway.

For details on the southern reaches of the Cardamom Mountains, which stretch all the way to the Gulf of Thailand, see p164.

Roads in the area are heavily rutted and some bridges have holes big enough to swallow a car. From Pursat, it's possible to find a taxi to Kravanh, Rovieng or Promoui: ask around at Psar Chaa in Pursat or enquire at your guesthouse.

CENTRAL CARDAMOMS PROTECTED FOREST (CCPF)

The CCPF's enforcement ranger teams get technical and financial support from **Conservation International** (CI; www.conservation.org). To coordinate a visit, arrange a guide or bed down at a **ranger station** (Kravanh or Rovieng), contact Conservation International's **Peau Somanak** (☎017 464663; lly@conservation.org).

Areas in and near the CCPF are still being de-mined, so stay on roads and well-trodden trails.

Rangers and military policemen based at **Kravanh** ranger station, deep in the Cardamoms jungle in the Tang Rang area south of Pursat, play an unending game of cat and mouse with loggers, poachers and encroachers. For information on trans-CCPF treks to/from Kravanh, see p166.

The most valuable contraband at the front-line **Rovieng** ranger station is aromatic *moras preuv* (sassafras, or safrole) oil, extracted from the roots of the endangered *Dysoxylum loureiri* tree. One tonne of wood produces just 30L of the oil, which has a delightful, sandalwood-like scent. Local people use it in traditional medicine, but it can also be used to make ecstasy.

A few kilometres from Rovieng (and 53km southwest of Pursat) are the **L'Bak Kamronh Rapids**, which attract Khmers on holidays. About 25km west of Rovieng, in Promoui Commune, the old-growth **Chhrok Preal Forest** can be visited with a guide.

PHNOM AURAL WILDLIFE SANCTUARY

Sadly, Phnom Aural Wildlife Sanctuary (2538 sq km), just east of the CCPF, is rapidly being destroyed from the south and the east by corrupt land speculation and rampant illegal logging.

Hiking up **Phnom Aural** (1813m), Cambodia's highest peak, takes at least two full days with an overnight at the summit. About halfway up is the site of a **crashed aircraft** that may have been bringing arms from China to the Khmer Rouge in the spring of 1975. Guides who know the way, and where to find water, can be hired in the village of Sra Ken. Travel from Phnom Penh to the town of Kompong Speu (45km) and arrange a moto onwards to Sra Ken.

PHNOM SAMKOS WILDLIFE SANCTUARY

Sandwiched between the CCPF and the Thai frontier, the Phnom Samkos Wildlife Sanctuary (3338 sq km) is well and truly out in the sticks. It is threatened by a copper-mining concession and the Chinese-built Atai hydroelectric dam, which will flood 52 sq km.

Boasting Cambodia's second-highest peak, **Phnom Samkos** (1717m), the sanctuary's main town is **Promoui** (Veal Veng), 125km and four hours from Pursat over a pretty rough road (see p211) that passes by Rovieng. This remote little outpost has three **guesthouses** (r US$5). Local moto drivers can take visitors to nearby ethnic minority villages.

A ruinous track heads south via **O Som** (where there's a CCPF ranger station and a local guesthouse) to Krong Koh Kong and the Koh Kong Conservation Corridor (see p165). In the dry season, it *may* be possible to hire a pick-up to the coast in Promoui.

BATTAMBANG PROVINCE

Battambang Province (ខេត្តបាត់ដំបង; Bat Dambang), said by proud locals to produce Cambodia's finest rice, sweetest coconuts and tastiest oranges (don't bring this up in Pursat), has a long border with Thailand and a short stretch of the Tonlé Sap shoreline. The region has an enduring tradition of producing many of Cambodia's best-loved singers and actors.

Battambang has passed from Cambodia to Thailand and back again several times over the past few centuries. Thailand ruled the area from 1794 to 1907 and again during WWII (1941 to 1946), when the Thais cut a deal with the Japanese and the Vichy French.

Battambang បាត់ដំបង

☎053 / POP 140,000

Battambang has a unique charm among Cambodia's larger urban centres. It seamlessly blends together the outlook of a modern city and small-town friendliness, set against the backdrop of some of Cambodia's best-preserved colonial architecture. Timeless hilltop temples and bucolic villages can be seen on leisurely day trips by bicycle or moto. The most scenic river trip in the country links Battambang with Siem Reap.

⊙ Sights

Colonial-Era Architecture   NEIGHBOURHOOD
Much of Battambang's special charm lies in its early-20th-century French architecture. Some of the finest **colonial buildings** are along the waterfront (St 1), especially just south of **Psar Nat**, itself quite an impressive structure. There are also some old **French shophouses** along St 3, including some just east of the train station. The two-storey **Governor's Residence**, with its balconies and wooden shutters, is another handsome legacy of the very early 1900s. Designed by an Italian architect for the last Thai governor, who departed in 1907, it has imposing balconies and a grand reception room with 5m ceilings. The interior is closed, but you can stroll the grounds.

Battambang Museum   MUSEUM
(St 1; admission US$1; ⊙8-11am & 2-5pm) This small museum displays fine Angkorian lintels and statuary from all over Battambang Province, including Phnom Banan and Sneng. Signs are in Khmer, English and French.

Wats   TEMPLES
Battambang's Buddhist temples survived the Khmer Rouge period relatively unscathed thanks to a local commander who ignored orders from on high. A number of the monks at **Wat Phiphétaram**, **Wat Damrey Sar** and **Wat Kandal** speak English and are glad for a chance to practise; they're often around in the late afternoon.

Train Station   TRAIN STATION
Here the time is always 8.02. Just along the tracks to the south, you can explore a treasure trove of crumbling, **French-era repair sheds**, warehouses and rolling stock.

🏃 Activities

Day trips out of town are one of the highlights here – see p220.

FREE **Heritage Walking Trail**   WALKING TOUR
(http://battambang-heritage.org/downloads .htm) Phnom Penh–based **KA Architecture Tours** (www.ka-tours.org) is highly regarded for its specialist tours in and around the capital and has collaborated with Battambang Municipality to create two heritage walks in the historic centre of Battambang. There are two downloadable PDFs including a colour map and numbered highlights. This is a great way to spend half a day exploring the city. Those with less time can rent a bicycle and run the combined routes in just an hour or so.

🚲**Soksabike**   CYCLING
(☑012-542019; www.soksabike.com; ⊙7.30am departures daily) Based at Street 1½ Cafe, Soksabike is a social enterprise aiming to connect visitors with the Cambodian countryside and its people. The half-day trip costs US$18 per person, covering about 30km, and the price includes a fresh coconut, seasonal fruits and a shot of rice wine.

🛶 **Green Orange Kayaks**   KAYAKING
(☑077-204121; feda@online.com.kh; ⊙7am-5pm Mon-Fri) One- to three-person kayaks can be rented from Green Orange Kayaks, run by an NGO (www.fedacambodia.org) that offers free English classes. The half-day trip from its grassy campus, 8km south of Battambang towards Phnom Banan, downriver to the city costs US$12 per person (including life jackets); an optional guide is US$3. To rent on Saturday or Sunday, make contact on a weekday.

Aerobics   HEALTH & FITNESS
(1000r) Head to Battambang's East Bank to see the locals burning off the rice carbs doing aerobics, from about 6am to 7am and 5pm to 7pm daily. Led by a local hunk with a portable sound system, just five minutes of

---

DON'T MISS

PHARE PONLEU SELPAK CIRCUS SCHOOL

Roll up, roll up, the circus is now in town every Monday and Thursday. **Phare Ponleu Selpak** (☑952424; www.phareps.org) is a multi-arts centre for disadvantaged children that hosts internationally acclaimed circus (*cirque nouveau*) performances (adult/child US$8/4), often preceded by dinner (US$6; book a day ahead). Time your visit to Battambang to catch the spectacle. During the day, it's often possible to observe circus, dance, music, drawing and graphic-arts **classes** (⊙8-11am & 2-5pm Mon-Fri). To get here from the Vishnu Roundabout on NH5, head west for 900m and then turn right (north) and continue another 600m.

NORTHWESTERN CAMBODIA BATTAMBANG

Battambang

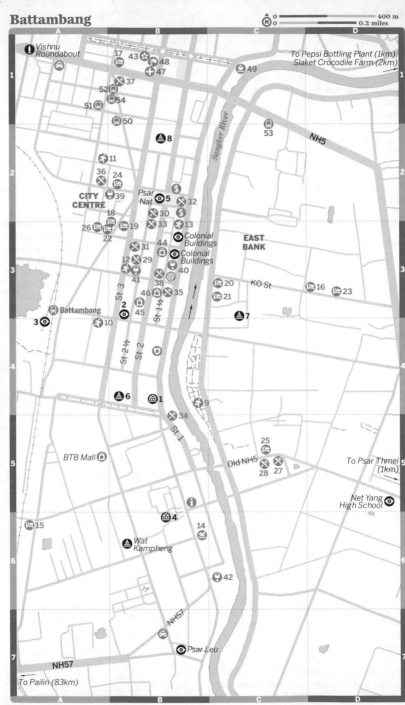

400 m
0.2 miles

Vishnu Roundabout

To Pepsi Bottling Plant (1km);
Slaket Crocodile Farm (2km)

17 43 48
47

37
52 54
51 50

8

11

36 24

CITY CENTRE
39 18 Psar Nat 5 32
30
26 19 33 13
22 31 44 Colonial Buildings
12 29 Colonial Buildings
41 40
38 @
Battambang 46 35
45
St 3 2 St 1½
10
St 2½ St 2

3

EAST BANK

KO St

20 16 23
21

7

Sangker River

NH5

53

NH5

6 1

34
St 1

9

25
Old NH5 28 27

To Psar Thmei (1km)

BTB Mall

Net Yang High School

15
4
14
Wat Kampheng

42

NORTHWESTERN CAMBODIA BATTAMBANG

NH57

Psar Leu

NH57

To Pailin (83km)

Battambang

working out should be enough to teach you some numbers in Khmer.

Victory Club FITNESS, SWIMMING
(☏017 530168; per day incl towel & locker US$2.50; ⊘6am-8pm) Has a 25m pool and fitness machines.

Seeing Hands Massage MASSAGE
(☏092-379903; per hr US$6; ⊘7am-10pm) Trained blind masseurs and masseuses offer soothing work-overs.

Volunteer English Teachers TEACHING
Teachers are welcomed by the Cambodian Education Center (p221) in Pheam Ek and the **Khmer New Generation Organization** (☏092-790597; www.kngo-home.org).

🎓 Courses

Smokin' Pot COOKING
(☏012 821400; vannaksmokingpot@yahoo.com; St 1½) Always wanted to learn how to prepare authentic family-style Khmer dishes? Daily from 9.30am to 12.30pm, Smokin' Pot offers

cooking classes (US$8) that start with a trip to Psar Nat and culminate in a three-course lunch (you eat what you cook). Reserve a day ahead.

Nary Kitchen COOKING
(✆012 763950; US$8) Another popular cooking class in town. It includes a visit to the local market, a three-course menu and a keepsake recipe book. Courses start at 9am and 4pm, lasting about three hours, plus time to eat your creations.

Australian Centres for Development LANGUAGE
(✆952370; acd@online.com.kh) Near the old train station; offers well-regarded Khmer language classes.

🛏 Sleeping

Battambang offers an excellent range of accommodation with some good-value guesthouses and an ever-increasing selection of boutique hotels.

CITY CENTRE
Most of the city's veteran hotels are within a few bustling blocks of Psar Nat. The rival Chhaya and Royal Hotels dominate the backpacker market and can help arrange guides and transport.

TOP CHOICE Chhaya Hotel & Apartments HOTEL $
(✆952170; www.chhayahotel.com; 118 St 3; dm US$1, r US$3-12, apartments US$15-25; ❇@🛜) One of the longest running budget hotels in Battambang, it has the cheapest beds in town if you don't mind a dorm. The new serviced apartments are incredible value, offering tasteful decoration, acres of space and a kitchen for self-catering.

TOP CHOICE Sanctuary Villa BOUTIQUE HOTEL $$
(✆012 206250; sanctuaryvilla.derlengtours.com; r from US$55; ❇@🛜) This intimate boutique resort is a tranquil hideaway in the suburban backstreets of Battambang. All accommodation is in attractive villas furnished with traditional woods and tasteful silks. Facilities include a swimming pool and an Asian-international restaurant. It lies a few hundred metres north of NH5 from St 3 and is signposted.

Royal Hotel HOTEL $
(✆016 912034; www.asrhotel.com.kh; r with fan/aircon from US$8/10; ❇@🛜) Deservedly popular with independent travellers, the 45-room

Royal doesn't have any bells and whistles, just clean, comfortable, spacious lodgings with fridge and TV.

Au Cabaret Vert BOUTIQUE HOTEL $$
(✆656 2000; www.aucabaretvert.com; r from US$50; ❇@🛜) Contemporary meets colonial, this pretty resort is located on the western edge of town. Rooms are stylish and include flat-screen TV and a rain shower. The swimming pool is a natural self-cleaning pond.

Banan Hotel HOTEL $$
(✆012 739572; www.bananhotel.doodlekit.com; NH5; r US$20-30; ❇@🛜) A modern hotel that combines two-star comfort with Khmer-style wooden decor. The 30 rooms come with all the mod cons, plus there is a new annexe with a rooftop pool.

Tomato Guesthouse GUESTHOUSE $
(✆6907374; r from US$3) A new budget crashpad with very few frills but the odd thrill. The friendly owners have opened a rooftop restaurant, which is a good place to relax after dark.

Lux Guesthouse GUESTHOUSE $
(✆092 335767; r US$8-18; ❇@🛜) Very centrally located, the five-storey Lux has 24 modern, comfortable rooms with top-notch furnishings. Good all-round value for money.

EAST BANK

TOP CHOICE Bambu Hotel HOTEL $$$
(✆953900; www.bambuhotel.com; KO St; r US$70-110; ❇@🛜) One of the newest boutique hotels in Battambang, Bambu is designed in Franco-Khmer style with spacious and stylish rooms. As well as the pool, it has a well-regarded restaurant and a bar that invites lingering.

Golden Land Hotel HOTEL $
(Sovanphoom Hotel; ✆6903790; sovanphoom@yahoo.com; Riverside Rd; r US$10-15; ❇@🛜) Still looking brand spanking new during our visit, this riverfront pad offers excellent value for money. Be a VIP for the night and enjoy space and a swish bathroom.

La Villa HOTEL $$$
(✆730151; www.lavilla-battambang.com; Riverside Rd; d US$55-85; ❇@🛜) One of the most romantic boutique hotels in Cambodia, this attractive hostelry occupies a French-era villa renovated in vintage 1930s style. The only drawback is that it has now been hemmed in by looming apartment blocks on both sides.

Phka Villa Hotel   BOUTIQUE HOTEL **$$**
(☎953255; KO St; r incl breakfast from US$50; ❄@☎☂) This homely boutique resort offers a series of tastefully decorated bungalows set around an inviting swimming pool. There is a small bar.

Spring Park Hotel   HOTEL **$**
(☎730999; spparkhotel@yahoo.com; Old NH5; r US$6-35; ❄@☎) This place keeps on improving and now offers 78 rooms running from basic fan jobs through to deluxe mini-suites. Excellent value all around.

✗ Eating
CITY CENTRE
At Psar Nat, you can dine cheaply in the area between the two buildings. A **night market** (⊙4-9pm) with barbecue chicken, frog and beef can be found in the market's northeast corner, facing Canadia Bank. The neon-lit **riverside night market** (St1; ⊙3pm-midnight) is across from the Battambang Museum.

🍃**Fresh Eats Café**   INTERNATIONAL **$**
(St 2½; mains US$1.50-3; ⊙6am-9pm; ☎) Run by an NGO that helps children whose families have been affected by HIV/AIDS, this little place serves cheap, tasty food, including Western breakfasts, bagels, fried spring rolls and Khmer curry.

Sunrise Coffee House   INTERNATIONAL **$**
(mains 8000-14,000r; ⊙6.30am-8pm Mon-Sat; ☎) Better than Starbucks, this is a great place for coffee, fresh-baked banana bread, California-style wraps, homemade tortillas, veggie or chicken quesadillas, and all-day breakfasts.

Gecko Café   INTERNATIONAL **$$**
(www.geckocafecambodia.com; St 3; mains US$2.75-5; ⊙8am-1pm; ☎) This is Battambang's answer to the Foreign Correspondents Club in Phnom Penh thanks to the glorious setting in an old French shophouse. Mellow and atmospheric, it's a good place for some international bites or an evening drink.

Pomme d'Amour   FRENCH **$$**
(63 St 2½; mains US$5-8.50; ⊙11am-10pm) The French-run 'Apple of Love' serves fine French cuisine at elegantly set tables. Specialties include local beef with black Kampot pepper sauce and authentic crêpes.

Vegetarian Foods Restaurant   VEGETARIAN **$**
(mains 1500-3000r; ⊙6am-11am; 🖉) Serves some of the most delicious vegetarian dishes

in Cambodia, including rice soup and homemade soy milk. Open only for breakfast and brunch, but tremendous value.

Lan Chov Khorko Miteanh   NOODLES **$**
(145 St 2; mains 4000-6000r; ⊙6.30am-9pm) More conveniently known as Chinese Noodle by resident foreigners, this is a cracking little noodle shop where the Chinese chef makes fresh noodles that are served a dozen or more ways including with pork or duck soup.

White Rose   CAMBODIAN **$**
(St 2; mains 7000-12000r; ⊙6.30am-10pm) One of the longest-running restaurants in town, with a menu of good-value Khmer, Chinese, Vietnamese and Thai dishes, including soups, veggie options and delicious *tukalok* (fruit shakes).

Smokin' Pot   CAMBODIAN **$**
(mains US$2-3.50; ⊙7am-11pm) This cheery, laid-back restaurant serves good Khmer, Thai and Western food – burgers and fried beef with ginger are popular choices. Offers cooking classes (US$8) every morning.

The Colonial   INTERNATIONAL **$$**
(mains US$3-6; ⊙11am-10pm) A new steakhouse in Battambang, this place has the atmosphere of a French bistro. There are four sauces to choose from, including green pepper or blue cheese. Pies and pasta also available. Near St 2.

Flavours of India   INDIAN **$**
(St 2½; mains US$3-6; ⊙11am-10pm) The new Battambang outpost of a popular Phnom Penh Indian restaurant, the inspiration for the opening came about when some curry-craving expats ordered takeaway from the capital, 293km to the southeast. Good value veggie thalis and the usual favourites.

EAST BANK
A lively restaurant scene is developing on the East Bank, especially along Old NH5.

Bamboo Train Cafe   INTERNATIONAL **$**
(Old NH5; mains 4000-24,000r; ⊙7am-10pm) The affable owner ensures this place is always popular. As well as an eclectic menu with pizzas, pastas, curries and a delicious tofu *amoc,* there is a pool table and regular movie screenings.

La Villa   FRENCH **$$**
(mains US$6-15; ⊙noon-2.30pm & 6-9pm; ❄) This is Battambang's finest restaurant. It

dishes up delectable Khmer, Vietnamese, French and Italian dishes, plus wines from around the world. House specials include a tender fish fillet in lemon sauce.

Battambang BBQ & Buffet ASIAN $
(Old NH5; US$4; ⊘11am-10pm) Offering an all-inclusive tabletop barbecue and serve-your-self buffet, this place is unbelievably popular with local Khmers and domestic tourists. Exceptional value.

🍸 Drinking

Riverside Balcony Bar BAR/RESTAURANT
(cnr St 1 & NH57; mains US$3.50-7.50; ⊘4pm-midnight Tue-Sun) Set in a gorgeous wooden house high above the riverfront, this is Battambang's original bar and still the best spot in town. Renowned for its burgers.

Cafe Eden BAR/RESTAURANT
(www.cafeedencambodia.com; 85 St 1; ⊘8am-9pm, closed Tue) Located in an old colonial block on the riverfront, this is a social enterprise offering a relaxed space for an afternoon drink, great food and an original boutique out the back.

Madison Corner BAR/RESTAURANT
(St 3; ⊘7am-11pm) A popular drinking hole for expats, this place has a pool table and welcoming vibe. The menu includes a host of DIY (design it yourself) crepes, and ice cream from the Blue Pumpkin in Siem Reap.

1½ Street Cafe CAFE
(www.kinyei.org; 1 St 1½; ⊘7am-7pm) The home base of Soksabike, this tiny cafe offers a welcome refuge from the backstreets of Battambang. Choose from global coffees, infused teas and some homemade cakes.

Battambang Comfort Inn BAR
(⊘6am-late) This small bar-restaurant near Psar Nat offers two-for-one cocktails on Friday night and is the most gay-friendly drinking spot in town.

☆ Entertainment

Centre Culturel Français CINEMA
(www.ccf-cambodge.org) Valiantly trying to keep French culture alive in the age of the Anglophones, the French Cultural Centre screens films from France (some with English subtitles) at 7pm on Friday. It also has an upstairs *médiathèque* (open 9am to noon and 3.30pm to 7pm Monday to Saturday) with books and DVDs.

🛍 Shopping

Sammaki Gallery ART
(sammaki.kinyei.org; St 2½; ⊘9am-9pm) New contemporary-art gallery showcasing the work of Battambang's diverse and eclectic artistic community.

Fresh Eats Café HANDICRAFTS
(St 2½; ⊘6am-9pm) Sells colourful purses, *kramas,* stuffed animals and other handicrafts made by vulnerable women.

Rachana Handicrafts TEXTILES
(⊘7.30am-5.30pm) A tiny NGO-run sewing workshop on the outskirts of town that trains disadvantaged women and sells purses, stuffed toys, kramas, and cotton and silk accessories. It's difficult to find, so it's best to go with a local moto driver.

Blue Lotus FASHION
(111 St 2; ⊘9am-7pm) New clothing shop, linked to the popular fair-trade Samatoa in Siem Reap. Promises tailor-made and adjusted clothing in just 24 hours.

Hat Bunthoeun SOUVENIRS
(88 St 1; ⊘7am-7pm) One of a cluster of shops along St 1 south of Psar Nat that sells wood and stone carvings, silver jewellery, drums and kitsch oil paintings for the domestic souvenir market.

Smiling Sky Bookshop BOOKS
(113 St 2; ⊘8am-7.30pm) Sells used books in English, French and German.

❶ Information

Battambang's city centre is on the west bank of the Sangker River; its focal point is Psar Nat (Meeting Market). St 1 runs along the riverfront, St 2 is one block inland and St 3 serves as the main commercial thoroughfare. In between are the comically named Sts 1½ and 2½.

Pick up a copy of *Battambang Buzz,* a local quarterly listings mag, available free at guesthouses, hotels and restaurants.

ANZ Royal Bank (St 1) Full international ATM, plus usual currency services.

Canadia Bank (Psar Thom) Free cash withdrawals and cash advances on plastic.

Emergency (☑952822; emergency@online.com.kh;⊘24hr for emergencies) This 70-bed, Italian-run 'surgical centre for war victims' (www.emergency.it) *cannot* help with tropical diseases or routine illness but may be able to save your life if you need emergency surgery. Has two ambulances. On the road to Pailin.

IN MEMORY OF THE BAMBOO TRAIN?

Battambang's **bamboo train** is one of the world's all-time classic rail journeys. From O Dambong, on the east bank 3.7km south of Battambang's old French bridge, the train bumps southeast to O Sra Lav along warped, misaligned rails and vertiginous bridges left by the French. Sadly the upgrade of the railway line may soon see the extinction of the bamboo train, but the Department of Tourism in Battambang has ambitious plans to relocate a section of track and continue this unique form of transport.

Each bamboo train – known in Khmer as a *norry* (*nori*) or *lorry* – consists of a 3m-long wooden frame, covered lengthwise with slats made of ultralight bamboo, that rest on two barbell-like bogies, the aft one connected by fan belts to a 6HP gasoline engine. Pile on 10 or 15 people or up to three tonnes of rice, crank it up and you can cruise along at about 15km/h.

The genius of the system is that it offers a brilliant solution to the most ineluctable problem faced on any single-track line: what to do when two trains going in opposite directions meet. In the case of bamboo trains, the answer is simple: one car is quickly disassembled and set on the ground beside the tracks so that the other can pass. The rule is that the car with the fewest passengers has to cede priority.

KOT Internet (⊙6am-8pm; per hr 1500r) Next to White Rose restaurant.

Polyclinique Visal Sokh (✆952401; NH5; ⊙24hr) For minor medical problems, including snake bites, malaria and rabies shots.

Tourist Information Office (✆730217; www .battambang-town.gov.kh; St 1; ⊙7.30am-5.30pm daily) Has brochures and maps of Battambang.

Vietnamese Consulate (✆952894; ⊙8-11am & 2-4pm Mon-Fri) Issues 15-day visas (US$35) in 15 minutes; one-month visas (US$40) take two or three days.

ⓘ Getting There & Away

Battambang is 290km northwest of Phnom Penh along NH5 and 80km northeast of Pailin along NH57 (formerly NH10).

Boat

The riverboat to Siem Reap (US$20, 7am) squeezes through narrow waterways and passes by protected wetlands, taking from five hours in the wet season to nine or more hours in the height of the dry season. Cambodia's most memorable boat trip, it's operated on alternate days by **Angkor Express** (✆012 601287) and **Chann Na** (✆012 354344). In the dry season, passengers are driven to a navigable section of the river. The best seats are away from the noisy motor. It may be possible to alight at the Prek Toal Bird Sanctuary (p113) and then be picked up there the next day for US$5 extra. Be aware that these fast boats are not always popular with local communities along the way, as the wake has caused small boats to capsize and fishing nets are regularly snagged. They can also be dangerously overcrowded and life jackets are a rare commodity.

Bus

Battambang does not have a central bus station. Rather, bus companies have offices and stops on or near NH5. All companies serve Phnom Penh (293km, 25,000r to 35,000r, five hours), Pursat (15,000r, two hours), Sisophon (10,000r, one hour) and Poipet (15,000r, three hours). Capitol and Neak Kror Horm have buses to Bangkok (US$15) and Siem Reap (20,000r); Paramount Angkor Express also goes to Siem Reap (20,000r). Phnom Penh Sorya has a service to Kompong Cham (35,000r).

Bus companies include the following:

Capitol Tour (✆953040)
Neak Kror Horm (✆953838)
Paramount Angkor Express (✆092 575572)
Phnom Penh Sorya (✆092 181804)
Ponleu Angkor Khmer (✆092 517792)
Rith Mony (✆012 823885)

Taxi

At the **taxi station** (NH5), share taxis to Poipet (20,000r), Sisophon (15,000r) and Siem Reap (30,000r) leave from the north side while taxis to Pursat (15,000r) and Phnom Penh (40,000r) leave from the southeast corner. Budget hotels can assist with arranging a private chartered taxi if you crave more space.

Share taxis to Pursat leave from **Psar Thmei** (NH5), 1km east of Ta Dambong Roundabout.

ⓘ Getting Around

A moto ride in town costs around 2000r, while a *remork* ride starts from US$1 (US$2 for several passengers).

Hiring a moto driver who speaks English or French costs US$6 to US$8 for a half-day in and around town and US$12 for a day trip out of the city. Many of the moto drivers who hang out at the Chhaya and Royal Hotels speak decent English.

Gecko Moto (☑089 924260; www.geckocafe cambodia.com; St 3; ☺8am-7pm) rents out 100cc/250cc motorbikes for US\$6/12 a day. The Chhaya Hotel charges US\$5/7 a day for an old/new motorbike, while the Royal Hotel charges US\$8.

Bicycles are a great way to get around and can be ridden along both banks of the river in either direction. They are available for US\$2 a day at Gecko Moto and the Royal Hotel.

Around Battambang

Before setting off on some adventures, try to link up with an English-speaking moto driver, as it really adds to the experience. Possible itineraries include a loop via Phnom Sampeau to Phnom Banan, with a winery visit on the way back. With your own wheels, Wat Phnom Sampeau and Sneng can be visited on the way to Pailin.

Admission to Phnom Sampeau, Phnom Banan and Wat Ek Phnom costs US\$2. If you purchase a ticket at one site, it's valid all day long at the other two.

A round trip to Phnom Sampeau, Phnom Banan or Wat Ek Phnom costs US\$5 to US\$7 by moto and US\$12 to US\$15 by *remork* (for one passenger). For a full-day trip to several sights, count on paying around US\$12 by moto and US\$20 to US\$25 by *remork*.

For details on sites not mentioned below, check out the guidebook *Around Battambang* (US\$10) by Ray Zepp, which has details on temples, wats and excursions in the Battambang and Pailin areas. Proceeds go to monks and nuns working to raise HIV/AIDS awareness and to help AIDS orphans.

PHNOM SAMPEAU   ភ្នំពេញ

At the summit of this fabled limestone outcrop, 12km southwest of Battambang along NH57 (towards Pailin), a complex of **temples** (admission US\$2) affords gorgeous views. Beware of the macaques that live around the summit, dining on bananas left as offerings, as some can be bad-tempered and aggressive. Access is via a steep staircase or, past the eateries, a cement road.

As you descend from the golden stupa at the summit, turn left under the gate decorated with a bas-relief of Eiy Sei (an elderly Buddha). A **deep canyon**, its vertical sides cloaked in greenery, descends steeply through a natural arch to a 'lost world' of stalactites, creeping vines and bats; two Angkorian warriors stand guard.

In the area between the two sets of antennas, two government **artillery pieces**, one with markings in Russian, the other in German, are still deployed. They point westwards towards **Phnom Krapeu** (Crocodile Mountain), a one-time Khmer Rouge stronghold.

About halfway up the hill, a road leads under a gate and 250m up to the **Killing Caves of Phnom Sampeau**, now a place of pilgrimage. An enchanted staircase, flanked by greenery, leads into a cavern where a golden reclining Buddha lies peacefully next to a glass-walled memorial filled with the bones and skulls of some of the people bludgeoned to death by Khmer Rouge cadres before being thrown through the overhead skylight. Next to the base of the stairway is the **old memorial**, a rusty cage made of chicken wire and cyclone fencing and partly filled with human bones.

At the base of the hill, a 30m-high **Buddha** is being carved out of the cliff face. Due to a lack of funds, only the top of the Buddha's head has been liberated from the natural rock outcrop.

PHNOM BANAN   ប្រាសាទបាណន់

Exactly 358 stone steps lead up shaded Phnom Banan, 28km south of Battambang, to **Prasat Banan** (admission US\$2), whose five towers are reminiscent of the layout of Angkor Wat. Indeed, locals claim it was the inspiration for Angkor Wat, but this seems an optimistic claim.

Udayadityavarman II, son of Suryavarman I, built Prasat Banan in the 11th century, and its hillside location offers incredible views across the surrounding countryside. There are impressive carved lintels above the doorways to each tower and bas-reliefs on the upper parts of the central tower. Many of this temple's best carvings are now in the Battambang Museum (p213).

From the temple, a narrow stone staircase leads south down the hill to three **caves**, which can be visited with a local guide.

WAT KOR VILLAGE

About 2km south of Battambang's Riverside Balcony Bar, on the road to Phnom Banan, is Wat Kor Village, known for its 21 **Khmer heritage houses**. Built of now-rare hardwoods almost a century ago and surrounded by orchard gardens, they have wide verandas and exude the ambience of another era.

CAMBODIA'S WINE COUNTRY

Midway between Battambang and Phnom Banan, in an area best known for its production of red hot chilli peppers (harvested from October to January), one of the world's most exclusive wines is grown on 4 hectares of vines and aged for a short time.

Prasat Phnom Banon Winery (☎012-665238; Bot Sala Village; ⊙6am-6pm), Cambodia's only wine-making enterprise, grows Shiraz and Cabernet Sauvignon grapes to make reds, and tropics-resistant Black Queen and Black Opal grapes to make rosés – liquids it's hard to describe without resorting to superlatives. Let's just say that both have a bouquet unlike anything you've ever encountered in a bottle with the word 'wine' on the label, and a taste as surprising as the aftertaste. Officially recognised by Cambodia's Ministry of Industry, Mines & Energy, Banon wines belong to that exclusive club of wineries whose vintages improve significantly with the addition of ice cubes. Also made here is Banon brandy, which has a heavenly bouquet and a taste that has been compared favourably to turpentine. Sampling takes place in an attractive garden pavilion, and you can visit the vineyards and production facilities.

The winery is 10km south of Battambang and 8km north of Phnom Banan.

One of the most interesting is **Khor Sang House** (☎017-529552, serey07@yahoo.com; admission US$1), its floors worn lustrous by a century of bare feet. Decorated with old furniture, family photos and old school certificates, it was built in 1907 by the French-speaking owner's grandfather, who served as a secretary to the province's last Thai governor. The back section dates from 1890. You can organise a **homestay** (per night US$6) here. Battambang's Tourist Information Office (p219) has details on more accommodation in Wat Kor.

WAT EK PHNOM   បាទ្ឯកភ្នំ

An atmospheric, partly collapsed 11th-century temple, **Wat Ek Phnom** (admission US$2) is surrounded by the remains of a laterite wall and an ancient *baray* (reservoir). A lintel showing the **Churning of the Ocean of Milk** can be seen above the eastern portal to the central temple. This is a very popular picnic and pilgrimage destination for Khmers, especially at festival times, and for women hoping to conceive.

On the way from Battambang by bicycle or moto, it's possible to make a number of interesting stops. About 1.2km north of Battambang's ferry landing is a 1960s **Pepsi bottling plant**, its logo faded but otherwise virtually unchanged since production ceased abruptly in 1975. You can still see the remains of the old production line (down an alley behind the cement water tanks) and, at the far end of the warehouse out back, thousands of dusty empties bearing Pepsi's old logo.

Drive 700m further, and at the sign for the Islamic Local Development Organisation, turn left (west). After 250m you'll get to a signless house, behind which is the **Slaket crocodile farm**. It's open all day, including mealtimes: the crocs are always happy to have tourists for lunch.

Return to the main road and drive another 3.5km, past several wats, to the village of **Pheam Ek**, whose speciality is making rice paper for spring rolls. All along the road, in family workshops, you'll see rice paste being steamed and then placed on a bamboo frame for drying in the sun. The coconuts grown in this area are said to be especially sweet. Wat Ek Phnom is 5.5km further on.

The nonprofit **Cambodian Education Center** in Pheam Ek, 13km from Battambang, provides free English instruction to local kids and is always looking for volunteer teachers (the Khmer staff are all volunteers, too). For details contact **Racky Thy** (☎092-301697; rith_gentleman@yahoo.com).

Wat Ek Phnom is 11km from Battambang's ferry landing by the shortest route and 21km if you go via the Pepsi plant and Pheam Ek. Combining both makes for a nice 32km circuit.

KAMPING POY   កំពីងពួយ

Also known as the Killing Dam, Kamping Poy, 27km west of Battambang (go via NH5 and follow the irrigation canal), was one of the many grandiose Khmer Rouge projects intended to recreate the sophisticated irrigation networks that helped Cambodia wax mighty under the kings of Angkor. As many as 10,000 Cambodians are thought to have perished during its construction, worked to death under the shadow of executions, malnutrition and disease. These days, thanks to the dam, the Kamping Poy area is one of the few parts of Cambodia to produce two rice crops a year.

Despite the lake's grim history, and the fact that there's little to see except the dam and its sluice gates, the area's eateries, dining platforms and row boats (10,000r for two or three hours) are a popular destination for Battambangers on weekends and holidays. It's easy to combine a visit here with a stop at Phnom Sampeau.

SNENG ស្នឹង
This town, located on NH57 20km southwest of Battambang towards Pailin, is home to two small yet interesting temples. **Prasat Yeay Ten**, dedicated to Shiva, dates from the end of the 10th century and, although in a ruinous state, has above its doorways three delicately carved lintels that somehow survived the ravages of time and war; the eastern one depicts the Churning of the Ocean of Milk. The temple is situated on the east side of the highway, so close to the road that it resembles an ancient Angkorian tollbooth.

Behind Prasat Yeay Ten, 200m to the east, is a contemporary wat; tucked away at the back of the wat compound are three **brick sanctuaries** that have some beautifully preserved carvings around the entrances.

PAILIN PROVINCE

Pailin is best known for its gem mines, now pretty much exhausted, a surfeit of landmines and being a refuge for Khmer Rouge pensioners.

During the civil war, the Pailin area's gem and timber resources – sold on international markets with help from Thai army generals – served as the economic crutch that kept the

LANDMINE ALERT!

Pailin and nearby parts of Battambang Province (especially the districts of Samlot and Rotanak Mondol) are some of the most heavily mined places in the world. In recent years, Krong Pailin has had more casualties from mines and unexploded ordnance, per square kilometre, than any other province in Cambodia.

Khmer Rouge war machine hobbling along. In the mid-1990s, it was a staging area for regular dry-season offensives that overran government positions as far east as Phnom Sampeau.

In 1996, the Khmer Rouge supremo in these parts, Ieng Sary or Brother Number Three during the Democratic Kampuchea regime, defected to the government side with 3000 heavily armed troops. His reward was amnesty and free reign in Krong Pailin, a mini-province carved out of Battambang Province to serve as a Khmer Rouge fiefdom. Only in late 2007 were Ieng and his wife arrested for war crimes and crimes against humanity. Ieng's son, Ieng Vuth, currently serves as deputy governor of Pailin.

Pailin ប៉ៃលិន
📍055 / POP 24,000
The remote Wild West town of Pailin has little to recommend it except a particularly colourful hilltop temple and its usefulness as a gateway to an adventurous trip across the Cardamom Mountains – unless you happen to be an ex-Khmer Rouge commander, in which case it's an ideal place to retire among friends.

◉ Sights & Activities

Wat Phnom Yat TEMPLE
From NH57, stairs lead through a garish gate up to Wat Phnom Yat, a psychedelic temple centred on an ancient *po* tree. A life-sized cement **tableau** shows naked sinners being heaved into a cauldron (for the impious), de-tongued (for liars) and forced to climb a spiny tree (for adulterers). Medieval European triptychs don't portray a hell that is nearly so scary. Nearby, the repentant pray for forgiveness, a highly pertinent message given who lives around here. The sunrises and sunsets up here are usually nice enough to take your mind off the fire and brimstone.

At the base of the hill, an impressive gate from 1968 leads to **Wat Khaong Kang**, an important centre for Buddhist teaching before the Khmer Rouge madness. The exterior wall is decorated with an especially long bas-relief of the Churning of the Ocean of Milk.

Waterfalls WATERFALL
Moto drivers can take you to several waterfalls outside town. The problem is that they're at their most impressive during the rainy season, when the roads are often im-

Pailin

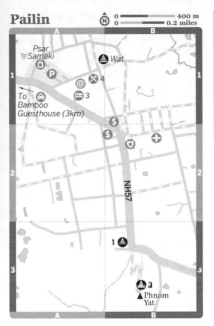

Pakard border crossing, this is one of several casino-hotels set up to milk cash from Thai gamblers. The chance to spin the wheel aside, the rooms are incredible value, including a VIP Suite for US$45.

Pailin Ruby Guesthouse GUESTHOUSE **$**
(☑636 3603; r US$7-15; 🌬) A good-value city-centre place with 48 clean, spacious rooms all kitted out with spring mattresses. It's worth paying US$2 extra for some natural light.

Leang Sreng Restaurant CAMBODIAN **$**
(meals US$1-3; ◷6am-11pm) This informal, open-fronted eatery is known for its steaming bowls of *pho*-style Vietnamese beef noodle soup. Just look for the sign decorated with a laughing cow.

ⓘ Information
Acleda Bank (NH57) With an ATM that handles Visa cash advances.
Boyada Phone Shop (◷7am-8pm) Has four internet computers.
Canadia Bank (NH57) Has an ATM offering free cash withdrawals.
Victoria Supermarket (Psar Pruhm; ◷7am-midnight) Internet access at the border.

ⓘ Getting There & Away
NH57 (sometimes still called Highway 10) from Battambang to Pailin (80km, 2½ hours) is now in excellent shape, making for a very straightforward journey by bus, car or motorbike.

In Battambang, taxis to Pailin leave from the west side of **Psar Leu** (southern end of St 3). A share taxi to Pailin town (1½ hours) costs 20,000r. A private taxi from Battambang direct to the border (oneway/return US$30/60) will give you the option of stopping off at Phnom Sampeau and Sneng. Paramount Angkor Express operate buses from Battambang (15,000r) at 7.30am, 9.30am, 10.30am and 1.30pm.

passable. When the rains dry up, so do the falls. Also they are not comfortable places to explore on foot due to the lingering presence of landmines.

🛏 Sleeping & Eating

TOP CHOICE Bamboo Guesthouse GUESTHOUSE **$$**
(☑012-405818; r US$12-25; 🌬🌐) Run with verve by a family from Kampot, Bamboo is located about 3km from the centre on the northwestern outskirts of town and is an oasis of calm. The 27 bungalows come with air-con, hot water, fridge and cable TV. Smarter options have a forest-lodge feel. The restaurant here serves Pailin's best Khmer and Thai food (mains 35B to 150B) in shaded outdoor pavilions.

Memoria Palace HOTEL **$$**
(☑055-636 3090; www.memoriapalace.com; r US$25; 🌬@🌐🏊) Located about 6km west of Pailin, this lodge-style resort has smart, spacious bungalows with flat-screen TV and DVD player. The hilltop swimming pool is a surprising bonus and there's a good restaurant.

Diamond Crown Hotel & Casino HOTEL **$$**
(☑012-400657; www.dchotelcasino.com; r US$15-45; 🌬@🌐) Located at the Psar Pruhm–Ban

The 22km road from Pailin to the Psar Pruhm-Ban Pakard border crossing is also in good shape. At the border, share taxis (25,000r to Battambang, 5000r or 50B to Pailin) stop near Victoria Supermarket. In Pailin, taxis and motos stop along NH57 just south of Psar Samaki. The 1.30pm Paramount Angkor Express bus from Battambang to Pailin continues to Psar Pruhm (5000r) at about 3pm daily.

A rough track goes from Treng District, about 25km east of Pailin, southward through the Cardamom Mountains to Koh Kong.

Samlaut

The northernmost tip of the Cardamom Mountains – home to elephants, gibbons, pangolins, hornbills and many other endangered creatures – covers the southern half of Krong Pailin (pretty much everything south of NH57). Known as the **Samlaut Multiple Use Area** (600 sq km), this expanse of forested mountains is contiguous with two Thai parks, including Namtok Klong Kaew National Park, with which it may soon be joined in a cross-border **Peace Park**, following a successful joint ranger-training initiative in December 2010. Countless landmines make the area too dangerous for ecotrekking.

Samlaut is administered and patrolled with help from the **Maddox Jolie-Pitt Foundation** (MJP; www.mjpasia.org), named after the adopted Cambodian-born son of its founder and president, the American actress Angelina Jolie.

BANTEAY MEANCHEY PROVINCE

Sandwiched between the casinos of Poipet, Cambodia's most important border crossing with Thailand, and the glories of Angkor, agricultural Banteay Meanchey Province (ខេត្តបន្ទាយមានជ័យ) often gets overlooked by travellers rushing on to Siem Reap or Battambang. Highlights include the Angkorian temple of Banteay Chhmar and the rare birds of Ang Trapeng Thmor Reserve (p116).

Poipet   ប៉ោយប៉ែត

☎054 / POP 50,000

Long the armpit of Cambodia, notorious for its squalor, scams and sleaze, Poipet (pronounced 'poi-*peh*' in Khmer) has recently splurged on a facelift and no longer looks like the post-apocalyptic place it once was.

Thanks mainly to the patronage of neighbouring Thais, whose own country bans gambling, its casino resorts – with names like Tropicana and Grand Diamond City – are helping turn the town into the Las Vegas of Cambodia. The casino zone, with its air-conditioned hotel-casinos, is basically an island of Thailand on Cambodian territory. It's a lot more family-oriented than you might expect, and better-off Khmer families come here to enjoy the feeling of being 'abroad'. However, beyond the border zone it's still a chaotic, trash-strewn strip mall sprinkled with dodgy massage parlours. The Khmers' gentle side is little in evidence, but don't worry, the rest of the country does not carry on like this.

The faster you get used to making quick conversions between Cambodian riel, US dollars and Thai baht, all of which are in use here, the easier: a good rule of thumb is 4000r = US$1 = 30B.

🛏 Sleeping & Eating

The modern megahotels in the casino zone offer three-star rooms starting at 1000B, including breakfast and 500B in casino chips. Cheap hotels and guesthouses, some of them brothels, are strung out along NH5 and around the bus station. However, as a general rule, unless you are an inveterate gambler, don't plan on sticking around.

Orkiday Angkor Hotel   HOTEL **$**
(☎967502; oa_tour@online.com.kh; NH5; r US$13-20; ❄) Right outside the casino zone, this hotel has rooms with terracotta floors, huge beds and hot water. There's no lift, so rates drop as you ascend the stairs.

The cheapest eats are around the market and along NH5. The casino zone's night market, a block north of NH5, has clean, well-lit restaurants and pubs. Some of the casino-zone hotels offer **all-you-can-eat buffets**, which are subsidised to encourage gamblers to stick around.

❶ Information

Poipet stretches from the border (the filthy O Chrou stream) and the clean, modern casino zone eastwards along NH5 for a few kilometres. Cambodian visas (see p350) are issued at the Visa Service, next to the ceremonial Kingdom of Cambodia gate – do not buy a visa anywhere else, no matter what the touts say, or you'll pay 1000B to 1300B instead of the official fee of US$20 (about 600B). Passports are stamped

LANDMINES: CAMBODIA'S UNDERGROUND WAR

Cambodia is a country scarred by years of conflict and some of the deepest scars lie just inches beneath the surface. The legacy of landmines in Cambodia is one of the worst anywhere in the world, with an estimated four to six million dotted about the countryside. Landmines are not just weapons of war, but weapons against peace, as they recognise no ceasefire. Although the conflict ended more than a decade ago, Cambodia's civil war is still claiming new victims: civilians who have stepped on a mine or been injured by unexploded ordnance (UXO), also known as explosive remnants of war (ERW).

The first massive use of mines came in the mid-1980s, when Vietnamese forces (using forced local labour) constructed a 700km-long minefield along the entire Cambodian–Thai border. After the Vietnamese withdrawal, more mines were laid by the Cambodian government to prevent towns, villages, military positions, bridges, border crossings and supply routes from being overrun, and by Khmer Rouge forces to protect areas they still held. Lots more government mines were laid in the mid-1990s in offensives against Khmer Rouge positions around Anlong Veng and Pailin.

Today, Cambodia has one of the world's worst land-mine problems and the highest number of amputees per capita of any country; more than 40,000 Cambodians have lost limbs due to mines and other military explosives. Despite extensive mine-risk-education (MRE) campaigns, an average of about 15 Cambodians are injured or killed every month. This is a vast improvement on the mid-1990s, when the monthly figure was more like 300, but it's still wartime carnage in a country officially at peace.

To make matters more complicated, areas that seem safe in the dry season can become dangerous in the wet season as the earth softens. It's not uncommon for Cambodian farmers to settle on land during the dry season, only to have their dreams of a new life shattered a few months later when a family member has a leg blown off.

A number of groups are working to clear mines. Between 1992 and 2008, 820,000 antipersonnel mines, 20,000 antitank mines and 1.77 million UXOs were removed from 486 sq km, but another 4000 sq km still need to be cleared. When travelling in the more remote parts of provinces such as Battambang, Banteay Meanchey, Krong Pailin, Oddar Meanchey, Preah Vihear and Pursat, you're likely to see de-mining teams run by the **Cambodian Mine Action Authority** (CMAA; www.cmaa.gov.kh), the **HALO Trust** (www.halotrust.org) and the **Mines Advisory Group** (MAG; www.maginternational.org) in action.

Some sage advice about mines:

» In remote areas, never leave well-trodden paths.

» Never touch anything that looks remotely like a mine or munitions.

» If you find yourself accidentally in a mined area, retrace your steps only if you can clearly see your footprints. If not, stay where you are and call for help – as advisory groups put it, 'better to spend a day stuck in a minefield than a lifetime as an amputee'.

» If someone is injured in a minefield, do *not* rush in to assist even if they are crying out for help – find someone who knows how to safely enter a mined area.

» Do not leave the roadside in remote areas, even for the call of nature. Your limbs are more important than your modesty.

In 1997 more than 100 countries signed a treaty banning the production, stockpiling, sale and use of landmines under any circumstances. However, the world's major producers refused to sign, including China, Russia and the USA. Cambodia was a signatory to the treaty, but mine clearance in Cambodia is, tragically, too often a step-by-step process. For the majority of Cambodians, the underground war goes on.

For more on the scourge of landmines, visit the Cambodian Land Mine Museum (p91) near Siem Reap.

200m further on, just beyond the big hotels and right before the 'big roundabout' that marks the eastern edge of the casino zone and, effectively, the western terminus of NH5. Poipet's market is about 1km east of the roundabout and a block north of NH5.

Don't change money at the places suggested by touts, no matter how official they look. In fact, there's no need to change money at all, as baht work just fine here.

ANZ Bank (NH5) Located 1.5km east of big roundabout. ATM here and in the casino zone.

Canadia Bank (NH5) About 1km east of big roundabout. ATM (24 hour) with free withdrawals.

Internet shops (casino zone) One block north of NH5, around the night market.

❶ Getting There & Away

Poipet is 48km west of Sisophon and 153km west of Siem Reap. NH5 between Poipet and Sisophon has at long last been paved.

For details on the Poipet–Aranya Prathet border crossing with Thailand, see p350.

The long-defunct railway line from Sisophon to Poipet is currently being refurbished.

Bus

If you are keen to avoid the official arrangements, some buses also pick up passengers at company offices, situated along NH5 near the turn-off to the bus station.

The many bus companies here including **Capitol Tour** (☑967350), **Phnom Penh Sorya** (☑092-181802) and **GST** (☑012 727771). Destinations include Sisophon (US$2 to US$3, 40 minutes), Siem Reap (US$5, 2½ to four hours), Battambang (US$3.75, two hours) and Phnom Penh (US$7.50, seven hours). Phnom Penh Sorya has a direct service to Kompong Cham. Almost all departures are between 6.15am and 10.30am, though the bus station monopoly (see box below) has afternoon buses to Siem Reap (US$9).

Several companies, including Capitol, offer mid-afternoon services to Bangkok (300B).

POIPET TRANSPORT HEADACHES

The moment you enter Cambodia at Poipet, whether you know it or not, you are the duly purchased client of a monopoly that has paid for the exclusive right to provide you with onward land transport.

Poipet now has two bus stations. The Poipet Tourist Passenger International Terminal, situated 9km east of town in the middle of nowhere, and the International Tourist Terminal, 1.5km east of the tourist zone. Posted fares at both these places are higher than the prices locals pay by up to 250%.

As you exit the immigration police office (where passports are stamped), fencing herds you into the 'Free Shuttle Bus Station', departure point for **OSP buses** (⊙7am-6pm) to the bus stations. OSP's job is straightforward: to cooperate with the international bus stations and make sure tourists get there.

Transport out of Poipet is orchestrated by three 'associations' that work out of the bus station on a rotational basis: each handles all buses and taxis for tourists on every third day. All charge the same fares, offering buses/four-passenger share taxis to Sisophon (US$5/5), Siem Reap (US$9/12), Battambang (US$10/10) and Phnom Penh (US$15/25).

For the cash-strapped traveller, the obvious solution is to find a taxi the way Cambodians do. The problem is that 'association' enforcers, with police backing often intervene to prevent independent taxi drivers from accepting foreign tourists. Readers report that when they declined OSP's shuttle offer, an 'association' agent followed them for blocks and intimidated any taxi driver they came upon. The trick, therefore, is to give the agent the slip, perhaps by saying you'll be overnighting in Poipet.

Remember, though, that once you've escaped the monopoly, you're on your own in dealing with the petty scams the monopolies were designed to end. Taxi drivers (especially at the big roundabout) may demand exorbitant sums to get you to Siem Reap, or a local tout may offer to help you find a taxi to Siem Reap and then overcharge, demanding, say, US$40 and then paying just US$20 to the driver.

The main result of these arrangements, other than the transfer of lucre into unseen pockets, is a lot of angry tourists. Some take out their frustrations on the taxi drivers, but these fellows have no choice but to accept work from the 'associations'. They're certainly not the ones getting rich from the whole enterprise.

Taxi

Six-person share taxis are available all day along NH5 about 1.3km east of the roundabout (near the bus station turn-off) if you can avoid the bus station 'associations'. Destinations include Sisophon (100B, 40 minutes), Siem Reap (250B, three hours), Battambang (200B, two hours) and Phnom Penh (500B). The usual fee for a private taxi is six times the single-seat fare, as Cambodian share taxis pack two and sometimes three passengers in front and four in back.

ⓘ Getting Around

Inside the casino zone, free casino-run shuttles whisk guests to and fro. Moto drivers wait at the big roundabout; a ride from the border to the bus station costs about 2000r (US$1 at night).

Sisophon   ស៊ីសុផុន
054 / POP 40,000

Sisophon (also confusingly known as Svay, Svay Sisophon, Srei Sophon and Banteay Meanchey) is strategically situated at northwest Cambodia's great crossroads, the intersection of NH5 and NH6. There is not a lot of reason to stick around the town, but some travellers use it as a base for exploring the Angkorian temples of Banteay Chhmar. It's arguably more rewarding to support the community homestay project (p229) operating in the village of Banteay Chhmar.

⊙ Sights & Activities

École d'Art et de Culture
Khmers   ARTS CENTRE
(School of Khmer Art & Culture; 017 449277; 7-11am & 2-5pm Mon-Fri, 7-11am Sat) Housed in a traditional Khmer-style building, this school teaches children traditional music, *apsara* dancing, painting, sculpture and shadow puppetry. It's usually possible to observe a class or see students practising.

🛏 Sleeping & Eating

Botoum Hotel   HOTEL $
(012 687858; r US$8-15; ✳@🛜) A new hotel near the Provincial Hall. The rooms are a real find compared with what is on offer elsewhere in town. The small coffee shop out front brews a good cuppa.

Golden Crown Guesthouse   HOTEL $
(958444; r US$6-13; ✳🛜) One of the most central hotels in town. Rooms are fair value, including hot-water showers and satellite

Sisophon

⊙ Sights
1 École d'Art et de Culture
    Khmers...B1

🛏 Sleeping
2 Botoum Hotel....................................A2
3 Golden Crown Guesthouse B1

🍽 Eating
4 Food Stalls..A2
5 Mirror Restaurant.............................B1
6 Psar Sisophon....................................A1

TV. Downstairs is a cheap and mildly cheerful restaurant.

Mirror Restaurant   CAMBODIAN $
(mains US$2-7) Quite a trendy little spot for backwater Sisophon, this modern diner offers traditional Cambodian *phnom pleung* (hill of fire or DIY barbecue) for 30,000r (US$7.50), plus sizzling barbecue chicken. The menu even includes ice cream.

ⓘ Information

NH6 (from Siem Reap and Phnom Penh) intersects NH5 (from Battambang and Phnom Penh) at the western tip of the triangular town centre.

Acleda Bank Not far from Botoum Hotel, Acleda has a 24-hour ATM that handles Visa cash advances.

Bayon Web (per hr 2000r; 7am-about 8pm) Internet access facing the Golden Crown Guesthouse.

Canadia Bank Full international ATM with free withdrawals.

NORTHWESTERN CAMBODIA SISOPHON

ⓘ Getting There & Away

Sisophon is 48km (40 minutes by car) east of Poipet, 105km west of Siem Reap, 61km south of Banteay Chhmar and 68km northwest of Battambang.

Long-haul buses and most share taxis stop at the bus and taxi station, about 400m south of NH6. Companies including **Capitol Tour**, **Rith Mony** and **Phnom Penh Sorya** serve Poipet (5000r to 10,000r), Siem Reap (15,000r to 20,000r), Battambang (7000r to 10,000r), Phnom Penh (US$5 to US$6) and Bangkok (US$10). Buses heading west depart between 6.30am and 10.30am; buses to Poipet and Bangkok leave in the early afternoon.

Share taxis link the bus station with Phnom Penh (US$10, five hours), Siem Reap (US$5) and Battambang (15,000r, one hour); a private taxi to Siem Reap costs about US$30. Share taxis to Poipet (10,000r) stop on NH5.

For details on transport to Banteay Chhmar, see p229.

Banteay Chhmar បន្ទាយឆ្មារ

The temple complex of Banteay Chhmar was constructed by Cambodia's most prolific builder, Jayavarman VII (r 1181–1219), on the site of a 9th-century temple and is one of the most impressive remote temple complexes beyond the Angkor area. The **Global Heritage Fund** (www.globalheritagefund.org) is assisting with conservation efforts and it is now a top candidate for Unesco World Heritage Site status. The nearby village is part of a worthwhile scheme to offer homestays to assist with community development.

◉ Sights

Banteay Chhmar   TEMPLE

(បន្ទាយឆ្មារ; admission US$5) Banteay Chhmar housed one of the largest and most impressive Buddhist monasteries of the Angkorian period and was originally enclosed by a 9km-long wall. Today it is one of the few temples to feature the enigmatic, Bayon-style, four-faced **Avalokiteshvaras**, with their mysterious and iconic smiles.

Banteay Chhmar is renowned for its 2000 sq metres of intricate carvings, including scenes of daily life. On the temple's east side, a huge **bas-relief** on a partly toppled wall dramatically depicts naval warfare between the Khmers (on the left) and the Chams (on the right), with the dead (some being devoured by crocodiles) at the bottom. Further south (to the left) are scenes of land warfare with infantry and elephants. There are more martial bas-reliefs along the exterior of the temple's south walls.

The once-grand entry gallery is now a jumble of fallen sandstone blocks, though elsewhere a few intersecting galleries have withstood the ravages of time, as have some almost-hidden 12th-century inscriptions. Sadly, all the *apsaras* (nymphs) have been decapitated by looters.

Unique to Banteay Chhmar was a sequence of eight **multiarmed Avalokiteshvaras** on the exterior of the southern section of the temple's western ramparts, but several of these were dismantled and trucked into Thailand in a brazen act of looting in 1998. The segments intercepted by the Thais are now on display in Phnom Penh's National Museum (p39); the two figures that remain in situ – one with 22 arms, the other with 32 – are truly spectacular.

Banteay Top   TEMPLE

Set among rice paddies southeast of Banteay Chhmar, Banteay Top (Fortress of the Army), may only be a small temple, but there's something special about the atmosphere here. Constructed around the same time as Banteay Chhmar, it may be a tribute to the army of Jayavarman VII, which confirmed Khmer dominance over the region by comprehensively defeating the Chams. One of the damaged towers looks decidedly precarious, like a bony finger pointing skyward. To get here from Banteay Chhmar, go south (towards Sisophon) along NH69 for 7km and then head east for 5km.

Other Temples   TEMPLES

There are nine fascinating satellite temples in the vicinity of Banteay Chhmar, all in a ruinous state and some accessible only if you chop through the jungle. These include Prasat Mebon, Prasat Ta Prohm, Prasat Prom Muk Buon, Prasat Yeay Choun, Prasat Pranang Ta Sok and Prasat Chiem Trey.

🏃 Activities

It is possible to see **silk** being woven and to purchase top-quality silk products destined for the French market at **Soieries du Mékong** (Mekong Silk Mill; www.soieriesdumekong.com, in French; ⊙7.30am-noon & 1.30-5pm Mon-Fri), 150m south of where NH69 from Sisophon meets the *baray*. It's affiliated with the French NGO **Enfants du Mékong** (☑012 307069; www.enfantsdumekong.com).

At the headquarters of the **Banteay Chhmar Protected Landscape** (☑012 197 1225),

2km towards Sisophon from town, it may be possible to hire a guide (non-English-speaking) for a nature walk.

🛏 Sleeping & Eating

Homestay Project HOMESTAY
(☑012 237605; cbtbanteaychhmar@yahoo.com; r US$7) Thanks to a pioneering community-based homestay project, it's possible to stay in Banteay Chhmar and three nearby hamlets. Rooms are inside private homes and come with mosquito nets, fans that run when there's electricity (6pm to 10pm) and downstairs bathrooms. Part of the income goes into a community development fund.

Banteay Chhmar Restaurant CAMBODIAN
(mains US$1.50-4) Near the temple's eastern entrance, this rustic restaurant is the only place to dine without pre-ordering. It serves really tasty Khmer food.

ℹ Information

Over the road and a bit south is the **community-based tourism office** (☑012 237605), which arranges homestays, ox-cart rides and rents bicycles (US$1.50 per day).

ℹ Getting There & Away

Banteay Chhmar is 61km north of Sisophon and about 50km southwest of Samraong along NH69, which is slowly but steadily being upgraded. However, renovations took a major hit during the flooding in the second half of 2011. The temple can be visited on a long day trip from Siem Reap.

From Sisophon's Psar Thmei (1km north of NH6), most northbound share taxis go only as far as Thmor Puok, although a few continue on to Banteay Chhmar (northbound/southbound 10,000r/15,000r, one hour). The few pick-ups that link Sisophon's Psar Thmei with Samraong pass through Banteay Chhmar. A moto from Sisophon to Banteay Chhmar should cost about US$12 to US$15 return.

The main road through town runs east-west south of the *baray* (the reservoir surrounding the temple) and then takes a 90-degree turn, heading north just east of the *baray*. The market and taxi park are at the turn; a few hundred metres north is the temple's main (eastern) entrance.

ODDAR MEANCHEY PROVINCE

The remote, dirt-poor province of Oddar Meanchey (ខេត្តឧត្តរមានជ័យ) produces very little apart from opportunities for aid organ-

LANDMINE ALERT!

Banteay Meanchey and Oddar Meanchey are among the most heavily mined provinces in Cambodia. Do not, under any circumstances, stray from previously trodden paths. If you've got your own wheels, travel only on roads or trails regularly used by locals.

isations. Khmer Rouge sites around Anlong Veng are starting to attract visitors, both foreign and Cambodian.

The province has two seldom-used international border crossings with Thailand: Choam-Choam Sa Ngam and O Smach-Chong Jom.

Anlong Veng   អន្លង់វែង

For almost a decade this was the ultimate Khmer Rouge stronghold, home to Pol Pot, Nuon Chea, Khieu Samphan and Ta Mok, among the most notorious leaders of Democratic Kampuchea. Anlong Veng fell to government forces in April 1998 and about the same time Pol Pot died mysteriously nearby. Soon after, Prime Minister Hun Sen ordered that NH67 be bulldozed through the jungle to ensure that the population didn't have second thoughts about ending the war.

Today Anlong Veng is a poor, dusty town with little going for it except the nearby Choam-Choam Sa Ngam border crossing, which connects with a pretty isolated part of Thailand. For those with an interest in contemporary Cambodian history, the area's Khmer Rouge sites are an important part of the picture. In this area, most of the residents, and virtually the entire political leadership and upper class, are ex-Khmer Rouge or their descendents.

Thanks in part to improved road connections to Siem Reap, the local economy is developing fast.

◉ Sights & Activities

TA MOK'S HOUSE & GRAVE

To his former supporters, many of whom still live in Anlong Veng, Ta Mok (Uncle Mok, aka Brother Number Five) was harsh but fair, a benevolent builder of orphanages and schools, and a leader who kept order, in stark contrast to the anarchic atmosphere that prevailed once government forces took over. But to most Cambodians, Pol Pot's military enforcer, responsible for thousands of deaths in successive purges during the terrible years of Democratic Kampuchea, was best known as 'the Butcher'. Arrested in 1999, he died in July 2006 in a Phnom Penh hospital, awaiting trial for genocide and crimes against humanity.

Ta Mok's House   MUSEUM
(admission US$2) On a peaceful lakeside site, is a Spartan structure with a bunker in the basement, five childish wall murals downstairs (one of Angkor Wat, four of Prasat Preah Vihear) and three more murals upstairs, including an idyllic wildlife scene. About the only furnishings that weren't looted are the floor tiles.

Swampy Ta Mok's Lake was created on Brother Number Five's orders, but the water killed all the trees, their skeletons a fitting monument to the devastation he and his movement left behind. In the middle of the lake, due east from the house, is a small brick structure, an outhouse and all that remains of Pol Pot's residence in Anlong Veng.

To get to Ta Mok's house, head north from the Dove of Peace Roundabout for about 2km, turn right and continue 200m past the so-called Tourism Information hut.

Ta Mok's Grave   MONUMENT
From the turn-off to Ta Mok's house, driving a further 7km north takes you to Tumnup Leu village, where a right turn and 400m brings you to Ta Mok's grave. Situated next to a very modest pagoda, it is now marked by an elaborate, Angkorian-style mausoleum built by his rich grandson in 2009. The cement tomb bears no name or inscription, but this doesn't seem to bother the locals who stop by to light incense and, in a bizarre local tradition, hope his spirit grants them a winning lottery number.

DANGREK MOUNTAINS
Further north, atop the Dangkrek Mountains, are a number of other key Khmer Rouge sites. For years the world wondered where Pol Pot and his cronies were hiding out: the answer was right here, close enough to Thailand that they could flee across the border if government forces drew nigh.

About 2km before the frontier, where the road splits to avoid a house-sized boulder, look out for a group of statues – hewn entirely from the surrounding rock by the Khmer Rouge – depicting a woman carrying bundles of bamboo sticks on her head and two uni-

formed Khmer Rouge soldiers (the latter were decapitated by government forces).

Near the border under a rusted corrugated iron roof and surrounded by rows of partly buried glass bottles, is the cremation site of Pol Pot, who was hastily burned in 1998 on a pile of rubbish and old tyres, a fittingly inglorious end, some say, given the suffering he inflicted on millions of Cambodians. Bizarre as it may sound, Pol Pot is remembered with affection by some locals, and people sometimes stop by to light incense. According to neighbours, every last bone fragment has been snatched from the ashes by visitors in search of good-luck charms. Pol Pot, too, is said to give out winning lottery numbers.

A few hundred metres north, next to a ramshackle smugglers' market, is the old Choam–Choam Sa Ngam border crossing (for more information, see p349). From the smugglers' market, a dirt road with potholes the size of parachutes, navigable only by 4WD vehicles and motorbikes, heads east, parallel to the escarpment. Domestic tourists head to Peuy Ta Mok (Ta Mok's Cliff) to enjoy spectacular views of Cambodia's northern plains, and some stay at the Khnong Phnom Dankrek Guesthouse (☎012 444067; r US$7.50), whose six rooms have mosquito nets and windows with shutters instead of glass.

From here the road continues northeast past slash-and-burn homesteads and army bases. After about 8km you come to Khieu Samphan's house, buried in the jungle on the bank of a stream, from where it's a few hundred metres along an overgrown road to Pol Pot's house. Surrounded by a cinder-block wall, the jungle hideout was comprehensively looted, though you can still see a low brick building whose courtyard hides an underground bunker.

The Choam border crossing is a good place to find a moto driver who knows the snaking route to Pol Pot's house (30,000r).

🛏 Sleeping

Monorom Guesthouse   HOTEL $
(☎012 603339; r with fan/air-con from US$6/15; ✳@🛜) Anlong Veng's finest hostelry has big, modern rooms with air-con and hot water. The new wing includes VIP rooms but is often full of visiting, well, VIPs.

Bot Ouddom Guesthouse   GUESTHOUSE $
(☎011 500507; r with fan/air-con from US$8/15; ✳) Owned by the family of the deputy gov-

ernor, this establishment has 40 spacious, spotless rooms, some with massive hardwood beds. The new annexe looks out on Ta Mok's Lake or swamp.

✖ Eating

South of the roundabout there are a few all-day eateries and a lively night market whose blazing braziers barbecue chicken, fish and eggs on skewers.

Phkay Preuk Restaurant   CAMBODIAN $
(NH67; mains 5000r-20,000r; ⊙6am-10pm) This popular eatery serves tasty, great-value Khmer dishes in private pavilions and is a good place to sup on a cold Angkor Beer. Situated about 2km north of town and a few buildings south of the turn-off to Ta Mok's house.

Sheang Hai Restaurant   CHINESE $
(mains US$2-6; ⊙5am-9pm) Named after the Chinese city of Shanghai (the Chinese-Cambodian owner's nickname), this canteen-like place serves Chinese and Khmer dishes, including fried rice and tom yam soup, on massive wooden tables. Avoid any bush meat that might be an endangered species.

❶ Information

The town's focal point is the Dove of Peace Roundabout, its monument a gift from Hun Sen. From here, roads lead north to the Choam border crossing, east to Sra Em and Prasat Preah Vihear, and south to Siem Reap (along NH67).

Acleda Bank (⊙7.30am-2pm Mon-Fri, 7.30am-noon Sat) The only bank in town; has an ATM.

VTC Computer (per hr US$1; ⊙6am-9pm) Anlong Veng's original internet shop.

❶ Getting There & Around

Anlong Veng is 124km north of Siem Reap along the excellent NH67, 16km south of the Choam-Choam Sa Ngam border crossing and about 90km west of Sra Em, the turn-off for Prasat Preah Vihear.

To Siem Reap, share taxis (20,000r, 1½ hours) and pick-ups (outside/inside 10,000r/15,000r) are most frequent in the morning, which is also when share taxis go east to Sra Em (20,000r, two hours).

Sheang Hai Restaurant sell tickets for GST buses to Siem Reap (15,000r, two hours, departure at 7.30am). There is no public transport to Banteay Chhmar.

To get from Anlong Veng to the Choam–Choam Sa Ngam border crossing, take a moto (15,000r oneway) or a private taxi (US$15).

To get to Ta Mok's house, locals pay 2000r for a moto. A moto circuit to the border, via Ta Mok's house and grave, costs 30,000r (60,000r including a tour of Pol Pot's house).

PREAH VIHEAR PROVINCE

Bordering Thailand and Laos to the north, vast Preah Vihear Province (ខេត្តព្រះវិហារ), much of it heavily forested and extremely remote, is home to three of Cambodia's most impressive Angkorian legacies. Prasat Preah Vihear, stunningly perched on a promontory high in the Dangkrek Mountains, became Cambodia's second Unesco World Heritage Site in 2008, sparking an armed stand-off with Thailand. The mighty Preah Khan isn't as far north, but is reachable only in the dry season. The 10th-century capital of Koh Ker (p154) is more accessible and lies a straightforward toll-road drive from Siem Reap, via Beng Mealea.

Preah Vihear Province, genuine 'outback' Cambodia, remains desperately poor, in part because many areas were under Khmer Rouge control until 1998, and in part because of the catastrophic state of the transport infrastructure. The needs of the Cambodian army in its confrontation with Thailand, and the patriotic fervour unleashed by the Prasat Preah Vihear crisis, seem to have had a dramatic effect on the implementation of long-promised road upgrades. A huge number of roads have been bulldozed through, graded and surfaced in the past couple of years, making travel a bit more straightforward, although public transport is still in short supply.

❶ Getting There & Around

The province's main transport artery, the north–south NH64 from Kompong Thom to Tbeng Meanchey (157km), is now surfaced, making

LANDMINE ALERT!

Preah Vihear Province, especially Choam Ksant district and Prasat Preah Vihear temple, is one of the most heavily mined provinces in Cambodia. Do not, under any circumstances, stray from previously trodden paths. Those with their own transport should travel only on roads or trails regularly used by locals.

access much easier. North of Tbeng Meanchey, roads to Prasat Preah Vihear, Choam Ksant and Anlong Veng have also been surfaced in the last year or two.

Tbeng Meanchey
ត្បូងមានជ័យ

📞064 / POP 25,000

Tbeng Meanchey, often referred to by locals as Preah Vihear (not to be confused with Prasat Preah Vihear), is one of Cambodia's sleepier provincial capitals. Sprawling and dusty red (or muddy red, depending on the season), it has the grid layout of a large city but, in fact, consists of little more than two parallel main roads, running north to south, on which dogs lounge in the middle of the day. There's very little to see or do here, but the town makes a good staging post for an overland journey to the mountain-top temple of Prasat Preah Vihear, 110km further north.

◉ Sights

🏴 Weaves of Cambodia   SILK WEAVING
(📞092-293342; www.weavescambodia.com) Originally established by the **Vietnam Veterans of America Foundation** (www.veteransfor america.org), Weaves of Cambodia, known locally as Chum Ka Mo, is a silk-weaving centre that provides work and rehabilitation for landmine and polio victims, widows and artisans. At their hand looms from 7am to 11am and 1pm to 5pm Monday to Friday and Saturday morning, produce silk scarves (US$25 to US$40) and sarongs (US$70) for export. It is now part of Vientiane-based American textile designer Carol Cassidy's silk empire. To get here from the hospital on Mlou Prey St, head half-a-block south and four anonymous blocks east.

🛏 Sleeping

Home Vattanak Guesthouse   GUESTHOUSE $$
(📞636 3000; St A14; r US$17-35; ✱@🙰) Wow, this is something a bit different for backwater Tbeng Meanchey. The 27 rooms include such luxuries as flat screen TVs and slick bathrooms. Standard rooms are US$17, or anoint yourself for a VIP for US$35.

Prom Tep Guesthouse   GUESTHOUSE $
(📞012 964645; Koh Ker St; r with fan/air-con US$6/16; ✱@) Large enough to be a hotel, this three-storey place has 25 big, impersonal rooms, all with cable TV and throne toilets. It was undergoing a major renova-

tion involving a garish green paint scheme during our visit.

Heng Heng Guesthouse   GUESTHOUSE $
(📞012 900992; Mlou Prey St; r with fan/air-con US$8/16; ✱) This 35-room place offers a good deal. Top-floor rooms have soaring ceilings and all include satellite TV, fridge and private bathroom.

🍴 Eating

Food stalls can be found along the northern side of **Psar Kompong Pranak** (Koh Ker St). There are several eateries facing the taxi park and around the corner on Koh Ker St.

Dara Raksmey Restaurant   CAMBODIAN $
(Mlou Prey St; mains 8000-20,000r; ⊙lunch & dinner) Tbeng Meanchey's finest and fanciest, with mirror-clad columns, massive wooden tables and the usual selection of popular Khmer dishes.

Mlop Dong Restaurant   CAMBODIAN $
(St A10; mains 5000-8000r; ⊙6am-7.30pm) This ramshackle local eatery serves up tasty Khmer staples, including flavoursome soups, barbecued meat and fried veggies.

ℹ Information

The centre of town, insofar as there is one, is around the taxi park and the market, a mass of low shacks on Koh Ker St known as Psar Kompong Pranak. A long block east, NH64 is known as Mlou Prey St in town.

Acleda Bank (Koh Ker St) Has a 24-hour ATM that offers Visa cash advances.

MSN Computer (Koh Ker St; ⊙7am-6pm) Internet access.

Tourist office (📞012 496154; Mlou Prey St; ⊙7.30-11.30am & 2-5pm Mon-Fri) A newish tourist information pavilion if you are lucky enough to find someone in residence.

ℹ Getting There & Around

Tbeng Meanchey is 157km north of Kompong Thom, 110km south of Prasat Preah Vihear, 72km east of Koh Ker and 185km northeast of Siem Reap. These roads are now all in good shape and surfaced for most of their length.

GST and Phnom Penh Sorya have 7am buses to Kompong Thom (20,000r, three hours) and Phnom Penh (25,000r, seven hours).

Share taxis, which leave from the **bus and taxi station** (St A10), go to Kompong Thom (25,000r, three hours) and, much less frequently, to Siem Reap (30,000r, departure at 7am), Choam Ksant (20,000r, two hours) and Sra Em (30,000r, two hours). Private taxis can be hired

Tbeng Meanchey

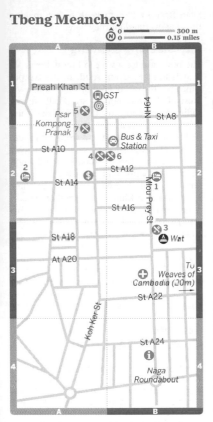

currently no public transport on this route, but it is possible to arrange space on an occasional pick-up truck or negotiate with Tbeng Meanchey moto drivers to undertake the long drive. Expect to pay about US$40 for the journey until the road settles down. It is about 110km and takes around four hours.

Prasat Preah Vihear

ប្រាសាទព្រះវិហារ

The most dramatically situated of all the Angkorian monuments, 800m-long **Prasat Preah Vihear** (www.preahvihearauthority.org; admission temporarily free) is perched high atop an escarpment in the Dangkrek Mountains (elevation 625m). The views are breathtaking: lowland Cambodia, 550m below, stretches as far as the eye can see, with the holy mountain of Phnom Kulen (p152) looming in the distance.

Prasat Preah Vihear, an important place of pilgrimage during the Angkorian period, was built by a succession of seven Khmer monarchs, beginning with Yasovarman I (r 889–910) and ending with Suryavarman II (r 1112–1152), builder of Angkor Wat. Like other temple-mountains from this period, it was designed to represent Mt Meru and was dedicated to the Hindu deity Shiva, though, unlike Angkor Wat, it's laid out along a north-to-south processional axis.

The best place to start a visit is at the bottom of the grey-sandstone **Monumental Stairway**. As you walk southward up the slope, you come to five cruciform *gopura* (pavilions), decorated with exquisite carvings and separated by esplanades up to 275m long. Delicate **Gopura V**, the first you come to, appears on the 1995-series 50,000r banknote and the 2008-series 2000r banknote. On the pediment above the southern door to **Gopura IV**; look for an early rendition of the Churning of the Ocean of Milk, a theme later depicted awesomely at Angkor Wat. The galleries around **Gopura I**, with their inward-looking windows, are in a remarkably good state of repair, but the Central Sanctuary is just a pile of rubble. Nearby, the cliff affords **stupendous views** of Cambodia's northern plains and is a fantastic spot for a picnic.

More recently the long-closed, 1800m **Eastern Stairway**, used for centuries by pilgrims climbing up from Cambodia's northern plains, was de-mined for reopening. To get there, turn north off the Sra Em-Kor Muy highway onto a paved road at a point

Tbeng Meanchey

🛏 Sleeping
1 Heng Heng Guesthouse	....	B2
2 Home Vattanak Guesthouse	....	A2

🍴 Eating
3 Dara Raksmey Restaurant	....	B3
4 Eateries	....	A2
5 Food Stalls	....	A1
6 Mlop Dong Restaurant	....	B2
7 Psar Kompong Pranak	....	A2

to Siem Reap (US$50 oneway), Kompong Thom (US$45 oneway) and Prasat Preah Vihear (oneway/return US$50/70).

A new road to link Tbeng Meanchey with Thala Boravit, across the Mekong from Stung Treng (see p257), is now under construction and when the bridges are finished this will eventually connect the temples of Angkor and Preah Vihear Province with Stung Treng, Ratanakiri and Champasak Province in southern Laos. There is

5km east of Kor Muy and 200m west of the big tree at the bend in the road.

The best guidebook to Prasat Preah Vihear's architecture and carvings is *Preah Vihear*, by Vittorio Roveda. These days it may be hard to find in Cambodia, as it was published in Thailand and the text is in English and Thai.

During our most recent visit in January 2012, there was still a large military presence in and around the temple. Ostensibly for security, it might make some visitors uncomfortable, and money or cigarettes are occasionally requested by soldiers. Always check the latest security situation when in Siem Reap or Phnom Penh before making the long overland journey here.

🛏 Sleeping & Eating

The best base for a visit to Prasat Preah Vihear is Sra Em, 27km south of the temple, which has the feel of a Wild West boomtown. Most of the guesthouses are, shall we say, rudimentary, and cater to soldiers and their families. **Sok San Guesthouse** (☑097 715 3839; r US$9-16; ❄@🤶) is cut from a different cloth and is the smartest (relatively speaking) in town. The 36 rooms include hot-water bathrooms, and remarkably for this remote outpost free wi-fi is available. There is also a decent Khmer restaurant attached.

Perhaps because Cambodia's army officers like to eat well, Sra Em has surprisingly good dining. **Pkay Prek Restaurant** (mains 4000-16,000r; ⏱6am-10pm) is famous for its delicious *phnom pleung* (hill of fire), which is served in open-air pavilions and which you barbecue yourself. Be sure not to order the meat of endangered animals, possibly poached by soldiers from the nearby forests.

❶ Getting There & Away

Normally, the easiest way to get to Prasat Preah Vihear is from Thailand, as there are paved roads from Kantharalak almost up to the Monumental Stairway. However, due to the long stand-off between Thailand and Cambodia (see the box, p236), the border has been sealed with concertina wire for several years. Until mid-2008, it was open for visa-free day trips (US$10) from the Thai side and may well reopen again during the lifetime of this book assuming relations between the two countries continue to improve.

The roads up here in this northernmost part of Cambodia are improving, as are the public-transport options. Share taxis now link the junction town of Sra Em, 27km from the temple, with Siem Reap (30,000r from Sra Em, US$10 from Siem Reap, three hours), Anlong Veng (20,000r, 1½ hours) and Tbeng Meanchey (25,000r, two hours). A private taxi from Siem Reap costs US$70 oneway. Some taxis also serve Kor Muy, at the base of the mountain. **GST** (☑077-881193) operates daily buses between Sra Em and Phnom Penh (40,000r) or Siem Reap (40,000r), both services departing at 7am.

For travel from Sra Em to Kor Muy (22km), a share taxi costs 10,000r per person, while a moto is more like US$10 following some serious negotiation. From there, the return trip up to the temple (5km each way), past sandbagged machine-gun positions, costs US$7 by moto or US$25 by jacked-up pick-up truck (the cement

Prasat Preah Vihear

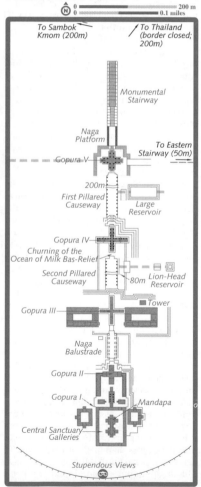

road is too steep for normal motorcars). Some moto drivers, many of whom are off-duty army officers, are happy to act as guides. A new, winding road with a more gentle gradient is currently under construction and will be completed during the lifetime of this book. Don't worry, a cable car is still light years away.

Chhep Vulture-Feeding Station

In order to save three critically endangered species, the white-rumped, slender-billed and red-headed vultures, the **Wildlife Conservation Society** (WCS; www.wcs.org) set up a 'vulture restaurant' at Chhep, on the edge of the ultra-remote Preah Vihear Protected Forest. With at least a week's advance coordination, visitors can observe these almost-extinct carrion eaters dining on the carcass of a domestic cow and, through fees, contribute to the project's funding.

The feeding station, accessible only in the dry season, and even then only by 4WD, is about 50km northeast of Tbeng Meanchey (80km in the wet season). To arrange a visit, contact the Siem Reap–based **Sam Veasna Center** (Map p92; ☑063-963710; www.samveasna.org). Accommodation is at a forest camp maintained by the WCS.

Preah Khan   ព្រះខន្ធ

Covering almost 5 sq km, **Preah Khan** (admission US$5) – not to be confused with a temple of the same name at Angkor – is the largest temple enclosure constructed during the Angkorian period, quite a feat when you consider the competition. Thanks to its back-of-beyond location, the site is astonishingly quiet and peaceful.

Preah Khan's history is shrouded in mystery, but it was long an important religious site, and some of the structures here date back to the 9th century. Both Suryavarman II, builder of Angkor Wat, and Jayavarman VII lived here at various times during their lives, suggesting that Preah Khan was something of a second city in the Angkorian empire. Originally dedicated to Hindu deities, it was reconsecrated to Mahayana Buddhist worship during a monumental reconstruction undertaken by Jayavarman VII in the late 12th and early 13th centuries.

At the eastern end of the 3km-long *baray* (reservoir) is a small pyramid temple called

LANDMINE ALERT!

Until as recently as 1998, landmines were used by the Khmer Rouge to defend Prasat Preah Vihear against government forces. During the past decade, demining organisations made real headway in clearing the site of these enemies within. However, the advent of a border conflict with Thailand led to this area being heavily militarised once again. Both sides denied laying new landmines during the armed stand-off between Cambodia and Thailand from 2008 to 2011, but rumours persist, as several Thai and Cambodian soldiers were killed by mines in the vicinity of the temple. So do not, under any circumstances, stray from marked paths.

Prasat Damrei (Elephant Temple). At the summit of the hill, two of the original exquisitely carved elephants can still be seen; two others are at Phnom Penh's National Museum (p39) and Paris' Musée Guimet.

In the centre of the *baray* is **Prasat Preah Thkol** (known by locals as Mebon), an island temple similar in style to the Western Mebon at Angkor. At the *baray's* western end stands **Prasat Preah Stung** (known to locals as Prasat Muk Buon or Temple of the Four Faces), perhaps the most memorable structure here because its central tower is adorned with four enigmatic Bayon-style faces of **Avalokiteshvara**.

It's a further 400m southwest to the walls of Preah Khan itself, which are surrounded by a moat similar to the one around Angkor Thom. Near the eastern *gopura* (entrance pavilion) there's a **dharmasala** (pilgrims' rest house). Much of this central area is overgrown by forest.

As recently as the mid-1990s, the central structure was thought to be in reasonable shape, but some time in the second half of the decade looters arrived seeking buried statues under each *prang* (temple tower). Assaulted with pneumatic drills and mechanical diggers, the ancient temple never stood a chance and many of the towers simply collapsed in on themselves, leaving the depressing mess we see today. Once again, a temple that had survived so much couldn't stand the onslaught of the 20th century and its all-consuming appetite.

THE FIGHT FOR PRASAT PREAH VIHEAR

For generations, Prasat Preah Vihear (Khao Phra Wiharn to the Thais) has been a source of tension between Cambodia and Thailand. This area was ruled by Thailand for several centuries, but was returned to Cambodia during the French protectorate, under the treaty of 1907. In 1959 the Thai military seized the temple from Cambodia and then-Prime Minister Sihanouk took the dispute to the International Court of Justice in the Hague, gaining worldwide recognition of Cambodian sovereignty in a 1962 ruling.

The next time Prasat Preah Vihear made international news was in 1979, when the Thai military pushed more than 40,000 Cambodian refugees across the border in one of the worst cases of forced repatriation in UN history. The area was mined and many – perhaps several hundred – refugees died from injuries, starvation and disease before the occupying Vietnamese army could cut a safe passage and escort them on the long walk south to Kompong Thom.

Prasat Preah Vihear hit the headlines again in May 1998 because the Khmer Rouge regrouped here after the fall of Anlong Veng and staged a last stand that soon turned into a final surrender. The temple was heavily mined during these final battles and demining was ongoing up until the outbreak of the conflict with Thailand. Remining seems to be the greater threat right now, with both sides accusing the other of using landmines.

In July 2008 Prasat Preah Vihear was declared Cambodia's second Unesco World Heritage Site. The Thai government, which claims 4.6 sq km of territory right around the temple (some Thai nationalists even claim the temple itself), initially supported the bid, but the temple soon became a pawn in Thailand's chaotic domestic politics. Within a week, Thai troops crossed into Cambodian territory, sparking an armed confrontation that has taken the lives of several dozen soldiers and some civilians on both sides. The Cambodian market at the bottom of the Monumental Stairway, which used to be home to some guesthouses, burned down during an exchange of fire in April 2009. In 2011, exchanges heated up once more and long-range shells were fired into civilian territory by both sides. The Thai army was accused by the Cambodians of using banned cluster munitions during some of the border skirmishes. The **Cluster Munitions Coalition** (CMC; www.stopclustermunitions.org) confirmed the use of cluster munitions after two investigations.

In July 2011, the International Court of Justice ruled that both sides should withdraw troops from the area to establish a demilitarised zone. With a new pro-Thaksin (therefore Hun Sen-friendly) government in Bangkok, the border dispute seems to have finally come to an end, helped in no small measure by the fact that both countries were heavily preoccupied with dealing with some of the most dramatic flooding in living memory.

Among the carvings found at Preah Khan was the bust of Jayavarman now in Phnom Penh's National Museum and widely copied as a souvenir for tourists. The body of the statue was discovered a few years ago by locals who alerted authorities, making it possible for a joyous reunion of head and body in 2000.

Most locals refer to this temple as Prasat Bakan; scholars officially refer to it as Bakan Svay Rolay, combining the local name for the temple and the district name. Khmers in Siem Reap often refer to it as Preah Khan-Kompong Svay.

Locals say there are no landmines in the vicinity of Preah Khan, but stick to marked paths just to be on the safe side.

🛏 Sleeping & Eating

Getting the most out of a visit to Preah Khan really requires an overnight stay. With a hammock and mosquito net, it's possible to camp within the Preah Khan complex, but it is best to coordinate a location with the tourist police, who will appreciate a small tip for their services. Or overnight in a simple family **homestay** (r US$3) in Ta Seng village, a rollercoaster 4km from the temple.

❶ Getting There & Away

Traditionally, Preah Khan has been the toughest of Preah Vihear Province's remote temples to reach, but new roads through Sangkum Thmey commune are slowly improving things. Unless you don't mind travelling by ox cart, it's virtually impossible to get to Preah Khan during the peak months of the wet season (roughly June to October). The best time to visit is from January to April, as the trails are reasonably dry at this time.

There's no public transport to Preah Khan, so your best bet is to hire a moto, a jacked-up Camry or a pick-up truck in Stoeng (on NH6), Kompong Thom (120km, five hours) or Tbeng Meanchey (four or five hours). With enough cash in hand, a 4WD is a good option for these tough roads.

Only experienced bikers should attempt to get to Preah Khan on rental motorcycles, as conditions range from difficult to extremely tough from every side. Take a wrong turn in this neck of the woods and you'll end up in the middle of nowhere, so consider bringing along a knowledgeable moto driver (US$15 a day plus petrol).

The better all-round option now is via the remote commune of Sangkum Thmey. This route lies about 93km north of Kompong Thom or about 64km south of Tbeng Meachey. Preah Khan temple is signposted 56km west of the main road. Until recently, this was a sea of sand and quite possibly the worst way to reach the temple. However, this road has recently been given an overhaul and is graded all the way to the village of Ta Seng, just 4km short of the temple. During the dry season, even minibuses can pass this way making a long day trip from Siem Reap an enticing possibility. It takes about two hours to the temple from the Svay Pak turn-off on NH64.

WORTH A TRIP

TMATBOEY: ON THE TRAIL OF THE GIANT IBIS

Cambodia's remote northern plains, the largest remaining block of deciduous dipterocarp forest, seasonal wetlands and grasslands in Southeast Asia, have been described as Southeast Asia's answer to Africa's savannahs. Covering much of northwestern Preah Vihear Province, they are one of the last places on earth where you can see Cambodia's national bird, the critically endangered giant ibis (nests from July to November). Other rare species that can be spotted here include the woolly-necked stork, white-rumped falcon, green peafowl, Alexandrine parakeet, grey-headed fish eagle and no less than 16 species of woodpecker, as well as owls and raptors. Birds are easiest to see from December to April.

In a last-ditch effort to ensure the survival of the giant ibis, protect the only confirmed breeding sites of the **white-shouldered ibis** (nests from December to March), and save the habitat of other globally endangered species, including the sarus crane (breeds June to October) and greater adjutant, the **Wildlife Conservation Society** (WCS; www.wcs.org) set up a pioneering community ecotourism project. Situated in the isolated village of Tmatboey (population 223 families) inside the **Kulen Promtep Wildlife Sanctuary**, the initiative provides local villagers with education, income and a concrete incentive to do everything possible to protect the ibis. Visitors agree in advance to make a donation to a village conservation fund, but only if they actually see one or more of the birds. The project was a 2007 winner of Wild Asia's **Responsible Tourism Award** (www.wildasia.net).

Tmatboey is about three to four hours from Siem Reap (via Beng Mealea and Koh Ker) and one hour north of Tbeng Meanchey. The site is accessible year-round, though at the height of the wet season the only way to get there may be by moto. To arrange a three-day, two-night visit (US$550 per person for a group of four, including accommodation, guides and food), contact the Siem Reap-based **Sam Veasna Center** (SVC; Map p92; ☎063-963710; www.samveasna.org). Visitors sleep in wooden bungalows with bathrooms and solar hot water.

For those wanting to explore the most remote corners of Cambodia, the Kulen Promtep Wildlife Sanctuary has a new birding site, about 60km from Tmatboey as the Giant Ibis flies, in the remote forest village of **Prey Veng**. The WCS and SVC aim to replicate the success of Tmatboey to ensure conservation of this habitat. Many of the same bird species from Tmatboey can be seen at Prey Veng, including the white-winged duck for serious enthusiasts. The campsite is situated on the banks of an Angkorian Baray similar in size to Rahal at Koh Ker, about 500m from an old temple. Prey Veng offers great opportunities for hiking through the open dry forest to a distant hilltop temple from the Angkor period. A three-day/two-night trip, including a visit to Beng Mealea and Koh Ker en route costs around $300 per person in a group of four. Contact SVC for details.

For motorbikers, the faster route used to be via Phnom Dek (on NH64 between Kompong Thom and Tbeng Meanchey), but this is pretty degraded these days due to heavy wet season storms and a lack of local maintenance. However, it does offer combinations with Sambor Prei Kuk (p240) on the way.

Coming from Siem Reap there are several options. If you've got four wheels, the most straightforward route is to take NH6 to Stoeng and then head north. By motorcycle, you can take NH6 to Kompong Kdei, head north to Khvau and then ride east. An amazing alternative is to approach from Beng Mealea along the ancient Angkor road (Cambodia's own Route 66 – NH66). You'll cross about 10 splendid Angkorian *naga* bridges, including the remarkable 77m-long **Spean Ta Ong**, 7km west of Khvau. The road from Beng Mealea to Khvau is now in fine condition and may well be turned into a Koh Ker–style toll road during the lifetime of this book.

The approach from the easterly direction via Kompong Thom or Tbeng Meanchey offers a couple of choices.

KOMPONG THOM PROVINCE

An easy stopover when travelling overland between Phnom Penh and Siem Reap, Kompong Thom Province (ខេត្តកំពង់ធំ) is drawing more visitors thanks to several unique sites near the provincial capital, Kompong Thom, including the pre-Angkorian temples of Sambor Prei Kuk and the extraordinary hilltop shrines of Phnom Santuk. The most noteworthy geographical feature in the province is Stung Sen, Cambodia's second-longest river, which eventually flows into Tonlé Sap River.

Kompong Thom came under US bombardment in the early 1970s in an effort to reopen the Phnom Penh-Siem Reap road severed by the Khmer Rouge.

Kompong Thom   កំពង់ធំ

🎵062 / POP 68,000

A bustling commercial centre, Kompong Thom is on NH6 midway between Phnom Penh and Siem Reap. It's a relaxed if uninspiring base from which to explore Sambor Prei Kuk (p240) and Phnom Santuk (p241).

⊙ Sights & Activities

On the river's south bank about 500m west of the bridge, next to the old **French governor's residence**, is the most extraordinary sight: hundreds of large **bats** (in Khmer, *chreoun*), with 40cm wingspans, live in three old mahogany trees. They spend their days suspended upside down like winged fruit, fanning themselves with their wings to keep cool. Around dusk (from about 5.30pm or 6pm) they fly off in search of food.

🛏 Sleeping

There are bargain-basement guesthouses on Dekchau Meas St, but some do most of their business as brothels by the hour and all are opposite the taxi park, which means early morning horn action.

TOP CHOICE **Sambor Village Hotel** BOUTIQUE HOTEL $$
(📞961391; Prachea Thepatay St; r US$50, ste US$80; ❄@🛜🏊) This atmospheric place brings boutique to Kompong Thom. Rooms are set in spacious bungalows and the verdant gardens include an inviting pool under the shade of a mango tree. International dishes at the restaurant. Located about 700m east of NH6, overlooking the river.

Arunras Hotel HOTEL $
(📞961294; 46 Sereipheap Blvd; r with fan/air-con US$6/15; ❄@🛜) Dominating the accommodation scene in Kompong Thom, this seven-

---

THE IRON KUY OF CAMBODIA

The Kuy are an ethnic minority found in northern Cambodia, Southern Laos and Northeastern Thailand. In Cambodia, the Kuy have long been renowned as smelters and smiths. It is thought that the Kuy may have produced iron – used for weaponry, tools and construction supports – since the Angkorian period.

The Kuy stopped smelting iron around 1950, but high-quality smithing continues to be practised in some communities. When travelling along NH64 between Kompong Thom and Tbeng Meanchey, it is possible to stop at Rumchek, about 2km south of the iron mines of Phnom Dek. Kuy smith Mr Ma Thean lives in Rumchek and can produce a traditional Kuy jungle knife in just one hour. The experience includes a chance to work the bellows and is a good way to support a dying art.

Kompong Thom

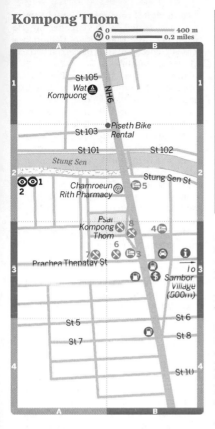

Kompong Thom

◉ Sights
  1 Bats...A2
  2 French Govenor's Residence.............A2

🛏 Sleeping
  3 Arunras Hotel......................................B3
  4 Bargain Basement
     Guesthouses B3
  5 Stung Sen Royal Garden Hotel B2

🍽 Eating
  6 American Restaurant B3
  7 Bayon Restaurant................................A3
  8 Psar Kompong Thom Night
     Market B3

Bayon Restaurant   CAMBODIAN $
(Prachea Thepatay St; mains incl rice 6000r; ☺5am-9pm) Lacking English signs or even a printed menu, this is a popular feeding station with locals, easily recognised by the signature Bayon faces. Situated one long block west of the Arunras Hotel.

Psar Kompong Thom Night Market   CAMBODIAN $
(NH6; mains 2000-4000r; ☺4pm-2am) Sit on a plastic chair at a neon-lit table and dig into chicken rice soup, chicken curry noodles, Khmer-style baguettes or a *tukalok* (fruit shake).

Arunras Hotel   CAMBODIAN $
(46 Sereipheap Blvd) The hotel's downstairs restaurant is very popular, with all the Phnom Penh–Siem Reap traffic stopping to feast on tasty Khmer fare. They serve Illy Coffee for caffeine cravers seeking a quality fix.

❶ Information

NH6 is oriented north-to-south as it passes through Kompong Thom. The town's focal point is the main market, Psar Kompong Thom. Other landmarks include the Arunras Hotel, which is 300m north of the Elephants and Tigers Statue and 300m south of the two bridges over Stung Sen.

Acleda Bank (NH6) Located 1km south of the centre, with a 24hr Visa ATM.

American Restaurant (Prachea Thepatay St; ☺7am-about 9pm) Internet access.

Canadia Bank (NH6) New branch in the middle of town with free cash withdrawals.

Chamroeun Rith Pharmacy (NH6; ☺6.30am-7.30pm or 8pm) Internet access as well as medications.

storey corner establishment has 58 smart, good-value rooms, as well as Kompong Thom's only lift. Operates the cheaper, 57-room Arunras Guesthouse next door.

Stung Sen Royal Garden Hotel   HOTEL $$
(☎961228; Stung Sen St; d/tr US$20/30; ❄) In an attractive riverside location, this is one of Kompong Thom's longest-running hotels, but it is a claim that is starting to wear thin. The 32 rooms offer jaded two-star comfort and roomy bathrooms.

✗ Eating

American Restaurant   INTERNATIONAL $
(Prachea Thepatay St; mains US$3-7.50; ☺7am-9pm; @) This outpost of culinary Americana specialises in thin-crust Neapolitan pizzas, spaghetti, sandwiches, burgers and homemade ice cream to accompany the unexpected waffles. Add to the mix Khmer dishes and freshly brewed coffee and it covers all bases.

Department of Tourism (Prachea Thepatay St; ☉8-11am & 2-5pm Mon-Fri) Upstairs in an old wooden building. May have handouts if open.

Im Sokhom Travel Agency (☏012 691527; guideimsokhom@yahoo.com) Runs guided tours, including cycling trips to Sambor Prei Kuk.

❶ Getting There & Around

Kompong Thom is 165km north of Phnom Penh, 147km southeast of Siem Reap and 157km south of Tbeng Meanchey.

Dozens of buses travelling between Phnom Penh (US$5, four hours) and Siem Reap (US$5, two hours) pass through Kompong Thom and can easily be flagged down outside the Arunras Hotel.

Share taxis are the fastest way to Phnom Penh (US$5) and Siem Reap (US$4) and also go to Kompong Cham (US$5); minibuses to Phnom Penh and Siem Reap cost US$3. Heading north to Tbeng Meanchey (often referred to as Preah Vihear), share taxis (25,000r) are popular on the new improved road. All services depart from the taxi park, one block east of NH6.

Moto drivers can be found across NH6 from the Arunras Hotel.

Bicycles can be rented at **Piseth Bike Rental** (☏012 835726; 295 St 103; 1/2/3 days US$2/2/3; ☉6am-5pm). For mountain bikes (US$5 a day), try the **American Restaurant** (Prachea Thepatay St). **Im Sokhom Travel Agency** (☏012 691527) rents bicycles (US$1 a day) and motorbikes (US$5 a day).

Around Kompong Thom

SAMBOR PREI KUK សំបូរព្រៃគុក
Cambodia's most impressive group of pre-Angkorian monuments, **Sambor Prei Kuk** (admission collected at bridge US$3; car parking 2000r) encompasses more than 100 mainly brick temples scattered through the forest, among them some of the oldest structures in the country. Originally called Isanapura, it served as the capital of Upper Chenla during the reign of the early 7th-century King Isanavarman and continued to serve as an important learning centre during the Angkorian era.

The main temple area consists of three complexes, each enclosed by the remains of two concentric walls. Their basic layout – a central tower surrounded by shrines, ponds and gates – may have served as an inspiration for the architects of Angkor five centuries later. Many of the original statues are now in the National Museum (p39) in Phnom Penh. The area's last mines were cleared in 2008.

For a **digital reconstruction** of Sambor Prei Kuk created by the Architecture Department of the University of California at Berkeley, check out http://steel.ced.berkeley.edu/research/sambor/.

Forested and shady, Sambor Prei Kuk has a serene and soothing atmosphere, and the sandy paths make for a pleasant stroll.

Isanborei Crafts Shop (☉closed in wet season), located past the ticket booth, sells a worthwhile English brochure (2000r), high-quality, handcrafted baskets and wood items, and T-shirts with original designs.

Isanborei Community Restaurant (set meals US$6, dishes US$2), not far from the crafts shop, is a small collection of bamboo and thatch outdoor eateries selling chicken-based dishes and cold drinks.

The principle temple group, **Prasat Sambor** (7th and 10th centuries) is dedicated to Gambhireshvara, one of Shiva's many incarnations (the other groups are dedicated to Shiva himself). Several of Prasat Sambor's towers retain brick carvings in fairly good condition, and there is a series of large *yonis* (female fertility symbols) around the central tower.

Prasat Yeai Poeun (Prasat Yeay Peau) is arguably the most atmospheric ensemble, as it feels lost in the forest. The eastern gateway is being both held up and torn asunder by an ancient tree, the bricks interwoven with the tree's extensive, probing roots. A truly massive tree shades the western gate.

Prasat Tao (Lion Temple), the largest of the Sambor Prei Kuk complexes, boasts excellent examples of Chenla carving in the form of two large, elaborately coiffed stone lions. It also has a fine, rectangular pond, **Srah Neang Pov**.

In the early 1970s, Sambor Prei Kuk was bombed by US aircraft in support of the Lon Nol government's doomed fight against the Khmer Rouge. Some of the craters, ominously close to the temples, can still be seen.

Visitors to Sambor Prei Kuk often find themselves accompanied by a gaggle of sweet but persistent local children selling colourful scarves (US$1). Some travellers find them a distraction, but others, after warming to their smiles, have been known to leave with a pile of cheap textiles.

❶ Getting There & Away

If you're interested in the chronological evolution of Cambodian temple architecture, it is advisable to see Sambor Prei Kuk before heading to Angkor.

To get here from Kompong Thom, follow NH6 north for 5km before continuing straight on NH64 towards Tbeng Meanchey (the paved road to Siem Reap veers left). After 11km turn right at the elaborate laterite sign and continue for 14km.

From Kompong Thom, a round-trip moto ride out here (under an hour) should cost US$10 (US$15 including Phnom Santuk). By car the trip takes about an hour.

PHNOM SANTUK ភ្នំល្ពួត

Its forested slopes adorned with Buddha images and a series of pagodas, **Phnom Santuk** (Phnom Sontuk; admission US$2) is the most important holy mountain (207m) in this region and a hugely popular site of Buddhist pilgrimage.

Santuk's extraordinary ensemble of wats and stupas is set high above the surrounding countryside, which means there are lots of stairs to climb – 809, in fact. You can wimp out and take the recently paved 2.5km road, but if you do, you'll miss the troupes of monkeys that await visitors along the stairway and the experience of winding up through the forest and emerging at a grouping of *prasat*-style wats (some of them still under construction) with more *nagas* and dragons than you can possibly imagine. Just beneath the southern summit, there are a number of **reclining Buddhas**; several are modern incarnations cast in cement, others were carved into the living rock in centuries past. A multitiered **Chinese pagoda** is decorated with porcelain figurines.

Phnom Santuk has an active wat and the local monks are always interested in receiving foreign tourists. Boulders located just below the summit afford **panoramic views** south towards Tonlé Sap.

For travellers spending the night in Kompong Thom, Phnom Santuk is a good place from which to catch a magnificent **sunset** over the rice fields, although this means descending in the dark (bring a torch/flashlight).

❶ Getting There & Away

The 2km paved road to Phnom Santuk intersects NH6 18km towards Phnom Penh from Kompong Thom; look for a sign reading 'Santuk Mountain Site'. From Kompong Thom, a round trip by moto costs about US$6.

KAKAOH

The village of Kakaoh is about 16km southeast of Kompong Thom in the direction of Phnom Penh. It is famous for its stonemasons, who fashion Buddha statues, decorative lions and other traditional Khmer figures with hand tools and a practised eye. It's fascinating to watch the figures, which range in height from 15cm to over 5m, slowly emerge from slabs of stone in five different hues: white, grey, red, yellow and green. A 2.5m-high Buddha carved from a single block of stone will set you back US$1800 to US$3500 depending on the quality of the materials, not including excess luggage charges. Statues produced here are often donated by wealthy Khmers to wats.

SANTUK SILK FARM

Situated 300m towards Kompong Thom from the paved access road to Phnom Santuk and 100m off NH6, the **Santuk Silk Farm** (☏012 906604; budgibb@yahoo.com; admission free; ☉during daylight) is one of the few places in Cambodia where you can see the entire process of silk production, starting with the seven-week lifecycle of the silkworm, a delicate creature that feeds only on mulberry leaves and has to be protected from predators such as geckos, ants and mosquitoes. Although most of the raw silk used here comes from China and Vietnam, the local worms produce 'Khmer golden silk', so-called because of its lush golden hue. You can watch artisans weaving scarves (US$20 to US$25) and other items by hand from 7am to 11am and 1pm to 5pm Monday to Friday and from 7am to 11am Saturday. The peaceful garden site has clean, top-quality

NORTHWESTERN CAMBODIA AROUND KOMPONG THOM

IN SEARCH OF THE BENGAL FLORICAN

The northeastern shores of Tonlé Sap lake are home to scores of bird species and some of them, such as the Bengal florican, are critically endangered. Sites in Kompong Thom Province that are gaining popularity with twitchers include the **Stoeng Chikrieng grasslands** and the **Boeng Tonlé Chhmar Wildlife Sanctuary** (one of Cambodia's three Ramsar wetland areas: see www.ramsar.org), both straddling the border between Kompong Thom Province and Siem Reap Province, and the **Kru Krom grasslands**, 25km due south of Kompong Thom town. The Siem Reap–based **Sam Veasna Center** (☏063-963710; www.samveasna .org) runs birding trips to these sites.

Western toilets; complimentary coffee, tea and cold water are on offer.

The farm is run by Budd Gibbons, an American Vietnam War veteran who's lived in Cambodia since 1996, and his Cambodian wife. If possible, call ahead a couple of hours before your visit.

PRASAT KUHA NOKOR

ប្រាសាទគុហានគរ

This 11th-century temple, constructed during the reign of Suryavarman I, is in ex-tremely good condition thanks to a lengthy renovation before the civil war. It is on the grounds of a modern wat and is an easy enough stop for those with their own transport. The temple is signposted from NH6 about 70km southeast of Kompong Thom and 22km north of Skuon and is 2km from the main road. From NH6, you can get a moto to the temple.

Eastern Cambodia

POP SIX MILLION / AREA 68,472 SQ KM

Best Places to Eat

» Destiny Coffee House (p247)

» Nature Lodge (p270)

» Terres Rouges Lodge (p262)

» Red Sun Falling (p252)

» Le Tonlé (p256)

Best Places to Stay

» Tree top Ecolodge (p261)

» Terres Rouges Lodge (p261)

» Elephant Valley Project (p259)

» Nature Lodge (p269)

» Koh Trong Community Homestay I (p254)

Why Go?

Home to diverse landscapes and peoples, the 'Wild East' shatters the illusion that the country is all paddy fields and sugar palms. There are plenty of those in the lowland provinces, but in the northeast they yield to the forested mountains of Mondulkiri and Ratanakiri Provinces, both up-and-coming ecotourism areas.

Rare forest elephants and vocal primates are found in the northeast, and the endangered freshwater Irrawaddy dolphin can be seen year-round near Kratie. Thundering waterfalls, crater lakes and meandering rivers characterise the landscape, and trekking, biking, kayaking and elephant experiences are all taking off. The rolling hills and lush forests also provide a home to many ethnic minority groups, known collectively as Khmer Leu (Upper Khmer) or *chunchiet* (ethnic minorities).

Picture it: this all adds up to an amazing experience.

When to Go

The elevated provinces of Mondulkiri and Ratanakiri are a few degrees cooler than lowland Cambodia; they're good places to escape the heat from March to May. Mondulkiri is particularly beautiful at the tail end of the wet season from September to November, when wildflowers give colour to the landscape.

When it comes to meandering along the Mekong, the ideal time is the dry season when the water levels drop. This makes dolphin-spotting around Kratie and the Lao border that much easier and reveals the Ramsar-recognised wetlands between Stung Treng and the Lao border.

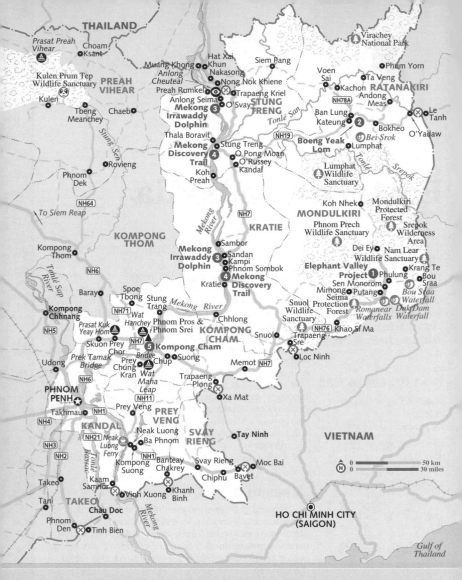

Eastern Cambodia Highlights

1 Observing elephants in their element at the **Elephant Valley Project** (p259) in Mondulkiri

2 Diving into the crystal-clear waters of the crater lake of **Boeng Yeak Lom** (p259) in Ratanakiri

3 Catching a glimpse of the rare freshwater **Mekong Irrawaddy dolphin** near Kratie (p255) or O'Svay (p257)

4 Experiencing the 'real Cambodia' on bike, foot or kayak along the **Mekong Discovery Trail** (p253) around Kratie and Stung Treng

5 Soaking up the charms of relaxing **Kompong Cham** (p245), gateway to historic temples, lush countryside and friendly locals

❶ Getting There & Away

Eastern Cambodia is home to several important international border crossings between Cambodia and its neighbours. The Mekong River border at Nong Nok Khiene-Trapaeng Kriel, shared with Laos to the north, is an ever-more-popular route for travellers. East of Phnom Penh are plenty of border crossings with Vietnam, including the old favourite Bavet–Moc Bai crossing on the road to Ho Chi Minh City, and the evocative Mekong River crossing at Kaam Samnor-Vinh Xuong. See p347 for more on border crossings in this region.

For those already in Cambodia, Phnom Penh is the usual gateway to the region, with a host of reliable roads fanning out to the major cities. The region's main north–south artery, National Highway 7 (NH7), is in great shape all the way to the Lao border. Sen Monorom (Mondulkiri) is now connected to NH7 by a newly sealed road that puts it within six hours of the capital. The road connecting NH7 to Ban Lung (Ratanakiri) is still under construction but will be completed during the lifetime of this book, bringing journey times down to eight hours.

At the time of writing there were no commercial flights to the region, although there are airstrips in Ban Lung and Sen Monorom.

❶ Getting Around

Eastern Cambodia is one of the more remote parts of the country and conditions vary widely between wet and dry seasons. Getting around the lowlands is easy enough, with buses, minibuses and taxis plying the routes between major towns.

Getting to off-the-beaten track locales is a different matter, as the punishing rains of the wet season leave rural roads in a state of disrepair. A good road can turn bad in a matter of weeks and journey times become hit and miss. Some 'roads', such as the infamous track linking Mondulkiri and Ratanakiri Provinces via Koh Nhek, are passable only by motorbike, which makes the region prime territory for off-road enthusiasts.

KOMPONG CHAM PROVINCE

Kompong Cham Province (ខេត្តកំពង់ចាម) draws a growing number of visitors thanks to its role as a gateway to the northeast. Attractions include several pre-Angkorian and Angkorian temples, as well as some atmospheric riverbank rides for cyclists and motorbikers. The provincial capital offers an accessible slice of the real Cambodia, a land of picturesque villages, pretty wats and fishing communities.

The most heavily populated province in Cambodia, Kompong Cham has supplied a steady stream of Cambodia's current political heavyweights, including Prime Minister Hun Sen and senate head Chea Sim. Most Kompong Cham residents enjoy quieter lives, living off the land or fishing along the Mekong River. Rubber was the major prewar industry and there are huge plantations stretching eastwards from the Mekong. Some of Cambodia's finest silk is also produced in this province and most of the country's *kramas* (scarves) originate here.

Kompong Cham កំពង់ចាម

📞 042 / POP 70,000

More a quiet town than a bustling city, Kompong Cham is a peaceful provincial capital spread along the banks of the Mekong. It was an important trading post during the French period, the legacy of which is evident as you wander through the streets of chastened yet classic buildings.

Long considered Cambodia's third city after Phnom Penh and Battambang, Kompong Cham has lately been somewhat left in

---

THE BOMBING OF NEAK LUONG

Neak Luong is depicted in the opening sequences of *The Killing Fields* (1984), the definitive film about Cambodia's civil war and genocide. In August 1973, American B-52s mistakenly razed the town to the ground in an attempt to halt a Khmer Rouge advance on Phnom Penh. The intensive bombardment killed 137 civilians and wounded 268. The US government tried to cover it up by keeping the media out, but Sydney Schanberg, played by Sam Waterstone in the film, managed to travel to the city by river and publicise the true scale of the tragedy. The US ambassador offered compensation of US$100 per family and the navigator of the B-52 was fined US$700.

Today, Neak Luong is the point at which travellers speeding between Phnom Penh and the Vietnamese border must stop to cross the mighty Mekong River. The car ferry chugs back and forth, giving kids ample time to try to sell you strange-looking insects and other unidentifiable food on sticks. This is all about to change, however, as a new bridge spanning the Mekong near Neak Luong is under construction.

Kompong Cham

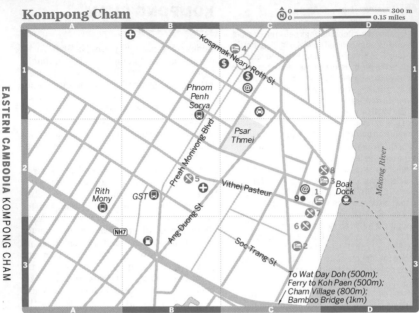

the dust by the fast-growing tourist towns of Siem Reap and Sihanoukville. However, Kompong Cham remains an important travel hub and acts as the gateway to eastern and northeastern Cambodia. This role has grown thanks to the first bridge to span the Mekong's width in Cambodia, dramatically cutting journey times to popular destinations such as Kratie and Mondulkiri.

☉ Sights & Activities

There's still a fair-sized population of Cham Muslims around (hence the name 'Kompong Cham'). One Cham village is on the left bank of the Mekong north of the French lighthouse. Its big, silver-domed mosque is clearly visible from the right bank. Another one is south of the bridge just beyond Wat Day Doh, which is worth a wander en route.

Line dancing takes place on the riverfront near the bridge at dusk if you want to get down with the locals.

Wat Nokor   TEMPLE
(វត្តនគរ; admission US$2) The original fusion temple, Wat Nokor is a modern Theravada Buddhist pagoda squeezed into the walls of an 11th-century Mahayana Buddhist shrine of sandstone and laterite. It is a kitsch kind of place and many of the older building's

archways have been incorporated into the new building as shrines for worship. On weekdays there are only a few monks in the complex and it's peaceful to wander among the alcoves and their hidden shrines. The entry price includes admission to Phnom Pros and Phnom Srei just outside town.

To get here, head out of town on the NH7 to Phnom Penh, and take the left fork at the large roundabout about 1km from town. The temple is at the end of this pretty dirt road.

Koh Paen   NEIGHBOURHOOD
For a supremely relaxing bicycle ride, it's hard to beat Koh Paen (កោះប៉ែន), a rural island in the Mekong River, connected to the southern reaches of Kompong Cham town by an elaborate bamboo bridge (500r to 1000r) in the dry season or a local ferry (with/without bicycle 1500/1000r) in the wet season. The bamboo bridge is an attraction in itself, totally built by hand each year and looking like it is made of matchsticks from afar. During the dry season, several sandbars, the closest thing to a beach in this part of Cambodia, appear around the island.

Old French Lighthouse   HISTORIC BUILDING
Looming over the Mekong River opposite town is an old French lighthouse (បមប្បារាំងចាស). For years it was an aban-

Kompong Cham

doned shell, but it's recently been renovated, including an incredibly steep metal stair case, more like a series of ladders. Don't attempt the climb if you are scared of heights. There are great views across the Mekong from the summit, especially at sunset.

👉 Tours

Lazy Mekong Daze   BOAT TOUR
(Riverside St) Runs sunset cruises on the Mekong in a traditional boat. These sometimes stop off at an interesting rural village on an island about 30 minutes upstream. The tours cost US$5 to US$7 per person, depending on the length of the cruise and how many people are on board (capacity is about 14 passengers).

🛏 Sleeping

Many visitors prefer to stay on the riverfront, with a view over the Mekong, but keep in mind that there is a lot of noise as soon as the sun comes up, including boat horns and the muezzin's drum from the Cham mosque across the river.

Monorom 2 VIP Hotel   HOTEL $$
(☎092 777102; Preah Bat Sihanouk St; r US$15-25; ❄🖵) Currently the smartest hotel in town. Rooms include heavy wood furnishings and inviting bathtubs. The lavish top-whack rooms have private balconies peering at the Mekong and large bathrooms loaded with toiletries. All rooms boast an eyebrow-raising painting of a half-nude Khmer princess. The US$15 rooms are windowless.

Mekong Hotel   HOTEL $
(☎941536; Preah Bat Sihanouk St; r with fan/air-con US$7/15; ❄) This old timer is still popular thanks to renovated rooms on the riverfront, which include satellite TV and hot water. The corridors are wide enough for an ultimate Frisbee tournament.

Mekong Sunrise   GUESTHOUSE $
(☎097 912 9280; www.mekong-sunrise.com; Preah Bat Sihanouk St; r US$5-7; 🖵) A new backpacker crashpad on the riverfront, Mekong Sunrise has spacious upper-floor rooms with access to a sprawling rooftop. Furnishings are sparse, but it's cheap enough.

Phnom Pros Hotel   HOTEL $
(☎941444; Kosamak Neary Roth St; phnompros hotel@yahoo.com; r US$6-12; ❄🖵) A large hotel in the centre of town, this place is owned by a nephew of Hun Sen, Cambodia's prime minister, so security is not generally a worry. The rooms include all the trimmings, such as satellite TV, fridge and hot water. Free internet in the lobby.

Rana Homestay   HOMESTAY $$
(☎012 686240; rana-ruralhomestay-cambodia.webs. com; per person US$25) Located in the country side beyond Kompong Cham, this homestay offers an insight into life in rural Cambodia. The price includes all meals and tours of the local area. There's a two-night minimum stay.

🍴 Eating

There are several good restaurants in town, including a couple of Western places, and a lot of cheaper hole-in-the-wall dives dotted around the market. Stalls line the newly refurbished waterfront, selling snacks and cold beers until late in the evening. Across the bridge over the Mekong on NH17 is a rash of Khmer restaurants, many of which have live bands or karaoke if you are in the mood for a little entertainment.

TOP CHOICE Destiny Coffee House   CAFE $
(12 Vithei Pasteur; mains US$2-5; ⏰7am-4.30pm Mon-Sat; 🖵) An unexpected oasis in little old Kompong Cham, this stylish cafe has relaxing sofas and a contemporary look. The international menu includes some delicious hummus with dips and lip-smacking home-made cakes and freshly prepared shakes.

Smile Restaurant   CAMBODIAN $
(Preah Bat Sihanouk St; www.bdsa-cambodia.org; mains US$2.50-4.50; 🖵) Run by the Buddhism

and Society Development Association, this nonprofit restaurant is a huge hit with the NGO crowd for its big breakfasts, healthy menu and free wi-fi.

Lazy Mekong Daze   INTERNATIONAL $
(Preah Bat Sihanouk St; mains US$2.50-4.50) With a pool table and a big screen for sports and movies, this is the place to be after dark. The menu parades a range of Khmer, Thai and Western food, and delicious Karem ice-cream is available.

Mekong Crossing   INTERNATIONAL $
(Preah Bat Sihanouk St; mains US$2-4) Occupying a prime corner on the riverfront, this old favourite serves an enticing mix of Khmer curries and Western favourites, such as big burgers and tasty sandwiches.

Hao An Restaurant   CAMBODIAN $
(Preah Monivong Blvd; mains US$2-7) The original Kompong Cham diner draws a legion of Khmers from across the country. The picture menu of Khmer and Chinese favourites has a huge array of images, including a cuddly baby goat on the raw-meat menu.

C@Moi   FRENCH $
(Vithei Pasteur; mains US$2-4.50) A French couple has retired here to cook a selection of modest but delicious French dishes such as *steak à cheval* (steak and egg) in a Khmer townhouse.

❶ Information

ANZ Royal Bank (Preah Monivong Blvd; ◷8.30am-4pm Mon-Fri) International banking in Kompong Cham, plus a working ATM, with a minimum US$4 charge for withdrawals.
Canadia Bank (Preah Monivong Blvd; ◷8.30am-3.30pm Mon-Fri) Free ATM withdrawals, plus free cash advances on credit card.
Sophary Internet Service (Vithei Pasteur; per hr 2000r) Internet access. Near Mekong Hotel.

❶ Getting There & Away

Phnom Penh is 120km southwest. NH7 is in excellent shape all the way to the Lao border.
 Phnom Penh Sorya (Preah Monivong Blvd), **Rith Mony** (NH7) and **GST** (Preah Monivong Blvd) all have regular air-con buses between Kompong Cham and Phnom Penh (16,000r, 2½ hours). **Rith Mony** has two direct trips to Siem Reap per day (US$5, five hours). GST has a daily trip to Battambang (30,000r, six hours). Share taxis (US$3.50) make the trip to Phnom Penh in under two hours from the taxi park near the New

Market (Psar Thmei), and overcrowded mini-buses also do the run (10,000r).
 Rith Mony buses from Phnom Penh to Sen Monorom (US$7.50), Ban Lung (US$10) and Stung Treng (US$7, six hours) pass through here, as do Sorya's buses to Stung Treng and Pakse in Laos. Most buses come through around 10am. Most buses bound for Stung Treng and Ban Lung stop in Kratie (US$4, three hours). Morning share taxis and minibuses get to Kratie in two hours via Chhlong, departing when full from the Caltex station at the main roundabout.
 For motorcyclists, there is a scenic dry-season route to Kratie that follows the Mekong River. Take the river road north out of Kompong Cham as far as Stung Trang (pronounced Trong) district and cross the Mekong on a small ferry before continuing up the east bank of the Mekong through Chhlong to Kratie. This is a very beautiful ride through small rural villages and takes about four hours on a trail bike. Better still, stay on the west bank as far north as Chhlong or even Kratie, as the villages and rural scenery are stunning in this area. However, it is quite difficult to navigate your way through the rubber plantations north of Stung Trang before reconnecting with the river.
 There are no longer any passenger boats running on the Mekong.

❶ Getting Around

Kompong Cham has a surplus of moto and *remork-moto* (túk-túk) drivers who speak great English and can guide you around the sites. If you sip a drink overlooking the Mekong, one of them will find you before too long. **Mr Vannat** (☏012 995890; vannat_kompongcham@yahoo. com) is the veteran of the group and has a 4WD for hire (he also speaks French), but all of these guys are pretty good and rates are extremely reasonable. Figure on US$10/15 or less per day for a moto/*remork* including gas (slightly more if including Wat Maha Leap in your plans).
 Moto journeys around town are only 1000r to 2000r, a little more at night. Most guesthouses or hotels can arrange motorbike rental. **Bophear Guesthouse** (Vithei Pasteur) rents bicycles for US$2 per day.

Around Kompong Cham
PHNOM PROS & PHNOM SREI
ភ្នំប្រុសភ្នំស្រី
'Man Hill' and 'Woman Hill' are the subjects of local legends with many variations, one of which describes a child taken away at infancy only to return a powerful man who falls in love with his own mother. Disbelieving her protestations, he demanded her hand in marriage. Desperate to avoid this disaster, the mother cunningly devised a deal: a com-

KRAMA CHAMELEON

The colourful checked scarf known as the *krama* is almost universally worn by rural Khmers and is still quite popular in the cities. The scarves are made from cotton or silk and the most famous silk *kramas* come from Kompong Cham and Takeo Provinces.

Kramas have a multitude of uses. They are primarily used to protect Cambodians from the sun, the dust and the wind, and it is for this reason many tourists end up investing in one during a visit. However, they are also slung around the waist as mini-sarongs, used as towels for drying the body, knotted at the neck as decorations, tied across the shoulders as baby carriers, placed upon chairs or beds as pillow covers, used to tow broken-down motorbikes and stuffed inside motorbike tyres in the advent of remote punctures – the list is endless.

Kramas are sold in markets throughout Cambodia and are an essential purchase for travellers using pick-up trucks or taking boat services. They have become very much a symbol of Cambodia and, for many Khmers, wearing one is an affirmation of their identity.

petition between her team of women and his team of men to build the highest hill by dawn. If the women won, she would not give her hand. As they toiled into the night, the women built a fire with the flames reaching high into the sky. The men, mistaking this for sunrise, lay down their tools and the impending marriage was foiled. Locals love to relay this tale, each adding their own herbs and spices as the story unfolds. Admission is US$2 and includes entry to Wat Nokor.

Phnom Srei has fine views of the countryside during the wet season and a very strokeable statue of Nandin (sacred bull that was Shiva's mount). Phnom Pros is a good place for a cold drink, among the inquisitive monkeys that populate the trees. The area between the two hills was once a killing field. A small, gilded brick stupa on the right as you walk from Man Hill to Woman Hill houses a pile of skulls.

The hills are about 7km out of town on the road to Phnom Penh. Opposite the entrance to Phnom Pros lies **Cheung Kok** village, home to a local ecotourism initiative, run by the NGO **Amica** (www.amica-cambodge .org, in French), aimed at introducing visitors to rural life in Kompong Cham. Villagers can teach visitors about harvesting rice, sugar palm and other crops. There is also a small shop in the village selling local handicraft products.

WAT MAHA LEAP   វត្ដ មហាលាភ
Sacred Wat Maha Leap is one of the last remaining wooden pagodas left in the country. More than a century old, it was only spared devastation by the Khmer Rouge because they converted it into a hospital. Many of the

Khmers who were put to work in the surrounding fields perished here; 500 bodies were thrown into graves on site, now camouflaged by a tranquil garden.

The pagoda itself is beautiful. The wide black columns supporting the structure are complete tree trunks, resplendent in gilded patterns. The Khmer Rouge painted over the designs to match their austere philosophies, but the monks have since stripped it back to its original glory.

The journey to Wat Maha Leap is best done by boat from Kompong Cham. You follow the Mekong downstream for a short distance before peeling off on a sublime tributary known as 'Small River', which affords awesome glimpses of rural Cambodian life. A 40HP outboard (US$40 per roundtrip including stops in nearby weaving villages) gets there in less than an hour each way, while slower long boats (US$30) take about 90 minutes. Hire boats on the river opposite the Mekong Hotel.

Small River is only navigable from about July to late December. At other times you'll have to go overland. It's pretty difficult to find on your own without some knowledge of Khmer, as there are lots of small turns along the way, so hire a moto (US$10 per roundtrip including a stop in Prey Chung Kran, one hour each way). It's 20km by river and almost twice that by road.

PREY CHUNG KRAN   ព្រៃចុងក្រោន
Kompong Cham is famous for high-quality silk. The tiny village of Prey Chung Kran is set on the banks of the river and nearly every household has a weaving loom. Under the cool shade provided by their stilted

homes, weavers work deftly to produce *kramas* that are fashionable and traditional. The most interesting thing to watch is the dyeing process, as the typical diamond and dot tessellations are formed at this stage. Prey Chung Kran is about 4km from Wat Maha Leap. There are additional weavers all along the road between Wat Maha Leap and Prey Chung Kran.

WAT HANCHEY   វត្តហាន់ជ័យ

Wat Hanchey is a hilltop pagoda that was an important centre of worship during the Chenla period when, as today, it offered some of the best Mekong views in Cambodia. During the time of the Chenla empire, this may have been an important transit stop on journeys between the ancient cities of Thala Boravit (near Stung Treng to the north) and Angkor Borei (near Takeo to the south), and Sambor Prei Kuk (near Kompong Thom to the west) and Banteay Prei Nokor (near Memot to the east).

Sitting in front of a large, contemporary wat is a remarkable brick sanctuary dating from the 8th century. The well-preserved inscriptions on the doorway are in ancient Sanskrit. A hole in the roof lets in a lone shaft of light. The foundations of several other 8th-century structures, some of them destroyed by American bombs, are scattered around the compound, along with a clutch of bizarre fruit and animal statues.

Moto drivers charge about US$7 return for the trip, which takes about 40 minutes each way from Kompong Cham. In the dry season, cycling here through the pretty riverbank villages is a good way to pass a day.

RUBBER PLANTATIONS   ចំការកៅស៊ូ

Kompong Cham was the heartland of the Cambodian rubber industry and rubber plantations still stretch across the province. Many of them are back in business and some of the largest plantations can be visited. Using an extended scraping instrument, workers graze the trunks until the sap appears, dripping into the open coconut shells on the ground. At **Chup Rubber Plantation**, about 15km east of Kompong Cham, you can observe harvesting in action and wander at will around the **factory** (admission US$1) where workers process the rubber.

KRATIE PROVINCE

Pretty Kratie Province (ខេត្តក្រចេះ) spans the Mekong, from which much of Kratie's population makes its living. Beyond the

---

INCY WINCY SPIDER

Locals in the small Cambodian town of Skuon (otherwise known affectionately as Spiderville) eat our eight-legged furry friends for breakfast, lunch and dinner. Most tourists travelling between Siem Reap and Phnom Penh pass through Skuon without ever realising they have been there. This is hardly surprising, as it has nothing much to attract visitors, but it is the centre of one of Cambodia's more exotic culinary delights – the deep-fried spider.

Buses usually make a bathroom stop in Spiderville, so take a careful look at the eight-legged goodies the food sellers are offering. The creatures, decidedly dead, are piled high on platters, but don't get too complacent, as there are usually live samples lurking nearby.

The spiders are hunted in holes in the hills to the northwest of Skuon in Kompong Thom Province and are quite an interesting dining experience. They are best treated like a crab and eaten by cracking the body open and pulling the legs off one by one, bringing the juiciest flesh out with them – a cathartic experience indeed for arachnophobes. They taste a bit like...um, chicken. Alternatively, for a memorable photo, just bite the thing in half and hope for the best. Watch out for the abdomen, which seems to be filled with some pretty nasty-tasting brown sludge, which could be anything from eggs to excrement – spider truffles, perhaps?

No one seems to know exactly how this microindustry developed around Skuon, although some have suggested that the population may have developed a taste for these creatures during the years of Khmer Rouge rule, when food was in short supply. Notorious celebrity chef Gordon Ramsay joined a spider hunt on his culinary journey of discovery through Cambodia in 2010. At the last count, deep-fried tarantula had not made it onto any of his Michelin three-star restaurants.

river, it's a remote and wild land that sees few outsiders. Most visitors are drawn to the rare freshwater Irrawaddy dolphins found in Kampi, about 15km north of the provincial capital. The town of Kratie is a little charmer and makes a good base from which to explore the surrounding countryside.

The provincial capital was one of the first towns to be 'liberated' by the Khmer Rouge (actually it was the North Vietnamese, but the Khmer Rouge later took the credit) in the summer of 1970. It was also one of the first provincial capitals to fall to the liberating Vietnamese forces in the overthrow of the Khmer Rouge on 30 December 1978.

In the past, getting about was easier by boat than by road, as most roads in the province were pretty nasty. However, Kratie is now connected by NH7 to Kompong Cham and Phnom Penh to the south and Stung Treng and the Lao border to the north, making it a major traveller crossroads.

Kratie

ក្រចេះ

072 / POP 42,000

Kratie is a thriving travel hub and the natural place to break the journey when travelling overland between Phnom Penh and Champasak in southern Laos. It is *the* place in the country to see Irrawaddy dolphins, which live in the Mekong River in ever-diminishing numbers. A lively riverside town, Kratie (pronounced kra-*cheh*) has an expansive riverfront and some of the best Mekong sunsets in Cambodia. There is a rich legacy of French-era architecture, as it was spared the wartime bombing that destroyed so many other provincial centres.

Sights & Activities

The main activity that draws visitors to Kratie is the chance to spot the elusive Irrawaddy dolphin (see p255).

Wat Roka Kandal TEMPLE
(www.cambodian-craft.com; admission 2000r) About 2km south of Kratie on the road to Chhlong is this beautiful little temple dating from the 19th century, one of the oldest in the region. To see the beautifully restored interior, which serves as a showroom for local wicker handicrafts, ask around for someone with the key. Plans are afoot to organise shadow-puppet shows in the temple grounds on a regularish basis. Check with CRDTours (p253) for an update on developments here.

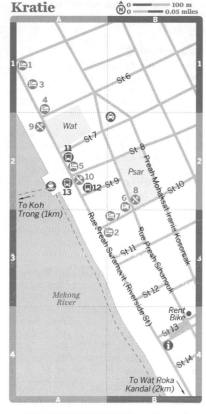

EASTERN CAMBODIA KRATIE

Kratie

Sleeping
1 Balcony Guesthouse A1
2 Heng Heng Guesthouse B3
3 Le Bungalow A1
4 Oudom Sambath Hotel A1
5 Santepheap Hotel A2
6 Star Guesthouse B2
7 You Hong II Guesthouse B3

Eating
8 Barbecue Stands B2
9 Food Stalls A2
  Le Bungalow .... (see 3)
10 Red Sun Falling A2

Transport
  GST .... (see 2)
11 Paramount Angkor A2
12 Phnom Penh Sorya A2
13 Rith Mony A2

The riverside road heading south from here towards Chhlong makes for a nice **bicycle ride**.

🛏 Sleeping

Most accommodation is on or near the riverfront. As well as the guesthouses and hotels covered below, there are also homestays and an upmarket lodge on the island of Koh Trong (see p254) opposite Kratie town.

Balcony Guesthouse   GUESTHOUSE $
(📱016 604036; www.balconyguesthouse.net; Rue Preah Suramarit; r US$3-20; 🕸@🛜) The sign proclaims it a Gust House, but don't be put off by the windbags, as this place attracts some bright young things thanks to good-value rooms and impressive food. The cheapest rooms have a shared bathroom with hot water. Doubles up as a popular little bar by night and is gay-friendly.

Le Bungalow   HOTEL $$
(📱089 758090; www.kohtrong.com; Rue Preah Suramarit; r incl breakfast US$40-70; 🕸@🛜) Akin to a boutique homestay, this small lodging opened in 2011 with three rooms decorated with Sino-Khmer furnishings from the colonial period. Two rooms are spacious with modern bathrooms, while the third is more suited to children travelling with their parents and has an outside bathroom.

Oudom Sambath Hotel   HOTEL $
(📱971502; Rue Preah Suramarit; r US$8-20; 🕸@🛜) Long one of the smartest hotels in town. There is a popular breakfast restaurant downstairs. Fan rooms are a good deal, but it's a long hike to the upper floors if you want the Mekong views.

Star Guesthouse   GUESTHOUSE $
(📱017 491906; khmermao@yahoo.com; Rue Preah Sihanouk; r US$3-5; 🕸🛜) Back under the stewardship of the original family, this budget crashpad looks set to take off again thanks to cheap rooms and wholesome meals. Popular spot for a beer or two at night.

You Hong II Guesthouse   GUESTHOUSE $
(📱085 885168; youhong_kratie@yahoo.com; St 10; r US$5-13; 🕸@🛜) A lively little shoes-off guesthouse between the market and the riverfront. As well as a good mix of rooms, there's a buzzing little bar-restaurant and internet access.

Heng Heng Guesthouse   GUESTHOUSE $
(📱971405; Rue Preah Suramarit; r US$10-15; 🕸🛜) One of the original guesthouses in Kratie, it

has recently been fully renovated, making it one of the smarter choices in town, complete with air-con, hot water and satellite TV. Popular local restaurant downstairs.

Santepheap Hotel   HOTEL $
(📱971537; santepheaphotel@yahoo.com; Rue Preah Suramarit; r US$5-20; 🕸🛜) The elder statesman of hotels in Kratie, this expansive place has large fan rooms at the back for just US$5 with TV and bathroom. Air-con rooms come in various shapes and sizes, some with plush wood trim and hot water.

✗ Eating & Drinking

Some of the best food in town is found at the aforementioned guesthouses, including Balcony Guesthouse, Star Guesthouse and You Hong II Guesthouse.

The food stalls that set up shop overlooking the Mekong are a fine spot for a cheap Cambodian meal or a sunset drink. It's easy to while away an evening just soaking up the atmosphere. Two famous Kratie specialties are on offer here: *krolan* (sticky rice, beans and coconut milk steamed inside a bamboo tube) and *nehm* (tangy, raw, spiced river fish wrapped in banana leaves). The south end of the *psar* (market) turns into a carnival of barbecue stands hawking meat-on-a-stick by night.

Red Sun Falling   INTERNATIONAL $
(Rue Preah Suramarit; mains 6000-14,000r) One of the liveliest spots in town, with a relaxed cafe ambience, used books for sale and a good selection of Asian and Western meals. By night it's a bar, but opening hours are somewhat erratic.

Le Bungalow   INTERNATIONAL $$
(Rue Preah Suramarit; mains US$4-16) The most sophisticated restaurant in town, offering a dash of Gallic cuisine (beef stewed in red wine), the most authentic pizzas in this corner of Cambodia and some Khmer favourites.

ℹ Information

You Hong II Guesthouse has a lively internet cafe and its walls are splattered with travel info. Most other recommended guesthouses are also pretty switched on to travellers' needs.

Acleda Bank (Rue Preah Sihanouk) Has an ATM that accepts Visa cards and can change travellers cheques (US dollars and Euros).

Cambodian Pride Tours (www.cambodianpride tours.com) Local tours website operated by two enthusiastic young guides from the Kratie area keen to promote real life experiences.

THE MEKONG DISCOVERY TRAIL

It's well worth sticking around Kratie for a couple of days to explore the various bike rides and activities on offer along the **Mekong Discovery Trail** (www.mekongdiscovery trail.com), an initiative to open up stretches of the Mekong River around Stung Treng and Kratie to community-based tourism. The project deserves support, as it intends to provide fishing communities an alternative income in order to protect the Irrawaddy dolphin and other rare species on this stretch of river.

A booklet with routes and maps outlining half-day to several-day excursions around Kratie is generally available in Kratie and Stung Treng. Ideal for cycling, it is being sign-posted so that travellers interested in pedalling their way through a slice of rural life can follow the trail for a few hours or several days, overnighting in village homestays. Routes criss-cross the Mekong frequently by ferry and traverse several Mekong islands, including Koh Trong (p254).

As well as homestays on Koh Trong, **CRDTours** can arrange homestays on **Koh Pdao**, an island 35km north of Kratie, and less popular **Koh Preah**, in southern Stung Treng Province. Participants do some serious interacting with locals and even get their hands dirty on volunteer building or farming projects. Diversions include cycling and dolphin-spotting from the shore. It costs US$35/50 for one/two nights, including all meals and transport.

Other popular destinations and activities further north along the trail include **kayaking** and **camping** trips through the **Ramsar wetlands** between Stung Treng and the Lao border, and homestays and dolphin-spotting around remote **Preah Rumkel** (p267) close to the border with Laos.

Canadia Bank (Rue Preah Suramarit) ATM offering free cash withdrawals, plus currency exchange.

CRDTours (☑099 834353; www.crdtours.org; Le Bungalow, Rue Preah Suramarit; ⊙7.30-11am & 1.30-5pm daily) The best source of information on the Mekong Discovery Trail and things to see and do around Kratie and north to Stung Treng. The place to book homestays on islands such as Koh Pdao and local tours that benefit local communities. Based at Le Bungalow, it is run to support local NGO the **Cambodian Rural Development Team** (CRDT; www.crdt.org).

Tourist office (Rue Preah Suramarit) A sleepy place that is rarely open, it supposedly stocks brochures and maps, plus information on the Mekong Discovery Trail.

❶ Getting There & Away

Kratie is 250km northeast of Phnom Penh via the Chhlong road and 141km south of Stung Treng.

Phnom Penh Sorya, Rith Mony, Paramount Angkor, and GST operate buses to Phnom Penh (29,000r, five hours) via Kompong Cham (19,000r, three hours). Trips are fairly frequent until about 1pm, when the last buses (originating at the Lao border) come through. Transfer in Skuon for Siem Reap.

Heading in the other direction are buses bound for Stung Treng (20,000r, 2½ hours), Ban Lung (US$10, six hours) in Ratanakiri, and Sen Monorom (25,000r) in Mondulkiri. There are also buses to the Lao border (US$8, 3½ hours) and Pakse (in Laos; US$17, six hours), which pass through from Phnom Penh between noon and 2pm.

Express minivans, which pick you up from your guesthouse at 6am, are the fastest and most comfortable way to get to Phnom Penh (US$8, four hours). Share taxis (US$10) and overcrowded minibuses (US$5) also head to Phnom Penh, usually between 6am and 8am. Additional rides depart after lunch.

❶ Getting Around

Most guesthouses can arrange motorbike hire (from US$6). An English-speaking *motodup* will set you back US$10 to US$15 per day. **Rent Bike** (Rue Preah Sihanouk) has bicycles available for 6000r per day.

Around Kratie

PHNOM SOMBOK   ភ្នំសំបុក
Phnom Sombok is a small hill with an active wat, located on the road from Kratie to Kampi. The hill offers the best views across the Mekong on this stretch of the river and a visit here can easily be combined with a trip to see the dolphins for an extra couple of dollars.

SAMBOR សំបូរ

Sambor was the site of a thriving pre-Angkorian city during the time of Sambor Prei Kuk and the Chenla empire. Not a stone remains in the modern town of Sambor, which is locally famous for having the largest wat in Cambodia, complete with 108 columns. Known locally as **Wat Sorsor Moi Roi** (100 Columns Temple), it was constructed on the site of a 19th-century wooden temple, a few pillars of which are still located at the back of the compound. This temple is a minor place of pilgrimage for residents of Kratie Province.

Mekong Turtle Conservation Centre (adult/child US$3/1.5; ☉8am-noon, 1.30-5pm) is located within the temple grounds. Established by **Conservation International** (www.conservation.org), it is home to several species of turtle, including the rare Cantor's softshell, which was only recently rediscovered along this stretch of the Mekong in 2007. One of the largest freshwater turtles, it can grow to nearly 2m in length. Hatchlings are nurtured here for 10 months before being released in the wild. If you look closely at the hatchling tanks notice the baby turtles staring back at you from out of the sand.

To get to Sambor, follow the Kampi road north to Sandan, before veering left along a reasonable 10km stretch of road – it's about 35km in total.

Chhlong ឈ្លង

Chhlong is a pleasant riverside port town that is finally on the map now that the road north to Kratie has finished being paved. The town's main attraction is the old governor's residence, a gorgeous, yellow-and-white French colonial mansion near the river that has been converted into high-end boutique hotel **Le Relais de Chhlong** (☎012 991801). The hotel is under new management and remained closed for extensive renovations (two years and counting) when we visited. If and when it reopens, it has a swimming pool and rooms are in the US$80 to US$100 range.

Not much else happens in Chhlong. A few decrepit French colonial buildings line the river. Architecture buffs might drop in at the **house of a hundred pillars** (1884), about 500m north of Le Relais. According to the house's owner, the Khmer Rouge removed many of the pillars so that today only 56 remain.

Chhlong is worth a wander if you are driving through with your own transport, but is probably not worth a special trip from Kratie. Keen cyclists might like to follow the old river road between Kratie and Chhlong, as it passes through some traditional Cham minority villages along the way.

STUNG TRENG PROVINCE

For a long while, poor Stung Treng Province (ខេត្តស្ទឹងត្រែង) was the neglected middle child, sandwiched between the luminary siblings of Ratanakiri Province and Kratie Province, not to mention the languid charms of Champasak in southern Laos. But

---

WORTH A TRIP

KOH TRONG, AN ISLAND IN THE MEKONG

Lying just across the water from Kratie is the island of Koh Trong, an almighty sandbar in the middle of the river. Cross here by boat and enjoy a slice of rural island life. This could be the Don Det of Cambodia in years to come. Attractions include an **old stupa** and a small **floating village**, as well as the chance to encounter one of the rare **Mekong mud turtles** who inhabit the western shore.

There are two homestays on the island. Best is **Koh Trong Community Homestay I** (per person US$4), set in an old wooden house, offering two proper bedrooms and fancy-pants bathrooms, meaning thrones not squats. It is located about 2km north of the ferry dock.

Sala Koh Trong (☎012 938984; www.kohtrong.com; r US$30-60) is a new lodge with attractive bungalows providing the best accommodation in the Kratie region. A swimming pool is planned during the lifetime of this book. Located at the northern tip of the island.

Catch the little ferry from the port (with/without bicycle 1000r/500r) in Kratie. Bicycle rental is available on the island for US$1.

DOLPHIN-WATCHING AROUND KRATIE

The freshwater Irrawaddy dolphin *(trey pisaut)* is an endangered species throughout Asia, with shrinking numbers inhabiting stretches of the Mekong in Cambodia and Laos, and isolated pockets in Bangladesh and Myanmar. The dark blue to grey cetaceans grow to 2.75m long and are recognisable by their bulging foreheads and small dorsal fins. They can live in fresh or salt water, although they are seldom seen in the sea. For more on this rare creature, see www.panda.org/greatermekong.

Before the civil war, locals say, Cambodia was home to as many as 1000 dolphins. However, during the Pol Pot regime, many were hunted for their oils, and their numbers continue to plummet even as drastic protection measures have been put in place, including a ban on fishing and motorised boat traffic on much of the Mekong between Kratie and Stung Treng. The dolphins continue to die off at an alarming rate, and experts now estimate that there are fewer than 70 Irrawaddy dolphins left in the Mekong between Kratie and the Lao border.

The place to see them is at Kampi, about 15km north of Kratie, on the road to Sambor. A moto/*remork* should be around US$5/10 return depending on how long the driver has to wait. Motorboats shuttle visitors out to the middle of the river to view the dolphins at close quarters. It costs US$9 per person for one to two persons and US$7 per person for groups of three or more. Encourage the boat driver to use the engine as little as possible once near the dolphins, as the noise is sure to disturb them. It is also possible to see them near the Lao border in Stung Treng province.

with a spiffy new border post and a network of recently upgraded roads now plugging Stung Treng into the rest of the country, the province may finally cash in on its tourism potential.

Much of that potential lies near the northern village of O'Svay, where several ecotourism initiatives have recently been launched on a sublime stretch of the Mekong. Here you can kayak out to a pod of rare Irrawaddy dolphins near the Lao border, passing islands, waterfalls, and bird-infested wetlands on the way.

The stretch of the Mekong between O'Svay and Stung Treng town can be explored by bicycle, boat or motorbike. From Stung Treng you can proceed by motorbike or boat to remote Siem Pang on the border of Virachey National Park, an area rich in birds and other wildlife.

Many more travellers are crossing the Cambodia–Laos border at Trapaeng Kriel, but few stop for long in Stung Treng. Those who do take some time to explore will be well ahead of the tourist pack.

Stung Treng   ស្ទឹងត្រែង
☎ 074 / POP 34,000

While new roads have helped put Stung Treng back on the map, they have also made it easier to pass through, and many travellers are no longer overnighting here. It is located on the banks of Tonlé San, which flows into the mighty Mekong on the western outskirts of the city. Some locals call Tonlé San the 'Tonlé Kong', as it merges with the Tonlé Kong 10km east of town. There is a major bridge across the San, which is a key link in the new road between Kratie and the Lao border, and there is now serious talk of an eventual bridge across the Mekong connecting Southern Laos with Preah Vihear and Siem Reap provinces.

◎ Sights & Activities

Thala Boravit   TEMPLE
Thala Boravit (ថាឡាបុរវិត) was an important Chenla-period trading town on the river route connecting the ancient city of Champasak and the sacred temple of Wat Phu with the southern reaches of the Chenla empire, including the ancient cities of Sambor Prei Kuk (Isanapura) and Angkor Borei. For all its past glories, there is very little to see today. It is hardly worth the effort for the casual visitor, but temple fiends may feel the urge to tick it off. Thala Boravit is on the west bank of the Mekong River and boats cross from Stung Treng roughly every 30 minutes throughout the day (3500/1500r with/without a motorbike).

🏠 Mekong Blue   SILK-WEAVING CENTRE
(មេគង្គប្លូ; ☎ 012 622096; www.mekongblue.com; ⊙ 7.30-11.30am & 2-5pm Mon-Sat) Part of the

Stung Treng

N 0 — 200 m
0 — 0.1 miles

Stung Treng

😴 Sleeping
1 Golden River Hotel.............................B1
2 Riverside Guesthouse.......................B1

🍴 Eating
3 Market Eateries.................................A2
4 Ponika's Place...................................B1
5 Street Vendors..................................A1

ℹ️ Information
6 Xplore-Asia..B1

ℹ️ Transport
7 GST..A2
8 Phnom Penh Sorya A2
9 Rith Mony..B1

Stung Treng Women's Development Centre, Mekong Blue is a silk-weaving centre on the outskirts of Stung Treng. Mekong Blue specialises in exquisite silk products for sale and export. At this centre it is possible to observe the dyers and weavers, most of whom come from vulnerable or impoverished backgrounds. There is a small showroom on site with a selection of silk on sale, plus a cafe. However, it only serves cold drinks unless you book a meal in advance. The centre is located about 4km east of the centre on the riverside road that continues under the bridge.

🛏️ Sleeping

TOP CHOICE Tonlé Tourism Training Centre
GUESTHOUSE $

(☏973638; fieldco@tourismforhelp.org; s/d from US$6/8) Located in a shady spot on the riverfront about 500m west of the ferry dock, this small guesthouse doubles as a training centre to help underprivileged locals get a start in the tourism industry. Rooms are simple but tastefully furnished. The four rooms share an immaculate bathroom and a comfy balcony with views of Tonlé San.

Golden River Hotel
HOTEL $$

(☏973790; r US$15-35; ❄️@🛜) The smartest hotel in town by some distance. Set on the riverfront, it has the province's only lift and 50 well-appointed rooms, many with panoramic vistas of the Mekong, although make sure you ask for a river view on check-in.

Riverside Guesthouse
GUESTHOUSE $

(☏012 439454; riverside.tour@yahoo.com; r US$5-7; @) Overlooking the riverfront area, the Riverside has long been a popular travellers' crossroads. Rooms are basic, but so are the prices. Good for travel information and there is a popular bar-restaurant downstairs.

Mekong Bird Lodge
GUESTHOUSE $

(☏099 709677; bungalows US$6-10) This self-styled ecolodge is situated on a bluff over a peaceful eddy of the Mekong, about 4km north of town. Pricier cottages have private balconies with hammocks and sunset views, but the place is rather showing its age. Power stops at 8pm. As the name suggests, the birdwatching is impressive.

🍴 Eating

On the riverside promenade west of the ferry dock, a handful of street-side vendors peddle cold beer and noodle soup until late in the evening. The southwest corner of the market has cheap-and-quick eateries with pots for your perusal.

Ponika's Place
INTERNATIONAL $

(mains US$2-5; ⊙6am-10pm) Need a break from *laab* after Laos? Burgers, pizza and English breakfast grace the menu, along with Indian food and wonderful Khmer curries. Affable owner Ponika speaks English.

🌿 Le Tonlé
INTERNATIONAL $

(mains US$2-5; ⊙6am-9pm) Part of the Tonlé Tourism Training Centre, Le Tonlé is a relaxed place to eat authentic Khmer dishes such as *amoc* (baked fish with lemongrass-based *kreung* paste, coconut and chilli in banana leaf), as well as some international specials and vegetarian meals. Good place for a good cause.

ℹ Information

Acleda Bank (half a block east of the market) Has an ATM for Visa only.

Canadia Bank (near market) Has a full international ATM with free withdrawals.

Internet Service (⏱7am-7pm) Internet access next to the GST bus office.

Mlup Baitong (☎012 425172; www.mlup.org) NGO organising dolphin-watching trips and homestays along the Mekong Discovery Trail.

Riverside Guesthouse Specialises in getting people to/from Laos, Siem Reap or just about anywhere else. Also runs boat tours, including trips to Kratie (four hours) and to the Lao border via the resident dolphin pod. English-speaking guides can take you places on motorbikes, including to Tbeng Meanchey.

Tourist Information Centre (☎638 8867; ⏱8-11am & 2.30-4pm) Inconveniently located near the new bridge, it's run by the ever-helpful Theany.

Xplore-Asia (☎012 675413) Doles out brochures, booklets and advice, and tailors one- to several-day cycling-and-kayak combo tours along the Mekong Discovery Trail. Rents out kayaks (US$30 per day), motorbikes (US$7 per day) and sturdy Trek mountain bikes (US$5 per day). One-way mountain bike rental to southern Laos and Phnom Penh is available.

ℹ Getting There & Away

NH7 south to Kratie (141km) and north to the Lao border is in great shape these days. Rith Mony, Phnom Penh Sorya and GST all have 7am buses to Phnom Penh (40,000r, nine hours) via Kratie (20,000r, two hours) and Kompong Cham (30,000r, six hours). Rith Mony has a 3pm bus to Ban Lung (20,000r). A few express minibuses do the trip to Phnom Penh via Chhlong, picking up from guesthouses and hotels around 4am (50,000r, seven hours). From the riverfront taxi park, share taxis and minibuses go to Phnom Penh (50,000r, eight hours) and Ban Lung (30,000r, four hours).

For the inside story on the border crossing with Laos, see p347. For getting to/from Ban Lung in Ratanakiri, see p263. There is a daily minibus to Ban Lung (US$6, three hours, 8am).

There is also a new road that leads across northern Cambodia from Stung Treng to either Tbeng Meanchey or Kompong Thom. Formerly a real ordeal, this road has now been significantly upgraded and is relatively straightforward in the dry season. Public transport is not yet available, but will no doubt start once the bridges are finished along this route. First, cross the Mekong to Thala Boravit, from where a jungle road leads west to the large village of Chhep. In the wet season, if you are crazy enough to try it during the rains, you may need to overnight in Chhep, but there are no guesthouses, just informal homestays. From Chhep, there is an old logging road west that joins with the main road from Kompong Thom to Tbeng Meanchey. A few moto drivers in Stung Treng brave this route, but it's pricey – at least US$40 to Tbeng Meanchey (more for an English-speaking guide/driver).

Around Stung Treng

O'SVAY & PREAH RUMKEL   អូរស្វាយ

These small villages are emerging as hotbeds of ecotourism thanks to their proximity to the Anlong Cheuteal Irrawaddy dolphin pool near the Lao border. Sightings of dolphins are practically guaranteed here, while sightings of other tourists are still relatively rare. With Ramsar-recognised wetlands, dozens of islands, a rich array of bird life and various rapids and waterfalls cascading down from Laos, this is one of the Mekong River's wildest and most beautiful stretches.

It is possible to hire longtailed boats in both O'Svay and Preah Rumkel (Anlong Seima) to explore the area and view the dolphins at Anlong Cheuteal. O'Svay is closer to Stung Treng but further from the dolphins. It's the better choice for those who want to observe a bit more of the river on their way out to the dolphins. Preah Rumkel is only 5km from the main Lao overland border crossing. Travellers coming in from Laos could get here in about 10 minutes on the back of a moto, spend a day on the river, and proceed to Stung Treng in the late afternoon.

Three-passenger boats cost US$13 from Anlong Seima and US$15 from O'Svay. There's an additional US$1 per person charge to see the dolphins. You can usually just show up and find a boat, or organise in advance through Mlup Baitong or Xplore-Asia in Stung Treng. Another option is to hire kayaks through Xplore-Asia and paddle out to the dolphins or join one of their two-day, one-night kayaking trips with an overnight camp on an island.

These trips all take place along the Mekong Discovery Trail (p253). **Homestays** (per person US$4) are a popular experience in this area, but facilities are still fairly basic and the level of English spoken by host families pretty rudimentary.

Mlup Baitong (www.mlup.org) organises homestays in Preah Rumkel and O'Russey Kandal, about 28km south of Stung Treng.

CRDTours (www.CRDTours.com) in Kratie (see p252) operates a homestay project in Koh Preah, about 15km south of Stung Treng.

CEPA (Culture & Environment Preservation Association; www.cepa-cambodia.org) can help organise a homestay in O'Svay.

SIEM PANG
POP 5000

សៀមប៉ាង

A relatively prosperous town that stretches for about 6km along the Tonlé Kong, Siem Pang is a good place to observe rural life or just relax by the riverside. This remote outpost in the far north of Stung Treng Province is now a little bit closer to civilisation thanks to a new road connecting it to the NH7 highway.

Siem Pang acts as the western gateway to Virachey National Park and is renowned for its rich wildlife. Rare giant ibises and white-shouldered ibises roost around here.

BirdLife International (☎092 994002, in Phnom Penh 023 993631; www.birdlife.org) runs a vulture-feeding station that attracts all three species of critically endangered vultures found in Cambodia. It's set up for research rather than tourism, but if you time your visit for the monthly 'feed', which involves killing a water buffalo or cow and leaving it in a field near an observation hideout, you may get a chance to spot the vultures. Or you can up the ante with US$150 to organise a private feed.

A ferry takes passengers (1000r) and motorbikes (2500r) across the river, where the scenic trail to Voen Sai in Ratanakiri starts. Theany Guesthouse (☎012 675413; r US$5) offers one-way motorbike rentals for this ride (US$25), along with simple rooms in a traditional wooden house.

A relaxing way to get to Siem Pang is on the slow boat from Stung Treng (US$5, eight hours), which departs daily at 7am in both directions. Otherwise, regular morning and occasional afternoon vans do the trip (US$5, 2½ hours). The trip from Stung Treng takes about two hours or so by motorbike. From Stung Treng, drive 55km north on NH7, turn right, and proceed another 52km on a rather sandy unsealed road.

RATANAKIRI PROVINCE

Popular Ratanakiri Province (ខេត្តរតនគិរី) is making a name for itself as a diverse region of outstanding natural beauty that provides a remote home for a mosaic of minority peoples. The Jarai, Tompuon, Brau and Kreung are the Khmer Leu (Upper Khmer) people, with their own languages, traditions and customs. There is also a large Lao population throughout the province and multiple languages will be heard in villages such as Voen Sai.

Adrenaline activities are abundant. Swim in clear volcanic lakes, shower under waterfalls, or trek in the vast Virachey National Park – it's all here. Tourism is set to take off, but that is if the lowland politicians and generals don't plunder the place first. Ratanakiri is the frontline in the battle for land, and the slash-and-burn minorities are losing out thanks to their tradition of collective ownership. The forest is disappearing at an alarming rate, being replaced by rubber plantations and cashew-nut farms. Hopefully someone wakes up and smells the coffee – there's plenty of that as well – before it's too late.

Gem mining is big business in Ratanakiri, hardly surprising given the name means 'hill of the precious stones'. There is good-quality zircon mined in several parts of the province, as well as other semiprecious stones. The prices are low compared with the West, but don't get suckered into a dream deal, as gem scams are as old as the hills themselves.

Ratanakiri Province played its part in the country's contemporary tragedy by serving as a base for the Khmer Rouge leadership during much of the 1960s. Pol Pot and Ieng Sary fled here in 1963 and established headquarters in Ta Veng in the north of the province.

Roads in Ratanakiri are not as impressive as the sights. In the dry season, prepare to do battle with the dust of 'red-earth Ratanakiri', which will leave you with orange skin and ginger hair. The roads look like a papaya shake during the wet season. The ideal time to explore is November, after the rains have stopped and before the dust begins to swirl.

Ban Lung
បានលុង

☎075 / POP 30,000

Affectionately known as 'dey krahorm' (red earth) after its rust-coloured affliction, Ban Lung provides a popular base for a range of Ratanakiri romps. It may look like autumn all year round, but it's just that the leaves, like everything else, are cloaked in a blanket of dust. Fortunately the dust is becoming less of a problem within town as more and more streets are sealed.

The town itself is busy and lacks the backwater charm of Sen Monorom in Mondulkiri, but with attractions such as Boeng Yeak Lom

THE ELEPHANT VALLEY PROJECT

For an original elephant experience, visit the **Elephant Valley Project** (☎099-696041; www.elephantvalleyproject.org). The project entices local mahouts to bring their over-worked or injured elephants to this sanctuary, where, in the words of project coordinator Jack Highwood, 'they can learn how to act like elephants again'.

A young Briton with a contagious passion for elephants, Highwood is on a mission to improve the lot of Mondulkiri's working elephants. While Bunong tradition calls for giving elephants a certain amount of down time, Highwood says that economic incentives to overwork elephants prove too great for the impoverished mahouts of Mondulkiri. In addi-tion to toting tourists around on their backs, elephants are hired to haul around anything and everything, including illegally cut timber. 'In Mondulkiri, the elephant is basically seen as a cheap tractor', he says.

Most tour companies in Mondulkiri make a point of stressing that their tours employ only humanely treated elephants. Highwood commends this, but wonders whether it's possible to know the truth. 'Most elephants in Mondulkiri are in a highly abused state', he says. 'They are beaten on the head and made to do things they aren't meant to be doing.'

Enter the Elephant Valley Project. Mahouts who bring their elephants here (there are six at the time of writing) are paid a competitive working wage to retire their elephants full time to ecotourism. Mahouts continue to work with their elephants, feeding and caring for them and making sure they don't escape into the wild. The elephants, for their part, can spend their days blasting through the forest in search of food, uprooting saplings to get to their yummy roots and hanging out by the river spraying mud on one another.

Highwood no longer allows visitors to ride the elephants here. Instead, you simply walk through the forest with them and observe them in their element. In the process you learn a lot about not only elephant behaviour but also Bunong culture and forest ecology.

If you do opt for an elephant-riding tour elsewhere, Highwood recommends inspect-ing the elephant closely for signs of abuse. Signs of malnourishment, such as protruding ribs, a protracted spine or abscesses on the back under the basket are clear signs that an elephant is being mistreated.

A two-day stay, including all meals, transport to the site and a night's accommoda-tion in exquisite bungalows tucked into the jungle on a ridge overlooking the valley, costs US$100 per person. A day trip costs US$50, but don't show up unannounced. The Bu-nong Place and Green House can handle bookings; for contact details, see p270. Short- and long-term volunteers who want to help the project while learning mahout skills are welcome, although volunteers must pay extra to cover training costs. The project does not take overnight visitors on Friday and Saturday nights and is not open to visitors on Saturday and Sunday.

just a short hop away, there is little room for complaint. Many of the minorities from the surrounding villages come to Ban Lung to buy and sell at the market. The town was originally known as Labansiek before the civil war, but the district name of Ban Lung has gradually slipped into use among locals.

⊙ Sights & Activities

There are no real sights in the centre of town. The big draw is Boeng Yeak Lom, while multiday treks around Ban Lung are picking up steam.

Boeng Yeak Lom   LAKE
At the heart of the protected area of **Yeak Lom** (admission US$1) is a beautiful blue cra-ter lake (បឹងយក្សឡោម) set amid the vivid greens of the towering jungle. The lake is believed to have been formed 700,000 years ago and some people swear it must have been formed by a meteor strike as the cir-cle is so perfect. The indigenous minority people in the area have long considered Yeak Lom a sacred place and their legends talk of mysterious creatures that inhabit the waters of the lake. It is one of the most peaceful, beautiful locations Cambodia has to offer and the water is extremely clear. Several wooden piers are dotted around the perimeter, making it perfect for swimming.

A small Cultural & Environmental Centre has information on ethnic minorities

RESPONSIBLE TREKKING AROUND RATANAKIRI

Overnight treks are very popular these days. Diehard trampers spend up to eight days sleeping in replica US Army hammocks and checking out some of the country's last virgin forest in and around Virachey National Park. Shorter trips are possible, as are several-day kayaking excursions on Tonlé San and overnight stays in ethnic-minority villages.

Keep in mind that trekking in Virachey National Park is the exclusive domain of **Virachey National Park Eco-Tourism Information Center** (Map p262; ✆weekdays 075-974013, weekends 077-965196; http://viracheyecotourism.blogspot.com; Department of Environment Compound, Ban Lung; ⊗8am-noon & 2-5.30pm Mon-Fri). Private tour operators also offer multiday treks, but these only go as far as the park's buffer zone. There's little forest left standing outside the park boundary, so be careful that you're not being taken for a loop – literally – around and around in the same small patch of forest.

Despite being shut out from the park, private operators can still design creative treks that take in minority villages and scenic spots around the province. Just be sure to make clear arrangements with your guide to ensure you get what is expected out of a trip.

Where possible, we recommend using indigenous guides for organised treks and other excursions around Ban Lung (see the box, p264). Unfortunately, the level of English among indigenous guides tends to be only fair. If you need a more fluent English guide, we suggest hiring both an English-speaking Khmer guide and a minority guide, if it's within your budget.

A newly formed association of **Tompuon guides** (yeak.loam@yahoo.com) is a good place to look for an indigenous guide. The association also runs an exclusive tour of several Tompuon villages around Boeng Yeak Lom. You can observe weavers and basket makers in action, learn about animist traditions and eat a traditional indigenous meal of bamboo-steamed fish, fresh vegetables, 'minority' rice and, of course, rice wine. The association also has English-teaching and other volunteer opportunities available.

Conservation International (CI: www.conservation.org) is in the process of supporting a range of community-based ecotourism products near Ban Lung in the Veun Sai-Siem Pang Conservation Area (VSSPCA), including overnight jungle treks and homestays. All will include a fee for conservation and development activities, which are determined by and for local communities. If you want to ensure your experience is a fair trek, talk to the local Ban Lung tour operators about undertaking a community trek to the VSSPCA. For more on the new Gibbon Trek, see p261.

Ban Lung places that run their own treks include Tree Top, Terres Rouges and Yaklom Hill Lodge. Terres Rouges offers treks with French-speaking guides, plus mountain-bike rides and even quad biking (ATVs). Norden House is the place to go for motorcycle tours on 250cc dirt bikes.

Day hikes, elephant rides, kayaking and overnight treks are offered by a number of tour companies:

» **DutchCo Trekking Cambodia** (✆097 679 2714; www.trekkingcambodia.com; ⊗closed Sep) One of the most experienced trekking operators in the province, run by – wait for it – a friendly Dutch couple. Opening a rustic camp in Voen Sai in 2012.

» **Parrot Tours** (✆012 764714; www.jungletrek.blogspot.com) Sitha Nan is a national-park-trained guide with expert local knowledge.

» **Smiling Tours** (✆012 247713; smeyadventure@gmail.com) Smey often hangs out at Tree Top Ecolodge and offers a range of trips and treks.

in the province, local handicrafts on display, suggested walks around the lake and **inner tubes** (per hr 4000r) for rent. The local Tompoun minority has a 25-year lease to manage the lake through to 2021, and proceeds from the entry fee go towards improving life in the nearby villages. However, developers, backed by local politicians, are actively trying to have the lease annulled to build hotels and a road around the lake, and a casino on a sacred mountain near the lake.

Boeng Yeak Lom is 5km east of Ban Lung's central roundabout. Turn right off the road to Bokheo at the statue of the minority family. Motos are available for around US$3 return, but expect to pay more if the driver has to wait. It takes almost an hour to reach on foot from Ban Lung.

Elephant Rides ELEPHANTS

Most guesthouses and hotels can arrange short elephant rides from nearby villages to local waterfalls. One of the most popular rides is from the village of Kateung to the spectacular waterfall of Ka Tieng. The ride takes about one hour, passing through beautiful rubber plantations. The usual charge is US$10 per person per hour. However, for a more responsible interaction with elephants, we suggest visiting the Elephant Valley Project in Mondulkiri Province (p259) and its unique 'walking with the herd' experience.

🛏 Sleeping

TOP CHOICE Terres Rouges Lodge BOUTIQUE HOTEL $$
(☏974051; www.ratanakiri-lodge.com; r US$40-85; ❄@🛅⛲) In a gorgeous lakeshore garden, this atmospheric complex has 23 rooms, including superb Balinese-style bungalows with open-plan bathrooms and antique decor. Amenities include a spa, Khmer sauna, an inviting swimming pool and even a pétanque (boules) track.

TOP CHOICE Tree Top Ecolodge GUESTHOUSE $
(☏012 490333; www.treetop-ecolodge.com; r US$7-15; 🕾) Setting the standard for budget digs in the northeast, Tree Top boasts rough-hewn walkways leading to all-wood bungalows with mosquito nets, thatch roofs and verandas with verdant valley vistas. The restaurant dangles over a lush ravine with great views of the hillside beyond. Up-to-date travel advice is plentiful, especially for those Laos bound.

Norden House LODGE $$
(☏690 0640; www.nordenhouseyaklom.com; r US$25; ❄@) In a peaceful spot on the road to Boeng Yeak Lom, the six international-standard, stylish bungalows here include embroidered linens, DVD players and bathrooms with solar hot water. The restaurant is renowned for its Swedish specialities.

Lakeside Hotel HOTEL $
(☏012 233312; r US$10-25; ❄@🕾) A new hotel next door to Chheng Lok. The architecture

---

AN ALTERNATIVE GIBBON EXPERIENCE

Many have heard of the Gibbon Experience in Northern Laos, but now Cambodia offers an alternative gibbon experience of its very own. While it doesn't offer ziplines and treetop accommodation, it does allow small, environmentally conscious groups of visitors to view and follow wild gibbons in their natural habitat within Veun Sai-Siem Pang Conservation Area (VSSPCA). Set up as a community-based ecotourism project by **Conservation International Cambodia** (www.conservation.org), this scheme offers three-day, two-night treks, which include a morning spent with the semi-habituated gibbons. Experiencing them waking the jungle with their haunting dawn call and seeing them swing through the canopy is memorable.

Visits are limited to a maximum of six people per time and the tours cost US$300 to US$350 per person depending on exact numbers. This includes entrance fees, guide fees, homestays and camps, and all meals. Community funds are used for conservation and development initiatives, so this is a very worthwhile way to contribute something positive to wildlife conservation and community development in northeast Cambodia.

Responsible tour operators working with Conservation International to promote this new gibbon project include the following:

DutchCo Trekking Cambodia (☏097 679 2714; www.trekkingcambodia.com) Ratanakiri-based operator working with independent travellers and walk-in visitors.

See Cambodia Differently (☏ UK 44 (0) 20 8150 5150, Cambodia 089 271715; www.see cambodiadifferently.com) UK-Cambodia-based operator working with overseas agents or independent travellers.

Due to the limited number of treks to the area, it is recommended that you book this experience well in advance.

CI is also setting up a range of community-based ecotourism products in the VSSPCA that can be booked through local trekking companies. For more on these initiatives, see p260.

Ban Lung

EASTERN CAMBODIA BAN LUNG

is an improvement on the mod-Khmer that predominates in town. Rooms include nice touches like silk hangings and a kettle. Opt for a balcony lakeview.

Lakeside Chheng Lok Hotel HOTEL $
(☏012 957422; lakeside-chhenglokhotel@yahoo. com; r US$5-20; ❄@🛜) Overlooking Boeng Kansaign lake, this 65-room hotel has a choice of attractive garden bungalows or clean, spacious rooms, all with cable TV. Good all-rounder.

Prak Dara Guesthouse HOTEL $
(☏666 6068; r with fan/air-con US$6/10; ❄@🛜) Another new place above the lake. Rooms here are cracking value given the cleanliness and comfort. Take advantage of the free wi-fi to plan your upcountry adventures.

Chay Veng Guesthouse GUESTHOUSE $
(☏012 686954; r with fan/air-con US$5/10; @) One of the better places to stay on the main

drag, Chay Veng is run by an energetic pair of young English-speaking brothers. Rooms are fairly standard Khmer fare, but are cleaner and brighter than most.

Yaklom Hill Lodge ECOLODGE $
(☏011 725881; www.yaklom.com; r incl breakfast & pick-up in town US$10-20) In lush forest 5km east of town, this ecolodge has all-wood bungalows that are atmospheric but starting to show their age. A generator enables hot showers from 6pm to 9pm.

🍴 Eating & Drinking

To get down with the locals, head to the lakefront near Coconut Shake Restaurant around sunset, plop down on a mat, and order cheap beer and snacks from waterfront shacks.

Terres Rouges Lodge CAMBODIAN, CHINESE $$
(www.ratanakiri-lodge.com; meals US$4-15) Terres Rouges is home to the most sophisticated

Ban Lung

restaurant in town, serving well-presented Khmer and Chinese dishes, as well as some imported lamb and beef with a distinctive French twist.

Gecko House INTERNATIONAL $
(mains 6000-18,000r; ⊙10am-11pm) A charming little restaurant-bar with inviting sofas, soft lighting and famously frosty beer mugs, this is a great place by day or night. The menu features Thai tastes, Khmer classics and some Western dishes.

Rik's Cafe Cambodge INTERNATIONAL $
(mains US$1.50-5.50) Run by the DutchCo team, one of the more experienced trekking outfits in Ratanakiri, this relaxed cafe offers great valley views. Good for coffee and light bites by day and a spot of pre- or post-trek beer drinking by night.

Sal's Restaurant & Bar INTERNATIONAL $
(mains US$1.75-5) This welcoming restaurant-bar, popular with Ban Lung's small expat community, is the place to come for comfort food from home, including Indian curries, spicy Mexican and great burgers. All dishes are freshly prepared, so order ahead if you don't want to wait around.

A'Dam Restaurant INTERNATIONAL $
(mains US$2-4; ⊙11am-3pm & 5.30pm-midnight) An animated bar by night thanks to a pool table and dart board that tempt barflies, this mellow restaurant warmly welcomes locals, expats and travellers.

Lay Lay Restaurant ASIAN $
(meals 4000-20,000r; ⊙7am-10pm) A new restaurant set in a cavernous yellow-green complex off the main drag, the big menu includes tasty Khmer, Chinese and Asian dishes.

Coconut Shake Restaurant CAFE $
(northeast cnr of Boeng Kansaign; meals 4000-12,000r; ⊙7am-8pm) The best coconut shakes in the northeast. Dare to try the 'fish and ship' or the friend toes (French toast?).

ⓘ Information

Visitors will find their guesthouse or hotel or the recommended tour companies (p260) to be most useful in the quest for local knowledge. Check out www.yaklom.com for more ideas on what to do in Ratanakiri.

Acleda Bank Has an ATM that accepts Visa cards only; changes travellers cheques and handles Western Union money transfers.

Redland Internet Café (⊙7am-8pm)

Tourist office (☑974125; ⊙7.30-11.30am & 2-5pm Mon-Fri) Brochures on Ratanakiri – that is, if you're lucky enough to find it open.

Virachey National Park Eco-Tourism Information Centre For park info.

ⓘ Getting There & Away

Ban Lung is 588km northeast of Phnom Penh and 150km east of Stung Treng. At the time of writing, Ratanakiri's airport had been closed to commercial flights for about five years, so don't expect them to resume any time soon.

Meanwhile, it's getting easier and easier to get to Ban Lung by road. Highway NH19 between Ban Lung and O Pong Moan (the junction 19km south of Stung Treng) is still being rebuilt at the time of writing and should be fully sealed by 2012. This has brought down journey times to around two hours to Stung Treng.

Buses to Phnom Penh (40,000r, 11 hours) operate only in the dry season for now. Phnom Penh Sorya and Rith Mony make the trip, with early-morning departures in either direction via Kratie and Kompong Cham. Long-distance bus services to Siem Reap or Pakse are also

EASTERN CAMBODIA BAN LUNG

promoted, but in reality this is a scam and you will be forced to buy another ticket in Kompong Cham or Stung Treng respectively.

Speedy express minibus services pick you up at your guesthouse at 6am and head to Phnom Penh (US$13, eight hours). Organise these through your guesthouse, or alternatively through **Sok Kun** (☎011-433939). Call Tree Top Ecolodge (p261) to arrange a pick-up if coming from Phnom Penh. Share taxis to Phnom Penh are losing popularity as the roads improve, while pick-up trucks are mainly a wet-season option.

Private minibus services offering guesthouse pick-ups also go to Stung Treng (US$6, 2½ hours). Otherwise take a share taxi (30,000r) or slower pick-up truck (inside/on the back 20,000/16,000r) from the taxi park.

There are also morning minibuses from the taxi park to the Cambodia–Vietnam border at O Yadaw-Le Thanh (US$7, two hours, 8am departure) for onwards travel to Pleiku, Quy Nhon and Hoi An. Guesthouses and hotels now offer through tickets to Pleiku (US$12, four hours), involving a change of minibus at the border.

ⓘ Getting Around

Motorbikes (US$5 to US$7), cars (from US$30) and 4WDs (from US$40) are available for hire from most guesthouses in town.

Norden House has well-maintained 250cc bikes for rent at US$25 per day. Local guides with motorbikes offer their services around the province and rates range from US$15 to US$20 per day for a good English-speaking driver-guide (less for a Khmer speaker).

For something cheaper and more environmentally friendly, consider a bicycle (US$1 to US$3 per day), available from some hotels and the cycle shops on the main drag.

Around Ban Lung

There are numerous waterfalls in the province, but many are difficult to reach in the wet season and lack water in the dry season. The three most commonly visited are **Chaa Ong**, **Ka Tieng** and **Kinchaan** (Kachang), all within 10km of town and attracting a 2000r admission fee.

TREAD LIGHTLY IN THE HILLS

Tourism can bring many benefits to highland communities: cross-cultural understanding, improved infrastructure, cheaper market goods, employment opportunities and tourist dollars supporting handicraft industries. However, there are also negatives, such as increased litter and pollutants, dependency on tourist dollars, and the erosion of local values and practices.

As tourism proliferates in the northeast, the negatives are beginning to outweigh the positives. Most of the benefits of increased tourism in Ratanakiri and Mondulkiri are not going to the ethnic-minority highlanders, but to the lowland Khmers who dominate the tourism industry. Khmer tour operators often pay lip service to responsible tourism, but ultimately their motivations are financial; they rarely encourage their clients to visit in a way that avoids corrupting indigenous communities.

That is why we recommend hiring indigenous guides directly. Not only does this ensure that your tourist dollars go directly to indigenous communities, it will also enrich your own visit. Indigenous guides can greatly improve your access to the residents of highland communities, who are animists and rarely speak Khmer. They also understand taboos and traditions that might be lost on Khmer guides. Their intimate knowledge of the forests is another major asset.

More tips on visiting indigenous communities responsibly:

Interaction

» Be polite and respectful – doubly so with elderly people.

» Dress modestly.

» Taste traditional wine if you are offered it, especially during a ceremony. Refusal will cause offence.

» Honour signs discouraging outsiders from entering a village, for instance during a spiritual ceremony. A good local guide will be able to detect these signs.

» Learn something about the community's culture and language and demonstrate something good about yours.

The most spectacular of the three is Chaa Ong, as it is set in a jungle gorge and you can clamber behind the waterfall or venture underneath for a power shower. However, it dries up from about February to May. Directions are signposted 3km west of town on the road to Stung Treng.

Ka Tieng is the most enjoyable, as it drops over a rock shelf allowing you to clamber all the way behind. There are some vines on the far side that are strong enough to swing on for some Tarzan action.

VOEN SAI វិនសៃ
POP 3000

Located on the banks of Tonlé San, Voen Sai is a cluster of Chinese, Lao and *chunchiet* villages. Originally, the town was located on the north bank of the river and known as Virachey, but these days the main settlement is on the south bank.

From the south side, cross the river on a small ferry (500/3000r without/with a motorbike) and walk west for a couple of kilometres, passing through the Khmer village, a Lao community and a small *chunchiet* area, before finally emerging in a wealthy Chinese village complete with large wooden houses and inhabitants who still speak Chinese. Note how neat and tidy it is compared with the surrounding communities.

Kachon is a 40-minute boat ride east of Voen Sai and has an impressive **Tompuon cemetery** (admission US$1). When a lengthy period of mourning is complete, villagers hold a big celebration and add two carved wooden likenesses of elephant tusks to the structures. Some of these tombs date back many years and have been abandoned to the jungle. Newer tombs of wealthy individuals have been cast in concrete and show some modern touches like shades and mobile phones. Remember that this is a sacred site for local Tompuon people – see the box text, p270, for advice on visiting *chunchiet* cemeteries responsibly.

The cemetery is in the old settlement of Kachon on the north bank of the Tonlé San. The cemetery in new Kachon on the south bank is off limits to outsiders. Expect

Gifts

» Individual gifts create jealousy and expectations. Instead, consider making donations to the local school, medical centre or community fund.

» If you do give individual gifts, keep them modest (such as matches).

» Do not give children sweets or money.

» Do not give clothes – communities are self-sufficient.

Shopping

» Haggle politely and always pay the agreed (and fair) price.

» Do not ask to buy a villager's personal household items, tools or the jewellery or clothes they are wearing.

» Don't buy village treasures, such as altar pieces or totems.

Photographs

» Do not photograph without asking permission first – this includes children. Some hill tribes believe the camera will capture their spirit.

» Don't photograph altars.

» Don't use a flash.

» Don't show up for 15 minutes and expect to be granted permission to take photos. Invest some time in getting to know the villagers first.

Travel

» Make a point of travelling in small, less disruptive groups.

» Try to spend some real time in minority villages – at least several hours if not an overnight. If you don't have a few hours to invest, don't go.

to pay around US$15 for the boat trip from Voen Sai to Kachon, including a jaunt to the Chinese and Lao villages opposite Voen Sai. Alternatively, travel to new Kachon by road from Voen Sai and pay a local a few thousand riel to take you across the river.

Voen Sai is 39km northwest of Ban Lung on a passable road. It is easy enough to get here under your own steam on a motorbike or with a vehicle. English-speaking guides ask US$10 to US$15 to take you out here on a moto.

Skilled motorbike and mountain-bike riders can ride from Voen Sai to Siem Pang in Stung Treng along a scenic trail that begins on the north side of the river. One-way motorbike rentals for the reverse trip are available in Siem Pang (see p258).

TA VENG   ទៃវ៉ែង

Ta Veng is an insignificant village on the southern bank of Tonlé San, but it acts as the main gateway to Virachey National Park and the base for many treks run by private operators in the park's buffer zone. It was in the Ta Veng district that Pol Pot, Ieng Sary and other leaders of the Khmer Rouge established their guerrilla base in the 1960s. Locals say nothing today remains of the remote base, although, in a dismal sign of decline, they point out that Ta Veng had electricity before the war.

Ta Veng is about 57km north of Ban Lung on a roller-coaster road through the mountains that affords some of the province's better views. The road passes through several **minority villages**, where it is possible to break the journey. There are some very steep climbs in sections, and for this reason, it wouldn't be much fun in the rain. Travel by motorbike or charter a vehicle.

It is possible to hire small boats in Ta Veng for river jaunts (US$10 to US$15 in the local area or US$70 to US$80 for the five-hour trip to Voen Sai).

ANDONG MEAS   អណ្ដូងមាស
POP 1500

Andong Meas district is popular thanks to a combination of minority villages, **Jarai cemeteries** and a short river trip, although the cemeteries were badly damaged by the ravages of typhoon Ketsana in 2009. There is a walkable trail from Andong Meas to a Jarai village and cemetery on the banks of the Tonlé San. It's two hours walking one-way or 30 minutes in a fast longtailed boat (US$15 return). Don't enter any Jarai cemetery without permission and a Jarai escort, and expect to pay up to US$3.

A visit here can be combined with a visit to the current hot spot for **gem mining** in Bokheo, 29km east of Ban Lung. Locals dig a large pit in the ground and then tunnel horizontally in their search for amethyst and zircon. When we visited, the mines were about 1km out of town on the road to Andong Meas, but they tend to move around.

Andong Meas lies 58km northeast of Ban Lung. Turn left off the sealed highway just before you enter Bokheo. From here, it's a straight shot on a reasonable dirt road. One way from Ban Lung should take about 1½ hours.

LUMKUT LAKE   ពីនទ្បុំគុត

Lumkut is a large crater lake hemmed in by dense forest on all sides, similar to the more illustrious and accessible Boeng Yeak Lom. If you want to have a dip, walk clockwise about a quarter of the way around the lake to a pier that allows easy access to the water. The lake is about 55km southeast of Ban Lung. Turn right off the road to O'Yadaw about 4km east of Bokheo.

VIRACHEY NATIONAL PARK
ឧទ្យានជាតិវីរ:ជ័យ

This **park** (admission US$5) is one of the largest protected areas in Cambodia, stretching for 3325 sq km east to Vietnam, north to Laos and west to Stung Treng Province. The park has never been fully explored and is home to a number of rare mammals, including elephants, clouded leopards, tigers and sun bears, although your chances of seeing any of these beasts are extremely slim. However, you'll probably hear endangered gibbons and might spot great hornbills, giant ibises, Germain's peacock-pheasants and other rare birds. So important is the park to the Mekong region that it was designated an Asean Heritage Park in 2003. However, the bad news is that it is seriously under threat from developers and Cambodian authorities have already sold more remote regions of the park to Vietnamese rubber plantation developers.

Virachey has one of the most organised ecotourism programs in Cambodia, focusing on small-scale culture, nature and adventure trekking. The program aims to involve and benefit local minority communities. All treks into the park must be arranged through the Virachey National Park Eco-Tourism Information Center in Ban Lung. The park

TREKS IN VIRACHEY NATIONAL PARK

There are two treks available in Virachey. Prices listed are per person for a group of two and include transport by moto to the trail head, park admission, food, guides, porters, hammocks and boat transport where necessary. Prices drop the larger the group.

Kalang Chhouy Sacred Mountain Trek (2 days US$59) This shorter trek starts from near Koklak village and includes a night by the Chai Chanang Waterfall. On the second day, continue to Phnom Gong, a sacred mountain for the Brau people, and swim at the Tju Preah rapids.

Phnom Veal Thom Wilderness Trek (7/8 days US$258/286) The longest trek into Virachey starts from Ta Veng with an overnight homestay in a Brau village. The trek goes deep into the heart of the Phnom Veal Thom grasslands, an area rich in wildlife such as sambar deer, gibbon, langur, wild pig, bear and hornbill. Trekkers return via a different route and pass through areas of evergreen forest.

offers two- to eight-day treks led by English-speaking, park-employed rangers. Private tour operators are forbidden from taking tourists into the park, but can make arrangements for you through the park office.

A section of the park is accessible from Siem Pang in Stung Treng district (p258). However, to legally enter the park in Siem Pang, you must still secure permits in Ban Lung.

LUMPHAT
លុមផាត់
POP 2000

The former provincial capital of Lumphat, on the banks of Tonlé Srepok, is something of a ghost town these days thanks to sustained US bombing raids in the early 1970s. This is also the last gasp of civilisation, if it can be called that, for hardcore bikers heading south on the tough trails to Mondulkiri Province.

The Tonlé Srepok is believed to be the river depicted in the seminal antiwar film *Apocalypse Now,* in which Martin Sheen's Captain Benjamin Willard goes upriver into Cambodia in search of renegade Colonel Kurtz, played by Marlon Brando.

Bei Srok (Tuk Chrouu Bram-pul; admission 2000r) is a popular waterfall with seven gentle tiers. It's about 20km east of Lumphat. Many Ban Lung tour companies offer it as a day tour (US$15 to US$20) combined with some abandoned gem mines nearby and bomb-crater spotting around Lumphat.

To get to Lumphat from Ban Lung, take the road to Stung Treng for about 15km before heading south. The 35km journey takes around an hour. Pick-ups leave early in the morning from Lumphat and return in the afternoon on most days.

MONDULKIRI PROVINCE

A world apart from lowland Cambodia, Mondulkiri Province (ខេត្តមណ្ឌលគីរី) is the original Wild East of the country. Climatically and culturally, it's also another world, which comes as a relief after the heat of the plains. Home to the hardy Bunong (Pnong) people and their noble elephants, it is possible to visit traditional villages and learn about elephants in their element at the Elephant Valley Project. The landscape is a seductive mix of pine clumps, grassy hills and windswept valleys that fade beguilingly into forests of jade green and hidden waterfalls. Wild animals, such as bears, tigers and especially elephants, are more numerous here than elsewhere, although sightings are usually limited to birds, monkeys and the occasional wild pig.

Mondulkiri means 'Meeting of the Hills', an apt sobriquet for a land of rolling hills. In the dry season it is a little like Wales with sunshine; in the wet season, like Tasmania with more rain. At an average elevation of 800m, it can get quite chilly at night, so carry something warm.

Mondulkiri is the most sparsely populated province in the country, with just four people per square kilometre. Almost half the inhabitants come from the Bunong minority group, with other minorities making up much of the rest of the population. There has been an influx of migrants in recent years, drawn to the abundant land and benign climate. Fruit and vegetable plantations are popping up, but hunting remains the profession of choice for many minorities. Conservationists have grand plans for the province, creating wildlife sanctuaries and

THE OVERLAND TRAIL RUNS DRY

Glance at a map and it seems obvious: the best way to visit both Mondulkiri and Ratanakiri without backtracking is to make a grand loop via the remote villages of Koh Nhek and Lumphat. Alas, while the road from Sen Monorom to Koh Nhek (93km) is in good shape and takes just a couple of hours, north of there – until Tonlé Srepok River – the road vanishes into a spider's web of ox-cart trails. Over the past few years, a handful of hardcore bikers have been using this route during the dry season (wet-season travel is close to impossible), but only attempt it if you have years of biking experience and an iron backside. A local guide who knows the route, spare parts for your bike, copious amounts of water and a compass should make for a smoother journey.

A few intrepid moto drivers in both Ban Lung and Sen Monorom ply this route. The journey takes about nine hours, with a few breaks along the way, and costs a hefty US$50 to US$70. A cheaper option is to use a minibus between Sen Monorom and Koh Nhek (15,000r) and charter a moto driver from there to Lumphat for about US$25. In the reverse direction, make your way to Lumphat and negotiate a moto south to Koh Nhek. Cheaper again but a little less adventurous is a combination of two buses via Kratie.

Work has started on upgrading the road and a new overland route should be up and running by 2013.

initiating sustainable tourism activities, but are facing off against speculators and industrialists queuing up for natural resources.

Roads are pretty poor throughout the province, but the main highway to Phnom Penh is now in superb shape, bringing the journey time down to six hours. The road to Koh Nhek is unrecognisable from the mess of bygone years. Improved access has fuelled an explosion of domestic tourists, so book ahead on weekends and during holidays.

Sen Monorom សែនមនោរម្យ

♩ 073 / POP 10,000

The provincial capital of Mondulkiri, Sen Monorom is really an overgrown village; a charming community set in the spot where the famous hills meet. In the centre of town are two lakes, leading some dreamers to call it 'the Switzerland of Cambodia'. The area around Sen Monorom is peppered with minority villages and picturesque waterfalls, making it the ideal place to spend some time. Many of the Bunong people from nearby villages come to here to trade, the distinctive baskets they carry on their backs making them easy to distinguish from the immigrant lowlanders. Set at more than 800m, when the winds blow it's notably cooler than the rest of Cambodia, so bring warm clothing.

◉ Sights & Activities

Not much happens in Sen Monorom itself, but there's plenty to see and do nearby,

including trips out to Bunong villages, elephant riding and an array of overnight treks.

There are a few worthwhile sights within a short motorbike ride or a long walk from town. **Monorom Falls** (admission free) is the closest thing to a public swimming pool for Sen Monorom. It has an attractive location in the forest, about 3km northwest of town. Motos can take people out here for about US$3 or so for the return trip.

Looming over the northeast corner of the air strip, **Wat Phnom Doh Kromom** has Mondulkiri's best sunset vista.

Check out the observation deck of **Phnom Bai Chuw** (Raw Rice Mountain), about 5km north of Wat Phnom Doh Kromom, for a jaw-dropping view of the emerald forest. It looks as though you are seeing a vast sea of treetops, hence the locals have named it Samot Cheur (Ocean of Trees).

⛳ Tours

As in Ratanakiri, multiday forest treks are becoming immensely popular in Mondulkiri. We recommend securing indigenous Bunong guides for these trips. They know the forests intimately and can break the ice with the locals in any Bunong villages you visit.

The Bunong Place (p270) employs several Bunong guides who can take you into Bunong villages and/or lead any of the popular day excursions. Other tour operators, such as Nature Lodge (p269) and Green House (p271), usually employ Bunong people as porters on longer excursions, but you should request this service.

Most of the guesthouses listed under Sleeping run the full gamut of treks and tours around Sen Monorom. Figure on about US$35 per person, per day for overnight trips, including all meals, transfer to the trail head by moto, and an English-speaking guide. Per-person prices drop for larger groups. The WWF runs its own set of tours north of Sen Monorom in the Mondulkiri Protected Forest (see p273).

Elephant Rides
ELEPHANTS

In general it is better to sign up for the humane and ecofriendly Elephant Valley Project experience (p259). However, elephant rides are possible in the villages of Phulung, 7km northeast of Sen Monorom, and Putang, 9km southwest of town. Treks cost US$20 to US$25 per person, including lunch and transport to and from the village. It can get pretty uncomfortable up on top of an elephant after a couple of hours; carry a pillow to ease the strain.

It is also possible to negotiate a longer trek with an overnight stay in a Bunong village, costing about US$50 per person.

🛏 Sleeping

Hot water is a nice bonus in chilly Mondulkiri, but you'll typically pay an extra US$5 for it. Places without hot-water showers can usually provide flasks of boiling water for bathing. There is rarely need for air-conditioning in this neck of the woods. The Elephant Valley Project (p259) offers an alternative lodging experience.

🔝 Nature Lodge
GUESTHOUSE $

(☎690 0442; www.naturelodgecambodia.com; r US$10-30; 🐕) Located on a windswept hilltop near town, this quirky ecoresort has basic bungalow accommodation with hot showers and some incredible Swiss Family Robinson-style chalets with sunken beds and hidden rooms.

Emario Mondulkiri Resort
HOTEL $$

(☎652 3344; r from US$35; ❄@🐕) Looking rather like a bungalow retirement community beamed down to Cambodia, this resort offers the smartest rooms in Mondulkiri with parquet flooring, comfortable beds and bathroom amenities.

Phanyro Guesthouse
GUESTHOUSE $

(☎017 770867; r US$8-12; 🐕) This is a favourite with visiting volunteers and NGOs, offering a clutch of cottages perched on a ridge overlooking the river valley. The rooms fail to exploit the views, but are clean with a capital C.

Sum Dy Guesthouse
HOTEL $

(☎099 250543; r US$12-30; ❄@🐕) Once occupied by mining conglomerate BHP Billiton, the rooms include sturdy wooden beds and slick if slightly uncoordinated bathroom decor. Fan rooms are a steal for US$12.

Long Vibol Guesthouse
GUESTHOUSE $

(☎012 944647; r US$5-20; 🐕) An attractive wooden resort with 20 rooms set amid a lush garden; staff here are knowledgeable about the area. Has a restaurant popular with

Sen Monorom

visiting Khmers. Vibol is the elder statesman among the tour guides of Mondulkiri, making this a top spot for information, although he no longer guides himself.

Mondulkiri Hotel
HOTEL **$$**

(☎390139; r US$15-30; ✳@🖥) It may look a little incongruous in this pristine land of rolling hills, but the hulking concrete exterior conceals some of the most modern and comfortable rooms in town. All are equipped with air-con, smart bathrooms, cable TV and fridge.

Pech Kiri Guesthouse
GUESTHOUSE **$**

(☎012 932102; r US$5-30; ✳🖥) Once upon a time, this was the only guesthouse in town and it is still going strong under the lively direction of Madame Deu. The cheap original rooms near reception are showing their age as management diverts attention to the opulent new digs at the back.

Boran Sortha Guesthouse
GUESTHOUSE **$**

(☎670 0111; r US$5-40; ✳🖥) A new guesthouse on the main strip, the friendly family here offer a wide range of rooms from singles with cold water right through to a two-bedroom family suite with air-con.

✘ Eating & Drinking

All the guesthouses have restaurants.

RESPECT THE DEAD

The *chunchiet* of Ratanakiri bury their dead amid the jungle, carving effigies of the deceased to stand guard over the graves. There are many cemeteries scattered throughout the forests of Ratanakiri, but most of them are strictly off limits to visitors. Enter *chunchiet* cemeteries only with permission from the village chief and preferably in the company of a local. If you are lucky enough to be allowed into a cemetery, touch nothing, act respectfully and ask permission before taking photos.

Unfortunately, there have been many reports of tourists ignoring clearly marked signs (in English) urging outsiders to abstain from entering *chunchiet* cemeteries. Worse, unscrupulous art collectors and amateur anthropologists from Europe have reportedly been buying up the old effigies from poor villagers.

Nature Lodge
CAMBODIAN, THAI **$$**

(www.naturelodgecambodia.com) This popular guesthouse has an inviting restaurant decorated with gnarly tree trunks. The menu includes a good range of affordable Khmer and Thai dishes, plus plenty of international fare from Israeli to Italian. By night it doubles as a bar and place to swap travel tales.

Khmer Kitchen
CAMBODIAN **$**

(mains US$2-4) This unassuming street-side eatery whips up some of the most flavoursome Khmer food in the hills. The *kari sait trey* (fish coconut curry) and other curries are particularly scrumptious.

Green House Restaurant & Bar
INTERNATIONAL **$**

(mains US$1.50-3.50) As well as internet access and tour information, the Green House is a popular place for inexpensive Khmer and Western dishes. By night, this place draws the drinkers to sup beers and cocktails against a backdrop of ambient reggae beats.

Bananas
INTERNATIONAL **$$**

(mains US$6.50-8; ⊙9am-10pm) Set in a small banana grove, this homey restaurant-bar has Mondulkiri's best Western cuisine, served table d'hôte-style, including coq au vin and Flemish stew.

🛍 Shopping

Bunong Place
HANDICRAFTS

(☎012 474879; www.bunongcenter.org; ⊙6am-6pm) Sells authentic Bunong textiles, and local coffee, sodas and beers are available.

Cambodian Indigenous Products
HANDICRAFTS

(⊙7.30am-5.30pm Mon-Sat) A fair-trade shop selling local Bunong weaving, scarves, bags, rattan items and a pick and mix of local products.

ℹ Information

The leading guesthouses in town are also good sources of information.

Acleda Bank (NH76) Changes major currencies and has a Visa-only ATM.

Bunong Place (☎012 474879; www.bunongcenter.org; ⊙6am-6pm) This NGO-run 'drop-in centre' for Bunong people is a good source of information on sustainable tourism, village homestays and elephant rides, and provides trained Bunong guides for local tours, costing US$15/25 per half/full day, including motorbike. Also sells handicrafts.

MONKEY BUSINESS IN MONDULKIRI

It is now possible to spot black-shanked doucs in their natural habitat around Andong Kraloung thanks to a new initiative to open up the northern highlands of the Seima Protected Forest to independent travellers. The scheme plans to provide local villagers with an incentive to conserve the doucs and protect their habitat. Day treks, overnight trips and three-day/two-night trails wind their way through mixed evergreen forest to distant waterfalls with a good chance of spotting the doucs along the way. Banteng (wild cattle) are also present, although not so commonly sighted, but the abundant bird life includes the spectacular giant hornbill and green peafowl.

Registered guides accompany visitors together with local Bunong guides from Andong Kraloung to identify the trails. A $10 conservation contribution is included in the cost of the trip, which supports village development projects. Sample prices are about $125 per person for a three-day/two-night trip, including all guides, accommodation and food. For information and booking contact **Green House Bar & Restaurant** (☎017 905659; sor.phouen@gmail.com) in Sen Monorom or the **Sam Veasna Center** (☎063 963710; bookings@samveasna.org) in Siem Reap.

Green House (☎017 905659; www.green house-tour.blogspot.com) Affable restaurant owner Sam Nang is the best source of information in town. He organises the standard treks and excursions to sights around Sen Monorom, plus tailored mountain-bike tours. Quality mountain bikes (per day US$5), motorbikes (US$6 to US$8) and a 250cc trail bike (US$15) are available for hire. He also arranges transport by moto to Ban Lung (US$60). Internet access available.

Veha Jungle Tours (☎011 500401; daung_veha@yahoo.com) Local tour guide based out of Long Vibol Guesthouse, offering trips around Mondulkiri.

WWF (☎012 466343; www.panda.org) Involved in a host of ecotourism initiatives around Mondulkiri.

ℹ Getting There & Away

Sen Monorom's airstrip has been closed to commercial flights for some time, so visitors who want to get to this unique region have to come overland, which these days is pretty straightforward. NH76 connecting Sen Monorom to Snuol and Phnom Penh (370km) beyond is now in fantastic shape, including some impressive bridges across the deep river valleys. Hardcore dirt bikers may still prefer the old French road heading east from Khao Si Ma, which runs roughly parallel to NH76.

Phnom Penh Sorya and Rith Mony run morning buses to/from Phnom Penh (30,000r, eight hours) and Kompong Cham (25,000r, five hours). Faster morning share taxis (50,000r) and minivans (40,000r) to Phnom Penh are best reserved a day in advance through a guesthouse or at the taxi park.

Minivans (departing from the taxi park) are the way forward to Kratie (30,000r, 4½ hours).

Count on at least one early-morning departure and two or three departures around 12.30pm. It's wise to reserve the morning van in advance.

To get to Ratanakiri, you must either backtrack to Snuol or Kratie and pick up transportation there, or brave the harsh trail north to Ban Lung; see p268 for more details on this hardcore route.

ℹ Getting Around

English-speaking moto drivers cost US$15 to US$20 per day. Sample round-trip moto prices for destinations around Sen Monorom are US$10 to Bou Sraa, US$8 to Dak Dam Waterfall and US$4 to Phnom Bai Chuw.

Most guesthouses rent out motorbikes for US$5 to US$8. Green House Restaurant has 250cc dirt bikes (US$15) for rent. Pick-up trucks and 4WDs can be chartered for the day. It costs about US$60 around Sen Monorom in the dry season, and more again in the wet season.

Around Sen Monorom

BOU SRAA WATERFALL ទឹកជ្រោះប៉ូស្រា
Plunging into the dense Cambodian jungle below, this is one of the country's most impressive **falls** (admission 5000r). Famous throughout the country, this double-drop waterfall has an upper tier of some 10m and a spectacular lower tier with a thundering 25m drop. To get to the bottom of the lower falls, cross the bridge over the river and follow a path to a precipitous staircase that continues to the bottom; it takes about 15 minutes to get down.

Bou Sraa is a 33km, one-hour journey east of Sen Monorom on a half-completed toll road. Prices are 3000r for a small motorbike,

5000r for a large motorbike and 15,000r for a car or 4WD. Hire a moto driver for the day or charter a car in a group. Basic snacks and drinks are available at the falls, but pack a picnic if you want something more sophisticated.

OTHER WATERFALLS

Other popular waterfalls in Mondulkiri include **Romanear Waterfall**, 18km southeast of Sen Monorom, and **Dak Dam Waterfall**, 25km southeast of Sen Monorom. Both are very difficult to find without assistance, so it's best to take a moto driver or local guide. Romanear is a low, wide waterfall with some convenient swimming holes. There is also a second Romanear Waterfall, known rather originally as **Romanear II**, which is near the main road between Sen Monorom and Snuol. Dak Dam is similar to the Monorom Falls (p268), albeit with a greater volume of water. The waterfall is several kilometres beyond the Bunong village of Dak Dam and locals are able to lead the way if you can make yourself understood.

BUNONG VILLAGES

Several Bunong villages around Sen Monorom make for popular excursions, although the frequently visited villages that appear on tourist maps have assimilated into modern society. In general, the further out you go, the less exposed the village. Trips to Bunong villages can often be combined with waterfalls or elephant treks. Each guesthouse has a preferred village to send travellers to, which is a great way to spread the wealth.

Seima Protection Forest
តំបន់ការពារព្រៃឈើកែវសីមា

This 3000-sq-km protected area may host the country's greatest treasure trove of mammalian wildlife. A recent World Conservation Society (WCS) study counted over 42,000 black-shanked doucs in Seima, the world's largest concentration, along with 2500 yellow-cheeked crested gibbons. An estimated 150 wild elephants – accounting for more than half of the total population in Cambodia – roam the park, along with bears and seven species of cat. The bird life is also impressive, and the jungle, which is lusher and denser than the dry forest in western Mondulkiri, has been relatively well preserved.

The park remains difficult to visit, however. The only way in is with WCS partner and birdwatching specialist **Sam Veasna Center** (☎063-963710; www.samveasna.org). Its bird guides are highly trained but expensive at US$100 per day, on top of a flat US$30-per-person conservation fee. Accommodation is in facilities run by the Forestry Administration that were, rather ironically, once part of a logging camp.

The WCS helps the Forestry Administration manage the park and maintains an office at the park headquarters, 5km east of Khao Si Ma. The elephants and other high-profile animals that dwell in Seima are shy and elusive; without guaranteed sightings, it's proving difficult to develop ecotourism in a way that will benefit the forest, the animals and the local Bunong community. 'We're still trying to find ways to crack the ecotourism nut', says Edward Pollard, a WCS technical advisor who works on site.

The road to Sen Monorom passes right through Seima Protection Forest – look out for monkeys above!

Mimong
មីមុង

Welcome to the Wild East, where the gold rush lives on. Mimong district is famous for its **gold mines** and this has drawn specula-

---

WORTH A TRIP

COMMUNITY HOMESTAYS IN MONDULKIRI

WWF (☎088 899 7060; www.mondulkiri tourism.org) has recently helped two villages launch projects geared towards giving tourists a glimpse into traditional Bunong lifestyles. In **Krang Te**, about 25km east of Sen Monorom, you can ride elephants, view traditional dancing, learn to weave baskets and buy locally produced honey, fruits and Bunong handicrafts. About 65km north of Sen Monorom on the road to Koh Nhek, the village of **Dei Ey** offers homestays, traditional meals, elephant rides, and trekking in surrounding Mondulkiri Protected Forest. Choose from day trips to two-day and three-day experiences; prices start from US$19 for a day trip rising to the US$150 mark for three-day adventures, depending on group sizes. Portions of the proceeds from these initiatives go into a community fund designed to improve local livelihoods and protect the forest.

MONDULKIRI PROTECTED FOREST: THE AFRICAN EXPERIENCE IN CAMBODIA

Before the civil war, the vast grasslands of northern Mondulkiri were home to huge herds of gaur, banteng and wild buffalo. Visitors lucky enough to witness their annual migrations compared the experience to the Serengeti and the annual wildebeest migrations. Sadly, the long civil war took its toll and, like Uganda and other African countries, thousands of animals were killed for bush meat.

WWF (☎088 899 7060; www.mondulkiritourism.org) has been working hard to return this area to its former glory through ecotourism initiatives in the Mondulkiri Protected Forest, one of the largest protected areas in Cambodia, which provides a home to tigers, leopards, bears, langurs, gibbons, wild cow and rare bird life. Ambitious plans for a high-end ecolodge in the heart of the protected area were scrapped, to be replaced by an upscale 'eco-tent camp' on an extremely remote stretch of the Tonlé Srepok in the northeast of the province. While the camp is finished, it remains mothballed until the WWF can find a suitable operator. Access is via a jungle trail that branches off the main road between Dei Ey and Koh Nhek.

One potential problem is that the cats, bears and other exotic prowlers that patrol the area are extremely difficult to spot. WWF hopes to increase the chance of sightings through night drives and strategically located hides. During our 2011 visit, we saw several herds of banteng, a rare type of wild cow, so there is still plenty of wildlife out there. Also on offer is primary-growth forest, river tours on the Srepok and plenty of bird life. Check with the WWF to find out the latest on the camp.

tors from as far away as Vietnam and China. Miners descend into the pits on ancient mine carts that are connected to dodgy-looking winches, sometimes going to a depth of 100m or more. It's not for the faint-hearted and several miners die in accidents each year. This place is very Wild East and visitors aren't exactly welcomed with open arms.

The main problem is getting here, as the road is so bad that it takes about four hours to cover the 47km from Sen Monorom, and few moto drivers make the trip. The road improves slightly on the other side of Mimong and it is possible to link up with NH7 to Kratie to the west (taking another four hours).

Koh Nhek កោះញែក

POP 6000

The final frontier as far as Mondulkiri goes, this village in the far north of the province is a strategic place on the challenging overland route between Sen Monorom and Ratanakiri Province (see p268 for the skinny on this route). Thanks to a new (unsealed) road covering the 93km from Sen Monorom, Koh Nhek is not quite the remote outpost it once was. An Acleda Bank (no ATM) is a sign of changing times.

There is a pair of unnamed **guesthouses** (r 20,000r) in town. The store on the northeast corner of the main intersection has food and some basic supplies, including cold beer – well earned by the time you get here.

Understand Cambodia

population per sq mile

CAMBODIA LAOS VIETNAM

≈ 30 people

Cambodia Today

The Khmer Rouge Tribunal

Sidelined by the politics of the Cold War for two decades, the Extraordinary Chambers in the Courts of Cambodia (ECCC) trial is finally under way after many a dispute between the Cambodian authorities and the international community. However, the wheels of justice may not turn fast enough to keep up with the ageing of the surviving Khmer Rouge leaders. (Military commander Ta Mok died in custody in 2006 and both Ieng Sary and Nuon Chea are in their 80s and suffering from health complications.) For more on the legacy of the Khmer Rouge and the trial, see p297.

» Bombs dropped on Cambodia: 539,000 tonnes

» Unexploded landmines: four to six million

» Number of landmine victims: 40,000

» Cost of victims' rehabilitation: US$120 million

Politics

The Cambodian People's Party (CPP) is making plans for the future with dynastic alliances between its offspring. Just look at the roll call of marriages in the past decade and it soon becomes apparent that senior leaders have their eyes firmly on a potential handover of power to the children of the party.

At the head of this elite is Prime Minister Hun Sen, who has proven himself a survivor, personally as well as politically, for he lost an eye during the battle for Phnom Penh in 1975. It would appear that, for the time being at least, with a poorly educated electorate and a divided opposition, 'in the country of the blind, the one-eyed man is king'.

Opposition leader Sam Rainsy continues to berate the country's rulers for their lack of leadership and has made real inroads in urban areas, setting the stage for some spicy showdowns with the CPP in the coming years. Sometimes they get a little too spicy; Rainsy and several of his fellow parliamentarians have been regularly stripped of their immunity from prosecution and charged with defamation. At the time of writing,

Useful Sites

» **Phnom Penh Post** (www.phnompenhpost.com) Recent events in Cambodia.

» **KI-Media** (http://ki-media.blogspot.com) Independent blog dedicated to keeping the Cambodian government on its toes.

Top Books

» **Voices from S-21** (David Chandler) A study of the Khmer Rouge's interrogation and torture centre.

» **The Gate** (François Bizot) Bizot was kidnapped by the Khmer Rouge, and later held by them in the French embassy.

» **Cambodia After the Khmer Rouge** (Evan Gottesman) Politics and life in Cambodia during the 1980s.

» **Cambodia Now** (Karen Coates) A no-holds-barred look at contemporary Cambodia through the eyes of its diverse population.

origin of visitors (%)

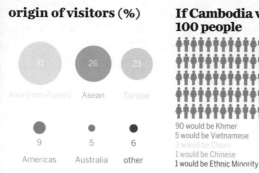

If Cambodia were 100 people

90 would be Khmer
5 would be Vietnamese
3 would be Cham
1 would be Chinese
1 would be Ethnic Minority

Rainsy remained in self-imposed exile to avoid charges of criminal damage for his efforts to move border posts with Vietnam in Svay Rieng Province in 2009.

Media

Cambodia's media scene looks to be in good shape on paper, with freedom of the press enshrined in the constitution, but the everyday reality is a different story. Opposition parties have far less access to the media than the CPP does, with many more pro-government newspapers and radio and TV stations.

Economy

Badly traumatised by decades of conflict, Cambodia's economy was long a gecko amid the neighbouring dragons. This has slowly started to change, as the economy has been liberalised and investors are circling to take advantage of the new opportunities. Asian investors are flocking to Phnom Penh, led by the South Koreans who have inked deals for skyscrapers all over the low-rise city. Westerners are starting to realise that they are on to something, and investment funds and venture capitalists are sniffing around.

Aid was long the mainstay of the Cambodian economy, supporting half the government's budget, and NGOs have done a lot to force important sociopolitical issues onto the agenda. The government, long shunned by international big business, is keen to benefit from all these newfound opportunities. Contracts are being signed off like autographs and there are concerns for the long-term development of the country. China has come to the table to play for big stakes, and it pledged US$1.1 billion in assistance in late 2009 – considerably more than all the other donors put together, and with no burdensome strings attached.

In a worrying trend, Cambodia dropped to 128 out of 175 countries in the *Press Freedom Index 2009* report prepared by Reporters Without Borders, its lowest ranking ever recorded; it was still at 128 in the 2010 index.

Ethical Clothing

The garment sector is important to the economy, with factories ringing the capital. Cambodia is trying to carve a niche for itself as an ethical producer, with good labour relations and air-conditioned factories.

Tourism

More than 2.5 million visitors arrived in 2010, a doubling of numbers in just a few years. Wages are low by regional standards, but tips can add up to a princely sum that might support an extended family.

Corruption

Anticorruption watchdog Transparency International rates Cambodia 154 out of 178 countries, tied with Central African Republic, Tajikistan and Papua New Guinea. Corruption is a major element of the economy and exists to some extent at all levels of government.

» Population:
14.75 million

» Life
expectancy:
63 years

» Infant
mortality:
55 per 1000
births

» GDP:
US$11.63 billion
(2010)

» Adult literacy
rate: 74%

However, Cambodia remains one of Asia's poorest countries. According to the UN Development Programme's Human Development Index for 2011, Cambodia remains in worse shape than Congo and Laos, just scraping in ahead of Swaziland. Income remains desperately low for many Khmers, with annual salaries in the hundreds rather than thousands of dollars, and public servants, such as teachers, are unable to eke out a living on their meagre wages.

Economy Versus Environment

Cambodia's pristine environment may be a big draw for adventurous ecotourists, but much of it is currently under threat. Ancient forests are being razed to make way for plantations, rivers are being sized up for major hydroelectric power plants and the South Coast is being explored by leading oil companies. All this adds up to an ever-stronger economy, but it's unlikely to encourage the ecotourism that is just starting to develop.

Key Films

The definitive film on the Khmer Rouge period in Cambodia, *The Killing Fields* (1985) tells the story of American journalist Sidney Schanberg and his Cambodian assistant Dith Pran during and after the war. In Francis Ford Coppola's master-piece *Apocalypse Now* (1979), a renegade colonel, played by Marlon Brando, goes AWOL in Cambodia. Martin Sheen plays a young soldier sent to bring him back, and the ensuing encounter makes for one of the most powerful indictments of war ever made.

Dancing King

Before assuming the throne, King Norodom Sihamoni lived in such diverse cities as Prague, Pyongyang and Paris, where he pursued a career as a ballet dancer and cultural ambassador to Unesco.

History

'The good, the bad and the ugly' is a simple way to sum up Cambodian history. Things were good in the early years, culminating in the vast Angkor empire, unrivalled in the region during four centuries of dominance. Then the bad set in, from the 13th century, as ascendant neighbours steadily chipped away at Cambodian territory. In the 20th century it turned downright ugly, as a brutal civil war culminated in the genocidal rule of the Khmer Rouge (1975–79), from which Cambodia is still recovering today.

The Origin of the Khmers

Like many legends, the one about the origin of Cambodia is historically opaque, but it does say something about the cultural forces that brought Cambodia into existence, in particular its relationship with its great subcontinental neighbour, India. Cambodia's religious, royal and written traditions stemmed from India and began to coalesce as a cultural entity in their own right between the 1st and 5th centuries AD.

Very little is known about prehistoric Cambodia. Much of the southeast was a vast, shallow gulf that was progressively silted up by the mouths of the Mekong, leaving pancake-flat, mineral-rich land ideal for farming. Evidence of cave-dwellers has been found in the northwest of Cambodia, and carbon dating on ceramic pots found in the area shows that they were made around 4200 BC. Examinations of bones dating back to around 1500 BC suggest that the people living in Cambodia at that time resembled the Cambodians of today. Early Chinese records report that the Cambodians were 'ugly' and 'dark' and went about naked. A healthy dose of scepticism may be required, however, when reading the reports of imperial China concerning its 'barbarian' neighbours.

The Early Cambodian Kingdoms

Cambodian might didn't begin and end with Angkor. There were a number of powerful kingdoms present in this area before the 9th century.

For the full flavour of Cambodian history, from humble beginnings in the prehistoric period through the glories of Angkor and right up to the present day, grab a copy of *The History of Cambodia* (1994), by David Chandler.

The ancient Khmers were like the Romans of Southeast Asia, building a network of long highways across the region to connect their regional cities.

TIMELINE	4200 BC	AD 100	245
	Cave-dwellers capable of making pots inhabit caves around Laang Spean; archaeological evidence suggests their vessels were similar to those still made in Cambodia today.	The religions, language and sculpture styles of India start to take root in Cambodia with the arrival of Indian traders and holy men.	The Chinese Wei emperor sends a mission to the countries of the Mekong region and is told that a barbarous but rich country called Funan exists in the Delta region.

THE LEGEND OF KAUNDINYA & THE NAGA PRINCESS

Cambodia came into being, so the legend says, through the union of a princess and a foreigner. The foreigner was an Indian Brahman named Kaundinya and the princess was the daughter of a *naga* (mythical serpent-being) king who ruled over a watery land. One day, as Kaundinya sailed by, the princess paddled out in a boat to greet him. Kaundinya shot an arrow from his magic bow into her boat, causing the fearful princess to agree to marriage. In need of a dowry, her father drank up the waters of his land and presented them to Kaundinya to rule over. The new kingdom was named Kambuja.

Founded by King Isanavarman I in the early 7th century, Sambor Prei Kuk was originally known as Isanapura and was the first major temple city to be constructed in Southeast Asia.

From the 1st century AD, the Indianisation of Cambodia occurred through trading settlements that sprang up on the coastline of what is now southern Vietnam, but was then inhabited by the Khmers. These settlements were important ports of call for boats following the trading route from the Bay of Bengal to the southern provinces of China. The largest of these nascent kingdoms was known as Funan by the Chinese, and may have existed across an area between modern Phnom Penh and the archaeological site of Oc-Eo in Kien Giang Province in southern Vietnam. Funan would have been a contemporary of Champasak in southern Laos (then known as Kuruksetra) and other lesser fiefdoms in the region.

Funan is a Chinese name and may be a transliteration of the ancient Khmer word *bnam* (mountain). Although very little is known about Funan, much has been made of its importance as an early Southeast Asian centre of power.

It is most likely that between the 1st and 8th centuries Cambodia was a collection of small states, each with its own elites who strategically intermarried and often went to war with one another. Funan was no doubt one of these states, and as a major sea port would have been pivotal in the transmission of Indian culture into the interior of Cambodia.

Cambodia's Funan-period trading port of Oc-Eo, now located in Vietnam's Mekong Delta, was a major commercial crossroads between Asia and Europe, and archaeologists there have unearthed Roman coins and Persian pottery.

The little that historians do know about Funan has mostly been gleaned from Chinese sources. These report that Funan-period Cambodia (1st century to 6th century AD) embraced the worship of the Hindu deities Shiva and Vishnu and, at the same time, Buddhism. The *linga* (phallic totem) appears to have been the focus of ritual and an emblem of kingly might, a feature that was to evolve further in the Angkorian cult of the god-king. The people practised primitive irrigation, which enabled successful cultivation of rice, and traded raw commodities such as spices and precious stones with China and India.

From the 6th century, Cambodia's population gradually concentrated along the Mekong and Tonlé Sap Rivers, where the majority of people remain today. The move may have been related to the development of wet-

600	**802**	**889**	**924**
The first inscriptions are committed to stone in Cambodia in ancient Khmer, offering historians the only contemporary accounts of the pre-Angkorian period other than from Chinese sources.	Jayavarman II proclaims independence from Java in a ceremony to anoint himself a *devaraja* (god-king) on the holy mount of Phnom Kulen, marking the birth of the Khmer Empire of Angkor.	Yasovarman I moves the capital from the ancient city of Hariharalaya (Roluos today) to the Angkor area, 16km to the northwest, and marks the location with three temple mountains.	Usurper king Jayavarman IV transfers the capital to Koh Ker and begins a mammoth building spree, but the lack of water sees the capital move back to Angkor just 20 years later.

rice agriculture. Between the 6th and 8th centuries, Cambodia was a collection of competing kingdoms, ruled by autocratic kings who legitimised their rule through hierarchical caste concepts borrowed from India.

This era is generally referred to as the Chenla period. Like Funan, this is a Chinese term and there is little to support the idea that Chenla was a unified kingdom that held sway over all of Cambodia. Indeed, the Chinese themselves referred to 'water Chenla' and 'land Chenla'. Water Chenla was located around Angkor Borei and the temple mount of Phnom Da (p202), near the present-day provincial capital of Takeo, and land Chenla in the upper reaches of the Mekong River and east of Tonlé Sap Lake, around Sambor Prei Kuk (p240), an essential stop on a chronological jaunt through Cambodia's history.

The Rise of the Angkorian Empire

Gradually the Cambodian region was becoming more cohesive. Before long the fractured kingdoms of Cambodia would merge to become a sprawling Asian empire.

A popular place of pilgrimage for Khmers today, the sacred mountain of Phnom Kulen (p152), northeast of Angkor, is home to an inscription that tells of Jayavarman II (r 802–50) proclaiming himself a 'universal monarch', or *devaraja* (god-king), in 802. It is believed that he may have resided in the Buddhist Shailendras' court in Java as a young man and was inspired by the great Javanese temples of Borobudur and Prambanan near present-day Yogyakarta. Upon his return to Cambodia, he instigated an uprising against Javanese control over the southern lands of Cambodia. Jayavarman II then set out to bring the country under his control through alliances and conquests, becoming the first monarch to rule most of what we call Cambodia today.

Jayavarman II was the first of a long succession of kings who presided over the rise and fall of the greatest empire mainland Southeast Asia has ever seen, one that was to bequeath the stunning legacy of Angkor. The key to the meteoric rise of Angkor was a mastery of water and an elaborate hydraulic system that allowed the ancient Khmers to tame the elements. The first records of the massive irrigation works that supported the population of Angkor date to the reign of Indravarman I (r 877–89), who built the *baray* (reservoir) of Indratataka. His rule also marks the flourishing of Angkorian art, with the building of temples in the Roluos area, notably Bakong (p148).

By the turn of the 11th century, the kingdom of Angkor was losing control of its territories. Suryavarman I (r 1002–49), a usurper, moved into the power vacuum and, like Jayavarman II two centuries before, re-unified the kingdom through war and alliances, stretching the frontiers of the empire. A pattern was beginning to emerge, which was repeated

India wasn't the only power to have a major cultural impact on Cambodia. The island of Java was also influential, colonising part of 'water Chenla' in the 8th century.

One of the definitive guides to Angkor is *A Guide to the Angkor Monuments* by Maurice Glaize, first published in the 1940s and now out of print. Download it free at www.theangkor guide.com.

HISTORY THE RISE OF THE ANGKOR AN EMPIRE

1002	1112	1152	1177
Suryavarman I comes to power and expands the extent of the kingdom by annexing the Buddhist kingdom of Louvo (known as Lopburi in modern-day Thailand). He also increases trade links with the outside world.	Suryavarman II commences the construction of Angkor Wat, the mother of all temples, dedicated to Vishnu and designed as his funerary temple.	Suryavarman II is killed in a disastrous campaign against the Dai Viet (Vietnamese), provoking this rising northern neighbour and sparking centuries of conflict between the two countries.	The Chams launch a surprise attack on Angkor by sailing up the Tonlé Sap. They defeat the powerful Khmers and occupy the capital for four years.

JAYAVARMAN VII

A devout follower of Mahayana Buddhism, Jayavarman VII (r 1181–1219) built the city of Angkor Thom (p135) and many other massive monuments. Indeed, many of the temples visited around Angkor today were constructed during Jayavarman VII's reign. However, Jayavarman VII is a figure of many contradictions. The bas-reliefs of the Bayon (p136) depict him presiding over battles of terrible ferocity, while statues of the king depict a meditative, otherworldly aspect. His program of temple construction and other public works was carried out in great haste, no doubt bringing enormous hardship to the labourers who provided the muscle, and thus accelerating the decline of the empire. He was partly driven by a desire to legitimise his rule, as there may have been other contenders closer to the royal bloodline, and partly by the need to introduce a new religion to a population predominantly Hindu in faith. However, in many ways he was also Cambodia's first progressive leader, proclaiming the population equal, abolishing castes and embarking on a program of school, hospital and road building.

throughout the Angkorian period: dislocation and turmoil, followed by reunification and further expansion under a powerful king. Architecturally, the most productive periods occurred after times of turmoil, indicating that newly incumbent monarchs felt the need to celebrate, even legitimise, their rule with massive building projects.

By 1066, Angkor was again riven by conflict, becoming the focus of rival bids for power. It was not until the accession of Suryavarman II (r 1112–52) that the kingdom was again unified. Suryavarman II embarked on another phase of expansion, waging costly wars in Vietnam and the region of central Vietnam known as Champa. Suryavarman II is immortalised as the king who, in his devotion to the Hindu deity Vishnu, commissioned the majestic temple of Angkor Wat (p125). For an insight into events in this epoch, see the bas-reliefs on the southwest corridor of Angkor Wat, which depict the reign of Suryavarman II.

Suryavarman II had brought Champa to heel and reduced it to vassal status, but the Chams struck back in 1177 with a naval expedition up the Mekong and into Tonlé Sap Lake. They took the city of Angkor by surprise and put King Dharanindravarman II to death. The following year a cousin of Suryavarman II rallied the Khmer troops and defeated the Chams in yet another naval battle. The new leader was crowned Jayavarman VII in 1181.

For more on the Angkorian period, see p119.

Decline & Fall of Angkor

Angkor was the epicentre of an incredible empire that held sway over much of the Mekong region, but like all empires, the sun was to eventually set.

1181

The Chams are vanquished as Jayavarman VII, the greatest king of Angkor and builder of Angkor Thom, takes the throne, changing the state religion to Mahayana Buddhism.

1219

Jayavarman VII dies aged in his 90s, and the empire of Angkor slowly declines due to a choking irrigation network, religious conflict and the rise of powerful neighbours.

» Statues of serpent-carrying giants, Angkor Thom (p135)

A number of scholars have argued that decline was already on the horizon at the time Angkor Wat was built, when the Angkorian empire was at the height of its remarkable productivity. There are indications that the irrigation network was overworked and slowly starting to silt up due to the massive deforestation that had taken place in the heavily populated areas to the north and east of Angkor. This was exacerbated by prolonged periods of drought in the 14th century, which was more recently discovered through the advanced analysis of dendrochronology, or the study of tree rings, in the Angkor area.

Massive construction projects such as Angkor Wat and Angkor Thom no doubt put an enormous strain on the royal coffers and on thousands of slaves and common people who subsidised them in hard labour and taxes. Following the reign of Jayavarman VII, temple construction effectively ground to a halt, in large part because Jayavarman VII's public works had quarried local sandstone into oblivion and left the population exhausted.

Another challenge for the later kings was religious conflict and internecine rivalries. The state religion changed back and forth several times during the twilight years of the empire, and kings spent more time engaged in iconoclasm, defacing the temples of their predecessors, than building monuments to their own achievements. From time to time this boiled over into civil war.

Angkor was losing control over the peripheries of its empire. At the same time, the Thais were ascendant, having migrated south from Yunnan, China, to escape Kublai Khan and his Mongol hordes. The Thais, first from Sukothai, later Ayuthaya, grew in strength and made repeated incursions into Angkor before finally sacking the city in 1431 and making off with thousands of intellectuals, artisans and dancers from the royal court. During this period, perhaps drawn by the opportunities for sea trade with China and fearful of the increasingly bellicose Thais, the Khmer elite began to migrate to the Phnom Penh area. The capital shifted several times over the centuries but eventually settled in present-day Phnom Penh.

From 1500 until the arrival of the French in 1863, Cambodia was ruled by a series of weak kings beset by dynastic rivalries. In the face of such intrigue, they sought the protection – granted, of course, at a price – of either Thailand or Vietnam. In the 17th century, the Nguyen lords of southern Vietnam came to the rescue of the Cambodian king in return for settlement rights in the Mekong Delta region. The Khmers still refer to this region as Kampuchea Krom (Lower Cambodia), even though it is well and truly populated by the Vietnamese today.

In the west, the Thais controlled the provinces of Battambang and Siem Reap from 1794 and held influence over the Cambodian royal family.

Chinese emissary Chou Ta Kuan lived in Angkor for a year in 1296, and his observations have been republished as *The Customs of Cambodia* (2000), a fascinating insight into life during the height of the empire.

HISTORY DECLINE & FALL OF ANGKOR

The commercial metropolis that is now Ho Chi Minh City (Saigon) in Vietnam was, in 1600, a small Cambodian village called Prey Nokor.

1253	1296	1353	1431
The Mongols of Kublai Khan sack the Thai kingdom of Nanchao in Yunnan, sparking an exodus southwards, which brings Thais into direct conflict with the weakening Khmer empire.	Chinese emissary Chou Ta Kuan spends one year living at Angkor and writes *The Customs of Cambodia*, the only contemporary account of life in the great Khmer capital.	Lao prince Chao Fa Ngum ends his Angkor exile and is sponsored by his Khmer father-in-law on an expedition to conquer the new Thai kingdoms, declaring himself leader of Lan Xang (Land of a Million Elephants).	The Thais sack Angkor definitively, carting off most of the royal court to Ayuthaya, including nobles, priests, dancers and artisans.

Indeed, one king was crowned in Bangkok and placed on the throne at Udong (p84) with the help of the Thai army. That Cambodia survived through the 18th century as a distinct entity is due to the preoccupations of its neighbours: while the Thais were expending their energy and resources fighting the Burmese, the Vietnamese were wholly absorbed by internal strife. The pattern continued for more than two centuries, the carcass of Cambodia pulled back and forth between two powerful tigers.

The French in Cambodia

The era of yo-yoing between Thai and Vietnamese masters came to a close in 1863, when French gunboats intimidated King Norodom I (r 1860–1904) into signing a treaty of protectorate. Ironically, it really was a protectorate, as Cambodia was in danger of going the way of Champa and vanishing from the map. French control of Cambodia developed as a sideshow to their interests in Vietnam, uncannily similar to the American experience a century later, and initially involved little direct interference in Cambodia's affairs. The French presence also helped keep Norodom on the throne despite the ambitions of his rebellious half-brothers.

By the 1870s, French officials in Cambodia began pressing for greater control over internal affairs. In 1884 Norodom was forced into signing a treaty that turned his country into a virtual colony, sparking a two-year rebellion that constituted the only major uprising in Cambodia before WWII. The rebellion only ended when the king was persuaded to call upon the rebel fighters to lay down their weapons in exchange for a return to the status quo.

During the following decades, senior Cambodian officials opened the door to direct French control over the day-to-day administration of the country, as they saw certain advantages in acquiescing to French power. The French maintained Norodom's court in splendour unseen since the heyday of Angkor, helping to enhance the symbolic position of the monarchy. In 1907 the French were able to pressure Thailand into returning the northwest provinces of Battambang, Siem Reap and Preah Vihear in return for concessions of Lao territory to the Thais. This meant Angkor came under Cambodian control for the first time in more than a century.

King Norodom I was succeeded by King Sisowath (r 1904–27), who was succeeded by King Monivong (r 1927–41). Upon King Monivong's death, the French governor-general of Japanese-occupied Indochina, Admiral Jean Decoux, placed 19-year-old Prince Norodom Sihanouk on the Cambodian throne. The French authorities assumed young Sihanouk would prove pliable, but this proved to be a major miscalculation (see the box, p287).

During WWII, Japanese forces occupied much of Asia, and Cambodia was no exception. However, with many in France collaborating with

The French did very little to encourage education in Cambodia, and by the end of WWII, after 70 years of colonial rule, there were no universities and only one high school in the whole country.

1594	**1772**	**1834**	**1863**
Temporary Cambodian capital of Lovek falls when, legend says, the Siamese fire a cannon of silver coins into its bamboo defences. Soldiers cut down the bamboo to retrieve the silver, leaving the city exposed.	Cambodia is caught between the powerful Vietnamese and Siamese, and the latter burn Phnom Penh to the ground, another chapter in the story of inflamed tensions, which persist today.	The Vietnamese take control of much of Cambodia during the reign of Emperor Minh Mang and begin a slow revolution to 'teach the barbarians their customs'.	The French force King Norodom I into signing a treaty of protectorate, which prevents Cambodia being wiped off the map and thus begins 90 years of French rule.

the occupying Germans, the Japanese were happy to let their new Vichy France allies control affairs in Cambodia. The price was conceding to Thailand (a Japanese ally of sorts) much of Battambang and Siem Reap Provinces once again, areas that weren't returned until 1947. However, after the fall of Paris in 1944 and with French policy in disarray, the Japanese were forced to take direct control of the territory by early 1945. After WWII, the French returned, making Cambodia an autonomous state within the French Union, but retaining de facto control. The immediate postwar years were marked by strife among the country's various political factions, a situation made more unstable by the Franco-Vietminh War then raging in Vietnam and Laos, which spilled over into Cambodia. The Vietnamese, as they were also to do 20 years later in the war against Lon Nol and the Americans, trained and fought with bands of Khmer Issarak (Free Khmer) against the French authorities.

The Sihanouk Years

The post-independence period was one of peace and prosperity. It was Cambodia's golden era, a time of creativity and optimism. Phnom Penh grew in size and stature, the temples of Angkor were the leading tourist destination in Southeast Asia and Sihanouk played host to a succession of influential leaders from across the globe. However, dark clouds were circling, as the American war in Vietnam became a black hole, sucking in neighbouring countries.

In late 1952 King Sihanouk dissolved the fledgling parliament, declared martial law and embarked on his 'royal crusade', a travelling campaign to drum up international support for his country's independence. Independence was proclaimed on 9 November 1953 and recognised by the Geneva Conference of May 1954, which ended French control of Indochina. In 1955, Sihanouk abdicated, afraid of being marginalised amid the pomp of royal ceremony. The 'royal crusader' became 'citizen Sihanouk'. He vowed never again to return to the throne. Meanwhile his father became king. It was a masterstroke that offered Sihanouk both royal authority and supreme political power. His newly established party, Sangkum Reastr Niyum (People's Socialist Community), won every seat in parliament in the September 1955 elections and Sihanouk was to dominate Cambodian politics for the next 15 years.

Although he feared the Vietnamese communists, Sihanouk considered South Vietnam and Thailand – both allies of the mistrusted USA – the greatest threats to Cambodia's security, even survival. In an attempt to fend off these many dangers, he declared Cambodia neutral and refused to accept further US aid, which had accounted for a substantial chunk of the country's military budget. He also nationalised many industries, including the rice trade. In 1965 Sihanouk, convinced that the USA had

For more on the incredible life and times of Norodom Sihanouk, read the biography *Prince of Light, Prince of Darkness* (1994) by Milton Osborne.

1884	1907	1942	1947
Rebellion against French rule in Cambodia erupts in response to a treaty giving French administrators wide-ranging powers. The treaty is signed under the watch of French gunboats in the Mekong River.	French authorities successfully negotiate the return of the northwest provinces of Siem Reap, Battambang and Preah Vihear, which have been under Thai control since 1794.	Japanese forces occupy Cambodia, leaving the administration in the hands of Vichy France officials, but fan the flames of independence as the war draws to a close.	The provinces of Battambang, Siem Reap and Sisophon, seized by the Thais during the Japanese occupation, are returned to Cambodia.

been plotting against him and his family, broke diplomatic relations with Washington and veered towards the North Vietnamese and China. In addition, he agreed to let the communists use Cambodian territory in their battle against South Vietnam and the USA. Sihanouk was taking sides, a dangerous position in a volatile region.

These moves and his socialist economic policies alienated conservative elements in Cambodian society, including the army brass and the urban elite. At the same time, left-wing Cambodians, many of them educated abroad, deeply resented his domestic policies, which stifled political debate. Compounding Sihanouk's problems was the fact that all classes were fed up with the pervasive corruption in government ranks, some of it uncomfortably close to the royal family. Although most peasants revered Sihanouk as a semi-divine figure, in 1967 a rural-based rebellion broke out in Samlot, Battambang, leading him to conclude that the greatest threat to his regime came from the left. Bowing to pressure from the army, he implemented a policy of harsh repression against left-wingers.

By 1969 the conflict between the army and leftist rebels had become more serious, as the Vietnamese sought sanctuary deeper in Cambodia. Sihanouk's political position had also decidedly deteriorated – due in no small part to his obsession with film-making, which was leading him to neglect affairs of state. In March 1970, while Sihanouk was on a trip to France, General Lon Nol and Prince Sisowath Sirik Matak, Sihanouk's cousin, deposed him as chief of state, apparently with tacit US consent. Sihanouk took up residence in Beijing, where he set up a government-in-exile in alliance with an indigenous Cambodian revolutionary movement that Sihanouk had nicknamed the Khmer Rouge (see also p297). This was a definitive moment in contemporary Cambodian history, as the Khmer Rouge exploited its partnership with Sihanouk to draw new recruits into their small organisation. Talk to many former Khmer Rouge fighters and they'll say that they 'went to the hills' (a euphemism for joining the Khmer Rouge) to fight for their king and knew nothing of Mao or Marxism.

Descent into Civil War

The lines were drawn for a bloody era of civil war. Sihanouk was condemned to death *in absentia,* a harsh move on the part of the new government that effectively ruled out any hint of compromise for the next five years. Lon Nol gave communist Vietnamese forces an ultimatum to withdraw their units within one week, which amounted to a declaration of war, as the Vietnamese did not want to return to the homeland to face the Americans.

On 30 April 1970, US and South Vietnamese forces invaded Cambodia in an effort to flush out thousands of Viet Cong and North Vietnamese

During the 1960s, Cambodia was an oasis of peace while wars raged in neighbouring Vietnam and Laos. By 1970 that had all changed. For the full story, read *Sideshow: Kissinger, Nixon and the Destruction of Cambodia*, by William Shawcross (1979).

Lon Nol's military press attaché was known for his colourful, even imaginative media briefings that painted a rosy picture of the increasingly desperate situation on the ground. With a name like Major Am Rong, few could take him seriously.

1953	1955	1962	1963
Sihanouk's royal crusade for independence succeeds and Cambodia goes it alone without the French on 9 November, ushering in a new era of optimism.	King Sihanouk abdicates from the throne to enter a career in politics; he founds the Sangkum Reastr Niyum (People's Socialist Community) party and wins the election with ease.	The International Court rules in favour of Cambodia in the long-running dispute over the dramatic mountain temple of Preah Vihear, perched on the Dangkrek Mountains on the border with Thailand.	Pol Pot and Ieng Sary flee from Phnom Penh to the jungles of Ratanakiri. With training from the Vietnamese, they launch a guerrilla war against Sihanouk's government.

SIHANOUK: THE LAST OF THE GOD-KINGS

Norodom Sihanouk has been a towering presence in the topsy-turvy world of Cambodian politics. A larger-than-life character of many enthusiasms and shifting political positions, amatory exploits dominated his early life. Later he became the prince who stage-managed the close of French colonialism, led Cambodia during its golden years, was imprisoned by the Khmer Rouge and, from privileged exile, finally returned triumphant as king. He is many things to many people, but whatever else he may be, he has proven himself a survivor.

Sihanouk, born in 1922, was not an obvious contender for the throne, as he was from the Norodom branch of the royal family. He was crowned in 1941, at just 19, with his education incomplete. In 1955 Sihanouk abdicated and turned his attention to politics, his party winning every seat in parliament that year. By the mid-1960s Sihanouk had been calling the shots in Cambodia for a decade.

The conventional wisdom was that 'Sihanouk is Cambodia', his leadership the key to national success. However, as the country was inexorably drawn into the American war in Vietnam and government troops battled with a leftist insurgency in the countryside, Sihanouk was increasingly seen as a liability.

On 18 March 1970, the National Assembly voted to remove Sihanouk from office. He went into exile in Beijing and joined the communists. Following the Khmer Rouge victory on 17 April 1975, Sihanouk returned to Cambodia as head of the new state of Democratic Kampuchea. He resigned after less than a year and was confined to the Royal Palace as a prisoner of the Khmer Rouge. He remained there until early 1979 when, on the eve of the Vietnamese invasion, he was flown back to Beijing.

Sihanouk never quite gave up wanting to be everything for Cambodia: international statesman, general, president, film director and man of the people. On 24 September 1993, after 38 years in politics, he settled once more for the role of king. On 7 October 2004 he once again abdicated, and his son King Sihamoni ascended to the throne. However, Sihanouk's place in history is assured, the last in a long line of Angkor's god-kings.

troops who were using Cambodian bases in their war to overthrow the South Vietnamese government. As a result of the invasion, the Vietnamese communists withdrew deeper into Cambodia, further destabilising the Lon Nol government. Cambodia's tiny army never stood a chance and within the space of a few months, Vietnamese forces and their Khmer Rouge allies overran almost half the country. The ultimate humiliation came in July 1970 when the Vietnamese occupied the temples of Angkor.

In 1969 the USA launched Operation Menu, the secret bombing of suspected communist base camps in Cambodia. For the next four years, until bombing was halted by the US Congress in August 1973, huge areas of the eastern half of the country were carpet-bombed by US B-52s,

1964	1969	1970	1971
After the US-sponsored coup against President Diem in South Vietnam, Sihanouk veers left, breaking diplomatic ties with the USA and nationalising the rice trade, antagonising the ethnic Chinese business community.	US President Nixon authorises the secret bombing of Cambodia, which starts with the carpet bombing of border zones, but spreads to the whole country, continuing until 1973 and killing up to 250,000 Cambodians.	Sihanouk throws in his lot with the Khmer Rouge after being overthrown by his cousin Prince Sirik Matak and military commander Lon Nol, and sentenced to death *in absentia*, marking the start of a five-year civil war.	Lon Nol, leader of the Khmer Republic, launches disasterous Chenla offensive against Vietnamese communists and their Khmer Rouge allies in Cambodia. He suffers a stroke, but struggles on as leader until 1975.

killing what is believed to be many thousands of civilians and turning hundreds of thousands more into refugees. Undoubtedly, the bombing campaign helped the Khmer Rouge in their recruitment drive, as more and more peasants were losing family members to the aerial assaults. While the final, heaviest bombing in the first half of 1973 may have saved Phnom Penh from a premature fall, its ferocity also helped to harden the attitude of many Khmer Rouge cadres and may have contributed to the later brutality that characterised their rule.

During the US bombing campaign, more bombs were dropped on Cambodia than were used by all sides during WWII.

Savage fighting engulfed the country, bringing misery to millions of Cambodians; many fled rural areas for the relative safety of Phnom Penh and provincial capitals. Between 1970 and 1975, several hundred thousand people died in the fighting. During these years, the Khmer Rouge came to play a dominant role in trying to overthrow the Lon Nol regime, strengthened by the support of the Vietnamese, although the Khmer Rouge leadership would vehemently deny this from 1975 onwards.

The leadership of the Khmer Rouge, including Paris-educated Pol Pot and Ieng Sary, had fled into the countryside in the 1960s to escape the summary justice then being meted out to suspected leftists by Sihanouk's security forces. They consolidated control over the movement and began to move against opponents before they took Phnom Penh. Many of the Vietnamese-trained Cambodian communists who had been based in Hanoi since the 1954 Geneva Accords returned down the Ho Chi Minh Trail to join their 'allies' in the Khmer Rouge in 1973. Many were dead by 1975, executed on the orders of the anti-Vietnamese Pol Pot faction. Likewise, many moderate Sihanouk supporters who had joined the Khmer Rouge as a show of loyalty to their fallen leader rather than a show of ideology to the radicals were victims of purges before the regime took power. This set a precedent for internal purges and mass executions that were to eventually bring the downfall of the Khmer Rouge.

It didn't take long for the Lon Nol government to become very unpopular as a result of unprecedented greed and corruption in its ranks. As the USA bankrolled the war, government and military personnel found lucrative means to make a fortune, such as inventing 'phantom soldiers' and pocketing their pay, or selling weapons to the enemy. Lon Nol was widely perceived as an ineffectual leader, obsessed by superstition, fortune tellers and mystical crusades. This perception increased with his stroke in March 1971 and for the next four years his grip on reality seemed to weaken as his brother Lon Non's power grew.

Despite massive US military and economic aid, Lon Nol never succeeded in gaining the initiative against the Khmer Rouge. Large parts of the countryside fell to the rebels and many provincial capitals were cut off from Phnom Penh. Lon Nol fled the country in early April 1975, leaving Sirik Matak in charge, who refused evacuation to the end. 'I

1973	1975	1977	1979
Sihanouk and his wife, Monique, travel down the Ho Chi Minh Trail to visit Khmer Rouge allies at the holy mountain of Phnom Kulen near Angkor, a propaganda victory for Pol Pot.	The Khmer Rouge march into Phnom Penh on 17 April and turn the clocks back to Year Zero, evacuating the capital and turning the whole nation into a prison without walls.	The Pol Pot faction of the Khmer Rouge launch their bloodiest purge against the Eastern Zone of the country, sparking a civil war along the banks of the Mekong and drawing the Vietnamese into the battle.	Vietnamese forces liberate Cambodia from Khmer Rouge rule on 7 January 1979, just two weeks after launching the invasion, and install a friendly regime in Phnom Penh.

cannot alas leave in such a cowardly fashion… I have committed only one mistake, that of believing in you, the Americans' were the words Sirik Matak poignantly penned to US ambassador John Gunther Dean. On 17 April 1975 – two weeks before the fall of Saigon (now Ho Chi Minh City) – Phnom Penh surrendered to the Khmer Rouge.

The Khmer Rouge Revolution

Upon taking Phnom Penh, the Khmer Rouge implemented one of the most radical and brutal restructurings of a society ever attempted; its goal was a pure revolution, untainted by those that had gone before, to transform Cambodia into a peasant-dominated agrarian cooperative. Within days of the Khmer Rouge coming to power, the entire population of Phnom Penh and provincial towns, including the sick, elderly and infirm, was forced to march into the countryside and work as slaves for 12 to 15 hours a day. Disobedience of any sort often brought immediate execution. The advent of Khmer Rouge rule was proclaimed Year Zero. Currency was abolished and postal services ground to a halt. The country cut itself off from the outside world.

In the eyes of Pol Pot, the Khmer Rouge was not a unified movement, but a series of factions that needed to be cleansed. This process had already begun with attacks on Vietnamese-trained Khmer Rouge and Sihanouk's supporters, but Pol Pot's initial fury upon seizing power was directed against the former regime. All of the senior government and military figures who had been associated with Lon Nol were executed within days of the takeover. Then the centre shifted its attention to the outer regions, which had been separated into geographic zones. The loyalist Southwestern Zone forces, under the control of one-legged general Ta Mok, were sent into region after region to 'purify' the population, a process that saw thousands perish.

The cleansing reached grotesque heights in the final and bloodiest purge against the powerful and independent Eastern Zone. Generally considered more moderate than other Khmer Rouge factions, the Eastern Zone was ideologically, as well as geographically, closer to Vietnam. The Pol Pot faction consolidated the rest of the country before moving against the east from 1977 onwards. Hundreds of leaders were executed before open rebellion broke out, sparking a civil war in the east. Many Eastern Zone leaders fled to Vietnam, forming the nucleus of the government installed by the Vietnamese in January 1979. The people were defenceless and distrusted – 'Cambodian bodies with Vietnamese minds' or 'duck's arses with chicken's heads' – and were deported to the northwest with new, blue *kramas* (scarves). Had it not been for the Vietnamese invasion, all would have perished, as the blue *krama* was a secret party sign indicating an eastern enemy of the revolution.

The Killing Fields (1985) is the definitive film on the Khmer Rouge period in Cambodia. It tells the story of American journalist Sidney Schanberg and his Cambodian assistant Dith Pran during and after the war.

HISTORY THE KHMER ROUGE REVOLUTION

1980

Cambodia is gripped by a terrible famine, as the dislocation of the previous few years means that no rice has been planted or harvested, and worldwide 'Save Kampuchea' appeals are launched.

1982

Sihanouk is pressured to join the Khmer Rouge as head of the Coalition Government of Democratic Kampuchea (CGDK), a new military front against the Vietnamese-backed government in Phnom Penh.

ANDREW BURKE/LONELY PLANET IMAGES ©

» One of Phnom Penh's French Colonial–style buildings

It is still not known exactly how many Cambodians died at the hands of the Khmer Rouge during the three years, eight months and 20 days of their rule. The Vietnamese claimed three million deaths, while foreign experts long considered the number closer to one million. Yale University researchers undertaking ongoing investigations estimated that the figure was close to two million.

Hundreds of thousands of people were executed by the Khmer Rouge leadership, while hundreds of thousands more died of famine and disease. Meals consisted of little more than watery rice porridge twice a day, but were meant to sustain men, women and children through a backbreaking day in the fields. Disease stalked the work camps, malaria and dysentery striking down whole families; death was a relief for many from the horrors of life. Some zones were better than others, some leaders fairer than others, but life for the majority was one of unending misery and suffering in this 'prison without walls'.

As the centre eliminated more and more moderates, Angkar (the organisation) became the only family people needed and those who did not agree were sought out and crushed. The Khmer Rouge detached the Cambodian people from all they held dear: their families, their food, their fields and their faith. Even the peasants who had supported the revolution could no longer blindly follow such insanity. Nobody cared for the Khmer Rouge by 1978, but nobody had an ounce of strength to do anything about it...except the Vietnamese.

To the End of Hell: One Woman's Struggle to Survive Cambodia's Khmer Rouge is the incredible memoir of Denise Affonço, one of the only foreigners to live through the Khmer Rouge revolution, due to her marriage to a senior intellectual in the movement.

Enter the Vietnamese

Relations between Cambodia and Vietnam have historically been tense, as the Vietnamese have slowly but steadily expanded southwards, encroaching on Cambodian territory. Despite the fact the two communist parties had fought together as brothers in arms, old tensions soon came to the fore.

From 1976 to 1978, the Khmer Rouge instigated a series of border clashes with Vietnam, and claimed the Mekong Delta, once part of the Khmer empire. Incursions into Vietnamese border provinces left hundreds of Vietnamese civilians dead. On 25 December 1978 Vietnam launched a full-scale invasion of Cambodia, toppling the Pol Pot government two weeks later. As Vietnamese tanks neared Phnom Penh, the Khmer Rouge fled westward with as many civilians as it could seize, taking refuge in the jungles and mountains along the Thai border. The Vietnamese installed a new government led by several former Khmer Rouge officers, including current Prime Minister Hun Sen, who had defected to Vietnam in 1977. The Khmer Rouge's patrons, the Chinese communists, launched a massive reprisal raid across Vietnam's northernmost border in early 1979 in an attempt to buy their allies time. It failed and after 17 days the Chinese

Only a handful of foreigners were allowed to visit Cambodia during the Khmer Rouge period of Democratic Kampuchea. US journalist Elizabeth Becker was one who travelled there in late 1978; her book *When the War Was Over* (1986) tells her story.

1984	1985	1989	1991
The Vietnamese embark on a major offensive in the west of Cambodia and the Khmer Rouge and its allies are forced to retreat to refugee camps and bases inside Thailand.	There is a changing of the guard at the top and Hun Sen becomes Prime Minister of Cambodia, a title he still holds today with the Cambodian People's Party.	As the effects of President Gorbachev's perestroika (restructuring) begin to impact on communist allies, Vietnam feels the pinch and announces the withdrawal of its forces from Cambodia.	The Paris Peace Accords are signed, in which all parties, including the Khmer Rouge, agree to participate in free and fair elections supervised by the UN.

THE POLITICS OF DISASTER RELIEF

The Cambodian famine became a new front in the Cold War, as Washington and Moscow jostled for influence from afar. As hundreds of thousands of Cambodians fled to Thailand, a massive international famine relief effort, sponsored by the UN, was launched. The international community wanted to deliver aid across a land bridge at Poipet, while the new Vietnamese-backed Phnom Penh government wanted all supplies to come through the capital via Kompong Som (Sihanoukville) or the Mekong River. Both sides had their reasons – the new government did not want aid to fall into the hands of its Khmer Rouge enemies, while the international community didn't believe the new government had the infrastructure to distribute the aid – and both fears were right.

Some agencies distributed aid the slow way through Phnom Penh, and others set up camps in Thailand. The camps became a magnet for half of Cambodia, as many Khmers still feared the return of the Khmer Rouge or were seeking a new life overseas. The Thai military convinced the international community to distribute all aid through their channels and used this as a cloak to rebuild the shattered Khmer Rouge forces as an effective resistance against the Vietnamese. Thailand demanded that, as a condition for allowing international food aid for Cambodia to pass through its territory, food had to be supplied to the Khmer Rouge forces encamped in the Thai border region as well. Along with weaponry supplied by China, this international assistance was essential in enabling the Khmer Rouge to rebuild its military strength and fight on for another two decades.

HISTORY ENTER THE VIETNAMESE

withdrew, their fingers badly burnt by their Vietnamese enemies. The Vietnamese then staged a show trial in Cambodia in which Pol Pot and Ieng Sary were condemned to death *in absentia* for their genocidal acts.

A traumatised population took to the road in search of surviving family members. Millions had been uprooted and had to walk hundreds of kilometres across the country. Rice stocks were decimated, the harvest left to wither and little rice planted, sowing the seeds for a widespread famine in 1979 and 1980.

As the conflict in Cambodia raged, Sihanouk agreed in 1982, under pressure from China, to head a military and political front opposed to the Phnom Penh government. The Sihanouk-led resistance coalition brought together – on paper, at least – Funcinpec (the French acronym for the National United Front for an Independent, Neutral, Peaceful and Cooperative Cambodia), which comprised a royalist group loyal to Sihanouk; the Khmer People's National Liberation Front, a non-communist grouping under former prime minister Son Sann; and the Khmer Rouge, officially known as the Party of Democratic Kampuchea and by far the most powerful of the three. The crimes of the Khmer Rouge were swept aside to ensure a compromise that suited the realpolitik of the day.

Cambodia's turbulent past is uncovered in a series of articles, oral histories and photos in an excellent website called *Beauty and Darkness: Cambodia, the Odyssey of the Khmer People*. Find it at www.mekong net/cambodia.

1993	1994	1995	1996
The pro-Sihanouk royalist party Funcinpec under the leadership of Prince Ranariddh wins the popular vote, but the communist CPP threaten secession in the east to muscle their way into government.	The Khmer Rouge target foreign tourists in Cambodia, kidnapping and killing groups travelling by taxi and train to the South Coast, reinforcing Cambodia's overseas image as a dangerous country.	Prince Norodom Sirivudh is arrested and exiled for allegedly plotting to kill Prime Minister Hun Sen, removing another potential rival from the scene.	British deminer Christopher Howes, working in Cambodia with the Mines Advisory Group (MAG), is kidnapped by the Khmer Rouge and later killed, together with his interpreter Houn Hourth.

For much of the 1980s Cambodia remained closed to the Western world, save for the presence of some humanitarian aid groups. Government policy was effectively under the control of the Vietnamese, so Cambodia found itself very much in the Eastern-bloc camp. The economy was in tatters for most of this period, as Cambodia, like Vietnam, suffered from the effects of a US-sponsored embargo.

In 1984, the Vietnamese overran all the major rebel camps inside Cambodia, forcing the Khmer Rouge and its allies to retreat into Thailand. From this time the Khmer Rouge and its allies engaged in guerrilla warfare aimed at demoralising their opponents. Tactics used by the Khmer Rouge included shelling government-controlled garrison towns, planting thousands of mines in rural areas, attacking road transport, blowing up bridges, kidnapping village chiefs and targeting civilians. The Khmer Rouge also forced thousands of men, women and children living in the refugee camps it controlled to work as porters, ferrying ammunition and other supplies into Cambodia across heavily mined sections of the border.

The Vietnamese, for their part, laid the world's longest minefield, known as K-5 and stretching from the Gulf of Thailand to the Lao border, in an attempt to seal out the guerrillas. They also sent Cambodians into the forests to cut down trees on remote sections of road to prevent ambushes. Thousands died of disease and from injuries sustained from landmines. The Khmer Rouge was no longer in power, but for many the 1980s were almost as tough as the 1970s, it was one long struggle to survive.

The Documentation Center of Cambodia is an organisation established to document the crimes of the Khmer Rouge as a record for future generations. Its excellent website is a mine of information about Cambodia's darkest hour. Take your time to visit www.dccam.org.

During much of the 1980s, the second-largest concentration of Cambodians outside Phnom Penh was in the Khao I Dang refugee camp on the Thai border.

The UN Comes to Town

The arrival of Mikhail Gorbachev in the Kremlin saw the Cold War draw to a close. It was the furthest-flung Soviet allies who were cut adrift first, leaving Vietnam internationally isolated and economically crippled. In September 1989, Vietnam announced the withdrawal of all of its troops from Cambodia. With the Vietnamese gone, the opposition coalition, still dominated by the Khmer Rouge, launched a series of offensives, forcing the now-vulnerable government to the negotiating table.

Diplomatic efforts to end the civil war began to bear fruit in September 1990, when a peace plan was accepted by both the Phnom Penh government and the three factions of the resistance coalition. According to the plan, the Supreme National Council (SNC), a coalition of all factions, would be formed under the presidency of Sihanouk. Meanwhile, the UN Transitional Authority in Cambodia (Untac) would supervise the administration of the country for two years, with the goal of free and fair elections.

Untac undoubtedly achieved some successes, but for all of these, it is the failures that were to cost Cambodia dearly in the 'democratic' era.

1997

Second Prime Minister Hun Sen overthrows First Prime Minister Norodom Ranariddh in a military coup, referred to as 'the events of 1997' in Cambodia.

1998

Pol Pot passes away on 15 April 1998 as Anlong Veng falls to government forces, and many observers ponder whether the timing is coincidental.

NICK RAY/LONELY PLANET IMAGES ©

» Decapitated Khmer Rouge statues, Anlong Veng (p229)

THE NAME GAME

Cambodia has changed its name so many times over the last few decades that there are understandable grounds for confusion. To the Cambodians, their country is Kampuchea. The name is derived from the word Kambuja, meaning 'those born of Kambu', the mythical founder of the country. It dates back as far as the 10th century. The Portuguese 'Camboxa' and the French 'Cambodge', from which the English name 'Cambodia' is derived, are adaptations of 'Kambuja'.

Since gaining independence in 1953, the country has been known in English by various names before coming full circle:

» The Kingdom of Cambodia

» The Khmer Republic (under Lon Nol, who ruled from 1970 to 1975)

» Democratic Kampuchea (under the Khmer Rouge, which controlled the country from 1975 to 1979)

» The People's Republic of Kampuchea (under the Vietnamese-backed government from 1979 to 1989)

» The State of Cambodia (from mid-1989)

» The Kingdom of Cambodia (from May 1993)

It was the Khmer Rouge that insisted the outside world use the name Kampuchea. Changing the country's official English name back to Cambodia was intended as a symbolic move to distance the present government in Phnom Penh from the bitter connotations of the name Kampuchea, which Westerners associate with the Khmer Rouge regime.

Untac was successful in pushing through many international human-rights covenants; it opened the door to a significant number of non-governmental organisations (NGOs); and, most importantly, on 25 May 1993, elections were held with an 89.6% turnout. However, the results were far from decisive. Funcinpec, led by Prince Norodom Ranariddh, took 58 seats in the National Assembly, while the Cambodian People's Party (CPP), which represented the previous communist government, took 51 seats. The CPP had lost the election, but senior leaders threatened a secession of the eastern provinces of the country. As a result, Cambodia ended up with two prime ministers: Norodom Ranariddh as first prime minister, and Hun Sen as second prime minister.

Even today, Untac is heralded as one of the UN's success stories. Another perspective is that it was an ill-conceived and poorly executed peace because so many of the powers involved in brokering the deal had their own agendas to advance. To many Cambodians who had survived

1999	2000	2002	2003
Cambodia finally joins Asean after a two-year delay, taking its place among the family of Southeast Asian nations, who welcome the country back onto the world stage.	The Cambodian Freedom Fighters (CFF) launch an 'assault' on Phnom Penh. Backed by Cambodian-American dissidents, the attackers are lightly armed, poorly trained and politically inexperienced.	Cambodia holds its first ever local elections at commune level, a tentative step toward dismantling the old communist system of control and bringing grass-roots democracy to the country.	The CPP wins the election, but political infighting prevents the formation of the new government for almost a year until the old coalition with Funcinpec is revived.

the 1970s, it was unthinkable that the Khmer Rouge would be allowed to play a part in the electoral process after presiding over a genocide.

The UN's disarmament program took weapons away from rural militias who for so long provided the backbone of the government's provincial defence network against the Khmer Rouge and this left communities throughout the country vulnerable to attack. Meanwhile the Khmer Rouge used the veil of legitimacy conferred upon it by the peace process to re-establish a guerrilla network throughout Cambodia. By 1994, when it was finally outlawed by the government, the Khmer Rouge was arguably a greater threat to the stability of Cambodia than at any time since 1979.

Untac's main goals had been to 'restore and maintain peace' and 'promote national reconciliation', and in the short term it achieved neither. It did oversee free and fair elections, but these were later annulled by the actions of Cambodia's politicians. Little was done during the UN period to try to dismantle the communist apparatus of state set up by the CPP, a well-oiled machine that continues to ensure that former communists control the civil service, judiciary, army and police today.

Western powers, including the USA and UK, ensured the Khmer Rouge retained its seat at the UN general assembly in New York until 1991, a scenario that saw those responsible for the genocide representing their victims on the international stage.

The Slow Birth of Peace

When the Vietnamese toppled the Pol Pot government in 1979, the Khmer Rouge disappeared into the jungle. The guerrillas eventually boycotted the 1993 elections and later rejected peace talks aimed at establishing a ceasefire. In 1994, the Khmer Rouge resorted to a new tactic of targeting tourists, with horrendous results for a number of foreigners in Cambodia. During 1994, three people were taken from a taxi on the road to Sihanoukville and subsequently shot. A few months later another three foreigners were seized from a train bound for Sihanoukville and in the ransom drama that followed they were executed as the army closed in.

The government changed course during the mid-1990s, opting for more carrot and less stick in a bid to end the war. The breakthrough came in 1996 when Ieng Sary, Brother No 3 in the Khmer Rouge hierarchy and foreign minister during its rule, was denounced by Pol Pot for corruption. He subsequently led a mass defection of fighters and their dependants from the Pailin area, and this effectively sealed the fate of the remaining Khmer Rouge. Pailin, rich in gems and timber, had long been the economic crutch that kept the Khmer Rouge hobbling along. The severing of this income, coupled with the fact that government forces now had only one front on which to concentrate their resources, suggested the days of civil war were numbered.

By 1997 cracks were appearing in the coalition and the fledgling democracy once again found itself under siege. But it was the Khmer Rouge that again grabbed the headlines. Pol Pot ordered the execution of Son Sen, defence minister during the Khmer Rouge regime, and many of

Journalist Henry Kamm spent many years filing reports from Cambodia and his book *Cambodia: Report from a Stricken Land* is a fascinating insight into recent events.

2004	2005	2006	2007
In a move that catches observers by surprise, King Sihanouk abdicates from the throne and is succeeded by his son King Sihamoni, a popular choice as Sihamoni has steered clear of politics.	Cambodia joins the WTO, opening its markets to free trade, but many commentators feel it could be counterproductive, as the economy is so small and there is no more protection for domestic producers.	Lawsuits and counter lawsuits see political leaders moving from conflict to courtroom in the new Cambodia. The revolving doors stop with opposition leader Sam Rainsy back in the country and Prince Ranariddh out.	Royalist party Funcinpec continues to implode in the face of conflict, intrigue and defections, with democrats joining Sam Rainsy, loyalists joining the new Norodom Ranariddh Party and others joining the CPP.

his family members. This provoked a putsch within the Khmer Rouge leadership, and the one-legged hardliner general Ta Mok seized control, putting Pol Pot on 'trial'. Rumours flew about Phnom Penh that Pol Pot would be brought there to face international justice, but events dramatically shifted back to the capital.

A lengthy courting period ensued in which both Funcinpec and the CPP attempted to win the trust of the remaining Khmer Rouge hardliners in northern Cambodia. Ranariddh was close to forging a deal with the jungle fighters and was keen to get it sewn up before Cambodia's accession to Asean, as nothing would provide a better entry fanfare than the ending of Cambodia's long civil war. He was outflanked and subsequently outgunned by Second Prime Minister Hun Sen. On 5 July 1997, fighting again erupted on the streets of Phnom Penh as troops loyal to the CPP clashed with those loyal to Funcinpec. The heaviest exchanges were around the airport and key government buildings, but before long the dust had settled and the CPP once again controlled Cambodia. Euphemistically known as the 'events of 1997' in Cambodia, much of the international community condemned the violence as a coup.

As 1998 began, the CPP announced an all-out offensive against its enemies in the north. By April it was closing in on the Khmer Rouge strongholds of Anlong Veng and Preah Vihear, and amid this heavy fighting Pol Pot evaded justice by dying a natural death on 15 April in the captivity of his former Khmer Rouge comrades. The fall of Anlong Veng in April was followed by the fall of Preah Vihear in May, and the surviving big three, Ta Mok, Khieu Samphan and Nuon Chea, were forced to flee into the jungle near the Thai border with their remaining troops.

The 1998 election result reinforced the reality that the CPP was now the dominant force in the Cambodian political system and on 25 December Hun Sen received the Christmas present he had been waiting for: Khieu Samphan and Nuon Chea were defecting to the government side. The international community began to pile on the pressure for the establishment of some sort of war-crimes tribunal to try the remaining Khmer Rouge leadership. After lengthy negotiations, agreement was finally reached on the composition of a court to try the surviving leaders of the Khmer Rouge. The CPP was suspicious of a UN-administered trial as the UN had sided with the Khmer Rouge-dominated coalition against the government in Phnom Penh, and the ruling party wanted a major say in who was to be tried and for what. The UN for its part doubted that the judiciary in Cambodia was sophisticated or impartial enough to fairly oversee such a major trial. A compromise solution – a mixed tribunal of three international and four Cambodian judges requiring a super majority of two plus three for a verdict – was eventually agreed upon. For more on the Khmer Rouge Tribunal, see p297.

Several of the current crop of Cambodian leaders were previously members of the Khmer Rouge, including Prime Minister Hun Sen and Head of the Senate Chea Sim, although there is no evidence to implicate them in mass killings.

When Jemaah Islamiyah (affiliated with Al Qaeda) bomber Hambali was arrested in Thailand in August 2003, it later surfaced that he had been living in a backpacker hostel on Doeng Kuk Lake for about six months.

2008 Elections are held and the CPP increases its share of the vote to 58%, while the opposition vote is split across several parties.

2009 Comrade Duch, aka Kaing Guek Eav, commandant of the notorious S-21 prison, goes on trial for crimes committed during the Khmer Rouge regime.

» A torture room at the S-21 prison (p40) in Phnom Penh

Early 2002 saw Cambodia's first-ever local elections to select village- and commune-level representatives, an important step in bringing grass-roots democracy to the country. Despite national elections since 1993, the CPP continued to monopolise political power at local and regional levels and only with commune elections would this grip be loosened. The national elections of July 2003 saw a shift in the balance of power, as the CPP consolidated their grip on Cambodia and the Sam Rainsy Party over-hauled Funcinpec as the second party. Today, the CPP commands enough of the vote to govern alone and the opposition remains divided and relatively weak. Elections are scheduled to be held once again in 2013. For more on the modern politics of Cambodia, see Cambodia Today (p276).

2010	2011	2012	2013
As the annual Bon Om Tuk (Water Festival) draws to a close on 22 November, more than 350 people die as revellers swarm across a narrow bridge in huge numbers.	The simmering border conflict over the ancient temple of Preah Vihear spills over into actual fighting between Cambodia and Thailand. A ceasefire is negotiated by Asean chair Indonesia.	Cambodia assumes the chair of Asean.	Another general election year for Cambodia, when all eyes will be on the credibility of the vote. As long as the opposition remain divided, a CPP victory looks assured.

Pol Pot & the Legacy of the Khmer Rouge

The Khmer Rouge controlled Cambodia for three years, eight months and 20 days, a periods etched into the consciousness of a generation of Cambodians who survived the Democratic Kampuchea regime. The Vietnamese ousted the Khmer Rouge on 7 January 1979, and the following summer staged a show trial in Phnom Penh in which Pol Pot and Ieng Sary were sentenced *in absentia* to death for the crime of genocide. With the world caught in the clutches of the Cold War, Cambodia's civil war rumbled on for another two decades before drawing to a close in 1999. Pol Pot had already evaded justice through his death in Anlong Veng on 15 April 1998, but many of the senior leadership were still alive. Finally, more than 20 years after the collapse of the Khmer Rouge regime, serious discussions began about a trial to bring those responsible for the deaths of about two million Cambodians to justice.

The Khmer Rouge period is politically sensitive in Cambodia, due in part to the connections the current leadership have with the communist movement – so much so that the history of the genocide was not taught in high schools until 2009.

The Khmer Rouge Tribunal

Case 001

Case 001, the trial of Kaing Guek Eav, aka Comrade Duch, began in 2009. Duch was seen as a key figure as he provided the link between the regime and its crimes in his role as head of S-21 prison. Duch was sentenced to 35 years in 2010, but this was reduced to just 19 years in lieu of time already served and his cooperation with the investigating team. For many Cambodians this was a slap in the face, as Duch had already admitted overall responsibility for the deaths of about 17,000 people. Convert this into simple numbers and it equates to about 10 hours of prison time per victim. However, an appeal verdict announced on 3 February 2012 extended the sentence to life imprisonment.

Case 002

Case 002 began in November 2011, involving the most senior surviving leaders of the Democratic Kampuchea (DK) era: Brother Number 2 Nuon Chea (age 84), Brother Number 3 and former foreign minister of Democratic Kampuchea Ieng Sary (age 83), and former DK head of state Khieu Samphan (age 79). Ieng Sary's wife and former DK Minister of Social Affairs Ieng Thirith (age 78) was ruled unfit to stand trial due to the onset of dementia. To keep abreast of developments in Case 002, visit the official ECCC website at www.eccc.gov.kh or the Cambodian Tribunal Monitor at www.cambodiatribunal.org.

Keep up to date with the latest developments in the Khmer Rouge trial by visiting the official website of the Cambodian Tribunal Monitor at www.cambodia tribunal.org.

Case 003

Case 003 against head of the DK navy, Meas Muth, and head of the DK air force, Sou Met, is politically charged; it threatened to derail the entire tribunal during 2011. Investigations into this case stalled back in 2009 under intense pressure from the Cambodian government, which wanted to draw a line under proceedings with the completion of Case 002. Prime Minister Hun Sen has made several public statements objecting to the continuation of Case 003 and the subsequent impasse has led to criticism from many quarters including Human Rights Watch. Many independent observers have called for the replacement of at least two Cambodian judges for their lack of political impartiality, and German judge Siegfried Blunk resigned under pressure for failing to conduct full investigations into Case 003. It remains to be seen who will prevail in this battle of wills, but to many observers the entire credibility of the trial is currently under threat.

Cost

In the meantime, the budget for the trial just keeps on rising. A total of US$100 million was spent in the first five years, against a backdrop of allegations of corruption on the Cambodian side. Some Cambodians feel the trial will send an important political message about accountability that may resonate with some of the Cambodian leadership today. However, others argue that the trial is a major waste of money given the overwhelming evidence against surviving senior leaders and that a truth and reconciliation commission may have provided more reaching answers for Cambodians who want to understand what motivated the average Khmer Rouge cadre.

To learn more about the origins of the Khmer Rouge and the Democratic Kampuchea regime, read *How Pol Pot Came to Power* (1985) and *The Pol Pot Regime* (1996), both written by Yale University academic Ben Kiernan.

Pol Pot & His Comrades

Pol Pot: Brother Number One

Pol Pot is a name that sends shivers down the spines of Cambodians and foreigners alike. It is Pol Pot who is most associated with the bloody madness of the regime he led between 1975 and 1979, and his policies heaped misery, suffering and death on millions of Cambodians.

Pol Pot was born Saloth Sar in a small village near Kompong Thom in 1925. As a young man he won a scholarship to study in Paris, and it is here that he came into contact with the Cercle Marxiste and communist thought, which he later transformed into a politics of extreme Maoism.

In 1963, Sihanouk's repressive policies sent Saloth Sar and comrades fleeing to the jungles of Ratanakiri. It was from this moment that he began to call himself Pol Pot. Once the Khmer Rouge was allied with Sihanouk, following his overthrow by Lon Nol in 1970 and subsequent exile in Beijing, its support soared and the faces of the leadership became familiar. However, Pol Pot remained a shadowy figure, leaving public duties to Khieu Samphan and Ieng Sary.

When the Khmer Rouge marched into Phnom Penh on 17 April 1975, few people could have anticipated the hell that was to follow. Pol Pot and his clique were the architects of one of the most radical and brutal revolutions in the history of mankind. It was Year Zero and Cambodia was on a self-destructive course to sever all ties with the past.

Pol Pot was not to emerge as the public face of the revolution until the end of 1976, after he returned from a trip to see his mentors in Beijing. He granted almost no interviews to foreign media and was seen only on propaganda movies produced by government TV. Such was his aura and reputation that, by the last year of the regime, a cult of personality was developing around him and stone busts were produced.

Pol Pot travelled up the Ho Chi Minh trail to visit Beijing in 1966 at the height of the Cultural Revolution there. He was obviously inspired by what he saw, as the Khmer Rouge went even further than the Red Guards in severing links with the past.

Pol Pot spent much of the 1980s living in Thailand and was able to rebuild his shattered forces and once again threaten Cambodia. His enigma increased as the international media speculated as to his real fate. His demise was reported so often that when he finally passed away on 15 April 1998, many Cambodians refused to believe it until they had seen his body on TV or in newspapers. Even then, many were sceptical and rumours continue to circulate about exactly how he met his end. Officially, he was said to have died from a heart attack, but a full autopsy was not carried out before his body was cremated on a pyre of burning tyres.

For more on the life and times of Pol Pot, pick up one of the excellent biographies written about him: *Brother Number One* by David Chandler or *Pol Pot: The History of a Nightmare* by Phillip Short.

Brother Number One (2011) is a feature-length documentary that follows New Zealand rower Rob Hamill on a personal journey to discover who was responsible for the murder of his brother Kerry Hamill in S-21 prison in 1978.

Nuon Chea: Brother Number Two

Long considered one of the main ideologues and architects of the Khmer Rouge revolution, Nuon Chea studied law at Bangkok's Thammasut University before joining the Thai Communist Party. He was appointed Deputy Secretary of the Communist Party of Kampuchea upon its secretive founding in 1960 and remained Pol Pot's second in command throughout the regime's rule with overall responsibility for internal security. He is currently on trial at the ECCC as part of Case 002.

Ieng Sary: Brother Number Three

One of Pol Pot's closest confidants, Ieng Sary fled to the jungles of Ratanakiri in 1963, where he and Pol Pot both underwent intensive guerrilla training in the company of North Vietnamese communist forces. Ieng Sary was one of the public faces of the Khmer Rouge and became foreign minister of Democratic Kampuchea. He maintains that he was not involved in the planning or execution of the genocide. However, he did invite many intellectuals, diplomats and exiles to return to Cambodia from 1975, the majority of whom were subsequently tortured and executed in S-21 prison. He helped hasten the demise of the Khmer Rouge as a guerrilla force with his defection to the government side in 1996. He was given an amnesty for his earlier crimes and is attempting to claim amnesty from prosecution in Case 002.

Enemies of the People (2010) follows Cambodian journalist and genocide survivor Thet Sambath as he wins the confidence of Brother Number Two in the Khmer Rouge, Nuon Chea, eventually coaxing him to give new testimony on his role in the genocidal regime.

Khieu Samphan: Brother Number Nine

Khieu Samphan studied economics in Paris and some of his theories on self-reliance were credited with inspiring Khmer Rouge economic policies. During the Sihanouk years of the 1960s, Khieu Samphan spent several years working with the Sangkum government and putting his more moderate theories to the test. During a crackdown on leftists in 1967, he fled to the jungle to join Pol Pot and Ieng Sary. During the DK period, he was made head of state from 1976 to 1979. He is currently on trial as one of the accused in Case 002.

Comrade Duch: Commandant of S-21

Born Kang Guek Iev in Kompong Thom in 1942, Duch initially worked as a teacher before joining the Khmer Rouge in 1967. Based in the Cardamom Mountains during the civil war of 1970–75, he was given responsibility for security and political prisons in his region, where he refined his interrogation techniques. Following the Khmer Rouge takeover, he was moved to S-21 prison and was responsible for the interrogation and execution of thousands of prisoners. He fled Phnom Penh as Vietnamese forces surrounded the city, and his whereabouts were unknown until he was discovered living in Battambang Province by British photojournalist Nic Dunlop. The first to stand trial and be sentenced in Case 001, Comrade Duch cooperated through the judicial process. He was sentenced to life in early 2012.

Khieu Samphan tries to exonerate himself in his 2004 publication, *Cambodia's Recent History and the Reasons Behind the Decisions I Made*.

POL POT & THE LEGACY OF THE KHMER ROUGE POL POT & HIS COMRADES

The Culture

The National Psyche

Since the glory days of the Angkorian empire, the Cambodian people have been on the losing side of many a historical battle, their country all too often a minnow amid the circling sharks. Popular attitudes have been shaped by this history, and the relationship between Cambodia and its neighbours Thailand and Vietnam is marked by a cocktail of fear, admiration and animosity.

Cambodian attitudes towards the Thais and Vietnamese are complex. The Thais aren't always popular, as some Cambodians feel the Thais fail to acknowledge their cultural debt to Cambodia and generally look down on their poorer neighbour. Cambodian attitudes towards the Vietnamese are more ambivalent. There is a certain level of mistrust, as many feel the Vietnamese are out to colonise their country. Many Khmers still call the lost Mekong Delta 'Kampuchea Krom', meaning 'Lower Cambodia'. However, this mistrust is balanced with a grudging respect for the Vietnamese role in Cambodia's 'liberation' from the Khmer Rouge in 1979 (see p290). But when liberation became occupation in the 1980s, the relationship soured once more.

Even the destructive Khmer Rouge paid homage to the mighty Angkor Wat on its flag, with three towers of the temple in yellow, set against a blood-red background.

At first glance, Cambodia appears to be a nation of shiny, happy people, but look deeper and it is a country of evident contradictions. Light and dark, rich and poor, love and hate, life and death – all are visible on a journey through the kingdom. Most telling of all is the evidence of the nation's glorious past set against the more recent tragedy of its present.

Angkor is everywhere: on the flag, the national beer, cigarettes, hotels and guesthouses – anything and everything. It's a symbol of nationhood and fierce pride, a two-fingered salute to the world – no matter how ugly things got in the bad old days, the Cambodians built Angkor Wat and it doesn't come bigger than that.

Jayavarman VII, Angkor's greatest king, is nearly as omnipresent as his temples. The man that vanquished the occupying Chams and took the empire to its greatest glories is a national hero.

Jayavarman VII was a Mahayana Buddhist and directed his faith towards improving the lot of his people, with the construction of hospitals, universities, roads and shelters.

Contrast this with the abyss into which the nation was sucked during the years of the Khmer Rouge. Pol Pot is a dirty word in Cambodia due to the death and suffering he inflicted on the country. Whenever you hear his name, it will be connected with stories of endless personal suffering, of dead brothers, mothers and babies, from which most Cambodians have never had the chance to recover. As the Khmer Rouge trial edges forward, no one has tasted justice, the whys and hows remain unanswered and the older generation must live in the shadow of this trauma.

If Jayavarman VII and Angkor are loved and Pol Pot and the Khmer Rouge despised, then the mercurial Sihanouk, the last of the god-kings who has ultimately shown his human side, is somewhere in between. Many Cambodians love him as the 'father of the nation', but to others he is the man who failed the nation by his association with the Khmer

Rouge. In many ways, his contradictions match those of contemporary Cambodia. Understand Sihanouk and what he has had to survive and you will understand much of Cambodia.

The Cambodian Way of Life

For many older Cambodians, life is centred on family, faith and food, an existence that has stayed the same for centuries. Family is more than the nuclear family we now know in the West, it's the extended family of third cousins and obscure aunts – as long as there is a bloodline, there is a bond. Families stick together, solve problems collectively, listen to the wisdom of the elders and pool resources. The extended family comes together during times of trouble and times of joy, celebrating festivals and successes, mourning deaths and disappointments. Whether the Cambodian house is big or small, there will be a lot of people living inside.

For the majority of the population still living in the countryside, these constants carry on as they always have: several generations sharing the same roof, the same rice and the same religion. But during the dark decades of the 1970s and 1980s, this routine was ripped apart by war and ideology, as the peasants were dragged from all they held dear to fight a bloody civil war and later forced into slavery. Angkar, the Khmer Rouge organisation, took over as the moral and social beacon in the lives of the people. Families were forced apart, children turned against parents, brother against sister. The bond of trust was broken and is only slowly being rebuilt today.

Faith is another rock in the lives of many older Cambodians, and Buddhism (mixed with a dash of Hinduism and animism for good measure) has helped them to rebuild their lives after the Khmer Rouge. Most Cambodian houses contain a small shrine to pray for luck and, come Buddha Day, the wats are thronged with the faithful.

Food is more important to Cambodians than to most, as they have tasted what it is like to be without. Famine stalked the country in the late 1970s and, even today, malnutrition and food shortages are common during times of drought. For country folk (still the majority of the population), their livelihood is their fields. Farmers are attached to their land, their very survival dependent on it, and the harvest cycle dictates the rhythm of rural life.

For the young generation, brought up in a post-conflict, post-communist period of relative freedom, it's a different story – arguably thanks to their steady diet of MTV and steamy soaps. Cambodia is experiencing its very own '60s swing, as the younger generation stands ready for a different lifestyle to the one their parents had to swallow. This creates plenty of friction in the cities, as rebellious teens dress as they like, date whom they want and hit the town until all hours. But few actually live on their own; they still come home to Ma and Pa at the end of the day (and the arguments start again).

CAMBODIAN GREETINGS

Cambodians traditionally greet each other with the *sompiah,* which involves pressing the hands together in prayer and bowing, similar to the *wai* in Thailand. The higher the hands and the lower the bow, the more respect is conveyed – important to remember when meeting officials or the elderly. In recent times this custom has been partly replaced by the handshake, but, although men tend to shake hands with each other, women usually use the traditional greeting with both men and women. It is considered acceptable (or perhaps excusable) for foreigners to shake hands with Cambodians of both sexes.

Cambodia is set for major demographic shifts in the next couple of decades. Currently, just 20% of the population lives in urban areas, which contrasts starkly with the country's more developed neighbours, such as Malaysia and Thailand. Increasing numbers of young people are likely to migrate to the cities in search of opportunity, forever changing the face of contemporary Cambodian society. However, for now at least, Cambodian society remains much more traditional than those of Thailand and Vietnam, and visitors need to keep this in mind.

Travellers crossing the border from liberal Thai islands such as Ko Pha Ngan or Ko Chang should remember they have crossed back in time as far as traditions are concerned, and that wandering around the temples of Angkor barechested (men) or scantily clad (women) will not be appreciated.

Multiculturalism

According to official statistics, more than 90% of the people who live in Cambodia are ethnic Khmers, making the country the most ethnically homogeneous in southeast Asia. However, unofficially, the figure is probably smaller due to a large influx of Chinese and Vietnamese in the past century. Other ethnic minorities include Cham, Lao and the indigenous peoples of the rural highlands.

Ethnic Khmers

The Khmers have inhabited Cambodia since the beginning of recorded regional history (around the 2nd century), many centuries before Thais and Vietnamese migrated to the region. Over the centuries, the Khmers have mixed with other groups residing in Cambodia, including Javanese and Malays (8th century), Thais (10th to 15th centuries), Vietnamese (from the early 17th century) and Chinese (since the 18th century).

There are just 20 female parliamentarians out of 123 seated in the National Assembly in Cambodia, making up just over 15% of MPs.

Ethnic Vietnamese

Vietnamese are one of the largest non-Khmer ethnic groups in Cambodia. According to government figures, Cambodia is host to around 100,000 Vietnamese. Unofficial observers claim that the real figure may be somewhere between half a million and two million. They play a big part in the fishing and construction industries in Cambodia. However, there is still some distrust between the Cambodians and the Vietnamese, even among those who have been living in Cambodia for generations.

Ethnic Chinese

The government claims that there are around 50,000 ethnic Chinese in Cambodia. Informed observers say there are more likely to be as many as half a million to one million in urban areas. Many Chinese Cambodians have lived in Cambodia for generations and have adopted the Khmer culture, language and identity. Until 1975, ethnic Chinese controlled the economic life of Cambodia. In recent years the group has re-emerged as a powerful economic force, mainly due to increased investment by overseas Chinese.

THE POPULATION OF CAMBODIA

Cambodia's second postwar population census was carried out in 2008 and put the country's population at about 13.5 million. The current population is estimated at nearly 15 million and, with a rapid growth rate of about 2% per year, the population is predicted to reach 20 million by 2025.

Phnom Penh is the largest city, with a population of 1.5 million. Other major population centres include the boom towns of Siem Reap, Sihanoukville, Battambang and Poipet. The most populous province is Kompong Cham, where more than 10% of Cambodians live.

The much-discussed imbalance of men to women due to years of conflict is not as serious as it was in 1980, but it is still significant: there are about 95 males to every 100 females, up from 86.1 to 100 in 1980. There is, however, a marked imbalance in age groups: more than 40% of the population is under the age of 16.

Ethnic Cham

Cambodia's Cham Muslims (known locally as the Khmer Islam) officially number around 200,000. Unofficial counts put the figure higher at around 500,000. The Cham live in villages on the banks of the Mekong and Tonlé Sap Rivers, mostly in the provinces of Kompong Cham, Kompong Speu and Kompong Chhnang. They suffered vicious persecution between 1975 and 1979, when a large part of their community was targeted. Many Cham mosques that were destroyed under the Khmer Rouge have since been rebuilt.

Ethno-Linguistic Minorities

Cambodia's diverse Khmer Leu (Upper Khmer) or *chunchiet* (ethnic minorities), who live in the country's mountainous regions, probably number around 100,000.

The majority of these groups live in the northeast of Cambodia, in the provinces of Ratanakiri, Mondulkiri, Stung Treng and Kratie. The largest group is the Tompuon (many other spellings are also used), who number nearly 20,000. Other groups include the Bunong, Kreung, Kavet, Brau and Jarai.

The hill tribes of Cambodia have long been isolated from mainstream Khmer society, and there is little in the way of mutual understanding. They practise shifting cultivation, rarely staying in one place for long. Finding a new location for a village requires a village elder to mediate with the spirit world. Very few of the minorities retain the sort of colourful traditional costumes found in Thailand, Laos and Vietnam.

Religion

Buddhism

Buddhism arrived in Cambodia with Hinduism but only became the official religion from the 13th and 14th centuries. Most Cambodians today practise Theravada Buddhism. Between 1975 and 1979 many of Cambodia's Buddhist monks were murdered by the Khmer Rouge and nearly all of the country's wats (more than 3000) were damaged or destroyed. In the late 1980s, Buddhism once again became the state religion and today young monks are a common sight throughout the country. Many wats have been rebuilt or rehabilitated and money-raising drives for this work can be seen on roadsides across the country.

The ultimate goal of Theravada Buddhism is nirvana – 'extinction' of all desire and suffering to reach the final stage of reincarnation. By feeding monks, giving donations to temples and performing regular worship at the local wat, Buddhists hope to improve their lot, acquiring enough merit to reduce their number of rebirths.

Every Buddhist male is expected to become a monk for a short period in his life, optimally between the time he finishes school and starts a career or marries. Men or boys under 20 years of age may enter the *sangha* (monastic order) as novices. Nowadays men may spend as little as 15 days to accrue merit as monks.

Hinduism

Hinduism flourished alongside Buddhism from the 1st century AD until the 14th century. During the pre-Angkorian period, Hinduism was represented by the worship of Harihara (Shiva and Vishnu embodied in a single deity). During the time of Angkor, Shiva was the deity most in favour with the royal family, although in the 12th century he was superseded by Vishnu. Today some elements of Hinduism are still incorporated into important ceremonies involving birth, marriage and death.

Among Cambodia's 24 provinces, Kandal has the densest population, with more than 300 people per sq km; Mondulkiri has the sparsest population, with just four people per sq km.

THE CULTURE RELIGION

The Cambodian and Lao people share a close bond, as Fa Ngum, the founder of the original Lao kingdom of Lan Xang (Land of a Million Elephants), was sponsored by his Khmer father-in-law.

Lowland Khmers are being encouraged to migrate to Cambodia's northeast where there is plenty of available land. But this is home to the country's minority peoples, who have no indigenous concepts of property rights or land ownership, so this may see their culture marginalised in coming years.

KHMER KROM

The Khmer Krom people of southern Vietnam are ethnic Khmers separated from Cambodia by historical deals and Vietnamese encroachment on what was once Cambodian territory. Nobody is sure just how many of them there are and estimates vary from one million to seven million, depending on who is doing the counting.

The history of Vietnamese expansion into Khmer territory has long been a staple of Khmer textbooks. King Chey Chetha II of Cambodia, in keeping with the wishes of his Vietnamese queen, first allowed Vietnamese to settle in the Cambodian town of Prey Nokor in 1623. It was obviously the thin end of the wedge, as Prey Nokor is now better known as Ho Chi Minh City (Saigon).

The Vietnamese government has pursued a policy of forced assimilation since independence, which has involved ethnic Khmers taking Vietnamese names and studying in Vietnamese. According to the Khmer Kampuchea Federation (KKF), the Khmer Krom continue to suffer persecution, including lack of access to health services, religious discrimination and outright racism. Several monks have been defrocked for nonviolent protests in recent years and the Cambodian government has even assisted in deporting some agitators, according to Human Rights Watch.

Many Khmer Krom would like to see Cambodia act as a mediator in the quest for greater autonomy and ethnic representation in Vietnam. The Cambodian government, for its part, turns a blind eye to the vast numbers of illegal Vietnamese inside its borders, as well as reports of Vietnamese encroachments on the eastern borders of Cambodia. The Cambodian government takes a softly, softly approach towards its more powerful neighbour, perhaps borne of the historic ties between the two political dynasties.

For more about the ongoing struggles of the Khmer Krom, visit www.khmerkrom.org.

Animism

Both Hinduism and Buddhism were gradually absorbed from beyond the borders of Cambodia, fusing with the animist beliefs already present among the Khmers before Indianisation. Local beliefs didn't disappear but were incorporated into the new religions to form something uniquely Cambodian. The concept of Neak Ta has its foundations in animist beliefs regarding sacred soil and the sacred spirit around us. Neak Ta can be viewed as a mother-earth concept, an energy force uniting a community with its earth and water. It can be represented in many forms, from stone or wood to termite hills – anything that symbolises both a link between the people and the fertility of their land.

Look out for Chinese and Vietnamese cemeteries dotting the rice fields of provinces to the south and east of Phnom Penh. Khmers do not bury their dead, but practise cremation, and the ashes may be interred in a stupa in the grounds of a wat.

Islam

Cambodia's Muslims are descendants of Chams, who migrated from what is now central Vietnam after the final defeat of the kingdom of Champa by the Vietnamese in 1471. Like Buddhists in Cambodia, the Cham Muslims call the faithful to prayer by banging a drum, rather than with the call of the muezzin.

Christianity

Christianity made limited headway into Cambodia compared with neighbouring Vietnam. There were a number of churches in Cambodia before the war, but many of these were systematically destroyed by the Khmer Rouge, including Notre Dame Cathedral in Phnom Penh. Christianity made a comeback of sorts throughout the refugee camps on the Thai border in the 1980s, as a number of food-for-faith-type charities set up shop dispensing religion with every meal. Many Cambodians changed their public faith for survival, before converting back to Buddhism on their departure from the camps, earning the moniker 'rice Christians'.

The Arts

The Khmer Rouge's assault on the arts was a terrible blow to Cambodian culture. Indeed, for a number of years the consensus among Khmers was that their culture had been irrevocably lost. The Khmer Rouge not only did away with living bearers of Khmer culture but also destroyed cultural artefacts, statues, musical instruments, books and anything else that served as a reminder of a past it was trying to efface. The temples of Angkor were spared as a symbol of Khmer glory and empire, but little else survived. Despite this, Cambodia is witnessing a resurgence of traditional arts and a growing interest in experimentation in modern arts and cross-cultural fusion.

Architecture

Khmer architecture reached its peak during the Angkorian era (9th to 14th centuries). Some of the finest examples of architecture from this period are Angkor Wat and the structures of Angkor Thom. See p124 for more information on the architectural styles of the Angkorian era.

Today, most rural Cambodian houses are built on high wood pilings (if the family can afford it) and have thatched roofs, walls made of palm mats and floors of woven bamboo strips resting on bamboo joists. The shady space underneath is used for storage and for people to relax at midday. Wealthier families have houses with wooden walls and tiled roofs, but the basic design remains the same.

The French left their mark in Cambodia in the form of some handsome villas and government buildings built in neoclassical style, Romanesque pillars and all. Some of the best architectural examples are in Phnom Penh, but most of the provincial capitals have at least one or two examples of architecture from the colonial period. Battambang and Kampot are two of the best-preserved colonial-era towns, with handsome rows of shophouses and the classic governor's residences.

During the 1950s and 1960s, Cambodia's so-called golden era, a group of young Khmer architects shaped the capital of Cambodia in their own image, experimenting with what is now called New Khmer Architecture. Vann Molyvann was the most famous of this school of architecture, designing a number of prominent Phnom Penh landmarks such as the Olympic Stadium, the Chatomuk Theatre and Independence Monument. The beach resort of Kep was remodelled at this time, as the emergent Cambodian middle class flocked to the beach, and there are some fantastic if dilapidated examples of New Khmer Architecture around the small town. Boutique hotels Knai Bang Chatt and Villa Romonea in Kep are both restored examples from this period.

To discover examples of New Khmer Architecture, visit the website of **KA Architecture Tours** (www.ka-tours.org) or sign up for one of its walking tours of Phnom Penh or Battambang. The website includes downloadable printouts for DIY tours of each city.

Cinema

Back in the 1960s, the Cambodian film industry was booming. Between 1960 and 1975, more than 400 films were made, some of which were exported all around Asia, including numerous films by then head-of-state Norodom Sihanouk. However, the advent of Khmer Rouge rule saw the film industry disappear overnight and it was not to recover for more than quarter of a century.

The film industry in Cambodia was given a new lease of life in 2000 with the release of *Pos Keng Kong* (The Giant Snake). A remake of a 1960s Cambodian classic, it tells the story of a powerful young girl born from a rural relationship between a woman and a snake king. It is an interesting

THE CULTURE THE ARTS

ANIMISM

The purest form of animism is practised among the minority people known as Khmer Leu. Some have converted to Buddhism, but the majority continue to worship spirits of the earth and skies and the spirits of their forefathers.

Friends of Khmer Culture (www .khmerculture .net) is dedicated to supporting Khmer arts and cultural organisations, and Reyum (p77, www.reyum .org), an exhibition space in Phnom Penh, promotes Khmer arts and culture.

love story, albeit with dodgy special effects, and achieved massive box-office success around the region.

The success of *Pos Keng Kong* heralded a mini revival in the Cambodian film industry and local directors turn out several films a year. However, many of these are amateurish horror films of dubious artistic value.

TOP 10 TIPS TO EARN THE RESPECT OF THE LOCALS

Take your time to learn a little about the local culture in Cambodia. Not only will this ensure that you don't inadvertently cause offence, but it will also ingratiate you with your hosts. Here are a few top tips to help you go native.

Dress Code
Respect local dress standards, particularly at religious sites. Covering the upper arms and upper legs is appropriate, although some monks will be too polite to enforce this. Always remove shoes before entering a temple, as well as hats. Nude sunbathing is considered *totally* inappropriate, even on beaches.

Make a Contribution
Since most temples are maintained through donations, remember to make a contribution when visiting a temple. When visiting a Khmer home, a small token of gratitude in the form of a gift is always appreciated.

Meet & Greet
Learn the Cambodian greeting, the *sompiah* (see p301), and use it when introducing yourself to new friends. When beckoning someone over, always wave towards yourself with the palm down, as palm up with fingers raised can be suggestive, even offensive.

A Woman's Touch
Monks are not supposed to touch or be touched by women. If a woman wants to hand something to a monk, the object should be placed within reach of the monk or on the monk's 'receiving cloth'.

Keep Your Cool
No matter how high your blood pressure rises, do not raise your voice or show signs of aggression. This will lead to a 'loss of face' and cause embarrassment to the locals, ensuring the situation gets worse rather than better.

It's on the Cards
Exchanging business cards is an important part of even the smallest transaction or business contact in Cambodia. Get some printed before you arrive and hand them out like confetti. Always present them with two hands.

Deadly Chopsticks
Leaving a pair of chopsticks sitting vertically in a rice bowl looks very much like the incense sticks that are burned for the dead. This is a powerful sign and is not appreciated in Asia.

Mean Feet
Cambodians like to keep a clean house and it's usual to remove shoes when entering somebody's home. It's rude to point the bottom of your feet towards other people. Never, ever point your feet towards anything sacred, such as an image of Buddha.

Hats off to Them
As a form of respect to the elderly or other esteemed people, such as monks, take off your hat and bow your head politely when addressing them. Never pat or touch an adult on the head – in Asia, the head is considered the most sacred part of the body.

Toothpicks
While digging out those stubborn morsels from between your teeth, it is polite to use one hand to perform the extraction and the other hand to cover your mouth.

SPORT IN CAMBODIA

The national sport of Cambodia is *pradal serey* (Cambodian kickboxing). It's similar to kickboxing in Thailand (don't make the mistake of calling it Thai boxing over here, though) and there are regular weekend bouts on CTN and TV5. It's also possible to go to the TV arenas and watch the fights live.

Football is another national obsession, although the Cambodian team is a real minnow, even by Asian standards. Many Cambodians follow the Premier League in England religiously and regularly bet on games.

The French game of *pétanque*, also called *boules*, is also very popular here and the Cambodian team has won several medals in regional games.

At least one overseas Cambodian director has enjoyed major success in recent years: Rithy Panh's *People of the Rice Fields* was nominated for the Palme d'Or at the Cannes Film Festival in 1995. The film touches only fleetingly on the Khmer Rouge, depicting the lives of a family eking out an arduous existence in the rice fields. His other films include *One Night after the War* (1997), the story of a young Khmer kickboxer falling for a bar girl in Phnom Penh; and the award-winning *S-21: The Khmer Rouge Killing Machine* (2003), a powerful documentary in which survivors from Tuol Sleng are brought back to confront their guards.

The definitive film about Cambodia is *The Killing Fields* (1985), which tells the story of American journalist Sydney Schanberg and his Cambodian assistant Dith Pran. Most of the footage was actually shot in Thailand, as it was filmed in 1984 when Cambodia was effectively closed to the West.

Quite a number of international films have been shot in Cambodia in recent years, including *Tomb Raider* (2001), *City of Ghosts* (2002) and *Two Brothers* (2004), all worth seeking out for their beautiful Cambodian backdrops. Australian independent feature film *Wish You Were Here,* partly shot in Cambodia in 2011, was nominated for the Sundance Festival 2012.

For more on Cambodian films and cinema, pick up a copy of *Kon. The Cinema of Cambodia* (2010), published by the Department of Media and Communication at the Royal University of Cambodia.

To learn more about New Khmer Architecture pick up a copy of *Building Cambodia: New Khmer Architecture 1953-1970* by Helen Grant Ross and Darryl Collins.

Dance

More than any of the other traditional arts, Cambodia's royal ballet is a tangible link with the glory of Angkor. Its traditions stretch long into the past, when the art of the *apsara* (nymph) resounded to the glory of the divine king. Early in his reign, King Sihanouk released the traditional harem of royal *apsara* that went with the crown.

Dance fared particularly badly during the Pol Pot years. Very few dancers and teachers survived. In 1981, with a handful of teachers, the University of Fine Arts was reopened and the training of dance students resumed.

Much of Cambodian royal dance resembles that of India and Thailand (the same stylised hand movements, the same sequined, lamé costumes and the same opulent stupa-like headwear), as the Thais incorporated techniques from the Khmers after sacking Angkor in the 15th century. Although royal dance was traditionally an all-female affair (with the exception of the role of the monkey), more male dancers are now featured. Known as *robam preah reachtrop* in Khmer, the most popular classical dances are the Apsara dance and the Wishing dance.

Folk dance is another popular element of dance performances that are regularly staged for visitors in Phnom Penh and Siem Reap. Folk dances draw on rural lifestyle and cultural traditions for their inspiration. One

The first major international feature film to be shot in Cambodia was *Lord Jim* (1964), starring Peter O'Toole.

of the most popular folk dances is *robam kom arek,* involving bamboo poles and some nimble footwork. Also popular are fishing and harvest-themed dances that include plenty of flirtatious interaction between male and female performers.

Other celebrated dances are only performed at certain festivals or at certain times of year. The *trot* is very popular at Khmer New Year to ward off evil spirits from the home or business. A dancer in a deer costume runs through the property pursued by a hunter and is eventually slain.

Chinese New Year (Tet to the Vietnamese in Cambodia) sees elaborate dragon dances performed all over Phnom Penh and other major cities in Cambodia.

Contemporary dances include the popular *rom vong* or circle dance, which is likely to have originated in neighbouring Laos. Dancers move around in a circle taking three steps forward and two steps back. Hip hop and break-dancing is fast gaining popularity among urban young-sters and is regularly performed at outdoor events.

Music

The bas-reliefs on some of the monuments in the Angkor region depict musicians and *apsara* holding instruments similar to the traditional Khmer instruments of today, demonstrating that Cambodia has a long musical tradition all of its own.

Customarily, music was an accompaniment to a ritual or performance that had religious significance. Musicologists have identified six types of Cambodian musical ensemble, each used in different settings. The most traditional of these is the *arek ka,* an ensemble that performs at weddings. The instruments of the *arek ka* include a *tro khmae* (three-stringed fiddle), a *khsae muoy* (single-stringed bowed instrument) and *skor areak* (drums), among others. *Ahpea pipea* is another type of wedding music that accompanies the witnessing of the marriage and *pin peat* is the music that is heard at ballet performances and shadow-puppet displays.

Much of Cambodia's golden-era music from the pre-war period was lost during the Pol Pot years. The Khmer Rouge targeted famous singers, and the great Sinn Sisamouth and female divas Ros Sereysothea and Pen Ron, Cambodia's most famous songwriters and performers, all disappeared in the early days of the regime.

After the war, many Khmers settled in the USA, where a lively Khmer pop industry developed. Influenced by US music and later exported back to Cambodia, it has been enormously popular.

A new generation of overseas Khmers growing up with influences from the West is producing its own sound. Cambodians are now returning to the homeland raised on a diet of rap in the US or France, and lots of new artists are breaking through, such as the ClapYaHandz collective started by Sok 'Cream' Visal.

There's also a burgeoning pop industry, many of whose stars perform at outdoor concerts in Phnom Penh. It's easy to join in the fun by visiting one of the innumerable karaoke bars around the country. Preap Sovath is the Robbie Williams of Cambodia and, if you flick through the Cambodian channels for more than five minutes, chances are he will be performing. Aok Sokun Kanha is one of the more popular young female singers, with a big voice, but it's a changeling industry and new stars are waiting in the wings.

Dengue Fever is the ultimate fusion band, rapidly gaining a name for itself beyond the USA and Cambodia. Cambodian singer Chhom Nimol fronts five American prog rockers who dabble in psychedelic sounds. Another fusion band fast gaining a name for itself is the Cambodian Space Project, comprising a mix of Cambodians and expats. They regularly play in Phnom Penh and are well worth catching if you happen to be in town.

The famous Hindu epic the *Ramayana* is known as the *Reamker* in Cambodia; Reyum Publishing has issued a beautifully illustrated book telling the story: *The Reamker* (1999).

Rithy Panh's 1996 film *Bophana* tells the true story of Hout Bophana, a beautiful young woman, and Ly Sitha, a regional Khmer Rouge leader, who fall in love and are executed for their 'crime'.

Amrita Performing Arts (www .amritaperform ingarts.org) has worked on a number of ground-breaking dance and theatre projects in Cambodia, including collaborations with French and Japanese performers.

One form of music unique to Cambodia is *chapaye,* a sort of Cambodian blues sung to the accompaniment of a two-stringed wooden instrument similar in sound to a bass guitar played without an amplifier. There are few old masters, such as Kong Nay (the Ray Charles of Cambodia), left alive, but *chapaye* is still often shown on late-night Cambodian TV before transmission ends. Kong Nay has toured internationally in countries such as Australia and the US, and has even appeared with Peter Gabriel at the WOMAD music festival in the UK.

For more on Cambodian music, pick up a copy of *Dontrey: The Music of Cambodia* (2011), published by the Department of Media and Communication at the Royal University of Cambodia.

Sculpture

The Khmer empire of the Angkor period produced some of the most exquisite carved sculptures found anywhere on earth. Even in the pre-Angkorian era, the periods generally referred to as Funan and Chenla, the people of Cambodia were producing masterfully sensuous sculpture that was more than just a copy of the Indian forms on which it was modelled. Some scholars maintain that the Cambodian forms are unrivalled, even in India itself.

The earliest surviving Cambodian sculpture dates from the 6th century AD. Most of it depicts Vishnu with four or eight arms. A large eight-armed Vishnu from this period is displayed at the National Museum in Phnom Penh.

Also on display at the National Museum is a statue of Harihara from the end of the 7th century, a divinity who combines aspects of both Vishnu and Shiva but looks more than a little Egyptian with his pencil moustache and long, thin nose – a reminder that Indian sculpture drew from the Greeks, who in turn were influenced by the Pharaohs.

Innovations of the early Angkorian era include freestanding sculpture that dispenses with the stone aureole that in earlier works supported the multiple arms of Hindu deities. The faces assume an air of tranquillity, and the overall effect is less animated.

The Banteay Srei style of the late 10th century is commonly regarded as a high point in the evolution of southeast Asian art. The National Museum has a splendid piece from this period: a sandstone statue of Shiva holding Uma, his wife, on his knee. Sadly, Uma's head was stolen some time during Cambodia's turbulent years. The Baphuon style of the 11th

---

Cambodia's great musical tradition was almost lost during the Khmer Rouge years, but the Cambodian Master Performers Program is dedicated to reviving the country's musical tradition. Visit its website at www .cambodian masters.org.

One of the greatest '70s legends to seek out is Nuon Sarath, the Jimi Hendrix of Cambodia, with his screaming vocals and wah-wah pedals. His most famous song, 'Chi Cyclo', is an absolute classic.

THE CULTURE THE ARTS

SIHANOUK & THE SILVER SCREEN

Between 1965 and 1969 Sihanouk (former king and head of state of Cambodia) wrote, directed and produced nine feature films, a figure that would put the average workaholic Hollywood director to shame. Sihanouk took the business of making films very seriously, and family and officials were called upon to play their part: the minister of foreign affairs acted as the male lead in Sihanouk's first feature, *Apsara* (1965), and his daughter Princess Bopha Devi, the female lead. When, in the same movie, a show of military hardware was required, the air force was brought into action, as was the army's fleet of helicopters.

Sihanouk often took on the leading role himself. Notable performances saw him as a spirit of the forest and as a victorious general. Perhaps it was no surprise, given the king's apparent addiction to the world of celluloid dreams, that Cambodia should challenge Cannes with its Phnom Penh International Film Festival. The festival was held twice, in 1968 and 1969. Perhaps unsurprisingly, Sihanouk won the grand prize on both occasions. He continued to make movies in later life and it is believed he has made around 30 films during his remarkable career. For more on the films of Sihanouk, visit the website www .norodomsihanouk.org.

century was inspired to a certain extent by the sculpture of Banteay Srei, producing some of the finest works to have survived today.

The statuary of the Angkor Wat period is felt to be conservative and stilted, lacking the grace of earlier work. The genius of this period manifests itself more clearly in the immense architecture and incredible bas-reliefs of Angkor Wat itself.

The final high point in Angkorian sculpture is the Bayon period from the end of the 12th century to the beginning of the 13th century. In the National Museum, look for the superb representation of Jayavarman VII, an image that projects both great power and sublime tranquillity.

As the state religion swung back and forth between Mahayana Buddhism and Hinduism during the turbulent 13th and 14th centuries, Buddha images and Bodhisattvas were carved only to be hacked out by militant Hindus on their return to power. By the 15th century stone was generally replaced by wood and polychrome as the material of choice for Buddha statues. A beautiful gallery of post-16th century Buddhas from around Angkor is on display in the National Museum.

Cambodian sculptors are rediscovering their skills now that there is a ready market among visitors for reproduction stone carvings of famous statues and busts from the time of Angkor.

Check out www.tinytoones.org for more on a hip-hop cooperative seeking to empower the youth of Cambodia to a healthier lifestyle free of drugs and exposure to HIV. Keep an eye out for their performances around Phnom Penh.

Food & Drink

It's no secret that the dining tables of Thailand and Vietnam are home to some of the finest food in the world, so it should come as no surprise to discover that Cambodian cuisine is also rather special. Unlike the culinary colossuses that are its neighbours, Cambodia is not that well known in international food circles, but all that looks set to change. Just as Angkor has put Cambodia on the tourist map, so too *amok* (baked fish with lemongrass-based *kreung* paste, coconut and chilli in banana leaf) could put the country on the culinary map.

Cambodia has a great variety of national dishes, some similar to the cuisine of neighbouring Thailand and Laos, others closer to Chinese and Vietnamese cooking, but all come with a unique Cambodian twist.

Freshwater fish forms a huge part of the Cambodian diet thanks to the natural phenomenon that is Tonlé Sap lake. The fish come in every shape and size, from the giant Mekong catfish to teeny-tiny whitebait, which are great beer snacks when deep-fried. The French left their mark, too, with baguettes becoming the national bread and Cambodian cooks showing a healthy reverence for tender meats.

Cambodia is a crossroads in Asia, the meeting point of the great civilisations of India and China, and, just as its culture has drawn on both, so too has its cuisine. Whether it is spring rolls or curry that takes your fancy, you will find it in Cambodian cooking. Add to this a world of dips and sauces to complement the cooking and a culinary journey through Cambodia becomes as rich a feast as any in Asia.

Staples & Specialities

No matter what part of the world you come from, if you travel much in Cambodia, you are going to encounter food that is unusual, strange, maybe even immoral, or just plain weird. The fiercely omnivorous Cambodians find nothing strange in eating insects, algae, offal or fish bladders. They will dine on a duck foetus, brew up some brains or snack on some spiders. They will peel live frogs to grill on a barbecue or down wine infused with snake to increase their virility.

To the Khmers there is nothing 'strange' about anything that will sustain the body. To them a food is either wholesome or it isn't; it's nutritious or it isn't; it tastes good or it doesn't. And that's all they worry about. They'll try anything once, even a burger.

As well as eating the notorious tarantulas of Skuon (p250), Cambodians also like to eat crickets, beetles, larvae and ants. Some scientists have suggested insect farms as a way to solve food problems of the future. For once, Cambodia may be ahead of the curve.

COOKING COURSES

If you are really taken with Cambodian cuisine, it is possible to learn some tricks of the trade by signing up for a cooking course. It's a great way to introduce your Cambodian experience to your friends; no one wants to sit through the slide show of photos, but offer them a mouth-watering meal and they will all come running.

There are courses available in Phnom Penh, Siem Reap, Battambang and Sihanoukville, and more are popping up all the time.

Rice, Fish & Soup

Cambodia's abundant waterways provide the fish that is fermented into *prahoc* (fermented fish paste), which forms the backbone of Khmer cuisine. Built around this are the flavours that give the cuisine its kick: the secret roots, the welcome herbs and the aromatic tubers. Together they give the salads, snacks, soups and stews a special aroma and taste that smacks of Cambodia.

Rice from Cambodia's lush fields is the principal staple, enshrined in the Khmer word for 'eating' or 'to eat', *nam bai* – literally 'eat rice'. Many a Cambodian, particularly drivers, will run out of steam if they run out of rice. It doesn't matter that the same carbohydrates are available in other foods, it is rice and rice alone that counts. Battambang Province is Cambodia's rice bowl and produces the country's finest yield.

For the taste of Cambodia in a bowl, try the local *kyteow,* a rice-noodle soup that will keep you going all day. This full, balanced meal will cost you just 5000r in markets and about US$2 in local restaurants. Don't like noodles? Then try the *bobor* (rice porridge), a national institution, for breakfast, lunch and dinner, and best sampled with some fresh fish and a splash of ginger.

A Cambodian meal almost always includes a *samlor* (traditional soup), which will appear at the same time as the other courses. *Samlor machou bunlay* (hot and sour fish soup with pineapple and spices) is popular.

Much of the fish eaten in Cambodia is freshwater, from the Tonlé Sap lake or the Mekong River. *Trey ahng* (grilled fish) is a Cambodian speciality (*ahng* means 'grilled' and can be applied to many dishes). Traditionally, the fish is eaten as pieces wrapped in lettuce or spinach leaves and then dipped into *teuk trey,* a fish sauce that is a close relative to Vietnam's *nuoc mam,* but with the addition of ground peanuts.

Teuk trey (fish sauce), one of the most popular condiments in Cambodian cooking, cannot be taken on international flights, in line with regulations on carrying strong-smelling or corrosive substances.

Salads

Cambodian salad dishes are popular and delicious, although they're quite different from the Western idea of a cold salad. *Phlea sait kow* is a beef and vegetable salad, flavoured with coriander, mint and lemongrass. These three herbs find their way into many Cambodian dishes.

Desserts & Fruit

Desserts can be sampled cheaply at night markets around the country. One sweet snack to look out for is the ice-cream sandwich. Popular with the kids, it involves putting a slab of homemade ice cream into a piece of sponge or bread.

Cambodia is blessed with many tropical fruits and sampling these is an integral part of a visit to the country. All the common fruits can be found in abundance, including *chek* (banana)*, menoa* (pineapple) and *duong* (coconut). Among the larger fruit, *khnau* (jackfruit) is very common, often weighing more than 20kg. The *tourain* (durian) usually needs no introduction, as you can smell it from a mile off; the exterior is green with sharp spines, while inside is a milky, soft interior regarded by

A popular food blog on Cambodia can be found at www.phnomenon.com, which covers Khmer food, surfing the streets and the up-and-coming dining scene. It's dated, but the archives are a treasure trove. For a more up-to-date food blog, check out Nyam Penh at nyampenh.com.

WE DARE YOU: TOP FIVE

» Crickets – anyone for cricket?

» Duck foetus – unborn duck, feathers and all.

» Durian – nasally obnoxious spiky fruit, banned on flights.

» *Prahoc* – fermented fish paste, almost a biological weapon.

» Spiders – just like it sounds, deep-fried tarantulas.

---

the Chinese as an aphrodisiac. It stinks, although some maintain it is an acquired taste...best acquired with a nose peg.

The fruits most popular with visitors include the *mongkut* (mangosteen) and *sao mao* (rambutan). The small mangosteen has a purple skin that contains white segments with a divine flavour. Similarly popular is the rambutan, with an interior like a lychee and an exterior covered in soft red and green spines.

Best of all, although common throughout the world, is the *svay* (mango). The Cambodian mango season is from March to May. Other varieties of mango are available year round, but it's the hot-season ones that are a taste sensation.

Drinks

Cambodia has a lively local drinking culture, and the heat and humidity will ensure that you hunt out anything on offer to quench your thirst. Coffee, tea, beer, wine, soft drinks, fresh fruit juices and some of the more exotic 'fire waters' are all widely available. Tea is the national drink, but these days it is just as likely to be beer in the glass.

Beer

It's never a challenge to find a beer in Cambodia and even the most remote village usually has a stall selling a few cans. Angkor is the national beer, produced in vast quantities in a big brewery down in Sihanoukville. It costs around US$2 to US$3 for a 660mL bottle in most restaurants and bars. Draught Angkor is available for around US$0.50 to US$1.50 in the main tourist centres. Other popular local brands include Kingdom Beer, newcomer Cambodia Beer and provincial favourite Crown Lager.

A beer brand from neighbouring Laos, Beerlao, is very drinkable and is also one of the cheapest ales available. Tiger Beer is produced locally and is a popular draught in the capital. Some Khmer restaurants have a bevy of 'beer girls', each promoting a particular beer brand. They are always friendly and will leave you alone if you prefer not to drink.

A word of caution for beer seekers in Cambodia: while the country is awash with good brews, there's a shortage of refrigeration in the countryside. Go native and learn how to say, '*Som teuk koh*' (Ice, please).

Wine & Spirits

Local wine in Cambodia generally means rice wine, it is popular with the minority peoples of the northeast. Some rice wines are fermented for months and are super strong, while other brews are fresher and taste more like a demented cocktail. Either way, if you are invited to join a session in a minority village, it's rude to decline. Other local wines include light sugar-palm wine and ginger wine.

In Phnom Penh and Siem Reap, foreign wines and spirits are sold in supermarkets at bargain prices, given how far they have to travel. Wines from Europe and Australia start at about US$5, while the famous names of the spirit world cost between US$5 and US$15.

Some Cambodian nightclubs allow guests to rent premium bottles of spirits, like Johnnie Walker Blue Label, to display on the table – a way of maintaining face despite the fact it's actually Johnnie Walker Red Label in the glass.

The local brew for country folk is sugar-palm wine, distilled daily direct from the trees and fairly potent after it has settled. Sold in bamboo containers off the back of bicycles, it's tasty and cheap, although only suitable for those with a cast-iron stomach.

BOTTOMS UP

When Cambodians propose a toast, they usually stipulate what percentage must be downed. If they are feeling generous, it might be just *ha-sip pea-roi* (50%), but more often than not it is *moi roi pea-roi* (100%). This is why they love ice in their beer, as they can pace themselves over the course of the night. Many a *barang* (foreigner) has ended up face down on the table at a Cambodian wedding when trying to outdrink the Khmer boys without the aid of ice.

FOOD GLOSSARY

Breakfast

bread	nohm paang	នំប៉័ង
butter	bœ	ប័រ
fried eggs	pohng moan chien	ពងមាន់ចៀន
rice porridge	bobor	បបរ
vegetable noodle soup	kyteow dak buhn lai	គុយទាវដាក់បន្លែ

Lunch & Dinner

beef	sait kow	សាច់គោ
chicken	sait moan	សាច់មាន់
crab	k'daam	ក្តាម
curry	karii	ការី
eel	ahntohng	អន្ទង់
fish	trey	ត្រី
fried	chien, chaa	ចៀន. ឆា
frog	kawng kaip	កង្កែប
grilled	ahng	អាំង
lobster	bawng kawng	បង្កង
noodles	mii (egg)	មី
	kyteow (rice)	គុយទាវ
pork	sait ch'ruuk	សាច់ជ្រូក
rice	bai	បាយ
shrimp	bawngkia	បង្គា
snail	kh'chawng	ខ្យង
soup	sup	ស៊ុប
spring rolls	naim (fresh)	ណែម
	chaa yaw (fried)	ឆាយ៉
squid	meuk	មឹក
steamed	chamhoi	ចំហុយ
vegetables	buhnlai	បន្លែ

Fruit

apple	phla i powm	ផ្លែប៉ោម
banana	chek	ចេក
coconut	duong	ដូង
custard apple	tiep	ទៀប
dragon fruit	phlai srakaa neak	ផ្លែស្រកានាគ
durian	tourain	ធូរេន
grapes	tompeang baai chuu	ទំពាំងបាជូរ
guava	trawbaik	ត្របែក

jackfruit	*khnau*	ខ្នុរ
lemon	*krow-it ch'maa*	ក្រូចឆ្មារ
longan	*mien*	មៀន
lychee	*phlai kuulain*	ផ្លែគុលែន
mandarin	*krow-it khwait*	ក្រូចខ្វិច
mango	*svay*	ស្វាយ
mangosteen	*mongkut*	មង្ឃុត
orange	*krow-it pow saat*	ក្រូចពោធិសាត
papaya	*l'howng*	ល្ហុង
pineapple	*menoa*	ម្នាស់
pomelo	*krow-it th'lohng*	ក្រូចថ្លុង
rambutan	*sao mao*	សាវម៉ាវ
star fruit (carambola)	*speu*	ស្ពឺ
watermelon	*euv luhk*	ឳឡឹក

Condiments

chilli	*m'teh*	ម្ទេស
fish sauce	*teuk trey*	ទឹកត្រី
garlic	*kh'tuhm saw*	ខ្ទឹមស
ginger	*kh'nyei*	ខ្ញី
ice	*teuk koh*	ទឹកកក
lemon grass	*sluhk kray*	ស្លឹកគ្រៃ
pepper	*m'rait*	ម្រេច
salt	*uhmbuhl*	អំបិល
soy sauce	*teuk sii iw*	ទឹកស៊ីអ៊ីវ
sugar	*skaw*	ស្ករ

Drinks

banana shake	*teuk kralohk*	ទឹកក្រឡុកចេក
beer	*bii-yœ*	បៀរ
black coffee	*kaa fey kh'mav*	កាហ្វេខ្មៅ
coffee	*kaa fey*	កាហ្វេ
iced coffee	*kaa fey teuk koh*	កាហ្វេទឹកកក
lemon juice	*teuk krow-it ch'maa*	ទឹកក្រូចឆ្មារ
mixed fruit shake	*teuk kralohk chek*	ទឹកក្រឡុកផ្លែឈើ
orange juice	*teuk krow-it pow sat*	ទឹកក្រូចពោធិសាត
tea	*tai*	តែ
tea with milk	*tai teuk dawh kow*	តែទឹកដោះគោ
water	*teuk*	ទឹក
white coffee	*kaa fey ohlay (ie café au lait)*	កាហ្វេអូលេ

Tea & Coffee

Chinese-style *tai* (tea) is a bit of a national institution, and in most Khmer and Chinese restaurants a pot will automatically appear for no extra charge as soon as you sit down. *Kaa fey* (coffee) is sold in most restaurants. It is either black or *café au lait,* served with dollops of condensed milk.

Water & Soft Drinks

Drinking tap water *must* be avoided, especially in the provinces, as it is rarely purified and may lead to stomach complications. Locally produced mineral water starts at 1000r per bottle at shops and stalls.

Although tap water should be avoided, it is generally OK to have ice in your drinks. Throughout Cambodia, *teuk koh* (ice) is produced with treated water at local ice factories, a legacy of the French.

All the well-known soft drinks are available in Cambodia. Bottled drinks are about 1000r, while canned drinks cost about 2000r, more again in restaurants or bars.

Teuk kalohk are popular throughout Cambodia. They are a little like fruit smoothies and are a great way to wash down a meal.

Dining Out

Whatever your taste, some eatery in Cambodia is sure to help out, be it the humble peddler, a market stall, a local diner or a slick restaurant.

It is easy to sample inexpensive Khmer cuisine throughout the country, mostly at local markets and cheap restaurants. For more refined Khmer dining, the best restaurants are in Phnom Penh and Siem Reap, where there is also the choice of excellent Thai, Vietnamese, Chinese, Indian, French and Mediterranean cooking. Chinese and Vietnamese food is available in towns across the country due to the large urban populations of both of these ethnic groups.

There are few Western fast-food chains in Phnom Penh as yet, with the exception of KFC, but there are a few local copycats. The most successful has been Lucky Burger, with lots of branches in the capital.

There are often no set hours for places to eat but, as a general rule of thumb, street stalls are open from very early in the morning until early evening, although some stalls specialise in the night shift. Most restaurants are open all day, while some of the fancier places are only open for lunch (usually 11am to 2.30pm) and dinner (usually 5pm to 10pm).

Friends (see the box, p63) is one of the best-known restaurants in Phnom Penh, turning out a fine array of tapas, shakes and specials to help street children in the capital. Its cookbook *The Best of Friends* is a visual feast showcasing its best recipes.

TOP FIVE REGIONAL RESTAURANTS HELPING CAMBODIA

There are lots of NGOs attempting to assist Cambodia as it walks the road to recovery. Some of these have established restaurants and eateries to raise funds and give young, disadvantaged Cambodians some experience in the hospitality sector. There are also several recommended restaurants in Phnom Penh (p63) and Siem Reap (p103) supporting good causes.

Epic Arts Café (p192) A lively little cafe in Kampot assisting the deaf community and promoting arts education for the disabled.

Fresh Eats Café (p217) A cosy place in Battambang that helps children from families affected by HIV/AIDS.

Gelato Italiano (p183) A modern *gelateria* staffed by students from Sihanoukville's Don Bosco Hotel School.

Smile Restaurant (p247) A non-profit restaurant in Kompong Cham; has big breakfasts, a healthy menu and free wi-fi.

Starfish Bakery & Café (p183) A homely cafe in Sihanoukville offering delectable cakes and light lunches, with all proceeds going to community projects.

Street Snacks

Street food is an important part of everyday Cambodian life. Like many southeast Asians, Cambodians are inveterate snackers. They can be found at impromptu stalls at any time of the day or night, delving into a range of unidentified frying objects. Drop into the markets for an even greater range of dishes and the chance of a comfortable seat. It's a cheap, cheerful and cool way to get up close and personal with Khmer cuisine.

In the Cambodian Kitchen

Enter the Cambodian kitchen and you will learn that fine food comes from simplicity. Essentials consist of a strong flame, clean water, basic cutting utensils, a mortar and pestle, and a well-blackened pot or two.

Cambodians eat three meals a day. Breakfast is either *kyteow* or *bobor*. Baguettes are available at any time of day or night, and go down well with a cup of coffee.

Lunch starts early, around 11am. Traditionally, lunch is taken with the family, but in towns and cities many workers now eat at local restaurants or markets.

Dinner is the time for family bonding. Dishes are arranged around the central rice bowl and diners each have a small eating bowl. The procedure is uncomplicated: spoon some rice into your bowl, and lay 'something else' on top of it.

When ordering multiple courses from a restaurant menu, don't worry – don't even think – about the proper succession of courses. All dishes are placed in the centre of the table as soon as they are ready. Diners then help themselves to whatever appeals to them, regardless of who ordered what.

Dining Out with Kids

Both Phnom Penh and Siem Reap have child-friendly eateries. Check out Le Jardin (p67) or Living Room (p67) in Phnom Penh, or Kanell (p106) or Tangram Garden (p106) in Siem Reap, and sit back and relax. Some of the fast-food places in the capital also have children's playgrounds.

Table Etiquette

Sit at the table with your bowl on a small plate, chopsticks or fork and spoon at the ready. Some Cambodians prefer chopsticks, some prefer fork and spoon, but both are usually available. Each place setting will include a small bowl, usually located at the top right-hand side for the dipping sauces.

When serving yourself from the central bowls, use the communal serving spoon so as not to dip your chopsticks or spoon into the food. To begin eating, just pick up your bowl with your left hand, bring it close to your mouth, and spoon in the rice and food.

Some dos and don'ts:
» *Do* wait for your host to sit first.
» *Don't* turn down food placed in your bowl by your host.
» *Do* learn to use chopsticks.
» *Don't* leave chopsticks in a V-shape in the bowl, a symbol of death.
» *Do* tip about 5% to 10% in restaurants, as wages are low.
» *Don't* tip if there is already a service charge on the bill.
» *Do* drink every time someone offers a toast.
» *Don't* pass out face down on the table if the toasting goes on all night.

Vegetarians & Vegans

Few Cambodians understand the concept of strict vegetarianism and many will say something is vegetarian to please the customer when in

Before it become a member of the WTO, copyright protection was almost unknown in Cambodia. During that period there were a host of copycat fast-food restaurants, including Khmer Fried Chicken, Pizza Hot and Burger Queen, all now sadly defunct.

One of the most popular street snacks in Cambodia is the unborn duck foetus. The white duck eggs contain a little duckling, feathers and all. Don't order *kaun pong tier* if you want to avoid this.

FOOD & DRINK IN THE CAMBODIAN KITCHEN

DUCK FOETUS

For the scoop on countryside cooking in Cambodia, pick up *From Spiders to Waterlilies* (2009), a cookbook produced by Romdeng restaurant (p64) in Phnom Penh.

fact it is not. If you are not a strict vegetarian and can deal with fish sauces and the like, you should have few problems ordering meals, and those who eat fish can sample Khmer cooking at its best. In the major tourist centres, many of the international restaurants feature vegetarian meals, although these are not budget options. In Khmer and Chinese restaurants, stir-fried vegetable dishes are readily available, as are vegetarian fried-rice dishes, but it is unlikely these 'vegetarian' dishes have been cooked in separate woks from other fish- and meat-based dishes. Indian restaurants in the popular tourist centres can cook up genuine vegetarian food, as they usually understand the vegetarian principle better than the *prahoc*-loving Khmers.

Environment

The Land

Cambodia's borders as we know them today are the result of a classic historical squeeze. As the Vietnamese moved south into the Mekong Delta and the Thais pushed west towards Angkor, Cambodia's territory – which in Angkorian times stretched from southern Burma to Saigon and beyond – began to shrink. Only the arrival of the French prevented Cambodia from going the way of the Chams, who became a people without a state. In that sense, French colonialism created a protectorate that actually protected.

Modern day Cambodia covers 181,035 sq km, making it a little more than half the size of Vietnam or about the same size as the US state of Washington, or England and Wales combined. To the west and northwest it borders Thailand, to the northeast Laos, to the east Vietnam, and to the south is the Gulf of Thailand.

Cambodia's two dominant geographical features are the mighty Mekong River and a vast lake, the Tonlé Sap: see p320 for more on this natural miracle. At Phnom Penh the Mekong splits into three channels: the Tonlé Sap River, which flows into, and out of, the Tonlé Sap lake; the Upper River (usually called simply the Mekong or, in Vietnamese, Tien Giang); and the Lower River (the Tonlé Bassac, or Hau Giang in Vietnamese). The rich sediment deposited during the Mekong's annual wet-season flooding has made central Cambodia incredibly fertile. This low lying alluvial plain is where the vast majority of Cambodians live, fishing and farming in harmony with the rhythms of the monsoon.

In Cambodia's southwest quadrant, much of the landmass is covered by mountains: the Cardamom Mountains (Chuor Phnom Kravanh), covering parts of the provinces of Koh Kong, Battambang, Pursat and Krong Pailin, which are now opening up to ecotourism; and, southeast of there, the Elephant Mountains (Chuor Phnom Damrei), situated in the provinces of Kompong Speu, Koh Kong and Kampot.

Cambodia's 435km coastline is a big draw for visitors on the lookout for isolated tropical beaches. There are islands aplenty off the coast of Sihanoukville, Kep and Koh Kong.

Along Cambodia's northern border with Thailand, the plains collide with a striking sandstone escarpment more than 300km long that towers up to 550m above the lowlands: the Dangkrek Mountains (Chuor Phnom Dangkrek). One of the best places to get a sense of this area is Prasat Preah Vihear.

In the northeastern corner of the country, the plains give way to the Eastern Highlands, a remote region of densely forested mountains that extends east into Vietnam's Central Highlands and north into Laos. The wild provinces of Ratanakiri and Mondulkiri provide a home for many minority (hill-tribe) peoples and are taking off as an ecotourism hot spot.

The Tonlé Sap provides a huge percentage of Cambodians' protein intake, 70% of which comes from fish. The volume of water in the Tonlé Sap can expand by up to a factor of 70 during the wet season.

Cambodia's highest mountain, at 1813m, is Phnom Aural in Pursat Province.

Wildlife

Cambodia's forest ecosystems were in excellent shape until the 1990s and, compared with its neighbours, its habitats are still relatively healthy. The years of war took their toll on some species, but others thrived in the remote jungles of the southwest and northeast. Ironically, peace brought increased threats as loggers felled huge areas of primary forest and the illicit trade in wildlife targeted endangered species. Due to years of inaccessibility, scientists are only just beginning to research and catalogue the country's plant and animal life.

Animals

Cambodia is home to an estimated 212 species of mammal, including tigers, elephants, bears, leopards and wild oxen. Some of the biggest characters, however, are the smaller creatures, including the binturong (nicknamed the bear cat), the pileated gibbon (the world's largest population lives in the Cardamoms) and the slow loris, which hangs out in trees all day. The country also has a great variety of butterflies.

Most of Cambodia's fauna is extremely hard to get a look at in the wild. The easiest way to see a healthy selection is to visit the Phnom Tamao Wildlife Rescue Centre near Phnom Penh, which provides a home for rescued animals and includes all the major species.

A whopping 720 bird species find Cambodia a congenial home, thanks in large part to its year-round water resources. Relatively common birds include ducks, rails, cranes, herons, egrets, cormorants, pelicans, storks and parakeets, with migratory shorebirds, such as waders, plovers and terns, around the South Coast estuaries. Serious twitchers should consider a visit to Prek Toal Bird Sanctuary; Ang Trapeng Thmor Reserve, home to the extremely rare sarus crane, depicted on the bas-reliefs at Angkor; or the Tmatboey Ibis Project, where the critically endangered giant ibis, Cambodia's national bird, can be seen. For details on birdwatching in Cambodia, check out the Siem Reap–based Sam Veasna Center (see p24).

Snake bites are responsible for more amputations in Cambodia than landmines these days. Many villagers go to the medicine man for treatment and end up with infection, gangrene and/or a funeral.

TONLÉ SAP: HEARTBEAT OF CAMBODIA

The Tonlé Sap, the largest freshwater lake in southeast Asia, is an incredible natural phenomenon that provides fish and irrigation waters for half the population of Cambodia. It is also home to 90,000 people, many of them ethnic Vietnamese, who live in 170 floating villages.

Linking the lake with the Mekong at Phnom Penh is a 100km-long channel known as the Tonlé Sap River. From June to early October, wet-season rains rapidly raise the level of the Mekong, backing up the Tonlé Sap River and causing it to flow northwestward into the Tonlé Sap lake. During this period, the lake surface increases in size by a factor of four or five, from 2500 sq km to 3000 sq km up to 10,000 sq km to 16,000 sq km, and its depth increases from an average of about 2m to more than 10m. An unbelievable 20% of the Mekong's wet-season flow is absorbed by the Tonlé Sap. In October, as the water level of the Mekong begins to fall, the Tonlé Sap River reverses direction, draining the waters of the lake back into the Mekong.

This extraordinary process makes the Tonlé Sap an ideal habitat for birds, snakes and turtles, as well as one of the world's richest sources of freshwater fish: the flooded forests make for fertile spawning grounds, while the dry season creates ideal conditions for fishing. Experts believe that fish migrations from the lake help to restock fisheries as far north as China.

This unique ecosystem was declared a Unesco Biosphere Reserve in 2001, but this may not be enough to protect it from the twin threats of upstream dams (see p323) and rampant deforestation.

You can learn more about the Tonlé Sap and its unique ecosystem at the Gecko Centre (p116) near Siem Reap.

Cambodia is home to about 240 species of reptile, including nine species of snake whose venom can be fatal, such as members of the cobra and viper families. The Sihanoukville NGO Hand of Help produces antivenins.

Endangered Species

Unfortunately, it is getting mighty close to checkout time for a number of species in Cambodia. The kouprey (wild ox), declared Cambodia's national animal by King Sihanouk back in the 1960s, and the Wroughton's free-tailed bat, previously thought to exist in only one part of India but recently discovered in Preah Vihear Province, are on the 'Globally Threatened: Critical' list, the last stop before extinction.

Other animals under serious threat in Cambodia include the Asian elephant, tiger, banteng, gaur, Asian golden cat, black gibbon, clouded leopard, fishing cat, marbled cat, sun bear, pangolin (see the box, p164), giant ibis and Siamese crocodile (see the box, p167).

Cambodia has some of the last remaining freshwater Irrawaddy dolphins (*trey pisaut* in Khmer), instantly identifiable thanks to their bulging forehead and short beak. Viewing them at Kampi (see the box, p300) is a popular activity.

In terms of fish biodiversity, the Mekong is second only to the Amazon, but dam projects threaten migratory species. The Mekong giant catfish, which can weigh up to 300kg, is critically endangered due to habitat loss and overfishing.

The following environmental groups – staffed in Cambodia mainly by Khmers – are playing leading roles in protecting Cambodia's wildlife:

Conservation International (www.conservation.org)
Flora & Fauna International (www.fauna-flora.org)
Maddox Jolie-Pitt Foundation (www.mjpasia.org)
Wildlife Alliance (formerly WildAid; www.wildlifealliance.org)
Wildlife Conservation Society (www.wcs.org)
WWF (www.worldwildlife.org)

Plants

No one knows how many plant species are present in Cambodia because no comprehensive survey has ever been conducted, but it's estimated that the country is home to 15,000 species, at least a third of them endemic.

In the southwest, rainforests grow to heights of 50m or more on the rainy southern slopes of the mountains, with montane (pine) forests in cooler climes above 800m and mangrove forests fringing the coast. In the northern mountains there are broadleaved evergreen forests, with trees soaring 30m above a thick undergrowth of vines, bamboos, palms and assorted woody and herbaceous ground plants. The northern plains support dry dipterocarp forests, while around the Tonlé Sap there are flooded (seasonally inundated) forests. The Eastern Highlands are covered with deciduous forests and grassland. Forested upland areas support many varieties of orchid.

The sugar palm, often seen towering over rice fields, provides fronds to make roofs and walls for houses, and fruit that's used to produce medicine, wine and vinegar. Sugar palms grow taller over the years, but their barkless trunks don't get any thicker, hence they retain shrapnel marks from every battle that has ever raged around them.

National Parks

In the late 1960s Cambodia had six national parks, together covering 22,000 sq km (around 12% of the country). The long civil war effectively

---

ENVIRONMENT NATIONAL PARKS

The *khting vor* (spiral-horned ox), so rare that no one had ever seen a live specimen, was considered critically endangered until DNA analysis of its distinctive horns showed that the creature had never existed – the 'horns' belonged to ordinary cattle and buffalos!

For a close encounter with tigers at the temples of Angkor, watch Jean-Jacques Annaud's 2004 film *Two Brothers*, the story of two orphaned tiger cubs during the colonial period.

Researchers estimate that about 50 to 100 wild elephants live in Mondulkiri Province. A similar number live in the Cardamom Mountains, including Botum Sakor National Park.

ENVIRONMENT ENVIRONMENTAL ISSUES

TIGER, TIGER, BURNING OUT?

In the mid-1990s, somewhere between 100 and 200 Cambodian tigers were being killed every year, their carcasses bringing huge sums around Asia (especially China) because of their supposed aphrodisiacal powers. By 1998 annual incidents of tiger poaching had dropped to 85 and in 2005 just two tigers were killed. Sadly, it's more likely that these estimates reflect a crash in tiger numbers rather than increased community awareness or more effective law enforcement.

Experts fear there may be only 50 of the big cats left in the wild in Cambodia. Numbers are so low that, despite repeated efforts, camera traps set by researchers in recent years have failed to photograph a single tiger, though footprints and other signs of the felines' presence have been recorded. As far as anyone can tell, the surviving tigers live in very low densities in very remote areas, making it difficult for both poachers and scientists to find them, and hard for environmentalists to protect them.

At present, tigers are known to inhabit two areas: the central part of the Cardamom Mountains and Mondulkiri Province. In addition, they are thought to be present in small numbers in Ratanakiri and Preah Vihear.

For insights, stories and links about tigers in Cambodia and what's being done to protect them, visit the website of the Cat Action Treasury at www.felidae.org.

Despite responsibility for nearly 20% of the Mekong River's waters, China is not a member of the Mekong River Commission (MRC) and has only recently begun to discuss its extensive dam developments with the MRC members downstream.

destroyed this system and it wasn't reintroduced until 1993, when a royal decree designated 23 areas as national parks, wildlife sanctuaries, protected landscapes and multiple-use areas. Several more protected forests were recently added to the list, bringing the area of protected land in Cambodia to over 43,000 sq km, or around 25% of the country.

This is fantastic news in principle, but in practice the authorities don't always protect these areas in any way other than drawing a line on a map. The government has enough trouble finding funds to pay the rangers who patrol the most popular parks, let alone to recruit staff for the remote sanctuaries, though in recent years a number of international NGOs have been helping to train and fund teams of enforcement rangers.

The Mondulkiri Protected Forest, at 4294 sq km, is now the largest protected area in Cambodia and is contiguous with Yok Don National Park in Vietnam. The Central Cardamoms Protected Forest, at 4013 sq km, borders the Phnom Samkos Wildlife Sanctuary to the west and the Phnom Aural Wildlife Sanctuary to the east, creating almost 10,000 sq km of designated protected land. The noncontiguous Southern Cardamoms Protected Forest (1443 sq km) is along the Koh Kong Conservation Corridor, whose ecotourism potential is as vast as its jungles are impenetrable.

Cambodia became the first southeast Asian country to establish a national park when it created a protected area in 1925 to preserve the forests around the temples of Angkor.

Environmental Issues

Logging

The greatest threat to Cambodia's globally important ecosystems is logging for charcoal and timber and to clear land for cash-crop plantations. During the Vietnamese occupation, troops stripped away swaths of forest to prevent Khmer Rouge ambushes along highways. The devastation increased in the 1990s, when the shift to a capitalist market economy led to an asset-stripping bonanza by well-connected businessmen.

International demand for timber is huge, and, as neighbouring countries such as Thailand and Vietnam began to enforce much tougher logging regulations, foreign logging companies flocked to Cambodia. At the height of the country's logging epidemic in the late 1990s, just under 70,000 sq km of the country's land area, or about 35% of its total surface area, had been allocated as concessions, amounting to almost all of

Cambodia's forest land except national parks and protected areas. However, even in these supposed havens, illegal logging continued. According to environmental watchdog **Global Witness** (www.globalwitness.org), the Royal Cambodian Armed Forces (RCAF) is the driving force behind much of the recent logging in remote border regions.

In the short term, deforestation is contributing to worsening floods along the Mekong, but the long-term implications of logging are hard to assess. Without trees to cloak the hills, rains will inevitably carry away large amounts of topsoil during future monsoons and in time this will have a serious effect on Tonlé Sap.

Since 2002, things have been looking up. Under pressure from donors and international institutions, all logging contracts were effectively frozen pending further negotiations with the government. However, small-scale illegal logging continued, including cutting for charcoal production and slash-and-burn for settlement.

The latest threat to Cambodia's forests comes from 'economic concessions' granted to establish plantations of cash crops such as rubber, mango, cashew and jackfruit, or agro-forestry groves of acacia and eucalyptus to supply wood chips for the paper industry.

Pollution

Phnom Penh's air isn't anywhere near as bad as Bangkok's, but as vehicles multiply it's getting worse. In provincial towns and villages, the smoke from garbage fires can ruin your dinner...or worse.

Cambodia has extremely primitive sanitation systems in urban areas, and nonexistent sanitary facilities in rural areas, with only a tiny percentage of the population having access to proper facilities. These conditions breed and spread disease: epidemics of diarrhoea are not uncommon and it is the number-one killer of young children in Cambodia.

Detritus of all sorts, especially plastic bags and bottles, can be seen in distressing quantities on beaches, around waterfalls, along roads and carpeting towns, villages and hamlets.

Dammed if You Do, Damned if You Don't

The Mekong rises in Tibet and flows for 4800km before continuing through southern Vietnam into the South China Sea. This includes

In September 2005, three enforcement rangers working with the NGO Flora & Fauna International to prevent illegal hunting and logging in the Cardamom Mountains were murdered In two separate incidents, apparently by poachers.

In the mid-1960s Cambodia was reckoned to have around 90% of its original forest cover intact. Estimates today vary, but 25% is common.

ENVIRONMENT ENVIRONMENTAL ISSUES

CAMBODIA'S MOST IMPORTANT NATIONAL PARKS

PARK	SIZE	FEATURES	ACTIVITIES	BEST TIME TO VISIT
Bokor	1581 sq km	ghost town, views, waterfalls, orange lichen	trekking, biking, wildlife watching	Nov–May
Botum Sakor	1834 sq km	mangroves, beaches, monkeys, dolphins, elephants	boat rides, swimming, hiking	Nov–May
Kirirom	350 sq km	waterfalls, vistas, pine forests	hiking, wildlife watching	Nov–Jun
Ream	150 sq km	beaches, islands, mangroves, dolphins, monkeys	boating, swimming, hiking, wildlife watching	Nov–May
Virachey	3325 sq km	unexplored jungle, waterfalls	trekking, adventure, wildlife watching	Nov–Apr

DOING YOUR BIT

Every visitor to Cambodia can make at least a small contribution to the country's ecological sustainability.

» Lead by example and dispose of your rubbish responsibly.

» Drink fresh coconuts, in their natural packaging, rather than soft drinks in throwaway cans and bottles.

» Choose trekking guides who respect both the ecosystem and the people who live in it.

» Avoid eating wild meat, such as bat, deer and shark fin.

» Don't touch live coral when snorkelling or diving – and don't buy coral souvenirs.

» If you see wild animals being killed, traded or eaten, take down details of what and where, and contact the Wildlife Alliance, an NGO that helps manage the government's **Wildlife Rapid Rescue Team** (012 500094; wildlifealliance@online.com.kh). Rescued animals are either released or taken to the Phnom Tamao Wildlife Rescue Centre.

Banned in Cambodia, the damning 2007 report *Cambodia's Family Trees*, by the UK-based environmental watchdog Global Witness (www.globalwitness.org), exposes Cambodia's most powerful illegal-logging syndicates.

almost 500km in Cambodia, where it can be up to 5km wide. With energy needs spiralling upwards throughout the region, it is very tempting for poor countries like Cambodia and its upstream neighbours to build hydroelectric dams on the Mekong and its tributaries.

Environmentalists fear that damming the mainstream Mekong may be nothing short of catastrophic for the flow patterns of the river, the migratory patterns of fish, the survival of the freshwater Irrawaddy dolphin and the very life of the Tonlé Sap. Plans now under consideration include the Sambor Dam, a massive 3300MW project 35km north of Kratie, and the Don Sahong (Siphandone) Dam just north of the Cambodia–Laos border.

Also of concern is the potential impact of dams on the annual monsoon flooding of the Mekong, which deposits nutrient-rich silt across vast tracts of land used for agriculture. A drop of just 1m in wet-season water levels on the Tonlé Sap would result in around 2000 sq km less flood area, with potentially disastrous consequences for Cambodia's farmers.

Overseeing development plans for the river is the **Mekong River Commission** (MRC; www.mrcmekong.org). Formed by the United Nations Development Programme and comprising Cambodia, Thailand, Laos and Vietnam, it is ostensibly committed to sustainable development.

Sand Extraction

Sand dredging in the estuaries of Koh Kong Province, including inside the protected Peam Krasaop Wildlife Sanctuary, threatens delicate mangrove ecosystems and the sea life that depends on them. Much of the sand is destined for Singapore. For details, see Global Witness' 2009 report *Country for Sale* (www.globalwitness.org/media_library_detail.php/713/en/country_for_sale).

Survival
Guide

Directory A–Z

Accommodation

Accommodation in Cambodia has improved immensely during the past decade and everything is available, from the classic budget crash pad to the plush palace. Most hotels quote in US dollars, but some places in the provinces quote in riel, while those near the Thai border quote in baht. We provide prices based on the currency quoted to us at the time of research.

In this guide, budget accommodation refers to guesthouses where the majority of rooms are within the US$2 to US$20 range, mid-range generally runs from US$20 up to US$80 and top end is considered US$80 and up, up, up.

Budget guesthouses used to be restricted to Phnom Penh, Siem Reap and Sihanoukville, but as tourism takes off in the provinces, they are turning up in most of the other provincial capitals. Costs hover around US$3 to US$10 for a bed. In many rural parts of Cambodia, the standard rate for cheap hotels is US$5, usually with bathroom and satellite TV.

In Phnom Penh, Siem Reap and the South Coast, which see a steady flow of tourist traffic, hotels improve significantly once you start spending more than US$10 a night. For US$15 it is usually possible to find an air-con room with satellite TV and attached bathroom. If you spend between US$20 and US$50 you can arrange something very comfortable with the possible lure of a swimming pool. Most smaller provincial cities also offer air-conditioned comfort in the US$10 to US$20 range.

There are now a host of international-standard hotels in Siem Reap, several in Phnom Penh and a couple on the coast in Sihanoukville and Kep. Some are operated by familiar international brands such as Orient Express and Raffles. Most quote hefty walk-in rates and whack 10% tax and 10% service on as well. Book via a hotel-booking website for a lower rate including taxes and service.

There are substantial low-season (April through September) rates available at major hotels in Phnom Penh, Siem Reap and Sihanoukville. Discounts of 50% or more are common, as are specials such as 'stay three, pay two'. Check hotel websites for details on any promos or offers.

Some guesthouses in Cambodia do not have hot water, but most places have at least a few more expensive rooms where it is available.

While many of the swish new hotels have lifts, older hotels often don't and the cheapest rooms are at the top of several flights of stairs. It's a win-win-win situation: cheaper rooms, a bit of exercise and better views.

Homestays

Homestays are popping up in the provinces and offer a good way to meet the local people and learn about the Cambodian lifestyle. There are several organised homestays around the country in provinces like Kompong Cham and Kompong Thom, as well as lots of informal homestays in out-of-the-way places such as Preah Vihear. In the minority areas of Mondulkiri and Ratanakiri, it is often possible to stay with tribal villagers. The Mekong Discovery Trail (p253) includes several homestays between Kratie and the Lao border.

Activities

Tourism in Cambodia is catching up fast and there

BOOK YOUR STAY ONLINE

For more accommodation reviews by Lonely Planet authors, check out http://hotels.lonelyplanet.com. You'll find independent reviews, as well as recommendations on the best places to stay. Best of all, you can book online.

are now more activities than ever to get that adrenaline buzz. Phnom Penh and Siem Reap remain the places with most of the action, but Sihanoukville and Kep are making a name for themselves for fun in the sun with water sports.

Birdwatching

Birdwatching is a big draw, as Cambodia is home to some of the region's rarest large waterbirds including adjutants, storks and pelicans. For more on the birds of Cambodia, see p320, and for the low-down on bird sanctuaries and birding opportunities around Siem Reap, see p112.

Boat Trips

With so much water around the country, it is hardly surprising that boat trips are popular with tourists. Some of these are functional, such as travelling up the Tonlé Sap River from Phnom Penh to Siem Reap (p79), or along the Sangker River from Siem Reap to Battambang (p219). Others are the traditional tourist trips, such as those available in Phnom Penh (p46), Siem Reap (p116) and Sihanoukville (p188), or check out dolphin-spotting boat trips in Kratie (p255).

Cycling

As Cambodia's roads continue to improve, cycling tourists are an increasingly common sight. It's a real adventure and brings visitors that much closer to the uber-friendly locals. Local kids will race you at any opportunity and families will beckon cyclists in for some fruit or hot tea. The most popular place for cycling is around the majestic temples of Angkor, where the roads are paved and the forest shade welcome. Bikes are available for hire in most towns in Cambodia for US$2 a day for a basic bike to around US$7 and up a day for a good imported mountain bike, but serious tourers should bring

their own wheels or purchase something in Bangkok or Phnom Penh.

Dirt Biking

For experienced riders, Cambodia is one of the most rewarding off-road biking destinations in the world. The roads are generally considered some of the worst in Asia (or best in Asia for die-hard biking enthusiasts). There are incredible rides all over the country, particularly in the north and northeast, but it is best to stay away from the main highways as traffic and dust make them a choking experience. For more on dirt biking, see p343, including recommended motorcycle-touring companies.

Diving & Snorkelling

Snorkelling and diving are available off the coast of

Sihanoukville. The jury is still out about the dive sites, as much is still to be explored, but while it may not be as spectacular as Indonesia or the Philippines, there is plenty in the deep blue yonder. It is best to venture further afield to dive sites such as Koh Tang and Koh Prins (p177), staying overnight on a boat. There are many unexplored areas off the coast between Koh Kong and Sihanoukville that could one day put Cambodia on the dive map of Asia.

Golf

Cambodia is an up-and-coming golfing destination thanks to several new courses in Siem Reap (p94), one of which now hosts an annual PGA event on the Asian tour. There are also a couple of courses in Phnom Penh (p47).

PRACTICALITIES

» **Newspapers** The *Phnom Penh Post* is now daily and offers the best balance of Cambodian and international news, including business and sport. The *Cambodia Daily* is another long-running English-language newspaper.

» **Magazines** *AsiaLife* is a free monthly listings magazine (a sort of *Time Out: Phnom Penh*). A variety of international magazines and newspapers are also widely available in Phnom Penh and Siem Reap.

» **TV** Cambodia has a dozen or so local Khmer-language channels, but most of them support the ruling CPP and churn out a mixture of karaoke videos, soap operas and ministers going about their business. Most midrange hotels have cable TV with access to between 20 and 120 channels, including some obscure regional channels, international movie channels and the big global news and sports channels such as BBC and ESPN.

» **Radio** BBC World Service broadcasts on 100.00FM in Phnom Penh. Cambodian radio and TV stations are mainly government-controlled and specialise in phone-ins and product placements.

» **Video** Cambodia uses the PAL and NTSC video systems.

» **Weights and measures** Cambodians use the metric system for everything except precious metals and gems, where they prefer Chinese units of measurement.

Trekking

Trekking is not the first activity most people would associate with Cambodia, due to the rather disconcerting presence of landmines, but there are several relatively safe areas of the country – including the nascent national parks – where walking can be enjoyed. The northeastern provinces of Mondulkiri and Ratanakiri were never mined, for example, and with their wild, natural scenery, abundant waterfalls and ethnic-minority populations, they are emerging as the country's leading trekking destinations.

Cambodia is steadily establishing a network of national parks with visitor facilities; Bokor National Park (p195), Kirirom National Park (p87) and Ream National Park (p188) all promise trekking potential, while Virachey National Park (p266) in Ratanakiri has multiday treks. Chi Phat and the Cardamom Mountains (p167) also offer the possibility of a walk on the wild side.

Angkor is emerging as a good place for gentle walks between the temples – one way to experience peace and solitude as visitor numbers skyrocket.

Water Sports

As the Cambodian coast takes off, there are more adrenaline buzzes available, including boating, windsurfing and kitesurfing off the beaches of Sihanoukville (p175).

Business Hours

Most Cambodians get up very early and it is not unusual to see people out and about exercising at 5.30am if you are heading home – ahem, sorry, getting up – at that time. Government offices, which are open from Monday to Friday and on Saturday mornings, theoretically begin the working day at 7.30am, break for a siesta from 11.30am to 2pm, and end the day at 5pm.

Banking hours vary slightly according to the bank, but most keep core hours of 8am to 3.30pm Monday to Friday, plus Saturday morning. Attractions such as museums are normally open seven days a week, and these days staff have had their arms twisted to stay open through lunch.

Local restaurants are generally open from about 6.30am until 9pm and international restaurants a little later. Local restaurants may stay open throughout, while international restaurants sometimes close between sittings. Many bars are open all day, but some open only for the night shift, especially if they don't serve food.

Local markets operate seven days a week and usually open and close with the sun, running from 6.30am to 5.30pm. Markets shut up shop for a few days during the major holidays of Chaul Chnam Khmer (Khmer New Year), P'chum Ben (Festival of the Dead) and Chaul Chnam Chen (Chinese New Year). Shops tend to open from about 8am until 6pm, sometimes later.

Customs Regulations

If Cambodia has customs allowances, it is closed-lipped about them. You are emtitled to bring into the country a 'reasonable amount' of duty-free items.

Climate

Phnom Penh

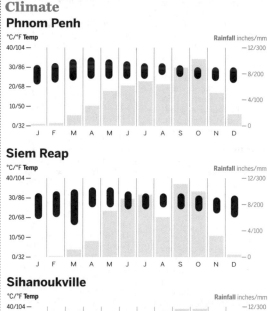

Siem Reap

Sihanoukville

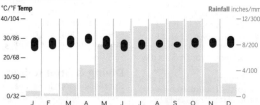

Travellers arriving by air might bear in mind that alcohol and cigarettes are on sale at prices well below duty free prices on the streets of Phnom Penh – a branded box of 200 cigarettes costs just US$10 and international spirits start as low as US$7 a litre.

Like any other country, Cambodia does not allow travellers to import any weapons, explosives or narcotics – some might say that there are more than enough in the country already.

It is illegal to take ancient stone sculptures from the Angkor period out of the country.

Discount Cards

Senior travellers and students are not eligible for discounts in Cambodia – all foreigners who are rich enough to make it to Cambodia are rich enough to pay, as far as Cambodians are concerned.

Electricity

230V/50Hz

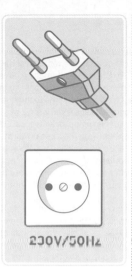

230V/50Hz

Embassies & Consulates

Quite a few countries have embassies in Phnom Penh, though some travellers will find that their nearest embassy is in Bangkok. It's important to realise what an embassy can and can't do to help if you get into trouble. Generally speaking, it won't be much help if the trouble is your own fault. Visitors are bound by the laws of the country they are in. The embassy won't be sympathetic if you end up in jail after committing a crime, even if such actions are legal in your own country.

In genuine emergencies assistance may be available, but only if all other channels have been exhausted. If you have all your money and documents stolen, the embassy can assist with getting a new passport, but a loan for onward travel is out of the question.

Embassies in Phnom Penh (☎023):

Australia (Map p43; ☎213413; 16 National Assembly St)

China (off Map p52; ☎720920; 256 Mao Tse Toung Blvd)

France (Map p36; ☎430020; 1 Monivong Blvd)

Germany (Map p43; ☎216381; 76-78 St 214)

India (off Map p52; ☎210912; 5 St 466)

Indonesia (off Map p52; ☎216148; 1 St 466)

Japan (off Map p43; ☎217161; 194 Norodom Blvd)

Laos (Map p52; ☎982632; 15-17 Mao Tse Toung Blvd)

Malaysia (off Map p43; ☎216177; 220 Norodom Blvd)

Myanmar (off Map p43; ☎223761; 181 Norodom Blvd)

Philippines (Map p52; ☎222303; 15 St 422)

Singapore (Map p43; ☎221875; 92 Norodom Blvd)

Thailand (Map p36; ☎726306; 196 Norodom Blvd)

UK (Map p36; ☎427124; 27-29 St 75)

USA (Map p48; ☎728000; 1 St 96)

Vietnam Phnom Penh (Map p52; ☎362531; 436 Monivong Blvd); Sihanoukville (off Map p184; ☎012-340495; Ekareach St)

Food

Cambodian cuisine may be less well known than that of its popular neighbours Thailand and Vietnam, but it is no less tasty. See p311 for the full story on Cambodian cuisine.

Price indicators ($, $$ or $$$) for Eating reviews in this book are as follows:

PRICE INDICATOR	COST PER MEAL
Budget ($)	<US$5
Midrange ($$)	US$5-10
Top End ($$$)	>US$10

Gay & Lesbian Travellers

While Cambodian culture is tolerant of homosexuality, the gay and lesbian scene here is certainly nothing like that in Thailand. The former

SPAS & MASSAGE

Reflecting Cambodia's newfound status as an international destination, there are some super-swish spas and a menu of massage styles to rival the dining options in cities like Phnom Penh and Siem Reap. Try Chinese acupuncture, Shiatsu from Japan, traditional Swedish, tough Thai or Vietnamese suction-cup massage to take out the bad winds.

Some masseurs are stronger than others, some techniques more persecution than pleasure, so only request a strong massage if you were a wrestler in an earlier life. Some of the more vigorous manoeuvres in this region include a judo-style throw of the body to each side or kneeling on your back while pulling the torso upwards with the hands behind the back. Ouch! But many of these are medicinal and you know what they say...no pain, no gain.

Foot-massage shops are popular and offer a range of remedies for dispirited soles. Plenty of pampering palaces offer mud baths, herbal saunas, floral plunges and seaweed wraps. There are also massages by the blind to help empower the visually-impaired community in Cambodia.

Some massage shops offer more 'services' than others. Gentleman should not be surprised to be offered a 'happy ending' in certain establishments, but the amount of make-up caking the face of the masseuse is usually a good indication that traditional massage may not be high on the agenda. That said, there is no real trick to selecting an authentic place, as we have heard stories of patrons at the smartest hotels in town being offered all sorts of unpublished extras.

King Norodom Sihanouk was a keen supporter of equal rights for same-sex partners and this seems to have encouraged a more open attitude among younger Cambodians. Both Phnom Penh and Siem Reap have a few gay-friendly bars, but it's a low-key scene compared with some parts of Asia.

With the vast number of same-sex travel partners – gay or otherwise – checking into hotels across Cambodia, there is little consideration over how travelling foreigners are related. However, it is prudent not to flaunt your sexuality. As with heterosexual couples, passionate public displays of affection are considered a basic no-no.

Cambodia Out (www.cambodiaout.com) Promoting the GLBT community in Cambodia and the gay-friendly Adore Cambodia campaign.

Sticky Rice (www.stickyrice.ws) Gay travel guide covering Cambodia and Asia.

Utopia (www.utopia-asia.com) Gay travel information and contacts, including some local gay terminology.

Insurance

Health insurance is essential; see p352 for details. Make sure your policy covers emergency evacuation: limited medical facilities mean that you may have to be airlifted to Bangkok in the event of serious injury or illness.

See p344 for motorcycle and car insurance.

Worldwide travel insurance is available at www.lonelyplanet.com/travel_services. You can buy, extend and claim online any time, even if you're already on the road.

Internet Access

Internet access is widespread and there are internet shops in all but the most remote provincial capitals. Charges range from 2000r to US$2 per hour. In this book, guesthouses and hotels that offer access to an online computer are indicated by an internet icon (@).

Many hotels, guesthouses, restaurants and cafes now offer wi-fi, although connections are easiest to find in Phnom Penh and Siem Reap. Places offering wi-fi are shown with the wi-fi icon (📶).

Language Courses

The only language courses available in Cambodia at present are in Khmer and are aimed at expat residents of Phnom Penh rather than travellers. If you are going to be based in Phnom Penh for some time, however, it would be well worth learning basic Khmer. Try the Institute of Foreign Languages at the **Royal University of Phnom Penh** (Map p36; 012866826; www.rupp.edu.kh; Russian Blvd). Also check out the noticeboards at popular guesthouses, restaurants and bars, where one-hour lessons are often advertised by private tutors. There are also regular listings under the Classifieds in the *Phnom Penh Post* and *Cambodia Daily*.

Legal Matters

Marijuana is not legal in Cambodia and police are beginning to take a harder line on it. There have been several busts (and a few set-ups, too) of foreigner-owned bars and restaurants where ganja was smoked – the days of free bowls in guesthouses are definitely history. Marijuana is traditionally used in some Khmer food, so it will continue to be around for a long time, but if you are a smoker, be discreet. It's probably only a matter of time before the Cambodian police turn the regular busting of foreigners into a lucrative sideline.

This advice applies equally to other narcotic substances, which are also illegal. And think twice about scoring from an unfamiliar moto driver, as it may end with you getting robbed after passing out.

Travellers should note that they can be prosecuted under the law of their home country regarding age of consent, even when abroad.

Maps

The best all-rounder for Cambodia is the Gecko *Cambodia Road Map*. At 1:750,000 scale, it has lots

PLANET OF THE FAKES

Cambodia is awash with pirated books and poor photocopies, including Lonely Planet titles. We know you wouldn't dream of buying a photocopied Lonely Planet guide, and that's very sensible given that old editions are sometimes wrapped in new covers, pages are bound in the wrong order and the type is so faded as to be almost unreadable. Be warned, if this is a photocopy, it may self-destruct in five seconds.

of detail and accurate place names. Other popular foldout maps include Nelles *Cambodia, Laos and Vietnam Map* at 1:1,500,000, although the detail is limited, and the Periplus *Cambodia Travel Map* at 1:1,000,000, with city maps of Phnom Penh and Siem Reap.

Lots of free maps, subsidised by advertising, are available in Phnom Penh and Siem Reap at leading hotels, guesthouses, restaurants and bars.

Money

Cambodia's currency is the riel, abbreviated in this guide by a lower-case 'r' written after the sum. Cambodia's second currency (some would say its first) is the US dollar, which is accepted everywhere and by everyone, though change may arrive in riel. Dollar bills with a small tear are unlikely to be accepted by Cambodians, so it's worth scrutinising the change you are given to make sure you don't have bad bills. In the west of the country, the Thai baht (B) is also commonplace. If three currencies seems a little excessive, perhaps it's because the Cambodians are making up for lost time: during the Pol Pot era, the country had *no* currency. The Khmer Rouge abolished money and blew up the National Bank building in Phnom Penh.

The Cambodian riel comes in notes of the following denominations: 50r, 100r, 200r, 500r, 1000r, 2000r, 5000r, 10,000r, 20,000r, 50,000r and 100,000r.

Throughout this book, prices are in the currency quoted to the average punter. This is usually US dollars or riel, but in the west it is sometimes baht. While this may seem inconsistent, this is the way it's done in Cambodia and the sooner you get used to thinking comparatively in riel, dollars or baht, the easier your travels will be.

For a listing of exchange rates at the time of going to print, see p13.

ATMs

There are now credit-card-compatible ATMs (Visa, MasterCard, JCB, Cirrus) in most major cities. There are also ATMs at the Cham Yeam, Poipet and Bavet borders if arriving by land from Thailand or Vietnam. Machines dispense US dollars. Large withdrawals of up to US$2000 are possible, providing your account can handle it. Stay alert when using ATMs late at night. ANZ Royal Bank has the most extensive network, including ATMs at petrol stations and popular hotels, restaurants and shops, closely followed by Canadia Bank. Acleda Bank has the widest network of branches in the country, including all provincial capitals, and has been upgrading ATMs to accept international cards, making far-flung travel that much easier to plan.

Bargaining

It is important to haggle over purchases made in local markets in Phnom Penh and Siem Reap, otherwise the stallholder may 'shave your head' (local vernacular for 'rip you off'). Bargaining is the rule in markets, when arranging share taxis and pick-ups, and in some guesthouses. The Khmers are not ruthless hagglers, so a persuasive smile and a little friendly quibbling is usually enough to get a fair price. Try to remember that the aim is not to get the lowest possible price, but a price that is acceptable to both you and the seller. Remember that in many cases a few hundred riel is more important to a Cambodian with a family to support than to a traveller on an extended vacation. After all, no one bargains over a beer in a busy backpacker bar, so why bargain so hard over a cheap bottle of water?

Cash

The US dollar remains king in Cambodia. Armed with enough cash, you won't need to visit a bank at all because it is possible to change small amounts of dollars for riel at hotels, restaurants and markets. It is always handy to have about US$10 worth of riel kicking around, as it is good for motos, *remork-motos* and markets. Pay for something cheap in US dollars and the change comes in riel. In remote areas of the north and northeast, locals only deal in riel or small dollar denominations.

The only other currency that can be useful is Thai baht, mainly in the west of the country. Prices in towns such as Krong Koh Kong, Poipet and Sisophon are often quoted in baht, and even in Battambang it is as common as the dollar.

In the interests of making life as simple as possible when travelling overland, organise a supply of US dollars before arriving in Cambodia. Cash in other major currencies can be changed at banks or markets in Phnom Penh or Siem Reap. However, most banks tend to offer a poor rate for any non-dollar transaction so it can be better to use moneychangers, which are found in and around every major market.

Western Union and MoneyGram are both represented in Cambodia for fast, if more expensive, money transfers. Western Union is represented by SBC and Acleda Bank, and MoneyGram is represented by Canadia Bank.

Credit Cards

Top-end hotels, airline offices and upmarket boutiques and restaurants generally accept most major credit cards (Visa, MasterCard, JCB and sometimes American Express), but many pass the charges straight on to the customer, meaning an extra 3% on the bill.

Cash advances on credit cards are available in Phnom Penh, Siem Reap, Sihanoukville, Kampot, Battambang, Kompong Cham and other major towns. Most banks advertise a minimum charge of US$5, but Canadia Bank offers this service for free.

Several travel agents and hotels in Phnom Penh and Siem Reap can arrange cash advances for about 5% commission; this can be particularly useful if you get caught short at the weekend.

Tipping

Tipping is not traditionally expected here, but in a country as poor as Cambodia, tips can go a long way. Salaries remain extremely low and service is often impressive. Many of the upmarket hotels levy a 10% service charge, but this doesn't always make it to the staff. If you stay a couple of nights in the same hotel, try to remember to tip the staff that clean your room. Consider tipping drivers and guides, as the time they spend on the road means time away from home and family.

It is considered proper to make a small donation at the end of a visit to a wat, especially if a monk has shown you around; most wats have contribution boxes for this purpose.

TIPPING TIPS

In many Cambodian restaurants, change will be returned in some sort of bill holder. If you leave the change there it will often be taken by the restaurant proprietor. If you want to make sure the tip goes to the staff who have served you, then leave the tip on the table or give it to the individuals directly.

Travellers Cheques

Acleda Bank now offers travellers-cheque encashment at most branches, bringing financial freedom to far-flung provinces like Ratanakiri and Mondulkiri. It is best to have cheques in US dollars. Expect to pay about 2% commission to change travellers cheques.

Photography

Many internet cafes in Cambodia will burn CDs or DVDs from digital images using card readers or USB connections. The price is about US$2.50 if you need a DVD or US$1.50 for a CD. Digital memory sticks are widely available in Cambodia and are pretty cheap. Digital cameras are a real bargain in Cambodia thanks to low tax and duty, so consider picking up a new model in Phnom Penh rather than Bangkok or Saigon.

Make sure you have the necessary charger, plugs and transformer for Cambodia. Take care with some of the electrical wiring in guesthouses around the country, as it can be pretty amateurish.

In Phnom Penh and Siem Reap, it is possible to obtain video tapes for most formats, but elsewhere around the country you are unlikely to find much of use.

Photographing People

The usual rules apply. Be polite about photographing people, don't push cameras into their faces, and have some respect for monks and people at prayer. In general, the Khmers are remarkably courteous people and if you ask nicely, they'll agree to have their photograph taken. The same goes for filming, although in rural areas you will often find children desperate to get in front of the lens and astonished at seeing themselves played back on an LCD screen. It is the closest most of them will get to being on TV. Some people will expect money in return for their photo being snapped; be sure to establish this before clicking away.

Post

The postal service is hit and miss from Cambodia; send anything valuable by courier or from another country. Ensure postcards and letters are franked before they vanish from your sight.

Letters and parcels sent further afield than Asia can take up to two or three weeks to reach their destination. Use a courier to speed things up; EMS (☎023-723511; www .ems.com.kh; Main Post Office, St 13) has branches at every major post office in the country.

Public Holidays

During public holidays and festivals, banks, ministries and embassies close down, so plan ahead if visiting Cambodia during these times. Cambodians also roll over holidays if they fall on a weekend and take a day or two extra during major festivals. Add to this the fact that they take a holiday for international days here and there and it soon becomes apparent that Cambodia has more public holidays than any other nation on earth!

International New Year's Day 1 January
Victory over the Genocide 7 January
International Women's Day 8 March
International Workers' Day 1 May
International Children's Day 8 May
King's Birthday 13-15 May
King Mother's Birthday 18 June
Constitution Day 24 September
King Father's Birthday 31 October

Independence Day 9 November
International Human Rights Day 10 December

Safe Travel

Cambodia is a pretty safe country for travellers these days, but remember the golden rule: *stick to marked paths in remote areas* (because of landmines).

The **Cambodia Daily** (www.cambodiadaily.com) and the **Phnom Penh Post** (www .phnompenhpost.com) are both good sources for breaking news. Check their websites before you hit the road.

Crime & Violence

Given the number of guns in Cambodia, there is less armed theft than one might expect. Still, hold-ups and motorcycle theft are a potential danger in Phnom Penh and Sihanoukville. There is no need to be paranoid, just cautious. Walking or riding alone late at night is not ideal, certainly not in rural areas.

There have been incidents of bag snatching in Phnom Penh in the last few years and the motorbike thieves don't let go, dragging passengers off motos and endangering lives.

Should anyone be unlucky enough to be robbed, it is important to note that the Cambodian police are the best that money can buy! Any help, such as a police report, is going to cost you.

FESTIVAL WARNING

In the run-up to major festivals such as P'chum Ben or Chaul Chnam Khmer, there is a palpable increase in the number of robberies, particularly in Phnom Penh. Cambodians need money to buy gifts for relatives or to pay off debts, and for some individuals theft is the quick way to get this money. Be more vigilant at night at these times and don't take valuables out with you unnecessarily.

The going rate depends on the size of the claim, but US$5 to US$20 is a common charge.

Violence against foreigners is extremely rare, but it pays to take care in crowded bars or nightclubs in Phnom Penh. If you get into a stand-off with rich young Khmers in a bar or club, swallow your pride and back down. Still think you can 'ave 'em? Many carry guns and have an entourage of bodyguards; enough said.

Mines, Mortars & Bombs

Never touch any rockets, artillery shells, mortars, mines, bombs or other war material

SHOPPING TIPS

High-quality handmade crafts, including silk clothing and accessories, stone and wood carvings, and silver, are widely available, especially in Siem Reap, Phnom Penh and towns with particular handicraft specialities. Hill tribes in Mondulkiri and Ratanakiri produce hand-woven cotton in small quantities. In the Phnom Penh and Siem Reap sections of this book, we focus on shops and organisations that contribute to reviving traditional crafts and support people who are disadvantaged or disabled.

GOVERNMENT TRAVEL ADVICE

Travel advisories on government-run websites update nationals on the latest security situation in any given country, including Cambodia. They are useful to check out for dangerous countries or dangerous times, but they tend to be pretty conservative.

Australia (www.smart raveller.gov.au)

Canada (www.voyage. gc.ca)

Germany (www. auswaertiges-amt.de)

Japan (www.anzen. mofa.go.jp)

Netherlands (www. minbuza.nl)

New Zealand (www. safetravel.govt.nz)

UK (www.fco.gov.uk/ travel)

USA (www.travel.state. gov)

you may come across. The most heavily mined part of the country is along the Thai border area, but mines are a problem in much of Cambodia. In short: *do not stray from well-marked paths under any circumstances*. If you are planning any walks, even in safer areas such as the remote northeast, it is imperative you take a guide as there may still be unexploded ordnance (UXO) from the American bombing campaign of the early 1970s.

Scams

Most scams are fairly harmless, involving a bit of commission here and there for taxi or moto drivers, particularly in Siem Reap.

There have been one or two reports of police set-ups in Phnom Penh, involving planted drugs. This seems to be very rare, but if you fall victim to the ploy, it may be best to pay them off before more police get involved at the local station, as the price will only rise when there are more officials to pay off.

There is quite a lot of fake medication floating about the region. Safeguard yourself by only buying prescription drugs from reliable pharmacies or clinics.

Telephone

Cambodia's landline system was totally devastated by the long civil war, leaving the country with a poor communications infrastructure. The advent of mobile phones has allowed Cambodia to catch up with its regional neighbours by jumping headlong into the technology revolution. Mobile phones are everywhere in Cambodia, but landline access in major towns is also improving, connecting more of the country to the outside world than ever before.

Landline area codes appear under the name of each city, but in many areas service is spotty. Mobile phones, whose numbers start with 01, 06, 07, 08 or 09, are hugely popular with both individuals and commercial enterprises. Foreigners need to present a valid passport to get a local SIM card.

The easiest way to make a local call in most urban areas is to head to one of the many small private booths on the kerbside, usually plastered with numbers like 012 and 016 and with prices around 300r. Many internet shops offer cheap international calls for 100r to 1000r per minute, though in places with broadband speeds you can Skype for the price of an internet connection (usually 2000r to 4000r *per hour*). International calls from mobile-phone shops cost about 1000r per minute.

For listings of businesses and government offices, check out www.yellowpages -cambodia.com.

Mobile Phones

When travelling with a mobile phone on international roaming, just select a network upon arrival, dial away and await a hefty phone bill once you return home. Note to self: Cambodian roaming charges are extraordinarily high.

Those who plan on spending longer in Cambodia should purchase a SIM card for one of the local service providers. Most mobile companies now offer cheap internet-based phone calls

YABA DABA DO? YABA DABA DON'T!

Watch out for *yaba*, the 'crazy' drug from Thailand, known rather ominously in Cambodia as *yama* (the Hindu god of death). Known as ice or crystal meth back home, it's not just any old diet pill from the pharmacist but homemade meta-amphetamines produced in labs in Cambodia and the region beyond. The pills are often laced with toxic substances, such as mercury, lithium or whatever else the maker can find. *Yama* is a dirty drug and more addictive than users would like to admit, provoking powerful hallucinations, sleep deprivation and psychosis. Steer clear of the stuff unless you plan on an indefinite extension to your trip.

Also be very careful about buying 'cocaine'. Most of what is sold as coke, particularly in Phnom Penh, is actually pure heroin and far stronger than any smack found on the streets back home.

DOMESTIC AREA CODES

Banteay Meanchey Province	☎054
Battambang Province	☎053
Kampot Province	☎033
Kandal Province	☎024
Kep Province	☎036
Koh Kong Province	☎035
Kompong Cham Province	☎042
Kompong Chhnang Province	☎026
Kompong Speu Province	☎025
Kompong Thom Province	☎062
Kratie Province	☎072
Mondulkiri Province	☎073
Oddar Meanchey Province	☎065
Phnom Penh	☎023
Preah Vihear Province	☎064
Prey Veng Province	☎043
Pursat Province	☎052
Ratanakiri Province	☎075
Siem Reap Province	☎063
Sihanoukville Province	☎034
Stung Treng Province	☎074
Svay Rieng Province	☎044
Takeo Province	☎032

accessed through a gateway number. Use the cheap prefix and calls will be just US 25¢ or less per minute.

M Fone offers a handy tourist SIM card. This costs US$10 and can be inserted into any unlocked phone. Calls are cheap at just US 25¢ per minute and the line is usually clear. The card lasts for seven days from activation.

Time

Cambodia, like Laos, Vietnam and Thailand, is seven hours ahead of Greenwich Mean Time or Universal Time Co-ordinated (GMT/UTC). When it is midday in Cambodia it is 10pm the previous evening in San Francisco, 1am in New York, 5am in London, 6am in Paris and 3pm in Sydney.

Toilets

Cambodian toilets are mostly of the sit-down variety. The occasional squat toilet turns up here and there, particularly in the most budget of budget guesthouses in the provinces.

The issue of toilets and what to do with used toilet paper is a cause for concern. Generally, if there's a waste-paper basket next to the toilet, that is where the toilet paper goes, as many sewerage systems cannot handle toilet paper. Toilet paper is seldom provided in the toilets at bus and train stations or in other public buildings, so keep a stash with you at all times.

Many Western toilets also have a hose spray in the bathroom, aptly named the 'bum gun' by some. Think of this as a flexible bidet, used for cleaning and ablutions as well as hosing down the loo.

Public toilets are rare, the only ones in the country being along Phnom Penh's riverfront and some beautiful wooden structures dotted about the temples of Angkor. The charge is usually 500r for a public toilet, although they are free at Angkor. Most local restaurants have some sort of toilet.

Should you find nature calling in rural areas, don't let modesty drive you into the bushes: *there may be landmines not far from the road or track*. Stay on the roadside and do the deed, or grin and bear it until the next town.

Tourist Information

Cambodia has only a handful of tourist offices, and those encountered by the independent traveller in Phnom Penh and Siem Reap are generally of limited help. However, in the provinces it is a different story, as the staff are often excited to see visitors. However, these offices generally have little in the way of brochures or handouts. You'll find some tourist offices listed in the relevant destination sections in this book, but lower your expectations compared with regional powerhouses like Malaysia and Singapore. Generally, fellow travellers, guesthouses, hotels, and free local magazines are more useful than tourist offices.

Cambodia has no official tourist offices abroad and it is unlikely that Cambodian embassies will be of much assistance in planning a trip, besides issuing visas, which are available on arrival anyhow.

Travellers with Disabilities

Broken pavements, potholed roads and stairs as

steep as ladders at Angkor ensure that for most people with mobility impairments, Cambodia is not going to be an easy country in which to travel. Few buildings have been designed with the disabled in mind, although new projects, such as the international airports at Phnom Penh and Siem Reap, and top-end hotels, include ramps for wheelchair access. Transport in the provinces is usually very overcrowded, but taxi hire from point to point is an affordable option.

On the positive side, the Cambodian people are usually very helpful towards all foreigners, and local labour is cheap if you need someone to accompany you at all times. Most guesthouses and small hotels have ground-floor rooms that are reasonably easy to access.

The biggest headache also happens to be the main attraction – the temples of Angkor. Causeways are uneven, obstacles common and staircases daunting, even for able-bodied people. It is likely to be some years before things improve, although some ramping is now being introduced at major temples.

Wheelchair travellers will need to undertake a lot of research before visiting Cambodia. There is a growing network of information sources that can put you in touch with others who have wheeled through Cambodia before. Try contacting the following:

Mobility International USA (☑54-1343 1284; www .miusa.org)

Royal Association for Disability and Rehabilitation (Radar; ☑020-7250 3222; www.radar.org.uk)

Society for Accessible Travel & Hospitality (SATH; ☑212-447 7284; www.sath.org)

The Thorn Tree travel forum on lonelyplanet.com is a good place to seek advice from other travellers.

Visas

Most visitors to Cambodia require a one-month tourist visa (US$20). Most nationalities receive this on arrival at Phnom Penh and Siem Reap airports, and at land borders, but do check if you are carrying an African, Asian or Middle Eastern passport, as there are restrictions and conditions for citizens of some countries in these regions. Citizens of Asean member countries do not require a visa to visit Cambodia. One passport-sized photo is required and you'll be 'fined' US$1 if you don't have one. It is also possible to arrange a visa through Cambodian embassies overseas or an online e-visa (US$20, plus a US$5 processing fee) through the **Ministry of Foreign Affairs** (www.mfaic.gov.kh).

Those seeking work in Cambodia should opt for the business visa (US$25) as it is easily extended for long periods, including multiple entries and exits. A tourist visa can be extended only once and only for one month, and does not allow for re-entry.

Travellers are sometimes overcharged when crossing at land borders with Thailand, as immigration officials demand payment in baht and round up the figure considerably. Overcharging is also an issue at the Laos border, but not usually at Vietnam borders. Arranging a visa in advance can help avoid overcharging.

Overstaying a visa currently costs US$5 a day.

Those intending to visit Laos should note that Lao visas are available in Phnom Penh for US$30 to US$42, depending on nationality, and take two working days. For Vietnam, one-month single-entry visas cost US$30 to US$35 and take just one day, faster still at the Vietnamese consulate in Sihanoukville.

Visa Extensions

Visa extensions are issued by the large immigration office located directly across the road from Phnom Penh International Airport.

There are two ways of getting an extension (one official and one unofficial) and, unsurprisingly, the time and money involved differ slightly. Officially, a one-month extension costs US$35, three months US$65, six months US$125, and one year US$200 (note that three-, six- and 12-month extensions are only available to those with a business visa); your passport will be held for 25 days and there will be more paperwork than a communist bureaucrat could dream up. This is fine for expats with an employer to make the arrangements, but those on their own really need to go unofficial. They don't call it corruption in Cambodia but 'under the table', and you can have your passport back the next day for the inflated prices of US$45 for one month, US$80 for three months, US$165 for six months and US$265 for one year. Once you are one of the 'unofficials', it is pretty straightforward to extend the visa *ad infinitum*. Travel agencies and some motorbike-rental shops in Phnom Penh can help with arrangements, sometimes at a discounted price.

Volunteering

There are fewer opportunities for volunteering than one might imagine in a country as impoverished as Cambodia. This is partly due to the sheer number of professional development workers based here, and development is a pretty lucrative industry these days.

Cambodia hosts a huge number of NGOs, some of whom do require volunteers from time to time. The best way to find out who is represented in the country is to drop in on the **Cooperation Committee for Cambodia** (CCC; ☑023-214152; www.ccc -cambodia.org; 9-11 St 476) in

Phnom Penh. This organisation has a handy list of all NGOs, both Cambodian and international, and is extremely helpful.

There are a couple of professional Siem Reap–based organisations helping to place volunteers. ConCERT (Map p92; ☎063-963511; www .concertcambodia.org) has a 'responsible volunteering' section on its website that offers some sound advice on preparing for a stint as a volunteer. Globalteer (☎063-761802; www.globalteer .org) coordinates the Cambodia Kids Project and offers volunteer placements with local orphanages and day centres, but this does involve a weekly charge.

The other avenue is professional volunteering through an organisation back home that offers one- or two-year placements in Cambodia. One of the largest organisations is Voluntary Service Overseas (VSO; www.vso.org.uk) in the UK, but other countries also have their own organisations, including Australian Volunteers International (AVI; www.australianvolunteers.com) and New Zealand's Volunteer Service Abroad (VSA; www.vsa.org.nz). The UN also operates its own volunteer program; details are available at www.unv.org. Other general volunteer sites with links all over the place include www .worldvolunteerweb.com and www.volunteerabroad.com.

For general tips on voluntourism in Cambodia, visit www.voluntourism101.org.

Women Travellers

Women will generally find Cambodia a hassle-free place to travel, although some of the guys in the guesthouse industry will try their luck from time to time. Foreign women are unlikely to be targeted by local men, but at the same time it pays to be careful. As is the case anywhere in the world, walking or riding a bike alone late at night is risky, and if you're planning a trip off the beaten trail it would be best to find a travel companion.

Despite the prevalence of sex workers and women's employment as 'beer girls', dancing companions and the like, foreign women will probably find Khmer men to be courteous and polite. It's best to live up things this way by being restrained in your dress. Khmer women dress fairly conservatively, and it's best to follow suit, particularly when visiting wats. In general, long-sleeved

---

THE PERILS OF ORPHANAGE TOURISM

In recent years, visiting orphanages in the developing world – Cambodia in particular – has become a popular activity, but is it always good for the children and the country in the longer run? Tough question. 'Orphan tourism' and all the connotations that come with it could be considered a disturbing development that is bringing unscrupulous elements into the world of caring for Cambodian children. There have already been reports of new orphanages opening up with a business model to bring in a certain number of visitors per month. In other cases, the children are not orphans at all, but are 'borrowed' from the local school for a fee.

In a report released in November 2009, Save the Children stated that most children living in orphanages throughout the developing world have at least one parent still alive. More than eight million children worldwide are living in institutions, with most sent there by their families because of poverty rather than the death of a parent. Many are in danger of abuse and neglect from carers, as well as exploitation and international trafficking, with children aged under three most at risk.

'One of the biggest myths is that children in orphanages are there because they have no parents. This is not the case,' the report states. 'Most are there because their parents simply can't afford to feed, clothe and educate them.' From 2005 to 2010, the number of orphanages in Cambodia almost doubled from 153 to 269. Of the 12,000 Cambodian children in institutions, only about 28% are genuine orphans without both parents.

Many orphanages in Cambodia are doing a good job in tough circumstances. Some are world class, enjoy funding and support from wealthy benefactors, and don't need visitors; others are desperate places that need all the help they can get. However, if a place is promoting orphan tourism, then proceed with caution, as the adults may not always have the best interests of the children at heart. Cambodia is a confusing and confounding place and it's not for us to play judge and jury, but we do believe travellers should be informed before they make a decision. Friends International and Unicef joined forces in 2011 to launch the 'Think Before Visiting' campaign. Learn more at www.thinkchildsafe. org/thinkbeforevisiting/before you inadvertently contribute to the problem.

shirts and long trousers or skirts are preferred. It is also worth having trousers for heading out at night on motos, as short skirts aren't too practical.

Tampons and sanitary napkins are widely available in the major cities and provincial capitals, but if you are heading into very remote areas for a few days, it is worth having your own supply.

Work

Jobs are available throughout Cambodia, but apart from teaching English or helping out in guesthouses, bars or restaurants, most are for professionals and are arranged in advance. There is a lot of teaching work available for English-language speakers; salary is directly linked to experience. Anyone with an English-language teaching certificate can earn considerably more than those with no qualifications.

For information about work opportunities with NGOs, call into the CCC (p336), which has a noticeboard for positions vacant. If you are thinking of applying for work with NGOs, you should bring copies of your education certificates and work references. However, most of the jobs available are likely to be on a voluntary basis, as most recruiting for specialised positions is done in home countries or through international organisations.

Other places to look for work include the classifieds sections of the *Phnom Penh Post* and the *Cambodia Daily,* and on the noticeboards at guesthouses and restaurants in Phnom Penh.

Do not expect to make a lot of money working in Cambodia, but if you want to learn more about the country and help the locals improve their standard of living, it can be a very worthwhile experience.

Transport

GETTING THERE & AWAY

Entering the Country

Cambodia has two international gateways for arrival by air, Phnom Penh and Siem Reap, and a healthy selection of land borders with neighbouring Thailand, Vietnam and Laos. Formalities at Cambodia's international airports are traditionally smoother than at land borders, as the volume of traffic is greater. Crossing at land borders is relatively easy, but immigration officers may try to wangle some extra cash, either for the visa or via some

other scam. Anyone without a photo for their visa form will be charged about US$1 at the airport, and as much as 100B at land borders with Thailand.

Arrival by air is popular for those on a short holiday, as travelling overland to or from Cambodia puts a dent in the time in-country. Travellers on longer trips usually enter and exit by land, as road and river transport is very reasonably priced in Cambodia.

Passport

Not only is a passport essential, but it needs to be valid for at least six months – Cambodian immigration will not issue a visa if there is less than six months' validity remaining.

It's also important to make sure that there is plenty of space left in the passport, as a Cambodian visa alone takes up one page.

Losing a passport is not the end of the world, but it is a serious inconvenience. To expedite the issuing of a new passport, keep a photocopy of passport details.

For the story on visas, see p336.

Air

Airports & Airlines

Phnom Penh International Airport (PNH; ☏023-890520; www.cambodia-airports.com) is the gateway to the Cambodian capital, while **Siem Reap International Airport** (REP; ☏063-380283; www.cambodia-airports.com) serves visitors to the temples of Angkor. Both airports have a good range of services, including restaurants, bars, shops and ATMs. **Sihanoukville International Airport** (KOS; www.cambodia-airports.com) may welcome its first international flights during the lifetime of this book.

Flights to Cambodia are expanding, but most connect only as far as regional capitals. However, budget airlines have taken off in recent years and are steadily driving down prices.

If you are heading to Cambodia for a short holiday and want a minimum of fuss, Thai Airways offers the easiest connections from major cities in Europe, the USA and

CLIMATE CHANGE & TRAVEL

Every form of transport that relies on carbon-based fuel generates CO_2, the main cause of human-induced climate change. Modern travel is dependent on aeroplanes, which might use less fuel per kilometre per person than most cars but travel much greater distances. The altitude at which aircraft emit gases (including CO_2) and particles also contributes to their climate change impact. Many websites offer 'carbon calculators' that allow people to estimate the carbon emissions generated by their journey and, for those who wish to do so, to offset the impact of the greenhouse gases emitted with contributions to portfolios of climate-friendly initiatives throughout the world. Lonely Planet offsets the carbon footprint of all staff and author travel.

Australia. Singapore Airlines' regional wing, Silk Air, and budget airline Jetstar offer at least one flight a day connecting Cambodia to Singapore. Other regional centres with flights to Cambodia are Ho Chi Minh City (Saigon), Hanoi, Vientiane, Luang Prabang, Pakse, Kuala Lumpur, Seoul, Taipei, Hong Kong, Guangzhou and Shanghai.

Domestic airlines in Cambodia tend to open up and close down regularly. Given the choice, enter the country on an international carrier rather than a local outfit.

Some airlines offer open-jaw tickets into Phnom Penh and out of Siem Reap, which can save some time and money. The majority of the following telephone numbers are for Phnom Penh offices (☏023). See the Siem Reap section for airline offices there (p111).

Airlines flying to/from Cambodia:

Air Asia (AK; ☏356011; www.airasia.com) Daily budget flights connecting Phnom Penh and Siem Reap to Kuala Lumpur and Bangkok.

Air France (AF; ☏965500; www.airfrance.com) Three flights a week to Paris via Bangkok.

Asiana Airlines (OZ; ☏890440; www.asiana.co.kr) Regular connections between Phnom Penh and Seoul.

Bangkok Airways (PG; ☏722545; www.bangkokair.com) Daily connections from Phnom Penh and Siem Reap to Bangkok.

Cambodia Angkor Airways (K6; ☏212564; www.cambodiaangkorair.com) Daily connections from Phnom Penh and Siem Reap to Ho Chi Minh City (Saigon).

China Eastern Airlines (MU; ☏063-965229; www.ce-air.com) Regular flights from Siem Reap to Kunming.

China Southern Airlines (CZ; ☏430877; www.cs-air.com) Regular flights from Phnom Penh to Guangzhou.

Dragon Air (KA; ☏424300; www.dragonair.com) Daily flights between Phnom Penh and Hong Kong.

Eva Air (BR; ☏219911; www.evaair.com) Daily flights between Phnom Penh and Taipei.

Jetstar (3K; ☏220909; www.jetstar.com) Daily budget flights from both Phnom Penh and Siem Reap to Singapore.

Korean Air (KE; ☏224047; www.koreanair.com) Regular flights connecting Phnom Penh and Siem Reap with Seoul and Incheon.

Lao Airlines (QV; ☏216563; www.laoairlines.com) Regular flights from Phnom Penh and Siem Reap to Pakse, Vientiane and Luang Prabang.

Malaysia Airlines (MY; ☏426688; www.malaysiaairlines.com) Daily connections from Phnom Penh and Siem Reap to Kuala Lumpur.

Myanmar Airways International (8M; ☏881178; www.maiair.com) Regular flights from Phnom Penh and Siem Reap to Yangon.

Shanghai Airlines (FM; ☏723999; www.shanghai-air.com) Regular flights linking Phnom Penh with Shanghai.

Silk Air (MI; ☏426807; www.silkair.com) Daily flights linking Phnom Penh and Siem Reap with Singapore, plus some flights between Siem Reap and Danang.

Thai Airways (TG; ☏214359; www.thaiair.com) Daily flights connecting Phnom Penh and Bangkok.

Vietnam Airlines (VN; ☏363396; www.vietnamair.com.vn) Daily flights linking both Phnom Penh and Siem Reap with both Hanoi and Ho Chi Minh City, as well as Phnom Penh with Vientiane, and Siem Reap with Luang Prabang.

Tickets

Buying direct from the airline is usually more expensive, unless the airline has a special promotion or you are flying with a budget carrier

offering online deals. As a rule, it is better to book as early as possible, as prices only get higher as the seats fill up.

The time of year has a major impact on flight prices. Starting out from Europe, North America or Australia, figure on prices rising dramatically over Christmas and during July and August, and dropping significantly during lax periods of business like February, June and October.

To research and buy a ticket on the internet, try these services:

Cheapflights (www.cheapflights.com) No-frills website with a number of destinations.

Kayak (www.kayak.com) Reliable fare-comparison website.

Lonely Planet (www.lonelyplanet.com) Use the Trip Planner service to book multi-stop trips.

Lowest Fare (www.lowestfare.com) They promise...'the lowest fares'.

STA Travel (www.statravel.com) Leading student-travel agency with cheap fares, plus separate websites for the UK, Australia and New Zealand.

Land

For all the juicy details on Cambodian land border crossings, see p347.

Tours

In the early days of tourism in Cambodia, organised tours were a near necessity. The situation has changed dramatically and it is now much easier to organise your own trip. Budget and midrange travellers in particular can go it alone, as arrangements are cheap and easy on the ground. If you are on a tight schedule, it can pay to book a domestic flight in advance if you're planning to link the temples of Angkor and

Siem Reap with Cambodia's capital, Phnom Penh. Once at Angkor, guides and all forms of transport under the sun are plentiful.

Shop around before booking a tour, as there is lots of competition and some companies, such as those listed here, offer more interesting itineraries than others. There are also several good companies based in Cambodia that are trying to put a little something back into the country.

Australia

Adventure World (☑02-8913 0755; www.adventure world.com.au) Offers adventure tours of Cambodia, as well as neighbouring Vietnam and Laos.

Intrepid Travel (☑1300 360 667; www.intrepidtravel.com .au) Small group tours for all budgets with an environmental, social and cultural edge.

Peregrine (☑02-9290 2770; www.peregrineadventures.com) Small group and private tours supporting responsible tourism.

Cambodia

About Asia (☑855-63 760190; www.asiatravel-cam bodia.com) Small bespoke travel company specialising in Siem Reap. Profits help build schools in Cambodia.

Hanuman (☑855-23 218396; www.hanuman.travel) Long-running locally owned, locally operated company with innovative tours like Temple Safari. Big supporter of responsible tourism initiatives.

Journeys Within (☑855-63 964748; www.journeys-within .com) A boutique tourism company offering trips to Cambodia and the Mekong region. Operates a charitable arm (see www.journeyswithin ourcommunity.org for more information) helping schools and communities.

Local Adventures (☑855-23 990460; www.cambodia .nl) Cambodian-based

company specialising in off-the-beaten-path tours to the less-visited regions of the country. Assists Cambodian children through the Cambodian Organisation for Learning and Training (www .colt-cambodia.org).

PEPY Ride (☑855-23 222804; www.pepyride.org) Specialist cycling company that runs adventurous bike rides through Cambodia to raise funds to build schools and improve education. Also offers non-cycling trips.

Sam Veasna Center (☑855-63 761597; www.sam veasna.org) Established ecotourism operator specialising in birdwatching tours around Cambodia. Supports conservation and education.

France

Compagnie des Indes & Orients (☑01-5363-3340; www.compagniesdumonde .com) Offers organised tours covering more of Cambodia than most.

Intermedes (☑01-4561-9090; www.intermedes.com) Offers specialised private tours.

La Route des Indes (☑01-4260-6090; www.larouterdesin des.com) High-end tours with an academic edge.

UK

Audley Travel (☑01604-234855; www.audleytravel .com) Popular tailor-made specialist covering Cambodia.

Bamboo Travel (☑020-7720 9285; www.bambootravel .co.uk) Offers innovative and off-the-beaten-track itineraries around Cambodia and Indochina.

Hands Up Holidays (☑0776-501 3631; www .handsupholidays.com) A popular company bringing guests closer to the people of Cambodia through its responsible holidays with a spot of volunteering.

Mekong Travel (☑01494-674456; www.mekong-travel .com) A name to inspire confidence in the Mekong region.

Symbiosis (☑020-7924 5906; www.symbiosis-travel .com) Small bespoke travel company with an emphasis on cycling and diving.

PHOTOGRAPHY TOURS

There are several professional photographers resident in Cambodia who offer classes and workshops from day trips through to guided country tours. This is a great way to improve your travel-photography skills and see some different angles through their eyes.

Eric de Vries (www.ericdevries.nl) Experienced Dutch photographer based in Siem Reap offering tours around the temples of Angkor and lifestyle experiences.

John McDermott (www.asiaphotos.net) American fine-art photographer who has taken iconic images of Angkor, offering more expensive group tours or one-on-one workshops.

Kevin Bolton (battambangbuzz.blogspot.com) Brit photographer based in Battambang, offering jeep-based rural lifestyle and temple trips.

Nathan Horton (www.nathanhortonphotography.com) Professional British photographer resident in Phnom Penh, offering a comprehensive program of day trips beyond the capital and multi-day tours around Angkor and beyond.

Wild Frontiers (☏020-7376 3968; www.wildfrontiers.co.uk) Adventure specialist with themed tours and innovative adventures.

USA

Asia Transpacific Journeys (☏800-642-2742, www.asiatranspacific.com) Group tours and tailor-made trips across the Asia-Pacific region.

Distant Horizons (☏800-333-1240; www.distanthorizons.com) Educational tours for discerning travellers.

Geographic Expeditions (☏800-777-8183; www.geoex.com) Well-established high-end adventure-travel company.

Myths & Mountains (☏800-670-6984; www.mythsandmountains.com) Voted one of Nat Geo Adventure's Top Ten Best Travel Companies.

Flights and tours can be booked online at lonelyplanet.com/bookings.

GETTING AROUND

Air

Airlines in Cambodia

Domestic flights offer a quick way to travel around the country. The problem is that the airlines themselves seem to come and go pretty quickly as well. There is currently only one fully-operational domestic airline, **Cambodia Angkor Airways** (K6; ☏023-212564; www.cambodiaangkorair.com; hub Phnom Penh), and this company operates almost as an offshoot of Vietnam Airlines. It serves the Phnom Penh to Siem Reap route with modern ATRs from France. Flights between Siem Reap and Sihanoukville have finally taken off after much travel-industry lobbying.

There are up to four flights a day between Phnom Penh and Siem Reap (from US$75

one way) and it is usually possible to get on a flight at short notice. Book ahead in peak season. There are currently three flights a week between Siem Reap and Sihanoukville (from US$85 one way).

Helicopter

Helicopters Cambodia (☏023-213706; www.helicopterscambodia.com) has offices in Phnom Penh and Siem Reap and operates reliable choppers that are available for charter. **Helistar** (☏088-8880017; www.helistarcambodia.com) is a newer company offering similar services.

Bicycle

Cambodia is a great country for adventurous cyclists to explore. Needless to say, given the country's legendary potholes, a mountain bike is the best bet. Top bikes, safety equipment and authentic spare parts are now readily available in Phnom Penh at very reasonable prices. Many roads remain in bad condition, but there is usually a flat unpaved trail along the side. Travelling at such a gentle speed allows for much more interaction with the locals. Although bicycles are common in Cambodian villages, cycling tourists are still very much a novelty and will be wildly welcomed in most small villages. In many parts of the country there are new dirt tracks being laid down for motorcycles and bicycles, and these are a wonderful way to travel into remote areas.

Much of Cambodia is pancake flat or only moderately hilly. Safety, however, is a considerable concern on the newer surfaced roads, as local traffic travels at high speed. Bicycles can be transported around the country in the back of pick-ups or on the roof of minibuses.

Cycling around Angkor is an awesome experience as it really helps to get a measure

of the size and scale of the temple complex. Mountain biking is likely to take off in Mondulkiri and Ratanakiri Provinces over the coming years, as there are some great trails off the beaten track. It is already a reality around Chi Phat (p167) in the Cardamom Mountains. Guesthouses and hotels throughout Cambodia rent out bicycles for around US$2 per day, or US$7 to US$10 for an imported brand.

For the full story on cycle touring in Cambodia, see Lonely Planet's *Cycling Vietnam, Laos & Cambodia,* which has the low-down on planning a major ride.

PEPY Ride (☏023-222804; www.pepyride.org) is a bicycle and volunteer tour company offering adventures throughout Cambodia. PEPY promotes 'adventurous living, responsible giving' and uses proceeds to help build schools in rural Cambodia and fund education programs.

Boat

Cambodia's 1900km of navigable waterways are not as important as they once were for the average tourist, given major road improvements. North of Phnom Penh, the Mekong is easily navigable as far as Kratie, but there are no longer regular passenger services on these routes, as buses have taken all the business. There are scenic boat services between Siem Reap and Battambang, and the Tonlé Sap lake is also navigable year-round, although only by smaller boats between March and July.

Traditionally the most popular boat services with foreigners are those that run between Phnom Penh and Siem Reap. The express services do the trip in as little as five hours, but it is not the most interesting boat journey in Cambodia, as the Tonlé Sap lake is like a vast sea, offering little scenery.

It's much smarter (and much cheaper) to take a bus on the paved road instead.

The small boat between Siem Reap and Battambang (p219) is more rewarding, as the river scenery is truly memorable, but it can take forever.

Bus

The range of road transport is extensive. On sealed roads, the large air-conditioned buses are the best choice. Elsewhere in the country, a shared taxi or minibus is the way to go.

Bus services have come on in leaps and bounds in the last few years and the situation is getting even better as more roads are upgraded. Bus travel is arguably the safest way to get around the country these days. The services used most regularly by foreigners are those from Phnom Penh to Siem Reap, Battambang, Sihanoukville, Kompong Cham and Kratie, and the tourist buses from Siem Reap to Poipet. Minibuses serve most provincial routes but are not widely used by Western visitors. They are very cheap but often uncomfortably overcrowded and sometimes driven by maniacs. Only really consider them if there is no alternative. 'Express minibuses' now connect Phnom Penh and northeastern destinations such as Stung Treng and Ban Lung. Usually Hyundai Starex people carriers, these can be a faster and more comfortable way to travel than old minibuses.

Car & Motorcycle

Car and motorcycle rental are comparatively cheap in Cambodia and many visitors rent a car or bike for greater flexibility to visit out-of-the-way places and to stop when they choose. Almost all car rental in Cambodia includes a driver, which is good news given the abysmal state of many roads, the lack of road signs and the prominence of the psychopathic driver gene among many Cambodian road users.

Driving Licence

A standard driving licence is not much use in Cambodia. In theory, to drive a car you need an International Driving Licence, usually issued through your automobile association back home, but Cambodia is not currently a recognised country. It is very unlikely that a driving licence will be of any use to most travellers, save for those coming to live and work in Cambodia.

When it comes to renting motorcycles, it's a case of no licence required. If you can drive the bike out of the shop, you can drive it anywhere, or so the logic goes.

Fuel & Spare Parts

Fuel is relatively expensive in Cambodia compared with other staples, at around 5000r (US$1.25) a litre. Fuel is readily available throughout the country, but prices generally rise in rural areas. Even the most isolated communities usually have someone selling petrol out of Fanta or Johnnie Walker bottles. Some sellers mix this fuel with kerosene to make a quick profit – use it sparingly, in emergencies only.

When it comes to spare parts, Cambodia is flooded with Chinese, Japanese and Korean motorcycles, so it is easy to get parts for Hondas, Yamahas or Suzukis, but finding a part for a Harley or a Ducati is another matter. The same goes for cars – spares for Japanese cars are easy to come by, but if you are driving something obscure, bring substantial spares.

Hire

CAR
Car hire is generally only available with a driver and is most useful for sightseeing around Phnom Penh and Angkor. Some tourists with a healthy budget also arrange cars or 4WDs with drivers for touring the provinces. Hiring a car with a driver is about US$30 to US$35 for a day in and around Cambodia's towns. Heading into the provinces it rises to US$50 or more, plus petrol, depending on the destination. Hiring 4WDs will cost around US$60 to US$120 a day, depending on the model and the distance travelled. Driving yourself is just about possible, but this is inadvisable due to chaotic road conditions, personal liability in the case of an accident and higher charges.

MOTORCYCLE
Motorcycles are available for hire in Phnom Penh and

ROAD SAFETY

Many more people are now killed and injured each month in traffic accidents than by landmines. While this is partly down to landmine awareness efforts and ongoing clearance programs, it is also down to a huge rise in the number of vehicles on the roads and drivers travelling at dangerous speeds. Be extremely vigilant when travelling under your own steam and take care crossing the roads on the high-speed national highways. It is best not to travel on the roads at night due to a higher prevalence of accidents at this time. This especially applies to bikers, as several foreigners are killed each year in motorbike accidents.

ROAD DISTANCES (KM)

	Phnom Penh	Siem Reap	Sihanoukville	Battambang
Siem Reap	316			
Sihanoukville	230	546		
Battambang	293	171	523	
Kratie	258	574	488	551

some other popular tourist destinations. In Siem Reap (and at times in Sihanoukville), motorcycle rental is forbidden, so anyone planning any rides around Siem Reap needs to arrange a bike elsewhere. In other provincial towns, it is usually possible to rent a small motorcycle after a bit of negotiation. Costs are US$3 to US$10 per day for a 100cc motorcycle and around US$10 to US$25 for a 250cc dirt bike.

Drive with due care and attention, as medical facilities and ambulances are less than adequate beyond Phnom Penh, Siem Reap and Battambang. If you have never ridden a motorcycle before, Cambodia is not the best place to start, but once out of the city it does get easier. If you're jumping in at the deep end, make sure you are under the supervision of someone who knows how to ride.

The advantage of motorcycle travel is that it allows for complete freedom of movement and you can stop in small villages that Westerners rarely visit. It is possible to take motorcycles upcountry for tours, but only experienced off-road bikers should take to these roads with a dirt bike. Anyone planning a longer ride should try out the bike around Phnom Penh for a day or so first to make sure it is in good health.

For those with experience, Cambodia has some of the best roads in the world for dirt biking, particularly in the provinces of Preah Vihear, Mondulkiri, Ratanakiri and the Cardamom Mountains.

There are several specialised dirt-bike touring companies:

Cambodia Expeditions (www.cambodiaexpeditions.com) This team has been running motorbike tours and rallies in Cambodia since 1998. Very professional with some great routes in the north of the country.

Dancing Roads (www.dancingroads.com) Offers motorbike tours around the capital and gentle tours further afield to the South Coast. Based in Phnom Penh, the driver-guides are fun and friendly.

Hidden Cambodia (www.hiddencambodia.com) A Siem Reap–based company specialising in motorcycle trips throughout the country, including the remote temples of northern Cambodia and beyond.

Red Raid Cambodia (www.motorcycletourscambodia.com) More expensive but experienced French-run outfit offering trips throughout Cambodia, including the Cardamoms.

Siem Reap Dirt Bikes (www.siemreapdirtbikes.com) Siem Reap based, as you might guess; offers everything from day trips to six-day remote temple adventures.

Insurance

If you are travelling in a tourist vehicle with a driver, then the car is usually insured. When it comes to motorcycles, many rental bikes are not insured and you will have to sign a contract agreeing to a valuation for the bike if it is stolen. Make sure you have a strong lock and always leave the bike in guarded parking where available.

Do not even consider hiring a motorcycle if you are daft enough to be travelling in Cambodia without medical insurance. The cost of treating serious injuries, especially if you require an evacuation, is bankrupting for budget travellers.

Road Conditions & Hazards

Whether travelling or living in Cambodia, it is easy to lull yourself into a false sense of security and assume that down every rural road is yet another friendly village. However, even with the demise of the Khmer Rouge, odd incidents of banditry and robbery do occur in rural areas. There have also been some nasty bike-jackings in Sihanoukville. When travelling in your own vehicle, and particularly by motorcycle in rural areas, make certain you check the latest security information in communities along the way.

Be particularly careful about children on the road – you'll sometimes find kids hanging out in the middle of a major highway. Livestock on the road is also a menace; hit a cow and you'll both be pizza.

Other general security suggestions for those travelling by motorcycle:

» Try to get hold of a good-quality helmet for long journeys or high-speed riding.

» Carry a basic repair kit, including some tyre levers, a puncture-repair kit and a pump.

» Always carry a rope for towing on longer journeys in case you break down.

» In remote areas always carry several litres of water, as you never know when you will run out.

» Travel in small groups, not alone.

» When in a group, stay close together in case of any incident or accident.

» Don't be cheap with the petrol – running out of fuel in a rural area could jeopardise your health, especially if water runs out, too.

» Do not smoke marijuana or drink alcohol and drive.

» Keep your eyes firmly fixed on the road; Cambodian potholes eat people for fun.

Road Rules

If there are road rules in Cambodia it is doubtful that anyone is following them. Size matters and the biggest vehicle wins by default. The best advice if you drive a car or ride a motorcycle in Cambodia is to take nothing for granted and assume that your fellow motorists are visually challenged psychopaths.

In Cambodia traffic drives on the right. There are some traffic lights at junctions in Phnom Penh, Siem Reap and Sihanoukville, but where there are no lights, most traffic turns left into the oncoming traffic, edging along the wrong side of the road until a gap becomes apparent. For the uninitiated it looks like a disaster waiting to happen, but Cambodians are quite used to the system. Foreigners should stop at crossings and develop a habit of constant vigilance. Never assume that other drivers will stop at red lights, these are considered optional by most Cambodians, especially at night.

Phnom Penh is the one place where, amid all the chaos, traffic police take issue with Westerners breaking even the most trivial road rules. Make sure you don't turn left at a 'no left turn' sign or travel with your headlights on during the day (although, strangely, it doesn't seem to be illegal for Cambodians to travel without headlights at night). New laws requiring that bikes have mirrors, and that drivers (not passengers, even children) wear helmets, are being enforced around the country by traffic police eager to levy fines. Foreigners are popular targets.

Local Transport

Bus

There are currently no local bus networks in Cambodia, even in the capital, Phnom Penh.

Cyclo

As in Vietnam and Laos, the *cyclo* (pedicab) is a cheap way to get around urban areas. In Phnom Penh *cyclo* drivers can either be flagged down on main roads or found loitering around markets and major hotels. It is necessary to bargain the fare if taking a *cyclo* from outside an expensive hotel or popular restaurant or bar. Fares range from 1000r to US$1 (about 4000r). There are few *cyclos* in the provinces, and in Phnom Penh the *cyclo* is fast losing ground to the moto.

Moto

Motos, also known as *moto-dups* (*môdning moto driver*), are small motorcycle taxis. They are a quick way of making short hops around towns and cities. Prices range from 1000r to US$1 or more, depending on the distance and the town; expect to pay more at night. It used to be that prices were rarely agreed in advance, but with the increase in visitor numbers, a lot of drivers have got into the habit of overcharging. It's probably best to negotiate up front, particularly in the major tourist centres, outside fancy hotels or at night.

Outboards

Outboards (pronounced 'outboor') are the equivalent of Venice's *vaporetto*, a sort of local river-bus or taxi. Found all over the country, they are

---

THE MOTO BURN

Be careful not to put your leg near the exhaust pipe of a moto after long journeys; many travellers have received nasty burns, which can take a long time to heal in the sticky weather, and often require antibiotics to recover.

WARNING

Moto drivers and *cyclo* riders with little or no English may not understand where you want them to go even though they nod vigorously. This is a particular headache in a big city like Phnom Penh – see the box, p82.

small fibreglass boats with 15HP or 40HP engines, and can carry up to six people for local or longer trips. They rarely run to schedules but usually wait patiently for them to fill up. Those with time on their hands can join the wait; those in a hurry can charter the whole boat and take off. Another variation are the longtail rocket boats imported from Thailand that connect small villages on the upper stretches of the Mekong. Rocket is the definitive word and their safety is questionable.

Remork-moto

The *remork-moto* is a large trailer hitched to a motorcycle and pretty much operates as a low-tech local bus with oh-so-natural air-conditioning. They are used throughout rural Cambodia to transport people and goods, and are often seen on the edge of towns ready to ferry farmers back to the countryside.

Most popular tourist destinations, including Phnom Penh, Siem Reap and the South Coast, have their very own tourist versions of the *remork-moto (remork)*, with a canopied trailer hitched to the back of the motorbike for two people in comfort or as many as you can pile on at night. Often referred to as túk-túks by foreigners travelling in Cambodia, they're a great way to explore temples, as you get the breeze of the bike but some protection from the elements.

REMORK VERSUS TÚK-TÚK

So just what are those motorbikes with the cute little carriages pulled behind? *Remork-motos? Remorks? Túk-túks?* The debate rumbles on. Officially, Cambodians call them *remork-motos,* which is often shortened to *remork.* In Thailand, the high-octane three-wheeled taxis in Bangkok are known as túk-túks, and this moniker has hopped across the border into common usage in Cambodia. However, some Cambodians take offence at the use of the name túk-túk, so for the time being we are opting for *remork.* Remorkable.

Rotei Ses

Rotei means 'cart' or 'carriage' and *ses* is 'horse', but the term is used for any cart pulled by an animal. Cambodia's original 4WD, ox carts, usually pulled by water buffalo or cows, are a common form of transport in remote parts of the country, as only they can get through thick mud in the height of the wet season. Some local community-tourism initiatives now include cart rides.

Taxi

Taxi hire in towns and cities is getting easier, but there are still very few metered taxis, with just a couple of operators in Phnom Penh. Guesthouses, hotels and travel agents can arrange cars for sightseeing in and around towns.

Share Taxi & Pick-Up Trucks

In these days of improving roads, pick-up trucks are losing ground to 'express minibuses' or pumped-up Toyota Camrys that have their suspension jacked up like monster trucks. When using share taxis or pick-ups, it is an advantage to travel in numbers, as you can buy spare seats to make the journey more comfortable. Double the price for the front seat and quadruple it for the entire back row. It is important to remember that there aren't necessarily fixed prices on every route, so you have to negotiate, and prices do fluctuate with the price of petrol.

Share taxis are widely available for hire. For major destinations they can be hired individually, or you can pay for a seat and wait for other passengers to turn up. Guesthouses are also very helpful when it comes to arranging share taxis, at a price, of course.

When it comes to pick-ups, passengers can sit in the cab or, if money is short and comfort an alien concept, out on the back; trucks depart when seriously full. Passengers sitting out back should carry a scarf to protect against the dust, and sunscreen to protect against the sun. In the wet season a raincoat is as good as compulsory.

Train

Cambodia's rail system is, like the old road network, one of the most notorious in Asia. There are currently no passenger services, but this may change during the lifetime of this book as the railway is overhauled by a private Australian company.

The railway is currently being rehabilitated to bring speeds up to 50km/h. Eventually, the Cambodian network will be plugged into the Trans-Asian Railway, which will eventually link Singapore and China, but connecting Phnom Penh with Ho Chi Minh City via a Mekong bridge will take a few years yet.

The rail network consists of about 645km of single-track metre-gauge lines. The 385km northwestern line, built before WWII, links Phnom Penh with Pursat and Battambang. The final stretch from Sisophon to Poipet was pulled up by the Khmer Rouge in the 1970s but is now being replaced. The 254km southwestern line, which was completed in 1969, connects Phnom Penh with Takeo, Kampot and Sihanoukville. The prettiest sections of the network are between Takeo and Kampot and from there to Sihanoukville.

Cambodia Border Crossings

During the bad old days of communism and the Cold War, pretty much no land borders were open to foreigners. Times have changed and there are now more than a dozen border crossings connecting Cambodia with its neighbours.

Cambodia shares one border crossing with Laos, six crossings with Thailand and eight with Vietnam. Cambodian visas are now available at all the land crossings with Laos, Thailand and Vietnam. Neighbouring visas are available on arrival in Laos and Thailand but are not available on arrival in Vietnam. Most borders are open during the core hours of 7am to 5pm. However, some of the most popular crossings are open later in the evening and other more remote crossings close for lunch.

There are few legal money-changing facilities at some of the more remote border crossings, so be sure to have some small-denomination US dollars handy.

Cambodian immigration officers at the land border crossings – especially with Thailand – have a bad reputation for petty extortion. Travellers are occasionally asked for a small 'immigration fee' of some kind. More serious scams include overcharging for visas by demanding payment in Thai baht (anywhere between 1000B and 1200B instead of 600B) and forcing tourists to change US dollars into riel at a poor rate. Hold your breath, stand your ground, don't start a fight and remember that not all Cambodians are as mercenary as the boys in blue.

In this book we give detailed instructions for every crossing open to foreigners. Before making a long-distance trip, be aware of border closing times, visa regulations and any transport scams. Border details change regularly, so ask around or check the Lonely Planet Thorn Tree (www .lonelyplanet.com/thorn tree). For the latest on Cambodian border crossings, check out the Immigration Department website at http://cambodia-immigra tion.com.

Laos

Cambodia and Laos share a remote frontier that includes some of the wildest areas of both countries. There is only one border crossing open to foreigners.

Trapaeng Kriel–Nong Nok Khiene

The border between Cambodia and Laos is officially open from 7am to 5pm daily. It is very popular as an adventurous and cheap way to combine travel to northeastern Cambodia and southern Laos.

To enter Cambodia using this route, visas are available on arrival at Trapaeng Kriel. Lao visas are also finally available on arrival, ranging from US$30 to US$42 depending on nationality. Both sides of the border charge a processing fee for those crossing. (US$2 at any time; US$3 to US$4 after hours).

To leave Cambodia, travel to the remote town of Stung Treng. From Stung Treng there are minibuses (US$5) heading north to the border at around 7am or so and again just after lunch, but as onward transport is almost nonexistent on the Lao side it may be best to book a transfer on to Ban Nakasong in Laos, which guesthouses can help arrange. There are also a couple of buses during the day, including Rith Mony at about 8am and Phnom Penh Sorya Transport (from Phnom Penh) after 3pm, the latter continuing to Pakse.

Heading south, most of the above can be done in reverse. The minibuses head back to Stung Treng any time after 8.30am and the buses both depart the border around 10am or so. If you're stuck, it might be possible to charter a minibus for about US$30 and a moto for around US$10 if you bargain hard.

Thailand

Cambodia and Thailand share an 805km border and there are now six legal international border crossings, and many more options

Border Crossings

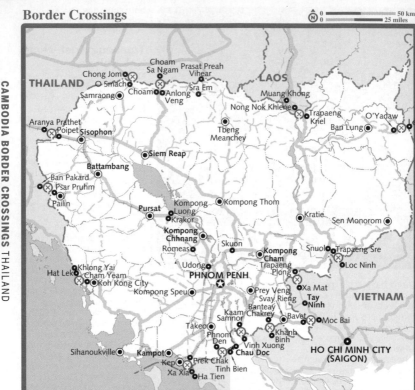

for locals. Tourist visas are available at all crossings for US$20. There are now clear signs displaying the US$20 charge, but many people are still charged 1000B or more.

Poipet–Aranya Prathet

The original land border crossing between Cambodia and Thailand has earned itself a bad reputation in recent years, with scams galore to help tourists part with their money.

There are two slow trains a day from Hualamphong train station in Bangkok to the Thai border town of Aranya Prathet (48B, six hours); take the 5.55am service unless you want to spend the night in a border town. There are also regular

bus services from Bangkok's Mo Chit northern terminal to Aranya Prathet (1st/2nd class 215/125B, four to five hours). From Aranya Prathet, take a túk-túk (motorised three-wheeled pedicab; 80B) or local bus (15B) for the final 6km to the border.

Once across the border, try not to get roped into the 'free' tourist shuttle to the 'International Tourist Terminals' (p226), which arrange transport to major cities, but at inflated prices: Phnom Penh (US$15, seven hours), Siem Reap (US$9, two hours) or Battambang (US$10, two hours). Stay solo and walk to the bus-company offices for cheaper fares. The vast majority of the buses depart very early in the morning (before 8am).

The road to Siem Reap (153km) is now in superb condition, making the on-ward journey just two hours in a private vehicle.

Leaving Cambodia, it is easy enough to get to Poipet from Siem Reap, Battam-bang or even Phnom Penh. By land there is no departure tax to leave Cambodia. From Poipet, take a túk-túk to Aranya Prathet, from where there are regular buses to Bangkok between 4am and 10pm or the slow train at 1.55pm.

Cham Yeam–Hat Lek

The Cham Yeam–Hat Lek border crossing, between Cambodia's Koh Kong and Trat in Thailand, is popular with travellers linking the beaches of Cambodia and

Thailand. It offers connections from Bangkok, Ko Samet and Ko Chang to the Cardamom Mountains, Sihanoukville and Phnom Penh.

Coming from Bangkok, take a bus to Trat (from 223B, five to six hours) from the city's Eastern or North and Northeastern bus stations. Buses depart regularly from 6am until 11.30pm. Another convenient option for travellers staying in the Khao San Rd area is to take one of the minibuses bound for Koh Chang, getting off at Trat.

From Trat, take a minibus straight to the Thai border at Hat Lek (120B). Once on the Cambodian side of the border you can take a moto (motorcycle with driver;

100B plus 11B toll) or taxi (200B plus 44B toll) to Koh Kong City.

Leaving Cambodia, take a taxi (US$10) or moto (US$3 or 100B) from Koh Kong across the toll bridge to the border. Once in Thailand, catch a minibus to Trat, from where there are regular buses to Bangkok.

Other Crossings

Several more out-of-the-way crossings are open for international traffic. The **O Smach–Chong Jom** crossing connects Cambodia's Oddar Meanchey Province and Thailand's Surin Province, but it is very remote. Share taxis link Siem Reap (90,000r, four hours) with Samraong

via NH68. From Samraong, take a moto (250B) or a charter taxi (US$25) for the punishing drive to O Smach (40km, nearly two hours) and its frontier casino zone. On the Thai side, it's easy, as *sawngthaew* (pick-ups) and motos take arrivals to the bus stop for Surin (70km, 1½ hours).

The **Choam–Choam Sa Ngam** crossing, a short distance from the site of Pol Pot's cremation, is 16km north of Anlong Veng or 134km north of Siem Reap. From Anlong Veng, a sealed road heads up to the border (US$3 to US$4 by moto). On the Thai side, you are in a pretty remote area, but there are some *sawngthaew* to Phusing, which has bus connections to Kantharalak or Si Saket. For transport options from Anlong Veng to Siem Reap (on a great new road), see p231; for Sra Em (near Prasat Preah Vihear), see p234.

The border at **Psar Pruhm–Ban Pakard** is 102km southwest of Battambang and 22km northwest of Pailin via rapidly improving roads. To travel this way independently, take a bus from Bangkok to Chanthaburi (160B, four hours) and then a minibus from there to Ban Pakard (150B, 1½ hours). A private taxi from Chanthaburi to Ban Pakard is about 1000B. On the Cambodian side, visas cost US$20 or 800B and the crossing is hassle-free. Cross the Cambodian border into the casino area and then arrange transport to Pailin (see p223).

There's also a crossing for visa-less day trips at **Prasat Preah Vihear**, the stunning Cambodian temple perched atop the Dangkrek Mountains. It is currently closed due to the earlier confrontation between Cambodia and Thailand over border demarcation in the area. However, it looks set to reopen during the lifetime of this book now that relations are thawing once more.

POPULAR LAND CROSSINGS

COUNTRY	BORDER CROSSING	CONNECTING TOWN	VISA ON ARRIVAL?
Cambodia	Trapeang Kriel	Stung Treng	Y (Cambodia)
Laos	Nong Nok Khiene	Si Phan Don	Y (Laos)
Cambodia	Poipet	Siem Reap	Y (Cambodia)
Thailand	Aranya Prathet	Bangkok	Y (Thailand)
Cambodia	Cham Yeam	Koh Kong	Y (Cambodia)
Thailand	Hat Lek	Trat	Y (Thailand)
Cambodia	O Smach	Samraong	Y (Cambodia)
Thailand	Chong Jom	Surin	Y (Thailand)
Cambodia	Psar Pruhm	Pailin	Y (Cambodia)
Thailand	Ban Pakard	Chanthaburi	Y (Thailand)
Cambodia	Bavet	Phnom Penh	Y (Cambodia)
Vietnam	Moc Bai	Ho Chi Minh City	N (Vietnam)
Cambodia	Kaam Samnor	Phnom Penh	Y (Cambodia)
Vietnam	Vinh Xuong	Chau Doc	N (Vietnam)
Cambodia	Prek Chak	Kep	Y (Cambodia)
Vietnam	Xa Xia	Ha Tien	N (Vietnam)
Cambodia	Phnom Den	Takeo	Y (Cambodia)
Vietnam	Tinh Bien	Chau Doc	N (Vietnam)
Cambodia	O Yadaw	Ban Lung	Y (Cambodia)
Vietnam	Le Tanh	Pleiku	N (Vietnam)

WELCOME TO SCAMBODIA

Poipet is a Wild West kind of place and has attracted a lot of unsavoury characters cling-ing to the coat-tails of the economic boom. Unfortunately, many of these are involved in the travel business and carry on like some sort of mafia, giving Cambodia a bad name. The Cham Yeam border, near Koh Kong, is not much better and notorious for overcharg-ing for visas. Below are some tips to navigate the maze, but rest assured that not every-one in Cambodia is out to scam you.

To avoid any visa overcharging at Cham Yeam and Poipet, it may be worth arranging an e-visa (www.mfaic.gov.kh; US$20 plus a processing fee of US$5) in advance. It takes three days to issue and you can exit at any land border crossing.

Poipet–Aranya Prathet

Right after you cross the stinky stream that marks the border, you come to 'Cambodian Visa Service', where the price of a tourist visa is posted as US$20. However, before you make it this far, plenty of enterprising people will have expended lots of creative energy in trying to make you part with up to double the actual cost of the visa.

A Cambodian 'consulate' has been set up inside Thailand, but there are no marked prices and 'officials' try to charge anywhere between 1000B and 1300B (US$33 to US$42) for the visa. Various techniques are employed, including the line that visas are no longer available at Poipet or that the visa will take two or three days to issue at the border. The trick is to survive the Thai side and make it to the 'Cambodian Visa Service' counter. Pay for the visa in US dollars only, as if you pay in Thai baht then the charge will immediately jump up to 800B to 1000B.

For more details on the Poipet shenanigans, see p226.

Cham Yeam–Hat Lek

Immigration officials at the Cham Yeam border are known to demand 1200B (US$42) for a tourist visa that should cost US$20. Government employees in Cambodia are notoriously underpaid and many 'buy' their jobs from senior officials. This involves a 'monthly fee' to keep the position and it seems tourists are being made to foot the bill.

We have heard reports of polite and persistent travellers who have managed to pay just US$25 or even US$20 (by claiming they only have US dollars, asking for a receipt or threatening to complain to the Ministry of Foreign Affairs or Interior in Phnom Penh), but these visas tend to be processed *very* slowly. Others have been told that if they don't pay the 1200B fee then they can go back to Thailand.

Vietnam

Cambodia and Vietnam share a long frontier with a bevy of border crossings. Foreigners are currently permitted to cross at eight places and there are new crossings opening every year. Cambodian visas are now available at all crossings. Vietnamese visas should be arranged in advance, as they are not available on arrival.

Bavet–Moc Bai

The original land crossing be-tween Vietnam and Cambo-dia has seen steady traffic for two decades. The trip by bus between Phnom Penh and Ho Chi Minh City takes about six to seven hours, including the border crossing, although it can take a lot longer before and after festivals. There are lots of companies offering direct services with no need to change buses. All charge between US$9 and US$12; see p80 for contact details.

Kaam Samnor–Vinh Xuong

This river border is very popular with independent travellers. It is a far more in-teresting trip than taking the road, as it involves a fast boat on the Mekong in Cambodia and travel along some very picturesque areas of the Me-kong Delta in Vietnam. Com-ing from Ho Chi Minh City, it is possible to book a cheap Mekong Delta tour through to Chau Doc and then make your own way from there.

There are several boat companies offering direct services between Phnom Penh and Chau Doc. Capitol Tour (Map p43; ☎023-217627; www.capitoltourscambodia .com; US$21) is the cheapest direct option to Chau Doc, departing at 8.30am daily. Hang Chau (☎023-631 4454; www.hangchautourist.com.vn; US$24) pulls out from Chau Doc at 7.30am and departs Phnom Penh at noon. The more upmarket Blue Cruiser (Map p48; ☎023-990441; www.bluecruiser.com; 93 Sisowath Quay, Phnom Penh;

US$35) departs Chau Doc at 8am and Phnom Penh at 1pm. Both take about three to four hours depending on the efficiency of the border crossing. **Victoria Hotels** (www.victoriahotels-asia .com; US$97) also has a boat making several runs a week between Phnom Penh and its Victoria Chau Doc Hotel. All of these boats depart from the Tourist Boat Dock (Map p48) in Phnom Penh.

There are several companies offering luxury cruises between Ho Chi Minh City and Siem Reap via this border crossing. International player **Pandaw Cruises** (www.pandaw.com) is an expensive option favoured by high-end tour companies. Cambodian company **Toum Teav Cruises** (www .cf-mekong.com) is smaller and is well regarded for its personal service and excellent food. **Heritage Line** (www.heritage-line.com) offers the most sophisticated cruise boats on this route with the original *Jayavarman VII* now complemented by the striking *Jahan*.

Prek Chak–Xa Xia

The easiest way to get to **Prek Chak** (open 6am to 5.30pm) and on to Ha Tien, Vietnam, is on a direct bus from Phnom Penh (US$16, five hours), Sihanoukville (US$16, five hours), Kampot (US$10, two hours), or Kep (US$8, 1½ hours). Virak Buntham has a bus from Phnom Penh; Virak Buntham and two other companies ply the Sihanoukville–Kampot–Kep–Ha Tien route.

A more flexible alternative from Phnom Penh or Kampot is to take any bus to Kompong Trach, then a moto (about US$3) for 15km, on a good road, to the frontier.

In Kep, tour agencies and guesthouses can arrange a direct moto (US$8, 40 minutes), *remork* (US$13, one hour) or taxi (US$20, 30 minutes). Rates and times are almost double from Kampot. Private vehicles take a new road that cuts south to the border 10km west of Kompong Trach.

At Prek Chak, motos ask US$5 to take you to the Vietnamese border post 300m past the Cambodian one, and then all the way to Ha Tien (7km). You'll save money walking across no-man's land and picking up a moto on the other side for US$2 to US$3.

As Ha Tien is a free economic zone, foreigners do not need a visa to visit, but they must limit their stay to 14 days and return via the same border. While technically you are required to have a visa to travel beyond the free economic zone, at the time of writing travellers were reportedly being allowed to travel on to Phu Quoc Island visa-free.

Vietnam visa holders bound for Phu Quoc should arrive in Ha Tien no later than 12.30pm to secure a ticket on the 1pm ferry (230,000r, 1½ hours). Extreme early risers may be able to make it to Ha Tien in time to catch the (slower) 8.20am car ferry to Phu Quoc. The scheduled buses from Cambodia to Ha Tien arrive before the 1pm boat departs.

Other Crossings

It's open season when it comes to border crossings between Cambodia and Vietnam, but many are a little out of the way for the average traveller.

The **Phnom Den–Tinh Bien** crossing (open 6am to 6pm) has been open for some time now but is rarely used, as most travellers prefer the Mekong crossing at Kaam Samnor or the newer Prek Chak crossing to the south. It lies about 60km southeast of Takeo town in Cambodia and offers connections to Chau Doc. Take a share taxi (10,000r), a chartered taxi (US$25) or a moto (US$10) from Takeo to the border (48km). When arriving from Vietnam, transport can be sporadic, but border police can radio for a taxi or moto.

There is a border crossing in Ratanakiri province at **O'Yadaw–Le Tanh** (open from 7am to 5pm), offering connections between Ban Lung and Pleiku, in Vietnam's central highlands. NH19 from Ban Lung to the O'Yadaw border is in good shape and traffic is picking up.

There is a cluster of border crossings in the east of Cambodia that connect obscure towns and are not really on the radar. The **Trapaeng Plong–Xa Mat** (open from 7am to 5pm) and **Trapaeng Sre–Loc Ninh** (7am to 5pm) crossings are both off NH7, and the Xa Mat crossing could be useful for those planning to visit the Cao Dai temple travelling to or from Ho Chi Minh City.

CAR & MOTORCYCLE

Car drivers and motorcycle riders will need registration papers, insurance documents and an International Driving Licence (although not officially recognised) to bring vehicles into Cambodia. It is complicated to bring in a car but relatively straightforward to bring in a motorcycle, as long as you have a *carnet de passage* (vehicle passport). This acts as a temporary import-duty waiver and should save a lot of hassles when dealing with Cambodian customs. Increasing numbers of international bikers are crossing into Cambodia, while most of the foreign cars that tend to make it are Thai-registered.

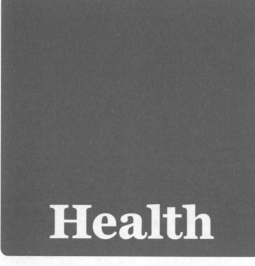

Health

General health is more of a concern in Cambodia than most other parts of southeast Asia, due to poor sanitation and a lack of effective medical-treatment facilities. Once you venture into rural areas you are very much on your own, although most towns have a reasonable clinic these days.

If you feel particularly unwell, try to see a doctor rather than visit a hospital; hospitals in rural areas are pretty primitive and diagnosis can be hit and miss. If you fall seriously ill in Cambodia you should head to Phnom Penh or Siem Reap (or Bangkok if it happens to be closer), as these are the only places in the country with decent emergency treatment. Pharmacies in the larger towns are remarkably well stocked and you don't need a prescription to get your hands on anything from antibiotics to antimalarials. Prices are also very reasonable, but do check the expiry date, as some medicine may have been on the shelves for quite a long time.

While the potential dangers can seem quite frightening, in reality few travellers experience anything more than an upset stomach. Don't let these warnings make you paranoid.

BEFORE YOU GO

Insurance

Do not visit Cambodia without medical insurance. Hospitals are extremely basic in the provinces and even in Phnom Penh the facilities are generally not up to the standards to which you may be accustomed. Anyone who has a serious injury or illness while in Cambodia may require emergency evacuation to Bangkok. With an insurance policy costing no more than the equivalent of a bottle of beer a day, this evacuation is free. Without an insurance policy, it will cost between US$10,000 and US$20,000 – somewhat more than a six-pack. Don't gamble with your health in Cambodia or you may end up another statistic.

Recommended Vaccinations

Plan ahead for getting your vaccinations (see the box, p352); some of them require more than one injection over a period of time, while others should not be given together.

Record all vaccinations on an International Certificate of Vaccination, available from your doctor. It is a good idea to carry this as proof of your vaccinations when travelling in Cambodia.

Medical Checklist

Following is a list of items you should consider including in your medical kit – consult your pharmacist for brands available in your country.

» aspirin or paracetamol – for pain or fever
» antihistamine – for allergies (such as hay fever), or to ease the itch from insect bites or stings
» cold and flu tablets, throat lozenges and nasal decongestant
» multivitamins – especially for long trips, when dietary vitamin intake may be inadequate
» loperamide or diphenoxylate – 'blockers' for diarrhoea
» rehydration mixture – to prevent dehydration, which may occur during bouts of diarrhoea
» insect repellent, sunscreen, lip balm and eye drops
» calamine lotion or aloe vera – to ease irritation from sunburn
» antifungal cream or powder – for fungal skin infections and thrush
» antiseptic (such as povidone-iodine) – for cuts and grazes
» bandages, plasters and other wound dressings
» water-purification tablets or iodine
» sterile kit (sealed medical kit containing syringes and needles) – highly recommended, as Cambodia has potential medical-hygiene issues

IN CAMBODIA

Availability & Cost of Health Care

Self-diagnosis and treatment of health problems can be risky, so you should always seek professional medical help.

Antibiotics should ideally be administered only under medical supervision. Take only the recommended dose at the prescribed intervals and use the whole course, even if the illness seems to be cured earlier. Stop immediately if there are any serious reactions, and don't use the antibiotic at all if you are unsure that you have the correct one.

The best clinics and hospitals in Cambodia are found in Phnom Penh and Siem

Reap. A consultation usually costs in the region of US$20 to US$40, plus medicine. Elsewhere, facilities are more basic, although a private clinic is usually preferable to a government hospital. For serious injuries or illnesses, seek treatment in Bangkok.

Infectious Diseases

Dengue

This viral disease is transmitted by mosquitoes. There is only a small risk to travellers, except during epidemics, which usually occur during and just after the wet season.

Unlike the malaria mosquito, the *Aedes aegypti* mosquito, which transmits the dengue virus, is most active during the day and is found mainly in urban areas.

Signs and symptoms of dengue fever include a sudden onset of high fever, headache, joint and muscle pains (hence its old name, 'breakbone fever'), plus nausea and vomiting. A rash of small red spots appears three to four days after the onset of fever. Dengue is commonly mistaken for other infectious diseases, including influenza.

Seek medical attention if you think you may be infected. A blood test can diagnose infection, but there is no specific treatment for the disease. Aspirin should be avoided, as it increases the risk of haemorrhaging, but plenty of rest is advised. Recovery may be prolonged, with tiredness lasting for several weeks.

There is no vaccine against dengue fever. The best prevention is to avoid mosquito bites at all times – see Malaria, p354, for more details.

Fungal Infections

Fungal infections occur more commonly in hot weather and are usually on the scalp, between the toes (athlete's foot) or fingers, in the groin and on the body (ringworm). Ringworm, a fungal infection, not a worm, is contracted from infected animals or other people. Moisture encourages these infections.

To prevent fungal infections wear loose, comfortable clothes, avoid artificial fibres, wash frequently and dry yourself carefully. If you do get an infection, wash the infected area at least once daily with a disinfectant or medicated soap and water, rinse and dry well.

Hepatitis

Hepatitis is a general term for inflammation of the liver. Several different viruses cause hepatitis, and they differ in the way that they are transmitted. The symptoms are similar in all forms of the illness, and include fever, chills, headache, fatigue, feelings of weakness, and aches and pains, followed by loss of appetite, nausea,

RECOMMENDED VACCINATIONS

Recommended vaccinations for a trip to Cambodia are listed here, but it is imperative that you discuss your needs with your doctor. For more details about the diseases themselves, see the individual entries later in this section.

» **Diphtheria and tetanus** – vaccinations for these two diseases are usually combined.

» **Hepatitis A** – this vaccine provides long-term immunity after an initial injection and a booster at six to 12 months. The hepatitis A vaccine is also available in a combined form with the hepatitis B vaccine – three injections over a six-month period are required.

» **Hepatitis B** – vaccination involves three injections, with a booster at 12 months.

» **Japanese B encephalitis** – three injections over 30 days.

» **Polio** – a booster every 10 years maintains immunity.

» **Rabies** – vaccination should be considered by those spending a month or longer in Cambodia. Vaccination involves having three injections over 21 to 28 days.

» **Tuberculosis** – vaccination against TB (BCG vaccine) is recommended for children and young adults who will be living in Cambodia for three months or more.

» **Typhoid** – vaccination against typhoid may be required if you are travelling for more than a couple of weeks in Cambodia.

vomiting, abdominal pain, dark urine, light-coloured faeces, jaundiced (yellow) skin and yellowing of the whites of the eyes.

Hepatitis A is transmitted by ingesting contaminated food or water. You should seek medical advice, but there is not much you can do apart from resting, drinking lots of fluids, eating lightly and avoiding fatty foods. Hepatitis E is transmitted in the same way as hepatitis A.

There are almost 300 million chronic carriers of hepatitis B in the world. It is spread through contact with infected blood, blood products or body fluids; for example, through sexual contact, unsterilized needles, blood transfusions or contact with blood via small breaks in the skin. Hepatitis C and D are spread in the same way as hepatitis B and can also lead to long-term complications.

HIV/AIDS

Infection with the human immunodeficiency virus (HIV) may lead to acquired immune deficiency syndrome (AIDS), which is a fatal disease. Any exposure to blood, blood products or body fluids may put the individual at risk.

The disease is often transmitted through sexual contact or dirty needles, so vaccinations, acupuncture, tattooing and body piercing can be potentially as dangerous as intravenous drug use.

Intestinal Worms

These parasites are most common in rural Cambodia. The various worms have different ways of infecting people. Some may be ingested in food such as undercooked meat (eg tapeworms) and some enter through your skin (eg hookworms). Consider having a stool test when you return home to check for worms and to determine the appropriate treatment.

Malaria

This serious and potentially fatal disease is spread by mosquitoes. If you are travelling in endemic areas it is extremely important to avoid mosquito bites and to take tablets to prevent the disease developing if you become infected. There is no malaria in Phnom Penh, Siem Reap and most other major urban areas in Cambodia, so visitors on short trips to the most popular places do not need to take medication. Malaria self-test kits are widely available in Cambodia, but are not that reliable.

Symptoms of malaria include fever, chills and sweating, headache, aching joints, diarrhoea and stomach pains, usually preceded by a vague feeling of ill health. Seek medical help immediately if malaria is suspected, as, without treatment, the disease can rapidly become more serious or even fatal.

Sexually Transmitted Infections (STIs)

Gonorrhoea, herpes and syphilis are among these infections. Sores, blisters or a rash around the genitals and discharges or pain when urinating are common symptoms. With some STIs, such as wart virus or chlamydia, symptoms may be less marked or not observed at all, especially in women. Syphilis symptoms eventually disappear completely, but the disease continues and can cause severe problems in later years. Reliable condoms are widely available throughout urban areas of Cambodia.

Typhoid

Typhoid fever is a dangerous gut infection caused by contaminated water and food. Medical help must be sought.

In its initial stages sufferers may feel they have a bad cold or flu on the way, as early symptoms are a headache, body aches and a fever that rises a little each day until it is around 40°C (104°F) or higher. There may also be vomiting, abdominal pain, diarrhoea or constipation.

In the second week, the high fever and slow pulse continue, and a few pink spots may appear on the body; trembling, delirium, weakness, weight loss and dehydration may occur.

Traveller's Diarrhoea

Simple things like a change of water, food or climate can all cause a mild bout of diarrhoea, but a few rushed toilet trips with no other symptoms are not indicative of a major problem. Almost everyone gets a mild bout of the runs on a longer visit to Cambodia.

Dehydration is the main danger with diarrhoea, particularly in children or the elderly as it can occur quite quickly. Under all circumstances *fluid replacement* is the most important thing to remember. Stick to a

EVERYDAY HEALTH

Normal body temperature is up to 37°C (98.6°F); more than 2°C (4°F) higher indicates a high fever. The normal adult pulse rate is 60 to 100 beats per minute (children 80 to 100, babies 100 to 140). As a general rule, the pulse increases about 20 beats per minute for each 1°C (2°F) rise in fever.

Respiration (breathing) rate is also an indicator of illness. Count the number of breaths per minute: between 12 and 20 is normal for adults and older children (up to 30 for younger children, 40 for babies). People with a high fever or serious respiratory illness breathe more quickly than normal. More than 40 shallow breaths a minute may indicate pneumonia.

bland diet as you recover. Commercially available oral rehydration salts are very useful; add them to boiled or bottled water.

Gut-paralysing drugs such as Lomotil or Imodium can be used to bring relief from the symptoms of diarrhoea, although they do not actually cure the problem. Only use these drugs if you do not have access to toilets and *must* travel.

Sometimes antibiotics may be required, for diarrhoea with blood or mucus (dysentery), any diarrhoea with fever, profuse watery diarrhoea, persistent diarrhoea not improving after 48 hours and severe diarrhoea. These suggest a more serious cause, and gut-paralysing drugs should be avoided.

Environmental Hazards

Food

There is an adage that says, 'If you can cook it, boil it or peel it you can eat it...otherwise forget it'. This is slightly extreme, but many travellers have found it is better to be safe than sorry. Vegetables and fruit should be washed with purified water or peeled where possible. Beware of ice cream that is sold in the street (or anywhere), as it might have been melted and refrozen. Shellfish such as mussels, oysters and clams should be avoided, as should undercooked meat, particularly in the form of mince.

Heat Exhaustion

Dehydration and salt deficiency can cause heat exhaustion. Take time to acclimatise to high temperatures, drink sufficient liquids and do not do anything too physically demanding.

Salt deficiency is characterised by fatigue, lethargy, headaches, giddiness and muscle cramps; salt tablets may help, but adding extra salt to your food is better.

CONTACT LENSES

People wearing contact lenses should be aware that Cambodia is an extremely dusty country and this can cause much irritation when travelling. It is generally bearable in cars, but when travelling by motorcycle or pick-up, it is most definitely not. Pack a pair of glasses.

Heatstroke can occur if the body's heat regulating mechanism breaks down, causing the body temperature to rise to dangerous levels. Long, continuous periods of exposure to high temperatures and insufficient fluids can leave you vulnerable to heatstroke.

Insect Bites & Stings

Bedbugs live in various places, but particularly in dirty mattresses and bedding, and are evidenced by spots of blood on bedclothes or on the wall. Bedbugs leave itchy bites in neat rows. Calamine lotion or Stingose spray may help.

All lice cause itching and discomfort. They make themselves at home in your hair (head lice), your clothing (body lice) or in your pubic hair (crabs). You catch lice through direct contact with infected people or by sharing combs, clothing and the like. Powder or shampoo treatment will kill the lice, and infected clothing should be washed in very hot, soapy water and left to dry in the sun.

Leeches may be present in damp rainforest conditions; they attach themselves to your skin to suck your blood. Trekkers often get them on their legs or in their boots. Salt or a lighted cigarette end will make them fall off.

Prickly Heat

Prickly heat is an itchy rash caused by excessive perspiration trapped under the skin. It usually strikes people who have just arrived in a hot climate. Keeping cool, bathing often, drying the skin, using a mild talcum or prickly heat powder, or finding air-conditioning, may help.

Snakes

To minimise the chances of being bitten by a snake, always wear boots, socks and long trousers when walking through undergrowth where snakes may be present.

Water

The number-one rule is *be careful of water and ice,* although both are probably factory produced, a legacy of the French. If you don't know for certain that the water is safe, assume the worst. Reputable brands of bottled water or soft drinks are usually fine, but you can't safely drink tap water. Only use water from containers with a serrated seal. Tea and coffee are generally fine, as they're made with boiled water.

Traditional Medicine

Traditional medicine or *thnam boran* is very popular in rural Cambodia. There are *kru Khmer* (traditional medicine men) in most districts of the country and some locals trust them more than modern doctors and hospitals. Working with tree bark, roots, herbs and plants, they boil up brews to supposedly cure all ills. However, when it comes to serious conditions like snake bites, their treatments can be counterproductive. Other popular traditional remedies, even in the city, include *kor kchoal,* a vigorous coin massage to take away the bad wind, and *chup kchoal,* a massage using heated vacuum cups. The first leaves red streaks on the torso like the patient has been flayed, the second large round circles like a contagious disease.

WANT MORE?

For in-depth language information and handy phrases, check out Lonely Planet's Southeast Asia Phrasebook. You'll find it at **shop.lonelyplanet.com**, or you can buy Lonely Planet's iPhone phrasebooks at the Apple App Store.

Language

The Khmer language is spoken by approximately nine million people in Cambodia, and is understood by many in neighbouring countries. Although Khmer as spoken in Phnom Penh is generally intelligible to Khmers nationwide, there are several distinct dialects in other parts of the country. Most notably, inhabitants of Takeo Province tend to modify or slur hard consonant/vowel combinations, especially those with 'r'. For example, *bram* (five) becomes *pe-am*, *sraa* (alcohol) becomes *se-aa*, and *baraang* (French for foreigner) becomes *be-ang*. In Siem Reap there's a Lao-sounding lilt to the local speech – some vowels are modified, eg *poan* (thousand) becomes *peuan*, and *kh'sia* (pipe) becomes *kh'seua*.

Though English is fast becoming Cambodia's second language, the Khmer population still clings to the Francophone pronunciation of the Roman alphabet and most foreign words. This is helpful to remember when spelling Western words and names aloud – 'ay-bee-see' becomes 'ah-bey-sey' and so on.

The pronunciation guides in this chapter are designed for basic communication rather than linguistic perfection. Read them as if they were English, and you shouldn't have problems being understood. Some consonant combinations are separated with an apostrophe for ease of pronunciation, eg 'j-r' in j'rook (pig) and 'ch-ng' in ch'ngain (delicious). Also note that k is pronounced as the 'g' in 'go'; kh as the 'k' in 'kind'; p as the final 'p' in 'puppy'; ph as the 'p' in 'pond'; r as in 'rum' (hard and rolling); t as the 't' in 'stand'; and th as the 't' in 'two'.

Vowels and vowel combinations with an h at the end are pronounced with a puff of air at the end. Vowels are pronounced as follows:

» a and ah shorter and harder than aa
» aa as the 'a' in 'father'
» ae as the 'a' in 'cat'
» ai as in 'aisle'
» am as the 'um' in 'glum'
» av like a nasal ao (without the 'v')
» aw as the 'aw' in 'jaw'
» awh as the 'aw' in 'jaw' (short and hard)
» ay as ai (slightly nasal)
» e as in 'they'
» eh as the 'a' in 'date' (short and hard)
» eu like 'oo' (with flat lips)
» euh as eu (short and hard)
» euv like a nasal eu (without the 'v')
» ey as in 'prey'
» i as in 'kit'
» ia as the 'ee' in 'beer' (without the 'r')
» ih as the 'ee' in 'teeth' (short and hard)
» ii as the 'ee' in 'feet'
» o as the 'ow' in 'cow'
» œ as 'er' in 'her' (more open)
» oh as the 'o' in 'hose' (short and hard)
» ohm as the 'ome' in 'home'
» ow as in 'glow'
» u as the 'u' in 'flute' (short and hard)
» ua as the 'ou' in 'tour'
» uah as ua (short and hard)
» uh as the 'u' in 'but'
» uu as the 'oo' in 'zoo'

BASICS

The Khmer language reflects the social standing of the speaker and the subject through personal pronouns and 'politeness words'. These range from the simple *baat* for men and *jaa* for women, placed at the end of a sentence and meaning 'yes' or 'I agree', to the very formal and archaic *Reachasahp* or 'royal language', a separate vocabulary reserved for addressing the king and very high officials. Many of the pronouns are determined on the basis of the subject's age and gender in relation to the speaker.

Foreigners are not expected to know all of these forms. The easiest and most general personal pronoun is *niak* (you), which may be used in most situations, for either gender. Men of your age or older may be called *lowk* (Mister). Women of your age or older can be called *bawng srei* (older sister) or, for more formal situations, *lowk srei* (Madam). *Bawng* is a good informal, neutral pronoun for men or women who are (or appear to be) older than you. For the third person (he/she/they), male or female, singular or plural, the respectful form is *koat* and the common form is *ke*.

Hello.	ជំរាបសួរ	johm riab sua
Goodbye.	លាសិនហើយ	lia suhn hao-y
Excuse me./ Sorry.	សុំទោស	sohm toh
Please.	សូម	sohm
Thank you.	អរគុណ	aw kohn
You're welcome.	អត់អីទេ/ សូមអញ្ជើញ	awt ei te/ sohm anjœ-in
Yes.	បាទ/ចាស	baat/jaa (m/f)
No.	ទេ	te

How are you?
អ្នកសុខសប្បាយទេ? niak sohk sabaay te

I'm fine.
ខ្ញុំសុខសប្បាយ kh'nyohm sohk sabaay

What's your name?
អ្នកឈ្មោះអ្វី? niak ch'muah ei

My name is ...
ខ្ញុំឈ្មោះ ... kh'nyohm ch'muah ...

Does anyone speak English?
ទីនេះមានអ្នកចេះ tii nih mian niak jeh
ភាសាអង់គ្លេសទេ? phiasaa awngle te

I don't understand.
ខ្ញុំមិនយល់ទេ/ kh'nyohm muhn yuhl te/
ខ្ញុំស្ដាប់មិនបានទេ kh'nyohm s'dap muhn baan te

ACCOMMODATION

Where's a hotel?
អ្នកតែលនៅឯណា? ohtail neuv ai naa

I'd like a room ...	ខ្ញុំសុំបន្ទប់ ...	kh'nyohm sohm bantohp ...
for one person	សំរាប់ មួយនាក់	samruhp muy niak
for two people	សំរាប់ ពីរនាក់	samruhp pii niak
with a bathroom	ដែលមាន បន្ទប់ទឹក	dail mian bantohp tuhk
with a fan	ដែលមាន កង្ហារ	dail mian dawnghahl
with a window	ដែលមាន បង្អួច	dail mian bawng-uit

How much is it per day?
តំលៃមួយថ្ងៃ damlay muy th'ngay
ប៉ុន្មាន? pohnmaan

DIRECTIONS

Where is a/the ...?
... នៅឯណា? ... neuv ai naa

How can I get to ...?
ផ្លូវណាទៅ ...? phleuv naa teuv ...

Go straight ahead.
ទៅត្រង់ teuv trawng

Turn left.
បត់ឆ្វេង bawt ch'weng

Turn right.
បត់ស្ដាំ bawt s'dam

at the corner
នៅកាច់ជ្រុង neuv kait j'rohng

behind
នៅខាងក្រោយ neuv khaang krao-y

in front of
នៅខាងមុខ neuv khaang mohk

next to
នៅជាប់ neuv joab

opposite
នៅទល់មុខ neuv tohl mohk

EATING & DRINKING

Where's a ...? ... នៅឯណា? ... neuv ai naa

food stall	កន្លែងលក់ម្ហូប	kuhnlaing loak m'howp
market	ផ្សារ	psar
restaurant	ភោជនីយដ្ឋាន	resturawn

Do you have a menu in English?
មានម៉ឺនុយជាភាសាអង់គ្លេសទេ? mien menui jea piasaa awnglay te

What's the speciality here?
ទីនេះមានម្ហូបអ្វីពិសេសទេ? tii nih mien m'howp ei piseh te

I'm vegetarian.
ខ្ញុំតមសាច kh'nyohm tawm sait

I'm allergic to (peanuts).
កុំដាក់ (សណ្ដែកដី) kohm dak (sandaik dei)

Not too spicy, please.
សូមកុំធ្វើហឹរពេក sohm kohm twœ huhl pek

This is delicious.
អានេះឆ្ងាញ់ណាស់ nih ch'ngain nah

The bill, please.
សូមគិតលុយ sohm kuht lui

Fruit & Vegetables

apple	ផ្លែប៉ោម	phla i powm
banana	ចេក	chek
coconut	ដូង	duong
custard apple	ទៀប	tiep
dragonfruit	ផ្លែស្រកានាគ	phlai srakaa neak
durian	ធុរេន	tourain
grapes	ទំពាំងបាយជូរ	tompeang baai juu
guava	ត្របែក	trawbaik
jackfruit	ខ្នុរ	khnau
lemon	ក្រូចឆ្មារ	krow-it ch'maa
longan	មៀន	mien
lychee	ផ្លែគូលេន	phlai kuulain
mandarin	ក្រូចខ្វិច	krow-it khwait
mango	ស្វាយ	svay

mangosteen	មង្ឃុត	mongkut
orange	ក្រូចពោធិសាត់	krow-it pow saat
papaya	ល្ហុង	l'howng
pineapple	ម្នាស់	menoa
pomelo	ក្រូចថ្លុង	krow-it th'lohng
rambutan	សាវម៉ាវ	sao mao
starfruit	ស្ពឺ	speu
vegetables	បន្លែ	buhn lai
watermelon	ឪឡឹក	euv luhk

Meat & Fish

beef	សាច់គោ	sait kow
chicken	សាច់មាន់	sait moan
crab	ក្ដាម	k'daam
eel	អន្ទង់	ahntohng
fish	ត្រី	trey
frog	កង្កែប	kawng kaip
lobster	បង្កង	bawng kawng
pork	សាច់ជ្រូក	sait j'ruuk
shrimp	បង្គា	bawngkia
snail	ខ្យង	kh'jawng
squid	មឹក	meuk

Other

bread	នំបុ័ង	nohm paang
butter	ប៊ឺរ	bœ
chilli	ម្ទេស	m'teh
curry	ការី	karii
fish sauce	ទឹកត្រី	teuk trey
fried	ឆៀន/ឆា	jien/chaa
garlic	ខ្ទឹមស	kh'tuhm saw
ginger	ខ្ញី	kh'nyei
grilled	អាំង	ahng
ice	ទឹកកក	teuk koh
lemongrass	ស្លឹកគ្រៃ	sluhk kray
noodles (egg/rice)	មី/គុយទាវ	mii/kyteow

pepper	ម្រេច	m'rait
rice	បាយ	bai
salt	អំបិល	uhmbuhl
soup	ស៊ុប	sup
soy sauce	ទឹកស៊ីអ៊ីវ	teuk sii iw
spring rolls (fresh/fried)	ណែម/ឆាយ៉	naim/chaa yaw
steamed	ចំហុយ	jamhoi
sugar	ស្ករ	skaw

Drinks

beer	បៀរ	bii-yœ
coffee	កាហ្វេ	kaa fey
lemon juice	ទឹកក្រូច ឆ្មារ	teuk krow-it ch'maa
orange juice	ទឹកក្រូច ពោធិសាត់	teuk krow-it pow sat
tea	តែ	tai
water	ទឹក	teuk

EMERGENCIES

Help!
ជួយខ្ញុំផង!   juay kh'nyohm phawng

Call the police!
ជួយហៅប៉ូលីសមក!   juay hav polih mao

Call a doctor!
ជួយហៅ   juay hav
គ្រូពេទ្យមក!   kruu paet mao

I've been robbed.
ខ្ញុំត្រូវចោរប្លន់   kh'nyohm treuv jao plawn

I'm ill.
ខ្ញុំឈឺ   kh'nyohm cheu

I'm allergic to (antibiotics).
ខ្ញុំមិនត្រូវធាតុ   kh'nyohm muhn treuv thiat
(អង់ទីប៊ីយោទិក)   (awntiibiowtik)

Where are the toilets?
បង្គន់នៅឯណា?   bawngkohn neuv ai naa

SHOPPING & SERVICES

I want to see the ...
ខ្ញុំចង់ទៅមើល ...   kh'nyohm jawng teuv mœl ...

What time does it open?
វាបើកម៉ោងប៉ុន្មាន?   wia baok maong pohnmaan

What time does it close?
វាបិទម៉ោងប៉ុន្មាន?   wia buht maong pohnmaan

I'm looking for the ... ខ្ញុំរក ...   kh'nyohm rohk ...

bank	ធនាគារ	th'niakia
post office	ប្រៃសណីយ៍	praisuhnii
public telephone	ទូរស័ព្ទ សាធារណៈ	turasahp saathiaranah
temple	វត្ត	wawt

How much is it?
នេះថ្លៃប៉ុន្មាន?   nih th'lay pohnmaan

That's too much.
ថ្លៃពេក   th'lay pek

No more than ...
មិនលើសពី ...   muhn lœh pii ...

What's your best price?
អ្នកដាច់ប៉ុន្មាន?   niak dait pohnmaan

I want to change US dollars.
ខ្ញុំចង់ដូរ   kh'nyohm jawng dow
ដុល្លាអាមេរិក   dolaa amerik

What is the exchange rate for US dollars?
មួយដុល្លា   muy dolaa
ដូរបានប៉ុន្មាន?   dow baan pohnmaan

TIME & DATES

What time is it?
ពេលវេលានេះម៉ោងប៉ុន្មាន? eileuv nih maong pohnmaan

in the morning	ពេលព្រឹក	pel pruhk
in the afternoon	ពេលរសៀល	pel r'sial
in the evening	ពេលល្ងាច	pel l'ngiat
at night	ពេលយប់	pel yohp

yesterday	ម្សិលមិញ	m'suhl mein
today	ថ្ងៃនេះ	th'ngay nih
tomorrow	ថ្ងៃស្អែក	th'ngay s'aik

Monday	ថ្ងៃចន្ទ	th'ngay jahn
Tuesday	ថ្ងៃអង្គារ	th'ngay ahngkia
Wednesday	ថ្ងៃពុធ	th'ngay poht
Thursday	ថ្ងៃព្រហស្បតិ៍	th'ngay prohoah
Friday	ថ្ងៃសុក្រ	th'ngay sohk
Saturday	ថ្ងៃសៅរ៍	th'ngay sav
Sunday	ថ្ងៃអាទិត្យ	th'ngay aatuht

TRANSPORT

Where's the ...?	... នៅឯណា?	... neuv ai naa
airport	វិមានយន្ត	wial yohn
	ហោះ	hawh
bus stop	ចំណត	jamnawt
	ឡានឈ្នួល	laan ch'nual
train station	ស្ថានីយ	s'thaanii
	រថភ្លើង	roht plœng

When does the ... leave?	... ចេញម៉ោង ប៉ុន្មាន?	... jein maong pohnmaan
boat	ទូក	duk
bus	ឡានឈ្នួល	laan ch'nual
train	រថភ្លើង	roht plœng
plane	យន្តហោះ	yohn hawh

What time does the last bus leave?
ឡានឈ្នួលចុងក្រោយ   laan ch'nual johng krao-y
ចេញទៅម៉ោងប៉ុន្មាន?   jein teuv maong pohnmaan

I want to get off (here).
ខ្ញុំចង់ចុះ(ទីនេះ)   kh'nyohm jawng joh (tii nih)

How much is it to ...?
ទៅ ... ថ្លៃប៉ុន្មាន?   teuv ... th'lay pohnmaan

Please take me to (this address).
សូមជូនខ្ញុំទៅ   sohm juun kh' nyohm teuv
(អាសយដ្ឋាននេះ)   (aasayathaan nih)

Here is fine, thank you.
ឈប់នៅទីនេះក5បាន   chohp neuv tii nih kaw baan

Numbers

Khmers count in increments of five – after reaching the number five *(bram)*, the cycle begins again with the addition of one, ie 'five-one' *(bram muy)*, 'five-two' *(bram pii)* and so on to 10, which begins a new cycle. For example, 18 has three parts: 10, five and three.

There's also a colloquial form of counting that reverses the word order for numbers between 10 and 20 and separates the two words with *duhn: pii duhn dawp* for 12, *bei duhn dawp* for 13 and so on. This form is often used in markets, so listen keenly.

1	មួយ	muy
2	ពីរ	pii
3	បី	bei
4	បួន	buan
5	ប្រាំ	bram
6	ប្រាំមួយ	bram muy
7	ប្រាំពីរ	bram pii
8	ប្រាំបី	bram bei
9	ប្រាំបួន	bram buan
10	ដប់	dawp
11	ដប់មួយ	dawp muy
12	ដប់ពីរ	dawp pii
16	ដប់ប្រាំមួយ	dawp bram muy
20	ម្ភៃ	m'phei
21	ម្ភៃមួយ	m'phei muy
30	សាមសិប	saamsuhp
40	សែសិប	saisuhp
100	មួយរយ	muy roy
1000	មួយពាន់	muy poan
1,000,000	មួយលាន	muy lian
1st	ទីមួយ	tii muy
2nd	ទីពីរ	tii pii
3rd	ទីបី	tii bei
4th	ទីបួន	tii buan
10th	ទីដប់	tii dawp

GLOSSARY

apsara – heavenly nymph or angelic dancer, often represented in Khmer sculpture

Asean – Association of Southeast Asian Nations

Avalokiteshvara – the Bodhisattva of Compassion and the inspiration for Jayavarman VII's Angkor Thom

baray – reservoir

boeng – lake

Chenla – pre-Angkorian period, 6th to 8th centuries

chunchiet – ethnic minorities

CPP – Cambodian People's Party

cyclo – pedicab, bicycle rickshaw

devaraja – cult of the god-king, established by Jayavarman II, in which the monarch has universal power

devadas – goddesses

EFEO – École Française d'Extrême Orient

essai – wise man or traditional medicine man

Funan – pre-Angkorian period, 1st to 5th centuries

Funcinpec – National United Front for an Independent, Neutral, Peaceful and Cooperative Cambodia; royalist political party

garuda – mythical half-man, half-bird creature

gopura – entrance pavilion in traditional Hindu architecture

Hun Sen – Cambodia's prime minister (1985–present)

Jayavarman II – the king (r 802–50) who established the cult of the god-king, kicking off a period

of amazing architectural productivity that resulted in the extraordinary temples of Angkor

Jayavarman VII – the king (r 1181–1219) who drove the Chams out of Cambodia before embarking on an ambitious construction program, including the walled city of Angkor Thom

Kampuchea – the name Cambodians use for their country; to non-Khmers, it is associated with the bloody rule of the Khmer Rouge, which insisted that the outside world adopt for Cambodia the name Democratic Kampuchea from 1975 to 1979

Khmer – a person of Cambodian descent; the language of Cambodia

Khmer Krom – ethnic Khmers living in Vietnam

Khmer Rouge – a revolutionary organisation that seized power in 1975 and implemented a brutal social restructuring, resulting in the suffering and death of millions of Cambodians during its four-year rule

kouprey – extremely rare wild ox of Southeast Asia, probably extinct

krama – scarf

linga – phallic symbols

Mahayana – literally, 'Great Vehicle'; a school of Buddhism (also known as the Northern School) that built upon and extended the early Buddhist teachings; see also *Theravada*

moto – small motorcycle with driver; a common form of transport in Cambodia

Mt Meru – the mythical dwelling of the Hindu god Shiva

naga – mythical serpent, often multiheaded; a symbol

used extensively in Angkorian architecture

nandi – sacred ox, vehicle of Shiva

NGO – nongovernmental organisation

NH – national highway

Norodom Ranariddh, Prince – son of King Sihanouk and former leader of *Funcinpec*

Norodom Sihanouk, King – former king, head of state, film director and a towering figure in modern-day Cambodia

Pali – ancient Indian language that, along with Sanskrit, is the root of modern *Khmer*

phnom – mountain or hill

Pol Pot – the former leader of the Khmer Rouge; responsible for the suffering and deaths of millions of Cambodians; also known as Saloth Sar

prasat – stone or brick hall with religious or royal significance

preah – sacred

psar – market

Ramayana – an epic Sanskrit poem composed around 300 BC featuring the mythical Ramachandra, the incarnation of the god Vishnu

remork-moto – trailer pulled by a motorcycle; often shortened to *remork*

rom vong – Cambodian circle dancing

Sangkum Reastr Niyum – People's Socialist Community; a national movement, led by King Sihanouk, that ruled the country during the 1950s and 1960s

Sanskrit – ancient Hindu language that, along with *Pali*, is the root of modern Khmer language

stung – river

Suryavarman II – the king (r 1112–52) responsible for building Angkor Wat and for expanding and unifying the Khmer empire

Theravada – a school of Buddhism (also known as the Southern School or Hinayana) found in Myanmar (Burma), Thailand, Laos and Cambodia; this school confined itself to the early Buddhist teachings; see also *Mahayana*

tonlé – large river

UNDP – UN Development Programme

Unesco – UN Educational Scientific and Cultural Organization

Untac – UN Transitional Authority in Cambodia

vihara – temple sanctuary

WHO – World Health Organization

Year Zero – 1975; the year the Khmer Rouge seized power

yoni – female fertility symbol

behind the scenes

SEND US YOUR FEEDBACK

We love to hear from travellers – your comments keep us on our toes and help make our books better. Our well-travelled team reads every word on what you loved or loathed about this book. Although we cannot reply individually to postal submissions, we always guarantee that your feedback goes straight to the appropriate authors, in time for the next edition. Each person who sends us information is thanked in the next edition – the most useful submissions are rewarded with a selection of digital PDF chapters.

Visit **lonelyplanet.com/contact** to submit your updates and suggestions or to ask for help. Our award-winning website also features inspirational travel stories, news and discussions.

Note: We may edit, reproduce and incorporate your comments in Lonely Planet products such as guidebooks, websites and digital products, so let us know if you don't want your comments reproduced or your name acknowledged. For a copy of our privacy policy visit lonelyplanet.com/privacy.

OUR READERS

Many thanks to the travellers who used the last edition and wrote to us with helpful hints, useful advice and interesting anecdotes:

Henri, Jaroslav, Markus, Rosalind, Saranya, Yoshiko, Olle Backgard, Kat Barseth, Nick Baum, Ayden C, Claudio Calcagno, Emma Casey, Daizhuo Chen, Claire Cody, Owen Davis, Bart De Pauw, Marine Douchin, Cedric Gasnier, Reto & Jennifer Gehr, Angela Guerrero, Mohamad Hafiz Zolkipli, Mark Harrison, Wendy Hodge, Helen Iveson, Ralpha Jacobson, Berthille Jarry, Ann Laherty-Hunt, Sophie Laurencin, Fergus Maclagan, Chung Man Po, Emilie Pavey, Nicola Peel, April Ratchta, Karen Schroeder-Ames, W Snyder, Ed Teja, Annieke & Lindy Ten Raa, Eline Thijssen, Louise Thoft Jensen, Christine Usher, Joris Jan Voermans, Holly Whitaker.

AUTHOR THANKS

Nick Ray

As always, a huge and heartfelt thanks to the people of the Mekong region, whose warmth and humour, stoicism and spirit make it a happy yet humbling place to be. Biggest thanks are reserved for my lovely wife, Kulikar Sotho, as without her support and encouragement the adventures would not be possible. And to our young children, Julian and Belle, for enlivening our lives immeasurably.

Many thanks to my mum and dad for their many visits to this part of the world. And thank you to my Cambodian family for welcoming me warmly and understanding my not-so-traditional lifestyle. Thanks to fellow travellers and residents, friends and contacts in the Mekong region who have helped shape my knowledge and experience in this country. There is no room to thank everyone, but you all know who you are, as we meet for beers regularly enough.

Thanks also to my co-author and good friend Greg Bloom for going the extra mile to ensure this is a worthy new edition. And to long-time author Daniel Robinson for his in-depth work on the 1st, 6th and 7th editions of this book. Finally, thanks to the Lonely Planet team who have worked on this title. The author may be the public face, but a huge amount of work goes into making this a better book behind the scenes and I thank everyone for their hard work.

Greg Bloom

The cumulative knowledge of 'the gang' in Phnom Penh was elemental in writing this book – you know who you are. Special thanks to Stephen and Rachel for snouting around Snooky with me. For tips and advice, thanks to Lina Goldberg, Steve Golden and colleague-slash-cagey-Phnom-Penh-vet

Nick. A nod to daughter Anna for her Phnom Tamao insight, and for enduring climbs up Phnom Chisor and Udong; and to her mama for holding down the fort.

ACKNOWLEDGMENTS

Climate map data adapted from Peel MC, Finlayson BL & McMahon TA (2007) 'Updated World Map of the Köppen-Geiger Climate Classification', *Hydrology and Earth System Sciences*, 11, 1633–44.

Cover photograph: Ruins of Angkor Wat, Jose Fuste Raga/Photolibrary ©. Many of the images in this guide are available for licensing from Lonely Planet Images: www.lonelyplanet images.com.

THIS BOOK

This 8th edition of Cambodia was researched and written by Phnom Penh residents and aficionados of all things Cambodia, Nick Ray and Greg Bloom. Nick coordinated the book and researched the Siem Reap, Temples of Angkor, South Coast, Northwestern Cambodia and Eastern Cambodia chapters. Nick updated the previous five editions. Greg researched and wrote the Phnom Penh chapter and the South Coast chapter.

This guidebook was commissioned in Lonely Planet's Melbourne office, and produced by the following:

Commissioning Editor Ilaria Walker

Coordinating Editors Sarah Bailey, Pat Kinsella

Coordinating Cartographer Marc Milinkovic

Coordinating Layout Designer Wibowo Rusli

Managing Editors Bruce Evans

Senior Editors Andi Jones, Martine Power

Managing Cartographer Shahara Ahmed

Managing Layout Designer Jane Hart

Assisting Editors Sam Trafford, Simon Williamson, Helen Yeates

Cover Research Naomi Parker

Illustrator Javier Martinez Zarracina

Internal Image Research Aude Vauconsant

Language Content Branislava Vladisavljevic

Thanks to Ryan Evans, Yvonne Kirk, Gerard Walker, Susan Paterson Trent Paton, Kirsten Rawlings, Juan Winata

NOTES

index

000 Map pages
000 Photo pages

how to use this book

These symbols will help you find the listings you want:

Sights	Tours	Drinking
Beaches	Festivals & Events	Entertainment
Activities	Sleeping	Shopping
Courses	Eating	Information/Transport

Look out for these icons:

TOP CHOICE — Our author's recommendation

FREE — No payment required

A green or sustainable option

Our authors have nominated these places as demonstrating a strong commitment to sustainability – for example by supporting local communities and producers, operating in an environmentally friendly way, or supporting conservation projects.

These symbols give you the vital information for each listing:

Telephone Numbers	Wi-Fi Access	Bus
Opening Hours	Swimming Pool	Ferry
Parking	Vegetarian Selection	Metro
Nonsmoking	English-Language Menu	Subway
Air-Conditioning	Family-Friendly	Tram
Internet Access	Pet-Friendly	Train

Reviews are organised by author preference.

Map Legend

Sights
- Beach
- Buddhist
- Castle
- Christian
- Hindu
- Islamic
- Jewish
- Monument
- Museum/Gallery
- Ruin
- Winery/Vineyard
- Zoo
- Other Sight

Activities, Courses & Tours
- Diving/Snorkelling
- Canoeing/Kayaking
- Skiing
- Surfing
- Swimming/Pool
- Walking
- Windsurfing
- Other Activity/Course/Tour

Sleeping
- Sleeping
- Camping

Eating
- Eating

Drinking
- Drinking
- Cafe

Entertainment
- Entertainment

Shopping
- Shopping

Information
- Bank
- Embassy/Consulate
- Hospital/Medical
- Internet
- Police
- Post Office
- Telephone
- Toilet
- Tourist Information
- Other Information

Transport
- Airport
- Border Crossing
- Bus
- Cable Car/Funicular
- Cycling
- Ferry
- Metro
- Monorail
- Parking
- Petrol Station
- Taxi
- Train/Railway
- Tram
- Other Transport

Routes
- Tollway
- Freeway
- Primary
- Secondary
- Tertiary
- Lane
- Unsealed Road
- Plaza/Mall
- Steps
- Tunnel
- Pedestrian Overpass
- Walking Tour
- Walking Tour Detour
- Path

Geographic
- Hut/Shelter
- Lighthouse
- Lookout
- Mountain/Volcano
- Oasis
- Park
- Pass
- Picnic Area
- Waterfall

Population
- Capital (National)
- Capital (State/Province)
- City/Large Town
- Town/Village

Boundaries
- International
- State/Province
- Disputed
- Regional/Suburb
- Marine Park
- Cliff
- Wall

Hydrography
- River, Creek
- Intermittent River
- Swamp/Mangrove
- Reef
- Canal
- Water
- Dry/Salt/Intermittent Lake
- Glacier

Areas
- Beach/Desert
- Cemetery (Christian)
- Cemetery (Other)
- Park/Forest
- Sportsground
- Sight (Building)
- Top Sight (Building)

OUR STORY

A beat-up old car, a few dollars in the pocket and a sense of adventure. In 1972 that's all Tony and Maureen Wheeler needed for the trip of a lifetime – across Europe and Asia overland to Australia. It took several months, and at the end – broke but inspired – they sat at their kitchen table writing and stapling together their first travel guide, *Across Asia on the Cheap*. Within a week they'd sold 1500 copies. Lonely Planet was born.

Today, Lonely Planet has offices in Melbourne, London and Oakland, with more than 600 staff and writers. We share Tony's belief that 'a great guidebook should do three things: inform, educate and amuse'.

OUR WRITERS

Nick Ray

Coordinating Author; Siem Reap, Temples of Angkor, Northwestern Cambodia, Eastern Cambodia A Londoner of sorts, Nick comes from Watford, the sort of town that makes you want to travel. He lives in Phnom Penh with his wife, Kulikar, and his young children, Julian and Belle. He has written for countless guidebooks on the Mekong region, including Lonely Planet's *Cambodia*, *Vietnam* and *Laos* books, as well as *Southeast Asia on a Shoestring*. When not writing, he is often out exploring the remote parts of Cambodia as a location scout and manager for the world of television and film, and he has been involved in movies including *Tomb Raider* and *Two Brothers*. Motorbikes are a part-time passion (riding them a passion, maintaining them part-time) and he has travelled through most of Indochina on two wheels.

Greg Bloom

Phnom Penh, South Coast After five years in Manila, Greg crossed the pond to 'small-town' Phnom Penh in 2008 and immediately took a liking to the city. He's spent ample time researching its restaurants and bars ever since. That said, he'd move to Cambodia's southern islands in a heartbeat if he had an excuse. When not writing about Cambodia and the Philippines for Lonely Planet, Greg might be found poking around the former Soviet Union (he was editor of the *Kyiv Post* in another life) or running around Asia's ultimate Frisbee fields. Read about his trips at www.mytripjournal.com/bloomblogs.

Read more about Greg at:
lonelyplanet.com/members/gbloom4

Published by Lonely Planet Publications Pty Ltd
ABN 36 005 607 983
8th edition – Jun 2012
ISBN 978 1 74179 965 1
© Lonely Planet 2012   Photographs © as indicated 2012
10 9 8 7 6 5 4 3 2 1
Printed in China

Although the authors and Lonely Planet have taken all reasonable care in preparing this book, we make no warranty about the accuracy or completeness of its content and, to the maximum extent permitted, disclaim all liability arising from its use.

All rights reserved. No part of this publication may be copied, stored in a retrieval system, or transmitted in any form by any means, electronic, mechanical, recording or otherwise, except brief extracts for the purpose of review, and no part of this publication may be sold or hired, without the written permission of the publisher. Lonely Planet and the Lonely Planet logo are trademarks of Lonely Planet and are registered in the US Patent and Trademark Office and in other countries. Lonely Planet does not allow its name or logo to be appropriated by commercial establishments, such as retailers, restaurants or hotels. Please let us know of any misuses: lonelyplanet.com/ip.